Oracle Integration Cookbook for Oracle ERP Cloud

A Hands-On Guide to Build Enterprise Integrations

Juan Jesús Montero Rodríguez
Sadia Tahseen

Apress®

Oracle Integration Cookbook for Oracle ERP Cloud: A Hands-On Guide to Build Enterprise Integrations

Juan Jesús Montero Rodríguez
Madrid, Spain

Sadia Tahseen
Dallas, TX, USA

ISBN-13 (pbk): 979-8-8688-3019-8
ISBN-13 (electronic): 979-8-8688-3020-4
https://doi.org/10.1007/979-8-8688-3020-4

Managing Director, Apress Media LLC: Welmoed Spahr
Acquisitions Editor: Shivangi Ramachandran
Editorial Assistant: Jessica Vakili

Cover designed by eStudioCalamar

Cover image designed by kjpargeter on Freepik

Distributed to the book trade worldwide by Springer Science+Business Media New York, 1 New York Plaza, New York, NY 10004. Phone 1-800-SPRINGER, fax (201) 348-4505, e-mail orders-ny@springer-sbm.com, or visit www.springeronline.com. Apress Media, LLC is a Delaware LLC and the sole member (owner) is Springer Science + Business Media Finance Inc (SSBM Finance Inc). SSBM Finance Inc is a Delaware corporation.

For information on translations, please e-mail booktranslations@springernature.com; for reprint, paperback, or audio rights, please e-mail bookpermissions@springernature.com.

Apress titles may be purchased in bulk for academic, corporate, or promotional use. eBook versions and licenses are also available for most titles. For more information, reference our Print and eBook Bulk Sales web page at http://www.apress.com/bulk-sales.

Any source code or other supplementary material referenced by the author in this book is available to readers on GitHub. For more detailed information, please visit https://www.apress.com/gp/services/source-code.

If disposing of this product, please recycle the paper

To Raquel, Carlota, and Adriana.

Table of Contents

About the Authors .... **xxi**

About the Technical Reviewer .... **xxiii**

Acknowledgments .... **xxv**

Introduction .... **xxvii**

Chapter 1: Introduction **1**

Background: From SOA to OIC 1

What Is OIC in Simple Terms? 1

Core Technologies 2

Book Focus 2

Basic Types of Integrations 3

Application Integration 3

Scheduled Integration 4

Event-Based Integration 4

Chapter 2: Adapters and Connections **5**

Our Approach 5

Adapters Available in Generation 3 5

What Is an Adapter? 7

Understanding Trigger and Invoke Roles 7

Trigger 8

Invoke 8

Connections Used in This Book....8
REST Connection....8
FTP Connection....10
Basic ERP Cloud Connection....11
ERP Cloud Events and Callbacks Connection....16
SOAP ExternalReportWSSService Connection....19
SOAP ScheduleService Connection....20
SOAP ErpObjectDFFUpdateService Connection....21
SOAP ErpIntegrationService Connection....22
ATP Database Connection....23
OCR Connection....27
Visual Builder Objects Connection....28
Object Storage Connection....30
REST API for ERP Integrations Connection....31
Chapter 3: Application Integration Types and Fault Handlers....33
Understanding OIC Gen3 Projects....33
What Is a Project?....33
What a Project Is NOT....34
Integration Patterns in OIC Gen3....34
Building Your First Application Integration....35
Preparation: Obtaining a Test Payload....35
Technical Reference....48
Advanced Flow Control: Switch and For-Each....48
Conclusion....55
Technical Reference....56
While Loops and Scope Activities....56
Understanding the Scope Component....56

Our Definition....56
Demonstration: Retry Logic with the While Loop....57
Testing the Retry Logic....58
Technical Reference....60

Chapter 4: Notification and Wait Activities....61
Overview....61
Configuring a Notification Activity....62
Configuration Fields....62
Email Body Options....63
Basic Notification Demo....63
Technical Reference....68

Chapter 5: JavaScript in OIC....69
Overview....69
Managing JavaScript Libraries....70
Example JavaScript Library....71
Uploading a JavaScript Library....71
Import or Manual Uploading of the JavaScript File....71
Using JavaScript Functions in Integrations....75
Technical Reference....76

Chapter 6: Mappings and XSLT....77
What Is XSLT?....77
Simple vs. Complex Mappings....78
Example Complex Mapping Requirements....79
Using XSLT Constructs....80
Direct XSLT Code Editing....81
Important Notes About Code Mode....82
Best Practices....82

Chapter 7: Projects and Packages....83

Overview....83

Our Perspective....83

Understanding Packages (Pre-Gen3)....84

Projects: The Gen3 Evolution....84

Considerations Before Adopting Projects....84

Important Limitations....85

Migration Challenges....85

Recommendation....86

Creating Projects from Packages....86

Chapter 8: Oracle Integration Limits....89

Understanding Service Limits....89

Our Perspective on Limits....89

Key Questions to Ask....89

No One-Size-Fits-All Solution....90

Design Strategies....90

Deciding Between Synchronous vs. Asynchronous Integrations....91

Chapter 9: Monitoring Capabilities in OIC....93

Our Perspective....93

Monitoring and Troubleshooting in OIC Gen3....94

Observability Dashboard....94

Projects Tab: Observe Subtab....94

Activity Stream (Instance Tracking)....95

Diagnostic Logs....96

Notifications and Alerts....96

Replay and Testing Capabilities....97

OCI Cloud Console 97
Alerting and Automation 98
Gen2 vs. Gen3 Monitoring Comparison 99
Key Gen3 Improvement 100
Chapter 10: OCR (Optical Character Recognition) 101
Introduction and Goal 101
Preparatory Steps 101
Testing with Postman 102
Sample PDF Document 104
Building the OIC Integration 105
OIC Integration Components 105
Testing the Integration 109
Conclusion 109
Technical Reference 110
Chapter 11: Visual Builder to OIC to SaaS: Create Invoices from Files with REST 111
Overview 111
Application Workflow 112
Summary of Features 113
Visual Builder Side 113
Oracle Integration Side 114
Oracle Integration Configuration 115
Connection Setup 115
Integration Flow Design 119
Inbound Parameters 119
Complete Integration Flow 119
Key Integration Activities 120

Visual Builder Configuration....................128
Backend Connection Setup....................128
Create an OIC Service Connection....................129
Test the Connection....................130
Business Object Definition....................132
Key Points to Consider....................132
Complete End-to-End Test....................136
Process Review Feature....................143
Error Handling....................144
Conclusion....................145
Technical Reference....................146
Chapter 12: Lookups....................147
Overview....................147
Common Use Cases for Lookups....................147
Advanced Demo: Reading Lookups As Tables....................150
The Challenge....................150
Use Case: Table-Like Iteration....................151
Solution Implementation....................151
Integration Design....................154
Overall Flow....................154
Key Implementation Steps....................154
Use Cases for Table-Based Lookup Access....................160
Technical Reference....................160
Chapter 13: OIC Integration using FBDI....................161
FBDI for Suppliers with Callback (Three Data Sources)....................161
Overview....................161
FBDI Basics....................161

FBDI File Structure 162

Integration 1: XX_DEMO_IMP_SUPP_FTP 163

Integration 2: XX_DEMO_IMP_SUPP_NO_FTP 165

Integration 3: XX_DEMO_IMP_SUPP_OB_STOR (Object Storage Approach) 167

Integration 4: XX_DEMO_IMP_SUPP_CB 172

Technical Reference 178

FBDI for Customers with File Management 178

Overview 178

Integration: XX_DEMO_AR_IMPORT_CUST 178

Technical Reference 184

Chapter 14: Other FBDI Interfaces 185

Overview 185

Finding Parameters 185

Suppliers Interface 186

Payables Invoices 187

Investigation Steps 187

Receivables Invoices 189

Investigation Steps 189

Items Import 191

Investigation Steps 191

Chapter 15: FTP Server and Stage Activity 193

Overview 193

FTP and Stage Activity Fundamentals 193

What Is Stage Activity? 193

Comparing FTP Server and Stage Operations 194

Key Differences 194

Example 1: Basic File Download 195
Example 2: FTP to Database Integration 197
Technical Reference 198
FTP Demo: Purge Files Based on Date 198
Introduction 198
Process Steps...199
Technical Reference 203

Chapter 16: ATP Database 205

Overview 205
Preparation 205
Basic Operations 207
ATP Insert Operation 207
ATP Update Operation 210
ATP Delete Operation 212
ATP Query with Parameter...212
Technical Reference 216

Chapter 17: Advanced REST: POC for Duplicating Receivables Transactions 217

Overview 217
Introduction 217
Business Requirements..217
Preparation 219
Auxiliary Integration: XX_DEMO_UPDATE_FLEX.......................................223
Main Integration: XX_DEMO_AR_TRX_DUPLICATE.......................................225
Process Flow Explanation..226
Section 1: Receive Parameters, Read Invoice, Create Copy 226
Section 2: Set Original Transaction As Incomplete and Update Flexfields...233

Section 3: Copy Attachments 236
Section 4: Return Response 237
Testing 237
Technical Reference 239

Chapter 18: SOAP ERP Demos 241

ErpIntegrationService 241
Overview 241
Integration Configuration 246
Technical Reference 252
ScheduleService 252
Overview 252
Preparation 256
Integration Setup 258
Additional Operations Examples 259
Technical Reference 264
ErpObjectDFFUpdateService 265
Overview 265
Oracle ERP Cloud Setup 265
OIC Integration Setup 269
Additional Resources 275
Technical Reference 275

Chapter 19: Attachments in Oracle ERP 277

Overview 277
Attachment Types 278
Manual Attachment Process 278
Automated Attachments with REST APIs 279
Example 1: File Attachment 280

Integration Overview 280

Connection Setup 280

Download File Activity 280

Create Attachment Activity 281

Mapping Configuration 283

Testing the Integration 287

Example 2: URL Attachment 288

Integration Overview 288

Mapping Configuration 288

Attachment Type 288

URL Mapping 289

Testing the Integration 289

Technical Reference 290

Chapter 20: Object Storage Upload 291

Overview 291

Object Storage Structure 292

Object Storage Hierarchy 293

Obtaining Connection Parameters 296

Integration to Upload a File to Object Storage 302

Technical Reference 306

Chapter 21: Read BI Publisher Reports and Multiple Verbs in REST 307

Overview 307

Reading BI Publisher Reports 307

Introduction and Goal 307

Important Considerations 309

Preparatory Steps 309

Testing the Integration 311

Multiple Verbs in REST API 316
Introduction and Goal 316
Technical Reference 321
Chapter 22: UCM Web Center Download/Upload 323
Overview 323
Download from UCM 323
Manual Upload for Testing 323
UCM Connection Configuration 327
Testing with SoapUI 327
Download Integration Example 329
Upload to UCM 331
Integration Overview 331
Technical Details 335
Chapter 23: Parallel Activity 337
Overview 337
Example: Calling Asynchronous Integrations 337
Example: Calling Synchronous Integrations 340
Technical Reference 342
Chapter 24: Data Stitch Activity and Global Variables 343
Demo Preparation 343
Global Variables 346
Data Stitch Activity 347
Business Requirement 347
Implementation Steps 348
Technical Reference 357

Chapter 25: REST API Tips 359

Overview 359

REST Request Headers: Critical Configuration 359

The Hidden Feature 359

Problem Scenario 359

Solution Discovery 361

OIC Implementation Fix 362

Chapter 26: B2B Basics 367

Introduction 367

What Is B2B Integration? 367

Common B2B Scenarios 368

Document Types 368

OIC B2B Activity 368

Implementation Steps 371

Chapter 27: Demo Control Dates Between OIC Runs, Using Delta Data Process 375

Overview 375

Solution Approach 375

General Integration Overview 376

Key Feature: Schedule Parameters 377

Testing and Execution 377

Execution Results 380

Date Range Logic 382

Benefits 383

Technical Reference 383

Chapter 28: Oracle ERP Cloud Business Events....385

Overview....385

Example: Purchase Order Events....386

Purchase Order Event Implementation....386

Setup Configuration....386

Event Filters....388

Testing the Integration....389

Event Payload Structure....391

Integration Actions....391

Technical Reference....392

Payables Invoice Event Implementation....392

Preparation: Enable Events....392

Integration Setup....393

Integration Overview....394

Event Payload Information....394

Technical Reference....398

Receivables Invoice Event Demo....398

Preparation: Enable Events....398

Integration Configuration....400

Testing....402

Execution Results....403

Available Event Information....404

Technical Reference....404

Chapter 29: Demo with Visual Builder, OIC, FTP, and ATP....405

Overview....405

Upload to an FTP Server....405

FTP Server Setup....407

ATP Database Setup....407

Database Connection....408
Oracle Integration Connections....409
Integration Steps....409
Visual Builder Steps....416
Conclusion....422
Download from an FTP Server Demo....423
Oracle Integration Steps....424
Visual Builder Steps....429
Conclusion....434
Technical Reference....435

Chapter 30: Massive Loads and Deletes in Visual Builder Business Objects: REST API Batch....437

Overview....437
Key Implementation Details....438
Preparation....439
Integration 1: XX_DEMO_FTP_2_DB_VB_SINGLE....439
General Overview....439
Setup....440
Integration 2: XX_DEMO_DB_VB_BATCH_DELETE....448
General Overview....448
Integration 3: XX_DEMO_FTP_2_DB_VB_BATCH....454
General Overview....454
The Key Components....455
Conclusion....464
Technical Reference....464

Chapter 31: Callback Advanced: Sending FBDI Files + Lookup........465

Introduction........465

Preparation........465

Integration 1: XX_DEMO_IMP_SUPP_CB........466

General Overview........466

Integration 2: XX_DEMO_SEND_FBDI_FILES........469

General Overview........469

File Processing........470

Lookup Setup........472

Testing........473

Email Notification........475

FTP Server Storage........476

Technical Reference........476

Chapter 32: OIC Generation 3 Events........477

Introduction........477

Basic Event Demonstration........477

Testing the Event Flow........485

Understanding Event Use Cases........487

What Are Events Used For?........487

Example Scenario........488

Important Limitation........488

Technical Reference........489

Appendix A: REST APIs and Postman........491

Appendix B: SOAP Web Services and SoapUI........493

Appendix C: SOAP Web Services Samples........501

Appendix D: Technical Tips and Best Practices................................511

Glossary..539

References..541

Index..543

About the Authors

Juan Jesús Montero Rodríguez is a seasoned Oracle Technology Professional with over 25 years of hands-on experience across enterprise applications and cloud platforms. He is recognized as an Oracle ACE. Currently he serves as Oracle ERP Cloud Senior Developer. He is deeply passionate about continuous learning, embracing emerging technologies, and exploring innovative technical paths to deliver impactful solutions. He is the author of many books currently published on Amazon, like *Oracle Visual Builder Redwood Cookbook* and others.

His core expertise lies in Oracle E-Business Suite (EBS), Oracle SaaS, ERP Cloud, Oracle Forms and Oracle Reports, Oracle Application Framework (OAF), Oracle Integration Cloud (Certified), Oracle Visual Builder, Oracle Redwood (Certified), Oracle Cloud Infrastructure (OCI), Artificial Intelligence (AI), BI Publisher, SAP, and JAVA.

Sadia Tahseen is a seasoned Oracle Technology Professional with over 17 years of experience, specializing in Oracle Cloud, Oracle Fusion Middleware, and Oracle Database technologies. She is recognized as an Oracle ACE. She currently serves as an Oracle Platform Lead, where she manages large-scale Oracle Fusion Cloud implementations, implements robust Oracle Integration solutions, delivers operational excellence, optimizes system performance, and helps define strategic technology roadmaps for large-scale enterprise clients. In addition to her technical leadership, she is an accomplished presenter and has shared her thought leadership and research articles and papers at many OATUG and IEEE conferences and various media publications.

Here core expertise lies in Oracle SaaS/PaaS, Oracle Enterprise Resource Planning (ERP), Oracle Integration Cloud (OIC) (Certified), Oracle Cloud Infrastructure (OCI) (Certified), Service-Oriented Architecture (SOA) (Certified), Oracle WebCenter Content/Imaging, Oracle WebLogic Server, Oracle Human Capital Management (HCM), and Artificial Intelligence (AI).

About the Technical Reviewer

Pramod Muppala is Vice President and Infrastructure Engineering Lead specializing in enterprise middleware, Oracle Fusion Middleware, DevOps automation, platform resilience, and infrastructure modernization. He has supported mission-critical systems across banking, financial services, telecommunications, insurance, and technology environments. His work focuses on improving the reliability, automation, scalability, and operational efficiency of enterprise platforms, with professional interests in Oracle middleware, cloud infrastructure, AI-enabled automation, and resilient system design.

LinkedIn profile: `https://www.linkedin.com/in/pramodmuppala/`

Acknowledgments

We are grateful to Arilds who provided help in difficult times.

Introduction

This book is a hands-on, practical guide designed for professionals working daily with Oracle Integration Cloud (OIC) and Oracle ERP Cloud. It is not intended to be an Oracle product documentation or reference guide; instead, it focuses on real-world, hands-on implementations to help readers understand and learn OIC functionality through practical use cases.

The book serves as a beginner-to-intermediate-level resource, emphasizing implementation-driven learning. While concepts are explained step by step, readers should expect to invest time and effort to fully understand and complete the exercises and examples presented throughout the book.

This book is suitable for

- Oracle Fusion/Oracle ERP Cloud SaaS developers who want to start or strengthen their skills in Oracle Integration Cloud while working with Oracle ERP Cloud
- Technical architects working with Oracle Fusion/ Oracle ERP Cloud SaaS who are looking for practical integration patterns and hands-on experience

This book is designed for a range of professionals working with Oracle ERP Cloud and Oracle Integration Cloud:

- **Oracle ERP Cloud SaaS Consultants—Technical**: Those looking to gain hands-on knowledge and practical skills for implementing and integrating OIC with Oracle ERP Cloud

- **Oracle ERP Cloud SaaS Consultants—Functional**: Professionals who want to understand the capabilities of the tools and how they can be applied to business processes
- **Managers and Architects**: Those who need a high-level reference to understand what the tools can achieve, enabling informed decision-making and planning

After completing some introductory readings or courses, this book will provide readers with

- **Real-world, practical examples** commonly encountered in daily Oracle ERP Cloud work
- **Step-by-step guidance** with detailed screenshots to ensure clarity and ease of learning
- **Multiple approaches** to solving different integration and implementation challenges
- **Focused content** exclusively on Oracle ERP Cloud and Oracle Integration Cloud, without covering other vendors
- **A pathway to advanced knowledge**, helping readers elevate their skills and confidently apply what they learn in real-world scenarios

All code used in demos in this book will be available in

https://github.com/juanjesusmontero/oic_for_erp_cookbook

Integrations can be found in the repository as OIC packages:

1. v22_XX_DEMO_COOKBOOK.par
2. v03_XX_DEMO_COOKBOOK_2.par

CHAPTER 1

Introduction

This book focuses on practical, real-world OIC implementations rather than repeating reference documentation already available on Oracle's websites and blogs. The content reflects what we use daily in production environments. While it doesn't cover every possible scenario, it addresses the most common requirements you'll encounter. The rest you'll need to investigate on a case-by-case basis.

Background: From SOA to OIC

Service-Oriented Architecture (SOA) and Oracle SOA Suite have been the industry standard for developing complex interfaces for many years, and we consider SOA Suite the parent of OIC. Oracle SOA Suite is robust, reliable, and scalable and continues to be used by companies worldwide.

What Is OIC in Simple Terms?

Oracle Integration Cloud (OIC) is an Oracle tool that has taken the essence of SOA Suite and made it significantly easier to learn. Most importantly, **OIC is pure cloud.**

While Oracle SOA tools can be deployed on-premises or in the cloud, OIC exists exclusively in the cloud. Oracle Integration Cloud is gaining momentum because it integrates seamlessly with Oracle ERP Cloud and many other cloud-based applications. Many artifacts seem specifically built to make these systems work together harmoniously.

J. J. Montero Rodríguez and S. Tahseen, *Oracle Integration Cookbook for Oracle ERP Cloud*,
https://doi.org/10.1007/979-8-8688-3020-4_1

OIC has a gentle learning curve, making it accessible to developers at various skill levels.

While Oracle Integration can be used for general purposes, **this book focuses specifically on Oracle ERP Cloud interactions**.

Core Technologies

To successfully work with OIC and ERP Cloud, you'll need to master these three fundamental technologies:

- **REST APIs**
- **SOAP web services**
- **FBDI (File-Based Data Import)**

These are the main building blocks you'll use to get jobs done.

Book Focus

This book is

- ✓ Learning-focused
- ✓ Practical and example-driven
- ✓ Based on real-world implementations

This book is NOT

- ✗ Exam certification–focused
- ✗ Focused on administrator tasks

If you're unfamiliar with REST APIs or SOAP web services, we strongly recommend learning as much as you can about both technologies before proceeding.

This book assumes someone else manages the OIC tenancies and assigns you the necessary roles. Oracle's reference documentation provides detailed information for administrative tasks.

Reference Documentation

For comprehensive OIC documentation, consult these resources:

- Oracle Integration User Guide
- Oracle Integration YouTube Playlist

Basic Types of Integrations

Oracle Integration Cloud supports three primary integration styles. For detailed information, see the Understand Integration Styles documentation.

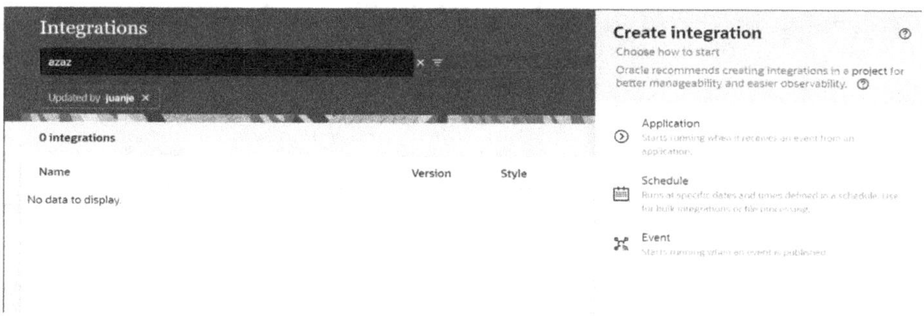

Figure 1-1. *Integration Style Selection Screen*

Application Integration

- Called by other applications or systems
- Can receive and return parameters of many types (when synchronous)
- Cannot be scheduled
- Used for real-time, on-demand processing

Scheduled Integration

- Used to schedule processes at specific times or dates
- Runs automatically based on defined schedules
- Often combined with application integrations for comprehensive solutions

Event-Based Integration

- Triggered by specific events in connected systems
- Provides real-time response to business events
- See Chapter 32 for detailed coverage

CHAPTER 2

Adapters and Connections

Our Approach

As stated in the Introduction: "While Oracle Integration can be used for general purposes, this book focuses specifically on Oracle ERP Cloud interactions."

This means we won't cover every OIC adapter Oracle provides. We'll focus on the adapters most relevant to ERP Cloud implementations.

Adapters Available in Generation 3

Oracle continuously expands the adapter library with each release. Below are examples of adapters available in Generation 3.

J. J. Montero Rodríguez and S. Tahseen, *Oracle Integration Cookbook for Oracle ERP Cloud*, https://doi.org/10.1007/979-8-8688-3020-4_2

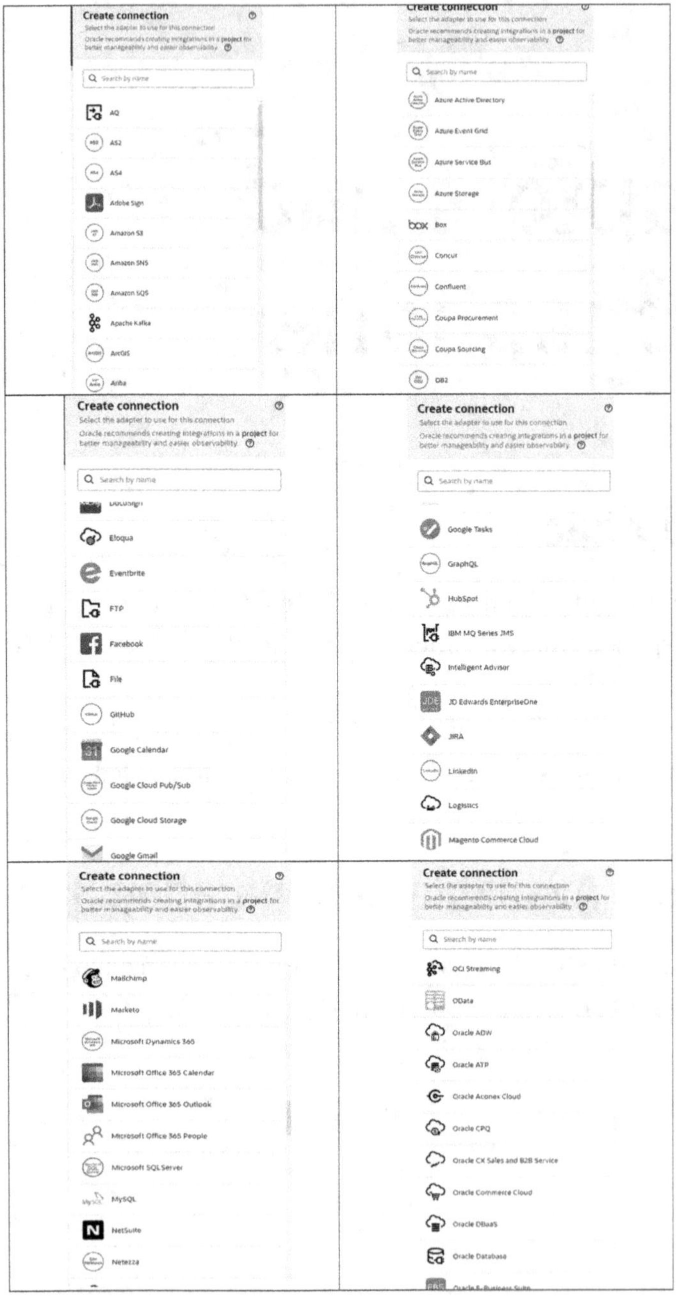

***Figure 2-1.** Adapter Categories*

What Is an Adapter?

Oracle's reference documentation provides various technical definitions of adapters. Here's our practical explanation:

Adapters are reusable, standardized artifacts that save you time by simplifying connections to different systems. They eliminate interface complexity and make your life easier as an OIC developer.

Adapters also solve secure connectivity challenges by providing multiple security options that vary by adapter type.

Adapter developers have pre-built functionality to accelerate your development work. For example, adapters typically include wizards that guide you through setup processes. After completing a wizard, you typically only need to

1. Map the input data.
2. Use the output data in subsequent steps.

For Advanced Users: Building Custom Adapters

Oracle allows experienced developers to create custom adapters using the Rapid Adapter Builder:

- Get Started with Rapid Adapter Builder

Understanding Trigger and Invoke Roles

Reference Documentation

- Understand Trigger and Invoke Connections (Oracle Docs)
- Oracle Integration Cloud: Trigger and Invoke (UnoGeeks)

Trigger

An external event or action initiates your integration. Examples include the following:

- A file arrives at an FTP server.
- A record is created in a database.
- A business event occurs in ERP Cloud.
- A scheduled time is reached.

Invoke

An invoke connection is used when OIC actively calls out to an external system or service. It represents the outbound (target) side of an integration. Invoke operations can be

- **Synchronous**: The process waits to finish and typically provides a response.
- **Asynchronous**: The process doesn't wait to finish and typically doesn't provide a response.

Connections Used in This Book

To follow the examples in this book, you'll need access to the following connections. We'll use these throughout our demonstrations.

REST Connection

Used to invoke integrations from other systems or test directly in the OIC console.

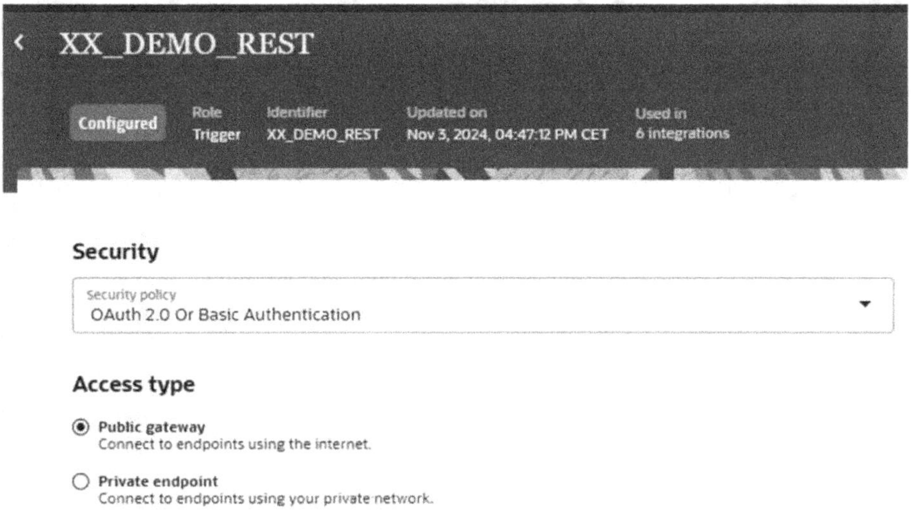

Figure 2-2. *REST Connection Configuration*

FTP Connection

Figure 2-3. FTP Connection Configuration

OIC Embedded File Server

OIC includes an optional embedded FTP server that's linked to but not enabled by default in your OIC instance. Up to 500 GB of storage is free (though standard message costs apply).

The embedded file server offers several advantages:

- Easy to use and configure
- Built-in security features

- Centralized control
- Supports SFTP clients
- Automatic encryption
- Comprehensive logging

Reference Documentation

- File Server Overview
- File Server FAQ

Basic ERP Cloud Connection

Set up with basic authentication security.

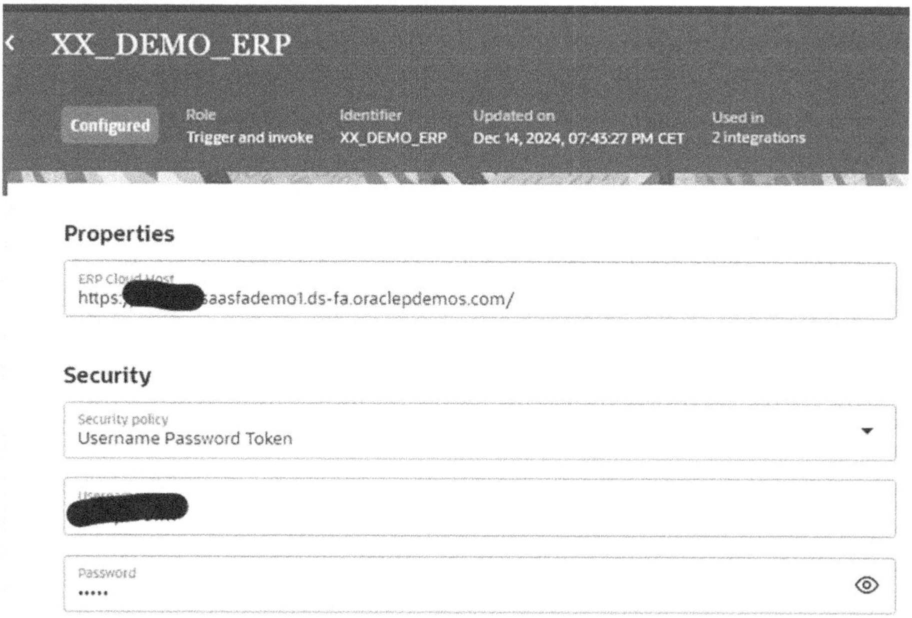

Figure 2-4. ERP Cloud Connection Configuration

This connection provides multiple action types.

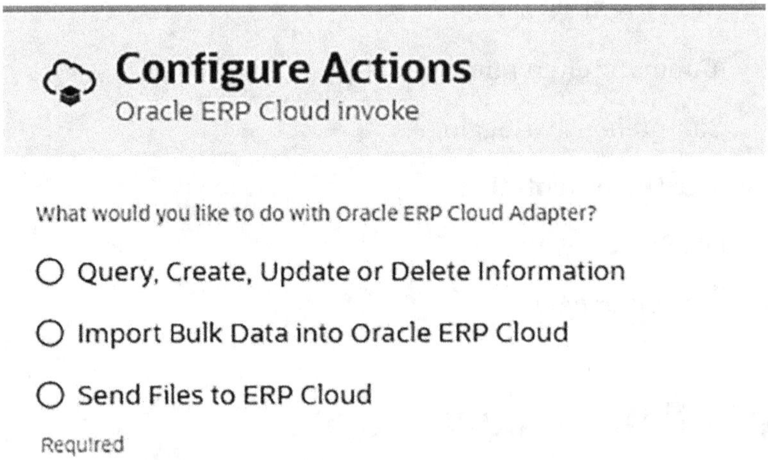

Figure 2-5. *ERP Cloud Actions Configuration*

Option 1: Query, Create, Update, or Delete Information

This option provides three sub-options.

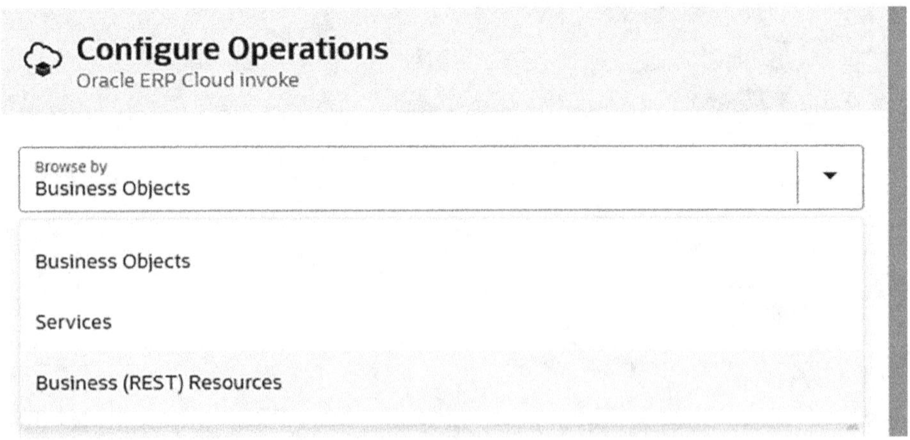

Figure 2-6. *ERP Cloud Connection Operation Types*

We have used mostly the following operations:

- **Services**: Select SOAP web services provided by Oracle.
- **Business (REST) Resources**: Select REST APIs provided by Oracle.

SOAP Web Services Used

- SOAP Web Services for Financials
- SOAP Web Services for SCM

REST APIs Used

- Financials REST API (25a)
- REST API for Oracle Fusion Cloud Financials - About the REST APIs
- REST API for Oracle Fusion Cloud SCM - Items Version 2 REST Endpoints

Option 2: Import Bulk Data into Oracle ERP Cloud

Provides a wizard to import FBDI (File-Based Data Import) files.

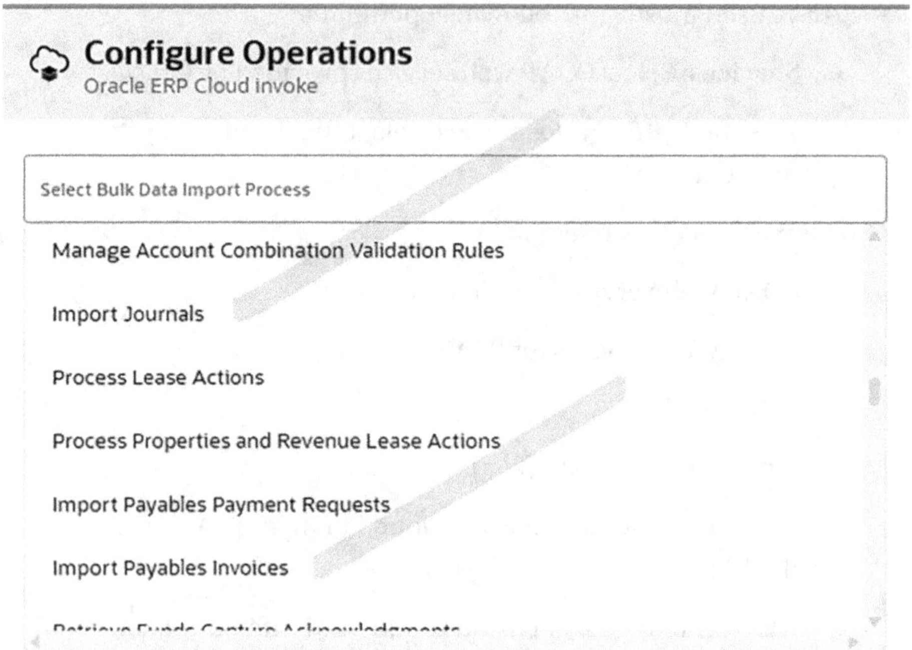

Figure 2-7. *FBDI Import Wizard*

See Chapter 14 for practical examples.

Option 3: Send Files to ERP Cloud

Used to upload files to UCM (Universal Content Management)/ WebCenter.

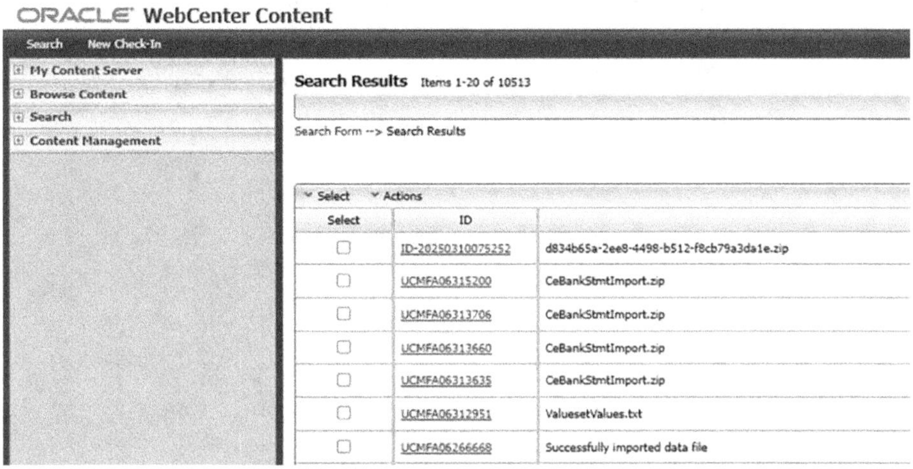

***Figure 2-8.** File Upload Configuration*

After selecting this option, you can choose the security group.

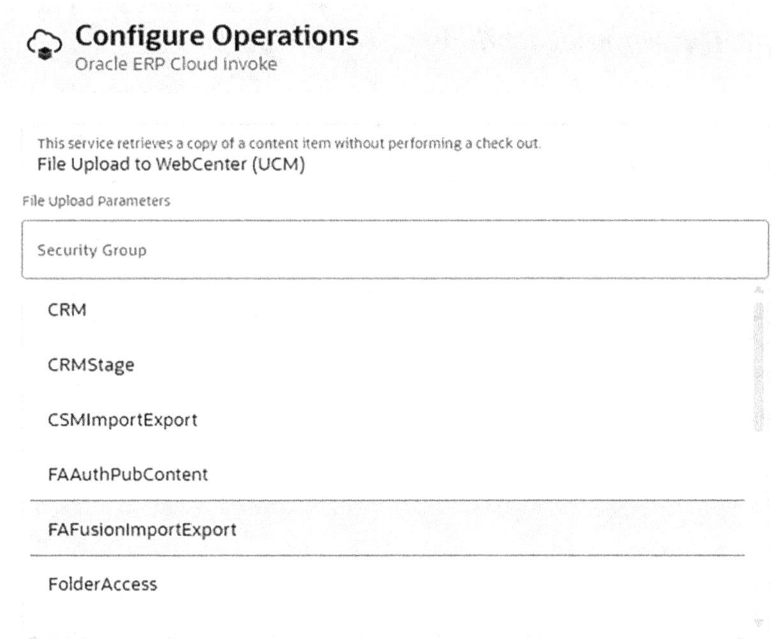

***Figure 2-9.** Security Group Selection*

In the mapping activity, you'll have these configuration options.

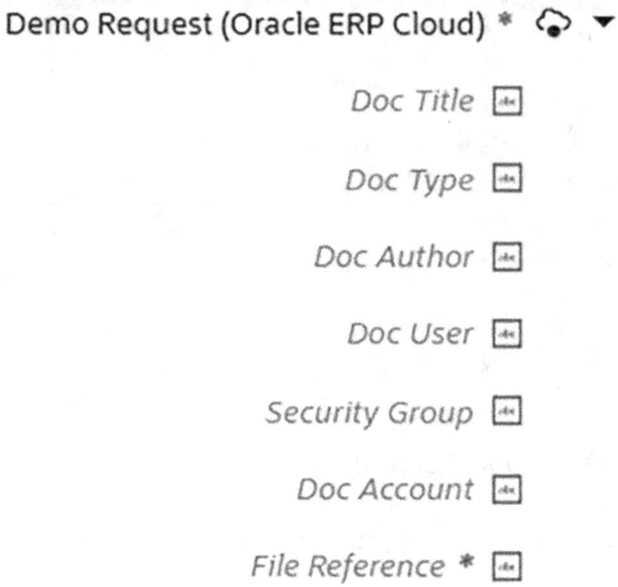

Figure 2-10. *Mapping Options for UCM Upload*

Practical examples are provided in Chapter 23.

Reference Documentation

Create ERP Cloud Connection

ERP Cloud Events and Callbacks Connection

This connection differs from the basic ERP Cloud connection and is specifically used for events and callbacks.

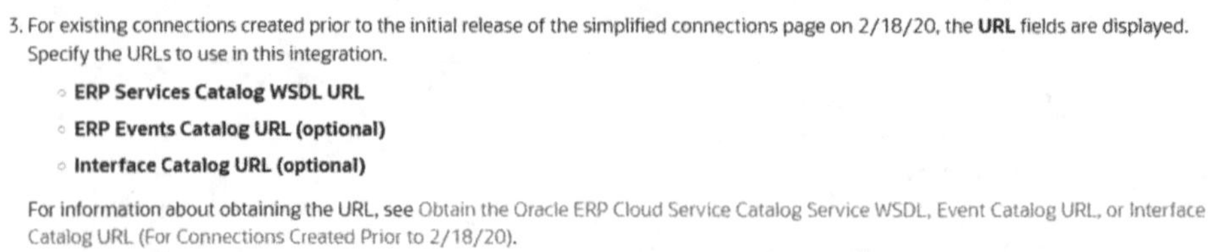

3. For existing connections created prior to the initial release of the simplified connections page on 2/18/20, the **URL** fields are displayed. Specify the URLs to use in this integration.
   - **ERP Services Catalog WSDL URL**
   - **ERP Events Catalog URL (optional)**
   - **Interface Catalog URL (optional)**

   For information about obtaining the URL, see Obtain the Oracle ERP Cloud Service Catalog Service WSDL, Event Catalog URL, or Interface Catalog URL (For Connections Created Prior to 2/18/20).

Figure 2-11. *ERP Cloud Events Connection Configuration*

Note These events differ from Generation 3 events explained in Chapter 11. For business events, see Chapter 29.

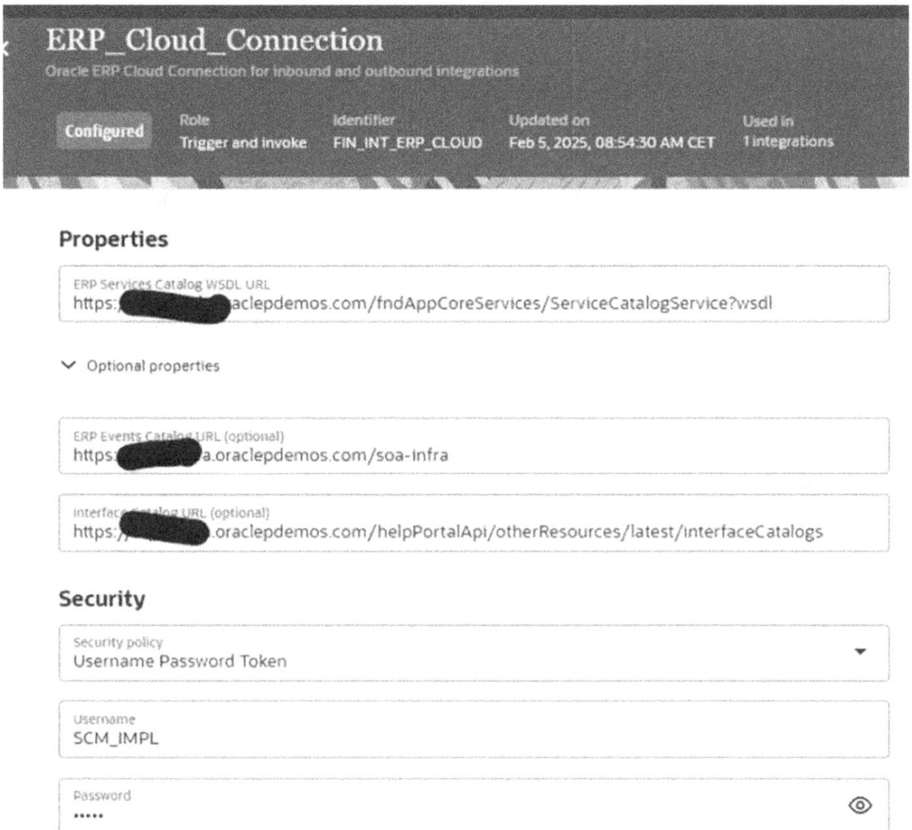

Figure 2-12. Events Connection Options

Here are available operations for this connection type.

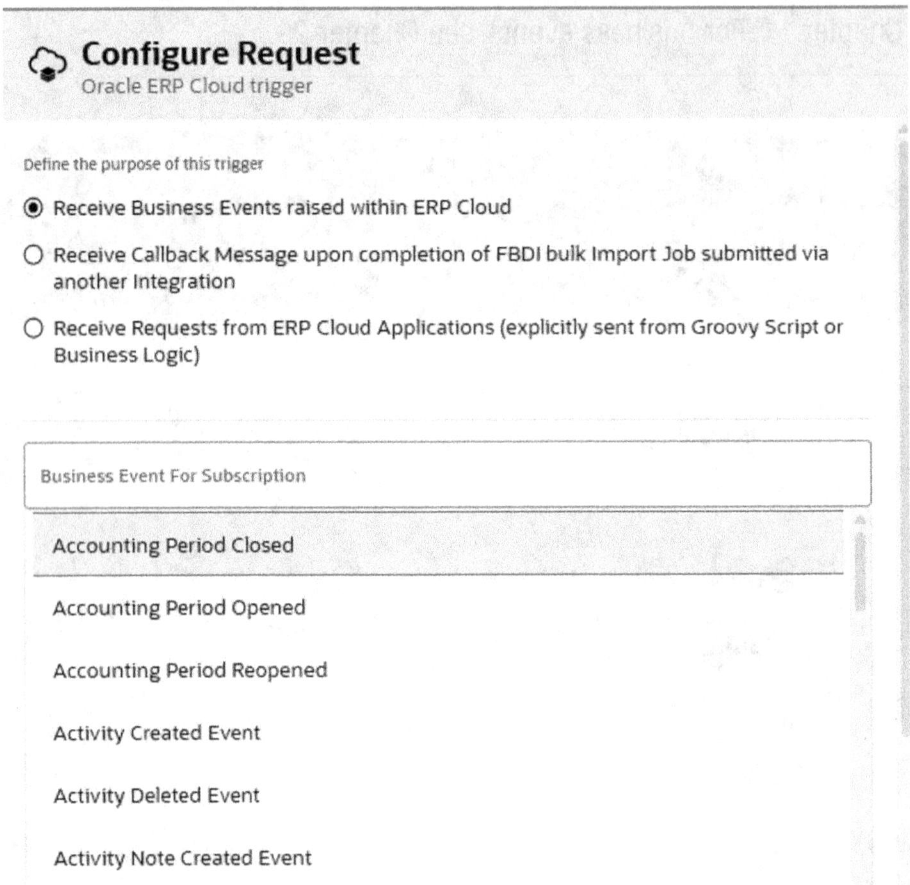

Figure 2-13. *Event Operations Menu*

SOAP ExternalReportWSSService Connection

Used to manage and run BI Publisher reports in Oracle ERP Cloud.

Figure 2-14. BI Publisher SOAP Connection

WSDL URL Format

```
https://fa-xxxx.ds-fa.oraclepdemos.com/xmlpserver/services/Exte
rnalReportWSSService?wsdl
```

SOAP ScheduleService Connection

Used to run, schedule, and manage BI Publisher jobs.

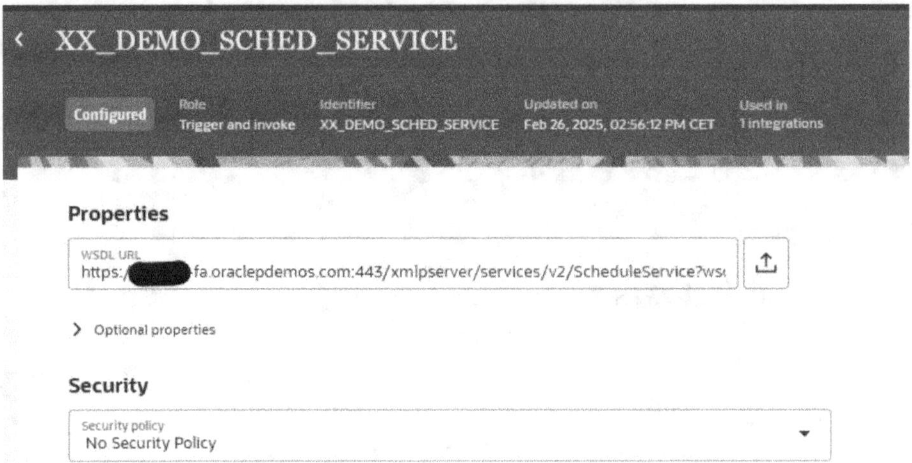

Figure 2-15. ScheduleService Connection

WSDL URL Format

```
https://xxxx.ds-fa.oraclepdemos.com:443/xmlpserver/services/v2/
ScheduleService?wsdl
```

Note This connection does not require a "Security Policy" setting.

SOAP ErpObjectDFFUpdateService Connection

Used to manage descriptive flexfields (DFFs) in ERP Cloud.

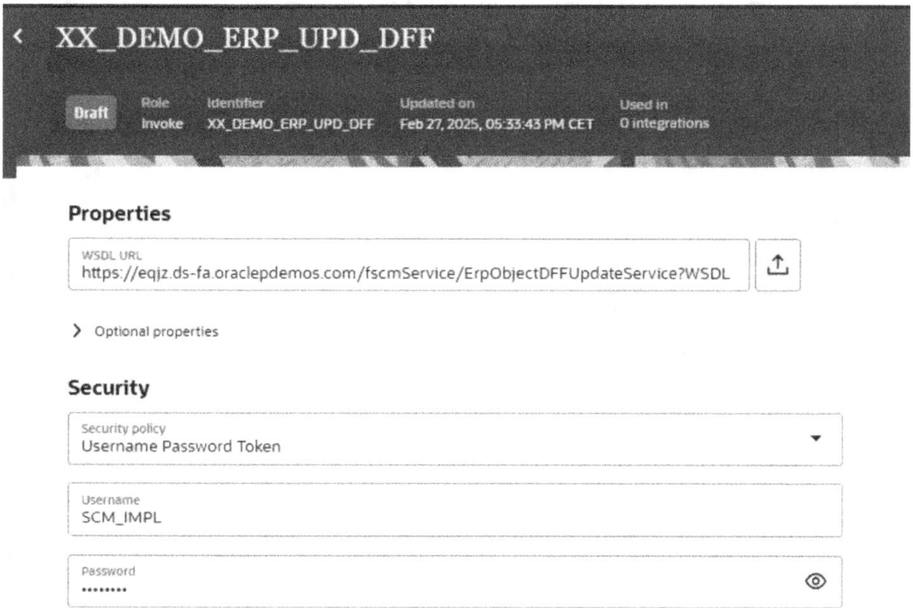

Figure 2-16. *DFF Update Service Connection*

WSDL URL Format

```
https://xxxx.ds-fa.oraclepdemos.com/fscmService/ErpObjectDFFUpd
ateService?WSDL
```

SOAP ErpIntegrationService Connection

Used to manage Oracle ERP Cloud integration jobs.

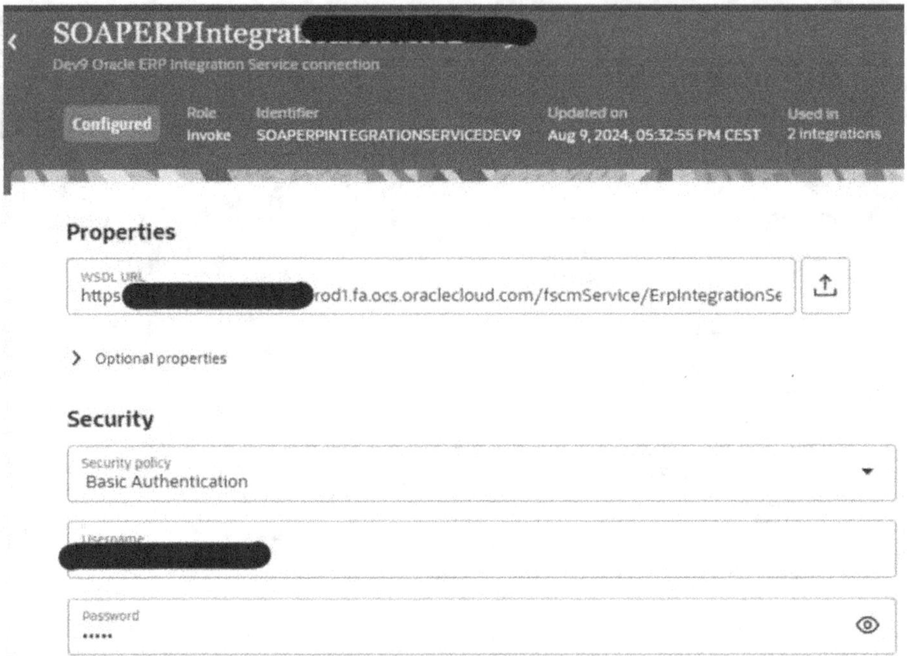

Figure 2-17. ErpIntegrationService Connection

This connection is configured as SOAP to access the web service.

WSDL URL Format

```
https://fa-xxxx-saasfaprod1.fa.ocs.oraclecloud.com/fscmService/
ErpIntegrationService?WSDL
```

ATP Database Connection

Note You can obtain a free Autonomous Transaction Processing (ATP) database and other cloud tools by creating an Oracle Cloud Free Tier account at oracle.com/cloud/free.

We'll use an ATP database for various examples. This connection uses our personal cloud environment.

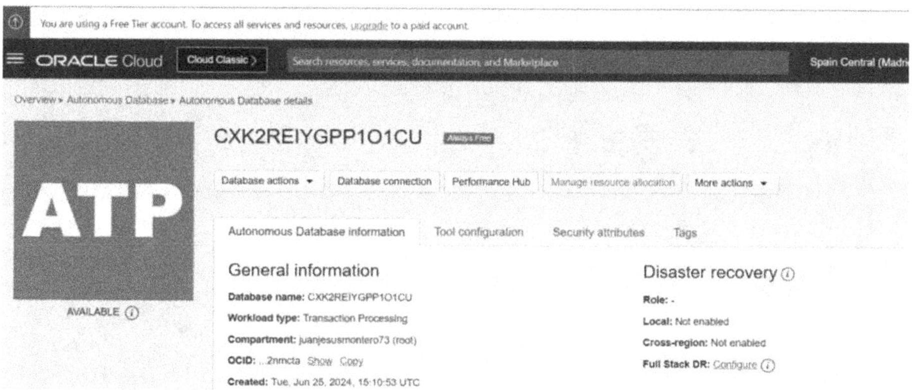

Figure 2-18. *ATP Database Connection—Part 1*

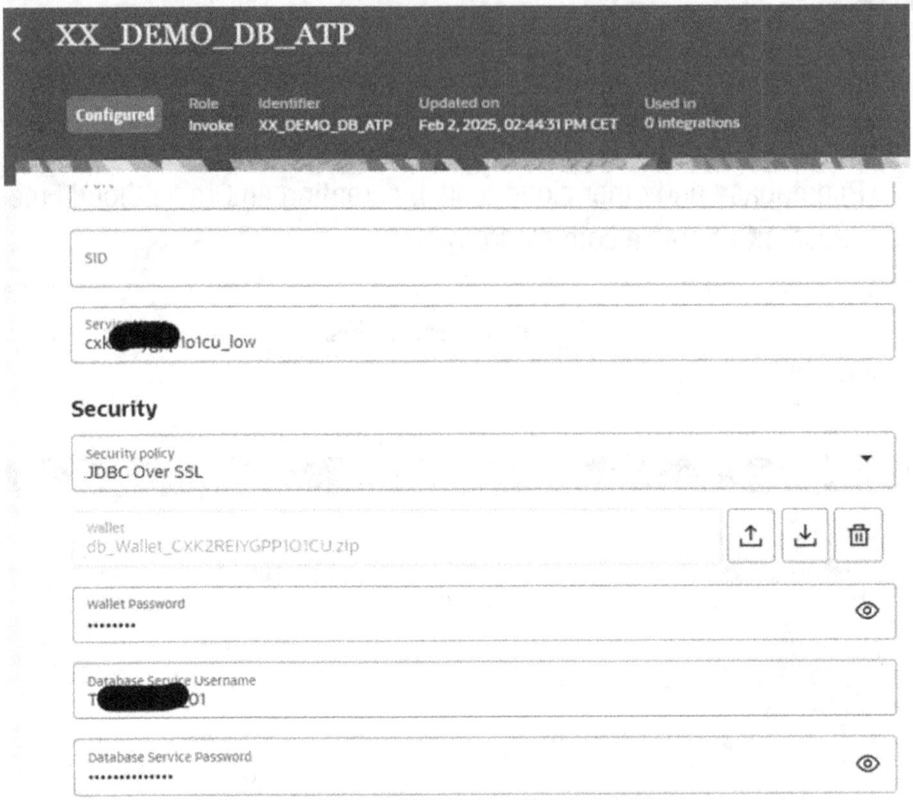

Figure 2-19. *ATP Database Connection—Part 2*

Obtaining the Wallet File and Password

Access the Oracle Cloud Infrastructure (OCI) console and follow these steps:

Step 1: Navigate to your database from the OCI console.

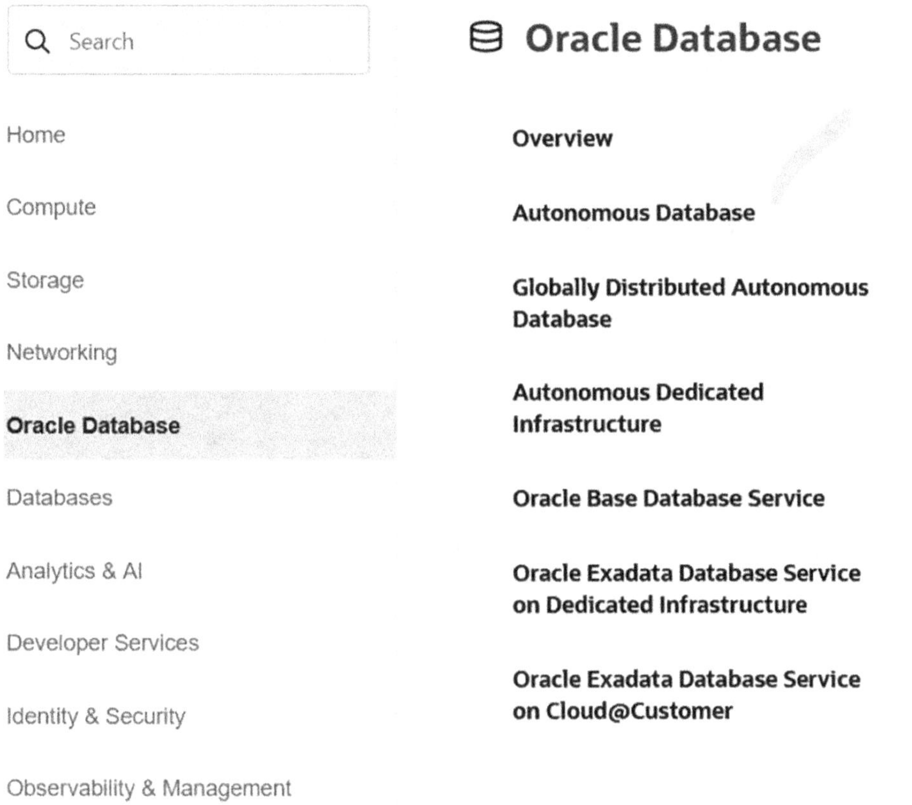

***Figure 2-20.** OCI Console Navigation*

Step 2: Select your database.

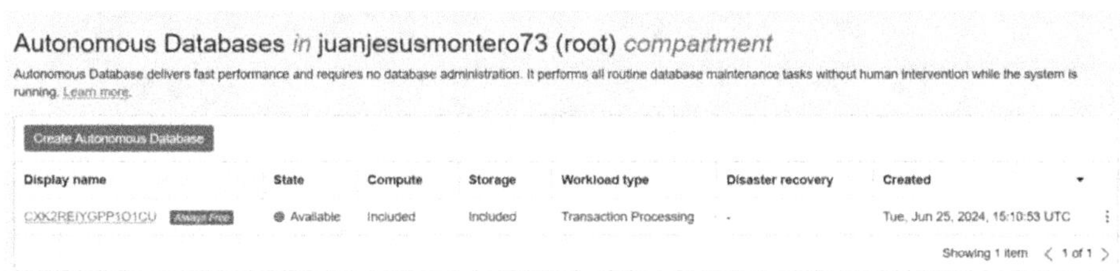

***Figure 2-21.** Database Selection*

Step 3: Click the "Database connection" button.

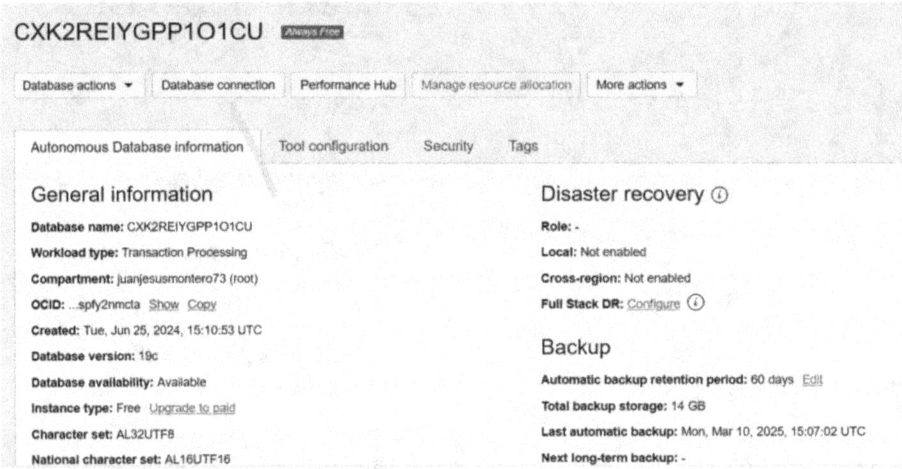

***Figure 2-22.** Database connection Button*

Step 4: Click "Download wallet."

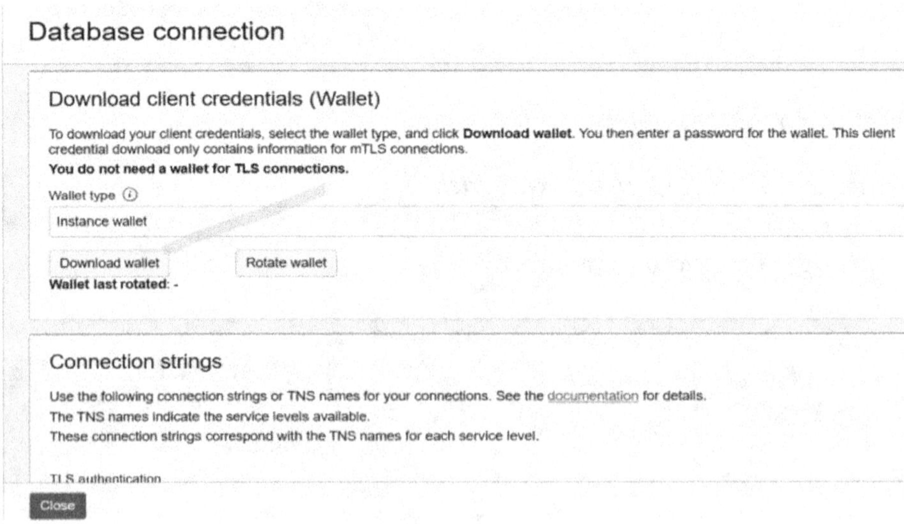

***Figure 2-23.** Download wallet Dialog*

Step 5: Assign a wallet password.

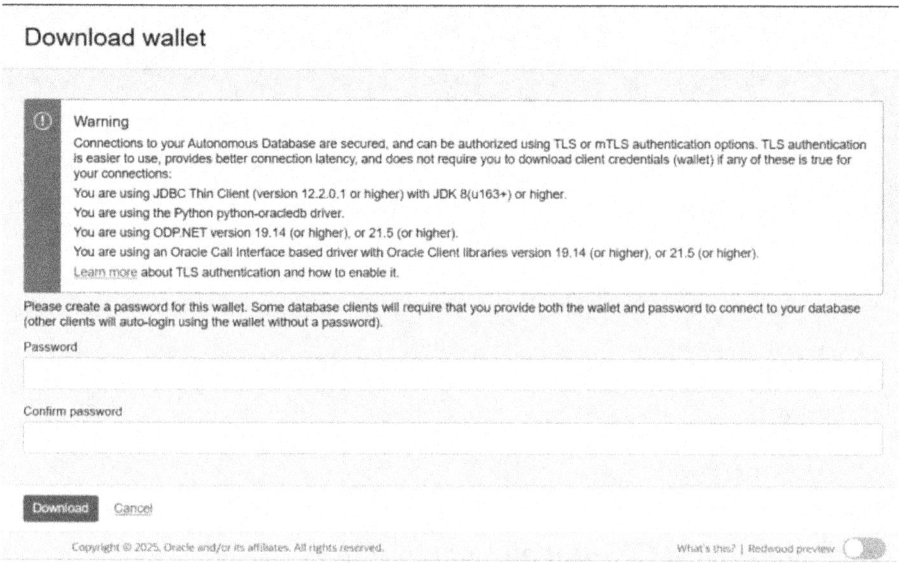

Figure 2-24. *Wallet Password Creation*

OCR Connection

Used for Optical Character Recognition (OCR) services.

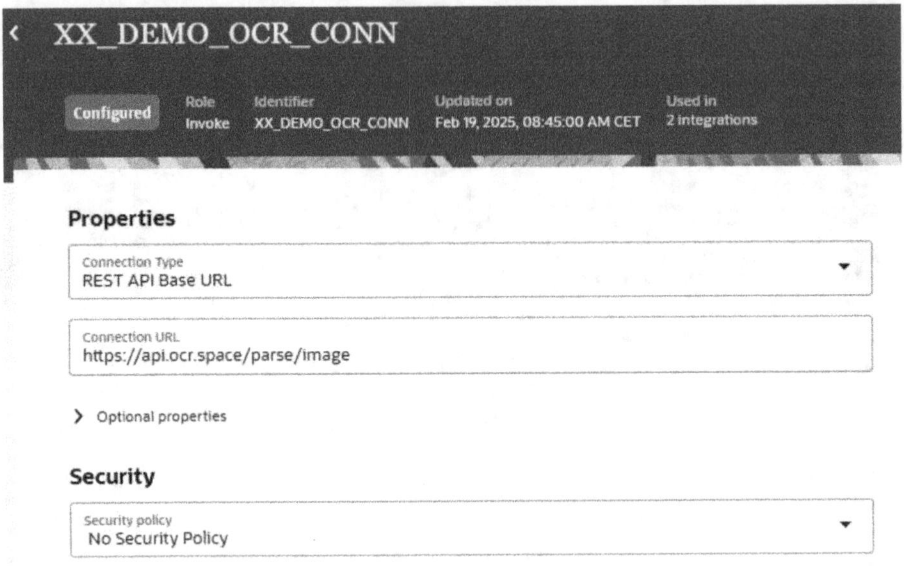

Figure 2-25. *OCR Connection Configuration*

Visual Builder Objects Connection

Set up this OIC connection after your Visual Builder application has been published.

After publishing, retrieve the connection URL as shown below by navigating from left to right in the Visual Builder interface.

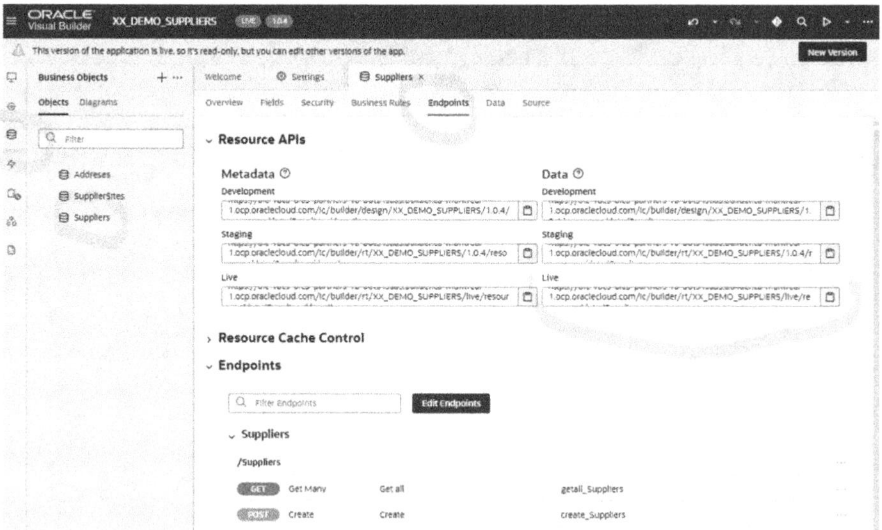

Figure 2-26. *Visual Builder Connection URL*

Example URL

```
https://xxx-vbcs-oic3-partners-vb-bots4saas.builder.ca-
montreal-1.ocp.oraclecloud.com/ic/builder/rt/XX_DEMO_SUPPLIERS/
live/resources/data/Suppliers
```

We typically split this URL into three parts:

For OIC Connection Base URL:

```
https://xxx-vbcs-oic3-partners-vb-bots4saas.builder.ca-
montreal-1.ocp.oraclecloud.com/ic/builder/rt
```

For Endpoint Path (Example):

/XX_DEMO_SUPPLIERS/live/resources/data

For Path Field in Batch Calls (Example):

/Suppliers

Other URL combinations are feasible, but these components form building blocks for constructing your API calls.

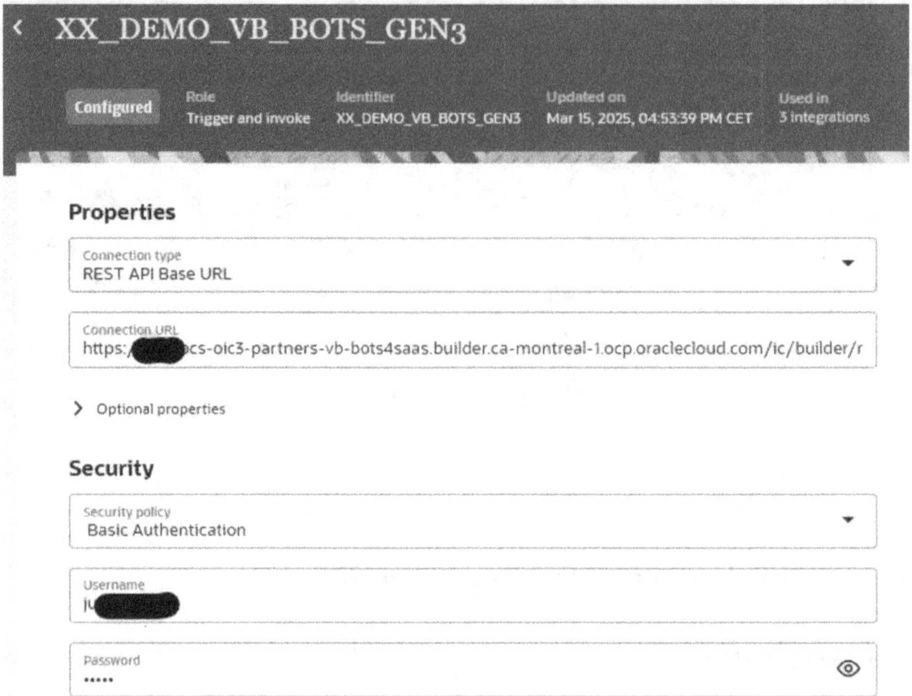

Figure 2-27. *Visual Builder Connection Setup in OIC*

Object Storage Connection

Note Oracle provides free Object Storage with an Oracle Cloud Free Tier account.

See Chapter 20 dedicated to Object Storage for detailed connection setup and useful implementation tips.

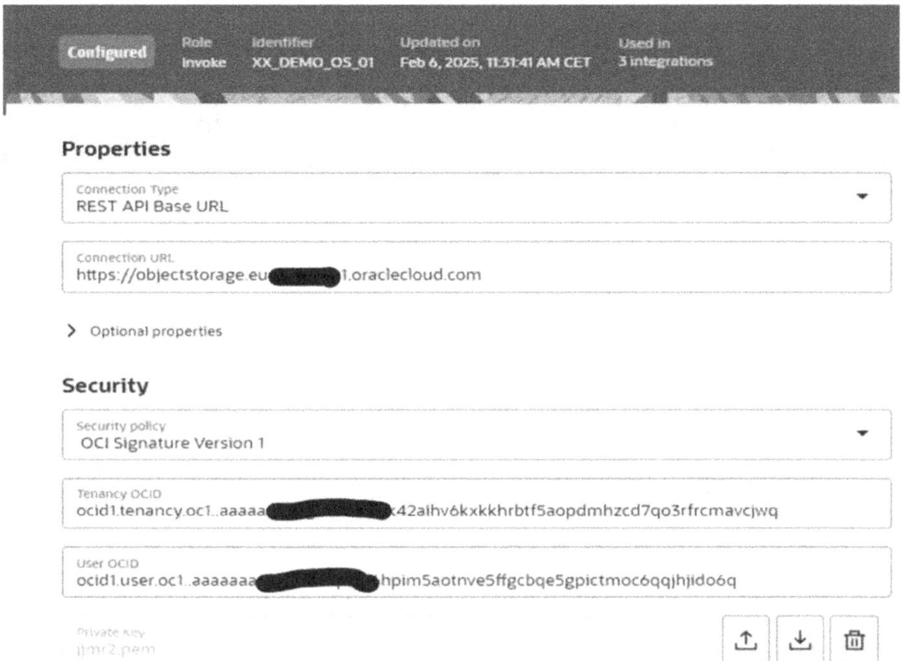

Figure 2-28. *Object Storage Connection Configuration*

REST API for ERP Integrations Connection

This connection uses the ERP Integrations REST API endpoint.

Reference Documentation

ERP Integrations POST Operation

API URL Format

```
https://xxxx-test.fa.em2.oraclecloud.com/fscmRestApi/
resources/11.13.18.05/erpintegrations
```

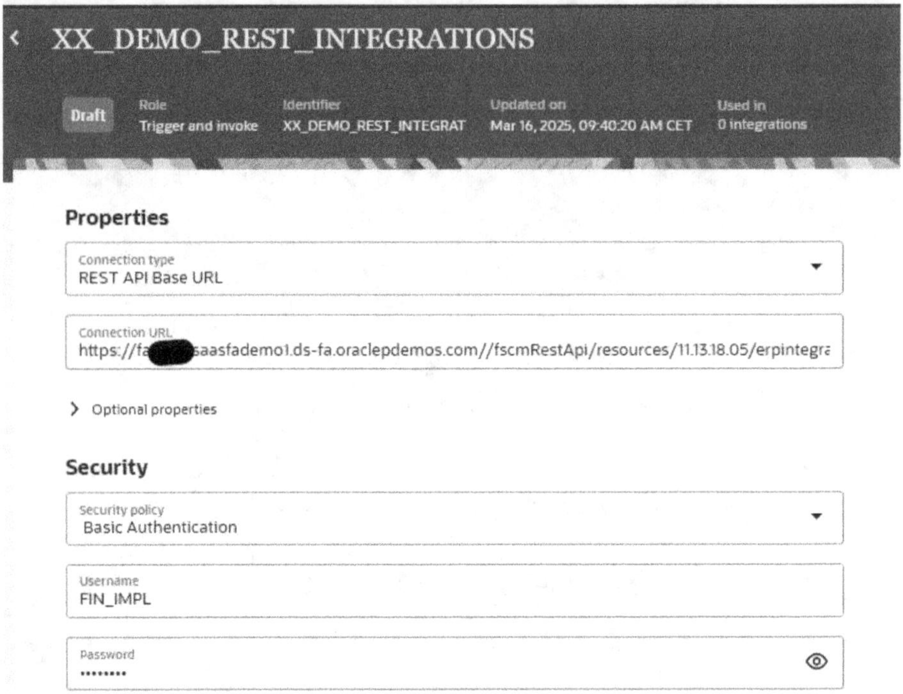

Figure 2-29. *ERP Integrations REST Connection*

CHAPTER 3

Application Integration Types and Fault Handlers

Before we start building integrations in OIC Gen3, let's understand briefly the concept of projects.

Understanding OIC Gen3 Projects

What Is a Project?

A project is a logical, governance-driven grouping of Oracle Integration Cloud Gen3 artifacts including

- Integrations
- Connections
- Lookups
- Insight models
- B2B (Business-to-Business) flows

J. J. Montero Rodríguez and S. Tahseen, *Oracle Integration Cookbook for Oracle ERP Cloud*, https://doi.org/10.1007/979-8-8688-3020-4_3

Projects are implemented within an OCI-native, containerized runtime to deliver a defined business capability or integration objective. They align to a business domain or integration use case and improve manageability and traceability.

What a Project Is NOT

✗ Not a single integration flow

✗ Not a tenant or instance

✗ Not just a folder or UI construct

✗ Not limited to one adapter or application

Integrations can be built inside projects or independently. More information about projects is shared in Chapter 7.

Integration Patterns in OIC Gen3

OIC Gen3 supports three primary integration patterns:

1. **Application integration**
2. **Scheduled integration**
3. **Event-based integration**

Note

1. **Event-based integrations (publish/subscribe)** cannot be created inside a project.
2. **B2B trading partner mode** integrations are not supported within projects—only B2B standalone mode is.

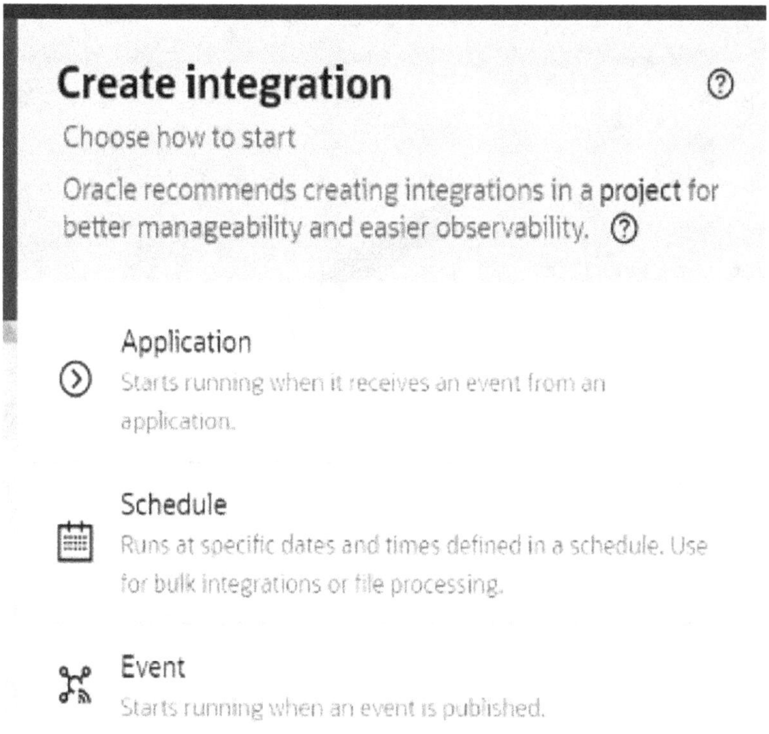

Figure 3-1. *Integration Pattern Selection*

Building Your First Application Integration

Preparation: Obtaining a Test Payload

For this demonstration, we'll use a REST API to retrieve sample data. If you need a refresher on REST basics, please review the Appendix.

Sample API Endpoint

```
https://zzz.oraclepdemos.com/fscmRestApi/resources/11.13.18.05/
purchaseOrders?onlyData=true&limit=5&expand=lines
```

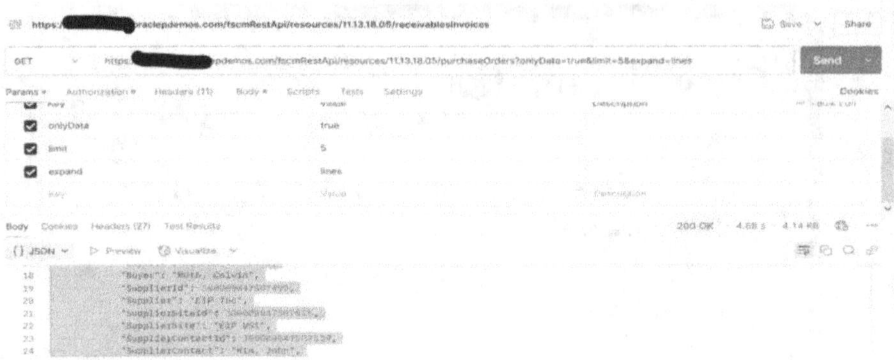

Figure 3-2. *Postman Test Request*

Keep the resulting payload from Postman available for the next steps.

Reference File: rest_sample_purchase_orders.json

Step 1: Create the Integration Inside Your Project

Provide a name for your integration: XX_DEMO_BASIC_01.

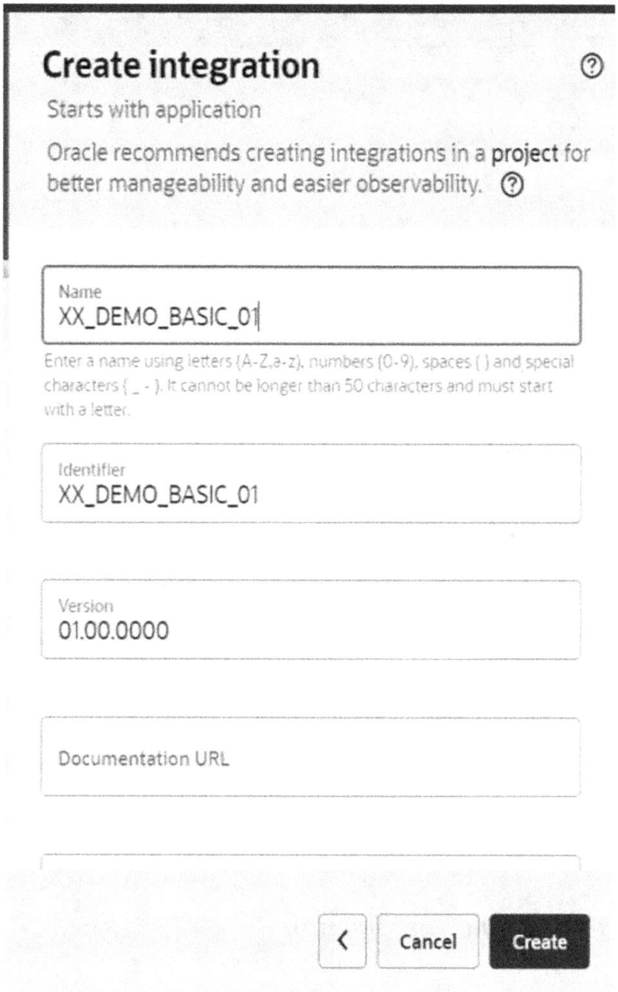

Figure 3-3. *Create integration Dialog*

Step 2: Configure the REST Trigger

When the configuration window opens, select your REST connection.

Figure 3-4. *Connection Selection*

Assign an endpoint name.

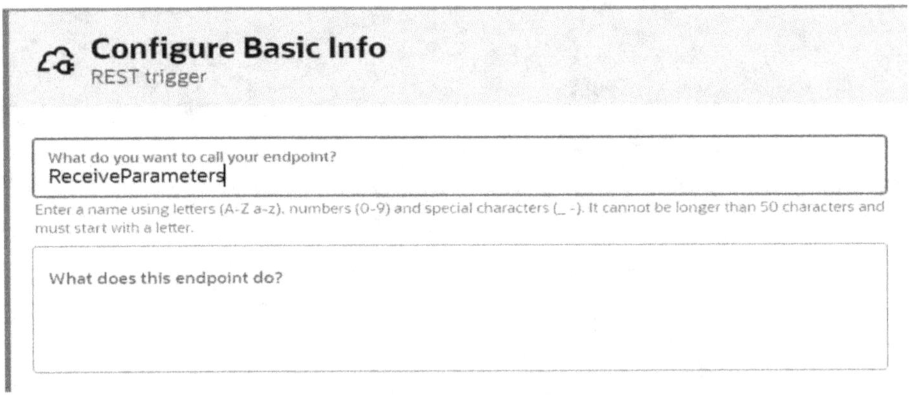

Figure 3-5. *Endpoint Configuration*

Click **Continue** and fill in the following configuration.

Note We'll use the POST action for convenience, as POST allows complex payloads for testing purposes.

Select the checkboxes to configure both request and response payloads.

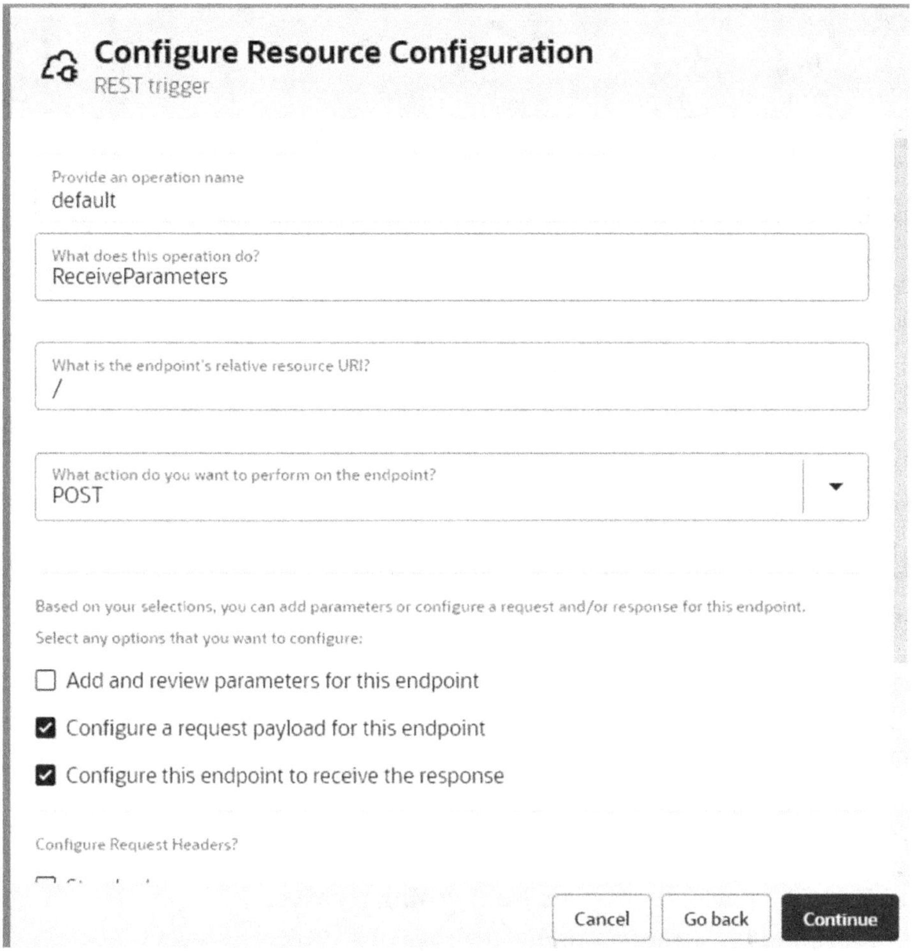

Figure 3-6. *Request and Response Configuration*

Step 3: Define the Request Payload

Click the link as shown to define the request payload structure.

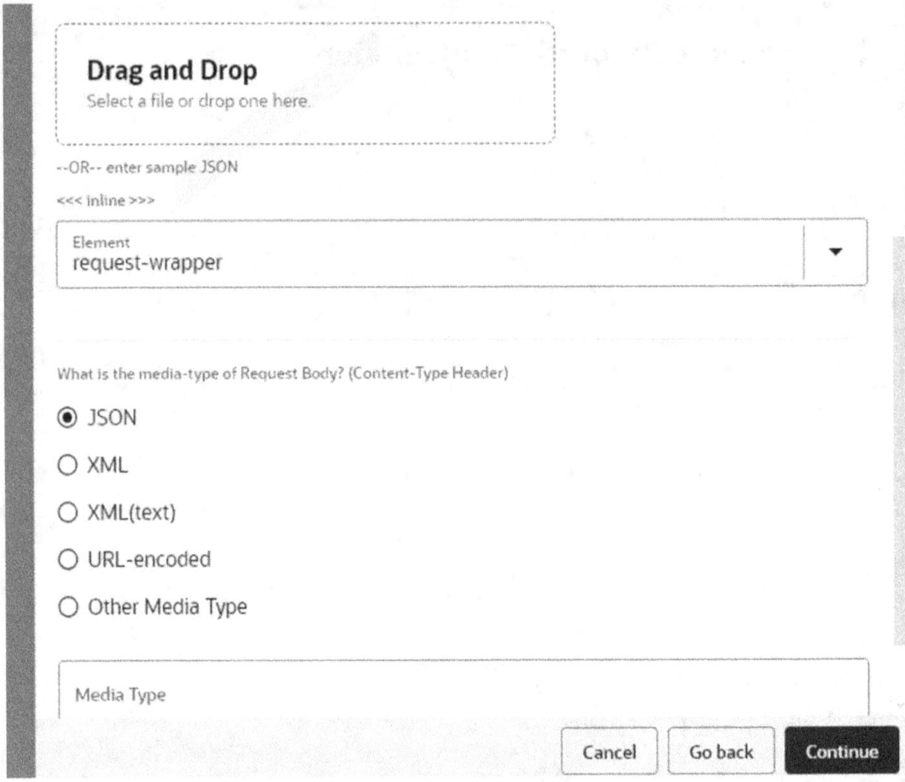

Figure 3-7. *Request Payload Link*

Paste the payload obtained from Postman earlier.

Sample File: sample_purchase_orders_rest.json

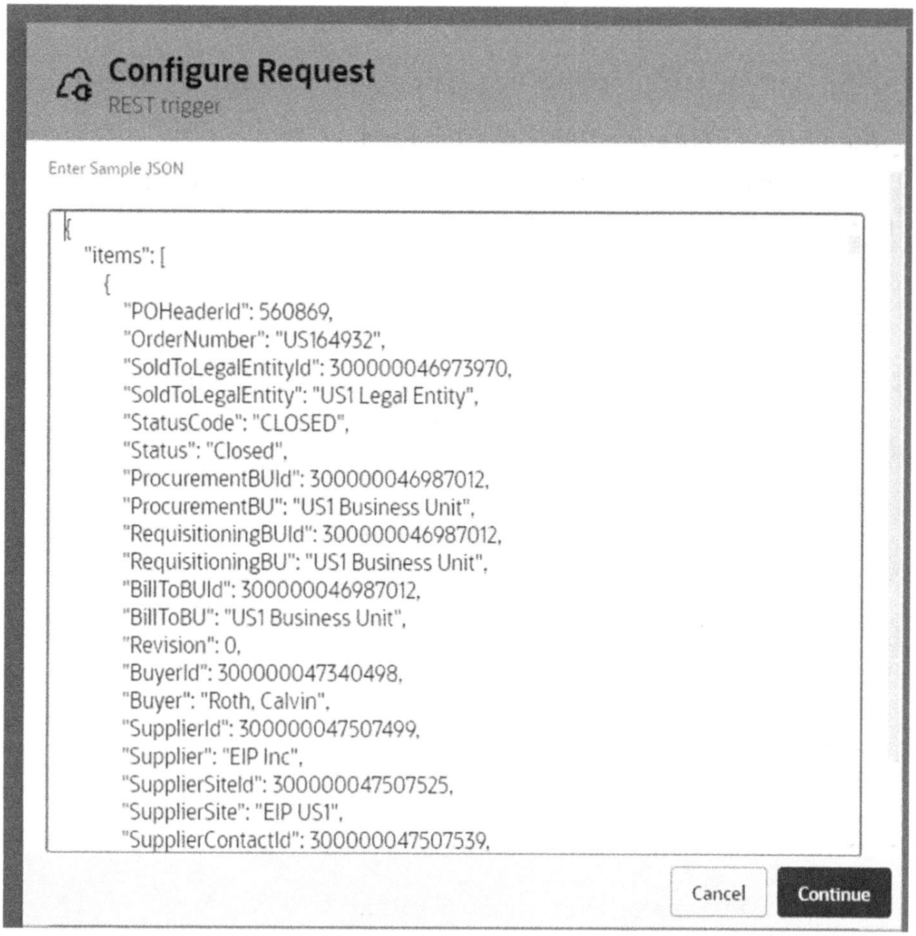

Figure 3-8. *Paste the Request Payload*

By providing a sample payload, we've enabled the integration to

- Generate an internal data structure based on the sample.
- Understand incoming data with the same structure in subsequent requests.

- Allow iteration through data, including child nodes.
- Enable mapping and data manipulation in later steps.

Step 4: Configure the Response Payload

For the response, we'll manually provide a sample payload to demonstrate the output structure.

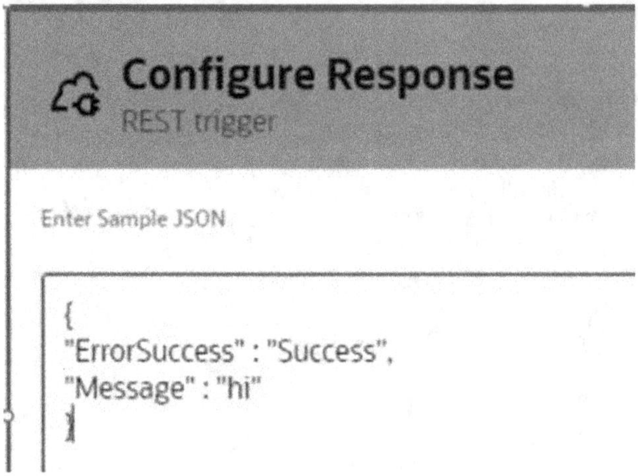

***Figure 3-9.** Response Payload Configuration*

At this point, we have a basic integration that

- Receives parameters in JSON format
- Returns sample dummy data

Step 5: Map the Response Data

Open the response mapping activity.

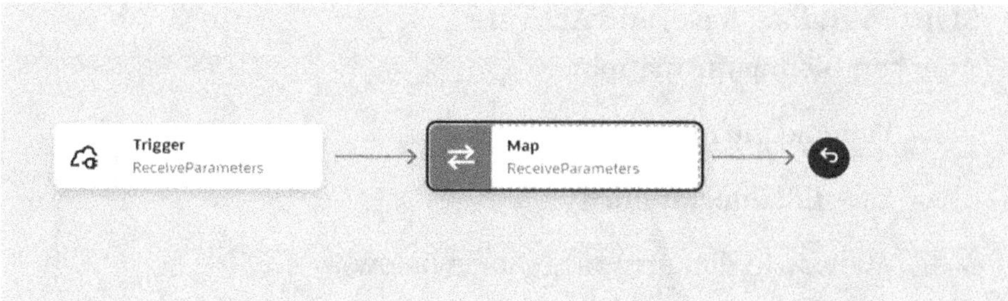

Figure 3-10. *Mapping Activity Location*

Configure the mapping to return dummy data.

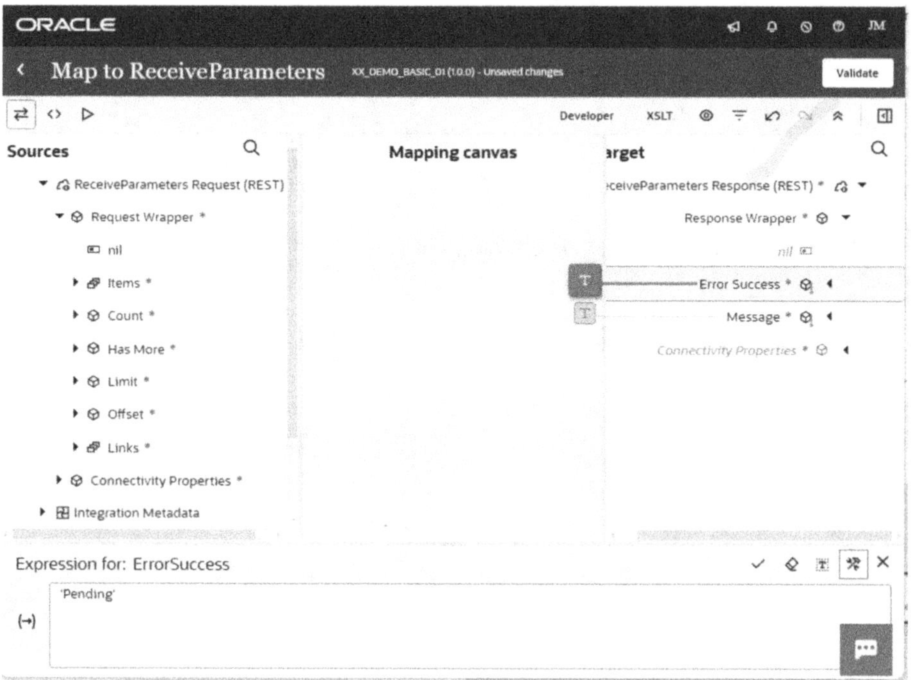

Figure 3-11. *Response Data Mapping*

Step 6: Validate, Save, and Activate

After completing the mapping:

1. Validate the mapping (shown above).
2. Save the integration.
3. Activate in debug mode (shown below).

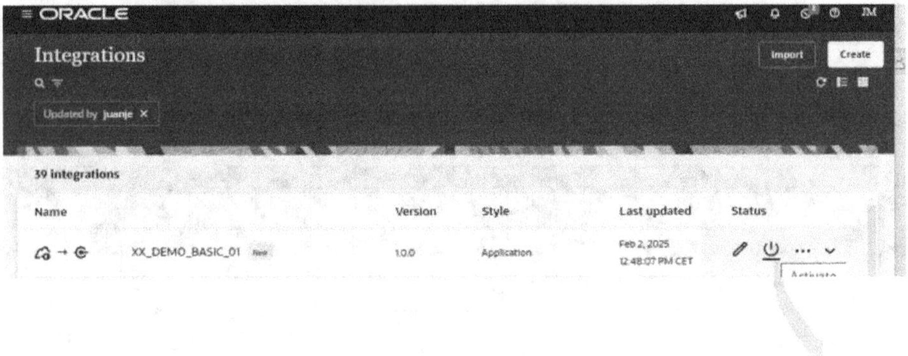

Figure 3-12. Integration Activation

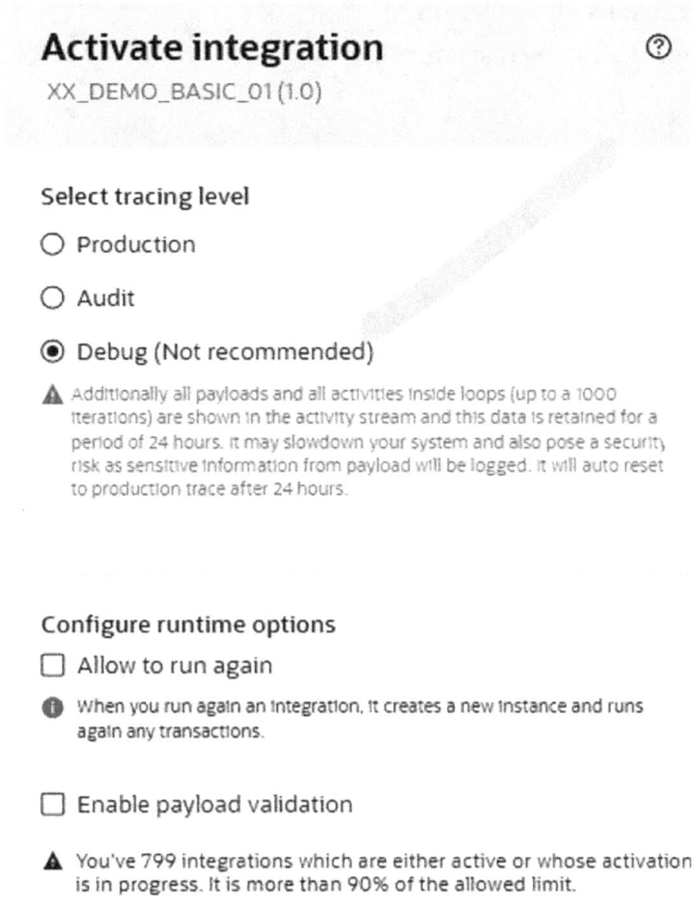

Figure 3-13. *Activation Confirmation*

Step 7: Test the Integration

Run a test using the test console.

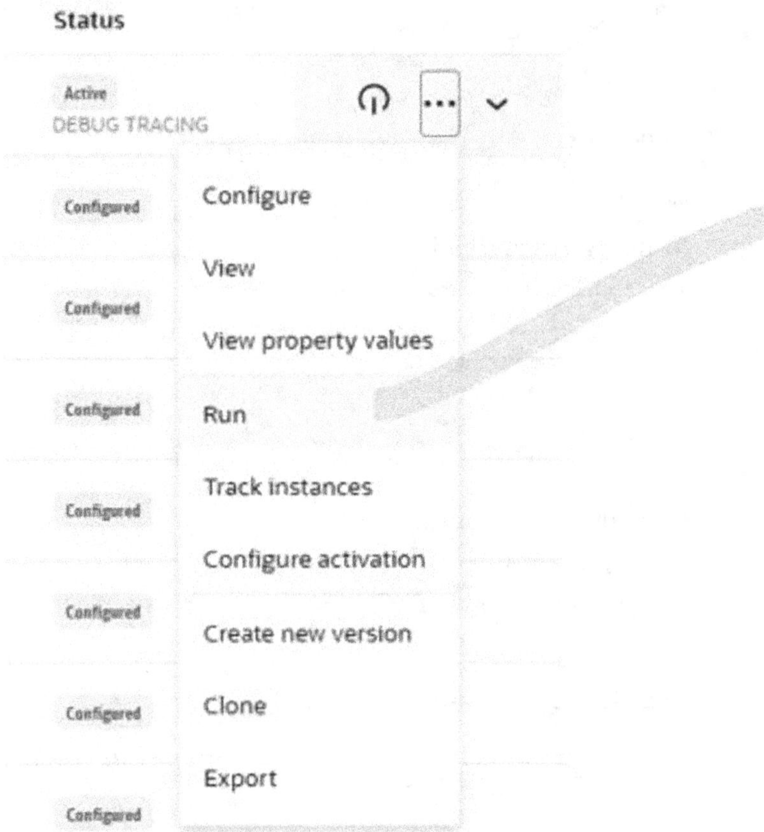

Figure 3-14. *Test Execution*

Review the results in the console.

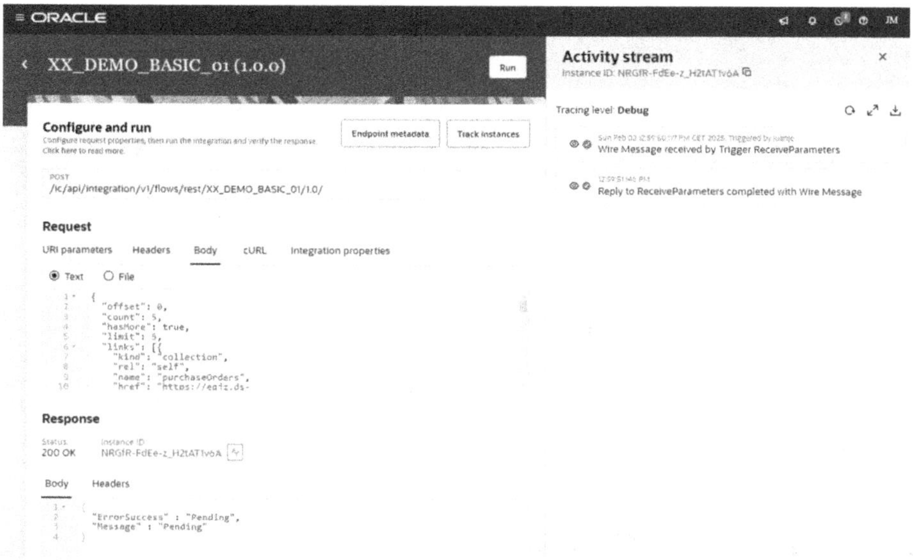

Figure 3-15. *Test Results—Console View*

For a graphical view, click the tracking link.

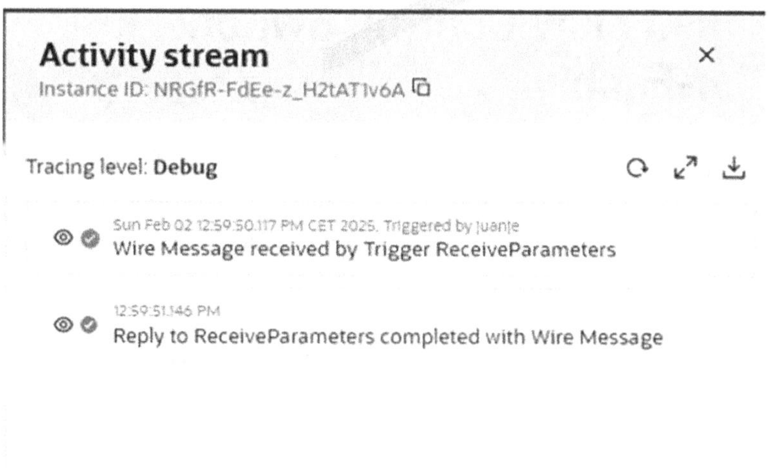

Figure 3-16. *Tracking Link*

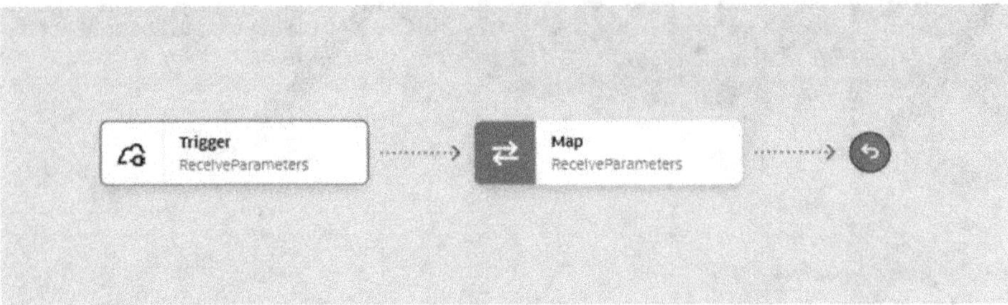

Figure 3-17. *Graphical Flow View*

Green components indicate the actual execution path the integration followed.

Technical Reference

Code Example	Comments
XX_DEMO_BASIC_01.iar	**Package File**: XX_DEMO_COOKBOOK.par

Advanced Flow Control: Switch and For-Each

This example demonstrates how to calculate the total amount of purchase orders for a specific supplier using conditional logic and loops.

Target Supplier We Used Here: "Office Depot"

We'll demonstrate how to

- Initialize variables.
- Loop through purchase orders.
- Apply conditional logic.
- Accumulate totals.

Step 1: Initialize Variables

"Supplier": "Office Depot".	Our example will show how to initialize variables.
	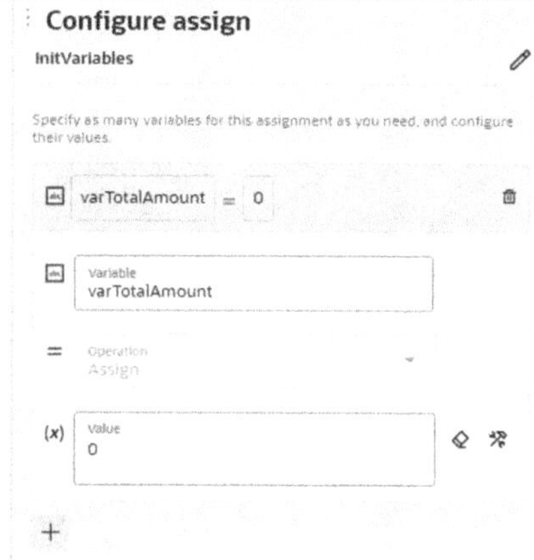

Figure 3-18. Initializing Variables

Step 2: Loop Through Purchase Orders by Adding a For-Each Loop

To iterate through purchase orders from the payload, add a For-Each loop action and assign as shown.

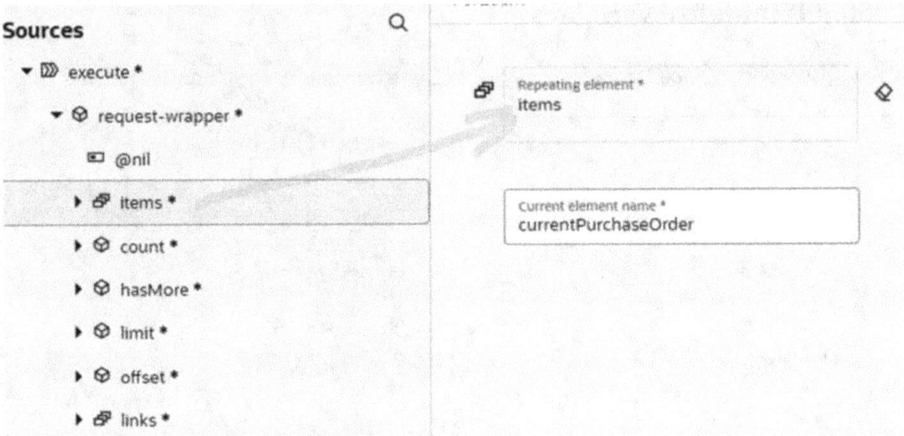

Figure 3-19. *Repeating Element Assignment*

Step 3: Add Conditional Logic with Switch

Use a Switch action to check if the supplier in the current purchase order matches “Office Depot”.

Ask with if the supplier read in variable “currentPurchaseOrder” is “Office Depot” with the action “Switch”.

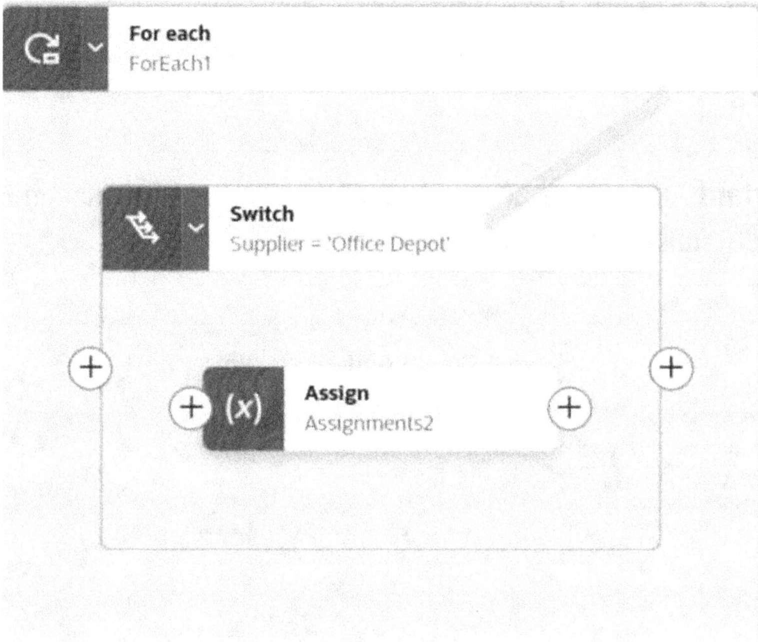

Figure 3-20. *For-Each and Switch Configuration*

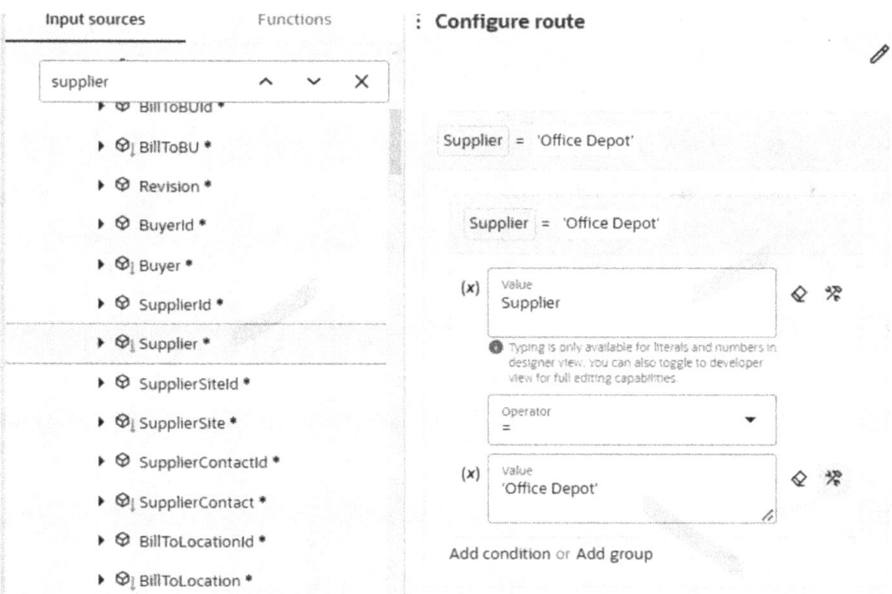

Figure 3-21. *Switch Variable Initialization*

Step 4: Accumulate the Total

Inside the Switch branch, accumulate the total in the varTotalAmount variable.

Important To ensure accurate numerical calculations, use the number() function as shown.

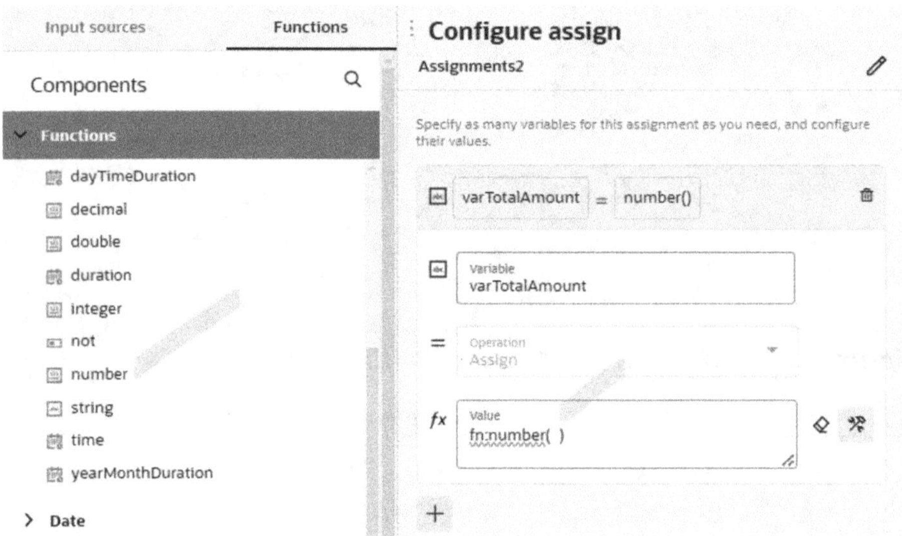

Figure 3-22. *Total Calculation Expression*

Here's the final assignment expression.

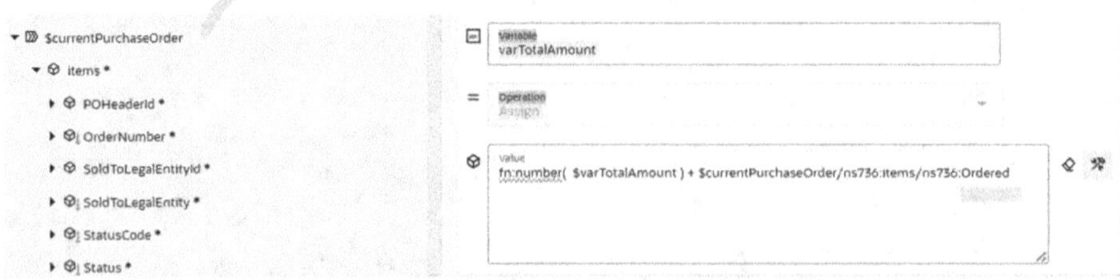

Figure 3-23. *Complete Assignment Using the fn:number() Statement*

Step 5: Assign Total to Response

Map the calculated total to the response variable.

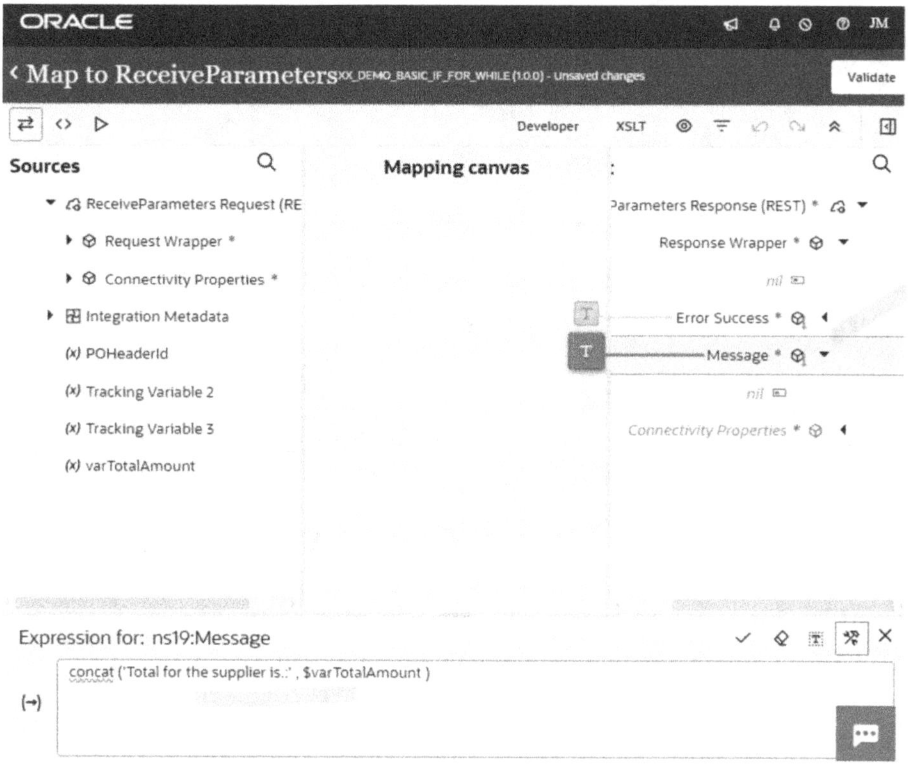

__Figure 3-24.__ Assignment Statement

Final Integration Overview

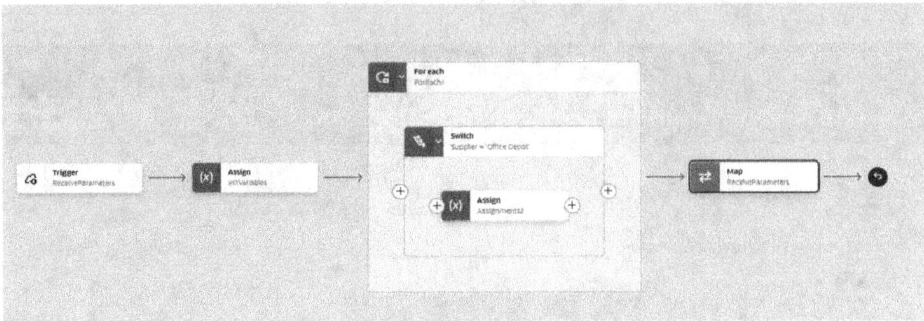

Figure 3-25. *Final Integration Flow*

Testing

Use the sample payload provided in GitHub: sample_for_REST_XX_DEMO_BASIC_IF_FOR_WHILE.json.

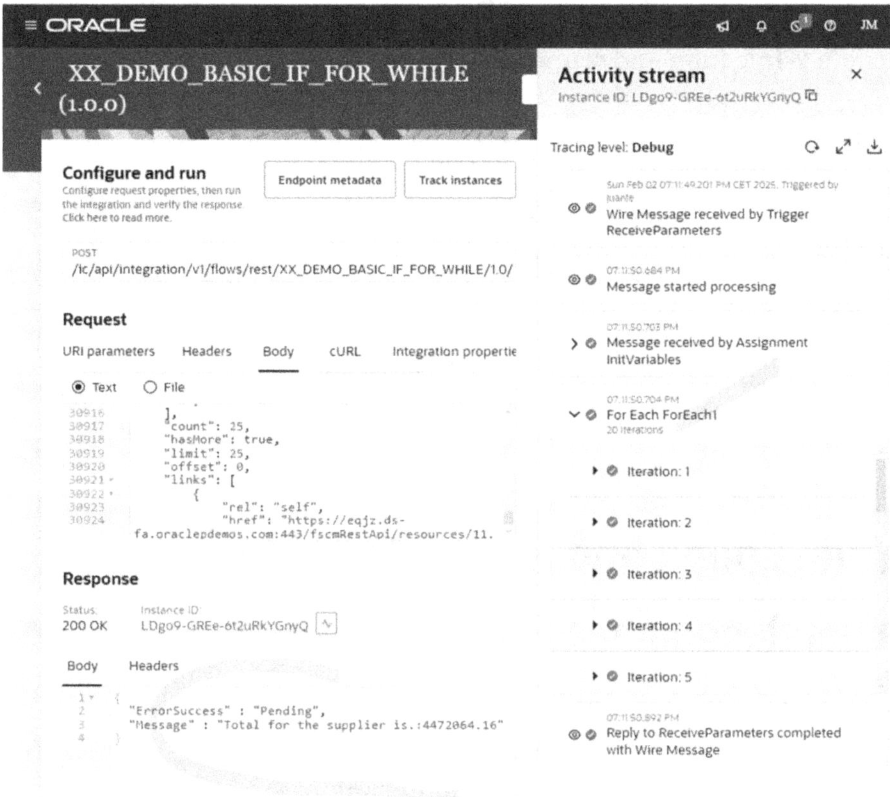

Figure 3-26. *Test Execution Results*

Conclusion

We've explored three fundamental OIC actions in the above section:

1. **Assign**: Variable assignment and manipulation
2. **For-Each**: Iteration through collections
3. **Switch**: Conditional logic (equivalent to if statements in programming languages)

We're going to explore another fundamental OIC action in the next section: **While loop and scope activities**.

Technical Reference

Code Example	Comments
XX_DEMO_BASIC_IF_FOR_WHILE.iar	**Package File**: XX_DEMO_COOKBOOK.par
sample_for_REST_XX_DEMO_BASIC_IF_FOR_WHILE.json	Sample payload for testing

While Loops and Scope Activities

Understanding the Scope Component

Reference Documentation

Using Integrations in Oracle Integration 3

According to above reference documentation:

> *"Scope" in the context of Oracle Integration Cloud (OIC) likely refers to a construct or component within Oracle Integration Cloud that defines a logical unit of work or a boundary for a set of integration-related actions.*

Our Definition

A scope is a component that

- Encapsulates a section of integration logic
- Enables error management through fault handlers

- Provides variable visibility control:
  - Global variables defined outside the scope are accessible within scope.
  - Local variables defined inside the scope are not accessible outside of scope.
- Can be nested for complex error handling scenarios

Demonstration: Retry Logic with the While Loop

This example demonstrates a retry mechanism that attempts to read a file from an FTP server up to three times before stopping.

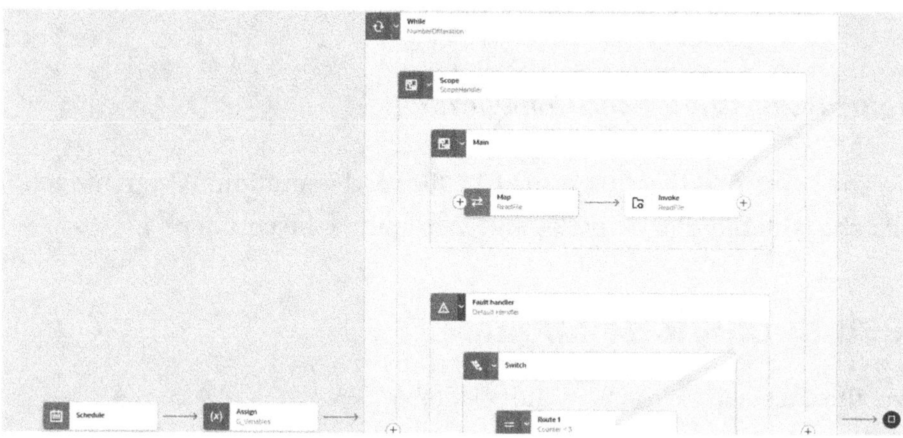

Figure 3-27. *Complete Integration Overview*

How It Works

1. The initial Assign activity initializes a counter variable.
2. A While loop attempts to read the file up to three times.

3. If the file read fails, the fault handler increments the counter.

4. After three failed attempts, the process stops.

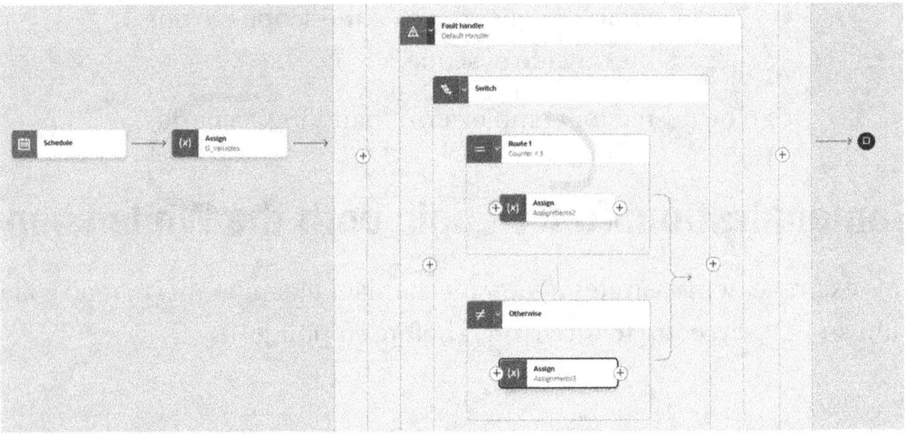

Figure 3-28. *While Loop Configuration*

The "controlled" action is the FTP file read operation. When this action fails, the fault handler activates and increments the counter.

Testing the Retry Logic

Execute a test where the file is not available.

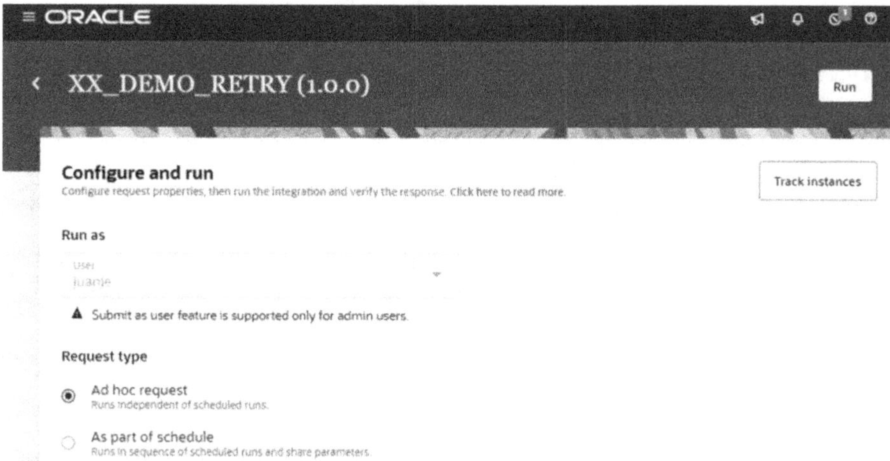

Figure 3-29. *Test Execution*

Notice the behavior after three iterations.

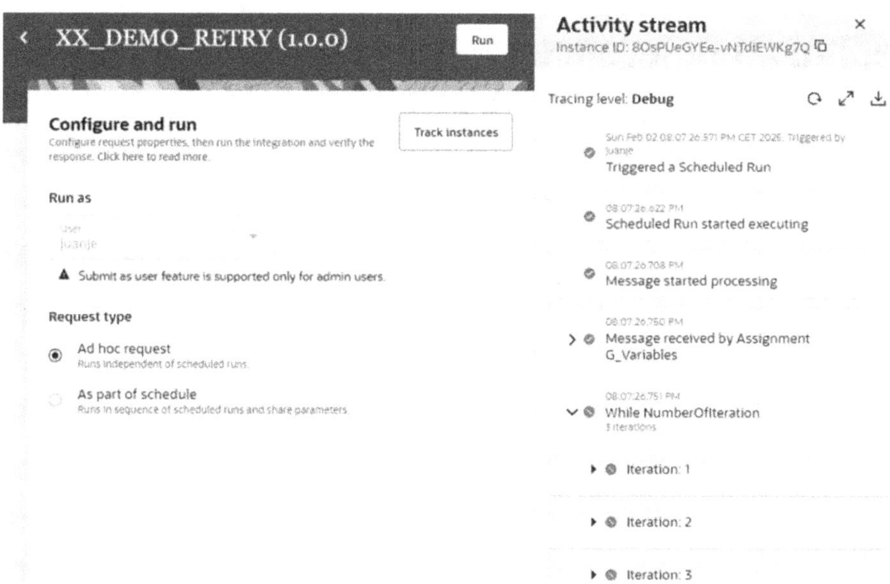

Figure 3-30. *Execution Results After Three Retries*

View the three iterations graphically in the activity stream.

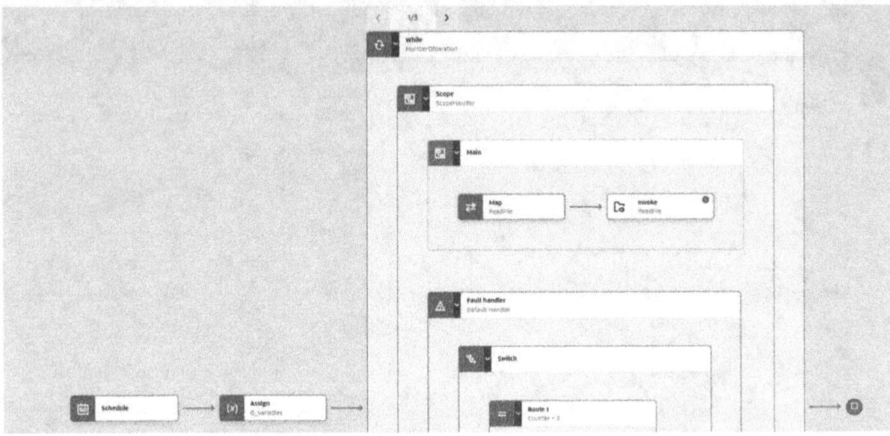

Figure 3-31. *Graphical View of Retry Attempts*

Technical Reference

Code Example	Comments
XX_DEMO_RETRY.iar	**Package File**: XX_DEMO_COOKBOOK.par

CHAPTER 4

Notification and Wait Activities

Overview

The notification feature in OIC provides a flexible way to send emails with optional file attachments. It's particularly useful for alerting users about integration status, errors, or completed processes.

Reference Documentation

- Configure Notification Emails (Oracle Docs)
- OIC Notification Activity (K21 Academy)
- Send Notification with Attachment (TechSupper)

Note The total size limit on a notification email is 1 MB for Oracle Integration (Gen3) and 2 MB for Oracle Integration Generation 2. Both the email body and attachment are considered in calculating the total size.

J. J. Montero Rodríguez and S. Tahseen, *Oracle Integration Cookbook for Oracle ERP Cloud*, https://doi.org/10.1007/979-8-8688-3020-4_4

Configuring a Notification Activity

The setup process is straightforward.

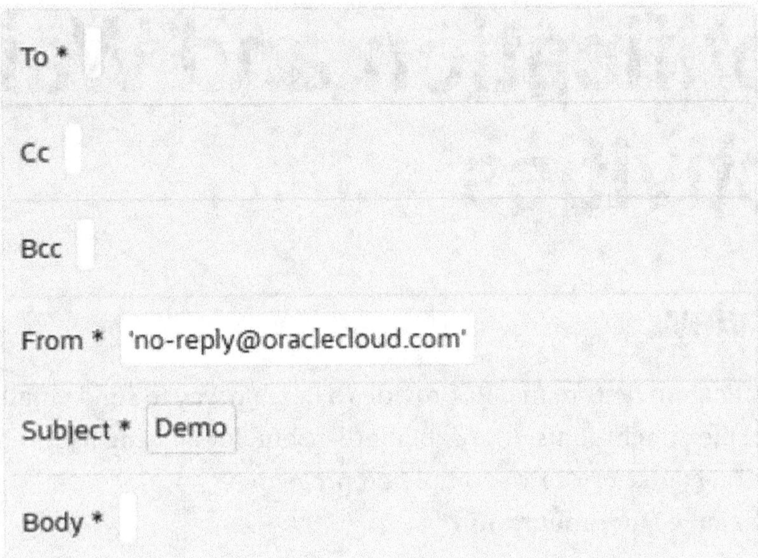

***Figure 4-1.** Notification Activity Configuration*

Configuration Fields

- **To:** Recipient email addresses (separate multiple addresses with commas)
- **From:** Sender email address (recommended: no-reply@oraclecloud.com)
- **Subject:** Email subject line
- **Body:** Plain text or HTML content
- **Attachments (Optional):** File references obtained in previous integration steps

Email Body Options

You can use plain text or HTML for the email body. Both formats support dynamic parameters.

HTML Example

Dear Receiver,

Please find the details of the Integration Run below

Start Time	{StartTime}
End Time	{EndTime}
Flow Id	{FlowId}

Integration Name	Message
Item Inbound Integration	Please find the details of Item Inbound Integration to Oracle and refer to the attached file for more details

Figure 4-2. *HTML Body with Parameters*

Basic Notification Demo

Preparation

Set up the integration with a Wait activity and two Assign variable activities.

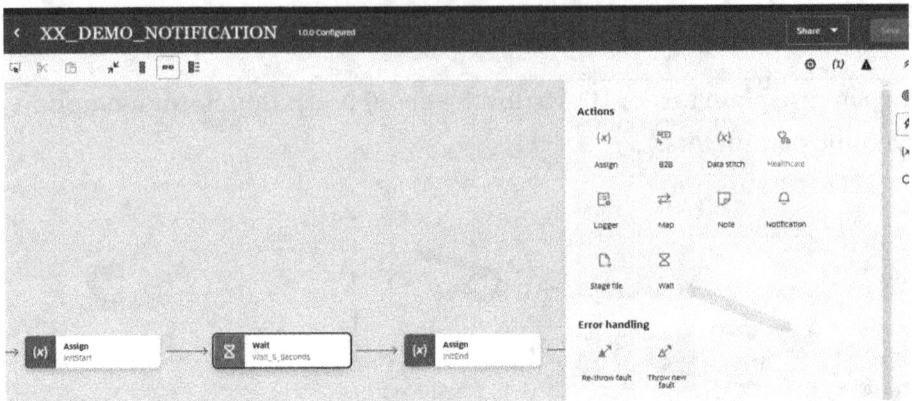

Figure 4-3. Integration Flow Setup

Notification Activity Setup

Configure the notification with recipient and content details.

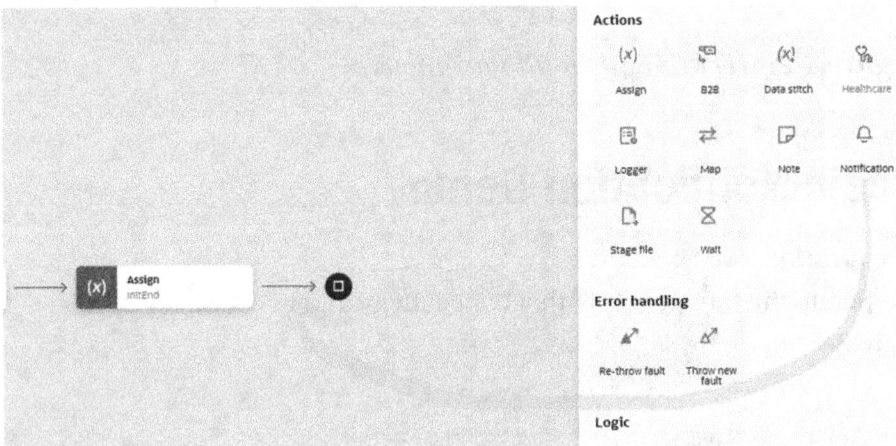

Figure 4-4. Notification Details

Assign Parameters

Map the variables to the email parameters.

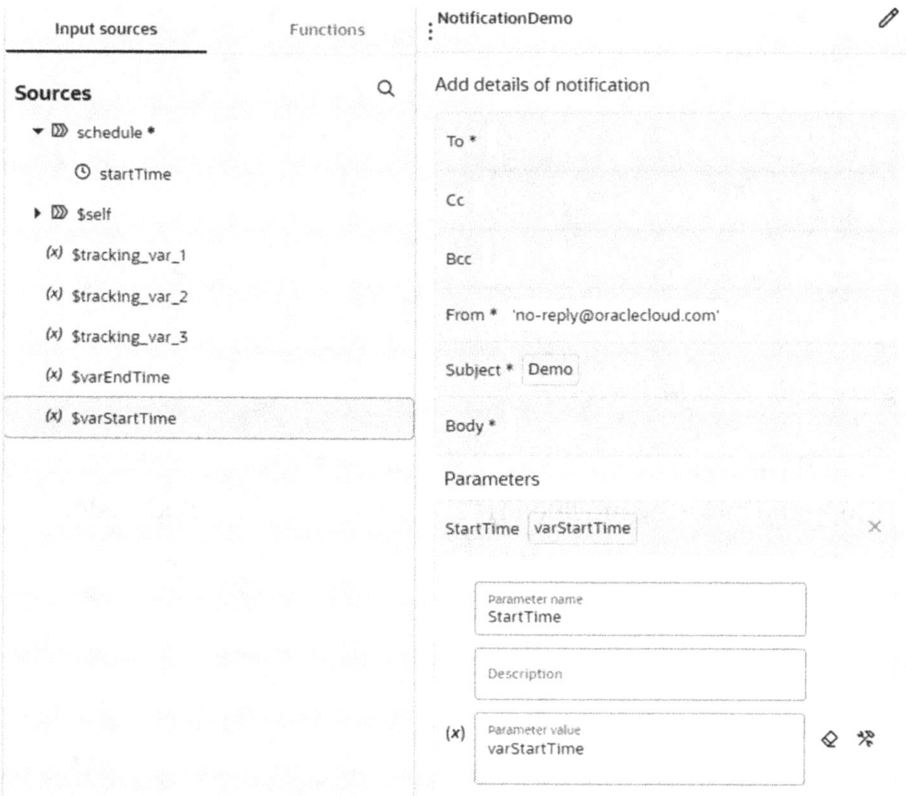

***Figure 4-5.** Parameter Mapping*

To retrieve the FlowId, follow this path.

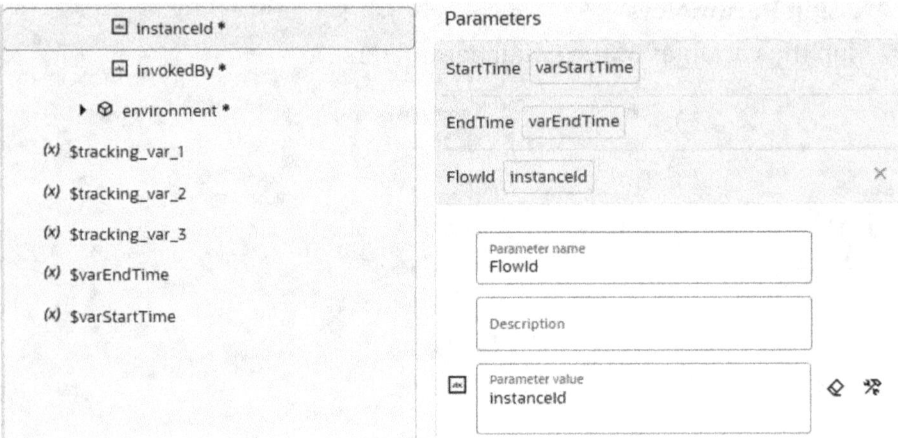

Figure 4-6. *FlowId Location*

Add HTML Body

Copy and paste the provided HTML template into the Body field.

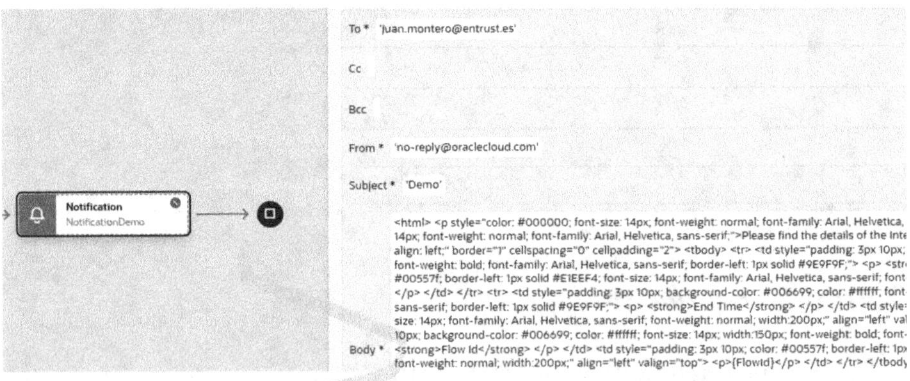

Figure 4-7. *HTML Body Configuration*

Activate and Test

Activate the integration and execute a test.

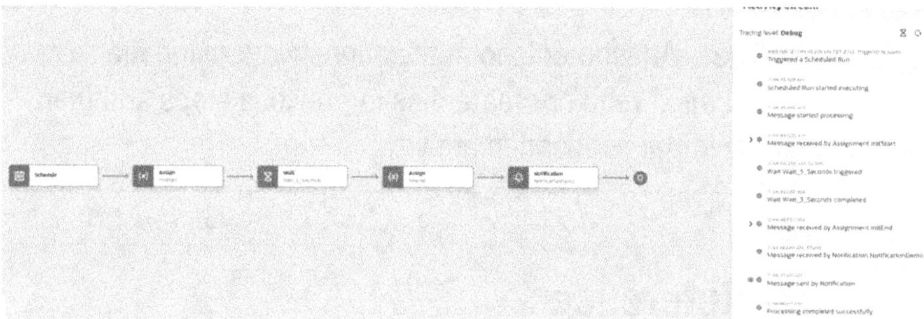

Figure 4-8. *Execution Flow*

Email Result

The recipient will receive an email like the following.

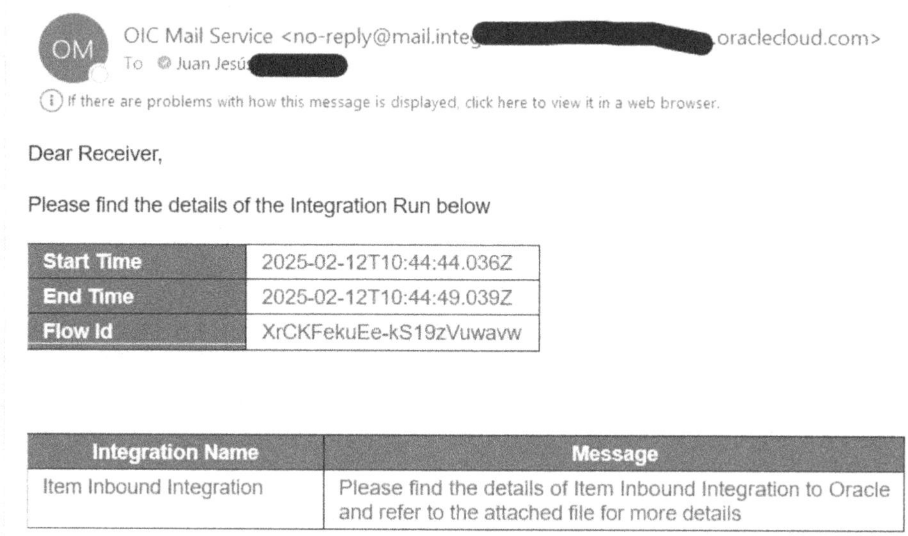

OIC Mail Service <no-reply@mail.inte[redacted].oraclecloud.com>
To Juan Jesú[redacted]

If there are problems with how this message is displayed, click here to view it in a web browser.

Dear Receiver,

Please find the details of the Integration Run below

Start Time	2025-02-12T10:44:44.036Z
End Time	2025-02-12T10:44:49.039Z
Flow Id	XrCKFekuEe-kS19zVuwavw

Integration Name	Message
Item Inbound Integration	Please find the details of Item Inbound Integration to Oracle and refer to the attached file for more details

Figure 4-9. *Sample Email Output*

Working with Attachments

For learning purposes, you can combine this example with the Stage file example to send email attachments.

Important Note Attachments in notifications work using file references. You must read or create files in previous steps and then reference them in the notification activity.

Technical Reference

Code Example	Comments
chapter_07_html.txt	Sample HTML template used in demo (contains three parameters to configure)
XX_DEMO_NOTIFICATION.iar	**Package File**: XX_DEMO_COOKBOOK.par

CHAPTER 5

JavaScript in OIC

Overview

Oracle Integration provides extensive out-of-the-box functions for data manipulation and transformation. However, when these standard functions don't meet your requirements, you can create custom JavaScript functions to fill the gaps.

Reference Documentation

Use Libraries to Manage Functions (Oracle Docs)

J. J. Montero Rodríguez and S. Tahseen, *Oracle Integration Cookbook for Oracle ERP Cloud*, https://doi.org/10.1007/979-8-8688-3020-4_5

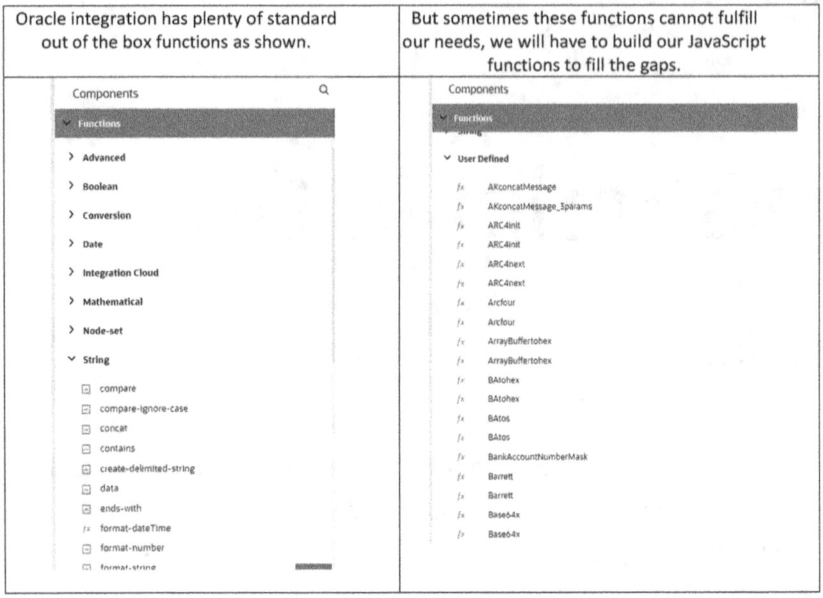

Figure 5-1. *Standard Functions vs. Custom JavaScript*

While OIC provides many standard functions, sometimes you need custom logic. JavaScript libraries enable you to create and reuse custom functions across multiple integrations.

Managing JavaScript Libraries

Access JavaScript libraries from the main menu.

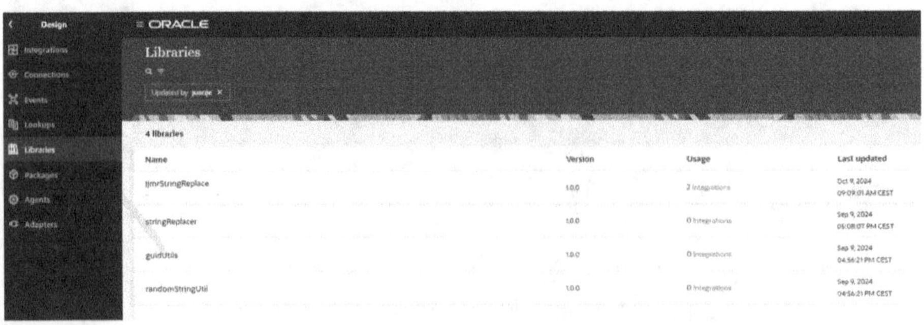

Figure 5-2. *JavaScript Library Menu Location*

Example JavaScript Library

Here's a sample JavaScript function that can be used in OIC.

```
function generateUniqueID() {
    var now     = new Date();
    var year    = now.getFullYear();
    var month   = now.getMonth()+1;
    var day     = now.getDate();
    var hour    = now.getHours();
    var minute  = now.getMinutes();
    var second  = now.getSeconds();
    if(month.toString().length == 1) {
        var month = '0'+month;
    }
    if(day.toString().length == 1) {
        var day = '0'+day;
    }
    if(hour.toString().length == 1) {
        var hour = '0'+hour;
    }
    if(minute.toString().length == 1) {
        var minute = '0'+minute;
    }
    if(second.toString().length == 1) {
        var second = '0'+second;
    }
    var UniqueID = year+''+month+''+day+''+hour+''+minute+''+second;
     return UniqueID;

}
```

Sample JavaScript Code

Uploading a JavaScript Library

Import or Manual Uploading of the JavaScript File

When you import an integration that contains JavaScript libraries, those libraries are automatically imported along with the integration. Oracle recommends creating the libraries inside a project, but we can create them independently also.

Follow these steps to manually upload a JavaScript library:

Step 1: Navigate to the Libraries section in your project and click **Import**.

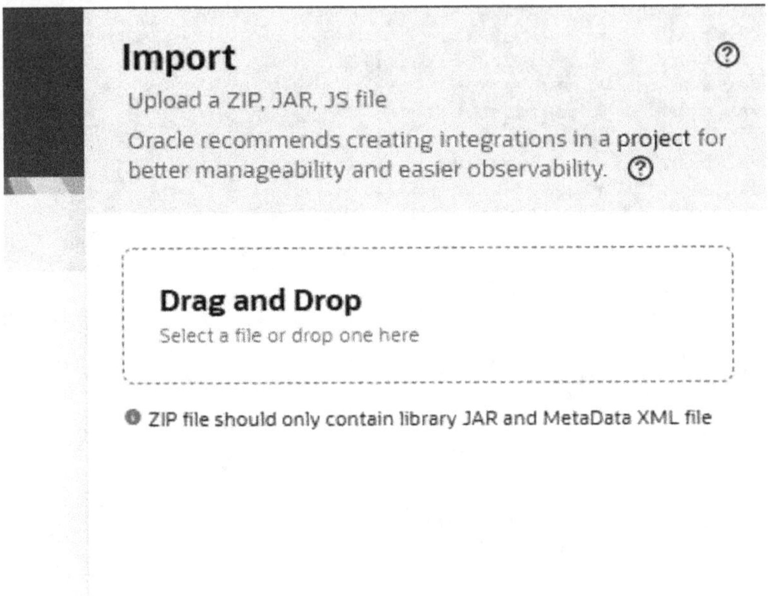

Figure 5-3. *Importing a Library*

Step 2: Select the JavaScript file.

Figure 5-4. *File Selection*

Step 3: Configure library details.

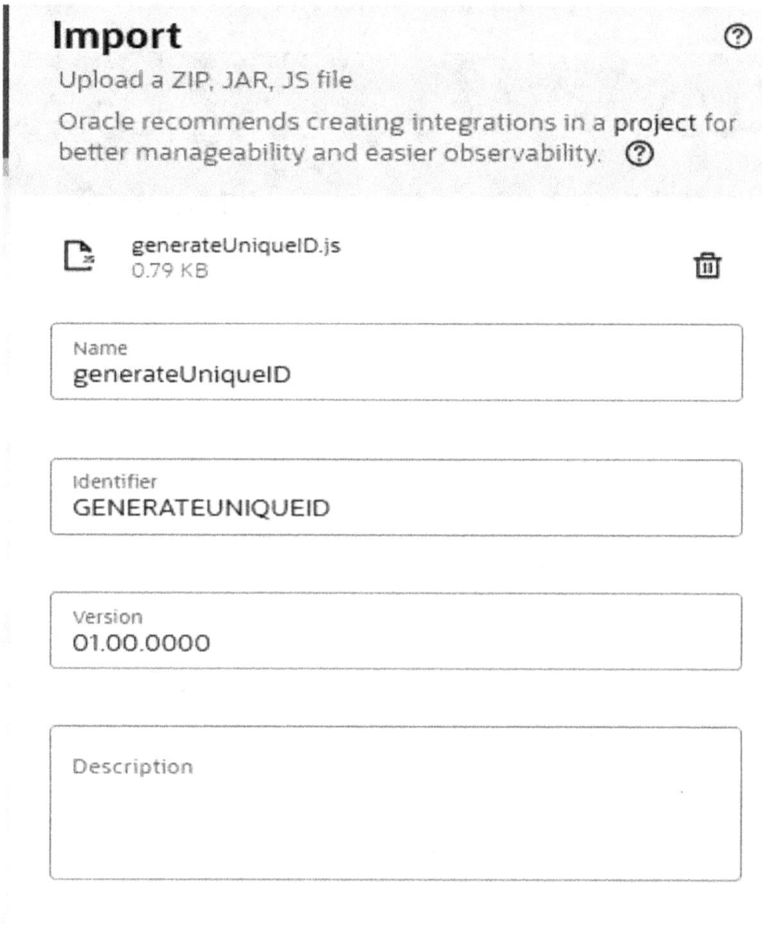

***Figure 5-5.** Library Configuration*

Step 4: Confirm creation.

Click the checkmark to create the library.

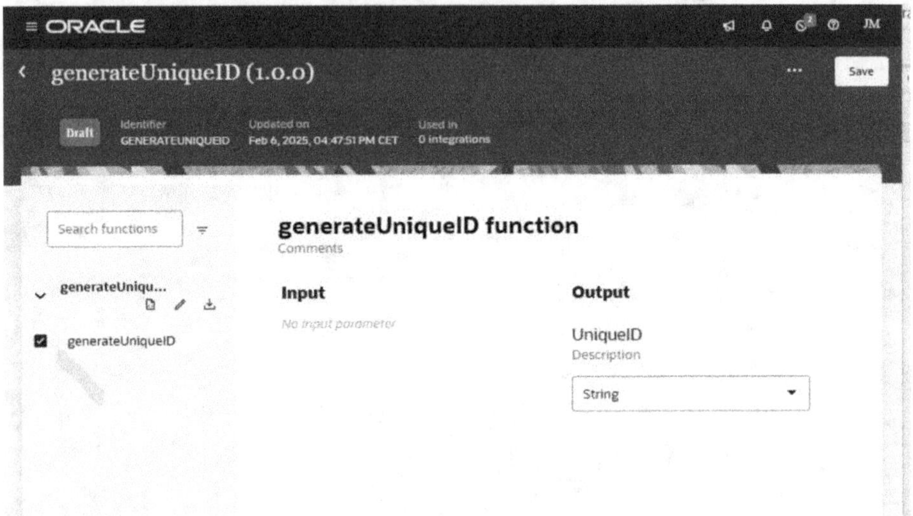

Figure 5-6. *Confirmation*

The library is now created and can be used in integrations like any other standard function.

Note OIC JavaScript functions have some important constraints. They

- Must be synchronous
- Cannot make external HTTP/network calls or perform I/O
- Must follow specific naming and return parameter conventions to be recognized by OIC.

Using JavaScript Functions in Integrations

For demonstration purposes, we'll create a basic integration that uses a custom JavaScript function.

Step 1: Create a Scheduled Integration

Create a scheduled integration and add an Assign activity.

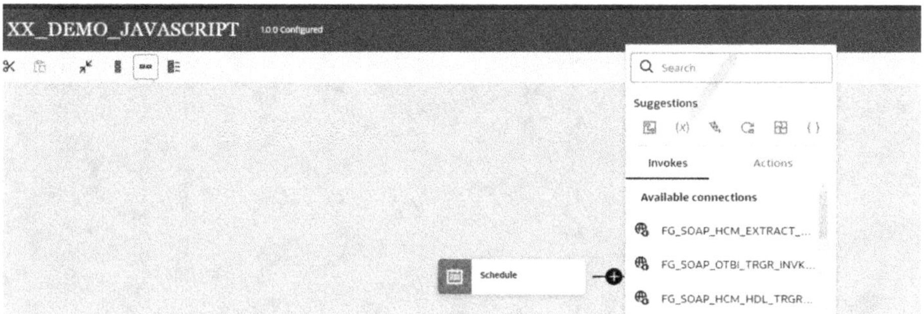

Figure 5-7. Integration with an Assign Activity

Step 2: Select the Custom Function

In the mapping editor, locate and select your custom JavaScript function.

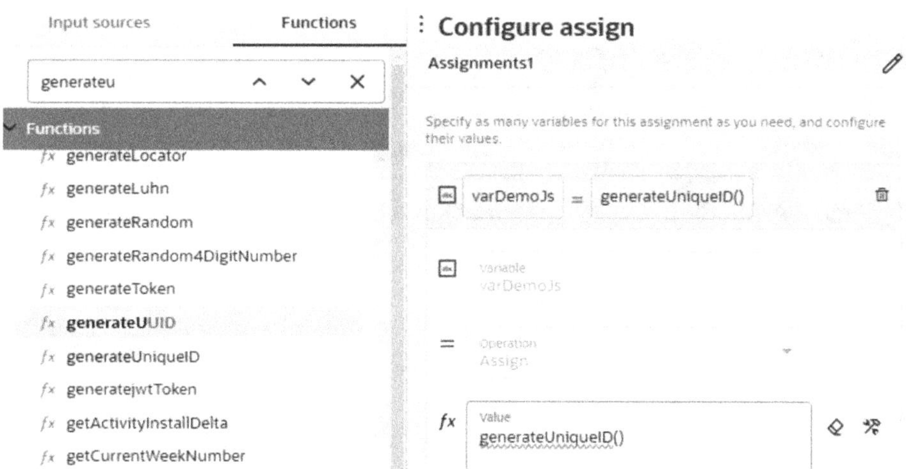

Figure 5-8. Function Selection

Step 3: Test the Integration

Activate the integration and run a test.

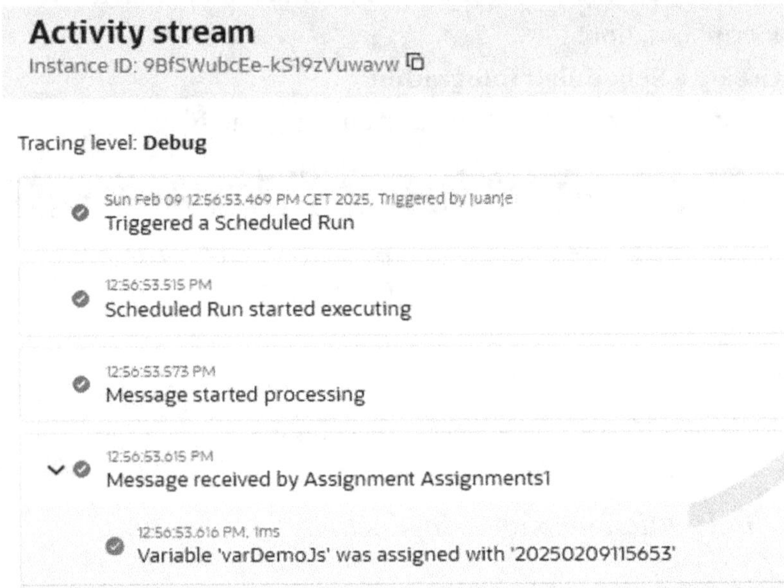

Figure 5-9. *Test Execution Results*

Technical Reference

Code Example	Comments
XX_DEMO_JAVASCRIPT	**Package File**: XX_DEMO_COOKBOOK.par

CHAPTER 6

Mappings and XSLT

What Is XSLT?

XSLT (Extensible Stylesheet Language Transformations) is the language that transforms one XML structure into XML, HTML, and plain text. It uses tags and templates to define the transformation rules.

In OIC, XSLT works behind the scenes for every mapping you create.

Note The OIC mapper supports XSL 2.0. XSL 1.0 is not supported.

Reference Documentation

- Oracle Integration Mapper Guide
- W3Schools XSL Tutorial

J. J. Montero Rodríguez and S. Tahseen, *Oracle Integration Cookbook for Oracle ERP Cloud*,
https://doi.org/10.1007/979-8-8688-3020-4_6

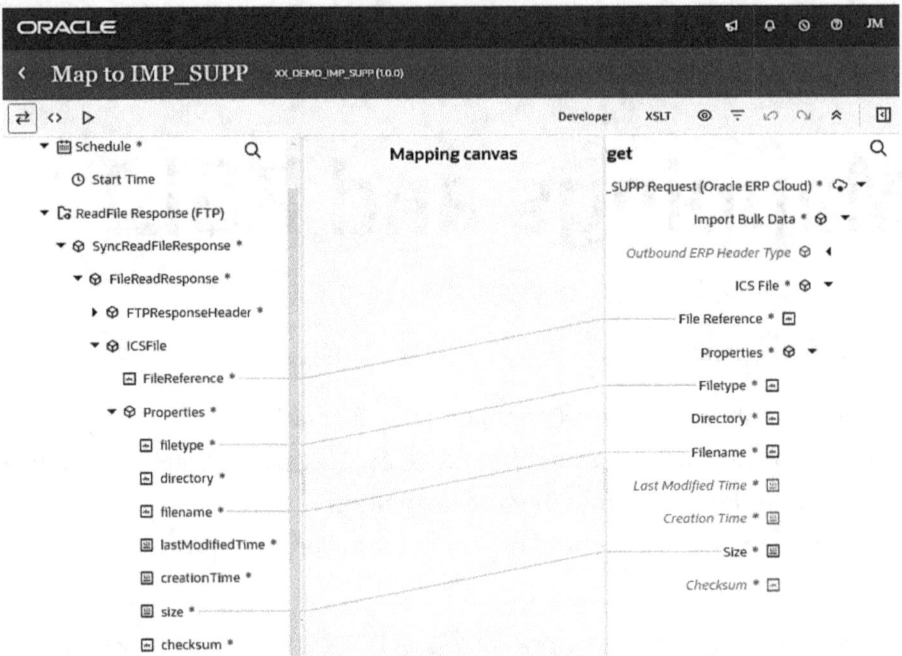

***Figure 6-1.** Mapping Editor Interface*

Simple vs. Complex Mappings

Drag-and-drop mapping is straightforward for simple transformations. However, when requirements become complex, you may need XSLT adjustments. Some adjustments can be done visually, while others require manual coding.

Example Complex Mapping Requirements

```
        <xsl:value-of select="nssrcmpr:ShipToPartyType" xml:id="id_100"/>
</tns:ShipToPartyType>
<xsl:choose xml:id="id_742">
        <xsl:when xml:id="id_743" test="($ReadBillToAddressFromBIP/nsmpr7:ReadResponse/ns53:GPDBillToAddress
                <tns:ShipToPartyIdentifier xml:id="id_744">
                        <xsl:value-of xml:id="id_745" select="$ReadBillToAddressFromBIP/nsmpr7:ReadResponse/ns53
                </tns:ShipToPartyIdentifier>
        </xsl:when>
        <xsl:otherwise xml:id="id_746">
                <tns:ShipToPartyIdentifier xml:id="id_747">
                        <xsl:value-of xml:id="id_748" select="''"/>
                </tns:ShipToPartyIdentifier>
        </xsl:otherwise>
</xsl:choose>
<xsl:choose xml:id="id_796">
        <xsl:when xml:id="id_797" test="$ReadBillToAddressFromBIP/nsmpr7:ReadResponse/ns53:GPDBillToAddressR
                <tns:ShipToPartyName xml:id="id_117">
                        <xsl:value-of xml:id="id_118" select="concat (nssrcmpr:ShipToPartyName, &quot;.&quot; )"
                </tns:ShipToPartyName>
        </xsl:when>
        <xsl:otherwise xml:id="id_800">
                <tns:ShipToPartyName xml:id="id_117">
                        <xsl:value-of xml:id="id_802" select="nssrcmpr:ShipToPartyName"/>
                </tns:ShipToPartyName>
        </xsl:otherwise>
</xsl:choose>
```

```
        <xsl:value-of select="nssrcmpr:BillToCountry" xml:id="id_63"/>
</tns:BillToCountry>
<tns:Payment xml:id="id_460"/>
<xsl:for-each select="nssrcmpr:OrderLineItems" xml:id="id_119">
        <tns:Line xml:id="id_83">
                <tns:SourceTransactionLineIdentifier xml:id="id_84">
                        <xsl:value-of select="nssrcmpr:SourceTransactionLineIdentifier" xml:id="id_85"/>
                </tns:SourceTransactionLineIdentifier>
                <tns:SourceTransactionScheduleIdentifier xml:id="id_86">
                        <xsl:value-of select="nssrcmpr:SourceTransactionScheduleIdentifier" xml:id="id_87"/>
                </tns:SourceTransactionScheduleIdentifier>
                <tns:SourceTransactionLineNumber xml:id="id_120">
                        <xsl:value-of select="nssrcmpr:SourceTransactionLineNumber" xml:id="id_121"/>
                </tns:SourceTransactionLineNumber>
                <tns:SourceTransactionScheduleNumber xml:id="id_122">
                        <xsl:value-of select="nssrcmpr:SourceTransactionScheduleNumber" xml:id="id_123"/>
                </tns:SourceTransactionScheduleNumber>
                <tns:ProductNumber xml:id="id_90">
                        <xsl:value-of select="nssrcmpr:ProductNumber" xml:id="id_91"/>
                </tns:ProductNumber>
```

Figure 6-2. *Manual XSLT Transformation Example*

Using XSLT Constructs

OIC provides built-in XSLT constructs that you can use visually.

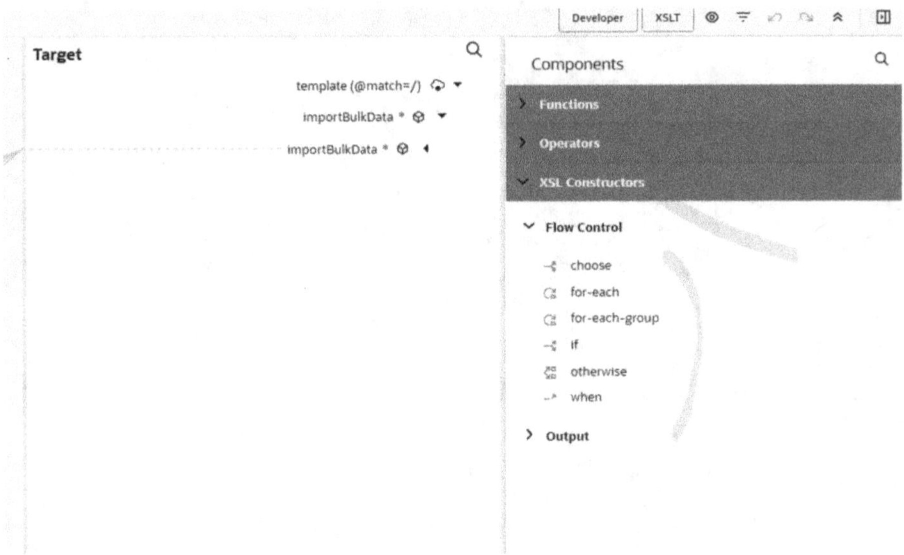

Figure 6-3. *XSLT Constructs Menu*

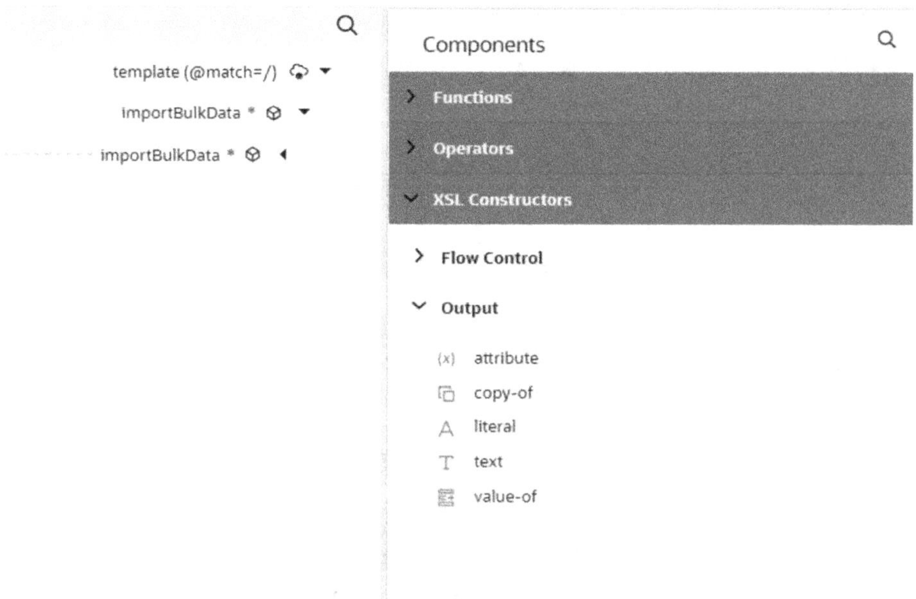

Figure 6-4. *XSLT Construct Selection*

Direct XSLT Code Editing

For advanced scenarios, you can switch to code mode and type XSLT directly.

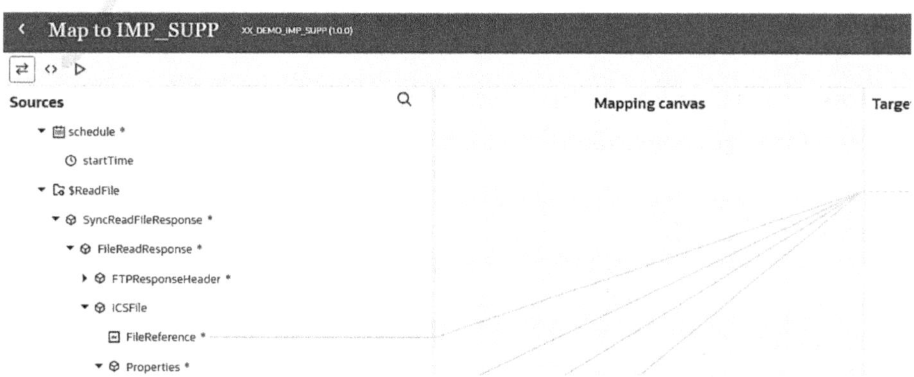

Figure 6-5. *Switch to Code View*

Figure 6-6. XSLT Code Editor

Important Notes About Code Mode

After making manual XSLT changes, OIC may not be able to return to Designer mode.

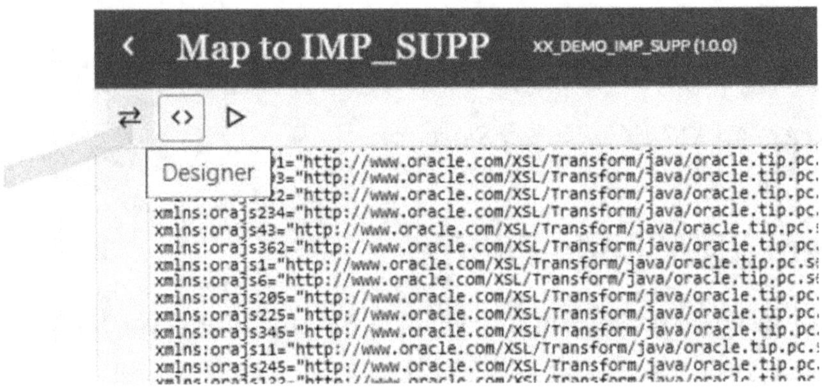

Figure 6-7. Designer Mode Unavailable Warning

Why This Happens: When XSLT constructs become too complex, the visual designer cannot accurately represent them graphically.

Best Practices

OIC experts understand that mastering XSLT is essential for handling truly complex mappings. While the visual mapper is excellent for straightforward transformations, advanced integration scenarios often require direct XSLT coding skills.

CHAPTER 7

Projects and Packages

Overview

Projects represent a significant new feature in OIC Gen3 that changes how you organize and manage integrations.

Reference Documentation

- OIC Gen3 Projects: Features, Limitations, and Advantages (Apps Associates)
- New Features in OIC Gen 3 Projects (Medium)
- OIC Gen3: Working with Projects & Packages (SoaLicious)

Our Perspective

Rather than repeating content from other sources, we'll share our practical insights.

J. J. Montero Rodríguez and S. Tahseen, *Oracle Integration Cookbook for Oracle ERP Cloud*,
https://doi.org/10.1007/979-8-8688-3020-4_7

Understanding Packages (Pre-Gen3)

If you're already familiar with OIC, you know how packages work:

- They group multiple integrations together.
- When exported, you get a .par file instead of individual .iar files.

Note Projects export as .car files, not .par files.

- Each integration can belong to only one package.

Projects: The Gen3 Evolution

Projects are a brand-new feature in Gen3 that extends the package concept with additional capabilities.

Considerations Before Adopting Projects

On paper, projects provide excellent features. **However**, there are important considerations.

We strongly recommend reading extensive documentation about projects before implementing them, as they require additional maintenance effort:

- **Access Control:** Managing user permissions at the project level. Enforces role-based access control (RBAC) and ensures environment-specific configurations and we can assign private endpoints for network isolation.

- **Versioning:** Tracking and managing integration versions inside the projects.
- **Deployment:** Coordinating deployment of integrations within the projects. Invoking one project from another project is not supported.
- **Monitoring:** Observe option to monitor integrations, instances, subscriptions, scheduled future runs, and audit records. Improves manageability and traceability.

Important Limitations

Be aware of these project constraints:

- Maximum 200 integrations per project
- Maximum 100 project deployments
- Maximum 100 connections per project
- Maximum 100 lookups per project
- Maximum 50 JavaScript libraries per project

Reference Documentation
Oracle Service Limits

Migration Challenges

Projects encapsulate objects, which creates challenges for existing implementations.

For customers with many integrations (we've seen 500+ in production environments) that share dozens of connections, migrating to a project-based approach is not trivial. The shared nature of existing integrations doesn't align easily with project boundaries.

Recommendation

The advantages must outweigh the increased maintenance effort. Evaluate your specific use case carefully before committing to project-based architecture.

Creating Projects from Packages

Note Oracle supports converting a package into a new project, but importing existing package integrations into an existing project is not supported.

Here's a useful tip from Srinanda Das in his blog on creating a project from an existing package.

Step 1: Right-Click the Package

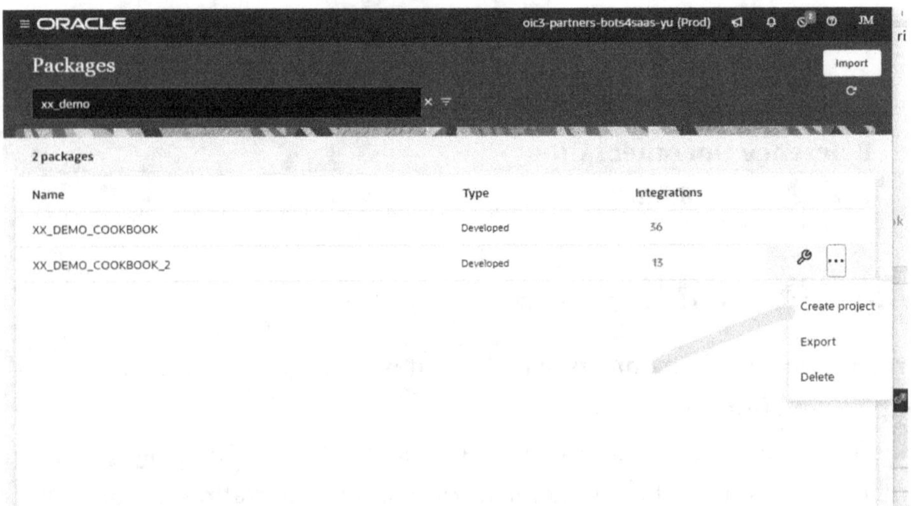

__Figure 7-1.__ Package Context Menu

Step 2: Configure a New Project

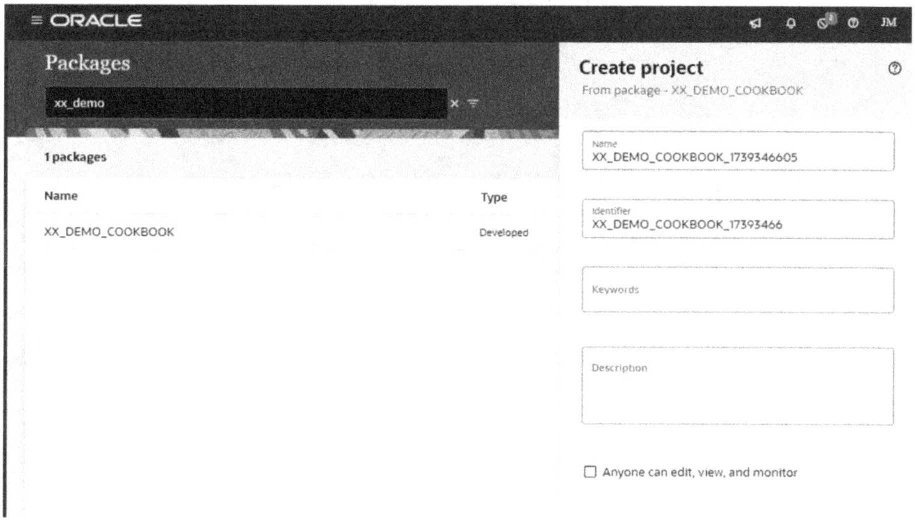

Figure 7-2. *Project Creation from the Package*

This feature provides a migration path for existing packages to the new project structure.

CHAPTER 8

Oracle Integration Limits

Understanding Service Limits

Rather than duplicating the comprehensive limits tables here, we recommend reviewing Oracle's official documentation.

Reference Documentation

Oracle Integration Service Limits

Our Perspective on Limits

Understanding OIC limits is crucial when designing integrations. You must consider these limits alongside expected workload volumes.

Key Questions to Ask

When gathering requirements, determine

- **Number of records** to process per run
- **Number of files** to handle
- **File sizes** (average and maximum)

J. J. Montero Rodríguez and S. Tahseen, *Oracle Integration Cookbook for Oracle ERP Cloud*, https://doi.org/10.1007/979-8-8688-3020-4_8

- **Payload sizes** for incoming and outgoing data
- **Time restrictions** (processing windows)
- **Timeframe restrictions** (batch windows, business hours)

No One-Size-Fits-All Solution

There's no magic formula for handling all scenarios. When any metric exceeds what you consider "substantial," review the limits table and adjust your design accordingly.

Design Strategies

Consider these approaches when facing limits:

1. **Parallel Processing:** Use parallel flows instead of sequential processing for large datasets.
2. **Database Staging:** For heavy processing, stage data in a database, process with PL/SQL, and then continue with OIC.
3. **Asynchronous Patterns:** Choose between synchronous and asynchronous based on expected response times.

Note Synchronous integrations must complete within **300 seconds (5 minutes)**. Oracle also recommends treating any integration likely to exceed **2 minutes** as asynchronous, and the default Oracle Public Cloud proxy has a **120-second** timeout.

Deciding Between Synchronous vs. Asynchronous Integrations

If estimated response time exceeds the synchronous timeout limits (see the reference documentation table), you must

- Design an asynchronous integration.
- Implement alternative notification methods for responses (callbacks, polling, notifications).
- Set appropriate expectations with users.

Bottom Line: Evaluate each integration on a case-by-case basis, considering both business requirements and technical constraints.

CHAPTER 9

Monitoring Capabilities in OIC

Reference Documentation

- Manage Errors in OIC
- Monitor Integrations at Runtime
- Monitor Integrations by Project
- Monitoring from OCI Cloud Console

Our Perspective

As an Oracle Integration Cloud (OIC) Gen3 developer or integration lead, ensuring the reliability, performance, and stability of live integrations is a critical responsibility. You must be able to proactively monitor execution health, quickly detect failures or latency issues, and efficiently trace errors to their root cause.

OIC Gen3 introduces enhanced observability and monitoring capabilities, including the Observability Dashboard, project-level monitoring, and the activity stream, enabling teams to move seamlessly from high-level health metrics to detailed, instance-level diagnostics.

J. J. Montero Rodríguez and S. Tahseen, *Oracle Integration Cookbook for Oracle ERP Cloud*,
https://doi.org/10.1007/979-8-8688-3020-4_9

Monitoring and Troubleshooting in OIC Gen3

Observability Dashboard

(Home ➤ Observability ➤ Dashboards)

The Observability Dashboard provides a **centralized, system-wide view** of integration health across all projects.

Key Capabilities

- Displays **overall execution health**, including
  - Success vs. failure trends
  - Execution volume over time
  - Error frequency by integration
- Helps identify **systemic issues** impacting multiple integrations
- Supports proactive monitoring and trend analysis
- Leverages date and time filters for better root cause analysis

Projects Tab: Observe Subtab

(Projects ➤ [Project Name] ➤ Observe)

The **Observe** subtab offers **real-time, project-specific observability**, making it ideal for structured, team-based integration development.

Key Features

- Live status of all integrations within the selected project
- Visual indicators highlighting
  - Failed or faulted instances

    - Long-running or slow executions
    - Backlogged, retrying, or suspended flows
- Drill-down access to
    - Integration run history
    - Fault and error locations within the flow
    - Input and output payloads for each instance

This view is especially effective when multiple teams own different integration flows in projects. Each team can monitor and troubleshoot only the integrations they are responsible for.

Activity Stream (Instance Tracking)

(Observability ➤ Instances or equivalent)

The activity stream enables **instance-level tracking and detailed execution analysis.**

Capabilities

- Filter integration instances by
    - Integration name
    - Execution status (completed, failed, in progress)
    - Date and time range
- Open individual instances to
    - View end-to-end execution flow
    - Inspect transformation logic and mapped values
    - Review detailed error messages and fault payloads
    - Access full input and output messages

Use the **Observability or project's Observe view** to identify problematic integrations quickly and then jump into the activity stream for **deep, instance-level diagnostics**.

Diagnostic Logs

Diagnostic logs provide **backend-level visibility** beyond what is available in instance tracking. This capability is especially valuable when troubleshooting issues related to **OCI networking, adapters, or runtime behavior**.

Best Used For

- Infrastructure-level issues
- Adapter connectivity problems
- Runtime or platform-related errors
- Intermittent failures not visible in integration instance logs

Search Options

- Integration name
- Flow or instance ID
- Timestamp ranges

Notifications and Alerts

To enable proactive issue management, OIC Gen3 supports alerting through

- Integration insight dashboards
- Custom notification logic (email, REST, OCI services)

Common Alert Scenarios

- Repeated or consecutive integration failures
- Unusually long-running integrations
- SLA or performance threshold breaches

Configure alerts for critical business integrations to reduce mean time to detection (MTTD) and resolution (MTTR).

Replay and Testing Capabilities

OIC Gen3 supports **replay of eligible failed integration instances**, allowing recovery without reprocessing entire workflows.

Key Capabilities

- Replay failed instances after correcting
  - Data issues
  - Mapping logic
  - External system availability
- Execute test runs directly from the integration canvas.
- Validate fixes before redeploying to production.

Replay and testing capabilities significantly reduce downtime and improve operational efficiency during incident resolution.

OCI Cloud Console

This provides **standard service metrics** for high-level metrics **and OCI logging analytics** for deep business insights.

OIC service metrics

- Provide standardized telemetry that **enables customers to monitor and analyze high-level usage patterns of Oracle Integration Cloud**
- Are presented on the Metrics subpage of individual OIC instances and are additionally available through the **Metrics Explorer and OCI dashboards** for deeper analysis

OCI logging analytics

- Introduces an **Oracle Integration Insight dashboard for OIC Gen3**, streamlining the monitoring and management of OIC integrations using **activity stream logs**
- Delivers **detailed insights into business metrics** configured in OIC and presents a visual sequence of the events and actions behind each integration flow

Alerting and Automation

OCI Monitoring Through Alarms: Which converts OIC metrics into alarms

Example: Failure count > threshold or latency exceeds SLA.

OIC Logs Can Be Streamed to OCI Logging: Which enables centralized log search and long term retention

OCI Notifications Through Email/Slack/Pager Alerts: Used for production incident responses

BEST Practices

- Define **business identifiers** in every integration.
- **Enable payload tracking** selectively.

- Set **alerts for recurring faults.**
- Monitor **agent backlog** for throughput issues.
- Use **Gen3 observability dashboards** for performance tuning.

Gen2 vs. Gen3 Monitoring Comparison

We want to highlight a significant improvement from Gen2 to Gen3.

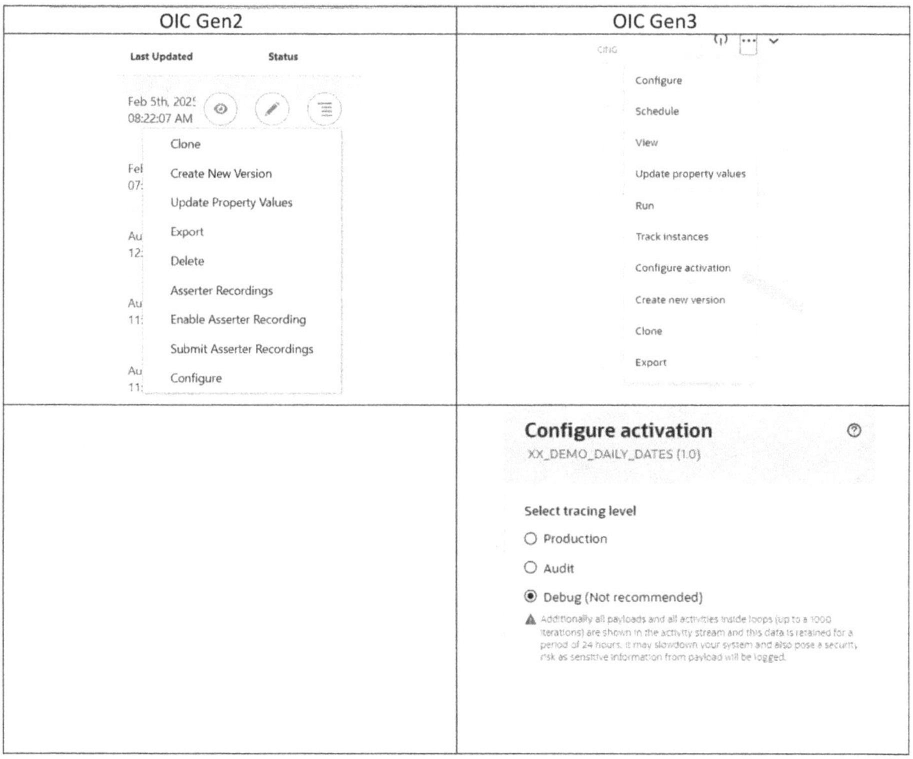

Figure 9-1. *OIC Gen2 Monitoring Interface*

Key Gen3 Improvement

Major Advantage: In Gen3, you no longer need to deactivate and reactivate integrations to change the tracing level. This significantly improves the debugging and monitoring experience without disrupting active integrations.

Reference Documentation

Manage Integrations

CHAPTER 10

OCR (Optical Character Recognition)

Introduction and Goal

This chapter demonstrates a basic OCR integration example. OCR tools read images or documents in various formats and extract text that can be used in subsequent integration steps.

Many OCR tools are available in the market with different features. We've selected one for learning purposes that offers a free trial.

Preparatory Steps

To follow this example, you'll need an API key from the OCR service.

Service URL: **`https://ocr.space/ocrapi`**

J. J. Montero Rodríguez and S. Tahseen, *Oracle Integration Cookbook for Oracle ERP Cloud*,
https://doi.org/10.1007/979-8-8688-3020-4_10

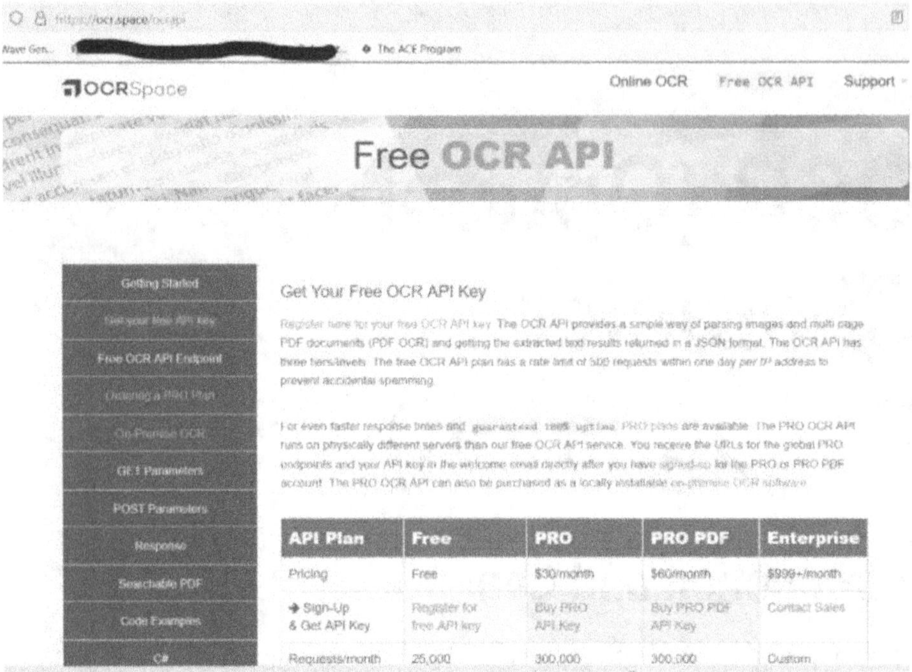

Figure 10-1. OCR Service Registration

Testing with Postman

Before building the OIC integration, let's understand how the OCR API works using Postman.

Step 1: Configure Headers

Set up the Headers section as shown.

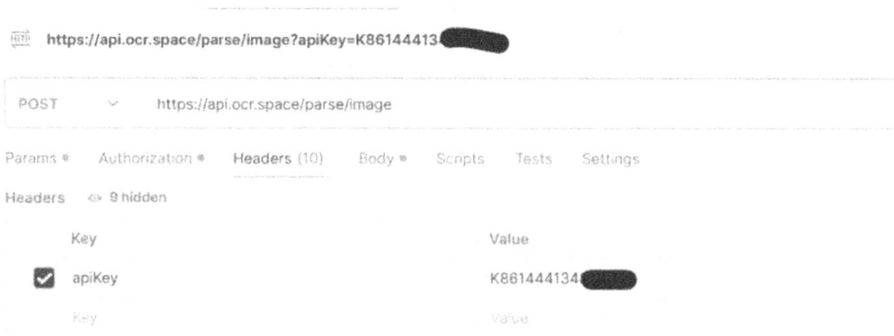

Figure 10-2. *Postman Headers Configuration*

Step 2: Configure Body

In the Body tab, configure the parameters and select the PDF file for testing.

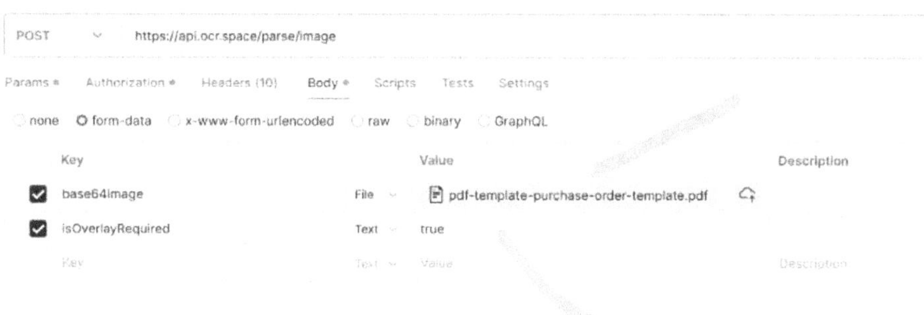

Figure 10-3. *Postman Body Configuration*

Step 3: Review Response

After executing the request, you'll receive a JSON response.

Figure 10-4. *OCR API Response*

Sample PDF Document

This is the dummy PDF used for demonstration (included in GitHub).

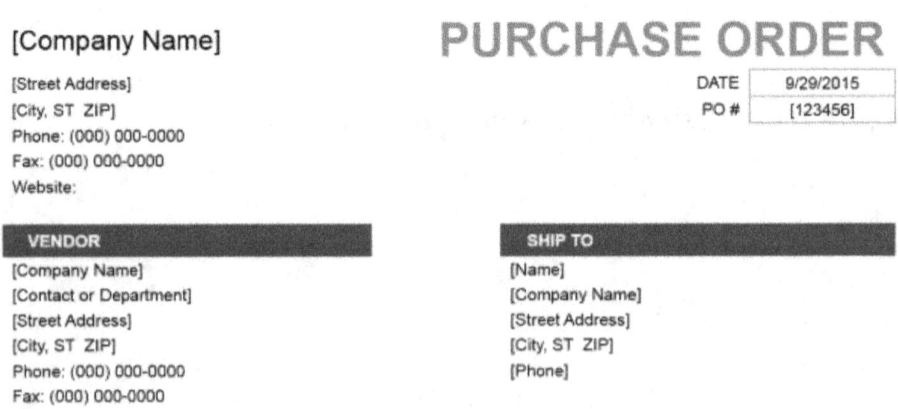

[Company Name]

[Street Address]
[City, ST ZIP]
Phone: (000) 000-0000
Fax: (000) 000-0000
Website:

PURCHASE ORDER

DATE	9/29/2015
PO #	[123456]

VENDOR

[Company Name]
[Contact or Department]
[Street Address]
[City, ST ZIP]
Phone: (000) 000-0000
Fax: (000) 000-0000

SHIP TO

[Name]
[Company Name]
[Street Address]
[City, ST ZIP]
[Phone]

Figure 10-5. *Sample PDF Content*

Building the OIC Integration

Now we'll convert the Postman test into an OIC integration.

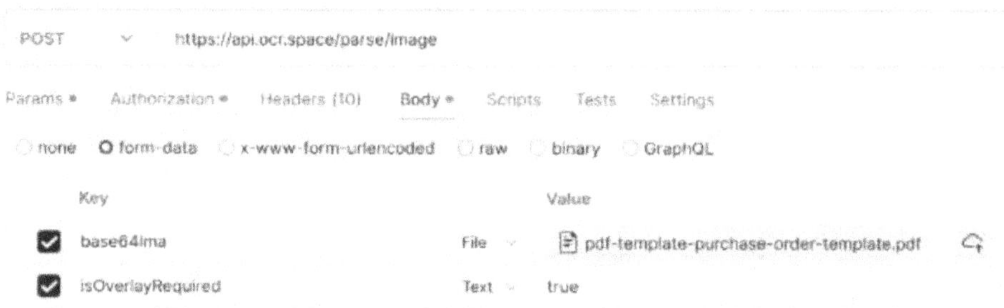

Figure 10-6. *Postman to OIC*

OIC Integration Components

1. **Connection Setup**
   Use connection XX_DEMO_OCR_CONN (see Chapter 2, section "OCR Connection").

2. **Integration Overview**

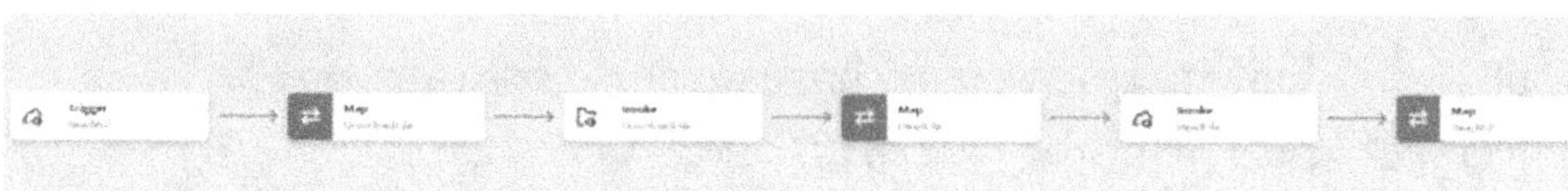

Figure 10-7. *Complete Integration Flow*

3. **ReadPdf Trigger Configuration**
   Configure the initial REST trigger to receive parameters.

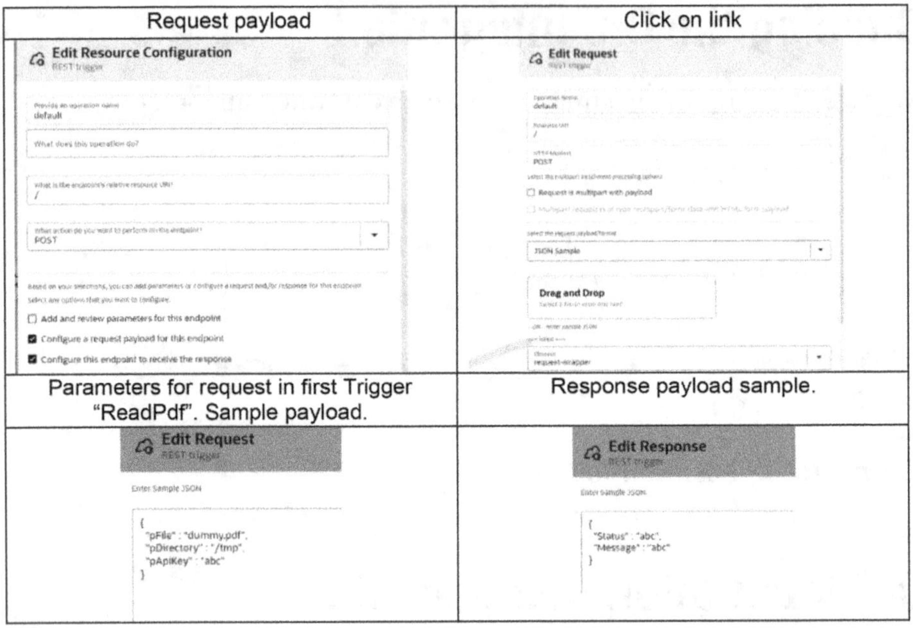

Figure 10-8. REST Trigger Setup

Sample Test Payload

```
{
  "pApiKey": " YOUR_OCR_API_KEY_HERE ",
  "pFile": "pdf-template-purchase-order-template.pdf",
  "pDirectory": "/home/jjmr_oic/demo"
}
```

1. **ReadFile Activity Invoke Configuration**

Call REST invoke	Detail Request
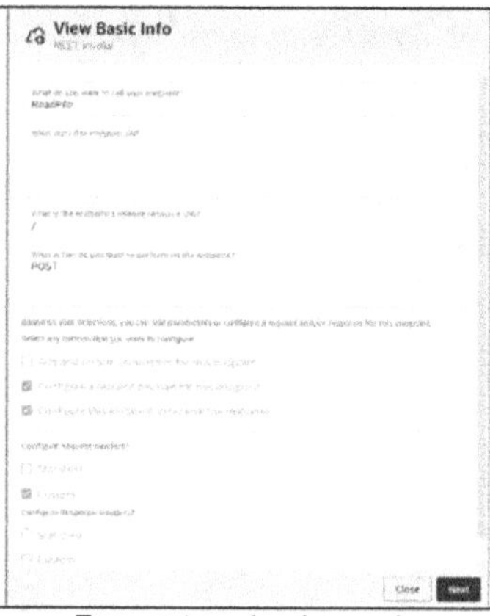	
Request payload sample	Headers
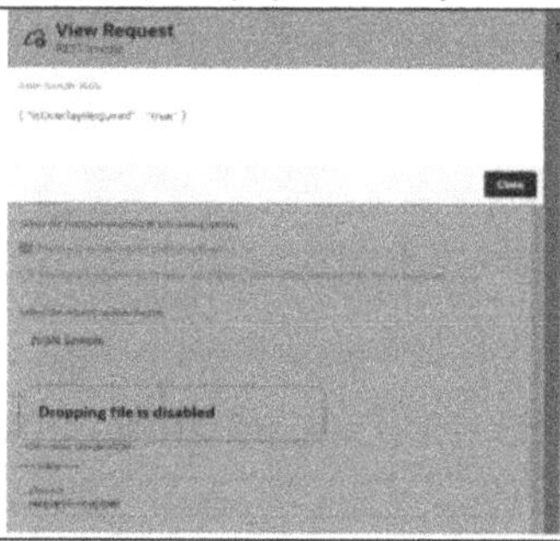	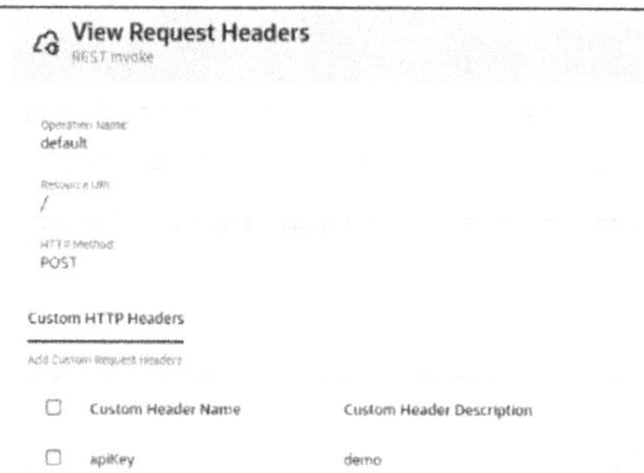
Detail response payload link.	Use the file provided as sample in GitHub: sample_ocr.json We got this file from Postman test response.

Figure 10-9. *REST Invoke Setup*

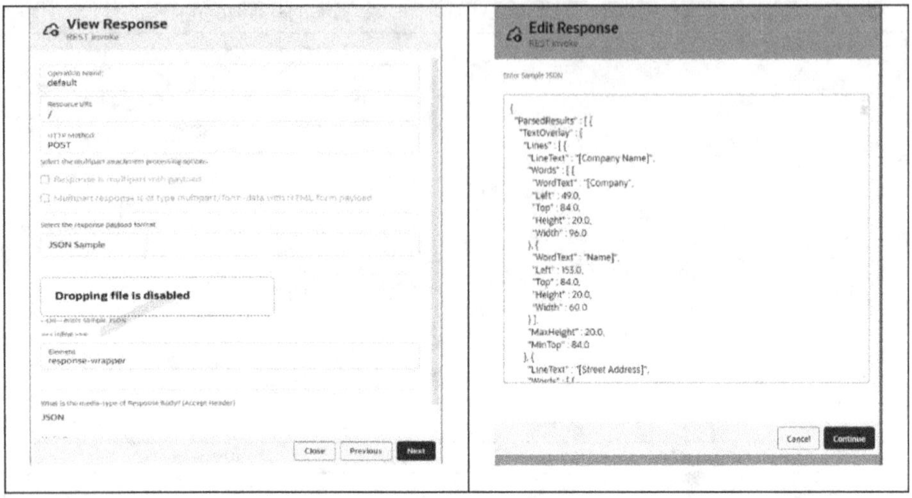

Figure 10-10. Response Configuration

Use the file provided in GitHub: sample_response_ocr.json.

Note This response sample was obtained from the Postman test response.

Testing the Integration

Execute a test run of the complete integration.

Figure 10-11. *Integration Test Execution*

Notice that the response contains formatted, readable information extracted from the PDF.

Conclusion

We've demonstrated how to set up, build, and test integration with an OCR tool available in the market.

Important This is a demonstration for learning purposes only. In production scenarios, you would need to

- Evaluate OCR accuracy for your specific document types.
- Consider error handling for failed extractions.
- Implement proper security for API keys.
- Handle various file formats and sizes.
- Plan for OCR service availability and rate limits.

Technical Reference

Code Example	Comments
sample_response_ocr.json	Sample response in JSON format
XX_DEMO_OCR	**Package File**: XX_DEMO_COOKBOOK.par

CHAPTER 11

Visual Builder to OIC to SaaS: Create Invoices from Files with REST

Overview

This chapter presents a real proof-of-concept (POC) developed for a customer in 2024. While the project was ultimately not implemented, it demonstrates a complete end-to-end integration workflow.

The application is a Redwood Guided Process with four steps designed to load Payables invoices from a CSV file selected in a Visual Builder (VB) page, using OIC to process and create the invoices in ERP Cloud.

J. J. Montero Rodríguez and S. Tahseen, *Oracle Integration Cookbook for Oracle ERP Cloud*,
https://doi.org/10.1007/979-8-8688-3020-4_11

Application Workflow

The process begins with this launch page.

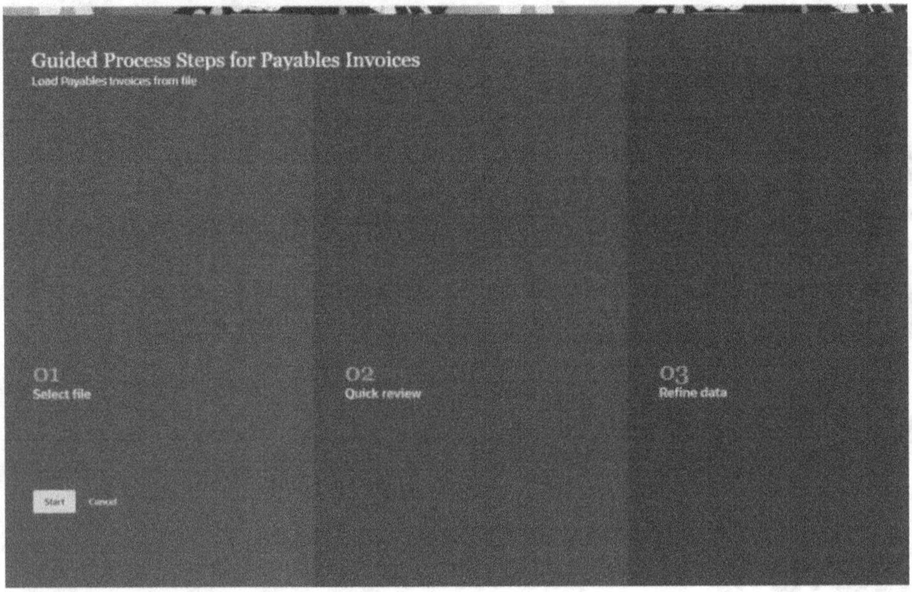

Figure 11-1. *Guided Process Launch Page*

Users then select a CSV file containing invoice data.

Figure 11-2. *File Selection Screen*

The remaining steps are shown at the end of this chapter.

At the completion of the process, Payables invoices are created in SaaS/Fusion Applications using the standard REST API integrated through OIC.

Summary of Features

Visual Builder Side

File Processing

- Load and parse data from CSV files.
- Validate and display data for user review.
- Store data in Visual Builder Business Objects.

Integration Execution

- Trigger OIC integration from Visual Builder.
- Pass batch processing parameters.
- Display processing results to users.

Reference Resource

For CSV parsing implementation, we used this blog post along with additional help from Oracle forums:

How to Parse CSV Data in Oracle Visual Builder Using JS Library

Oracle Integration Side

Invoice Creation

- Create Payables invoices using SaaS/Fusion Applications REST API.
- Handle batch processing of multiple invoices.
- Implement error handling for individual invoice failures.

Business Object Updates

- Update Visual Builder Business Objects from Oracle Integration.
- Log success/error status after REST API calls.
- When successful, record additional metadata including invoice IDs and timestamps.

Oracle Integration Configuration

Connection Setup

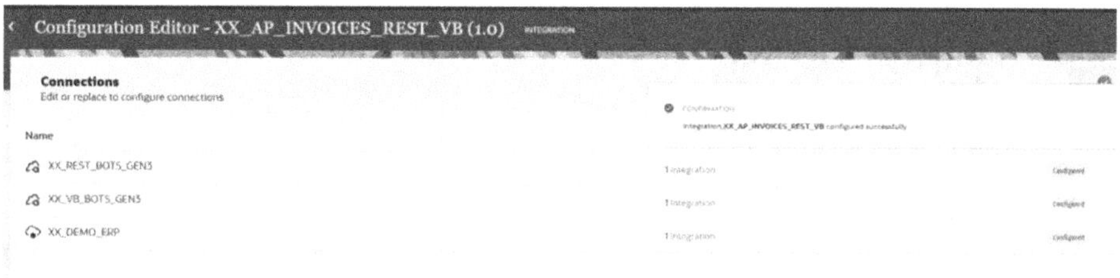

Figure 11-3. *OIC Connection Overview*

Visual Builder Business Object Connection

Obtain the connection URL from the Visual Builder application.

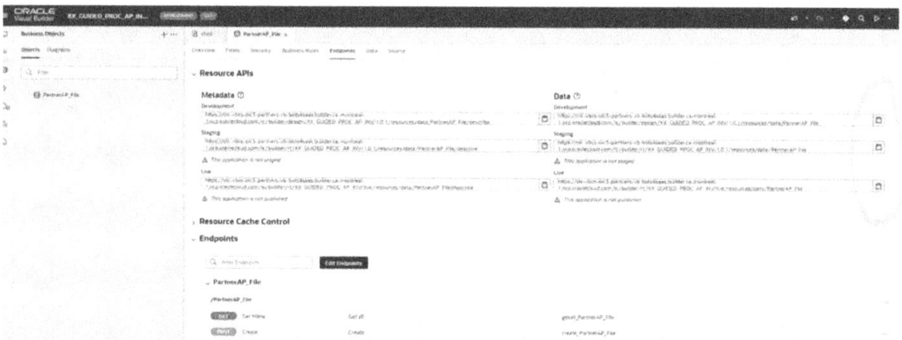

Figure 11-4. *Visual Builder URL Configuration*

On the right side, you'll find URLs corresponding to the three deployment stages:

- Design
- Stage
- Live (Published)

For learning purposes, we'll use the **Design** stage. (*Warning: The Design stage URL is for development and demo purposes only. Always use Stage or Live URLs with appropriate authentication in non-development environments.*)

Example URL Format

```
https://oic-xxxx-xxxx-redwood_demo-1.ocp.oraclecloud.com/ic/
builder/design/XX_GUIDED_PROC_AP_INV/1.0.3/resources
```

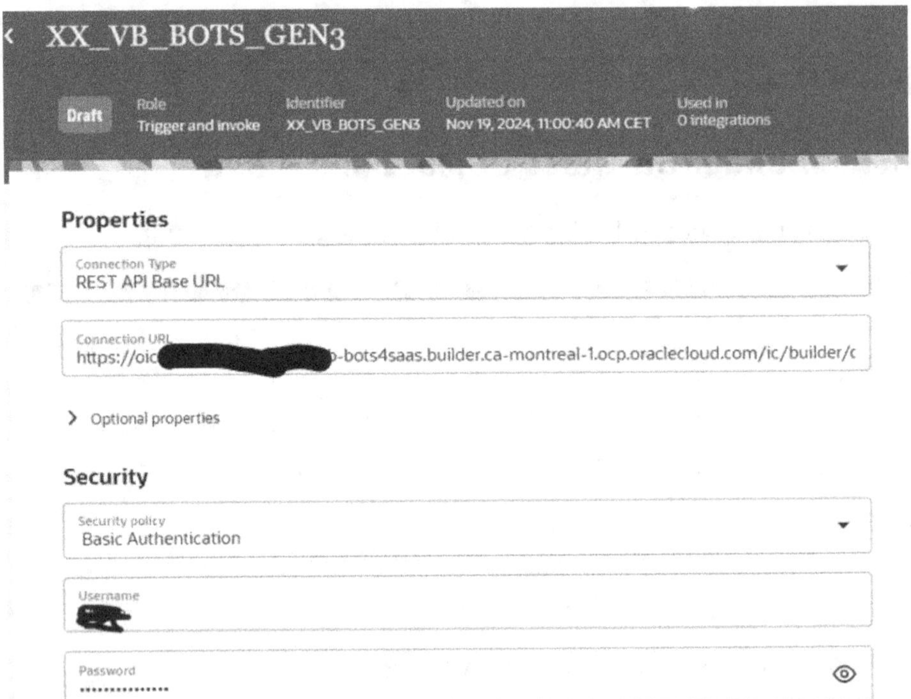

***Figure 11-5.** Visual Builder Connection Configuration*

Important Note on Versioning

Version numbers (1.0, 1.0.1, 1.0.2, etc.) apply only when **not** in Live mode.

URL Structure with Version

```
https://oic-xxx-cccc-redwood_demo-1.ocp.oraclecloud.com/ic/
builder/design/XX_GUIDED_PROC_AP_INV/1.0.3/resources
```

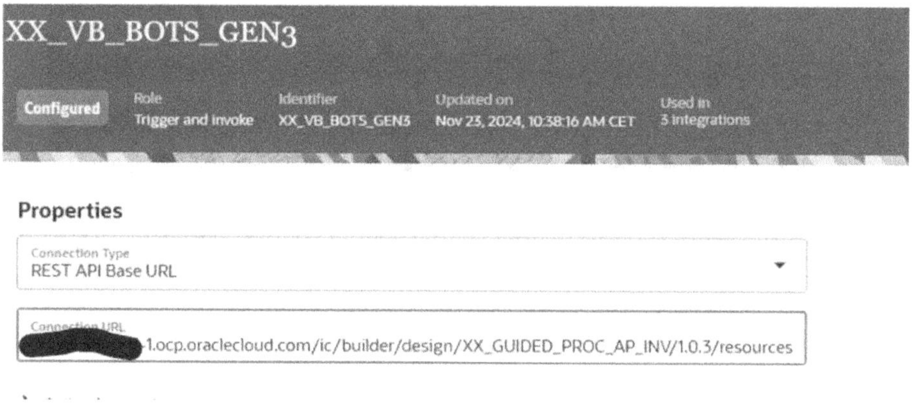

Figure 11-6. *Version Selection in URL*

REST Connection (Internal)

This connection enables Visual Builder to call OIC integrations.

Figure 11-7. Internal REST Connection

Base URL

```
https://oic3-xxxx-cccc-yu.integration.ca-montreal-1.ocp.
oraclecloud.com
```

SaaS/Fusion Applications Connection

Use the standard ERP Cloud connection described in Chapter 2, section "Basic ERP Cloud Connection."

Integration Flow Design

Inbound Parameters

The integration accepts these parameters.

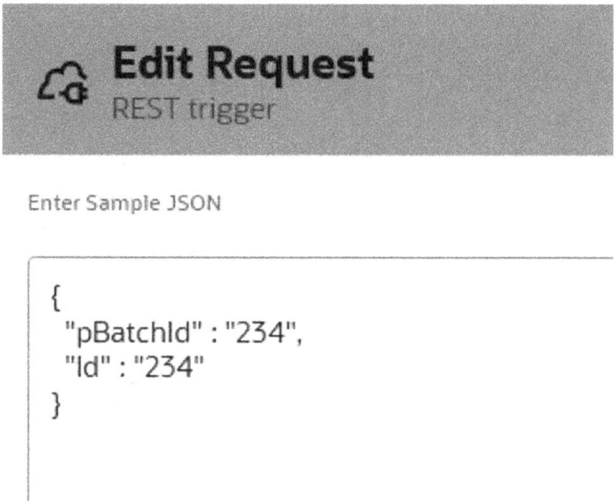

Figure 11-8. *Integration Input Parameters*

Complete Integration Flow

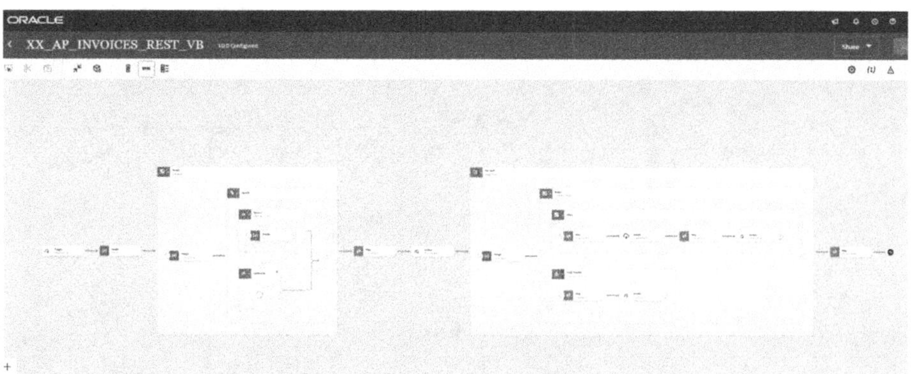

Figure 11-9a. *Integration Overview—Initial Steps*

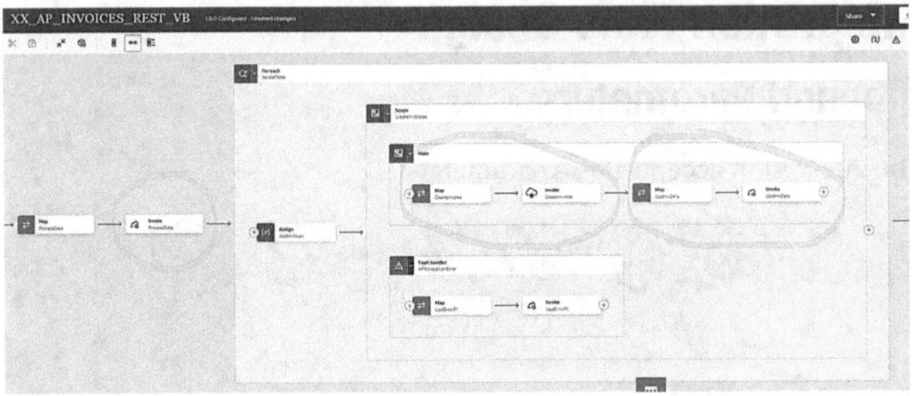

Figure 11-9b. *Integration Overview—Processing Loop*

Key Integration Activities

Read Visual Builder Business Object Data

The **ProcessData** invoke activity reads invoice records from the Visual Builder Business Object, filtering by the batch_id parameter received.

Process Each Invoice

The **IterateTable** loop processes each invoice record.

Invoice Creation

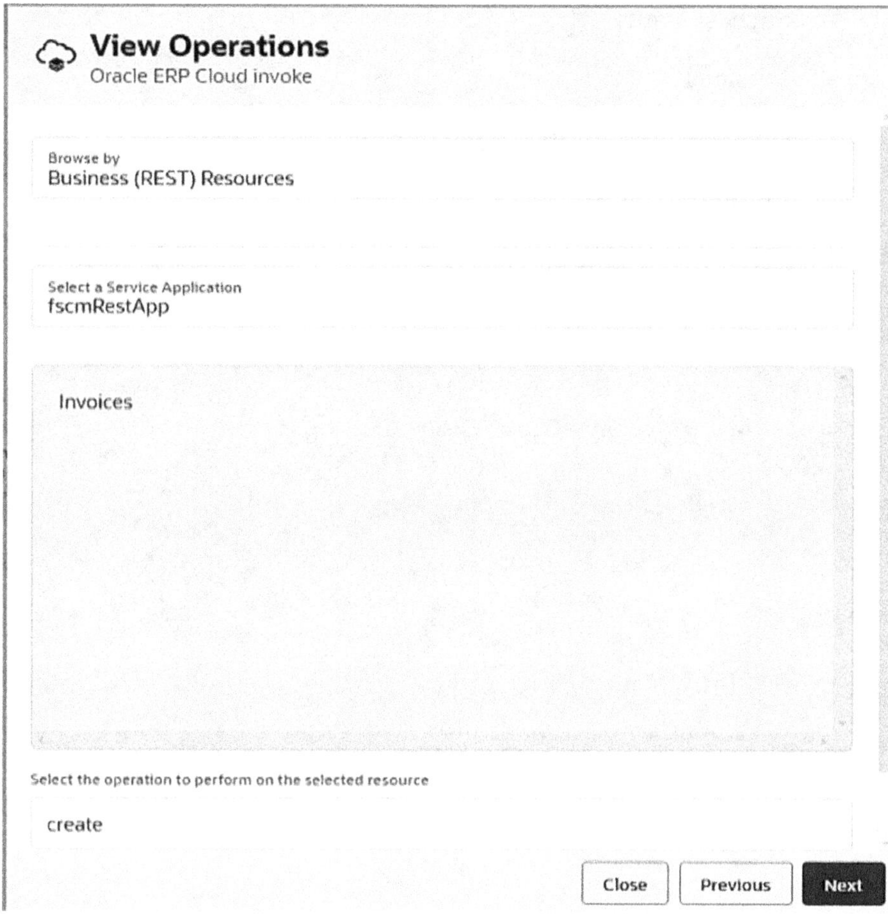

Figure 11-10. *Create Invoice REST Call Configuration*

The **CreateInvoice** invoke calls the ERP Cloud REST API to create each invoice.

Update Success Status

After successful invoice creation, the **UpdateInvData** invoke updates the Visual Builder Business Object with

- Success status
- Invoice ID
- Creation timestamp
- Additional metadata

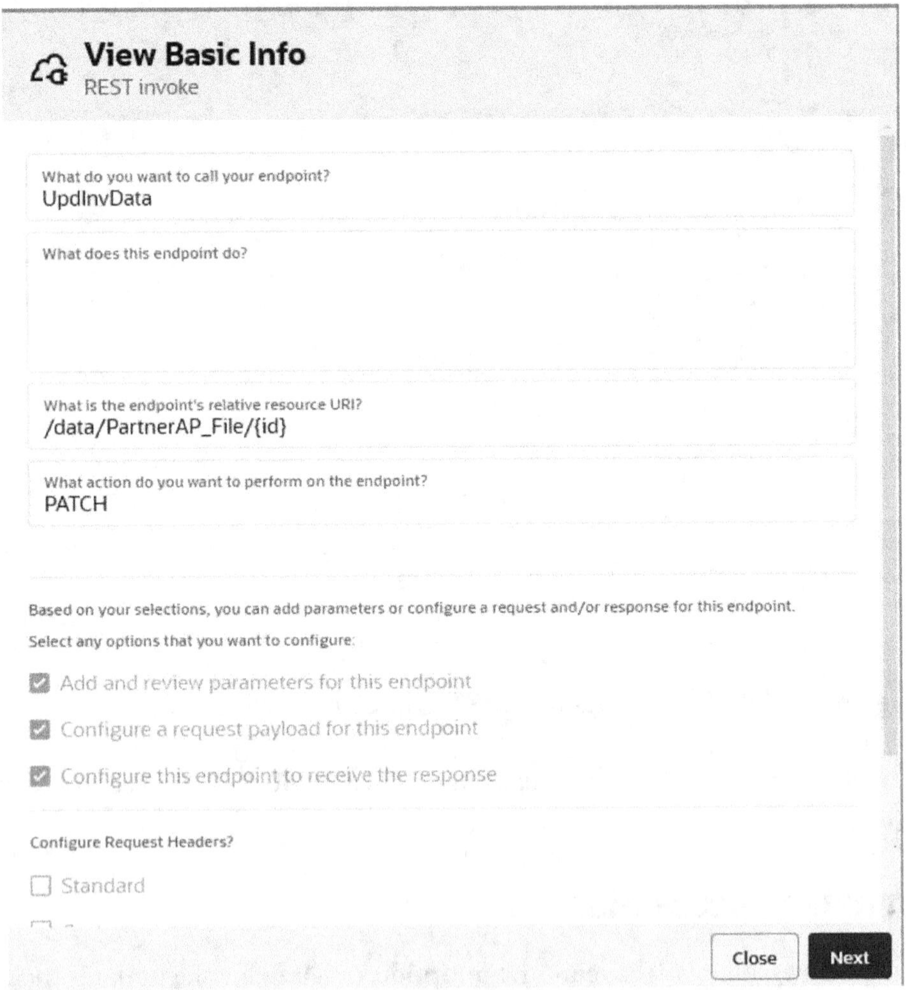

Figure 11-11. *Success Status Update Configuration*

Invoice Creation Mapping

The mapping transforms Visual Builder data to the ERP Cloud invoice structure.

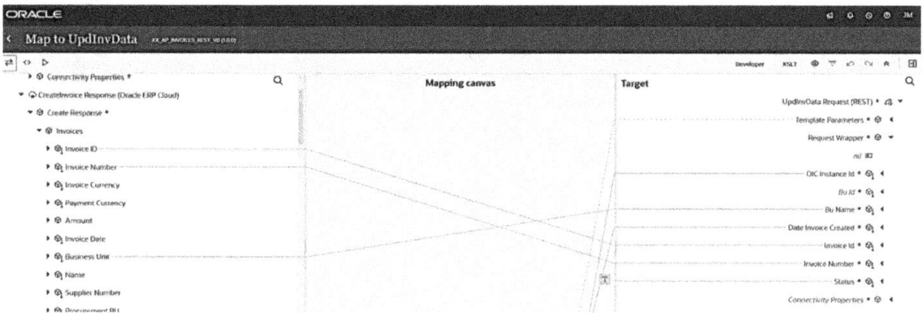

Figure 11-12. *Invoice Creation Mapping*

Error Handling

In case of errors, the integration updates the Business Object with error details.

Figure 11-13. *Error Status Update Flow*

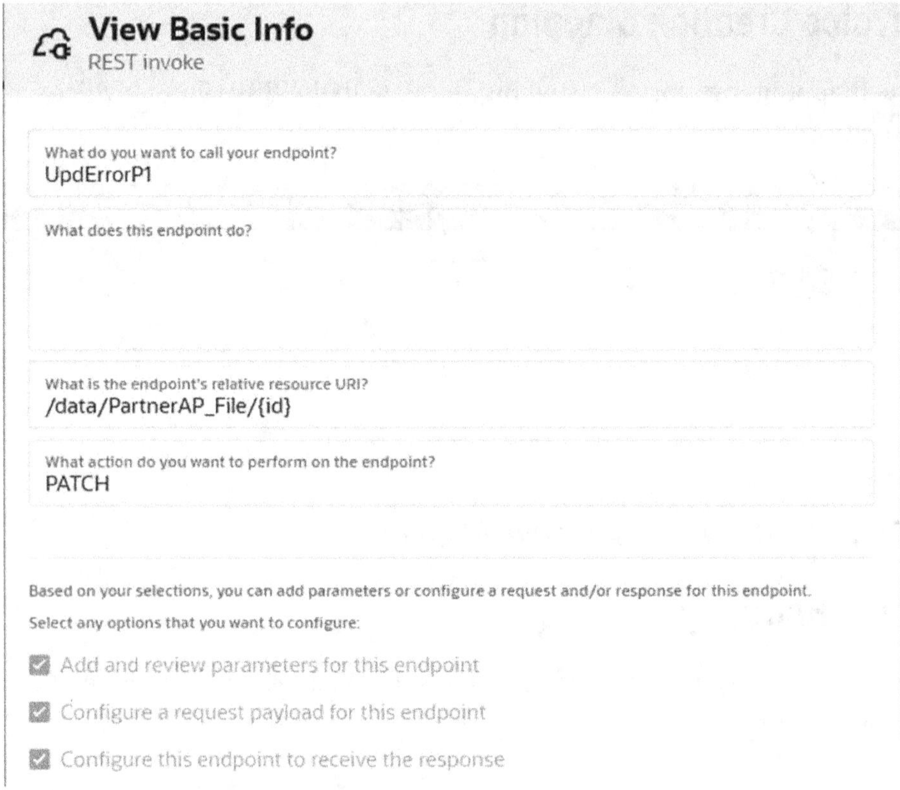

***Figure 11-14.** Error Mapping Configuration*

Example Error Mapping

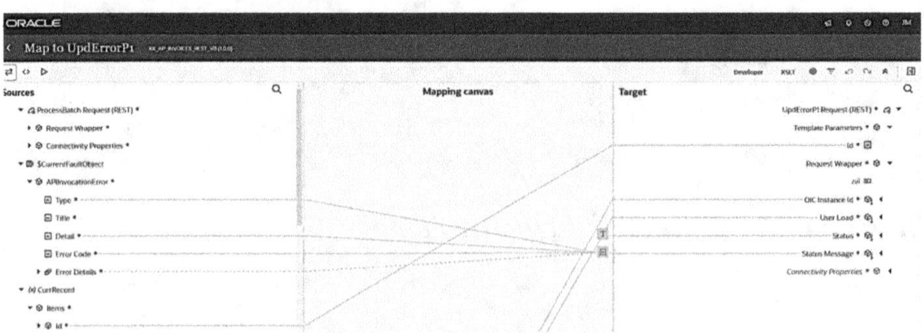

***Figure 11-15.** Error Update Mapping Details*

Response Design

Synchronous Processing

The integration operates synchronously, returning status and results at completion.

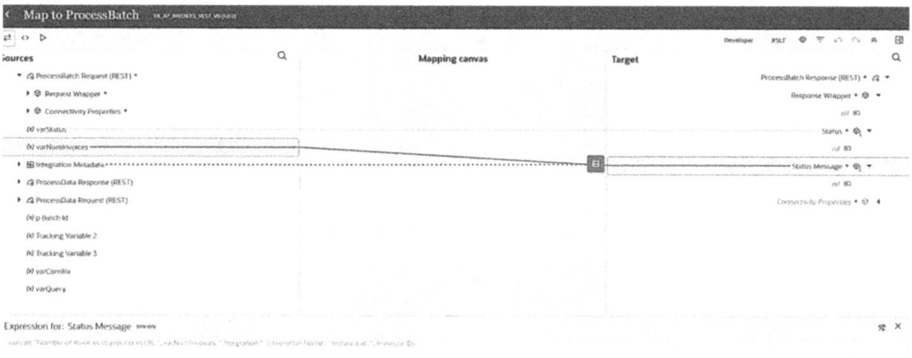

Figure 11-16. *Response Mapping*

This is a POC assuming a limited number of records per file (not thousands). For high-volume scenarios, we can consider asynchronous processing and batch size limits with callback notifications.

Testing the Oracle Integration

Test Data Setup

For this test, we'll use data with the following batch ID in the Visual Builder Business Object.

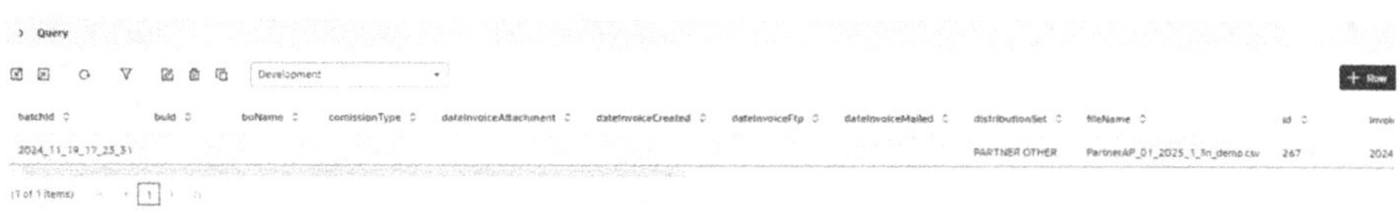

Figure 11-17. *Test Data in the Business Object*

Execute the Integration Test

Figure 11-18. *Integration Test Execution*

Review ERP Cloud API Request

Internal request payload sent to ERP Cloud for invoice creation (visible in OIC debug logs).

Figure 11-19. *REST API Request to ERP Cloud*

Review ERP Cloud API Response

Response received after successful invoice creation.

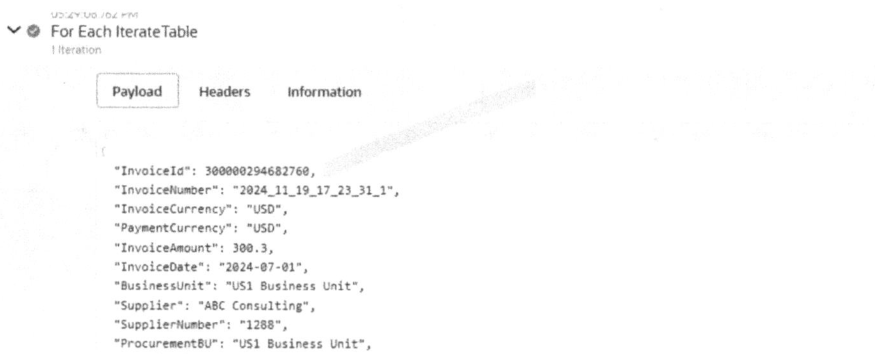

***Figure 11-20.** REST API Response from ERP Cloud*

Verify Business Object Updates

After processing, the Visual Builder Business Object is updated with results.

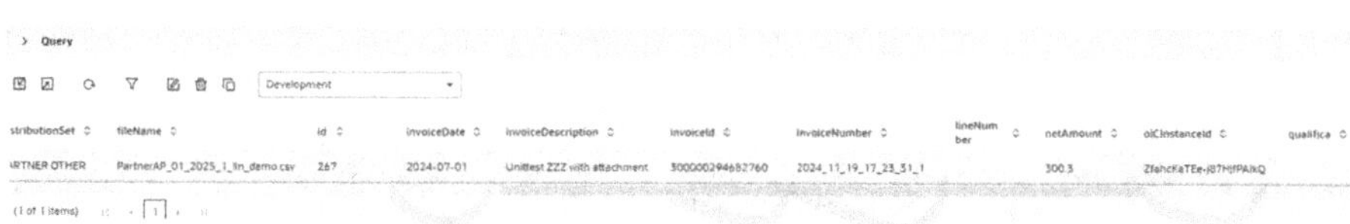

***Figure 11-21.** Updated Business Object Record—Status*

***Figure 11-22.** Updated Business Object Record—Details*

Visual Builder Configuration

Backend Connection Setup

Navigate to the Backends section.

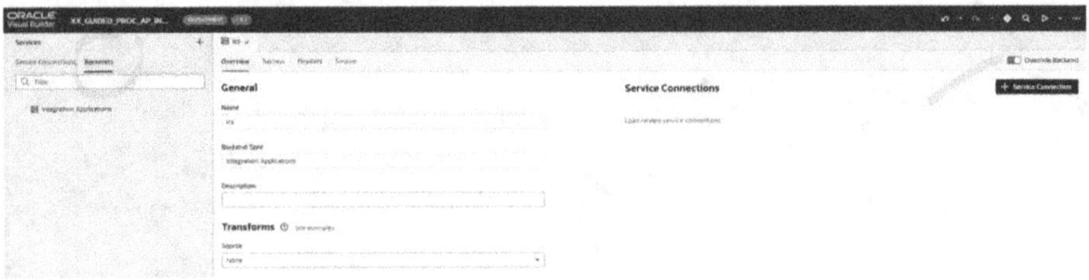

Figure 11-23. *Visual Builder Backends Menu*

Click **Override** and navigate to the **Servers** tab.

Figure 11-24. *Server Configuration*

Edit the server configuration and select **Delegate Authentication**.

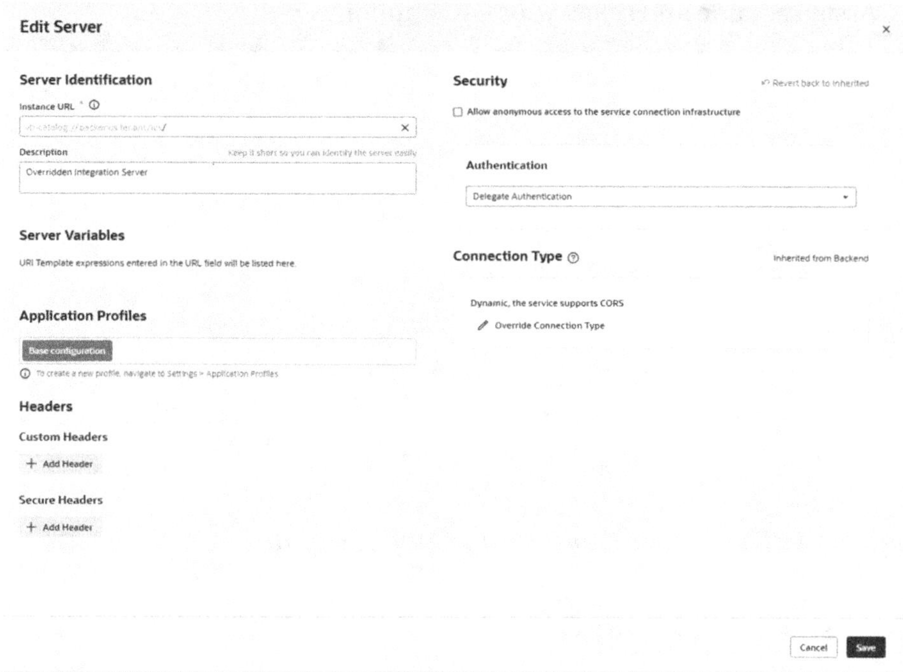

Figure 11-25. Authentication Configuration

Create an OIC Service Connection

After configuring authentication, create a connection to OIC from the backend.

Figure 11-26. Create a Service Connection

Assign a name and select your OIC endpoint.

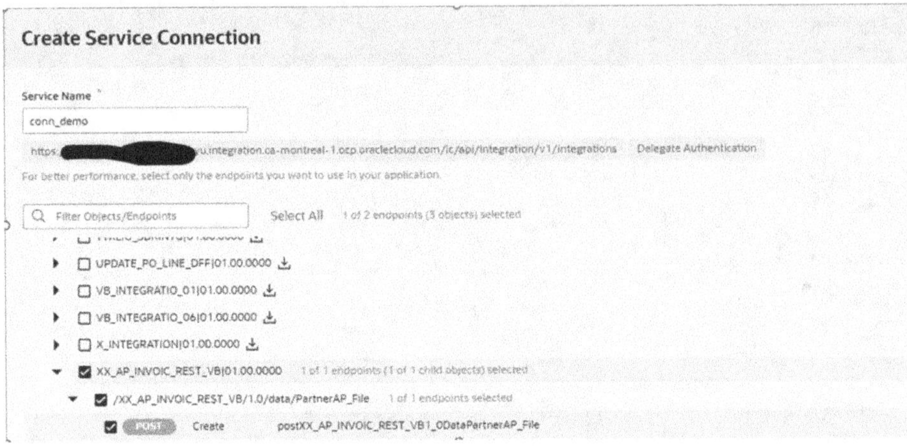

Figure 11-27. *Service Connection Configuration*

Test the Connection

Test the Visual Builder to OIC REST API connection.

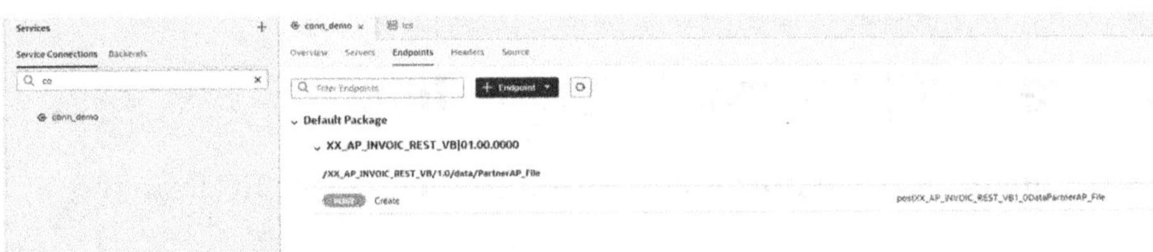

Figure 11-28. *Connection Test Interface*

Example Test Payload

File: 21_sample_1.txt

```
{
  "pBatchId": "2024_11_19_17_23_31",
  "Id": "267"
}
```

Execute a quick test from Visual Builder.

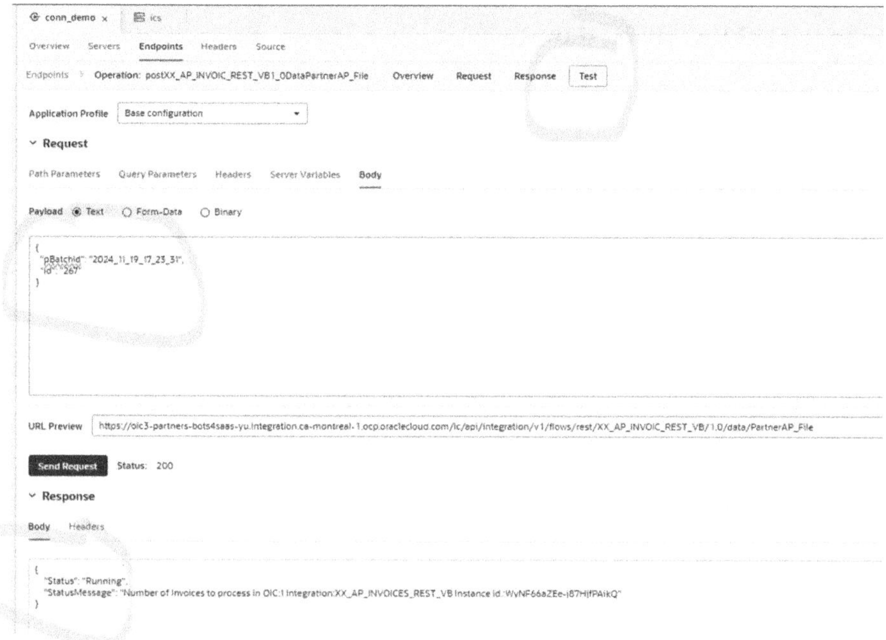

Figure 11-29. *Test Execution Results*

Business Object Definition

PartnerAP_File Fields: Part 1

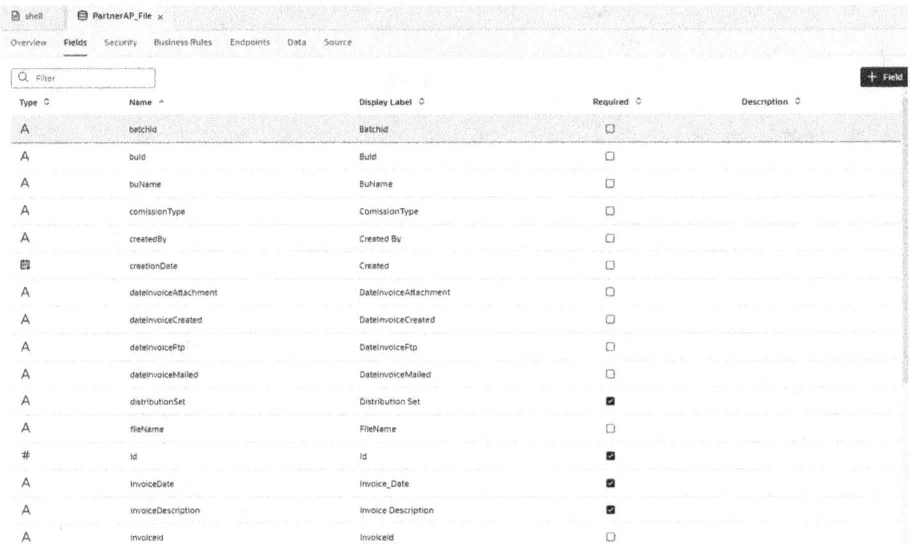

Figure 11-30. *PartnerAP_File Fields*

Note This Business Object has no relationship with other Business Objects, keeping the design simple for this POC.

Key Points to Consider

This chapter doesn't provide step-by-step instructions (as that would require many pages) but instead highlights the main features and areas to investigate in the provided code.

Complete code for all components is provided on GitHub.

JavaScript Library to Include in the JSON Tab in the Root Node

Include this library in the JSON tab of the root node for managing CSV file import.

Figure 11-31. *JavaScript Library in JSON Configuration*

JavaScript Library to Include in the HTML in the Root Node

Include this library in the HTML of the root node to manage CSV import.

***Figure 11-32.** JavaScript Library in HTML Configuration*

Page-Level JavaScript Code

Custom JavaScript code on the upload page (also provided in files).

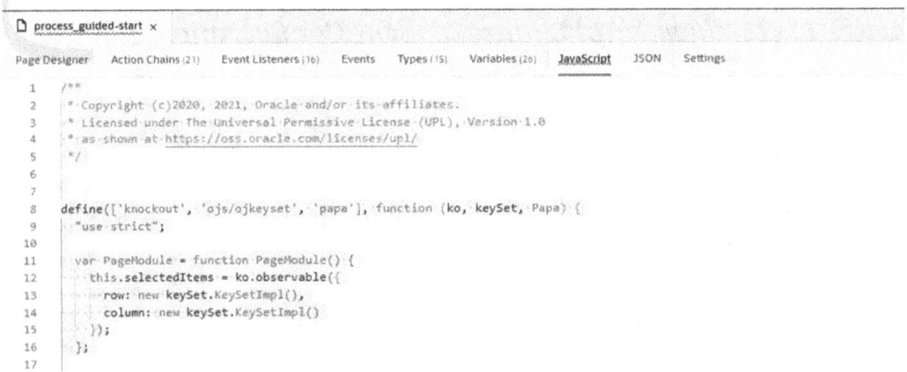

***Figure 11-33.** Page JavaScript Code Location*

Code Reference: 21_sample_2.txt

Call Oracle Integration REST API

Configure the Action Chain to invoke the OIC integration.

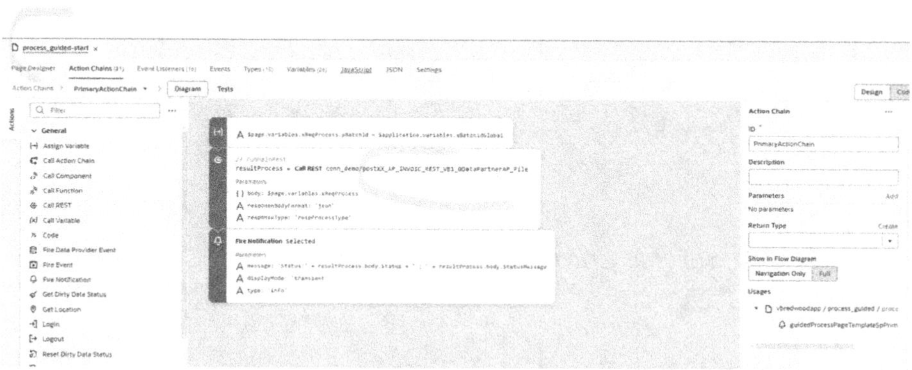

Figure 11-34. *Action Chain Configuration*

Code Mapping

The endpoint configuration must match between Visual Builder and OIC.

```
$page.variables.xReqProcess.pBatchId = $application.variables.xBatchIdGlobal;

// runMainRest
const resultProcess = await Actions.callRest(context, {
  endpoint: 'conn_demo/postXX_AP_INVOIC_REST_V81_0DataPartnerAP_File',
  responseBodyFormat: 'json',
  responseType: 'respProcessType',
  body: $page.variables.xReqProcess,
}, { id: 'runMainRest' });
```

Figure 11-35. *Endpoint Code Configuration*

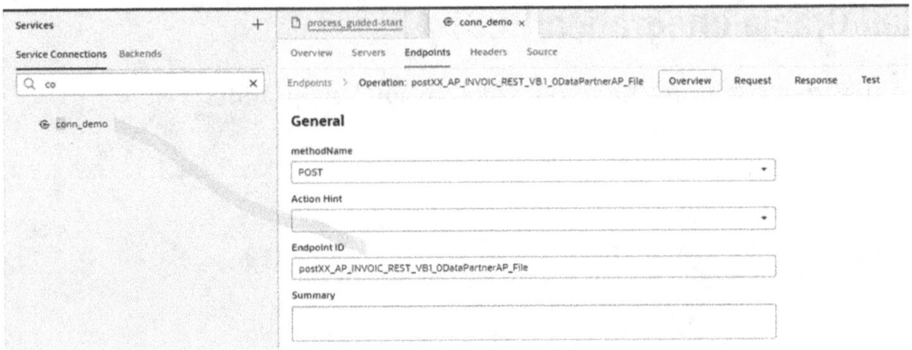

Figure 11-36. Service Connection Endpoint

Complete End-to-End Test

Step 1: Launch the Application

Preview the Guided Process page.

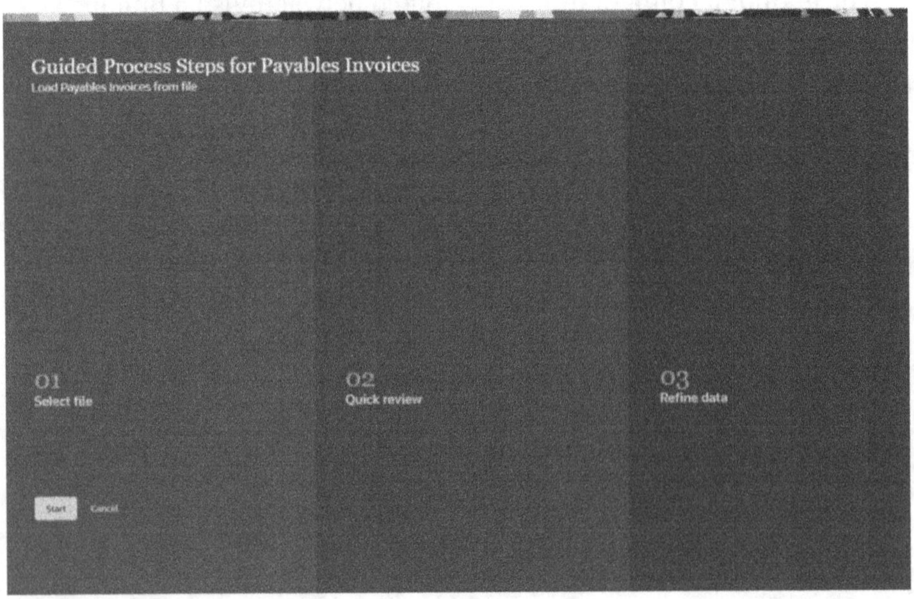

Figure 11-37. Application Launch Screen

Step 2: Load the CSV File

Select and upload the CSV file.

Test File: 21_PartnerAP_01_2025_1_lin_demo.csv

File Contents:

Vendor_Name,Vendor Number,Vendor_Address_Code,Invoice_Date,Distribution Set,Net Amount,qualifica,Invoice Description

ABC Consulting,1288,ABC US1,2024-07-01,PARTNER OTHER,300.30,ABCD,Unittest ZZZ with Appendix

Figure 11-38. File Selection Interface

Step 3: Generate a Batch ID

Click **Continue** to generate a unique batch ID for this processing run.

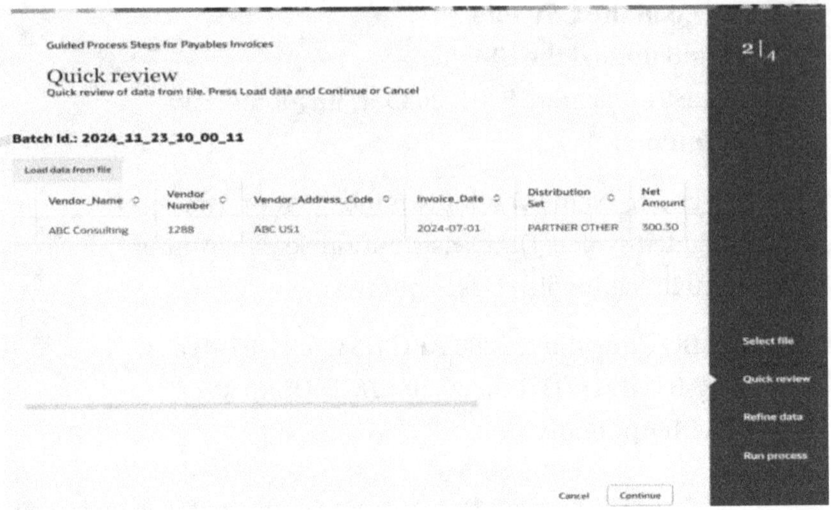

Figure 11-39. *Batch ID Generation*

Step 4: Load Data from the File

Click the **Load data from file** button to parse and store CSV data in the Business Object.

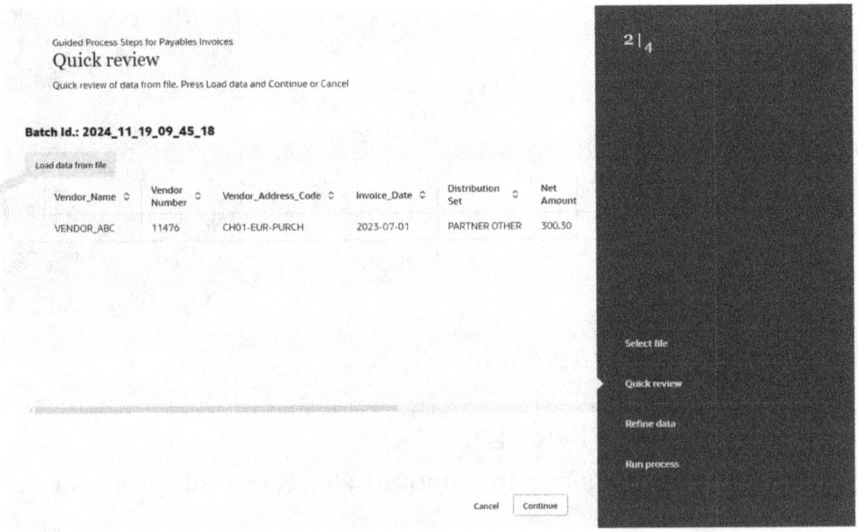

Figure 11-40. *Load data from file Button*

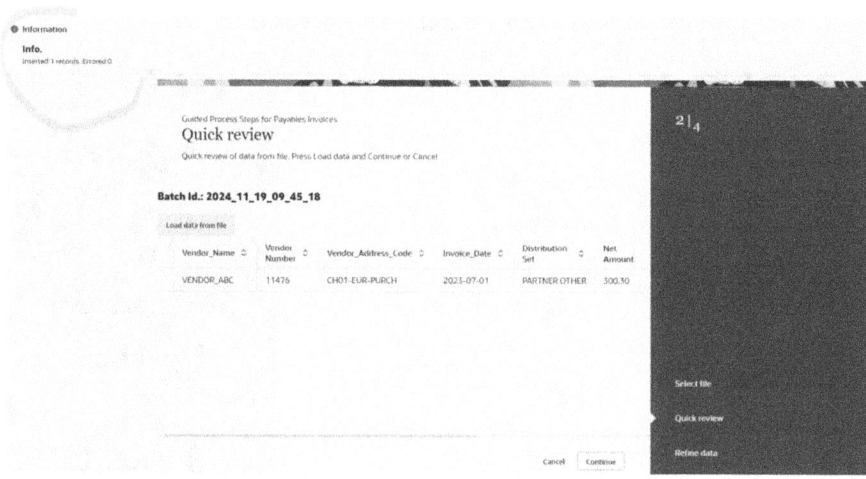

Figure 11-41. *Data Load Confirmation*

Step 5: Review and Edit Data

Before processing, review the loaded data and make corrections if necessary.

Figure 11-42. *Data Review Screen*

Edit data if needed, and then click the **Run Process** button.

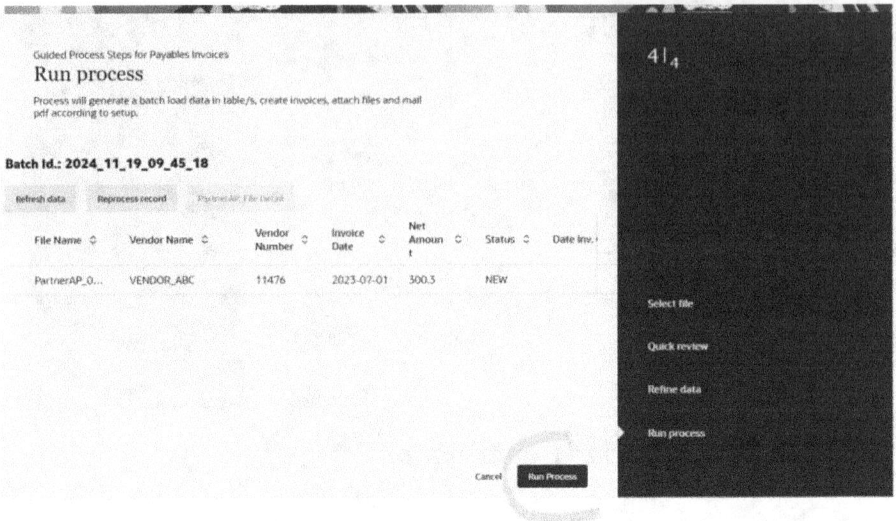

Figure 11-43. Edit and Run the Process

Step 6: Process Execution

At this point:

1. OIC integration executes.
2. The REST API creates Payables invoices in ERP Cloud.
3. Results (success/error) are written back to the Visual Builder Business Object.
4. Additional metadata is stored, including Invoice Number, Date Invoice created, Date Invoice attached, etc.

Figure 11-44. Processing Status Display

Figure 11-45. Processing Complete

Step 7: Review Results

View detailed results for each processed invoice.

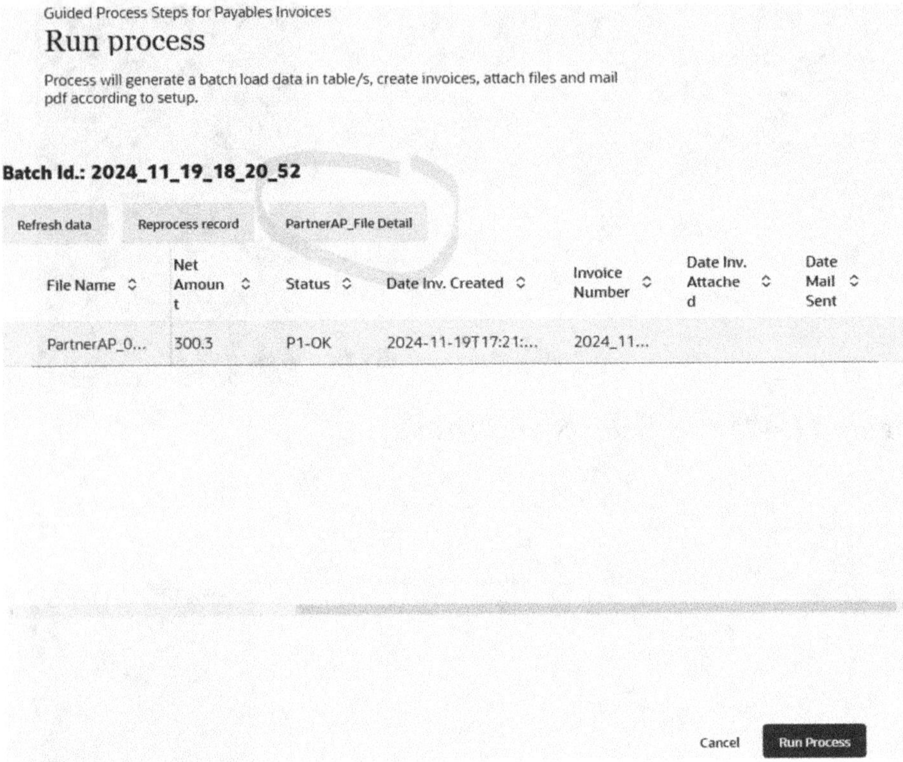

Figure 11-46. *Results Detail View*

Notice the invoice ID generated by ERP Cloud.

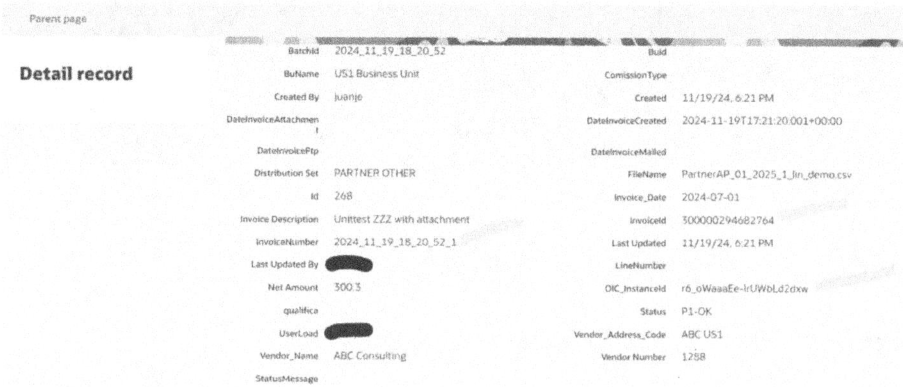

Figure 11-47. *Detailed Record*

Step 8: Verify in ERP Cloud

Confirm the invoice was created successfully in SaaS/Fusion Applications.

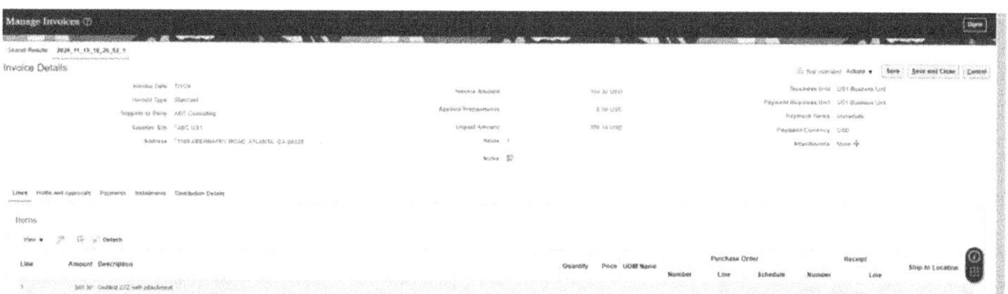

Figure 11-48. *Invoice in ERP Cloud*

Process Review Feature

The application includes a process review screen accessible via the **Review Processes** button.

Figure 11-49. *Review Processes Navigation*

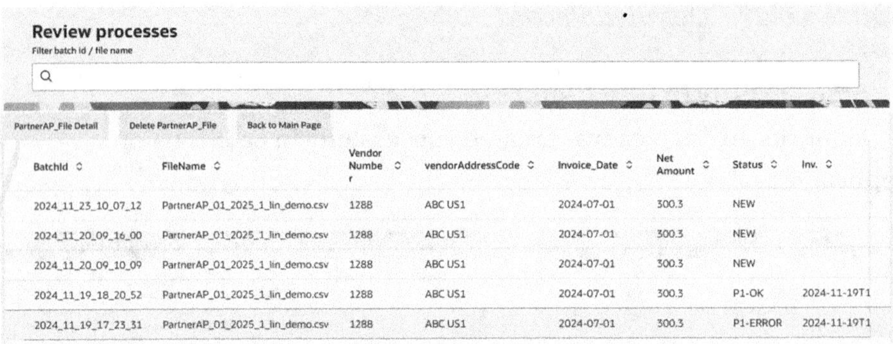

Figure 11-50. *Process Review Screen*

Error Handling

In case of processing errors, review detailed error information in the Business Object.

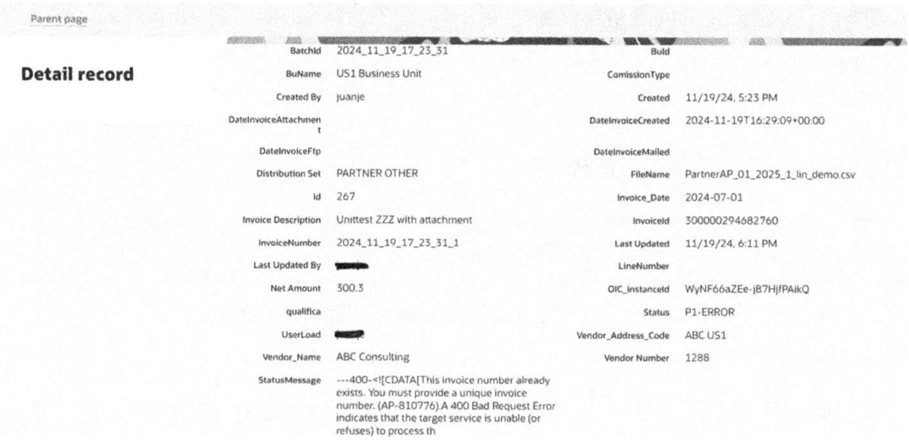

Figure 11-51. *Error Details Display*

Conclusion

This chapter has demonstrated a complete proof-of-concept (POC) that uses **Visual Builder** for user interface and data staging and **Oracle Integration Cloud** for orchestration and transformation to create **SaaS/ Fusion Applications** invoice payables from a CSV file and updating data in Visual Builder Business Objects.

The solution showcases

- CSV file parsing and validation
- Business Object data management
- REST API integration with ERP Cloud
- Bidirectional data updates between Visual Builder and OIC
- Error handling and status tracking
- User-friendly Guided Process workflow

This pattern can be adapted for other FBDI-style interfaces or data loading scenarios.

Technical Reference

Code Example	Comments
XX_AP_INVOIC_REST_VB_01.00.0001.iar	Oracle Integration used in demo
21_GUIDED_PROC_AP_INV-1.0.3.zip	Visual Builder application used in demo
21_PartnerAP_01_2025_1_lin_demo.csv	Sample CSV file for testing
21_PapaParse-1.0.zip	Visual Builder application for CSV parsing learning (based on Satish Kumar's Tutorial and GitHub Repository)
21_sample_1.txt	Sample test payload for OIC integration
21_sample_2.txt	JavaScript code for page-level CSV handling

CHAPTER 12

Lookups

Overview

Lookups in OIC serve multiple important purposes in integration development. They provide a flexible, maintainable way to manage reference data and configuration values without hardcoding inside the integration code.

Reference Documentation

- Managing Lookups in OIC
- Service Limits

Common Use Cases for Lookups

Value Mapping Between Systems

Lookup excels at translating values between different systems that use different codes for the same fields.

Example: Status Code Mapping

J. J. Montero Rodríguez and S. Tahseen, *Oracle Integration Cookbook for Oracle ERP Cloud*,
https://doi.org/10.1007/979-8-8688-3020-4_12

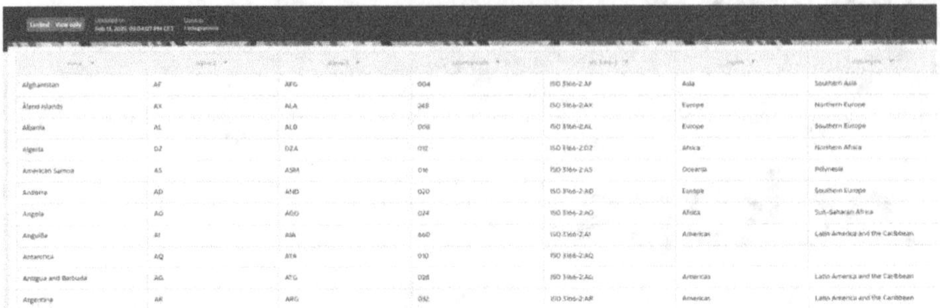

Figure 12-1. *Value Mapping Lookup*

This allows you to map "ACTIVE" in System A to "A" in System B or "PENDING" to "P", maintaining system independence while ensuring accurate data translation.

Avoiding Hardcoded Values

Store configuration values like email distribution lists to avoid hardcoding them in integrations.

Example: Notification Email Lists

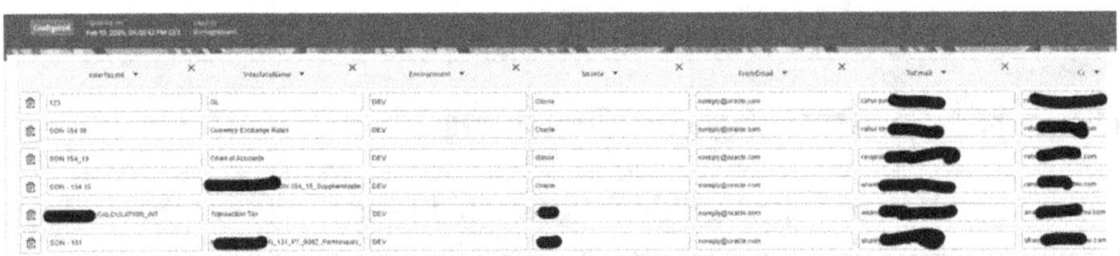

Figure 12-2. *Email Distribution List Lookup*

This approach allows you to update email recipients without modifying and redeploying integrations.

Example: HTML Message Templates

Figure 12-3. *HTML Template Lookup*

Store complete HTML templates in lookups for consistent, maintainable notification formatting.

Complex Mapping Logic Simplification

Lookups can replace complex JavaScript code or database queries, especially when database access isn't available.

Figure 12-4. *Complex Mapping Lookup*

Important Lookup Limitations

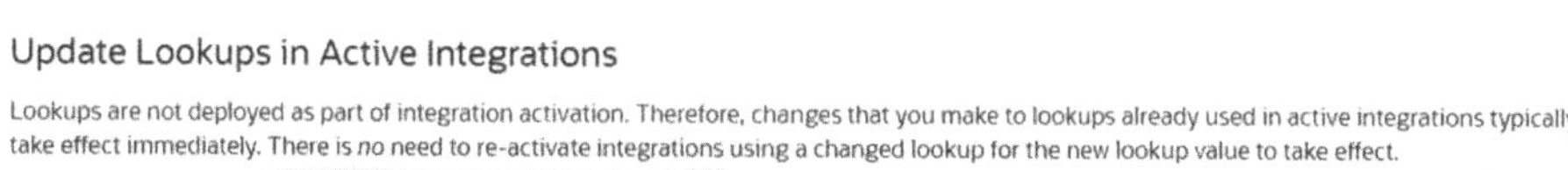

Update Lookups in Active Integrations

Lookups are not deployed as part of integration activation. Therefore, changes that you make to lookups already used in active integrations typically take effect immediately. There is *no* need to re-activate integrations using a changed lookup for the new lookup value to take effect.

Figure 12-5. *Lookup Limitations Notice*

Key Limitations

- Maximum lookup import limit size is 100 MB.
- There is no maximum limit for the number of rows in a lookup table.
- Maximum number of 100 columns in a lookup table.
- Performance degradation with large lookups.
- Not suitable for frequently changing data.
- Best for relatively static reference data.

Consider these limitations when designing your lookup strategy. For large or frequently changing datasets, consider alternative approaches like database tables or caching mechanisms.

Advanced Demo: Reading Lookups As Tables

The Challenge

Typically, lookups are accessed in a cell-by-cell manner, requiring

a) Lookup code

b) Domain code to search in

c) Domain code for response value

d) Parameter value to search for

This standard approach works well for single-value lookups but becomes cumbersome when you need to iterate through all rows of a lookup table.

Use Case: Table-Like Iteration

Sometimes you need to treat a lookup as a complete dataset to iterate through.

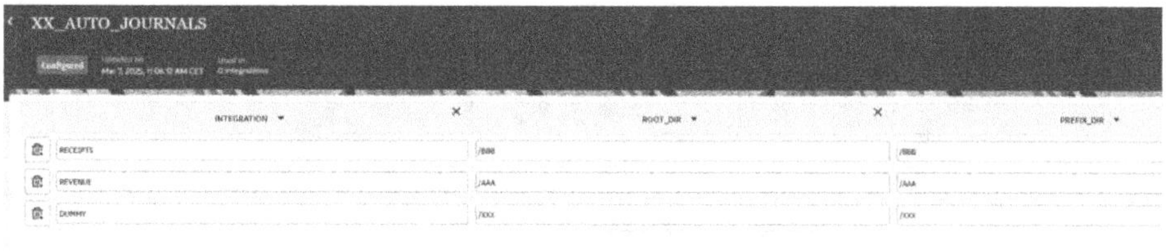

Figure 12-6. *Lookup As Table Structure*

This use case isn't straightforward with standard OIC lookup functions. We've developed a solution to address this need.

Solution Implementation

Prerequisites

OAuth Connection Setup

For Gen3, you need an OAuth connection configured as shown.

Figure 12-7. OAuth Connection Configuration

Important Contact your IT department for this setup, as it requires OIC administrative expertise

- Appropriate credentials and permissions
- OAuth token management configuration

Why OAuth Is Required

We need to access the OIC REST API endpoint for lookups. In Gen2, a basic username/password connection sufficed, but Gen3 requires OAuth for enhanced security.

Reference

Get Lookup Archive API

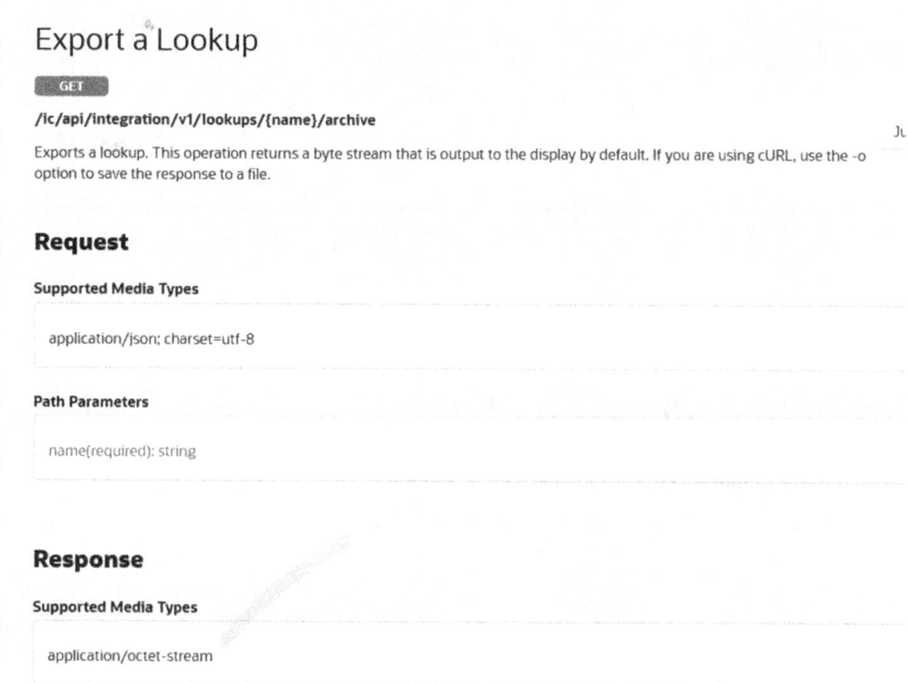

***Figure 12-8.** Lookup API Response Format*

Note The API returns data as application/octet-stream, requiring specific handling.

Integration Design

Overall Flow

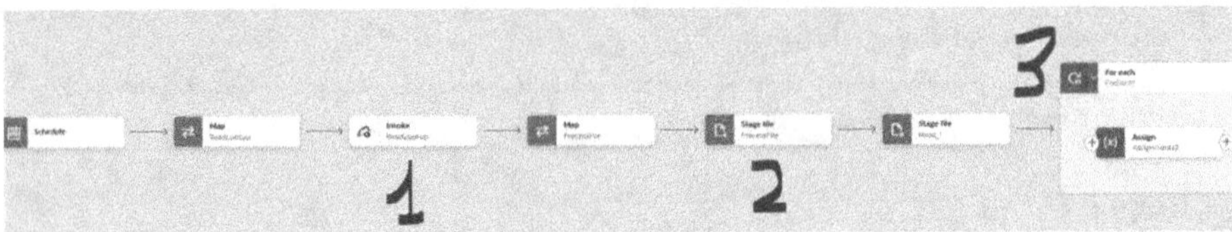

Figure 12-9. Read Lookup As Table Integration

Key Implementation Steps

Step 1: Read Lookup Data via REST API

Call the REST API to retrieve the lookup data.

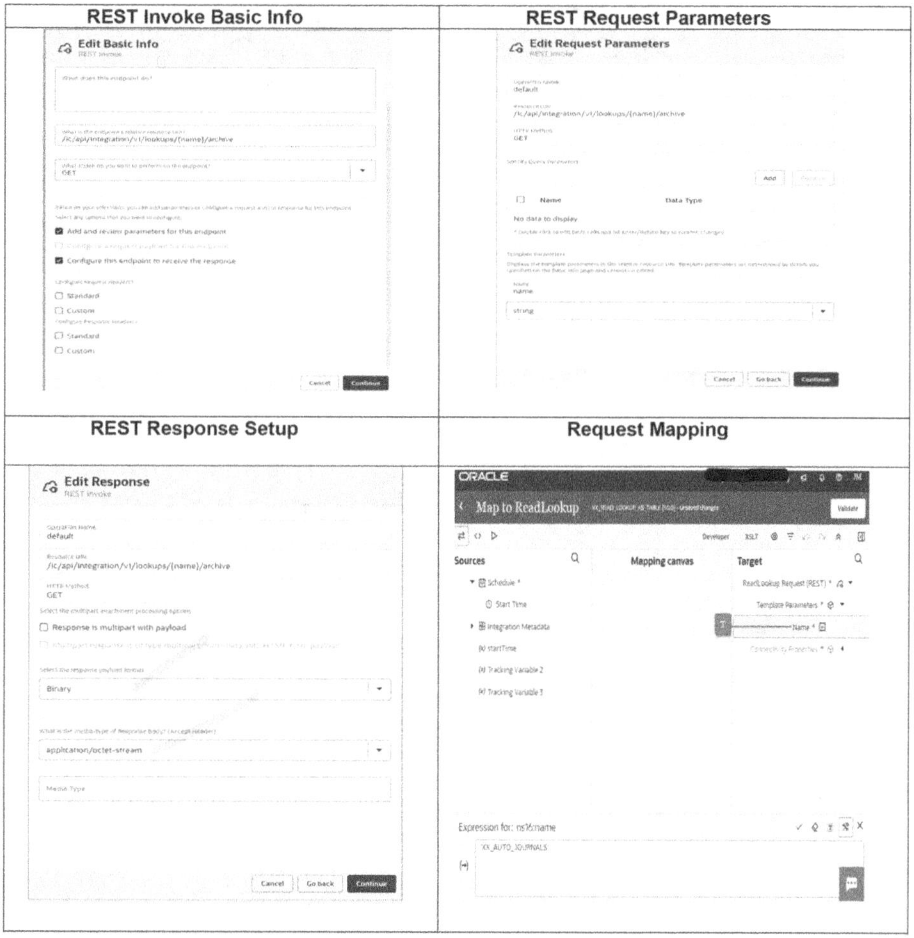

Figure 12-10. *Basic Configuration*

Step 2: Write File Reference

Write the received data reference to VFS (Virtual File System) using Stage Write file action.

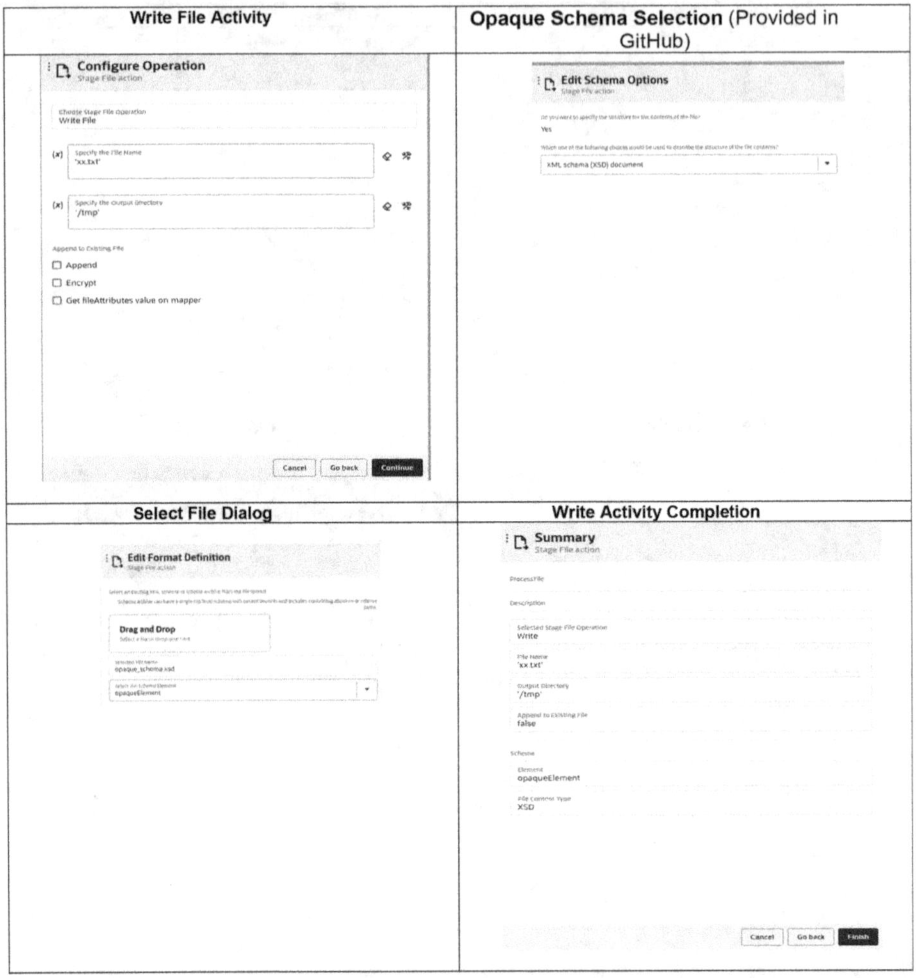

***Figure 12-11.** Stage Write File Configuration*

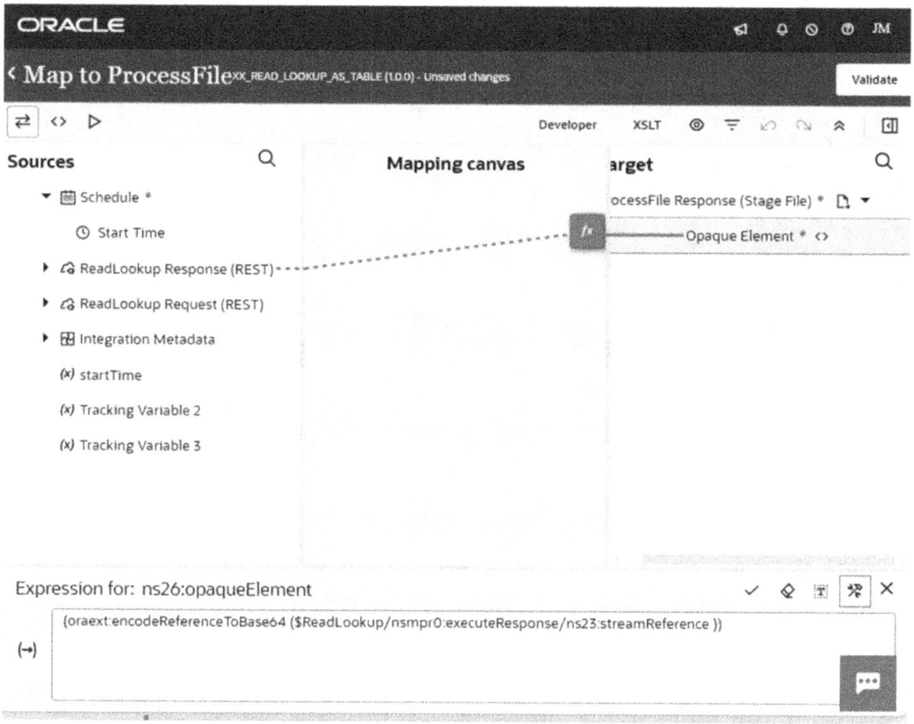

***Figure 12-12.** Stage Write File Mapping*

Step 3: Read CSV File

Read the CSV file for processing using Stage Read file action.

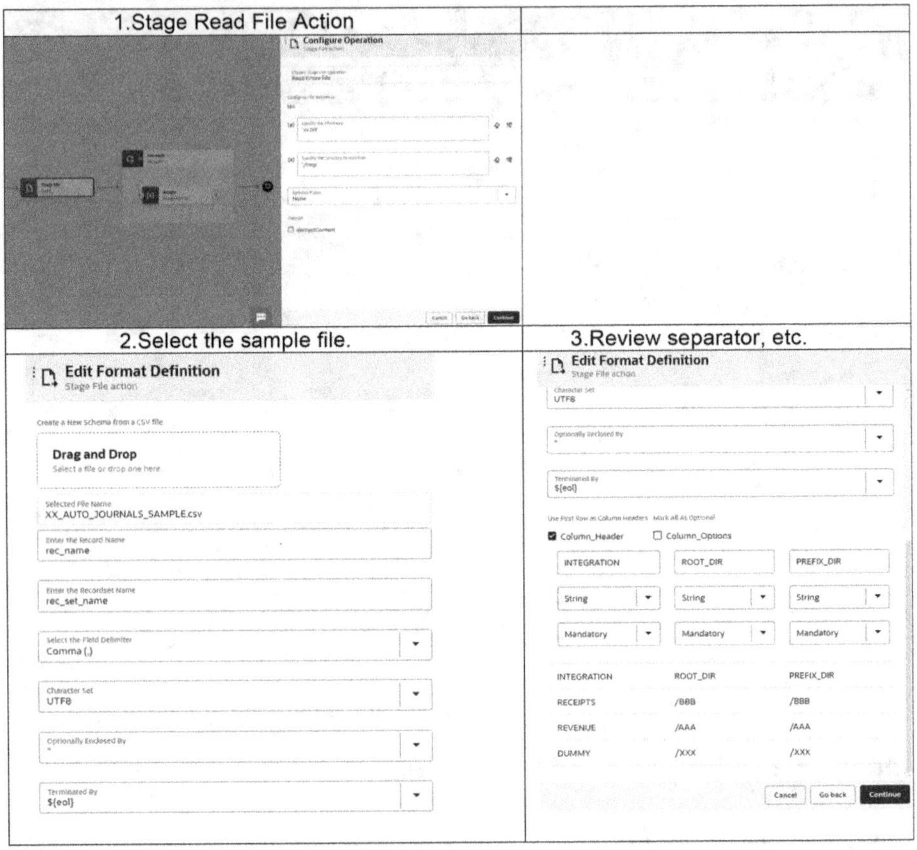

Figure 12-13. *Read File Activity*

Figure 12-14. *Select Sample CSV File—XX_AUTO_JOURNALS_SAMPLE.csv*

Sample File Reference: XX_AUTO_JOURNALS_SAMPLE.csv

Note the two-line structure (headers + data) shown in the configuration above.

Step 4: Access Column Values

Demonstrate accessing specific column values from the lookup table.

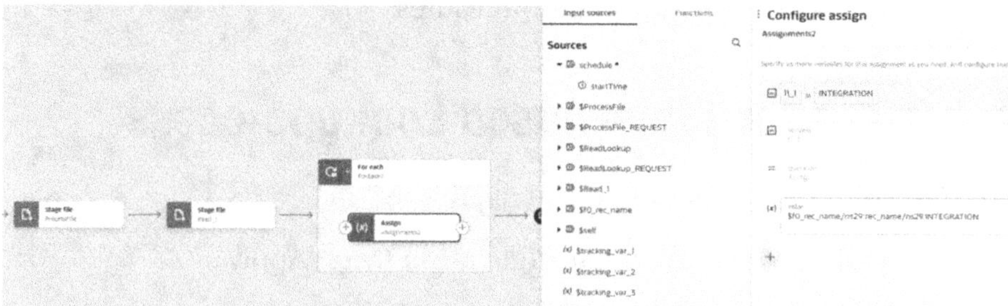

Figure 12-15. *Column Value Access*

Step 5: Testing the Integration

Execute a test to iterate through the lookup table and access row and column values.

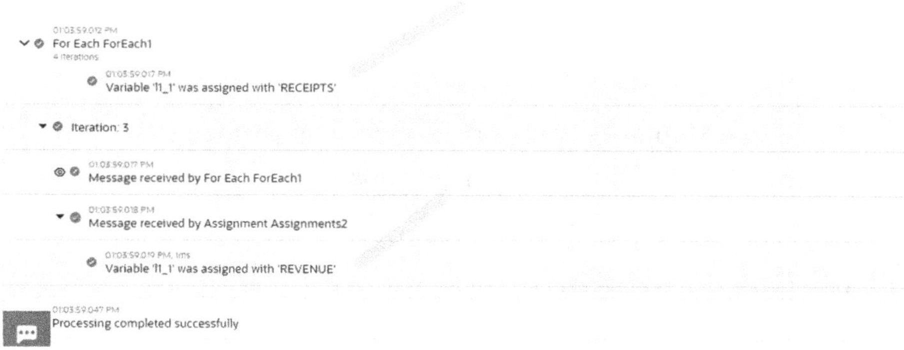

Figure 12-16. *Test Execution Results upon Table Iteration to Access Each of the Row–Column Values*

The test demonstrates successful

- Retrieval of lookup data via API
- Conversion to processable CSV format
- Iteration through all rows
- Access to individual column values

Use Cases for Table-Based Lookup Access

This approach is valuable when you need

1. **Bulk Processing of Configuration Data:** Apply rules or transformations based on entire lookup contents.
2. **Dynamic Configuration:** Load complete configuration sets at integration startup.
3. **Data Validation:** Check incoming data against entire reference datasets.
4. **Report Generation:** Include complete lookup contents in reports or logs.
5. **Batch Mapping:** Transform multiple values in one pass rather than individual lookups.

Technical Reference

Code Example	Comments
XX_AUTO_JOURNALS.csv	Lookup export file
XX_AUTO_JOURNALS_SAMPLE.csv	Sample file for Step 2 schema definition
XX_READ_LOOKUP_AS_TABLE	**OIC Integration—Package File**: XX_DEMO_COOKBOOK_2.par

CHAPTER 13

OIC Integration using FBDI

FBDI for Suppliers with Callback (Three Data Sources)

Overview

This section demonstrates File-Based Data Import (FBDI) for suppliers using three different data source approaches, plus a callback integration to handle processing results.

Reference Documentation

- FBDI Overview

FBDI Basics

Users can manually upload supplier data using Oracle-provided Excel templates to generate FBDI files. However, OIC adapters automate this process.

The ERP Cloud adapter for FBDI is streamlined—you simply provide a correctly formatted ZIP file, and OIC+ERP handle the rest.

J. J. Montero Rodríguez and S. Tahseen, *Oracle Integration Cookbook for Oracle ERP Cloud*,
https://doi.org/10.1007/979-8-8688-3020-4_13

FBDI File Structure

Required Components

Your ZIP file must contain

1. CSV data files
2. A ". properties" file with processing instructions

Figure 13-1. *FBDI ZIP File Contents*

Properties File Content

The properties file is an important file that contains crucial information of the adapter.

Figure 13-2. *Properties File Contents*

Key Information Included

- File path
- Program to execute
- Batch ID for tracking
- Processing options
- Additional parameters specific to the interface

Our Implementation Approach

We'll create four integrations demonstrating different data source approaches:

1. **XX_DEMO_IMP_SUPP_FTP:** Import files from an FTP server for FBDI process.
2. **XX_DEMO_IMP_SUPP_NO_FTP:** Create FBDI files "on the fly" using Stage operations.
3. **XX_DEMO_IMP_SUPP_OB_STOR:** Import files from Object Storage for FBDI.
4. **XX_DEMO_IMP_SUPP_CB:** Callback integration triggered when FBDI processing completes in ERP.

Required Connections

- **FBDI Processing:** Use "Basic ERP-CLOUD connection (3)" from Chapter 2.
- **Callback:** Use "ERP CLOUD events and Callback connection (4) " from Chapter 2.

Integration 1: XX_DEMO_IMP_SUPP_FTP

Integration Overview

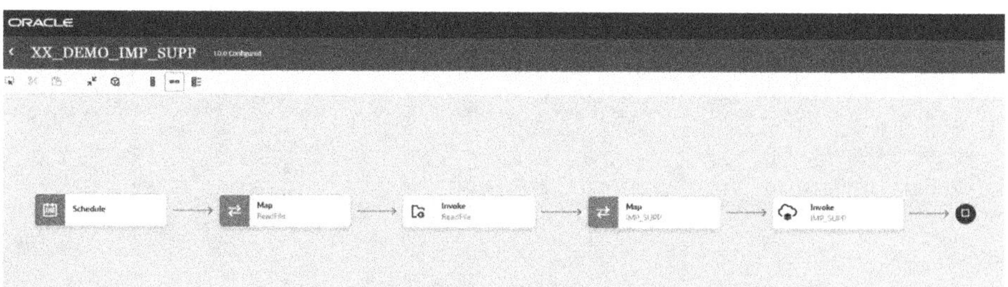

***Figure 13-3.** FTP-Based FBDI Integration Flow*

Configuration

For learning purposes, the filename is hardcoded.

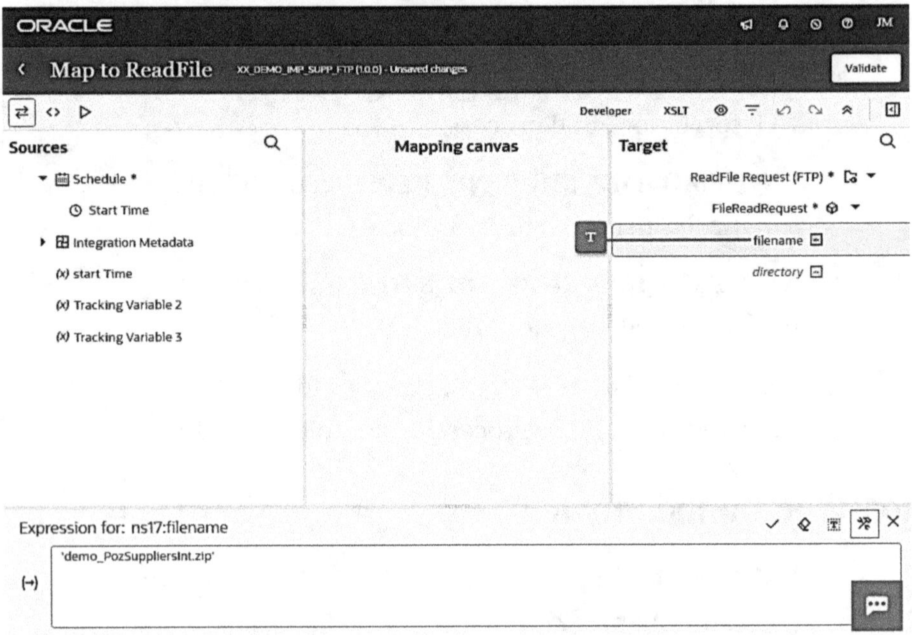

Figure 13-4. *Hardcoded Filename Configuration*

Testing

Prerequisites: Ensure the sample file exists on the FTP server before running.

Figure 13-5. *File on FTP Server*

Execute the Test:

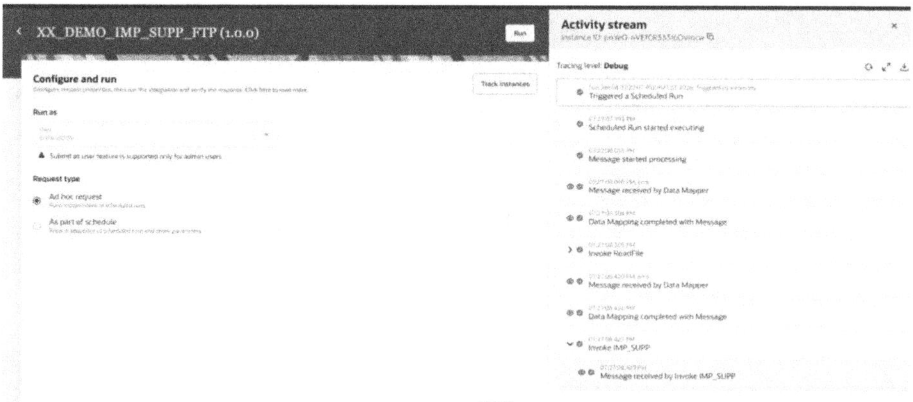

Figure 13-6. *Test Execution*

Verify Submission:

Check OIC Instance for successful run	Verify in Supplier creation in the ERP suppliers
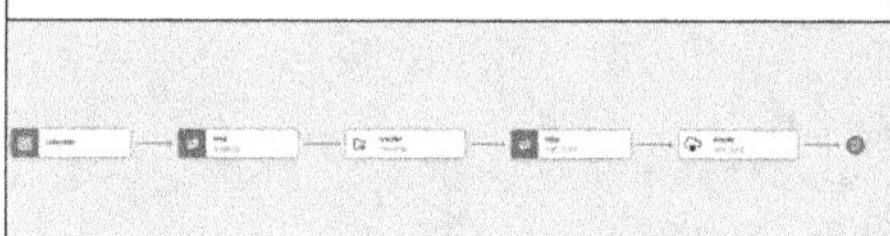	

Figure 13-7. *FBDI Job Submission Confirmation*

Integration 2: XX_DEMO_IMP_SUPP_NO_FTP

Integration Overview

This approach generates FBDI files dynamically using Stage operations, eliminating the need for a pre-existing file.

Figure 13-8. *Stage-Based FBDI Integration Flow*

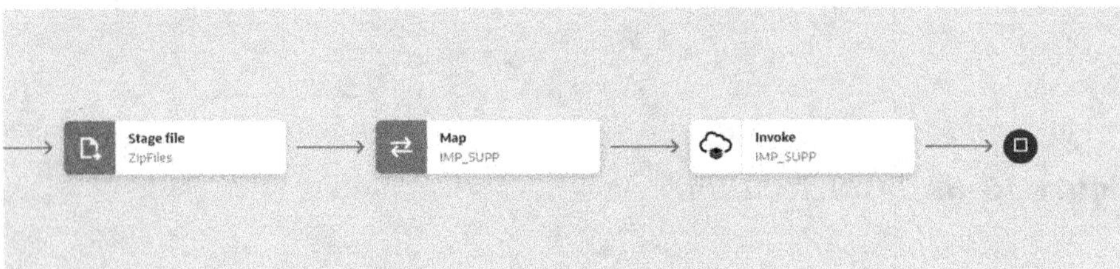

Figure 13-9. *File Creation with Stage Operations*

Testing

Execute the integration directly—no file preparation required.

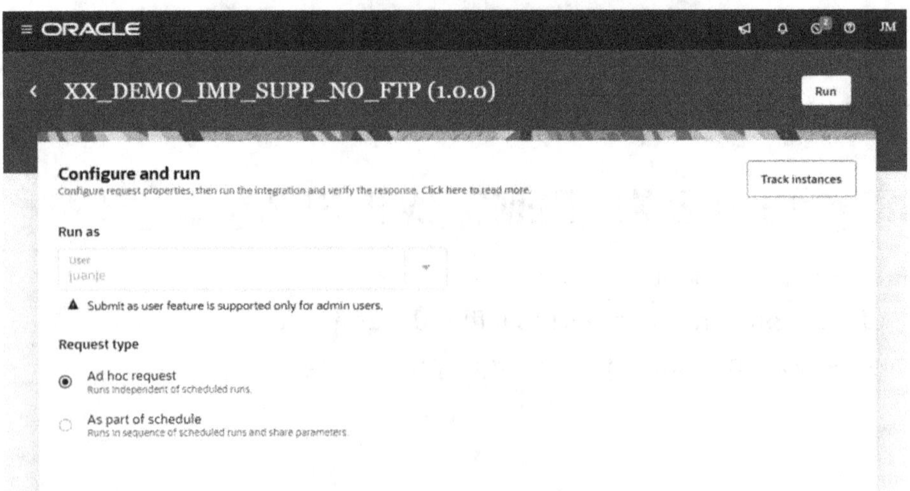

Figure 13-10. *Test Execution*

Integration 3: XX_DEMO_IMP_SUPP_OB_STOR (Object Storage Approach)

Integration Overview

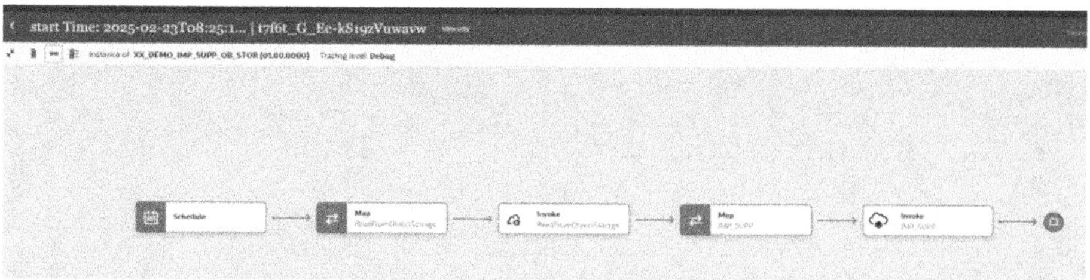

Figure 13-11. *Object Storage FBDI Integration Flow*

Object Storage Configuration

Resource URI Structure

The Object Storage resource URI follows this pattern:

```
/n/{namespaceName}/b/{bucketName}/o/{objectName}
```

Example Values:

- namespaceName="ax0t86rokvk3"
- bucketName="bucket-standard-jj1"
- objectName="demo_PozSuppliersInt.zip"

Invoke Activity Setup

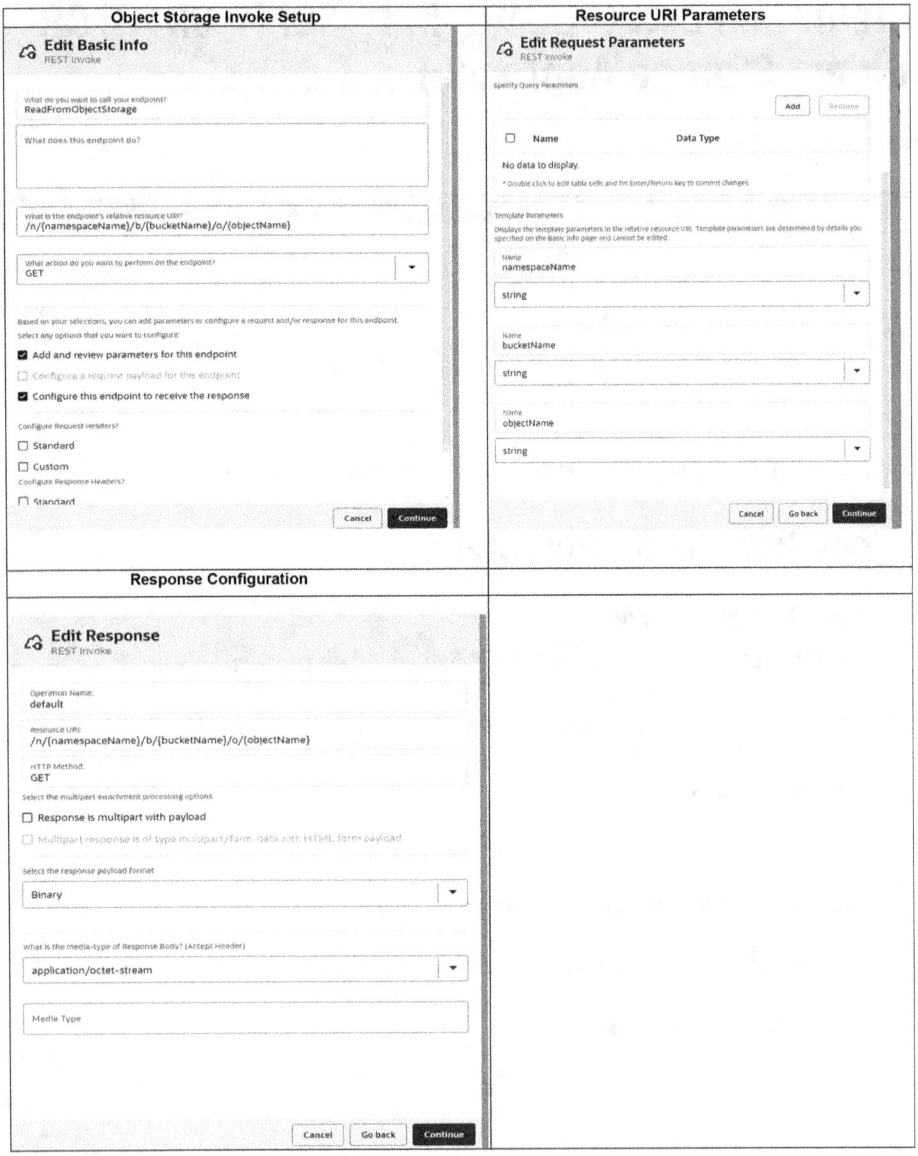

Figure 13-12. Invoke Activity for Object Storage

Mapping Configurations

Mapping 1: To Object Storage

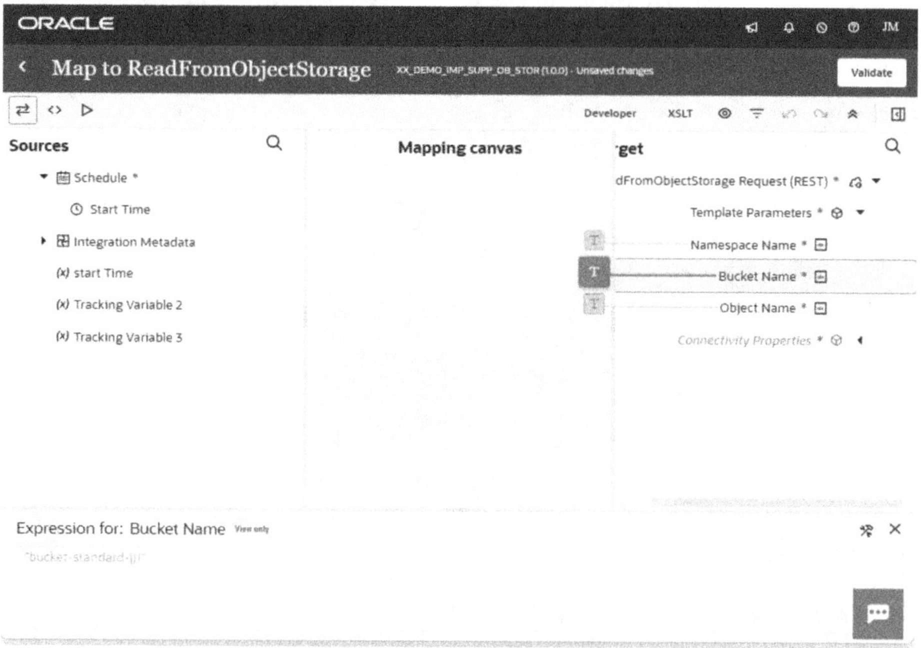

Figure 13-13. Object Storage Request Mapping

Mapping 2: To Import Suppliers

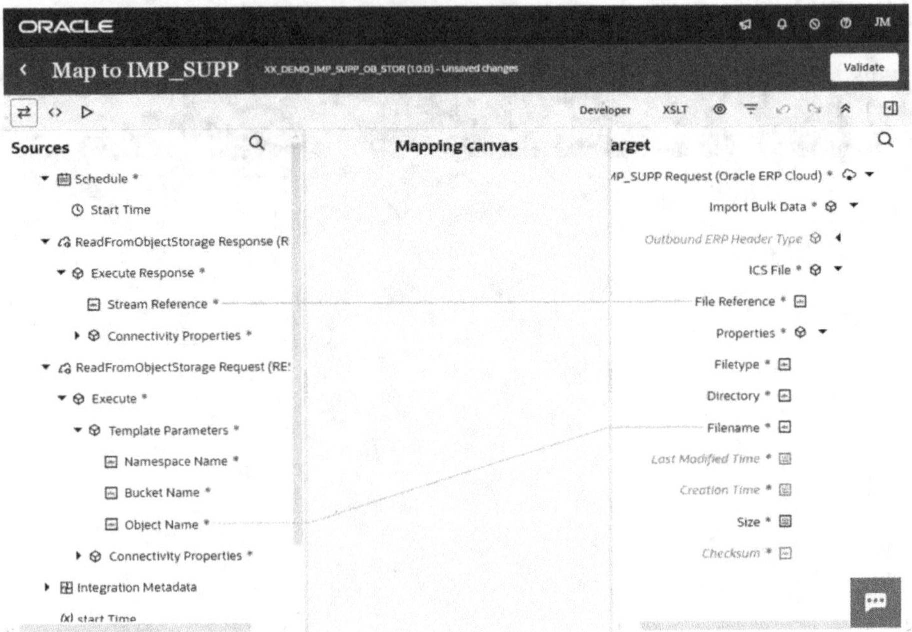

Figure 13-14. FBDI Submit Mapping

Testing

Execute the integration.

Locate the request ID in OIC logs.

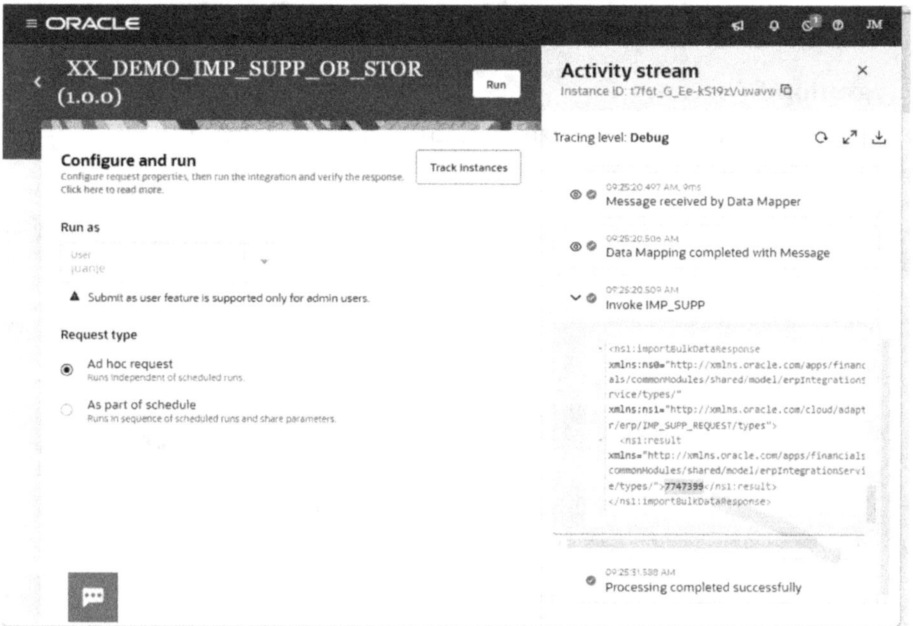

Figure 13-15. *Request ID in the Activity Stream*

Verify in ERP Cloud.

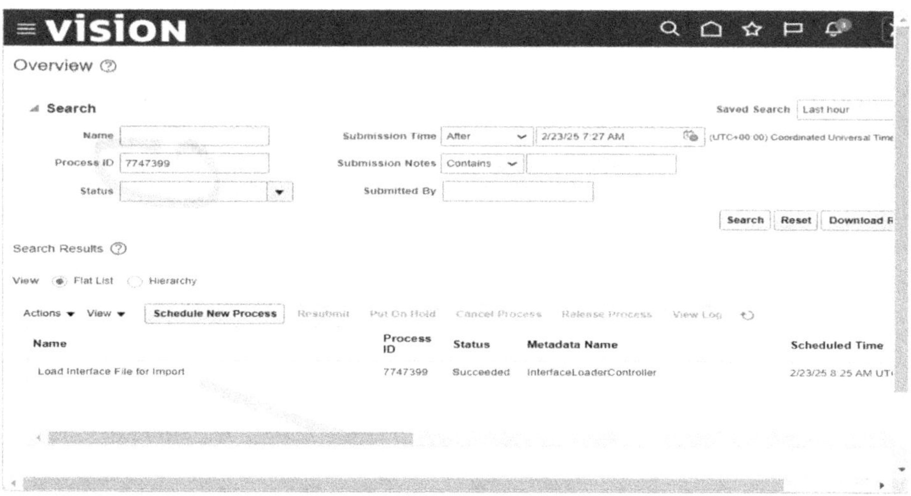

Figure 13-16. *Job in Scheduled Processes*

Integration 4: XX_DEMO_IMP_SUPP_CB

Integration Overview

The callback integration executes automatically when the FBDI process completes in ERP Cloud, providing real-time status updates.

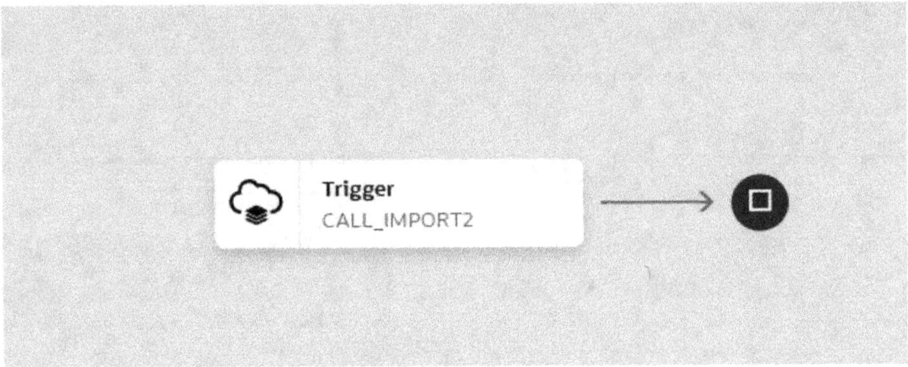

Figure 13-17. *Callback Integration Flow*

Event Filter Configuration

Configure a filter to process only relevant events.

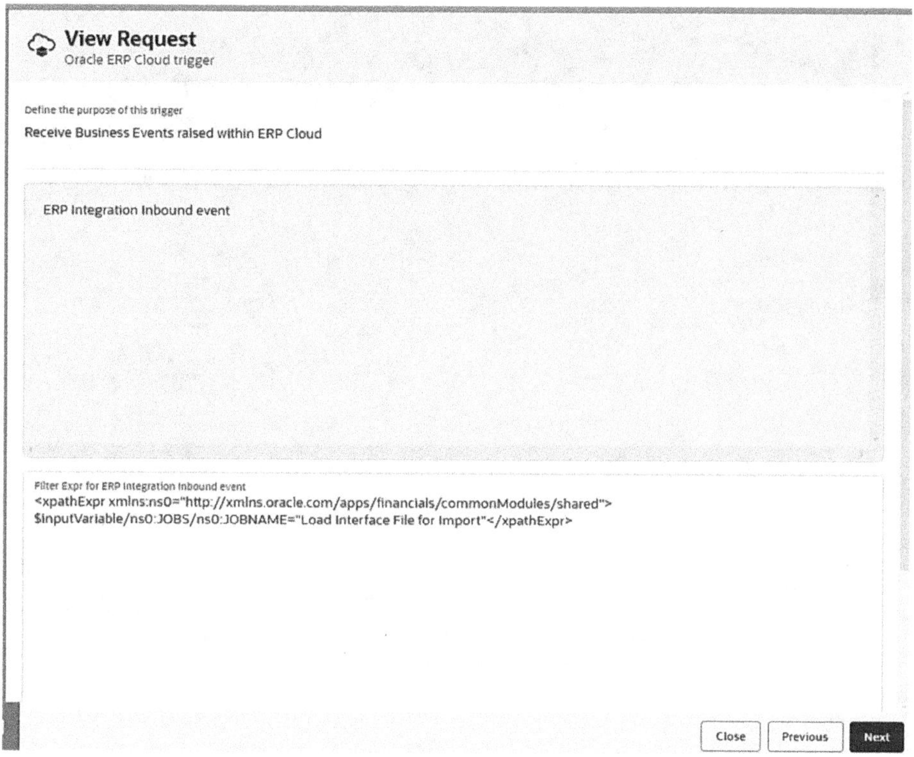

Figure 13-18. *Callback Event Filter*

This filter ensures the callback only processes supplier import completion events, ignoring other ERP jobs.

Reviewing Callback Integration

Monitor Callback Instances:

After running any of the three main integrations, the callback integration should trigger automatically when processing completes.

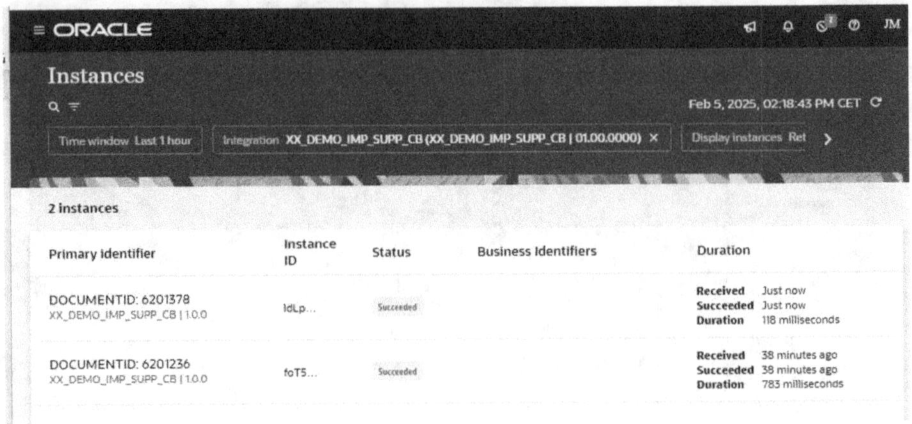

Figure 13-19. *Callback Integration Executions*

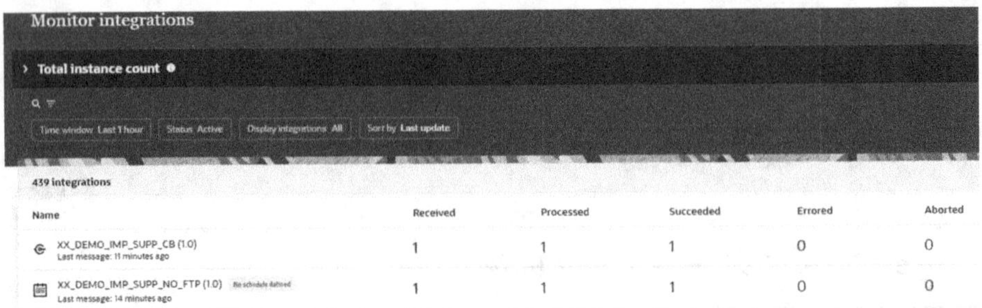

Figure 13-20. *Monitoring Integrations*

View Callback Details:

Click a succeeded instance to view details.

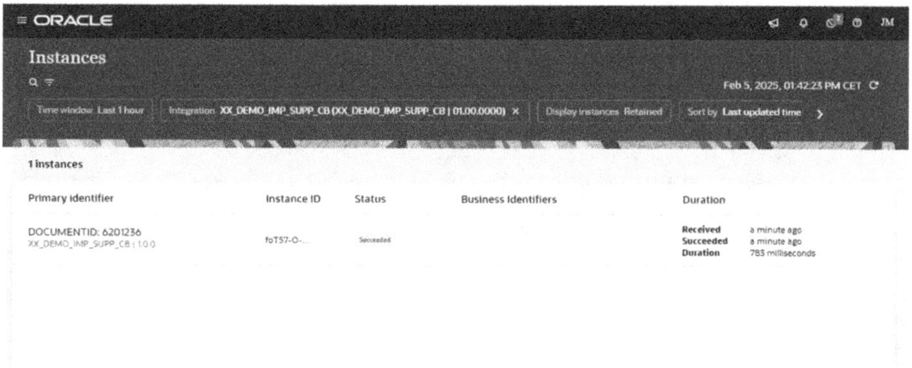

Figure 13-21. Succeeded Instance Details

ERP Payload Structure:

OIC-ERP provides a comprehensive payload with job details.

Figure 13-22. Callback Payload

Sample Payload Structure:

```
<ns0:JOBS>
    <ns0:CHILD>

      <ns0:JOBPATH>/oracle/apps/ess/financials/common
      Modules/shared/common/interfaceLoader</ns0:JOBPATH>
      <ns0:REQUESTID>7648988</ns0:REQUESTID>
      <ns0:JOBNAME>Transfer File</ns0:JOBNAME>
      <ns0:STATUS>SUCCEEDED</ns0:STATUS>
    </ns0:CHILD>
    <ns0:CHILD>
      <ns0:JOBPATH>/oracle/apps/ess/financials/common
      Modules/shared/common/interfaceLoader</ns0:JOBPATH>
      <ns0:REQUESTID>7648989</ns0:REQUESTID>
      <ns0:JOBNAME>Load File to Interface</ns0:JOBNAME>
      <ns0:STATUS>SUCCEEDED</ns0:STATUS>
    </ns0:CHILD>
    <ns0:JOBPATH>/oracle/apps/ess/financials/commonModules/
    shared/common/interfaceLoader</ns0:JOBPATH>
    <ns0:REQUESTID>7648987</ns0:REQUESTID>
    <ns0:JOBNAME>Load Interface File for Import</
    ns0:JOBNAME>
    <ns0:DOCUMENTNAME>zzzPozSuppliersInt.zip</
    ns0:DOCUMENTNAME>
    <ns0:STATUS>SUCCEEDED</ns0:STATUS>
  </ns0:JOBS>
  <ns0:JOBS>
    <ns0:JOBPATH>/oracle/apps/ess/prc/poz/supplierImport</
    ns0:JOBPATH>
    <ns0:REQUESTID>7648990</ns0:REQUESTID>
    <ns0:JOBNAME>Import Suppliers</ns0:JOBNAME>
    <ns0:STATUS>ERROR</ns0:STATUS>
```

```
      </ns0:JOBS>
      <ns0:JOBS>
        <ns0:JOBPATH>/oracle/apps/ess/financials/commonModules/
        shared/common/interfaceLoader</ns0:JOBPATH>
        <ns0:REQUESTID>7648992</ns0:REQUESTID>
        <ns0:JOBNAME>Upload Interface Error and Job Output File
        to Universal Content Management</ns0:JOBNAME>
        <ns0:STATUS>SUCCEEDED</ns0:STATUS>
      </ns0:JOBS>
    </ns0:ErpImportBulkDataEvent>
  </env:Body>
</env:Envelope>
```

(Note: This sample represents a failed import scenario. The callback integration should inspect the STATUS value before sending notifications.)

With this payload we could notify the users using "Notification" activity, for example, or run another process.

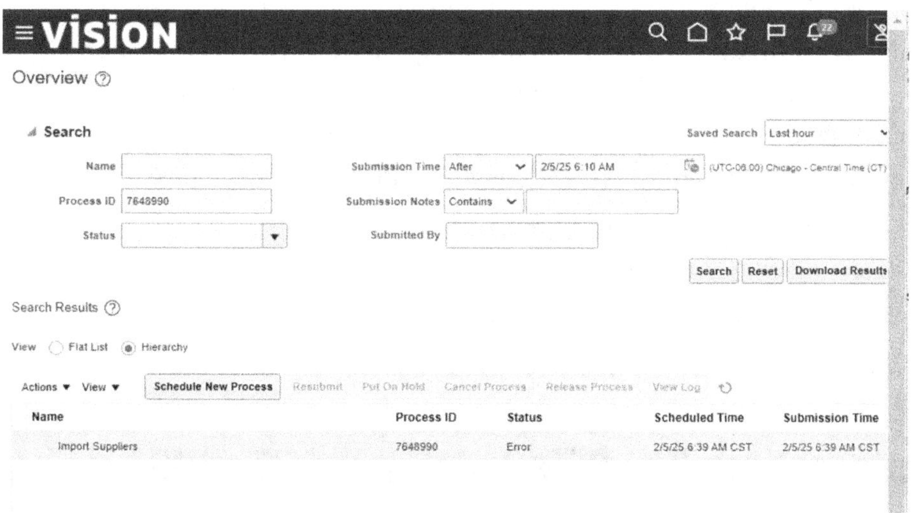

Figure 13-23. *Review ERP-SaaS*

Technical Reference

Code Example	Comments
XX_DEMO_IMP_SUPP_FTP	Package file XX_DEMO_COOKBOOK_2.par
XX_DEMO_IMP_SUPP_NO_FTP	Package file XX_DEMO_COOKBOOK_2.par
XX_DEMO_IMP_SUPP_OB_STOR	Package file XX_DEMO_COOKBOOK_2.par
XX_DEMO_IMP_SUPP_CB Version 1.0	Package file XX_DEMO_COOKBOOK_2.par
demo_PozSuppliersInt.zip	File demo for upload

FBDI for Customers with File Management

Overview

This section demonstrates a basic flow to import customers and related data with enhanced file management capabilities. The process reads multiple files, processes them, and moves them to either an "error" or "success" directory based on the processing result. The integration waits for the process to complete and retrieves the result via a SOAP web service.

Reference Documentation

Customer Import FBDI

> **Note** This interface does not require a ".properties" file.

Integration: XX_DEMO_AR_IMPORT_CUST

General Integration Flow

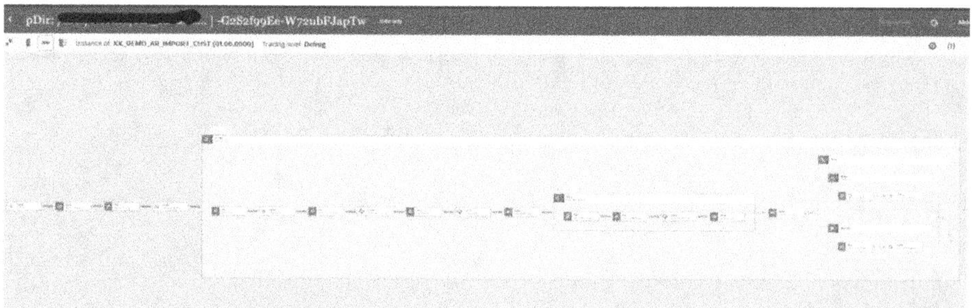

Figure 13-24. Integration Overview

Main Process Steps

Step 1: Receive Parameters and Initialize Variables

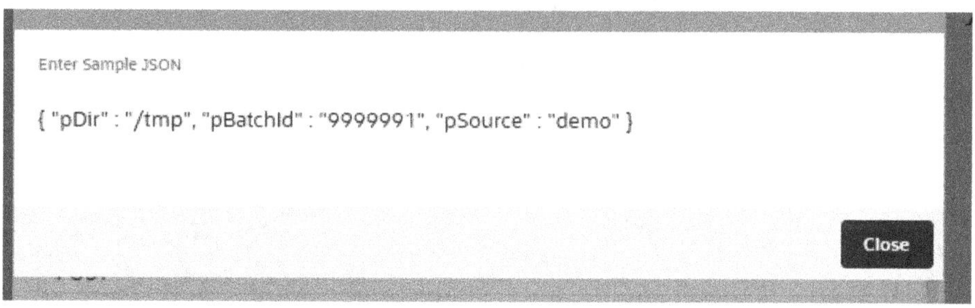

Figure 13-25. Parameter Configuration

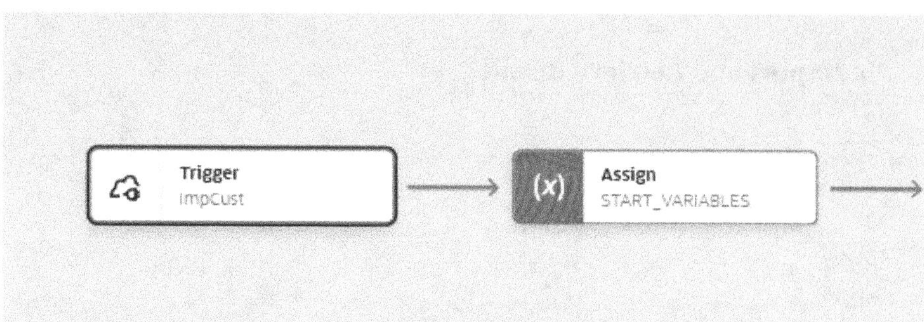

Figure 13-26. Variable Initialization

Step 2: List Files in the Directory

The integration lists all files in the directory sent as a parameter.

Figure 13-27. Directory File Listing

Step 3: Process Files in Loop

3a. Download the File and Send to UCM

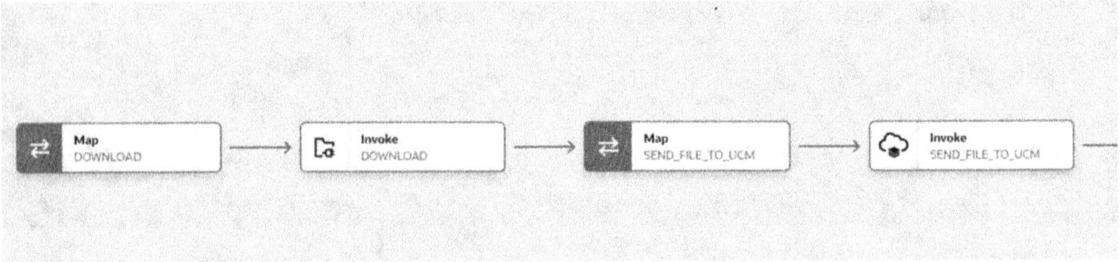

Figure 13-28. File Download and UCM Upload

3b. Import and Retrieve Result

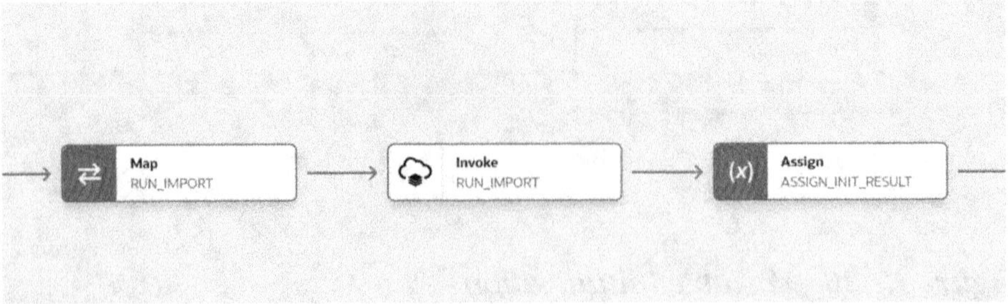

Figure 13-29. Import Process Flow

Mapping Configuration:

```
<xsl:template match="/" xml:id="id_11">
    <nstrgmpr:submitESSJobRequest xml:id="id_12">
        <nstrgmpr:jobPackageName xml:id="id_106">
            <xsl:value-of xml:id="id_231" select="$selfProperties/nsmpr7:properties/nsmpr7:x_job_path"/>
        </nstrgmpr:jobPackageName>
        <nstrgmpr:jobDefinitionName xml:id="id_108">
            <xsl:value-of xml:id="id_232" select="$selfProperties/nsmpr7:properties/nsmpr7:x_job_name"/>
        </nstrgmpr:jobDefinitionName>
        <nstrgmpr:paramList xml:id="id_56">
            <xsl:value-of xml:id="id_279" select="/ns48:execute/ns49:request-wrapper/ns49:pBatchId"/>
        </nstrgmpr:paramList>
        <nstrgmpr:paramList xml:id="id_56">
            <xsl:value-of xml:id="id_484" select="$SEND_FILE_TO_UCM/nsmpr2:FileUploadResponse/nsmpr2:docID"/>
        </nstrgmpr:paramList>
        <nstrgmpr:paramList xml:id="id_56">
            <xsl:value-of xml:id="id_525" select="/ns48:execute/ns49:request-wrapper/ns49:pBatchId"/>
        </nstrgmpr:paramList>
        <nstrgmpr:paramList xml:id="id_56">
            <xsl:value-of xml:id="id_327" select="'CREATE'"/>
        </nstrgmpr:paramList>
    </nstrgmpr:submitESSJobRequest>
```

Figure 13-30. *Mapping Configuration*

In this parameter, we send the reference to the file.

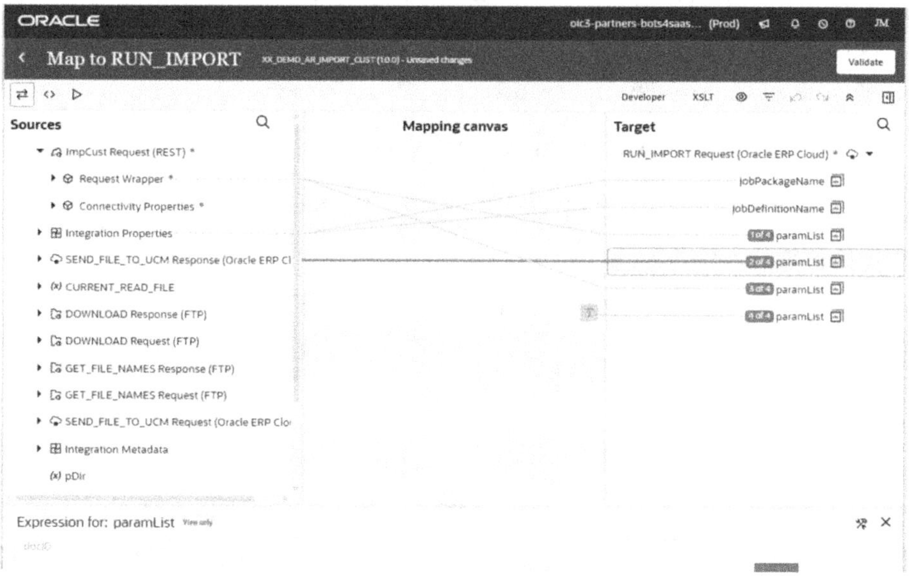

Figure 13-31. *File Reference Parameter*

3c. Wait for Process Completion

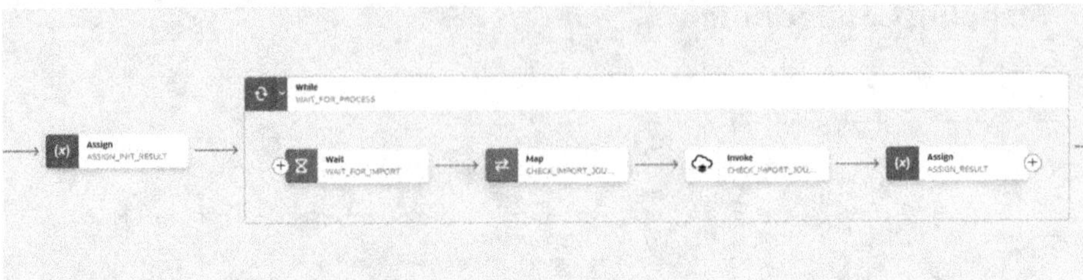

Figure 13-32. *Wait for Completion.*

Note In this implementation, the process waits indefinitely. As an exercise, you must add a counter and error path in any non-demo implementation and exit after ten retries.

3d. Capture Result and Move Files

Based on the processing result:

- **Success:** Move the file to the "success" directory.
- **Error:** Move the file to the "error" directory.

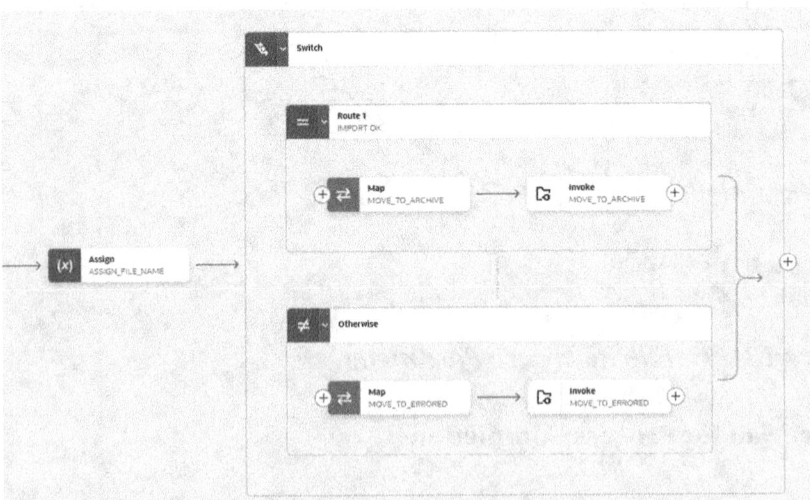

Figure 13-33. *Result Handling*

Testing

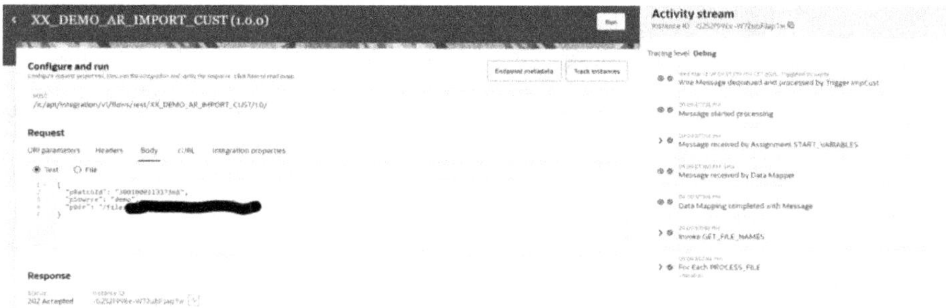

Figure 13-34. Test Configuration

We have provided a dummy .zip file (see below). The instance may not be able to process it successfully.

Figure 13-35. Sample File

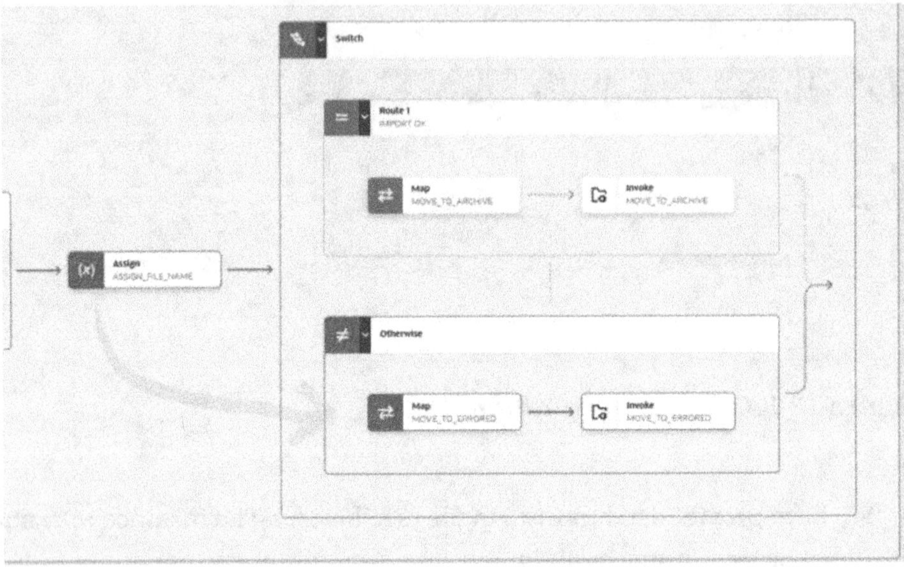

Figure 13-36. *Test Results*

Note This is a basic demo for learning purposes. Feel free to improve and add validations.

Technical Reference

Code Example	Comments
XX_DEMO_AR_IMPORT_CUST	**Package File**: XX_DEMO_COOKBOOK_2.par
arcustomerimport.zip	Demo file for upload

CHAPTER 14

Other FBDI Interfaces

Overview

The previous chapter demonstrated a basic flow to import suppliers and customers. Note that not all ERP interfaces require properties files and finding detailed information to compose these files is not always straightforward.

Finding Parameters

Sometimes we need to refer to Oracle Support for samples or investigate the job configuration directly. To determine the correct order of parameters:

1. Run the import process manually.
2. Review the Scheduled Processes page.

J. J. Montero Rodríguez and S. Tahseen, *Oracle Integration Cookbook for Oracle ERP Cloud*, https://doi.org/10.1007/979-8-8688-3020-4_14

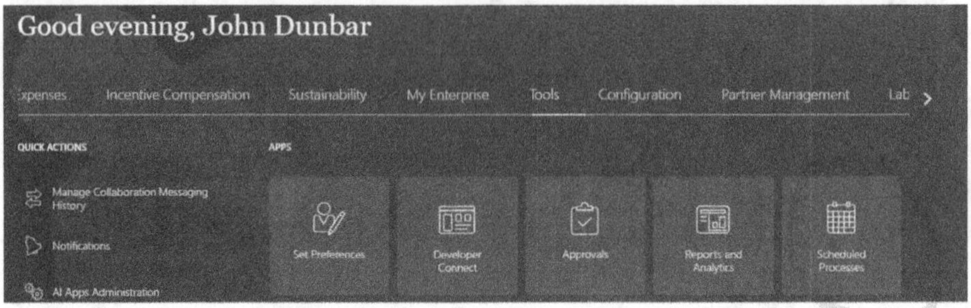

Figure 14-1. Scheduled Processes Page

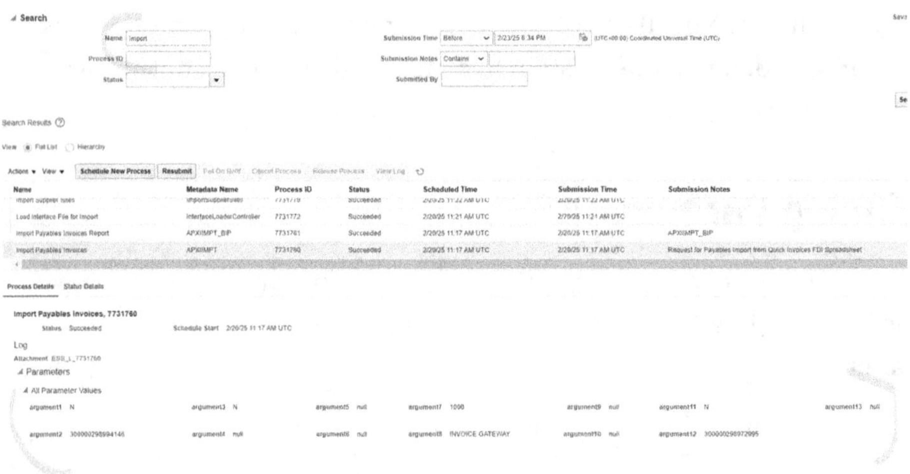

Figure 14-2. Process Parameters

This chapter provides additional properties file examples for various FBDI interfaces.

Suppliers Interface

The Suppliers interface consists of several sub-interfaces. Below are the properties file structure samples:

Interface	Sample
Suppliers	/oracle/apps/ess/prc/poz/supplierImport/,ImportSuppliers,suppliers, ALL,N,999999
Addresses	/oracle/apps/ess/prc/poz/supplierImport/,ImportSupplierAddresses,a ddresses,ALL,N,999999
Supplier Sites	/oracle/apps/ess/prc/poz/supplierImport/,ImportSupplierSites,sites, ALL,N,999999
Site Assignments	/oracle/apps/ess/prc/poz/supplierImport/,ImportSupplierSiteAssignm ents,site_assig,ALL,N,999999
Contacts	/oracle/apps/ess/prc/poz/supplierImport/,ImportSupplierContacts,co ntacts,ALL,N,999999
Bank Accounts	/oracle/apps/ess/financials/payments/fundsDisbursement/payments /,ImportSuppBankAccounts,sup_bank_accounts,ALL,N,999999

Payables Invoices

Reference Documentation: Payables Standard Invoice Import

Properties File Sample:

/oracle/apps/ess/financials/payables/invoices/transactions/,APXII MPT,apinvoiceimport,#NULL,300000001596022,N,#NULL,#NULL,#NUL L,1000,INVOICE GATEWAY,#NULL,N,N,300000001594026,#NULL,1

Investigation Steps

In Oracle ERP, navigate to **Menu ➤ Setup and Maintenance ➤ Search ➤ "Manage Enterprise Scheduler Job Definitions and Job Sets for Financial, Supply Chain Management, and Related Applications".**

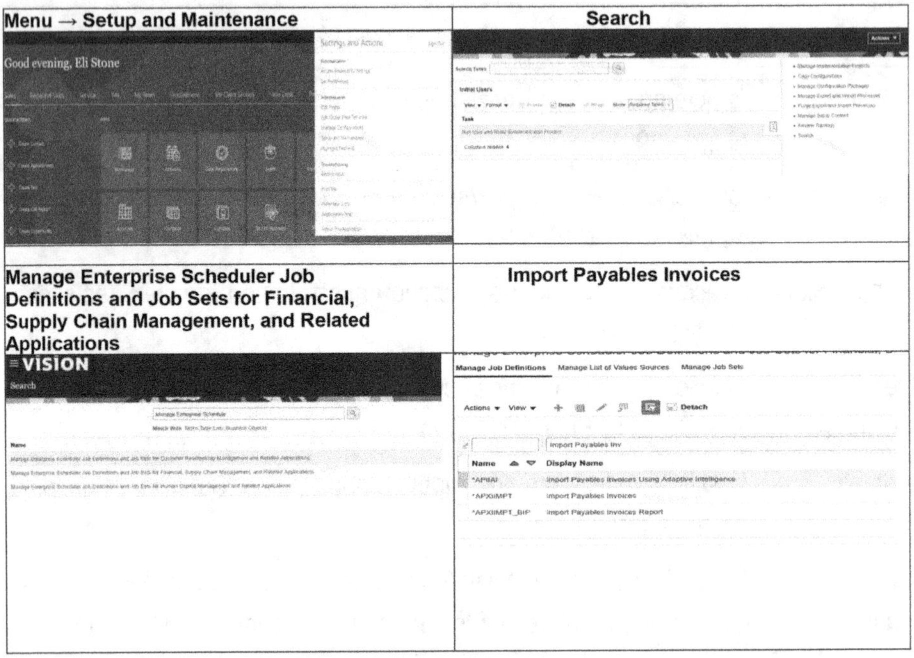

Figure 14-3. *Oracle ERP Navigation Steps*

Then filter by "Import Payables Invoices".

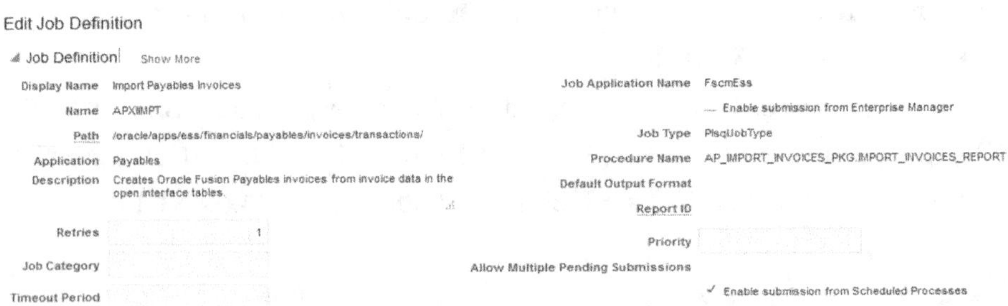

Figure 14-4. *Job Definition Search*

Parameter Prompt	Data Type	Page Element	Default Value
ATTRIBUTE1	String	Text box	
ATTRIBUTE2	Numeric	Choice list	
ATTRIBUTE3	String	Text box	N
Accounting Date	DateTime	Date Picker	
Hold	String	Choice list	
Hold Reason	String	Text box	
ATTRIBUTE7	Numeric	Text box	1000
Source	String	Choice list	
Import Set	String	Text box	
Purge	String	Choice list	
Summarize Report	String	Choice list	
ATTRIBUTE12	java.math.BigDecimal	Choice list	
Invoice Group	String	Text box	
Number of Parallel Processes	java.lang.Integer	Text box	1

***Figure 14-5.** Parameter Setup*

More Parameters

Number of Parallel Processes	java.lang.Integer	Text box	1
Ledger	String	List of values	
Business Unit	String	List of values	
HOLD	String	Text box	
SOURCE	String	List of values	
SummarizeReport	String	Text box	

Receivables Invoices

Reference Documentation: AutoInvoice Import

Properties File Sample:

/oracle/apps/ess/financials/receivables/transactions/autoInvoices/,AutoInvoiceImportEss,AutoInvoiceImport,300000001596022,Management,2025-10-03,#NULL,#NULL,#NULL,#NULL,#NULL,#NULL,#NULL,#NULL,#NULL,#NULL,#NULL,#NULL,#NULL,#NULL,#NULL,#NULL,#NULL,#NULL,#NULL,Y,#NULL

Investigation Steps

Navigate to **Menu ➤ Setup and Maintenance ➤ Search ➤ "Manage Enterprise Scheduler Job Definitions and Job Sets for Financial, Supply Chain Management, and Related Applications".**

Then filter by "Import AutoInvoice".

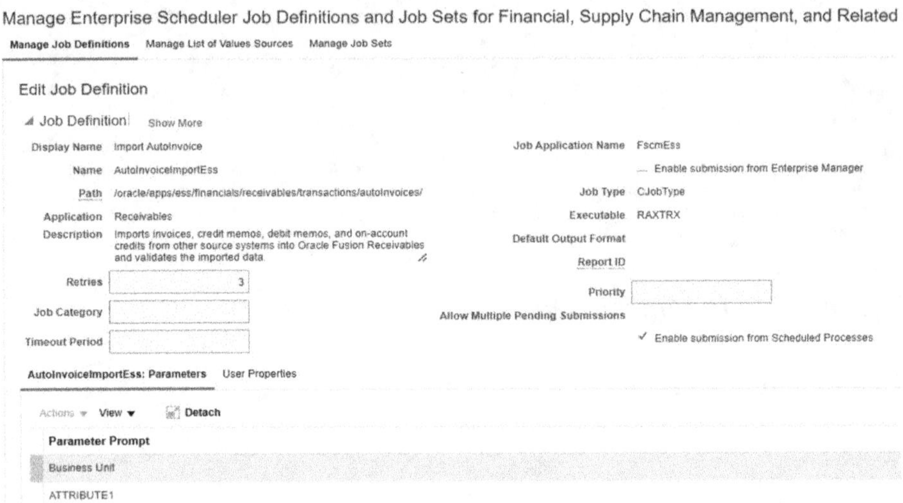

Figure 14-6. *AutoInvoice Job Definition*

Figure 14-7. *AutoInvoice Parameters—Part 1*

Figure 14-8. *AutoInvoice Parameters—Part 2*

Items Import

Reference Documentation: Item Import

Investigation Steps

Navigate to **Menu ➤ Setup and Maintenance ➤ Search ➤ "Manage Enterprise Scheduler Job Definitions and Job Sets for Financial, Supply Chain Management, and Related Applications".**

Then filter by "Item Import".

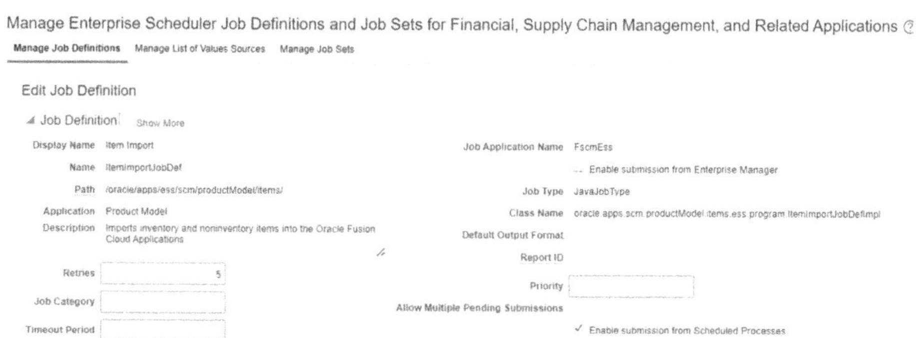

Figure 14-9. *Item Import Job Definition*

Parameters

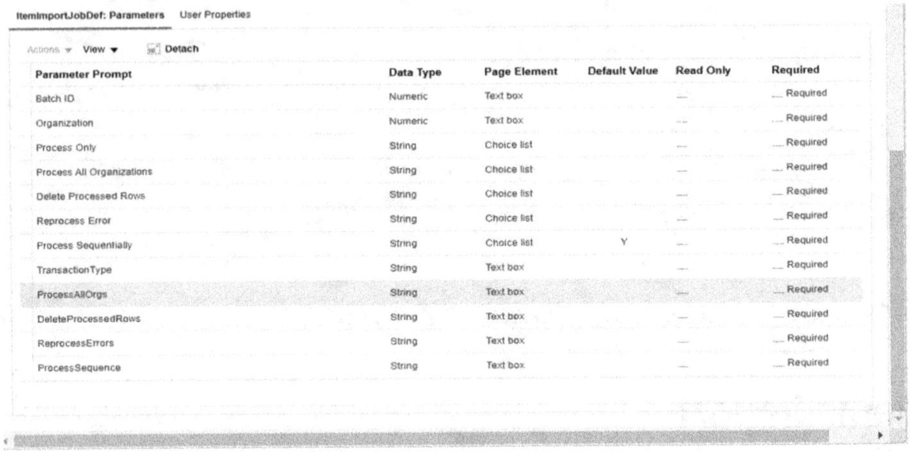

ItemImportJobDef: Parameters | User Properties

Actions ▾ View ▾ Detach

Parameter Prompt	Data Type	Page Element	Default Value	Read Only	Required
Batch ID	Numeric	Text box		—	Required
Organization	Numeric	Text box		—	Required
Process Only	String	Choice list		—	Required
Process All Organizations	String	Choice list		—	Required
Delete Processed Rows	String	Choice list		—	Required
Reprocess Error	String	Choice list		—	Required
Process Sequentially	String	Choice list	Y	—	Required
TransactionType	String	Text box		—	Required
ProcessAllOrgs	String	Text box		—	Required
DeleteProcessedRows	String	Text box		—	Required
ReprocessErrors	String	Text box		—	Required
ProcessSequence	String	Text box		—	Required

Figure 14-10. *Item Import Parameters*

CHAPTER 15

FTP Server and Stage Activity

Overview

This chapter provides examples of FTP server connections and Stage activity usage for learning purposes.

FTP and Stage Activity Fundamentals

What Is Stage Activity?

Oracle's official Gen3 documentation describes Stage as follows: "*The stage file action can read (and remove any trailer), write, zip, unzip, encrypt, decrypt, and list files in a staged location known to Oracle Integration.*"

Stage operations simplify OIC development by allowing you to read, write, and .zip files. Files in "Stage" locations are automatically removed after the integration finishes.

Note Stage Write with schema supports a maximum file size of 10 MB. For larger files, use write file reference (opaque) instead.

J. J. Montero Rodríguez and S. Tahseen, *Oracle Integration Cookbook for Oracle ERP Cloud*, https://doi.org/10.1007/979-8-8688-3020-4_15

Reference Documentation

Component: Integrations

Comparing FTP Server and Stage Operations

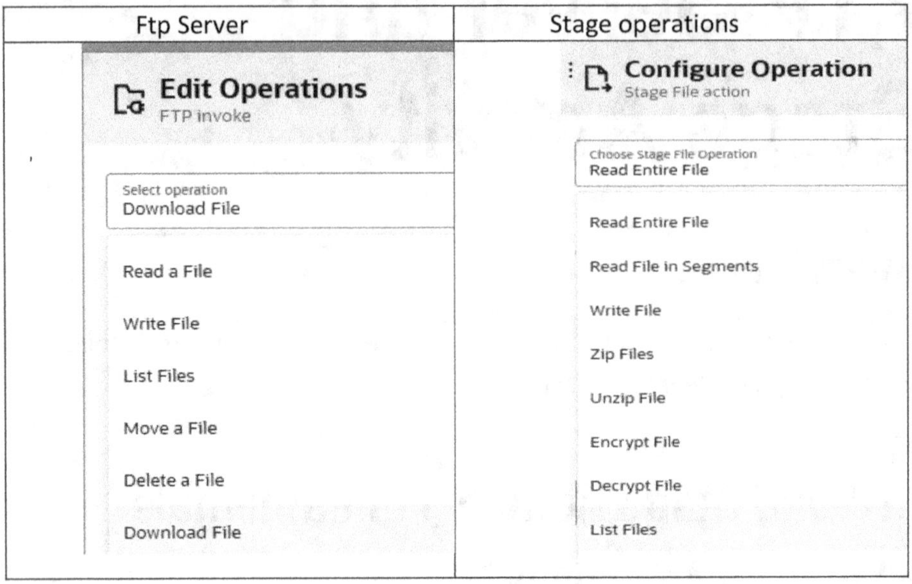

***Figure 15-1.** Comparing FTP Server and Stage Operations*

Key Differences

1. **Read a File in Segments:** Stage activity offers an option for handling large files efficiently.

2. **Delete Operation:** Stage does not have a delete operation because all files are automatically deleted when the integration completes.

3. **Special Stage Operations:**

    - Zip/unzip
    - Encrypt/decrypt

Example 1: Basic File Download

This integration receives directory and filename as parameters, downloads the file, and returns the reference.

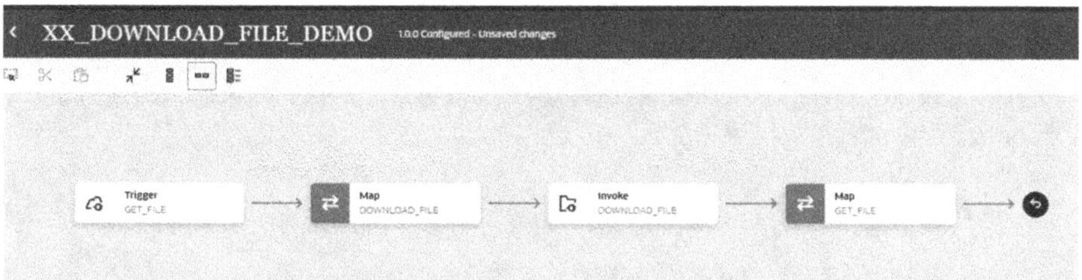

Figure 15-2. *Basic File Download Integration*

Trigger Definition: Parameters

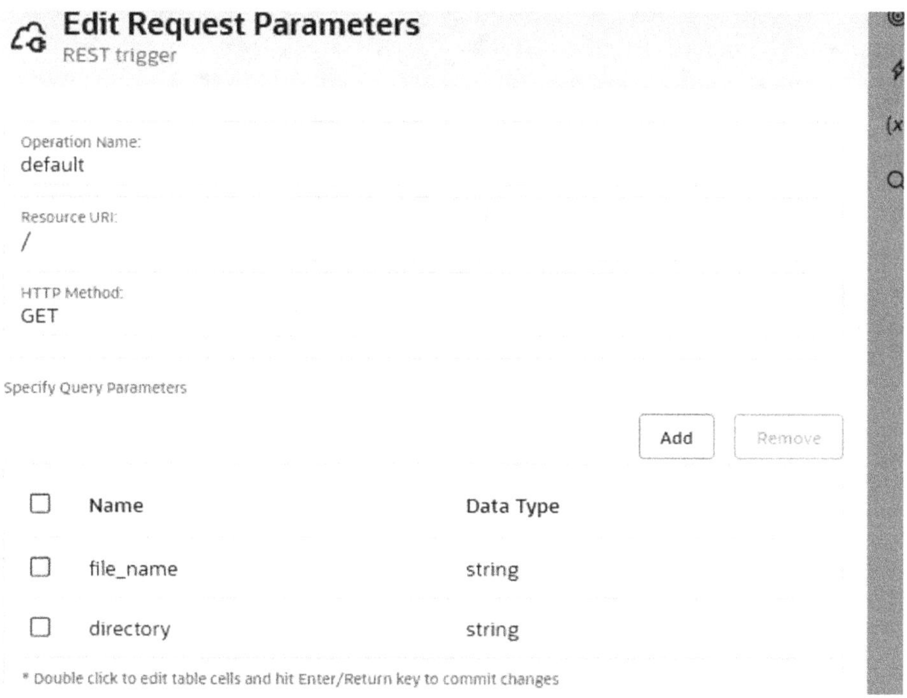

Figure 15-3. *Trigger Parameters*

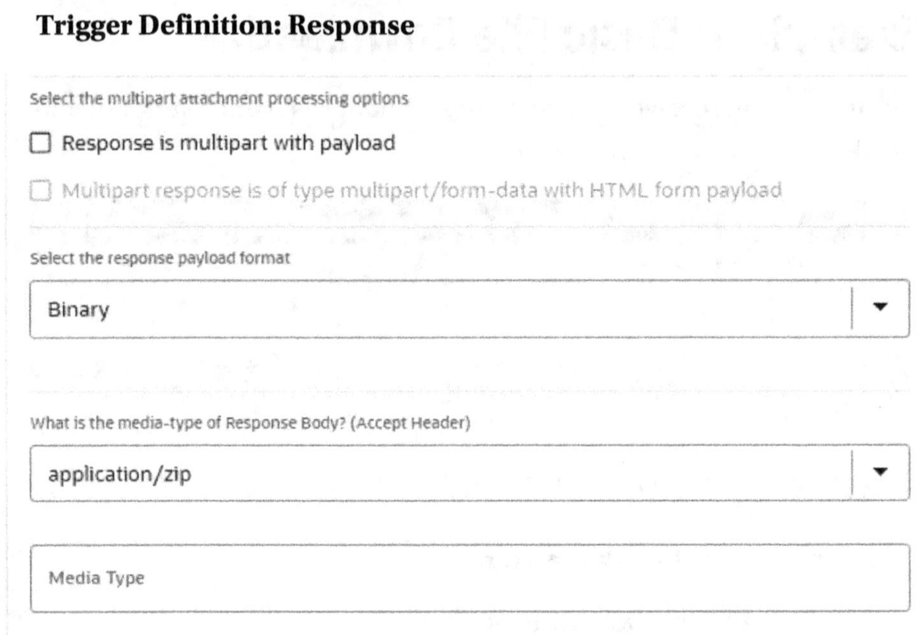

Figure 15-4. *Trigger Response*

Return Mapping

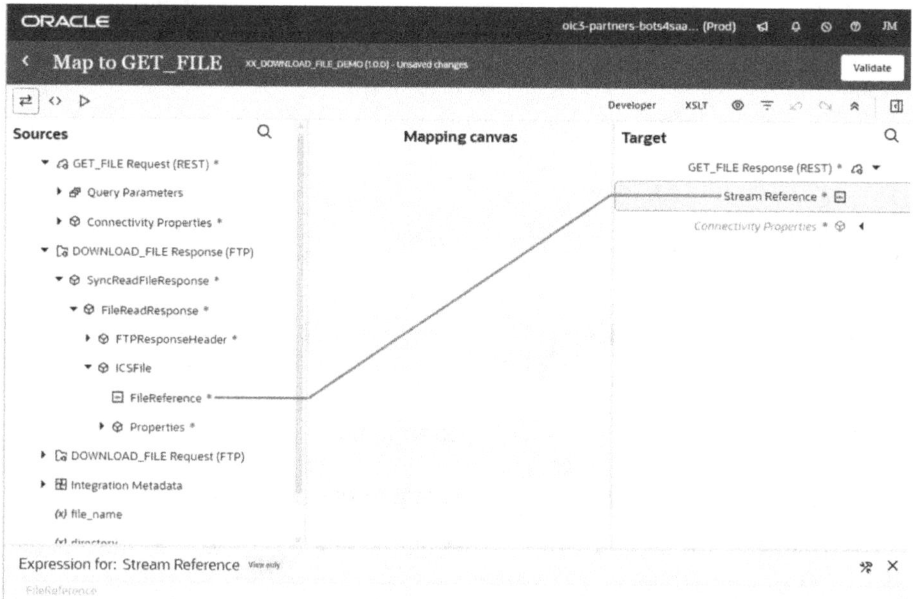

Figure 15-5. Return Mapping

Example 2: FTP to Database Integration

This integration downloads a file from FTP, reads it using Stage, and inserts the data into a Visual Builder Business Object.

Note More details are available in Chapter 30.

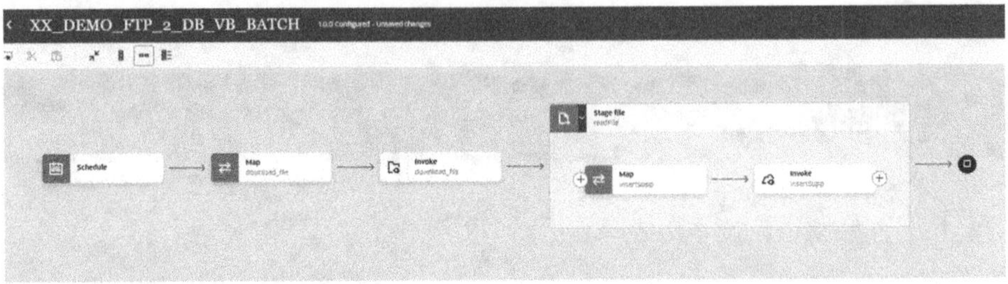

***Figure 15-6.** FTP to Database Integration*

Technical Reference

Code Example	Comments
XX_DOWNLOAD_FILE_DEMO	**Package File**: XX_DEMO_COOKBOOK.par
XX_DEMO_FTP_2_DB_VB_BATCH	**Package File**: XX_DEMO_COOKBOOK.par

FTP Demo: Purge Files Based on Date

Introduction

This exercise demonstrates FTP operations combined with JavaScript date manipulation. The integration purges files modified before "n" days.

Connections Required

- FTP server connection available in your system
- Internal REST connection

Integration Architecture

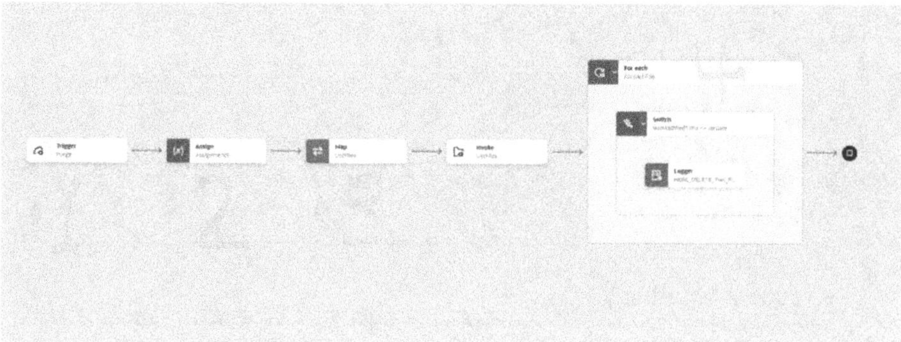

Figure 15-7. Integration Overview

Process Steps

Step 1: Receive Parameters

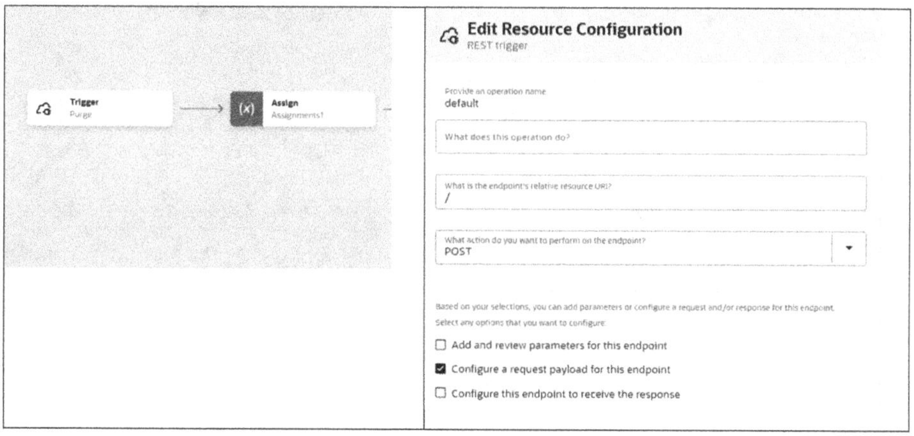

Figure 15-8. Parameter Configuration

Access to apply your sample for request.

Figure 15-9. Request Sample

Paste your sample request.

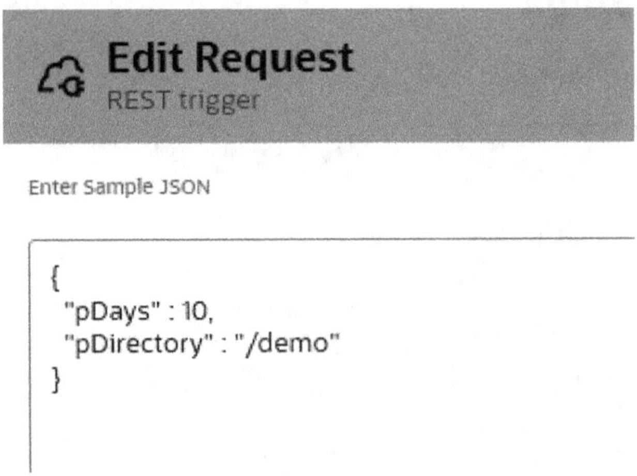

Figure 15-10. Sample Request Access

Step 2: Calculate Target Date

The integration calculates the target date using the system date and the days parameter.

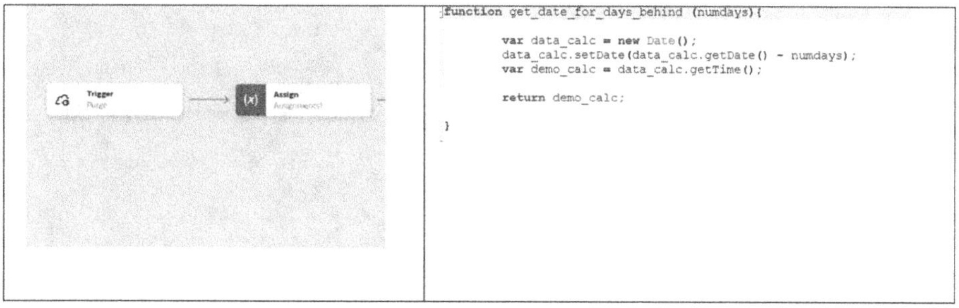

***Figure 15-11.** Date Calculation and Date Function*

Code Reference: DEMO_DATE_FOR_DAYS_BEHIND.js

Step 3: Filter Files

Filter files in the directory received as a parameter.

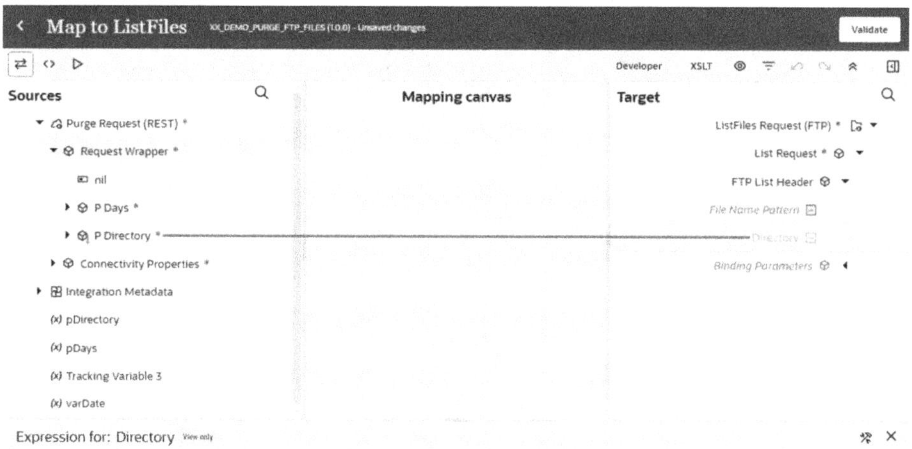

***Figure 15-12.** File Filtering Mapping*

Step 4: Check Last Modified Date

Compare the last modified date with the calculated date from Step 2.

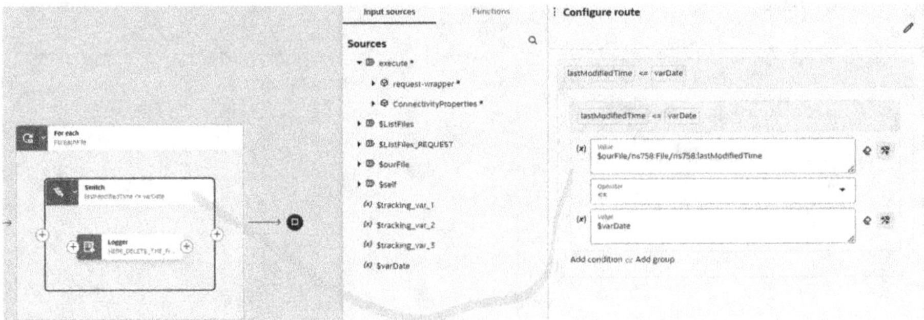

Figure 15-13. *Date Comparison*

Step 5: Log Results

In this exercise, we do not delete files. Feel free to complete the implementation with the deletion action (be very careful when testing).

The integration logs the filename and last modified date.

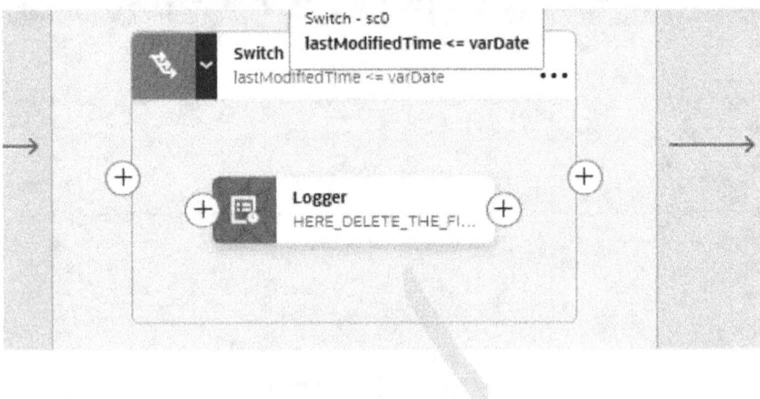

Figure 15-14. *Result Logging*

Testing

Test Directory:

Figure 15-15. *Test Directory*

Test Results:

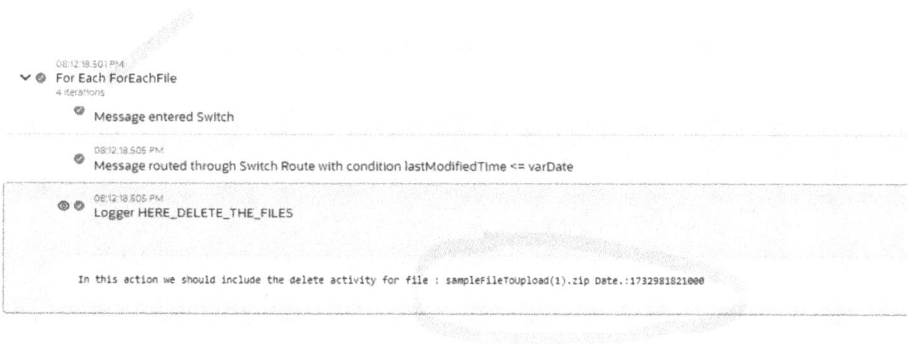

Figure 15-16. *Test Results*

Technical Reference

Code Example	Comments
XX_DEMO_PURGE_FTP_FILES	**Package File**: XX_DEMO_COOKBOOK.par

CHAPTER 16

ATP Database

Overview

There are numerous blogs covering this feature. This chapter provides basic examples and some advanced scenarios for completeness.

Reference Documentation

Blog Reference: OIC DB Adapter – Overcoming 10 MB Limit

Preparation

For your ATP database, we provide a script (see section "Technical Reference") to create the sequences and tables needed for these examples.

J. J. Montero Rodríguez and S. Tahseen, *Oracle Integration Cookbook for Oracle ERP Cloud*,
https://doi.org/10.1007/979-8-8688-3020-4_16

```
END;
/
ALTER TRIGGER "TEST_USER_01"."DEPT_TRG" ENABLE;
CREATE TABLE "TEST_USER_01"."EMP"
        (
                "EMPNO"     NUMBER(4,0) NOT NULL ENABLE                    ,
                "ENAME"     VARCHAR2(100 BYTE) COLLATE "USING_NLS_COMP",
                "JOB"       VARCHAR2(100 BYTE) COLLATE "USING_NLS_COMP",
                "MGR"       NUMBER(4,0)                                    ,
                "HIREDATE"  DATE                                           ,
                "SAL"       NUMBER(7,2)                                    ,
                "COMM"      NUMBER(7,2)                                    ,
                "DEPTNO"    NUMBER(2,0)                                    ,
                CONSTRAINT "EMP_PK" PRIMARY KEY ("EMPNO") USING INDEX PCTFREE 10 INITRANS
        )
DEFAULT COLLATION "USING_NLS_COMP" SEGMENT CREATION DEFERRED PCTFREE 10 PCTUSED 40 INITRAN
/
CREATE
OR REPLACE EDITIONABLE TRIGGER "TEST_USER_01"."EMP_TRG" BEFORE
INSERT  ON EMP FOR EACH ROW
BEGIN
        <<COLUMN_SEQUENCES>>
                BEGIN
                        IF
                                INSERTING
                                AND :NEW.EMPNO IS NULL
                        THEN
                                SELECT
                                        EMP_SEQ.NEXTVAL
                                INTO
                                        :NEW.EMPNO
                                FROM
                                        SYS.DUAL;
                        END IF;
                END COLUMN_SEQUENCES;
END;
/
ALTER TRIGGER "TEST_USER_01"."EMP_TRG" ENABLE;
create or replace type short_string_tt
        as table of varchar2(100);
        /
```

Figure 16-1. *Database Script*

Feel free to adapt the script to your requirements.

Basic Operations

ATP Insert Operation

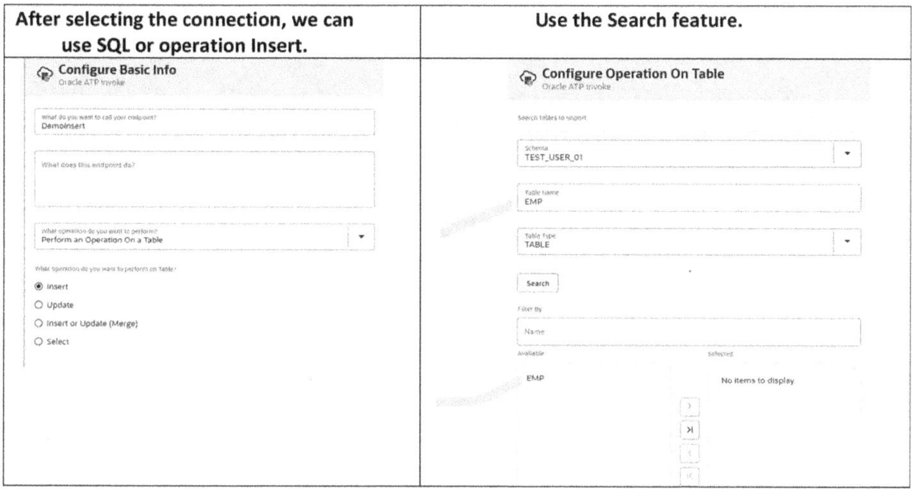

Figure 16-2. Insert Operation

Move the table to the right, click "Import Tables," and continue.

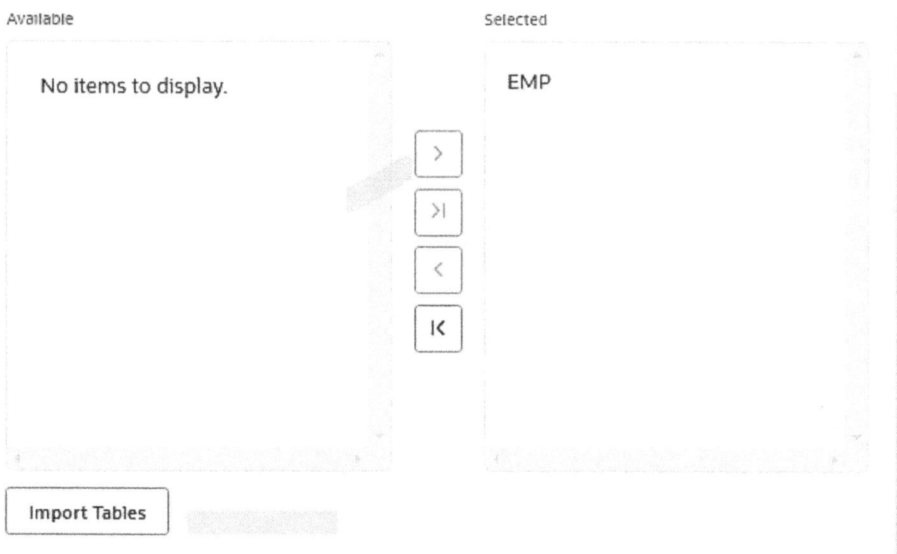

Figure 16-3. Import Tables

Map hardcoded values for a basic learning example.

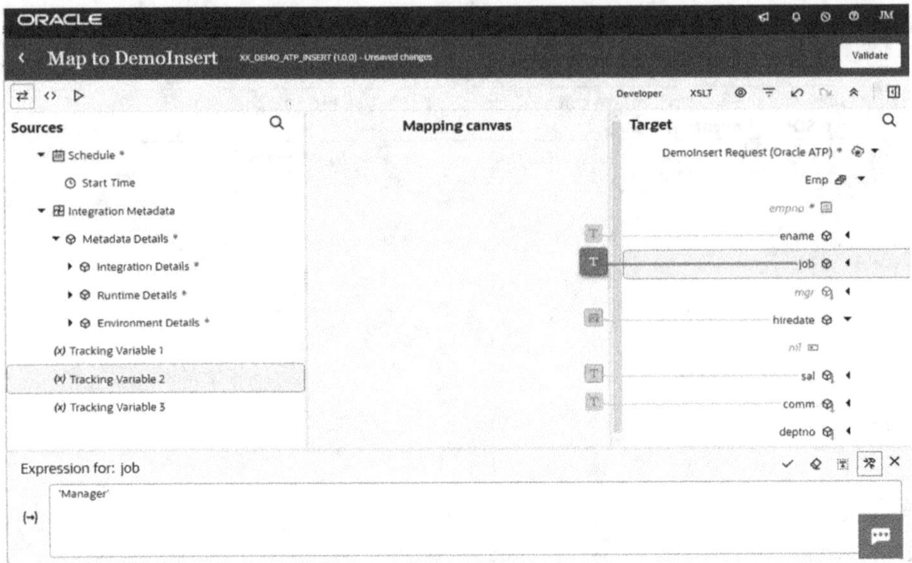

Figure 16-4. Insert Mapping

After Testing:

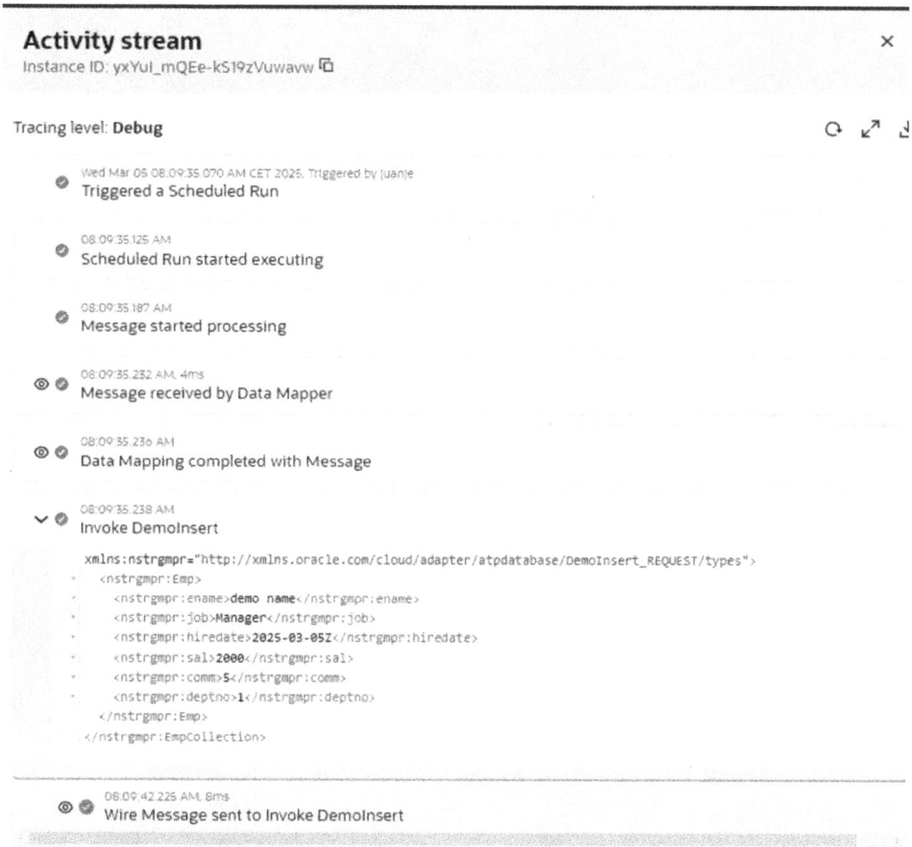

Figure 16-5. *Insert Test Result*

Database Result:

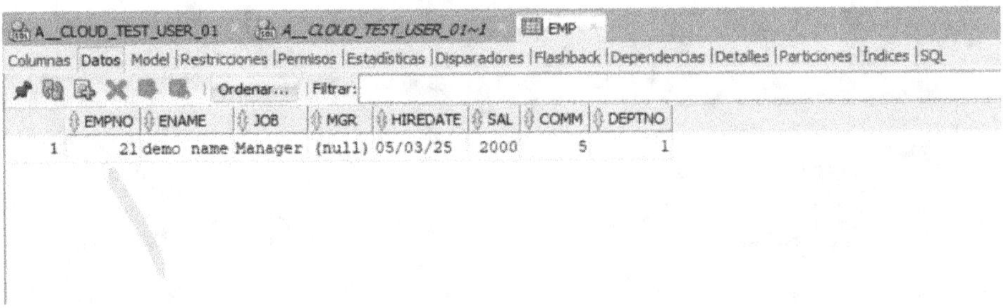

Figure 16-6. *Database Record*

The record is created with the proper database sequence.

ATP Update Operation

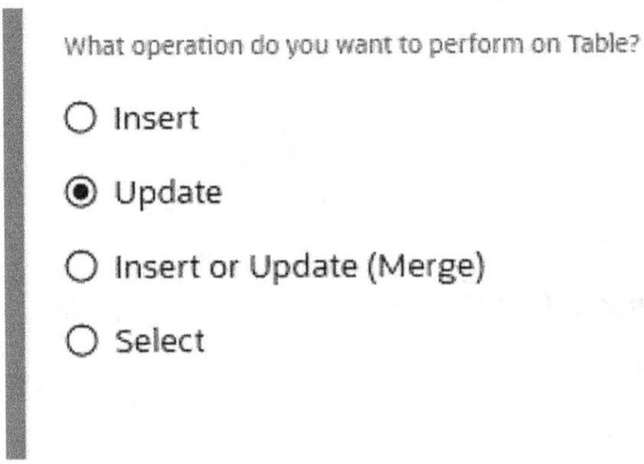

Figure 16-7. *Update Operation*

The process is like an insert operation, but OIC automatically provides the correct mapping for updates.

Note The mapping requires the "empno" key to identify the record to update.

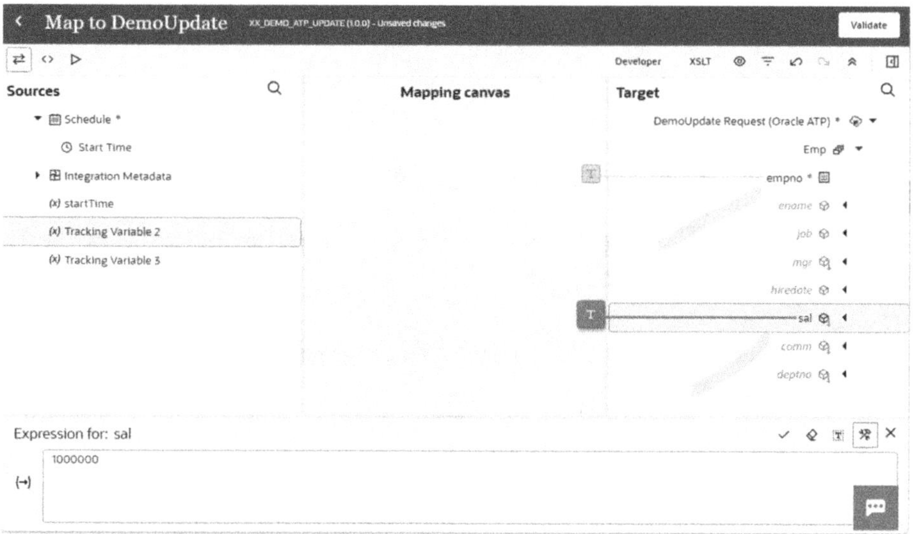

Figure 16-8. Update Mapping

Console Review After Testing:

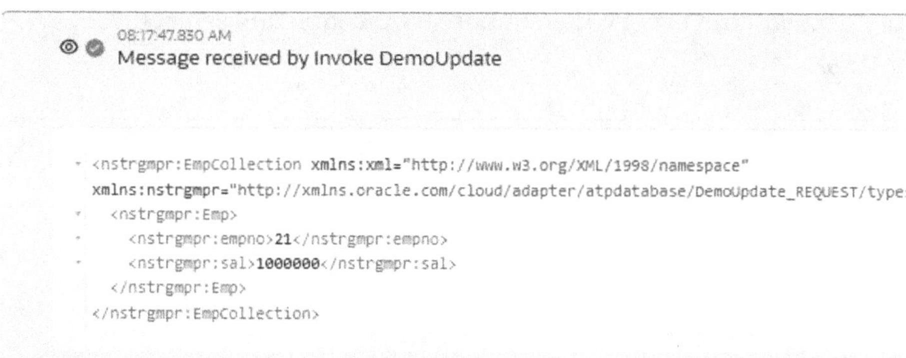

Figure 16-9. ATP Update Console Result

Database Result:

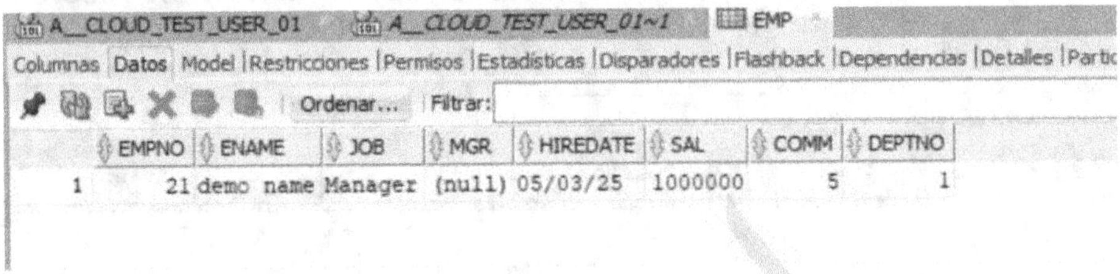

Figure 16-10. Updated Record

ATP Delete Operation

The delete operation is similar to the update operation. The mapping requires the "empno" column to delete.

ATP Query with Parameter

Note This example would be for any DML operation.

Create integration using your database connection and select these options.

Important Parameters use the "#" notation.

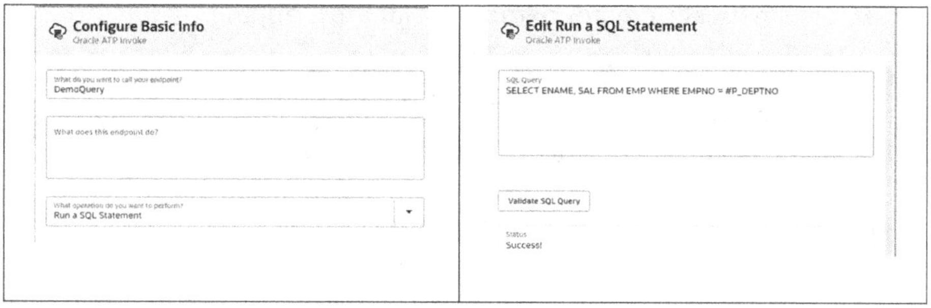

Figure 16-11. *ATP Invoke*

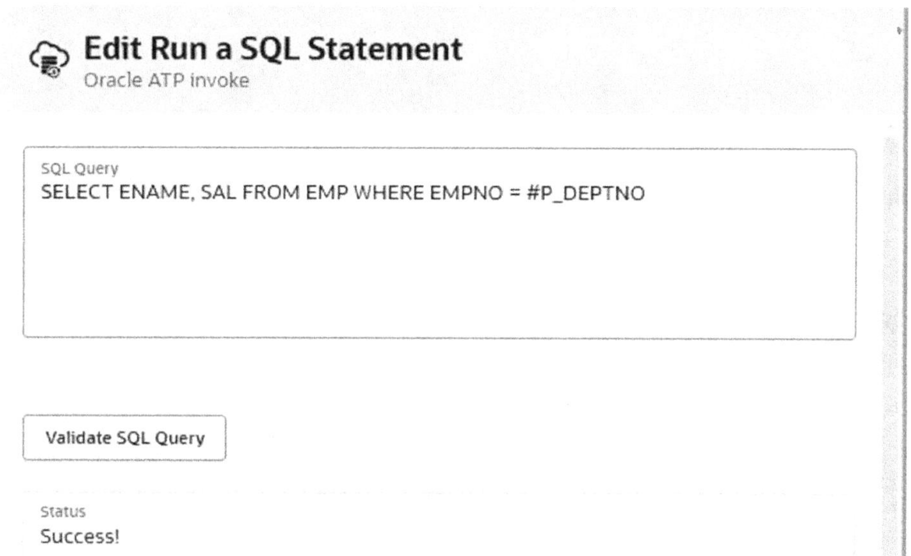

Figure 16-12a. *Run the SQL Statement.*

Important The query or SQL statement cannot contain carriage returns or special characters. Write the entire statement as a single line of text.

OIC automatically creates parameters in the mapping.

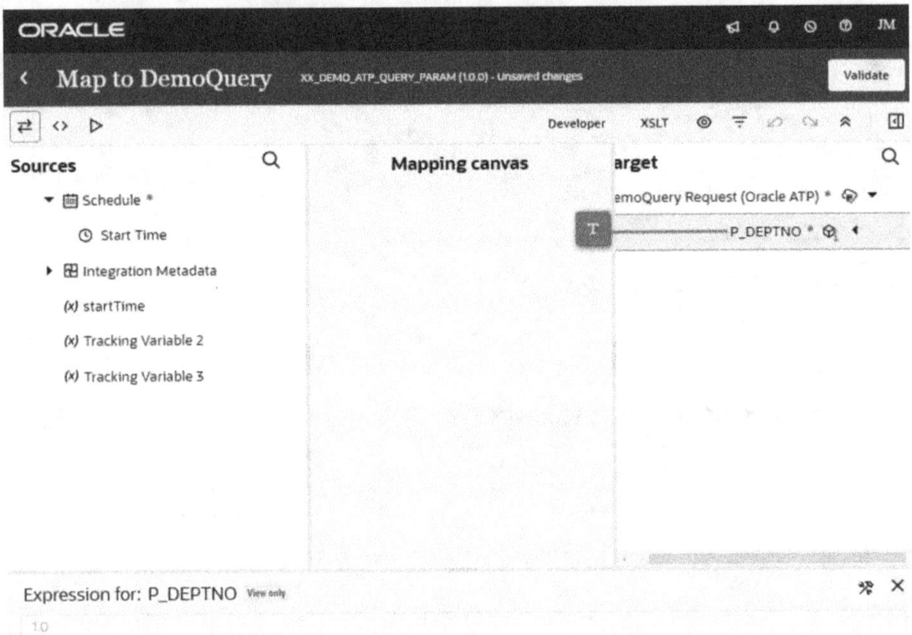

Figure 16-12b. *Query Mapping*

Processing Results:

In the flow, you can access retrieved records using a “For” loop activity for further processing.

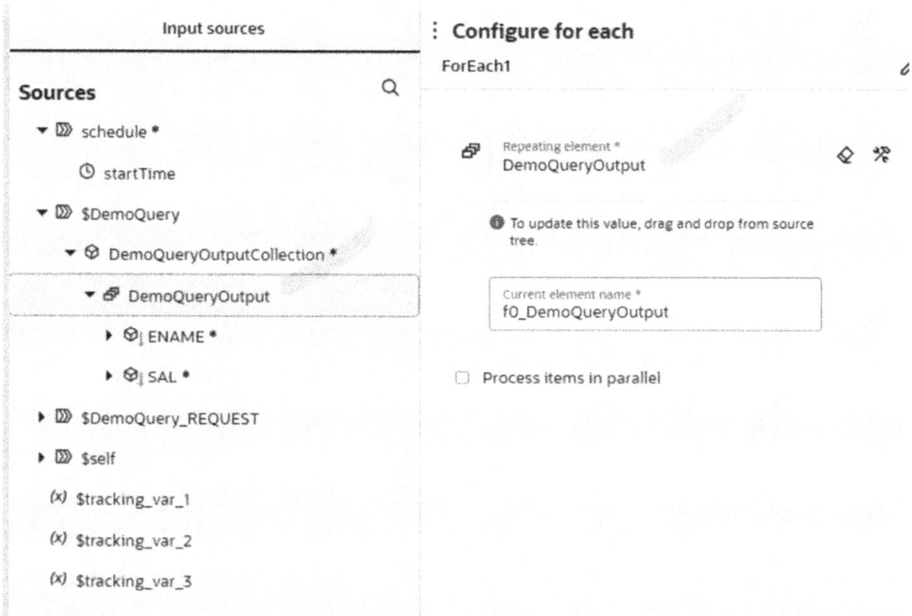

Figure 16-13. *Query Results*

For this example, we display the names of selected records.

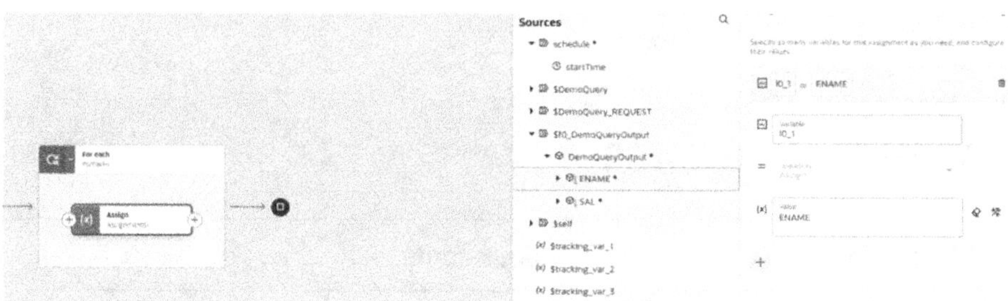

Figure 16-14. *Display Names*

Test Results:

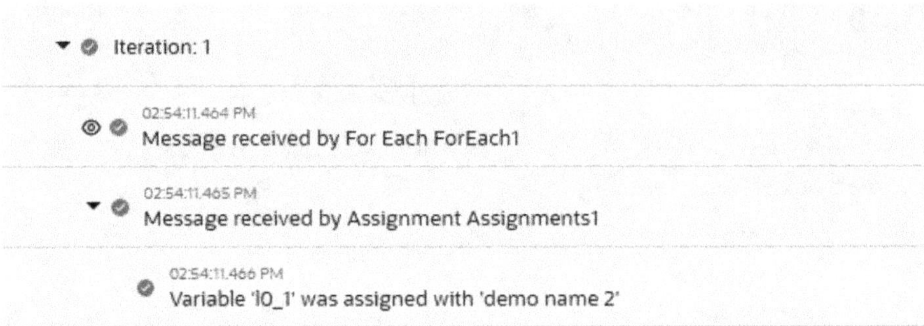

Figure 16-15. *Test Execution*

Database Data:

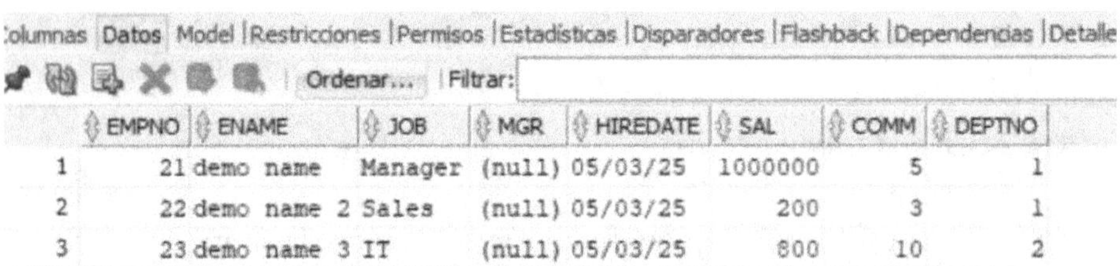

	EMPNO	ENAME	JOB	MGR	HIREDATE	SAL	COMM	DEPTNO
1	21	demo name	Manager	(null)	05/03/25	1000000	5	1
2	22	demo name 2	Sales	(null)	05/03/25	200	3	1
3	23	demo name 3	IT	(null)	05/03/25	800	10	2

Figure 16-16. *Source Data*

Technical Reference

Code Example	Comments
ATP_SCRIPT_DEPT_EMP_01.sql	Script to create sample tables and code
XX_DEMO_ATP_INSERT	**Package File**: XX_DEMO_COOKBOOK.par
XX_DEMO_ATP_UPDATE	**Package File**: XX_DEMO_COOKBOOK.par
XX_DEMO_ATP_QUERY_PARAM	**Package File**: XX_DEMO_COOKBOOK.par

CHAPTER 17

Advanced REST: POC for Duplicating Receivables Transactions

Overview

Introduction

This advanced exercise is based on a proof-of-concept (POC) that was not implemented in production. It demonstrates complex REST API operations for learning purposes.

Business Requirements

The requirements were approximately as follows:

> *A receivables transaction originates from a different ERP module. It arrives with missing information that we need in the workflow, but we cannot add this information in the source system. The import process is fully managed by Oracle ERP, and modification of the original transaction is not possible.*

J. J. Montero Rodríguez and S. Tahseen, *Oracle Integration Cookbook for Oracle ERP Cloud*,
https://doi.org/10.1007/979-8-8688-3020-4_17

Challenge: The required information cannot be added to or modified in the original transaction because it originates from another module and the system does not permit modifications.

Solution: While a standard solution was eventually provided, a "Plan B" approach was developed in parallel, which is presented here.

Approach: Duplicate the transaction to add the required information, and then void the original transaction.

Note This solution is presented for learning purposes only.

Solution Components

The integration developed here can duplicate a receivables transaction including

- Basic date
- Attachments
- Descriptive flexfields

Connections Required

Figure 17-1. *Required Connections*

Preparation

Step 1: Find a Receivables Transaction in Oracle ERP

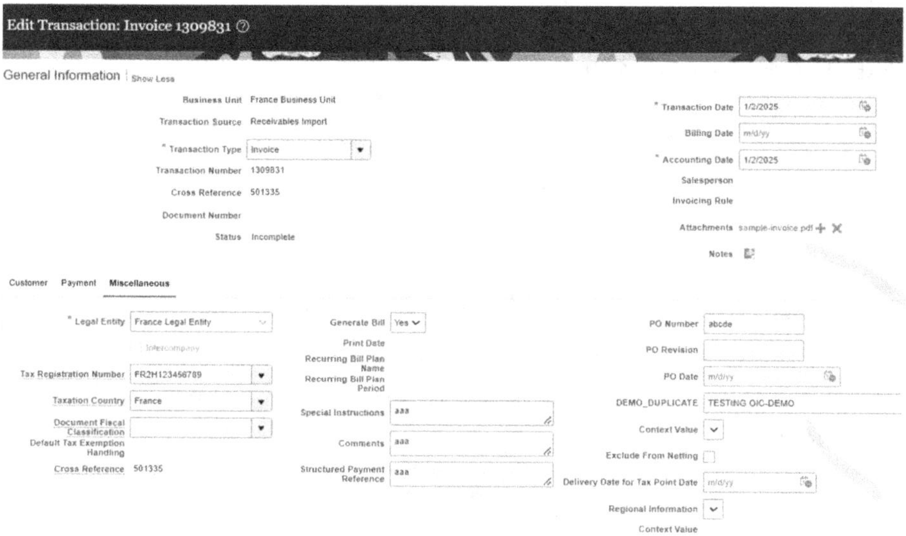

Figure 17-2. *Sample Transaction*

Step 2: Add Attachment

Add an attachment manually to the original transaction.

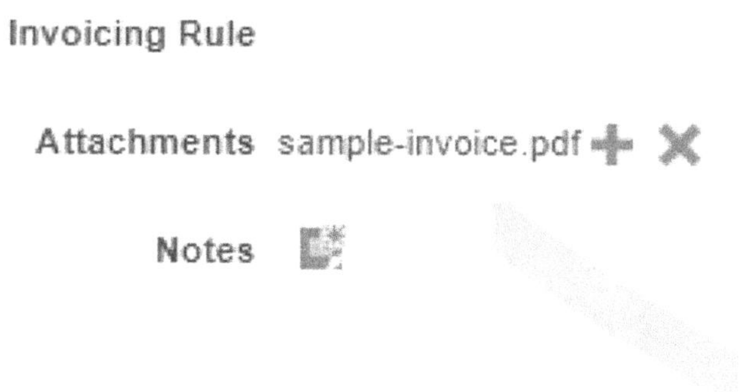

Figure 17-3. *Add Attachment*

Step 3: Retrieve the Transaction ID

To find the customer_trx_id value, use this query in BI Publisher:

```
SELECT CUSTOMER_TRX_ID
FROM RA_CUSTOMER_TRX_ALL
WHERE TRX_NUMBER = '1309831';
```

Example Values:

- **Transaction Number**: 1309831
- **Customer Transaction ID**: 1114425

The customer_trx_id value is required for REST API mapping in OIC.

Step 4: Configure a Descriptive Flexfield

In this instance, we need to set up a new descriptive flexfield.

Navigation:

1. In Oracle ERP, access **Menu ➤ Setup and Maintenance**.
2. Click the link as shown.

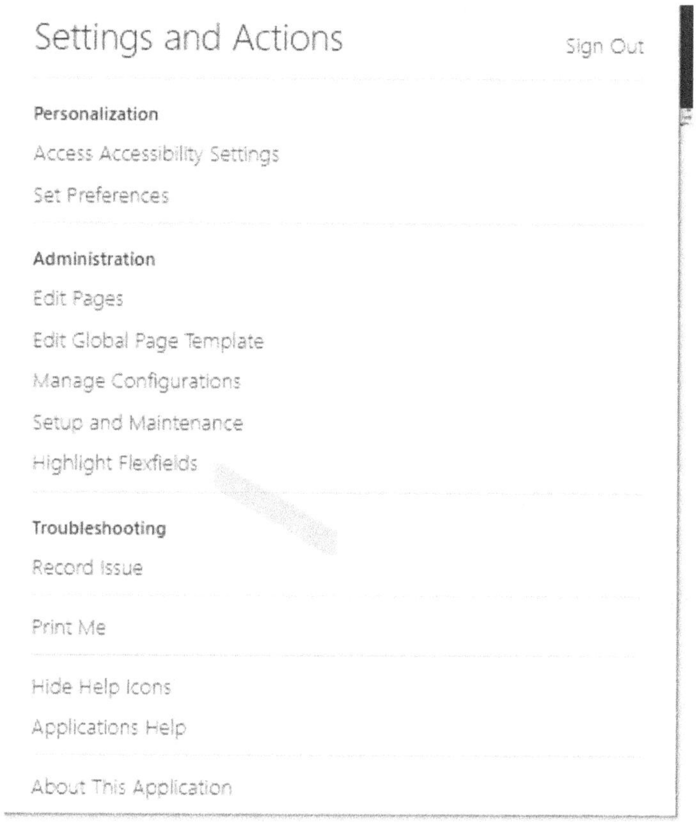

Figure 17-4. *Setup and Maintenance*

3. In the receivables invoice, navigate to **Show More ➤ Miscellaneous tab**.
4. Click the **Descriptive Flexfield** icon (on the right).

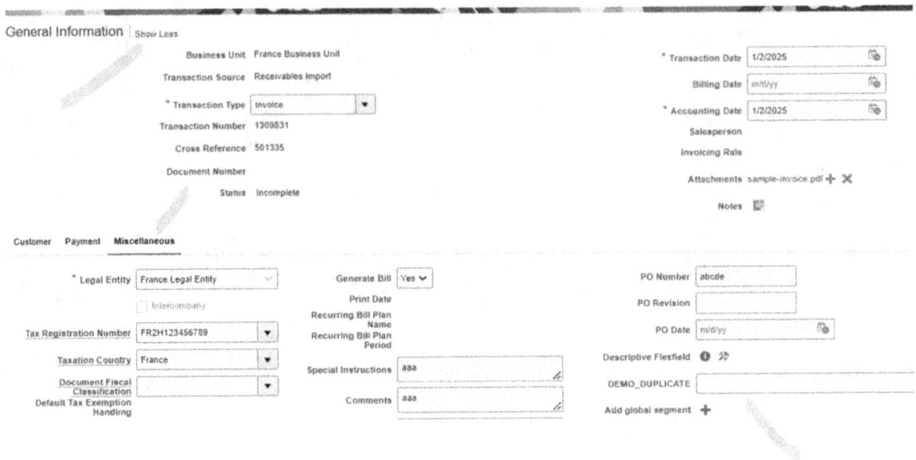

Figure 17-5. *Descriptive Flexfield Access*

5. Edit using the icon shown.

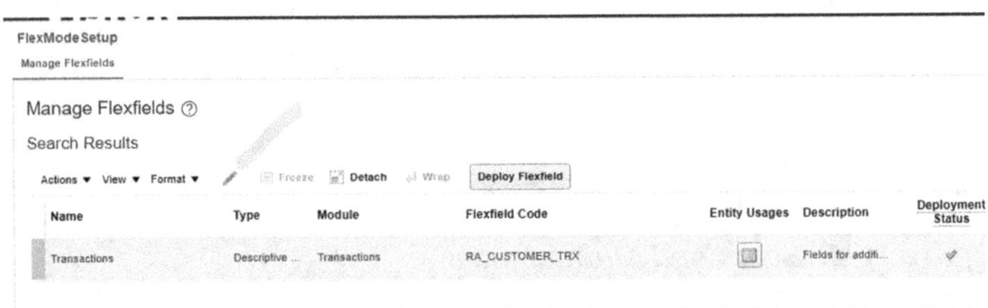

Figure 17-6. *Edit the Flexfield*

6. Add using "ATTRIBUTE1".

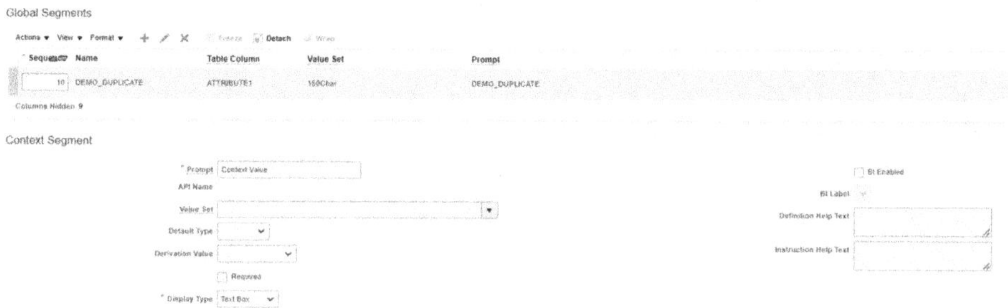

Figure 17-7. *Add an Attribute*

7. Click **Deploy Flexfield.**

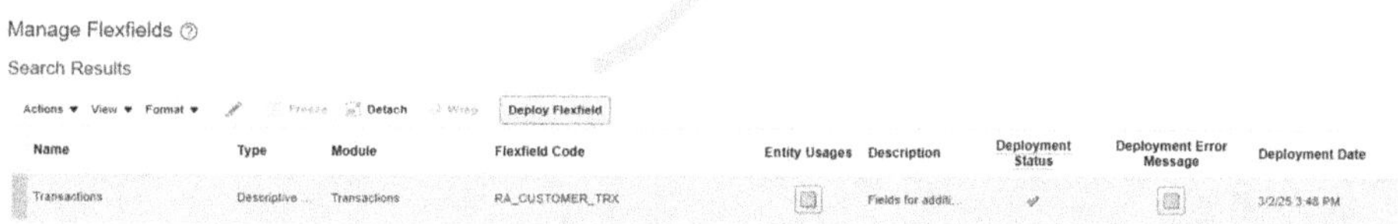

Figure 17-8. *Deploy Flexfield*

These steps enable you to add additional information to the receivables transaction header.

Auxiliary Integration: XX_DEMO_UPDATE_FLEX

This integration adds flexfield data for learning purposes.

Note This data can also be added in the main REST API when creating the new transaction.

Purpose: Update "ATTRIBUTE1" in the new copied transaction with the customer_trx_id of the original transaction.

General Overview

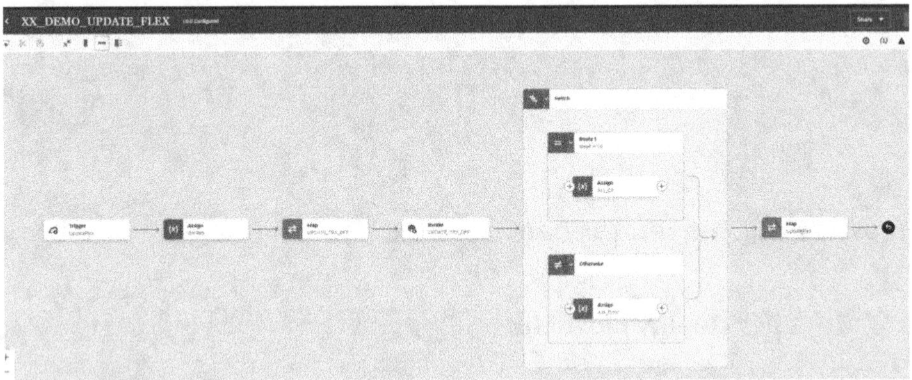

Figure 17-9. *Update Flex Overview*

Parameters

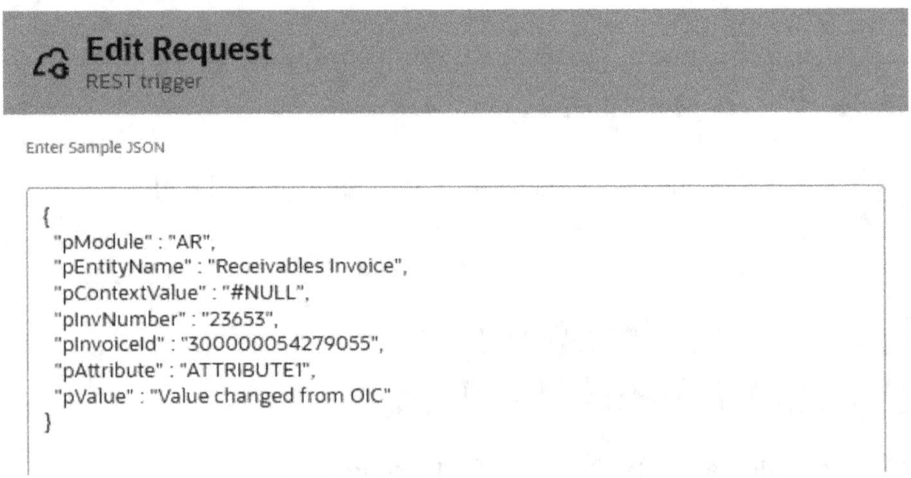

Figure 17-10. *Update Flex Parameters*

Connection

SOAP ErpObjectDFFUpdateService connection (see Chapter 2)

Main SOAP Invoke

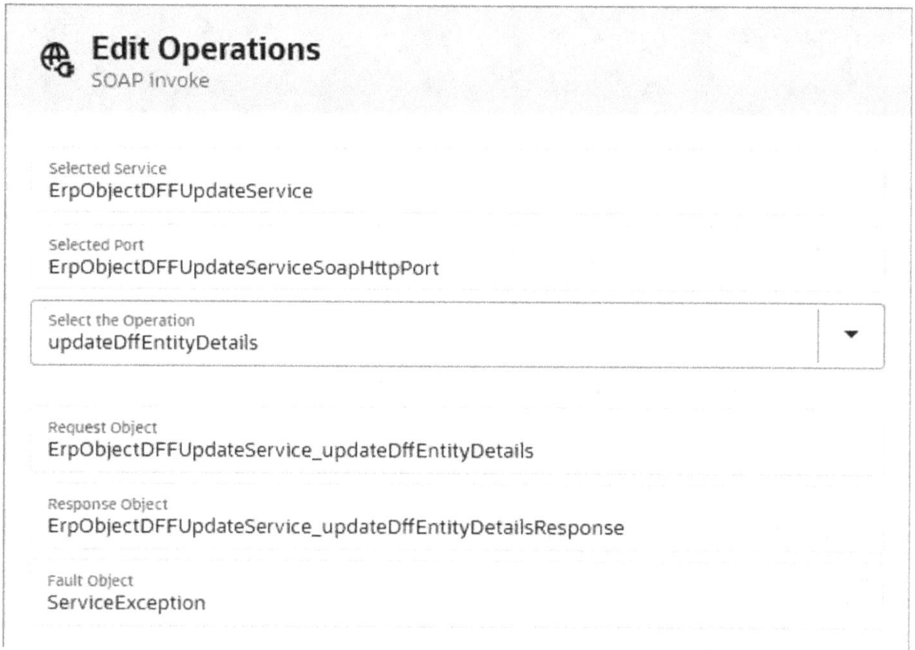

Figure 17-11. *SOAP Invoke*

Mapping: Use parameters received from parent integration XX_DEMO_AR_TRX_DUPLICATE.

Main Integration: XX_DEMO_AR_TRX_DUPLICATE

General Overview

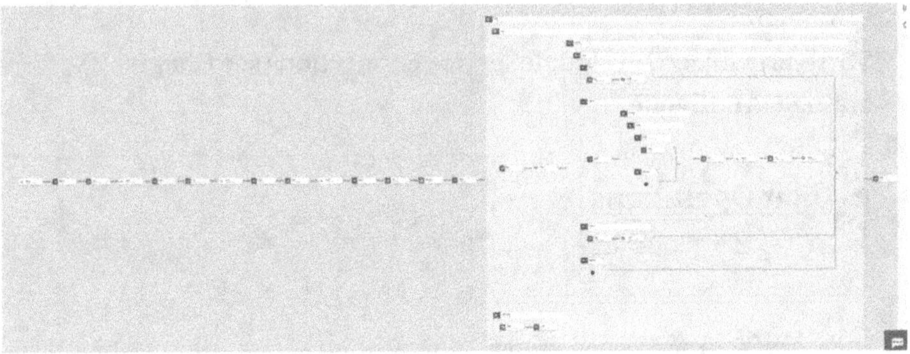

***Figure 17-12.** Main Integration Overview*

Note The right side handles attachments.

Process Flow Explanation

Section 1: Receive Parameters, Read Invoice, Create Copy

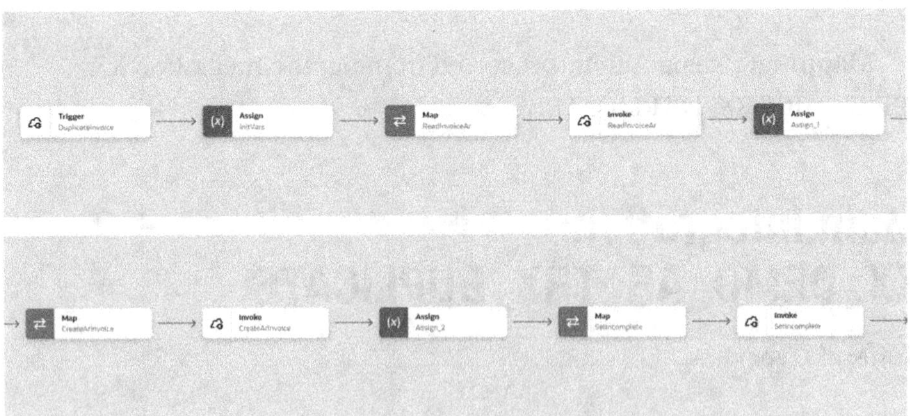

***Figure 17-13.** Receive Parameters, Read Invoice, Create Copy*

These steps receive parameters, read the original invoice, and create a copy (basic data only for learning purposes—feel free to add more information).

Receive Parameters

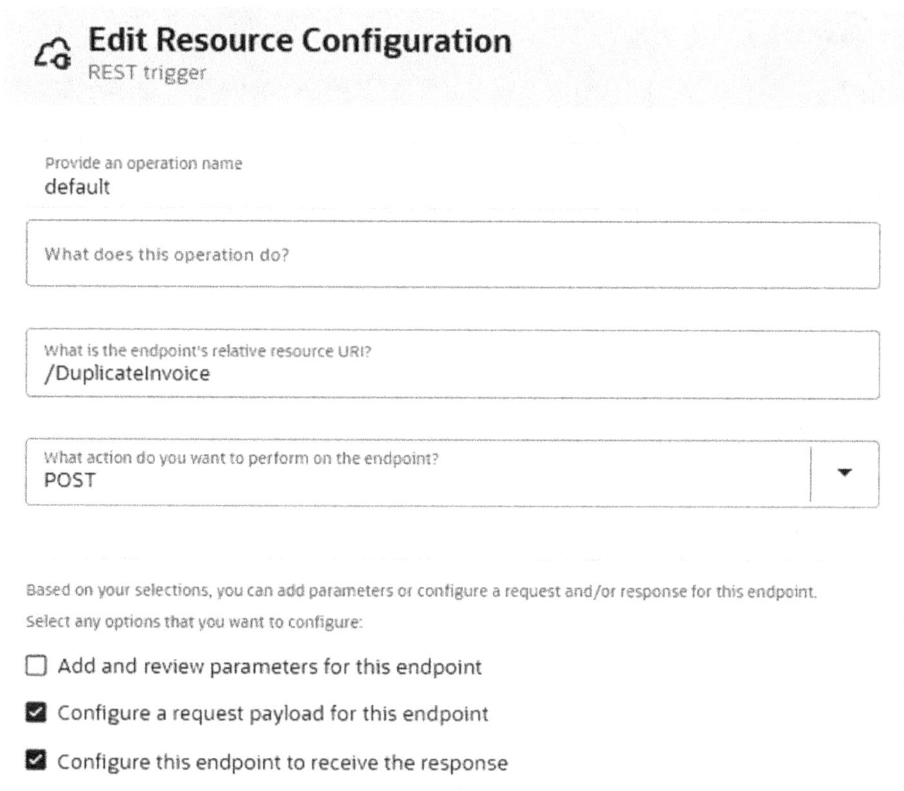

Figure 17-14. *Receive Parameters*

Set Up Sample Payload:

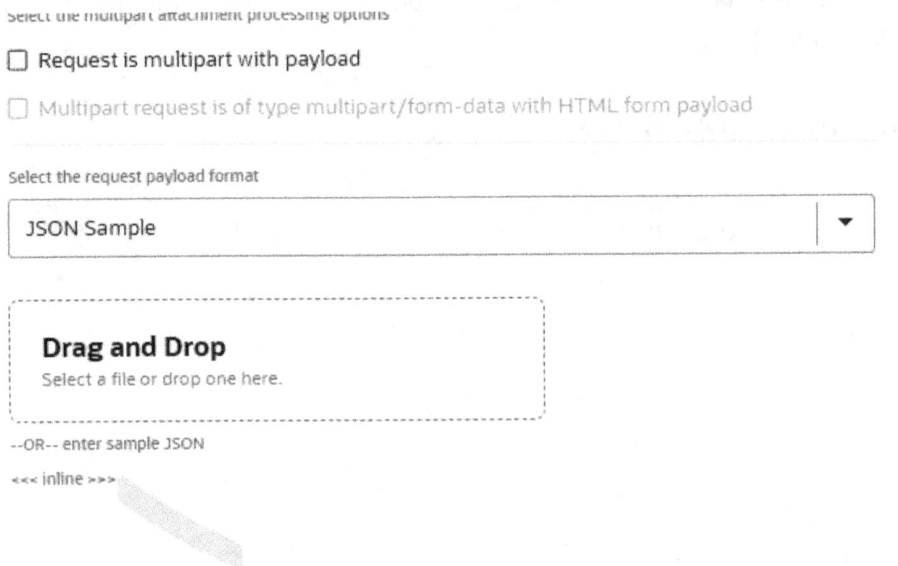

Figure 17-15. *Sample Payload*

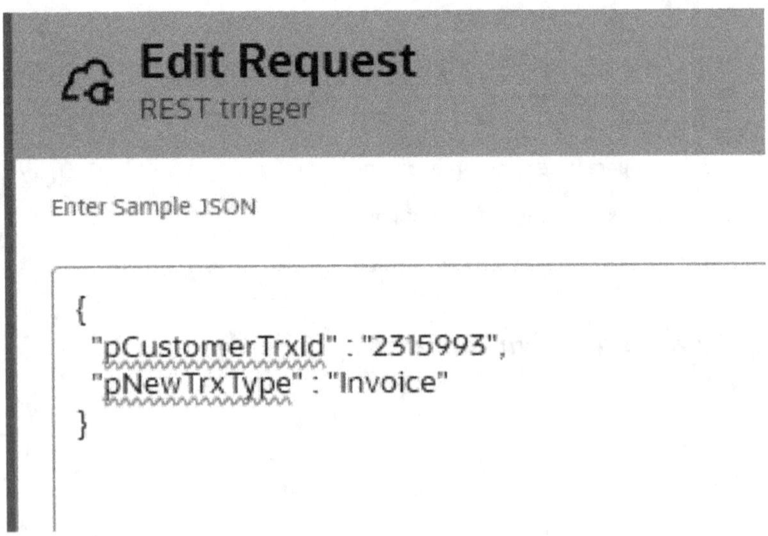

Figure 17-16. *Payload Configuration*

Read Source Transaction

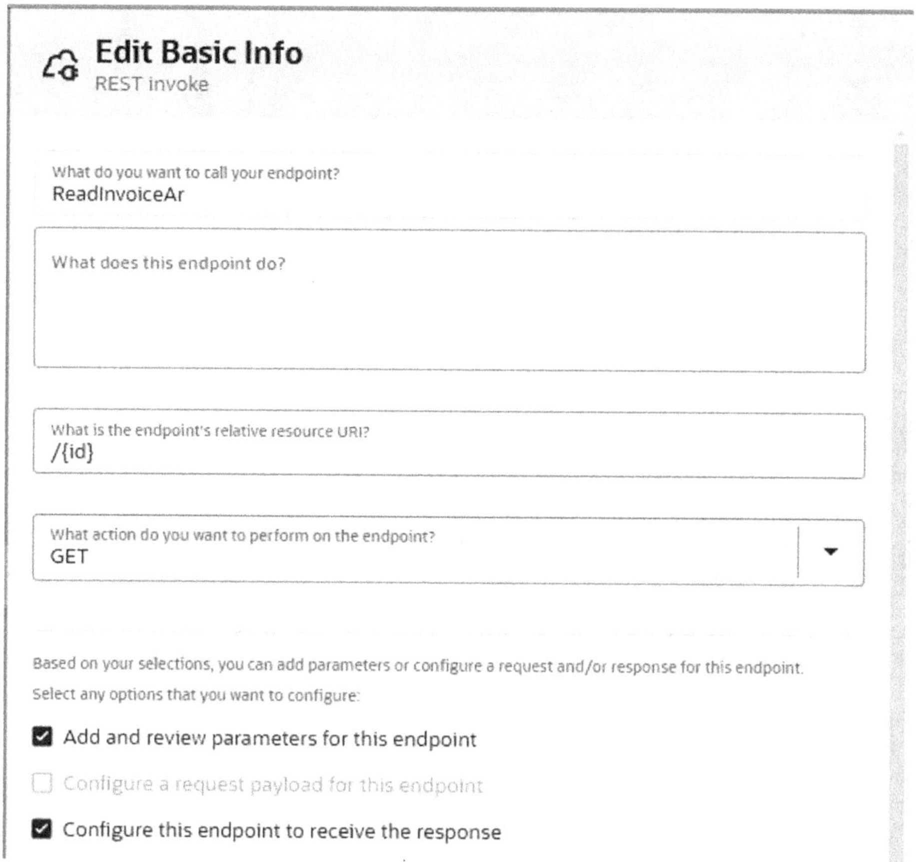

Figure 17-17. *Read Transaction*

For the response data, use Postman to obtain a sample.

API Endpoint:

https://fa-zzzz-saasfademo1.ds-fa.oraclepdemos.com/fscmRestApi/resources/11.13.18.05/receivablesInvoices/1114425?expand=receivablesInvoiceLines,receivablesInvoiceDFF,receivablesInvoiceTransactionDFF,receivablesInvoiceDistributions,receivablesInvoiceGdf,receivablesInvoiceLines.receivablesInvoiceLineTransactionDFF&onlyData=true

Get the Sample:

Figure 17-18. Postman Sample

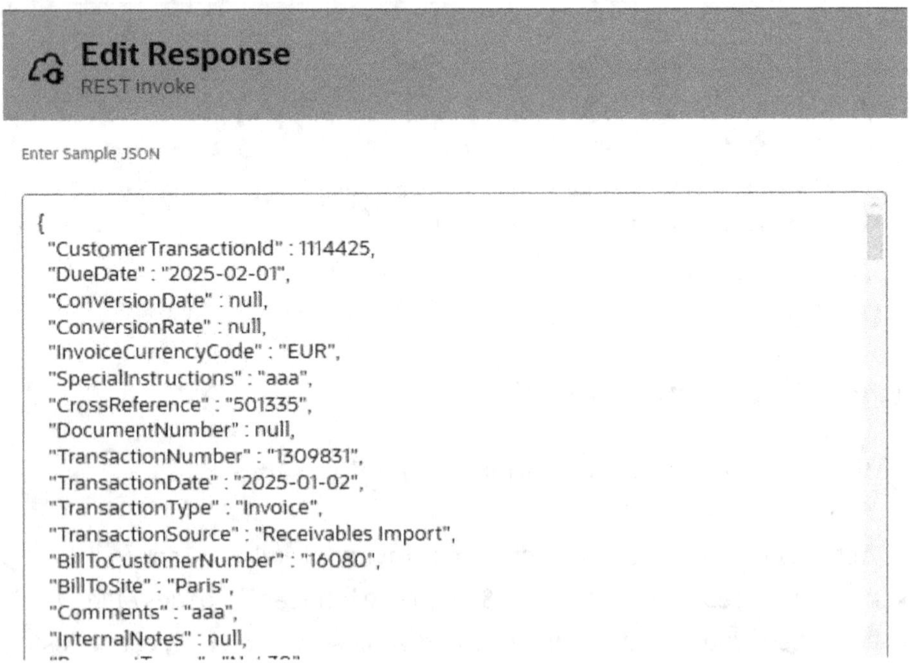

Figure 17-19. Sample Response

Create Invoice with REST API

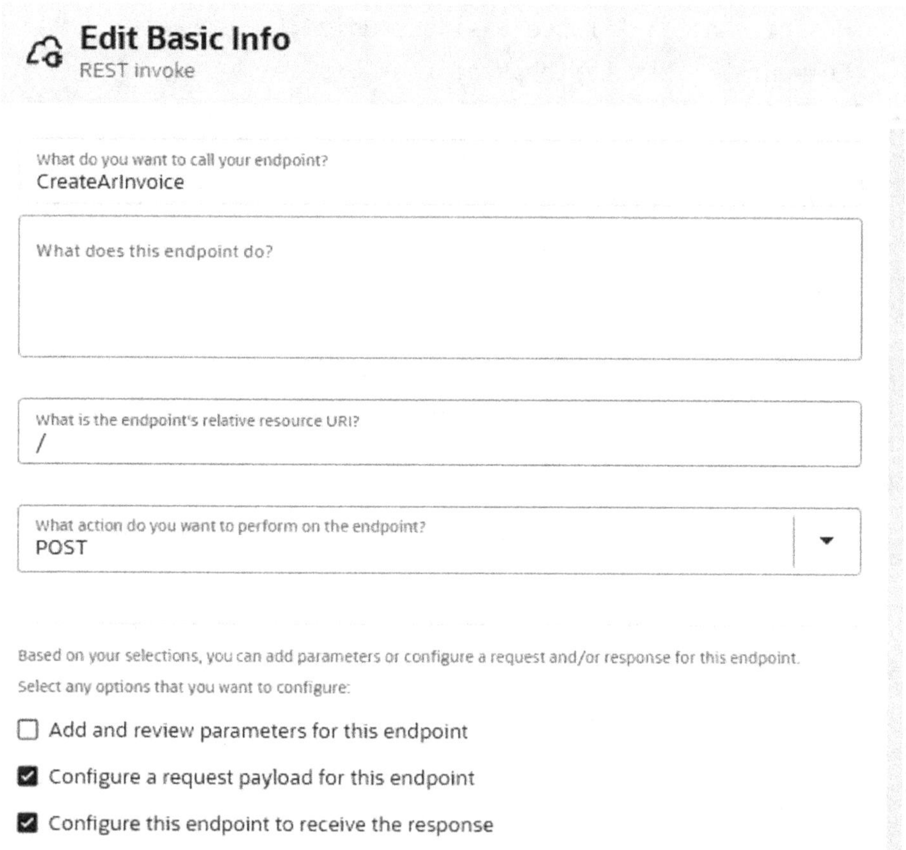

Figure 17-20. *Create Invoice*

Request Payload Sample (tested in Postman):


```
{
    "BusinessUnit": "France Business Unit",
    "Comments": "New Laptop Promotion",
    "DueDate": "2025-02-21",
    "InternalNotes": "Best Priced item",
    "InvoiceCurrencyCode": "USD",
    "PaymentTerms": "Net 30",
    "TransactionDate": "2024-12-23",
    "TransactionSource": "Manual",
    "BillToCustomerName": "Business World",
    "BillToCustomerNumber": "16080",
    "BillToSite": "Paris",
    "TransactionType": "Invoice",
    "receivablesInvoiceLines": [
        {
            "Description": "Laptop",
            "LineNumber": 1,
            "Quantity": 2,
            "UnitSellingPrice": 1
        },
        {
            "Description": "Battery",
            "LineNumber": 2,
            "Quantity": 2,
            "UnitSellingPrice": 2
        },
        {
```

```
            "Description": "Charger",
            "LineNumber": 3,
            "Quantity": 4,
            "UnitSellingPrice": 3
        }
    ]
}
```

Section 2: Set Original Transaction As Incomplete and Update Flexfields

Figure 17-21. *Initial Integration*

These steps set the original transaction as "Incomplete" and call the auxiliary integration to add descriptive flexfield data (ATTRIBUTE1 only—feel free to expand).

Set Original Transaction As Incomplete

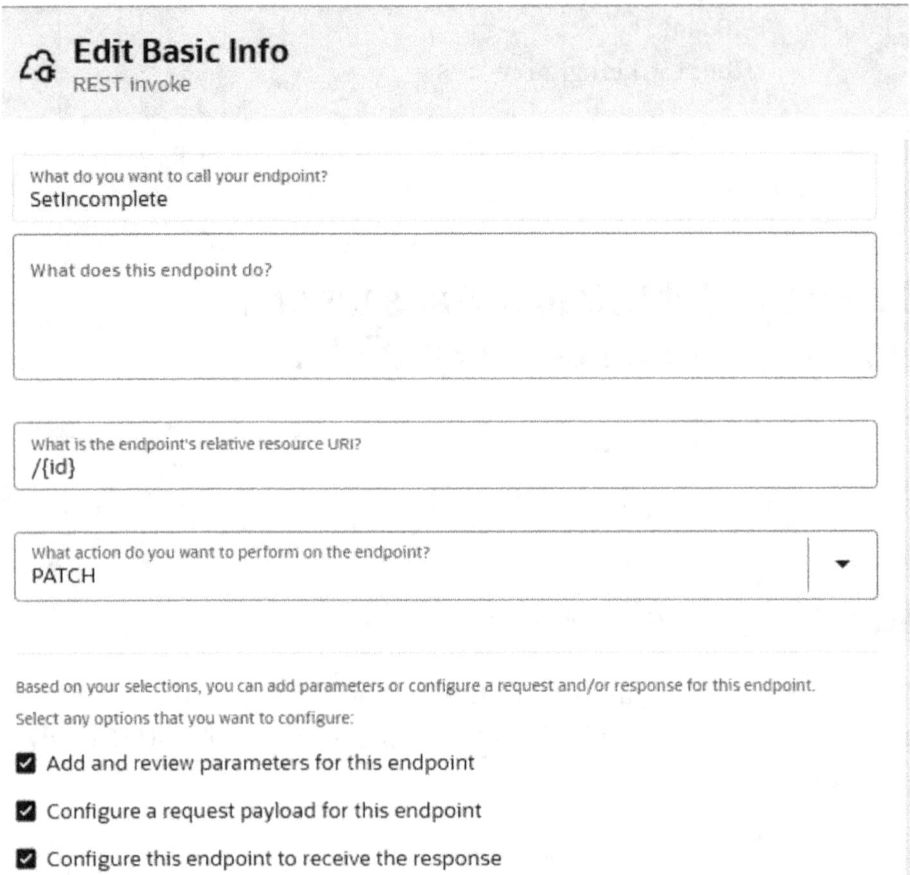

Figure 17-22. *Set Incomplete*

Request Payload Sample:

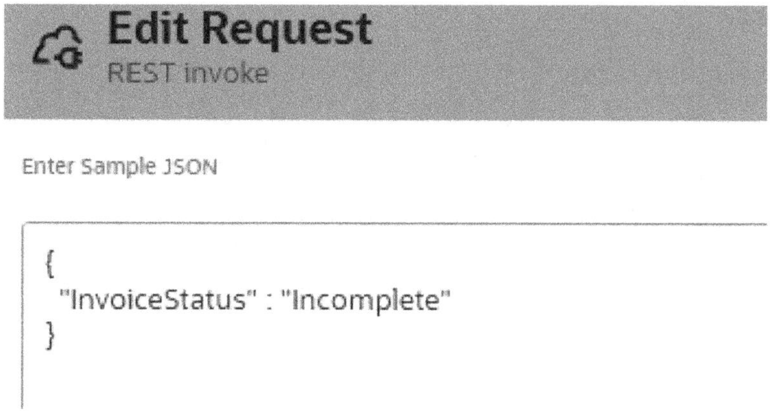

Figure 17-23. *Incomplete Payload*

The response payload is the same as used for creation (see "Create Invoice with REST API" under Section 1).

Update Flexfields

Call the auxiliary integration XX_DEMO_UPDATE_FLEX with the following parameters.

```
<xsl:template match="/" xml:id="id_11">
    <nstrgmpr:POST xml:id="id_12">
        <nstrgmpr:components.schemas.request-wrapper xml:id="id_56">
            <ns46:pModule xml:id="id_57">
                <xsl:value-of xml:id="id_58" select="'AR'"/>
            </ns46:pModule>
            <ns46:pEntityName xml:id="id_59">
                <xsl:value-of xml:id="id_60" select="'Receivables Invoice'"/>
            </ns46:pEntityName>
            <ns46:pContextValue xml:id="id_69">
                <xsl:value-of xml:id="id_111" select="'#NULL'"/>
            </ns46:pContextValue>
            <ns46:pInvNumber xml:id="id_67">
                <xsl:value-of xml:id="id_112" select="$CreateArInvoice/nsmpr0:executeResponse/ns40:response-wrapper/ns40:TransactionNumber"/>
            </ns46:pInvNumber>
            <ns46:pInvoiceId xml:id="id_66">
                <xsl:value-of xml:id="id_72" select="$CreateArInvoice/nsmpr0:executeResponse/ns40:response-wrapper/ns40:CustomerTransactionId"/>
            </ns46:pInvoiceId>
            <ns46:pAttribute xml:id="id_61">
                <xsl:value-of xml:id="id_62" select="'ATTRIBUTE1'"/>
            </ns46:pAttribute>
            <ns46:pValue xml:id="id_63">
                <xsl:value-of xml:id="id_110" select="concat (&quot;Source customer_trx_id is .: &quot;, /nssrcmpr:execute/ns21:request-wrapper/ns21:pCustomerTrxId )"/>
            </ns46:pValue>
        </nstrgmpr:components.schemas.request-wrapper>
    </nstrgmpr:POST>
</xsl:template>
</xsl:stylesheet>
```

Figure 17-24. *Update the Flexfield Call*

Section 3: Copy Attachments

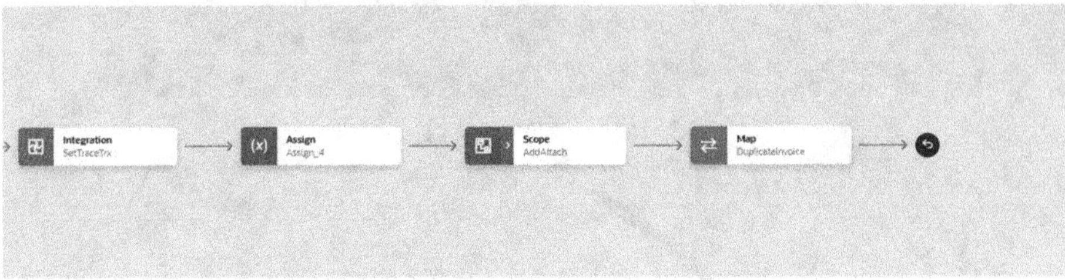

Figure 17-25. *Copy Attachments*

Different approaches apply depending on the attachment type.

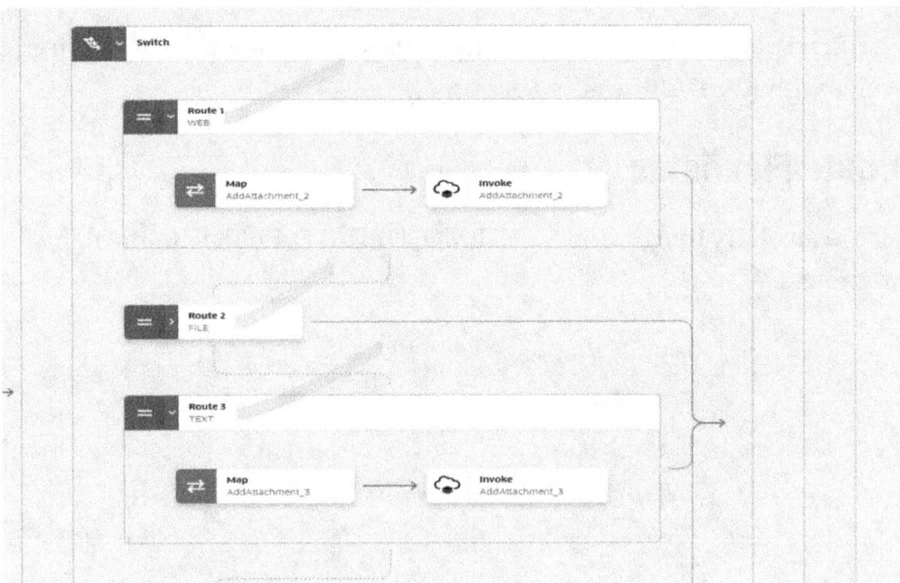

Figure 17-26. *Attachment Types*

Section 4: Return Response

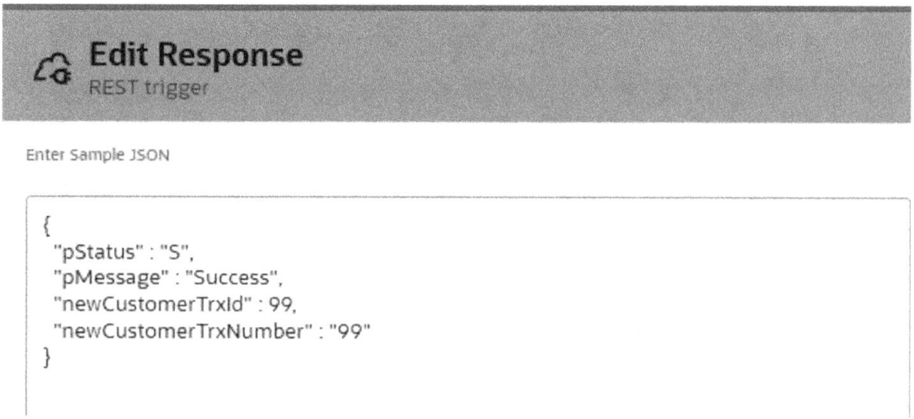

Figure 17-27. Return Response

Return the response payload defined in Section 1.

Testing

Step 1: Run the Integration

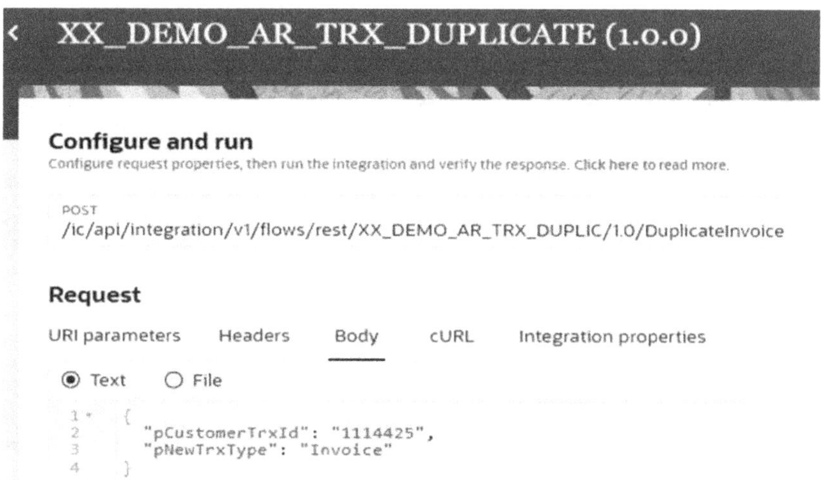

Figure 17-28. Run Integration

Step 2: Review Parent Integration

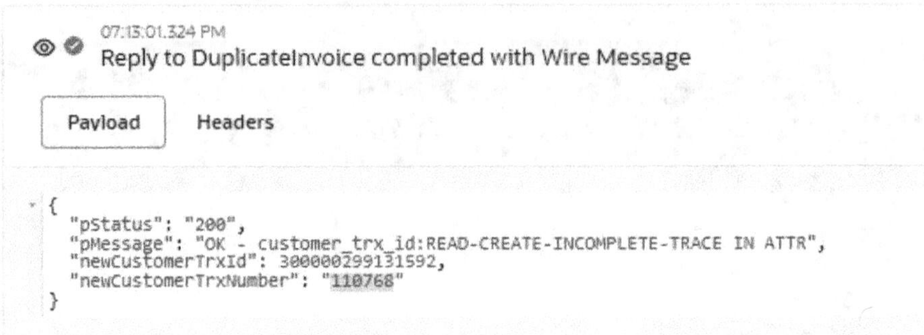

***Figure 17-29.** Parent Integration Review*

Step 3: Review Child Integration

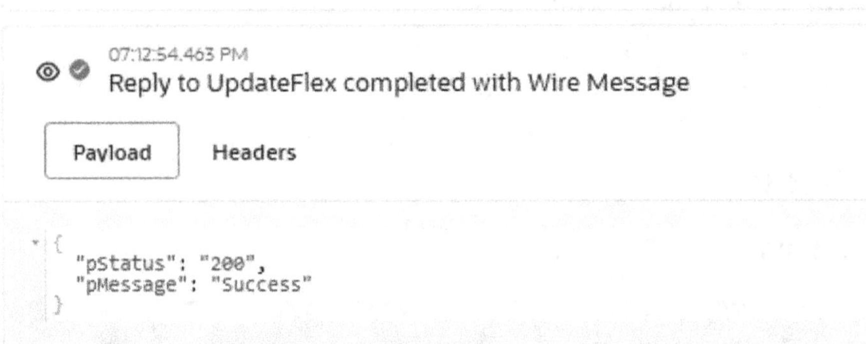

***Figure 17-30.** Child Integration Review*

Step 4: Review in Oracle ERP

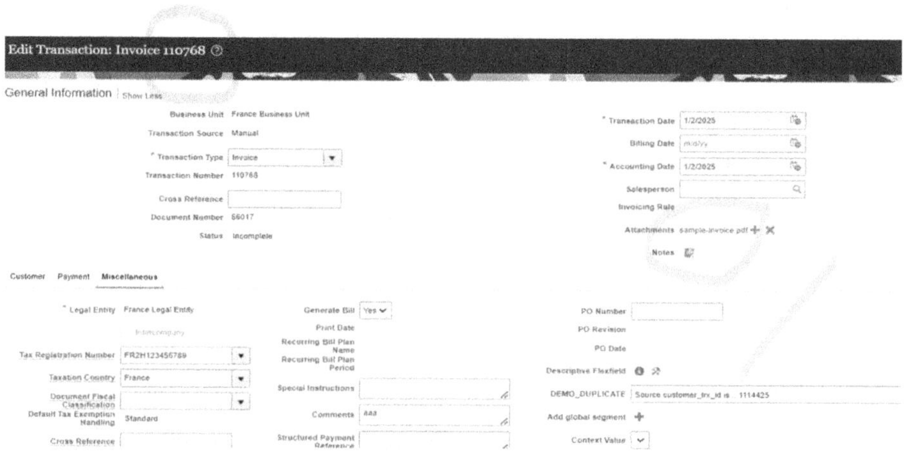

Figure 17-31. ERP Verification

Technical Reference

Code Example	Comments
XX_DEMO_UPDATE_FLEX	**Package File**: XX_DEMO_COOKBOOK.par
XX_DEMO_AR_TRX_DUPLICATE	**Package File**: XX_DEMO_COOKBOOK.par

CHAPTER 18

SOAP ERP Demos

ErpIntegrationService

Overview

The ErpIntegrationService is a SOAP web service provided by Oracle that enables interaction with Oracle ERP Cloud jobs. This service provides comprehensive operations for managing Enterprise Scheduler Service (ESS) jobs, document management, and data import/export processes.

Reference Documentation

Oracle Financials 26B—Get Started

Available Operations

The ErpIntegrationService supports 20 operations, with the most commonly used ones highlighted below.

Job Management Operations:

1. **getESSJobStatus**: Retrieve the current status of an ESS job.

2. **submitESSJobRequest**: Submit a new ESS job request.

3. **submitJobWithOutput**: Submit a job and retrieve output.

J. J. Montero Rodríguez and S. Tahseen, *Oracle Integration Cookbook for Oracle ERP Cloud*, https://doi.org/10.1007/979-8-8688-3020-4_18

4. **downloadESSJobExecutionDetails**: Download execution details for a job.
5. **getESSExecutionDetails**: Get detailed execution information.

Document Management Operations:

1. **getDocumentIdsForFilePrefix**: Retrieve document IDs by file prefix from a UCM account.
2. **getDocumentForDocumentId**: Get a specific document by document ID from UCM.
3. **getDocumentsForFilePrefix**: Retrieve documents by file prefix from a UCM account.
4. **uploadFileToUcm**: Upload files to Universal Content Management.

Data Import/Export Operations:

1. **loadAndImportData**: Uploads a file into a UCM server and submits an ESS job to load and import uploaded files to an application table. It is deprecated now so use importBulkData instead.
2. **importBulkData**: Uploads a file into a UCM server and submits an ESS job to load and import files to an application table.
3. **exportBulkData**: Submits an ESS job to export data from ERP Cloud and uploads the job output file to UCM. Used for outbound data extracts.
4. **extractAndPurge**: Submits an ESS job to load and import uploaded files to application tables and then purges the interface tables. Similar to importBulkData but includes automatic interface table cleanup.

5. **downloadExportOutput**: Download ESS job output and logs as .zip. This is deprecated; use downloadESSJobExecutionDetails instead.

Other Operations:

1. **appendFileComment**: Add comments to a document.
2. **confirmExtractConsumption**: Acknowledges and confirms that download for data extract is completed.
3. **updateInterfaceData**: Updates error data in interface tables.
4. **getDfltObjAttrHints**: Retrieve user interface hints.
5. **getServiceLastUpdateTime**: Retrieve the date and time when schema files were last changed.
6. **getEntityList**: Get a list of service data objects associated with ERP integration service.

WSDL Endpoint

```
https://[your-instance].ds-fa.oraclepdemos.com/fscmService/
ErpIntegrationService?WSDL
```

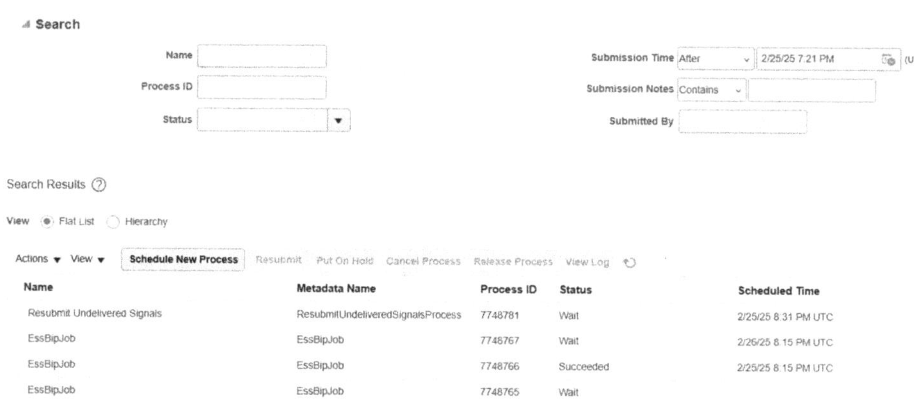

***Figure 18-1.** ErpIntegrationService Operations Overview*

You can test the ErpIntegrationService operations using Postman by creating a SOAP request. *(**Note**: The following example is a simplified illustration.)*

Figure 18-2. *Postman SOAP Request Configuration*

Sample Response

When calling the getESSExecutionDetails operation, the response provides detailed information about the job execution:

```
<env:Envelope xmlns:env="http://schemas.xmlsoap.org/soap/
envelope/"xmlns:wsa="http://www.w3.org/2005/08/addressing">
  <env:Header>
    <wsa:Action>http://xmlns.oracle.com/apps/financials/
    commonModules/shared/model/erpIntegrationService/
    ErpIntegrationService/getESSExecutionDetailsResponse</
    wsa:Action>
    <wsa:MessageID>urn:uuid:10dfa34d-4afd-46c5-9aa4-
    df61281e6a92</wsa:MessageID>
  </env:Header>
```

```
  <env:Body>
    <ns0:getESSExecutionDetailsResponse xmlns:ns0="http://
    xmlns.oracle.com/apps/financials/commonModules/shared/
    model/erpIntegrationService/types/">
      <result xmlns="http://xmlns.oracle.com/apps/financials/
      commonModules/shared/model/erpIntegrationService/types/">
        {
          "JOBS": {
            "JOBNAME": "Coordinate File Import Artifact
            Generation",
            "JOBPATH": "/oracle/apps/ess/crmCommon/core/
            fileImport",
            "REQUESTID": "7743389",
            "STATUS": "SUCCEEDED",
            "CHILD": [
              {
                "JOBNAME": "Generate File Import Artifact",
                "JOBPATH": "/oracle/apps/ess/crmCommon/core/
                fileImport",
                "REQUESTID": "7743390",
                "STATUS": "SUCCEEDED"
              }
            ]
          }
        }
      </result>
    </ns0:getESSExecutionDetailsResponse>
  </env:Body>
</env:Envelope>
```

Integration Configuration

Required Connections

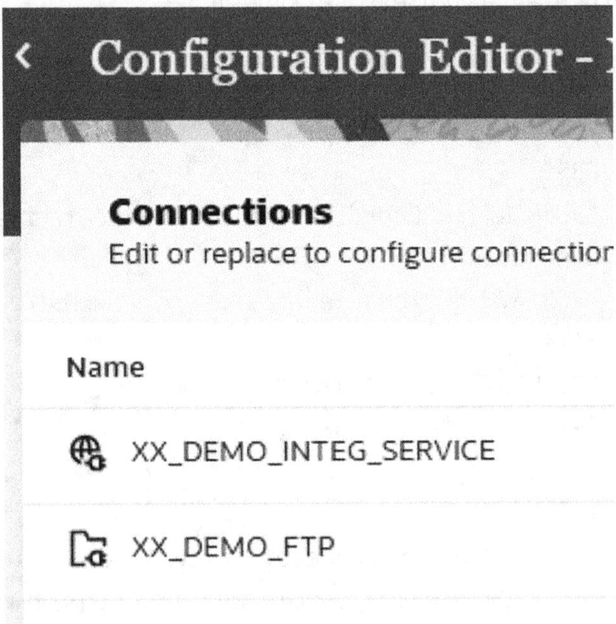

Figure 18-3. *Required Integration Connections*

Integration requires two connections:

1. **FTP Server Connection**: For file operations (explained in previous chapters)

2. **SOAP ErpIntegrationService Connection (8)**: For accessing the web service

Integration Design

This example demonstrates retrieving detailed information for job ID 7743389.

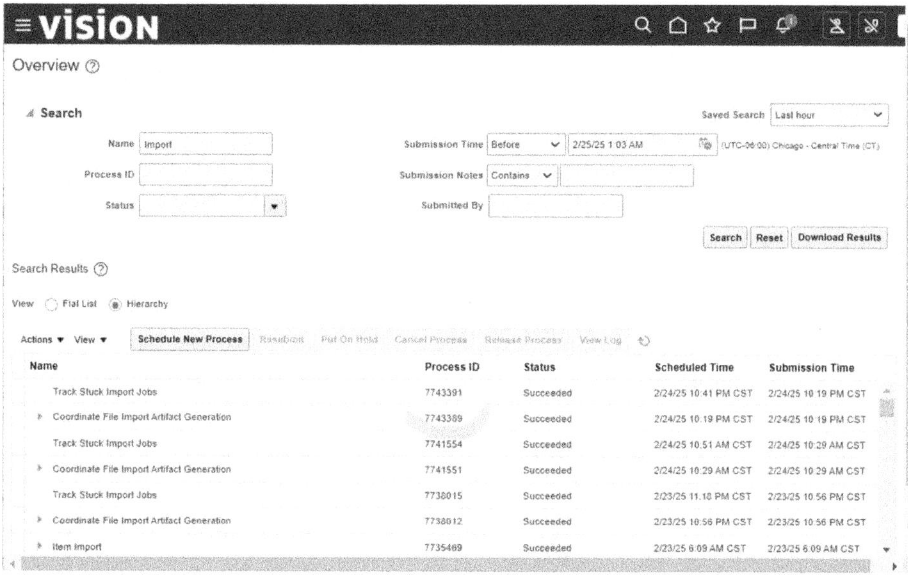

Figure 18-4. *Job Details in Oracle ERP Cloud*

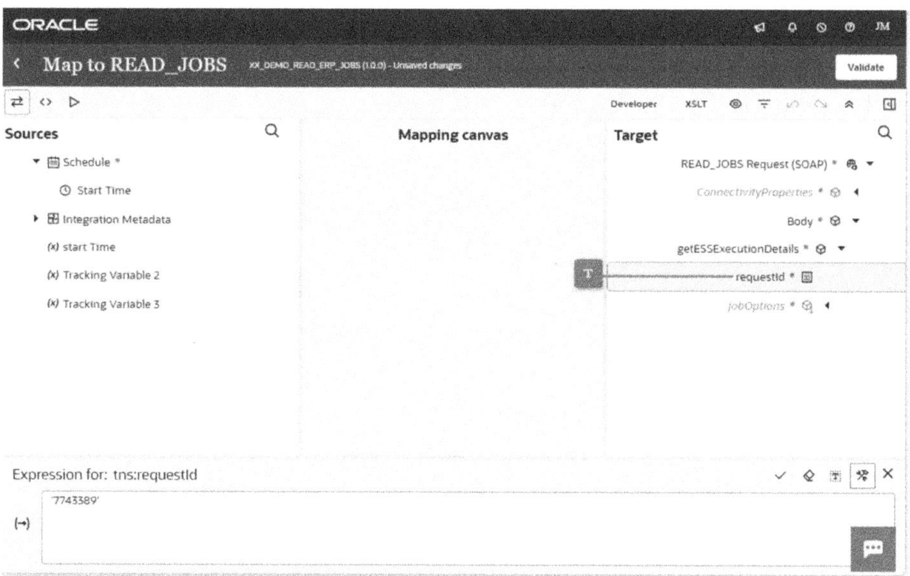

Figure 18-5. *Job Execution Details*

Integration Overview

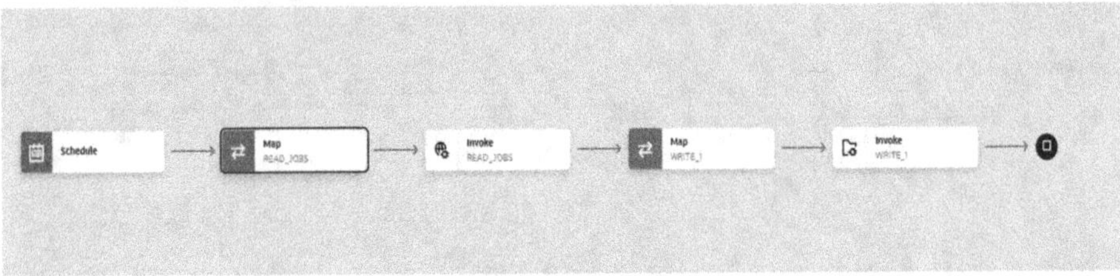

Figure 18-6. *Integration Flow Overview*

The integration performs the following steps:

1. Invokes the ErpIntegrationService to retrieve job execution details
2. Processes the response
3. Writes the result to an FTP server for further processing

Write Activity Configuration

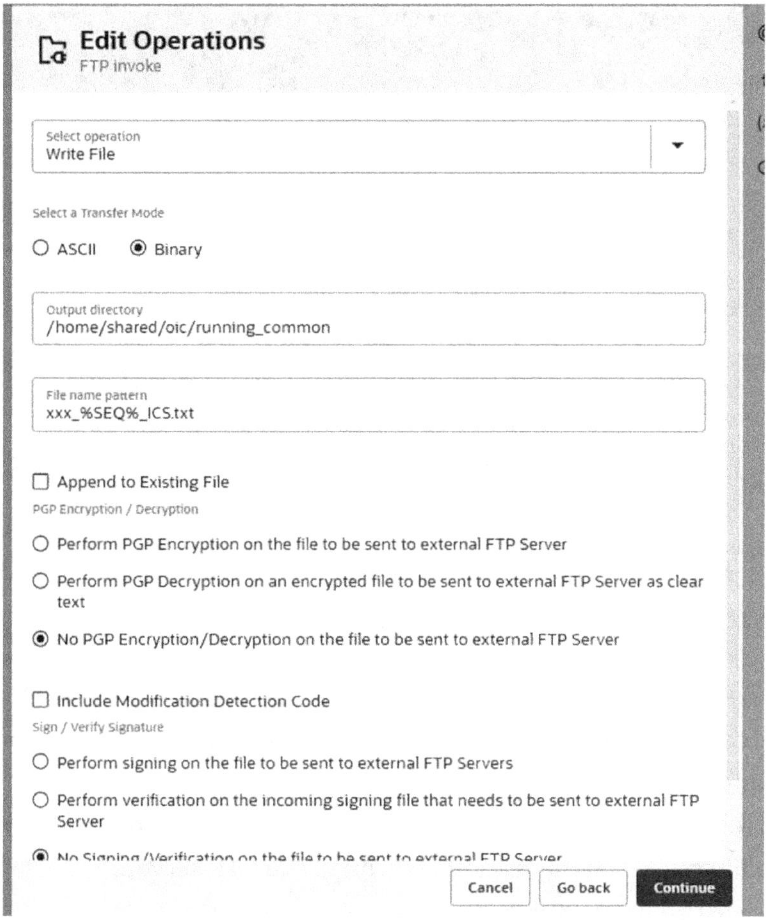

Figure 18-7. *Write Activity Properties*

Mapping Configuration

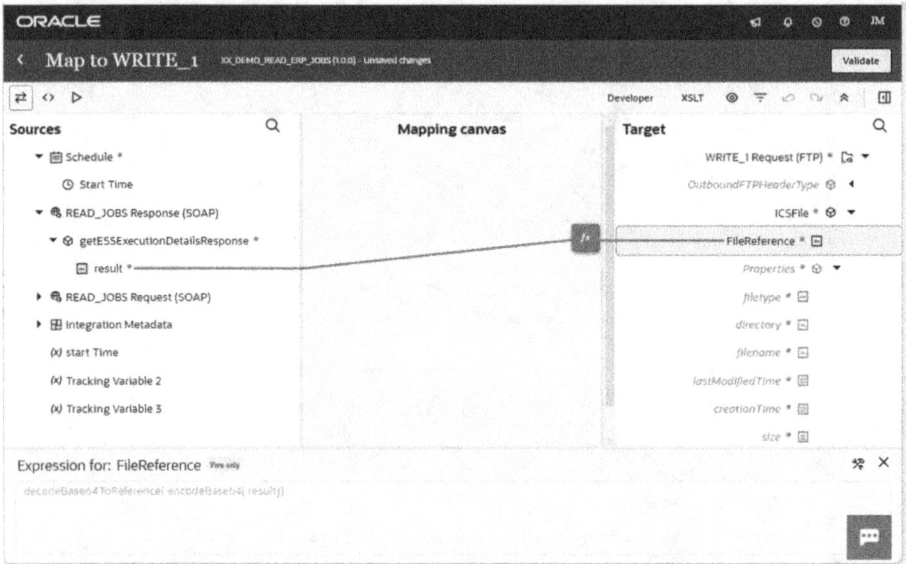

Figure 18-8. *Write Activity Mapping*

The key mapping expression used is **oraext:decodeBase64ToReference(oraext:encodeBase64($READ_JOBS/nsmpr1:getESSExecutionDetailsResponse/nsmpr1:result))**.

This expression encodes the result to Base64 and then decodes it to create a file reference that can be written to the FTP server.

Testing the Integration

When testing the integration, a file is created on the FTP server containing the job execution details. While ideally the integration would parse the output for further processing, this example demonstrates the basic concept of retrieving and storing job information.

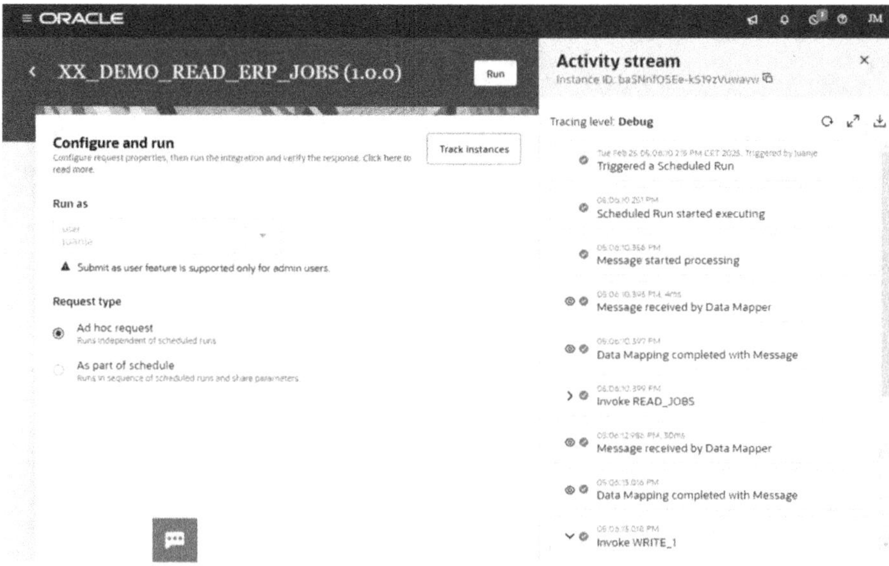

***Figure 18-9.** Integration Test Results*

FTP Server Contents

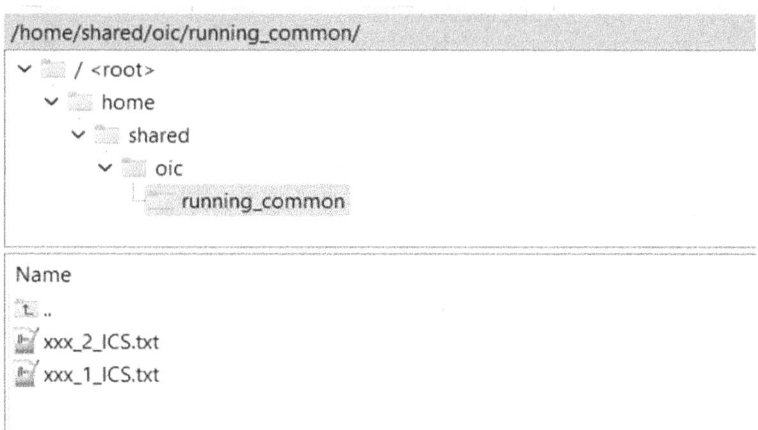

***Figure 18-10.** File Created on the FTP Server*

File Contents


```
{
    "JOBS": {
        "JOBNAME": "Coordinate File Import Artifact Generation",
        "JOBPATH": "/oracle/apps/ess/crmCommon/core/fileImport",
        "REQUESTID": "7743389",
        "STATUS": "SUCCEEDED",
        "CHILD": [
            {
                "JOBNAME": "Generate File Import Artifact",
                "JOBPATH": "/oracle/apps/ess/crmCommon/core/fileImport",
                "REQUESTID": "7743390",
                "STATUS": "SUCCEEDED"
            }
        ]
    }
}
```


Figure 18-11. *Job Execution Details in the File*

Technical Reference

Code Example	Comments
XX_DEMO_READ_ERP_JOBS	Integration included in package XX_DEMO_COOKBOOK.par

ScheduleService

Overview

The ScheduleService is a SOAP web service provided by Oracle for managing scheduled reports and jobs in Oracle ERP Cloud. This service is particularly useful for automating report generation and delivery processes.

Important Note This web service uses username/password in the payload, which is not a security best practice. However, it is included here for completeness and educational purposes. Recommend using the service only over HTTPS and using a dedicated service account with minimal privileges.

Reference Documentation

WSDL Endpoint:

```
https://xxxx.ds-fa.oraclepdemos.com/xmlpserver/services/v2/
ScheduleService?wsdl
```

Sample payloads are provided in the GitHub repository.

Available Operations

The ScheduleService provides 38 operations for comprehensive schedule management.

Schedule Management:

1. **cancelSchedule()**: Cancel a scheduled report.
2. **cancelScheduleInSession()**: Cancel a schedule within a session.
3. **deleteSchedule()**: Delete a scheduled report.
4. **deleteScheduleInSession()**: Delete a schedule within a session.
5. **resumeSchedule()**: Resume a suspended schedule.
6. **resumeScheduleInSession()**: Resume a schedule within a session.
7. **suspendSchedule()**: Suspend a scheduled report.
8. **suspendScheduleInSession()**: Suspend a schedule within a session.

9. **scheduleReport()**: Schedule a new report.
10. **scheduleReportInSession()**: Schedule a report within a session.

Job History Management:

1. **deleteJobHistory()**: Delete job history records.
2. **deleteJobHistoryInSession()**: Delete job history within a session.
3. **purgeJobHistory()**: Purge old job history.
4. **purgeJobHistoryInSession()**: Purge job history within a session.

Report Information Retrieval:

1. **getAllScheduledReport()**: Get all scheduled reports.
2. **getAllScheduledReportHistory()**: Get all scheduled report history.
3. **getAllScheduledReportHistoryInSession()**: Get report history within a session.
4. **getAllScheduledReportInSession()**: Get all scheduled reports within a session.
5. **getScheduledJobInfo()**: Get information about a scheduled job.
6. **getScheduledJobInfoInSession()**: Get job info within a session.
7. **getScheduledReportDeliveryInfo()**: Get report delivery information.
8. **getScheduledReportDeliveryInfoInSession()**: Get delivery info within a session.

9. **getScheduledReportOutputInfo()**: Get report output information.

10. **getScheduledReportOutputInfoInSession()**: Get output info within a session.

Document and Data Operations:

1. **downloadDocumentData()**: Download document data.

2. **downloadDocumentDataInSession()**: Download document data within a session.

3. **downloadXMLData()**: Download XML data.

4. **downloadXMLDataInSession()**: Download XML data within a session.

5. **getDocumentData()**: Get document data.

6. **getDocumentDataInSession()**: Get document data within a session.

7. **getXMLData()**: Get XML data.

8. **getXMLDataInSession()**: Get XML data within a session.

Delivery Service:

1. **deliveryService()**: Execute delivery service.

2. **deliveryServiceInSession()**: Execute delivery service within a session.

3. **getDeliveryServiceDefinition()**: Get delivery service definition.

4. **getDeliveryServiceDefinitionInSession()**: Get delivery definition within a session.
5. **resendScheduledReport()**: Resend a scheduled report.
6. **resendScheduledReportInSession()**: Resend a report within a session.

Preparation

BI Report Setup

You need a BI Publisher report with parameters in the following folder structure.

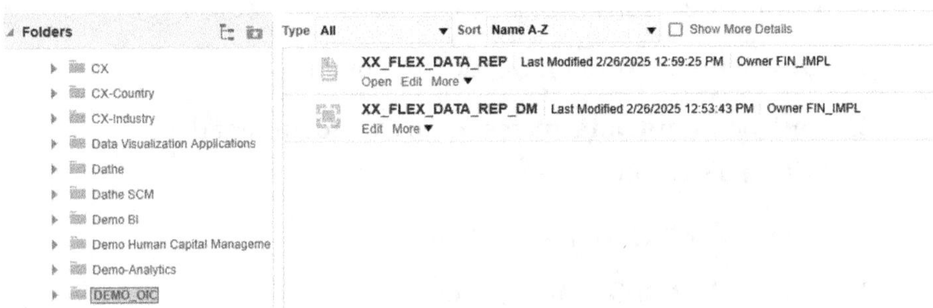

***Figure 18-12.** BI Report Folder Structure*

Folder Location: /shared/Custom/DEMO_OIC

Report Name: XX_FLEX_DATA_REP (provided in DEMO_OIC.catalog on GitHub)

SoapUI Project Setup

Create a SoapUI project with the ScheduleService WSDL:

```
https://xxxx.ds-fa.oraclepdemos.com/xmlpserver/services/v2/
ScheduleService?wsdl
```

Testing with Postman

Schedule Report Operation:

Figure 18-13. *Schedule Report Request in Postman*

```
        </v2:wccOptions>
    </v2:deliveryChannels>
    <v2:reportRequest>
        <v2:attributeFormat>HTML</v2:attributeFormat>
        <v2:attributeLocale>en-US</v2:attributeLocale>
        <v2:attributeTemplate>XX_FLEX_DATA</v2:attributeTemplate>
        <v2:reportAbsolutePath>/Custom/DEMO_OIC/XX_FLEX_DATA_REP.xdo</v2:reportAbsolutePath>
        <v2:sizeOfDataChunkDownload>-1</v2:sizeOfDataChunkDownload>
        <v2:parameterNameValues>
            <v2:listOfParamNameValues>
                <v2:item>
                    <v2:name>P_EXT_SOURCE</v2:name>
                    <v2:values>
                        <v2:item>DEMO1</v2:item>
                    </v2:values>
                </v2:item>
            </v2:listOfParamNameValues>
        </v2:parameterNameValues>
    </v2:reportRequest>
    <v2:notifyWhenFailed>true</v2:notifyWhenFailed>
```

Figure 18-14. *Schedule Report Payload*

When you execute the Postman web service call, the report is scheduled and executed in Oracle ERP Cloud.

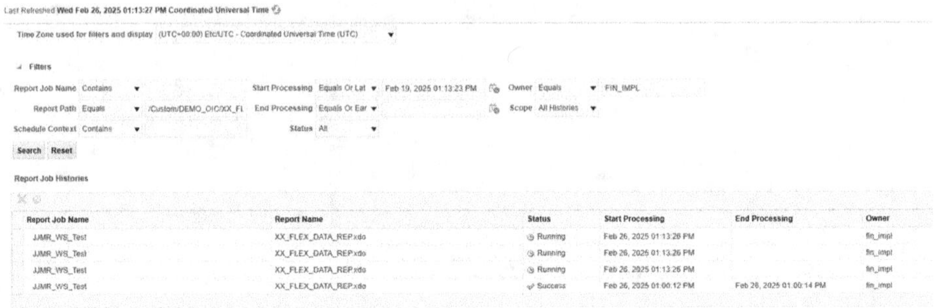

***Figure 18-15.** Report Execution in Oracle ERP Cloud*

Integration Setup

Connection Configuration

Refer to Chapter 2 for detailed connection setup instructions.

Create an Integration

Create an integration using the Schedule type.

***Figure 18-16.** Schedule Integration Type*

Test the Integration

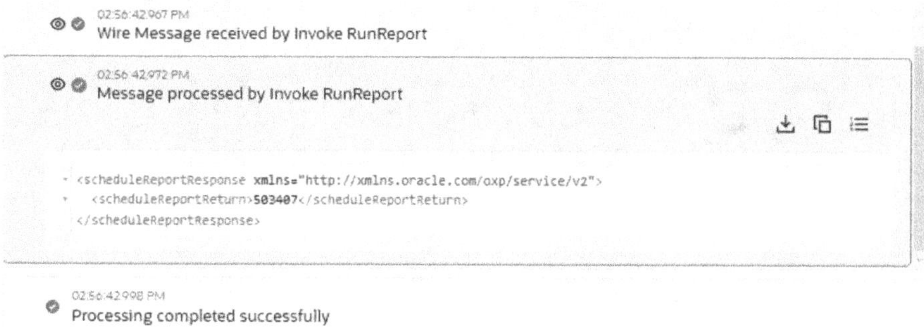

Figure 18-17. *Integration Test Execution*

Additional Operations Examples

Get Scheduled Job Info

Figure 18-18. *getScheduledJobInfo Operation*

Get Scheduled Report Status

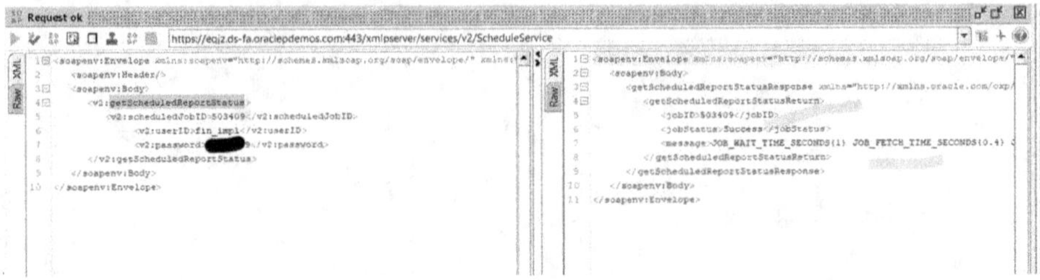

Figure 18-19. *getScheduledReportStatus Operation*

Get All Job Instance IDs

This operation is particularly useful as it provides the IDs needed for other operations.

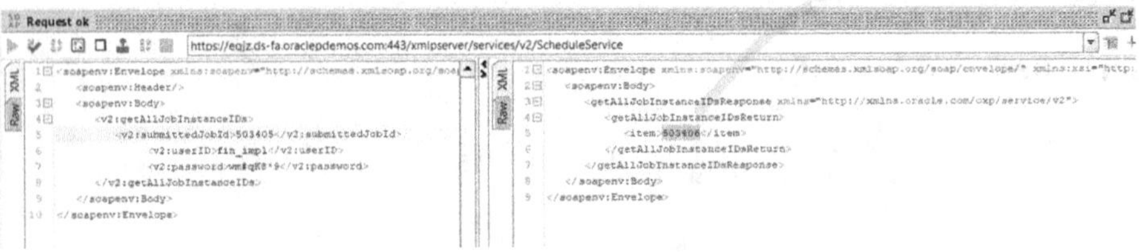

Figure 18-20. *getAllJobInstanceIDs Operation*

Get XML Data

Here's an example of retrieving XML data using the job instance ID.

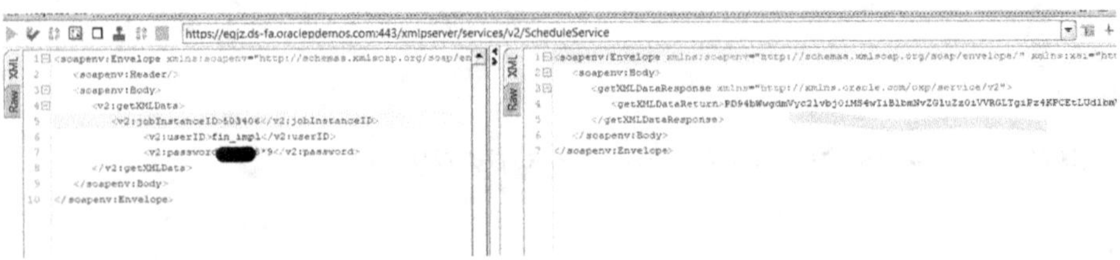

Figure 18-21. *getXMLData Operation*

Get All Scheduled Report History

Figure 18-22. *getAllScheduledReportHistory Operation*

Get Scheduled Report Output Info

Figure 18-23. *getScheduledReportOutputInfo Operation*

Get Document Data

This operation uses the document ID from the previous operation to retrieve the actual report output.

Figure 18-24. *getDocumentData Operation*

Complete Integration Example

The following example demonstrates a comprehensive integration that uses multiple ScheduleService operations.

Step 1: Get Instance

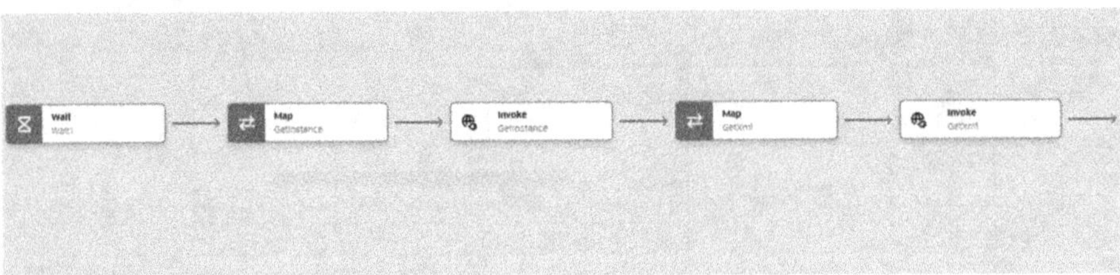

Figure 18-25. *Get Job Instance Step*

Step 2: Get XML Data

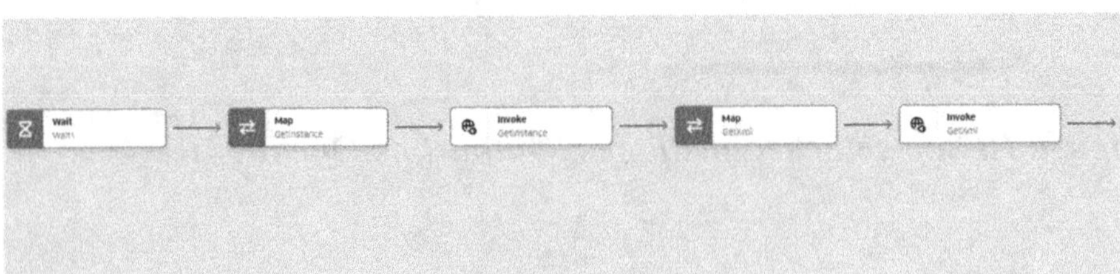

Figure 18-26. *Get XML Data Step*

Step 3: Get Report ID

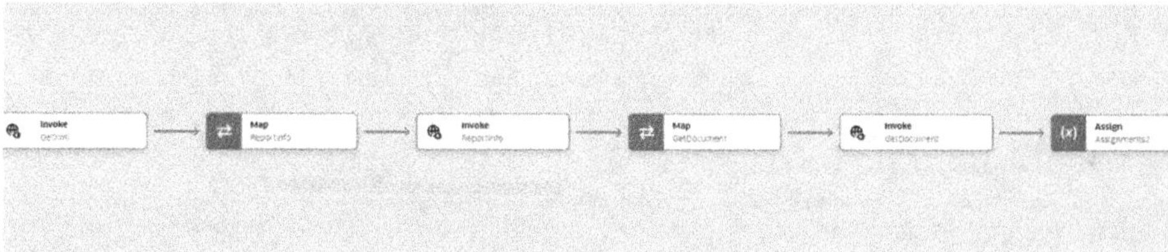

Figure 18-27. *Get Report ID Step*

Step 4: Get Report Document

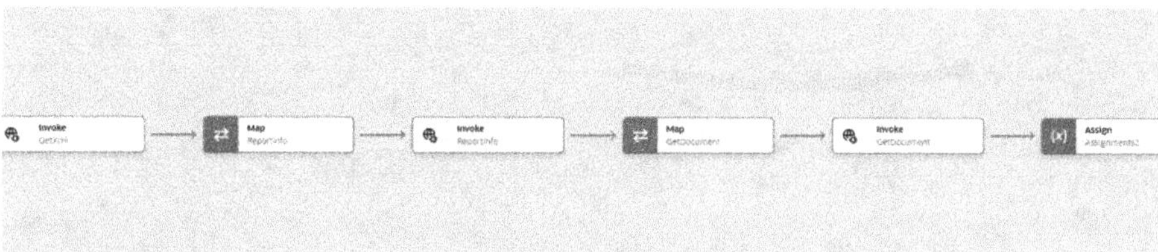

Figure 18-28. *Get Report Document Step*

Final Output

For demonstration purposes, the integration displays two variables containing the decoded content.

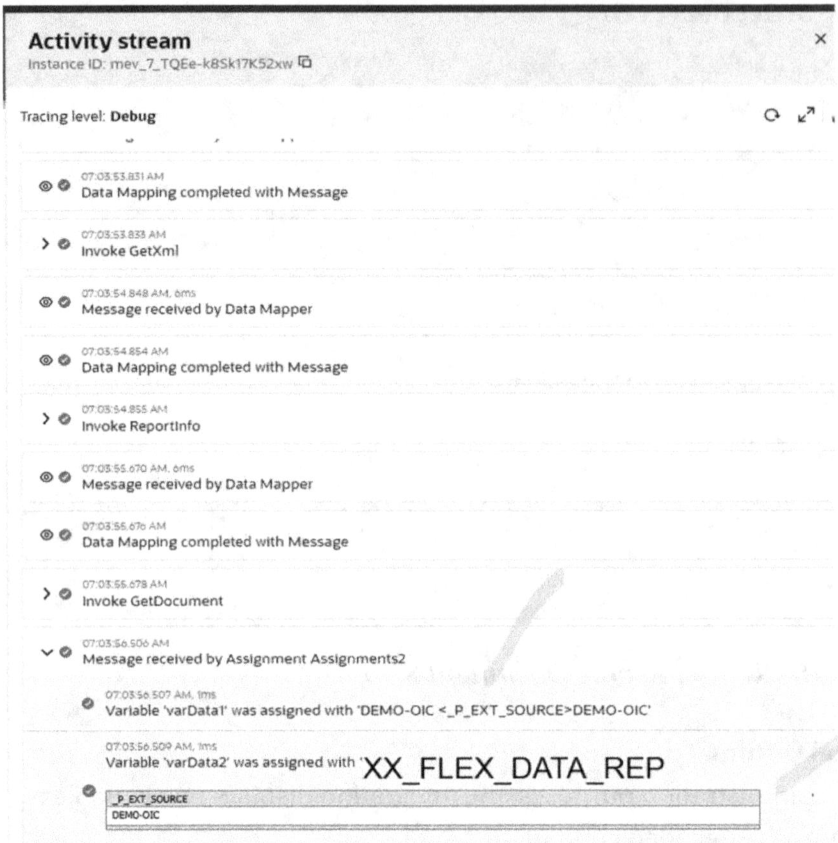

Figure 18-29. Integration Output Variables

Technical Reference

Code Example	Comments
XX_DEMO_SCHED_SERVICE_01.iar	Integration included in package XX_DEMO_COOKBOOK.par
XX_FLEX_DATA_REP	Report included in file DEMO_OIC.catalog
XX_FLEX_DATA_REP_DM	Data model included in file DEMO_OIC.catalog

ErpObjectDFFUpdateService

Overview

The ErpObjectDFFUpdateService is a SOAP web service provided by Oracle that enables programmatic updates to descriptive flexfields (DFFs) and global descriptive flexfields (GDFs) in Oracle ERP Cloud. This service is essential for automating the maintenance of flexible field data across various ERP modules.

Reference Documentation

- ERP Object Descriptive Flexfield Update Service
- Payload to Update AR Invoice DFF

Oracle ERP Cloud Setup

Before using the service, you must configure and deploy the DFF in Oracle ERP Cloud.

Step 1: Navigate to Flexfield Configuration

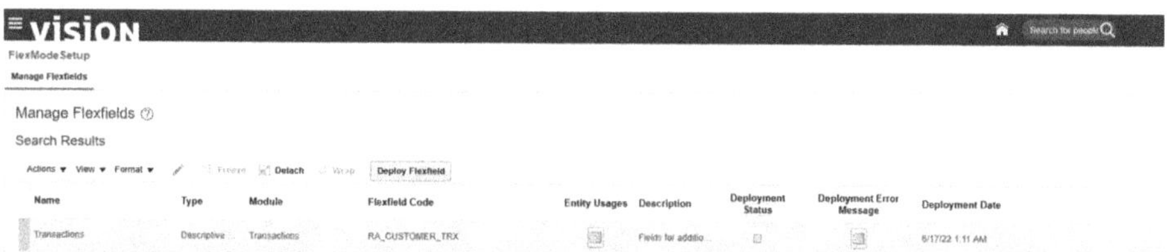

Figure 18-30. Manage Descriptive Flexfields

Step 2: Configure Context

Figure 18-31. *Configure DFF Context*

Step 3: Deploy the Flexfield

Click the "Deploy Flexfield" button to make the configuration active.

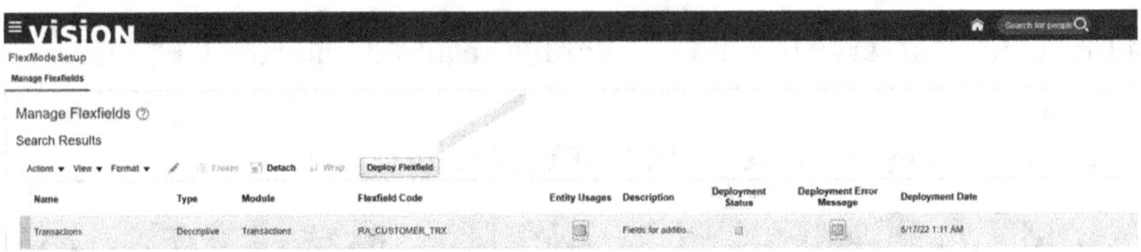

Figure 18-32. *Deploy Flexfield*

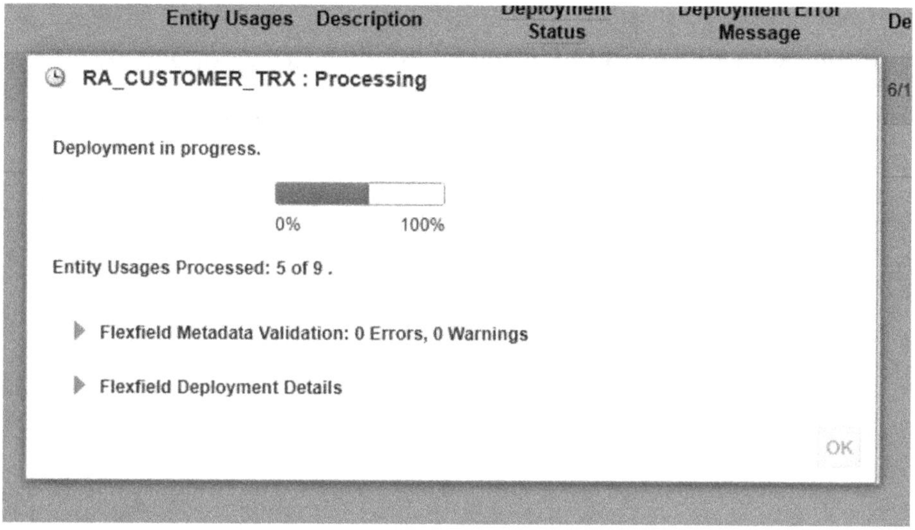

Figure 18-33. *Deployment Confirmation*

Step 4: Verify Deployment

After reconnecting to the instance, verify the DFF appears in the transaction form.

Figure 18-34. *DFF in the Transaction Form*

Testing with Postman

Create a SOAP project in Postman with the WSDL endpoint:

```
https://xxxx.ds-fa.oraclepdemos.com/fscmService/ErpObjectDFFUpd
ateService?WSDL
```

Figure 18-35. *Postman SOAP Request*

Response Interpretation:

- A response of "1" indicates the update was successful.
- Any other response indicates an error occurred.

Verification in ERP Cloud

After a successful update, requery the transaction page to see the updated field.

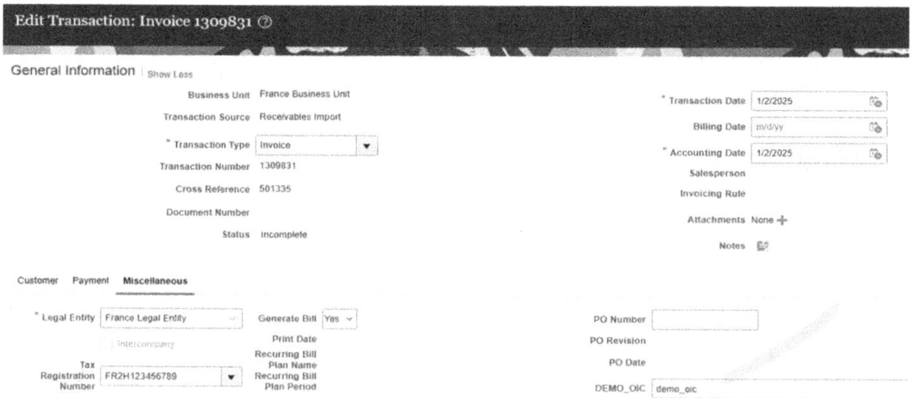

***Figure 18-36.** Updated DFF Value*

OIC Integration Setup

Create a Schedule Integration

Create a basic integration using the Schedule trigger type.

Select an Operation

Choose the ErpObjectDFFUpdateService connection and select the appropriate operation.

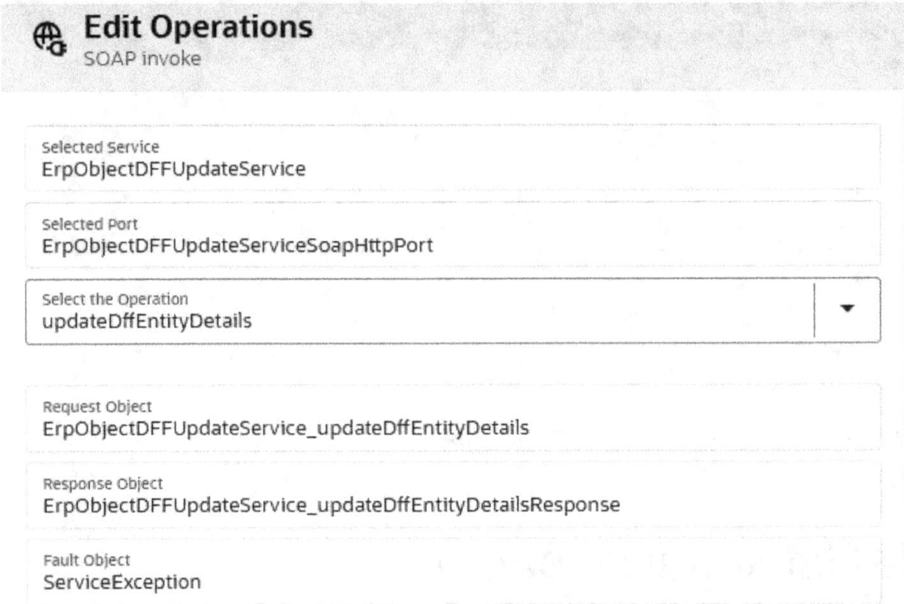

Figure 18-37. *Select an Update Operation*

Integration Overview

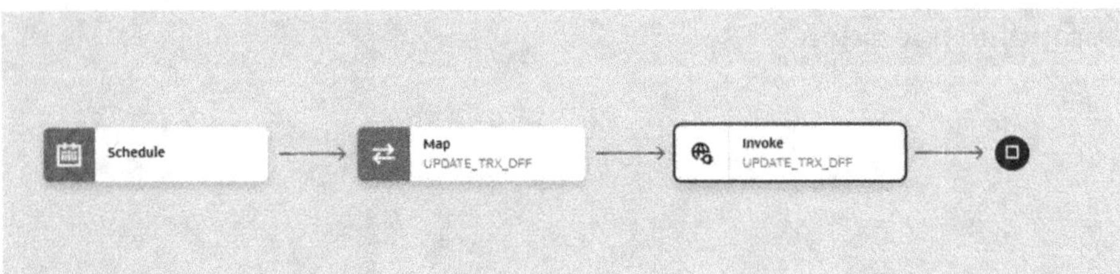

Figure 18-38. *Integration Flow Overview*

Mapping Configuration

For learning purposes, values are hardcoded in the mapping. In production, these would be dynamically populated.

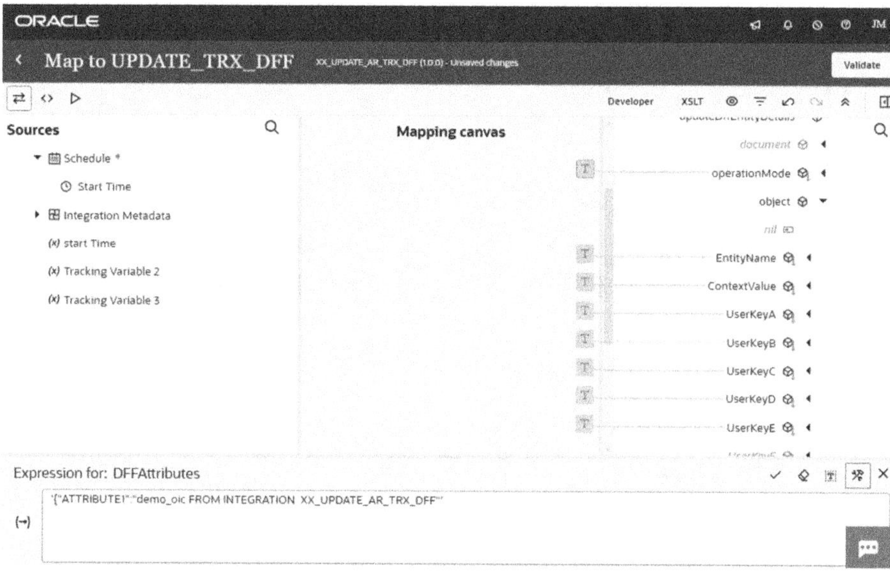

Figure 18-39. Mapping Configuration

Code View

Figure 18-40. Mapping in Code Mode

Testing the Integration

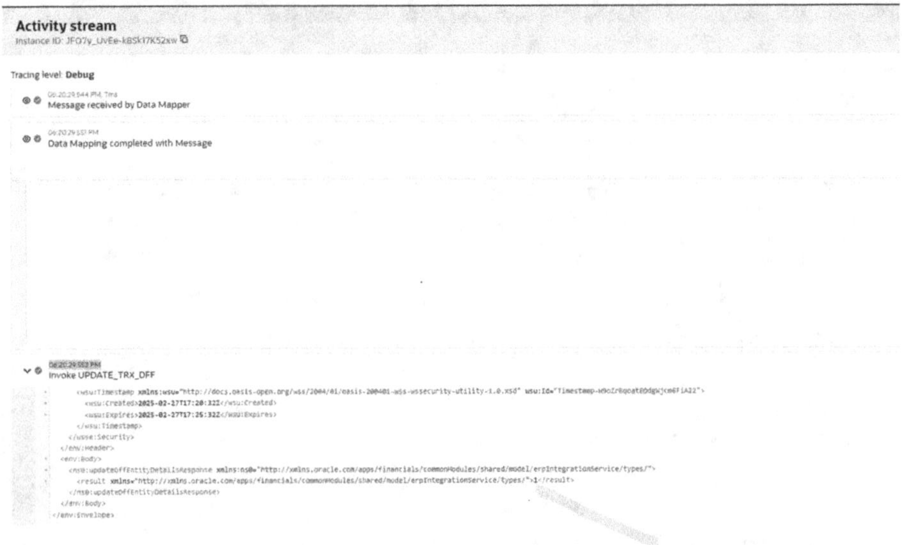

Figure 18-41. Integration Test Results

A response of "1" confirms the update was successful.

Verify in ERP Cloud

Requery the transaction to confirm the field was updated.

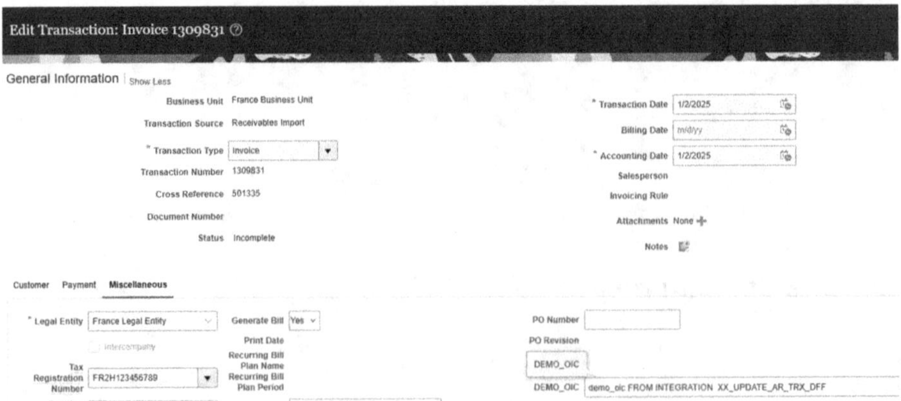

Figure 18-42. Verified Update in ERP Cloud

User Key Configuration

When updating DFFs, you need to provide the correct user keys to identify the record. The following table shows the user keys for Accounts Receivable invoices:

User Key	Details	Comments
User Key A	Transaction Number	Primary identifier
User Key B	Batch Source Name	Not mandatory if Transaction Number is unique
User Key C	Set Name	Not mandatory if Transaction Number is unique
User Key D	Transaction Identifier	**Technical Attribute**: CustomerTrxId. Not visible in UI; retrieve via BI Publisher report

Payables Invoice Lines Example

The process for updating Payables invoice line DFFs is similar. The key is obtaining a working sample using SoapUI first.

***Figure 18-43.** Payables Invoice DFF Update*

A response of "1" indicates success.

Sample Payload: Available on GitHub as soap_sample_update_dff_payables_inv_line.xml


```xml
<!--DOCID METALINK (Doc ID 2546651.1) -->
<!--
https://cloudcustomerconnect.oracle.com/posts/a2489bd8fc
 Line Number in User Key A
 Invoice Number in User Key B
 Business Unit Name in User Key C
 Supplier Name in User Key D
 Supplier Number in User Key E
 Supplier Site Name in User Key F
 Invoice Identifier in User Key G-VOUCHER NUMBER?
 -->
<soap:Body>
    <ns1:updateDffEntityDetails xmlns:ns1="http://xmlns.oracle.com/apps/financials/commonModules/shared/model/erpIntegrationService/types/">
        <ns1:document xmlns:ns2="http://xmlns.oracle.com/apps/financials/commonModules/shared/model/erpIntegrationService/">
            <ns2:Content>NULL</ns2:Content>
            <ns2:FileName>#NULL</ns2:FileName>
            <ns2:ContentType>#NULL</ns2:ContentType>
            <ns2:DocumentTitle>#NULL</ns2:DocumentTitle>
            <ns2:DocumentAuthor>#NULL</ns2:DocumentAuthor>
            <ns2:DocumentSecurityGroup>#NULL</ns2:DocumentSecurityGroup>
            <ns2:DocumentAccount>#NULL </ns2:DocumentAccount>
            <ns2:DocumentName/>
            <ns2:DocumentId/>
        </ns1:document>
        <ns1:operationMode>single</ns1:operationMode>
        <ns1:object xmlns:ns2="http://xmlns.oracle.com/apps/financials/commonModules/shared/model/erpIntegrationService/">
            <ns2:EntityName>Payables Invoice Lines</ns2:EntityName>
            <ns2:ContextValue>#NULL</ns2:ContextValue>
            <ns2:UserKeyA>1</ns2:UserKeyA>
            <ns2:UserKeyB>TEST00012</ns2:UserKeyB>
            <ns2:UserKeyC>ZZZ XKX Spain SAU</ns2:UserKeyC>
            <ns2:UserKeyD>IBERICA, S.R.L.</ns2:UserKeyD>
            <ns2:UserKeyE>11622</ns2:UserKeyE>
            <ns2:UserKeyF>ACREEDOR</ns2:UserKeyF>
            <ns2:UserKeyG>#NULL</ns2:UserKeyG>
            <ns2:UserKeyH>#NULL</ns2:UserKeyH>
            <ns2:DFFAttributes>{"ATTRIBUTE4":"123123-1"}</ns2:DFFAttributes>
        </ns1:object>
        <ns1:notificationCode>#NULL</ns1:notificationCode>
        <ns1:callbackURL>#NULL</ns1:callbackURL>
    </ns1:updateDffEntityDetails>
</soap:Body>
</soap:Envelope>
```


***Figure 18-44.** Payables DFF Payload Details*

Note Determining the correct values for each node is not always straightforward. Refer to Oracle Support notes for specific module guidance.

Additional Resources

Oracle Support Notes

- **Customers:** NOTE:2563101.1—how to update Accounts Receivable receipt DFFs using ErpObjectDFFUpdateService
- **Receipts:** Doc ID 2563101.1—how to update receipt DFFs using the updateDffEntityDetails operation

Technical Reference

Code Example	Comments
XX_UPDATE_AR_TRX_DFF	Integration included in package XX_DEMO_COOKBOOK.par
XX_UPDATE_AR_TRX_DFF_SII	Integration with mapping example for Spanish SII global attributes, included in package XX_DEMO_COOKBOOK.par

CHAPTER 19

Attachments in Oracle ERP

Overview

Attachments in Oracle ERP Cloud are a widely used feature that allows users to associate various types of content with Business Objects. Users can attach desktop files, text notes, and URLs to ERP transactions such as receivables invoices, purchase orders, and many other entities.

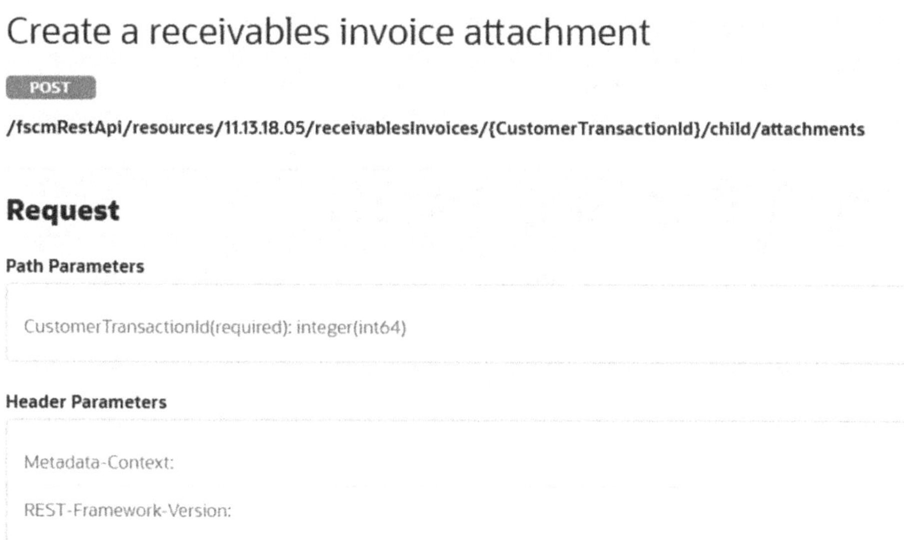

***Figure 19-1.** Create a receivables invoice attachment*

J. J. Montero Rodríguez and S. Tahseen, *Oracle Integration Cookbook for Oracle ERP Cloud*,
https://doi.org/10.1007/979-8-8688-3020-4_19

Attachment Types

Oracle ERP Cloud supports several attachment types.

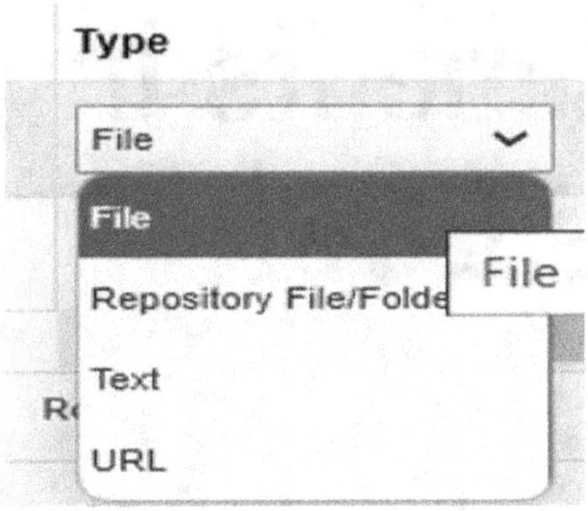

Figure 19-2. *Available Attachment Types*

1. **File**: Upload documents from your computer.
2. **Text**: Add text notes directly.
3. **URL**: Link to web pages or external resources.

Manual Attachment Process

Users can manually add attachments through the ERP Cloud interface. For example, in the Receivables Transactions page, see Figure 19-3.

Figure 19-3. Attachments Link in Receivables Transaction

Automated Attachments with REST APIs

REST APIs enable programmatic attachment creation, allowing OIC to automate this process. This chapter demonstrates how to use OIC to automatically attach files and URLs to receivables transactions.

Note *REST API–based file attachments have a size limit. Oracle Fusion REST APIs for attachments typically enforce a payload size limit (commonly 10 MB for the overall request). For large file attachments, the approach of Base64-encoding file content and including it directly in the REST payload will fail. For larger files, the UCM upload approach (upload to UCM first, and then reference the document ID) is needed.*

Example 1: File Attachment

Integration Overview

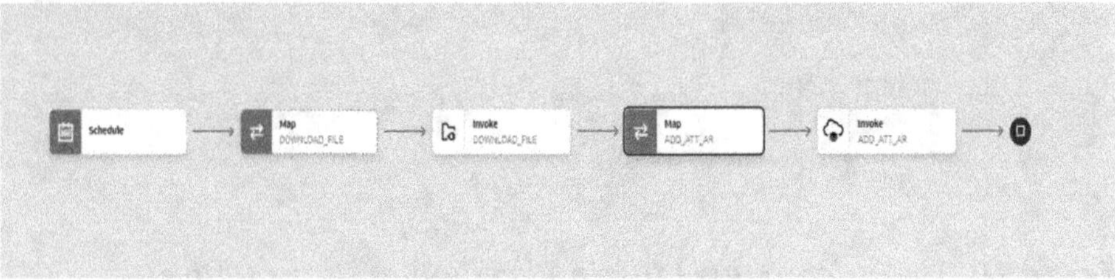

Figure 19-4. *File Attachment Integration Flow*

Connection Setup

Use a standard Oracle ERP Cloud connection (refer to Chapter 2 for detailed setup).

Download File Activity

Configure the FTP download activity to retrieve the file.

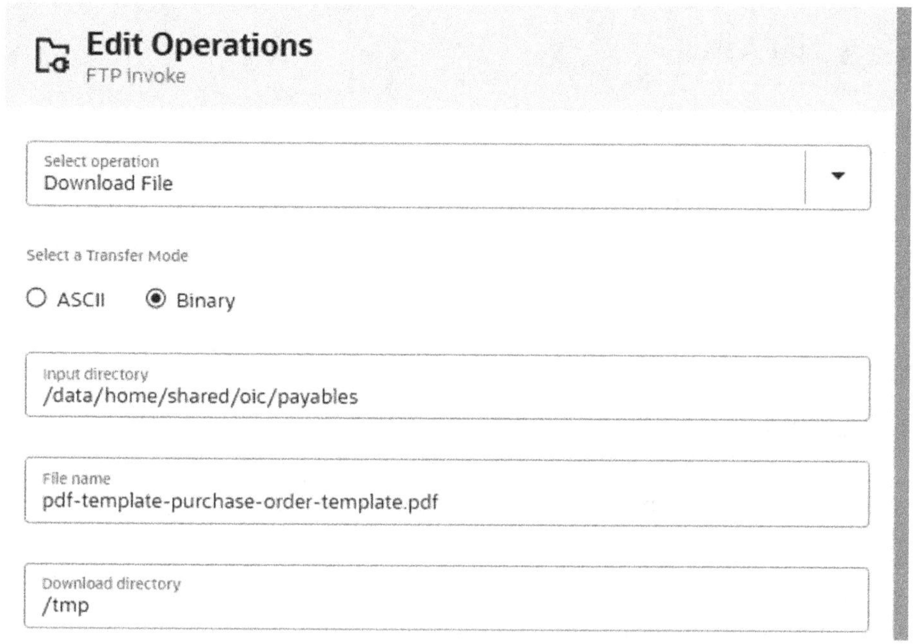

Figure 19-5. *Download File Activity Configuration*

Create Attachment Activity

Step 1: Add REST Invoke

Drag and drop the Oracle ERP Cloud connection and select the following option.

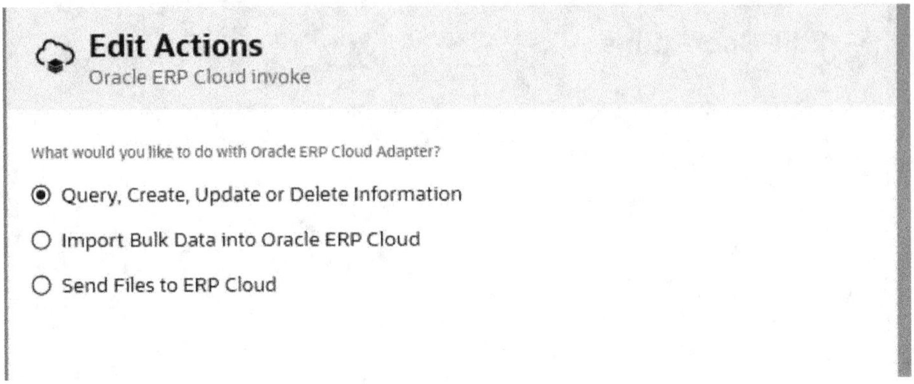

Figure 19-6. *Select the REST Resource Option*

Step 2: Select Business Resources

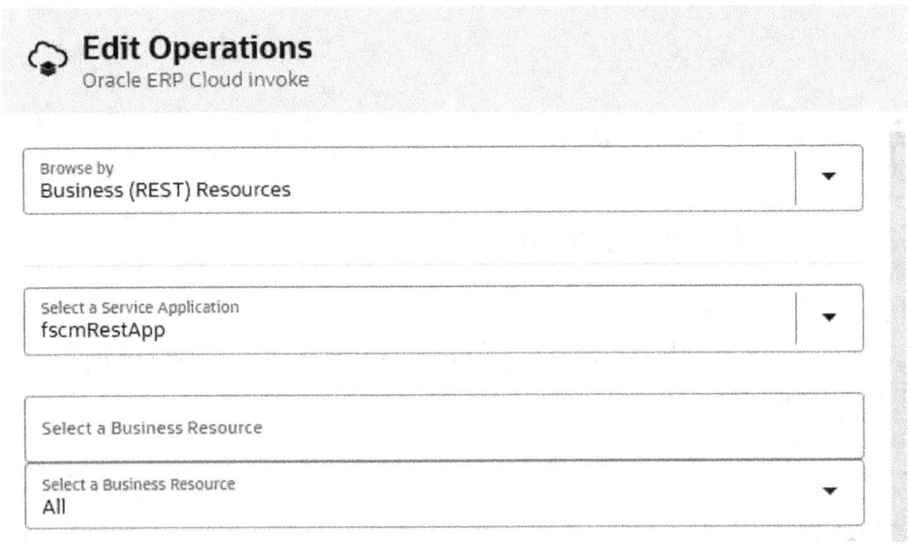

Figure 19-7. *Business Resources Selection*

Step 3: Configure Endpoint

In the final step, you will see the attachment endpoint configuration.

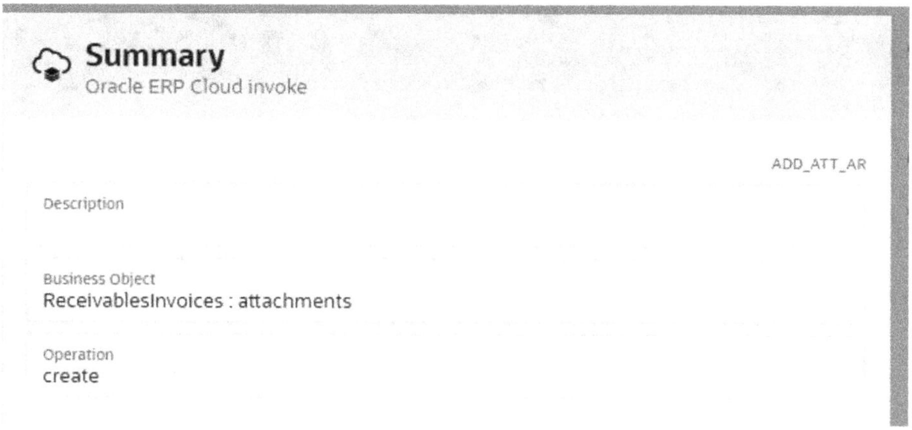

Figure 19-8. *Attachment Endpoint Configuration*

Mapping Configuration

Transaction ID Mapping

First, map the customer transaction ID (from the CUSTOMER_TRX_ID column in the RA_CUSTOMER_TRX_ALL table).

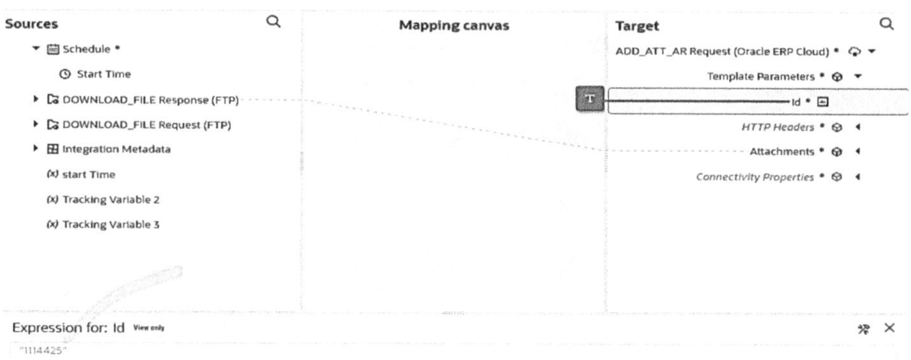

Figure 19-9. *Transaction ID Mapping*

Finding the Transaction ID

You can find the customer transaction ID in Oracle ERP Cloud.

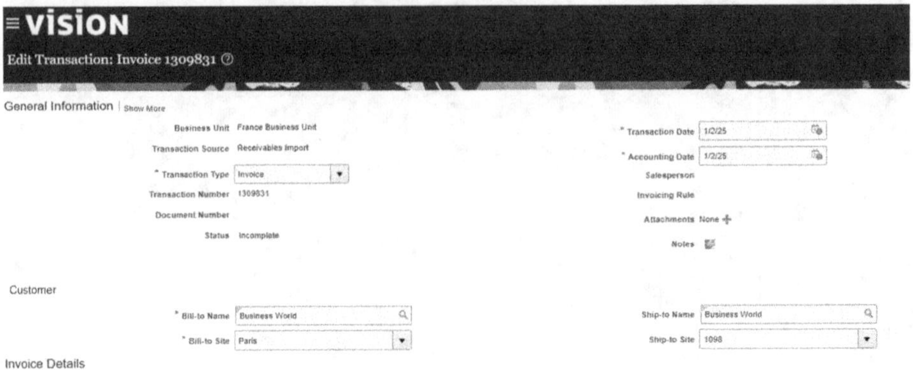

Figure 19-10. Transaction in ERP Cloud

Use the following BI Publisher query:

```
SELECT CUSTOMER_TRX_ID
FROM RA_CUSTOMER_TRX_ALL
WHERE TRX_NUMBER = '1309831';
```

Example Values:

- **Transaction Number**: 1309831
- **Customer Transaction ID**: 1114425

Attachment Details Mapping

Map the filename, category, and other attachment properties.

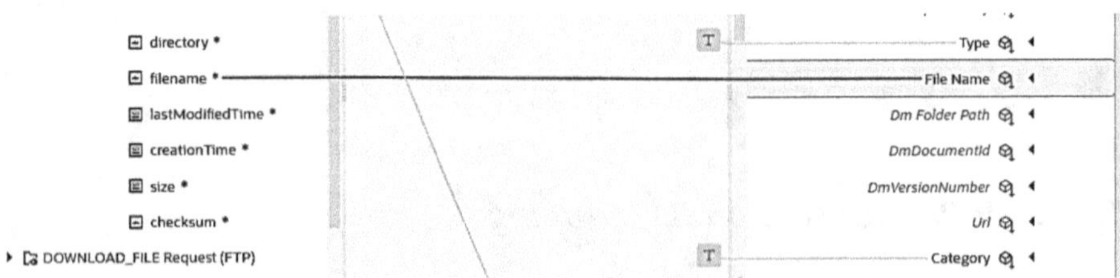

Figure 19-11. Attachment Details Mapping

File Contents Mapping

Map the file contents using the Base64 encoding function.

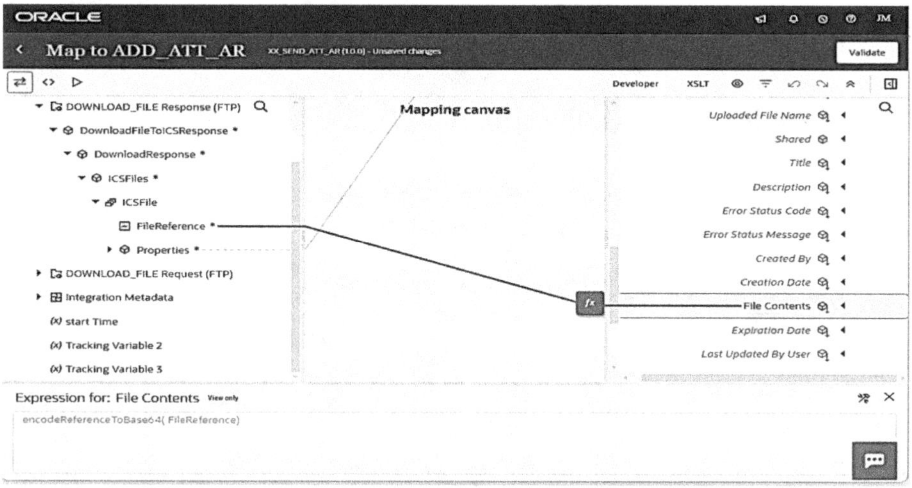

Figure 19-12. *File Contents Mapping with Encoding*

When testing, before running our test, this value is the one needed in mapping, as shown. Hardcode for learning purposes.

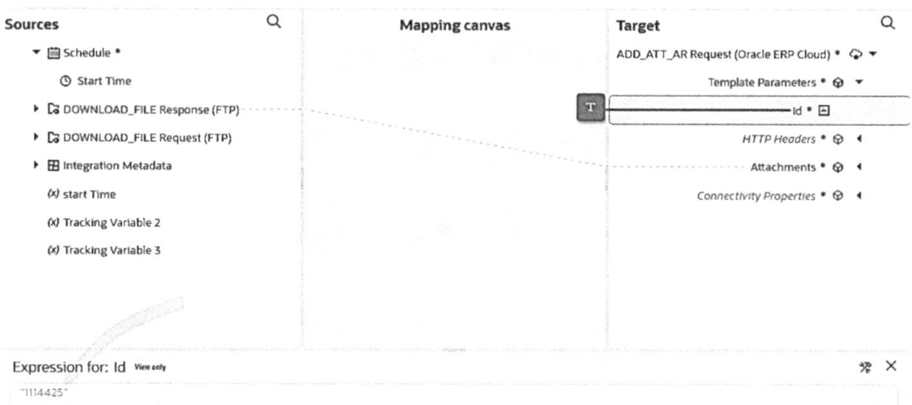

Figure 19-13. *Hardcode the ID Value*

Here's the BI Publisher data model provided on GitHub: XX_DEMO_AR_ATTACHMENTS_DM.xdm.catalog.

Alternative Method: Using REST API

You can also retrieve the customer transaction ID using REST API.

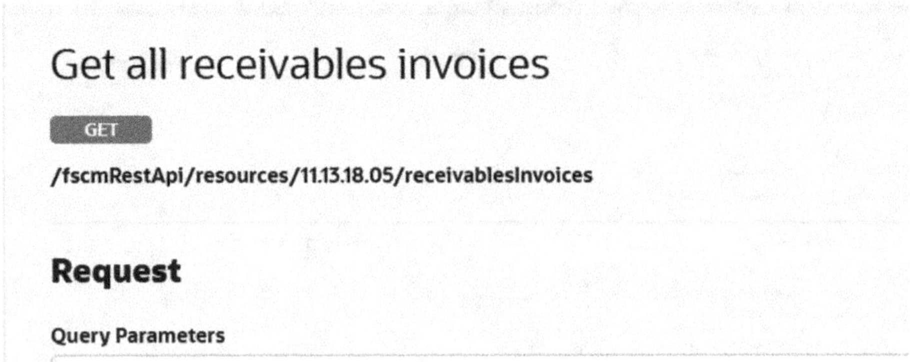

Figure 19-14. *REST API to Get the Transaction ID*

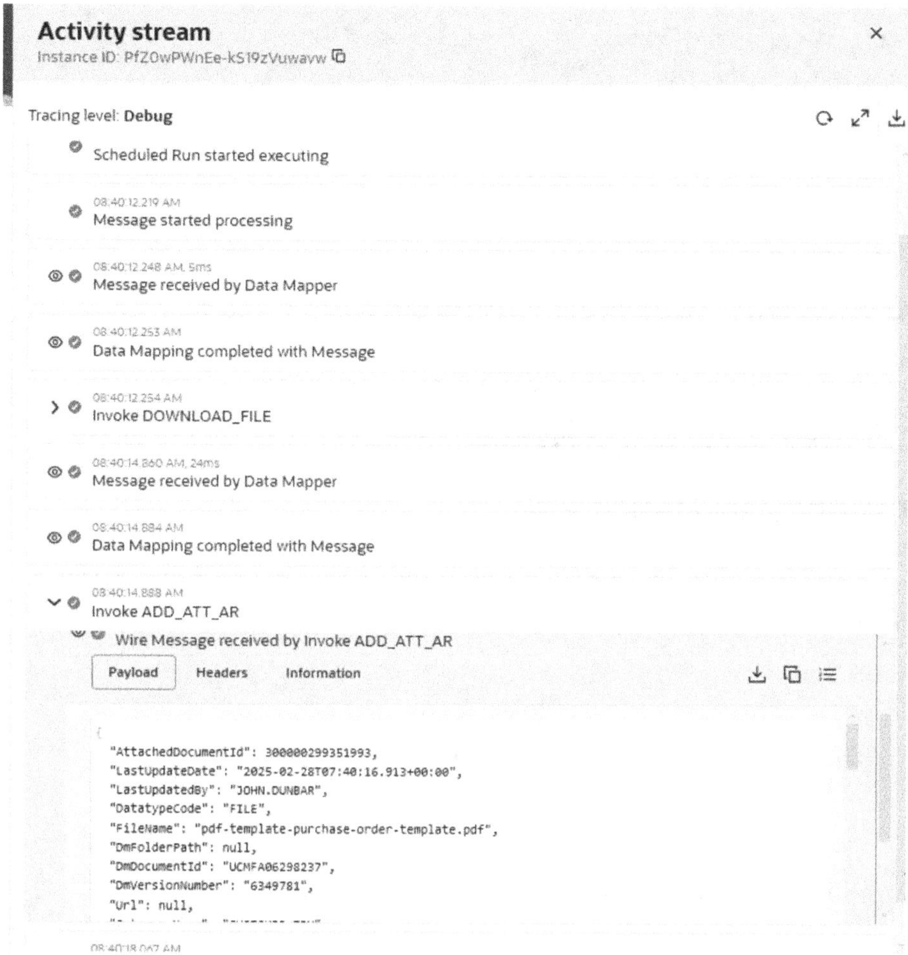

Figure 19-15. *REST API Response*

Testing the Integration

Before Execution

The transaction has no attachments.

After Execution

The attachment appears in the transaction.

Figure 19-16. Transaction with Attachment

Example 2: URL Attachment

Integration Overview

For learning purposes, this example clones Example 1 and removes the Download activity.

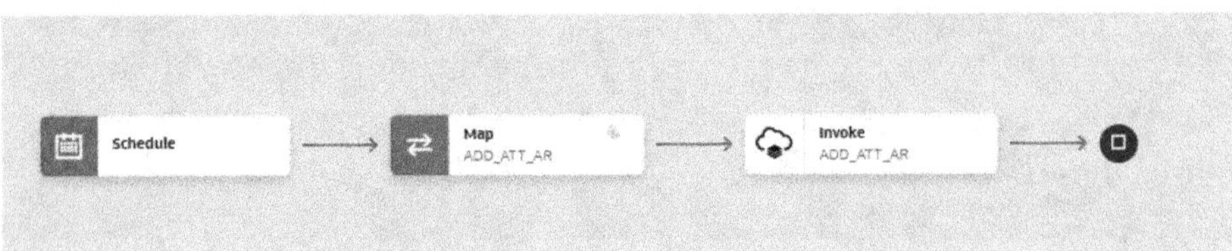

Figure 19-17. URL Attachment Integration Flow

Mapping Configuration

The mapping differs in two key areas.

Attachment Type

Set the type to "WEB_PAGE".

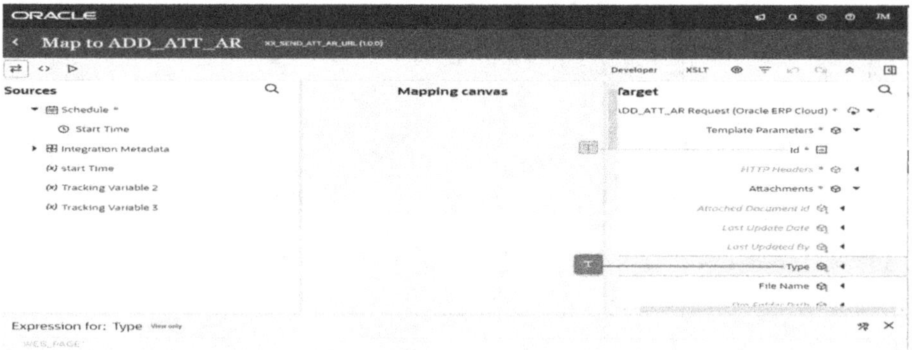

Figure 19-18. *URL Attachment Type Mapping*

URL Mapping

Provide the web page URL.

Figure 19-19. *URL Mapping*

Testing the Integration

After Execution

The URL attachment appears in the transaction.

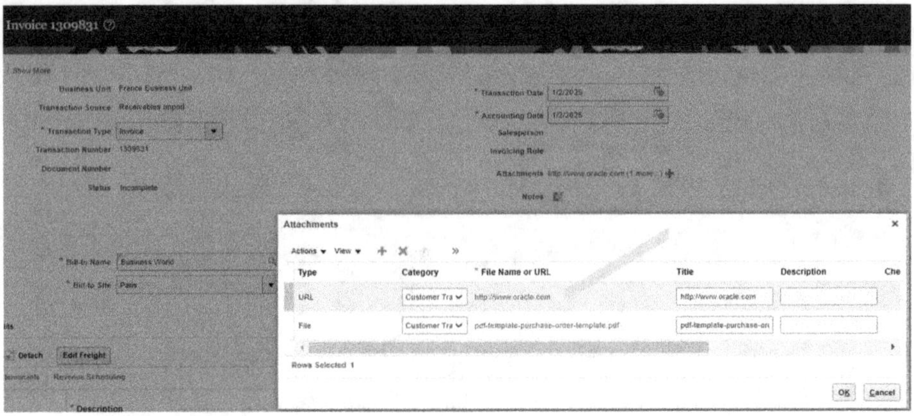

Figure 19-20. *Transaction with URL Attachment*

Technical Reference

Code Example	Comments
XX_SEND_ATT_AR	File attachment integration, included in package XX_DEMO_COOKBOOK.par
XX_SEND_ATT_AR_URL	URL attachment integration, included in package XX_DEMO_COOKBOOK.par

Note Additional examples can be found in Chapter 13.

CHAPTER 20

Object Storage Upload

Overview

According to Oracle's documentation:

> Oracle Cloud Infrastructure (OCI) Object Storage provides scalable, durable, and low-cost storage for any type of data. It offers "11 nines of durability" and can scale storage to nearly unlimited capacity for unstructured data.

In simple terms, Object Storage is like a REST API–based storage service where files are stored as objects in buckets, accessible via HTTP operations (PUT, GET, DELETE), and we can do manual file uploads/downloads through the OCI console.

Prerequisites

- Access to the OCI (Oracle Cloud Infrastructure) console.
- System administrator assistance may be required for credential setup.

J. J. Montero Rodríguez and S. Tahseen, *Oracle Integration Cookbook for Oracle ERP Cloud*,
https://doi.org/10.1007/979-8-8688-3020-4_20

Object Storage Structure

Accessing the OCI Console

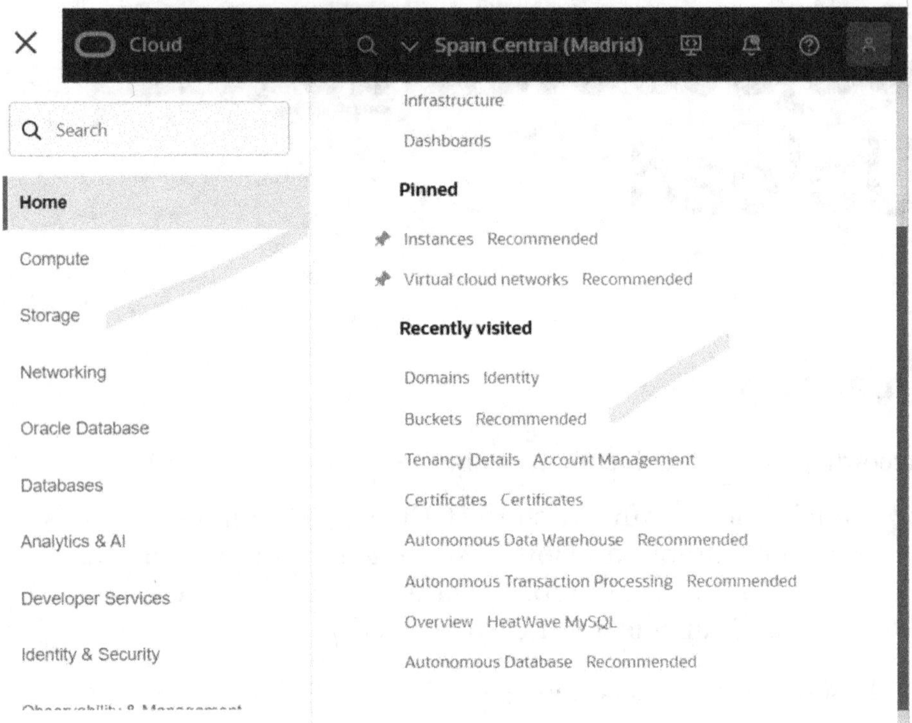

Figure 20-1. *OCI Console Access*

Buckets View

Object Storage organizes data in buckets.

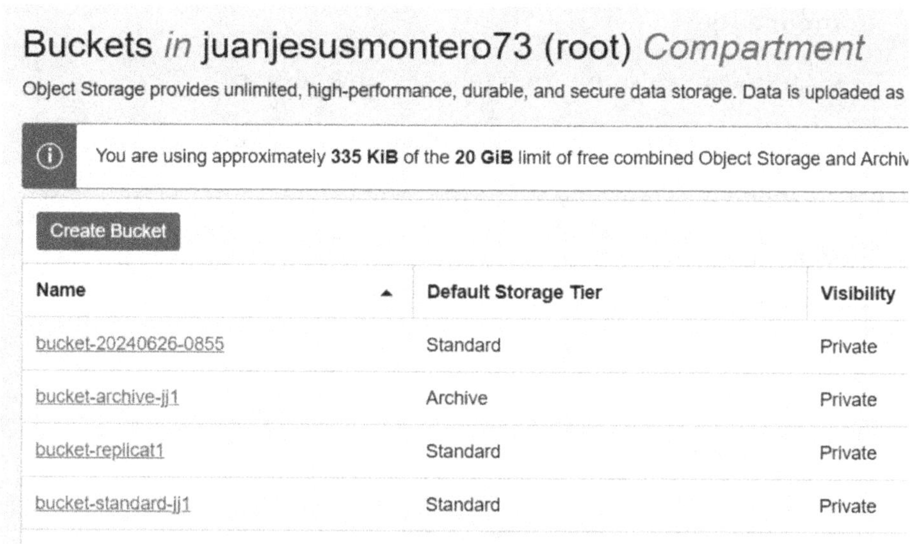

Figure 20-2. *Object Storage Buckets*

Bucket Contents

Buckets can contain files and folders.

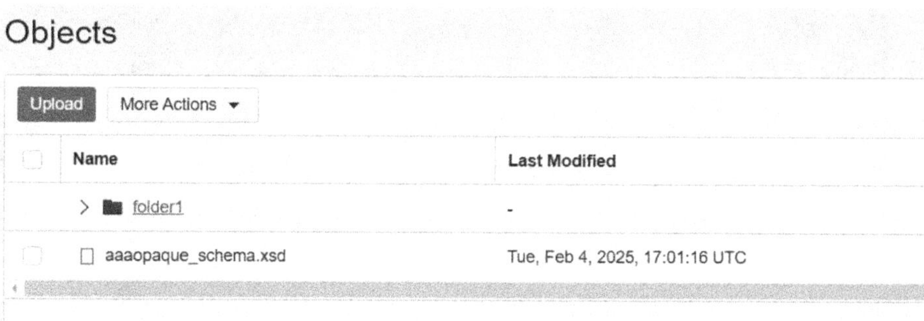

Figure 20-3. *Bucket Contents*

Object Storage Hierarchy

To access objects/files in Object Storage, you need three required levels:

```
/n/{namespaceName}/b/{bucketName}/o/{objectName}
```

Components:

- **namespaceName**: Your tenancy's namespace
- **bucketName**: The bucket containing your objects
- **objectName**: The specific file or object

Finding the Namespace

The namespace can be found in the OCI console.

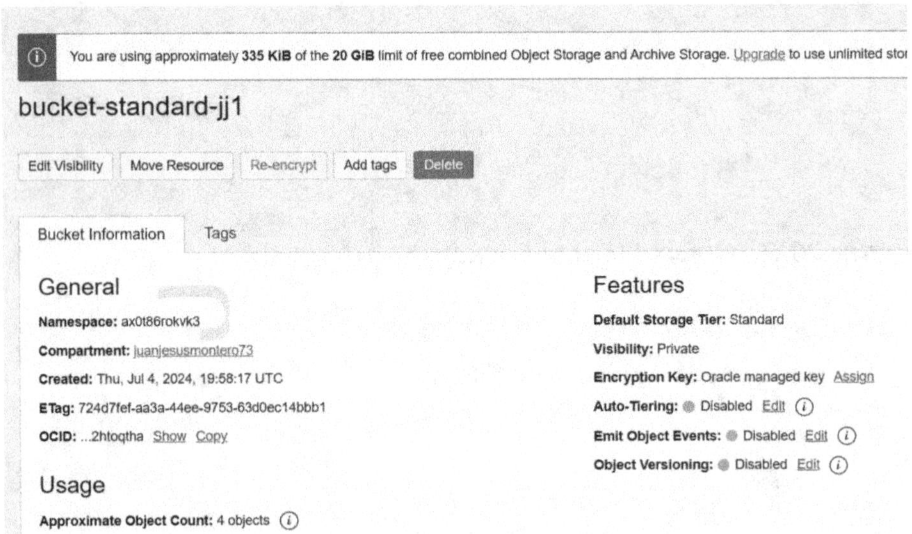

***Figure 20-4.** Namespace Location in the OCI Console*

Note Bucket and object names are self-explanatory from the previous screenshots.

Connection Setup

REST Connection Configuration:

While there is no strict rule, developers typically receive Object Storage connections pre-configured. This section provides guidance for setting up the connection yourself if you have OCI console access.

Reference Documentation:

- **Video Tutorial**: `https://www.youtube.com/watch?v=2RztbTusekI`
- OCI Signature Guide
- Troubleshooting

Connection Example:

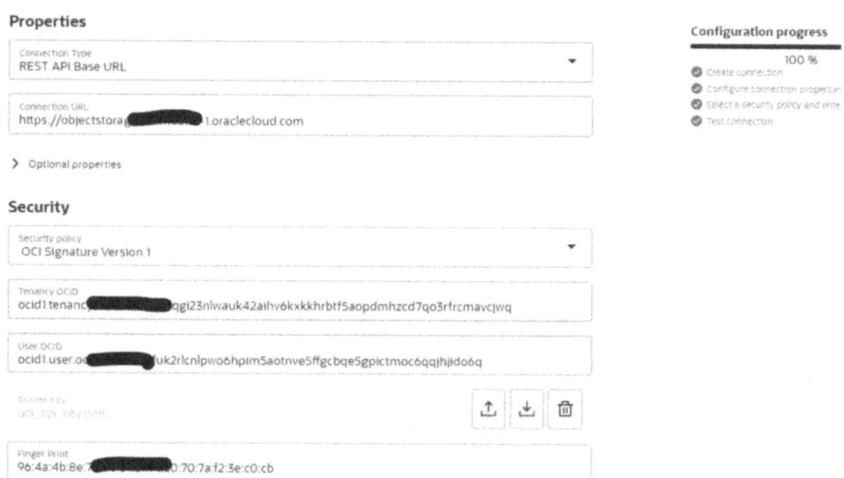

***Figure 20-5.** Object Storage REST Connection*

Note See Chapter 2 for detailed information.

Reference Connection XX_DEMO_OS_01

Obtaining Connection Parameters

Additional Resource: `https://www.techsupper.com/2021/03/accessing-object-storage-from-oracle-integration/`

Connection URL

Obtain the connection URL from the bucket details page.

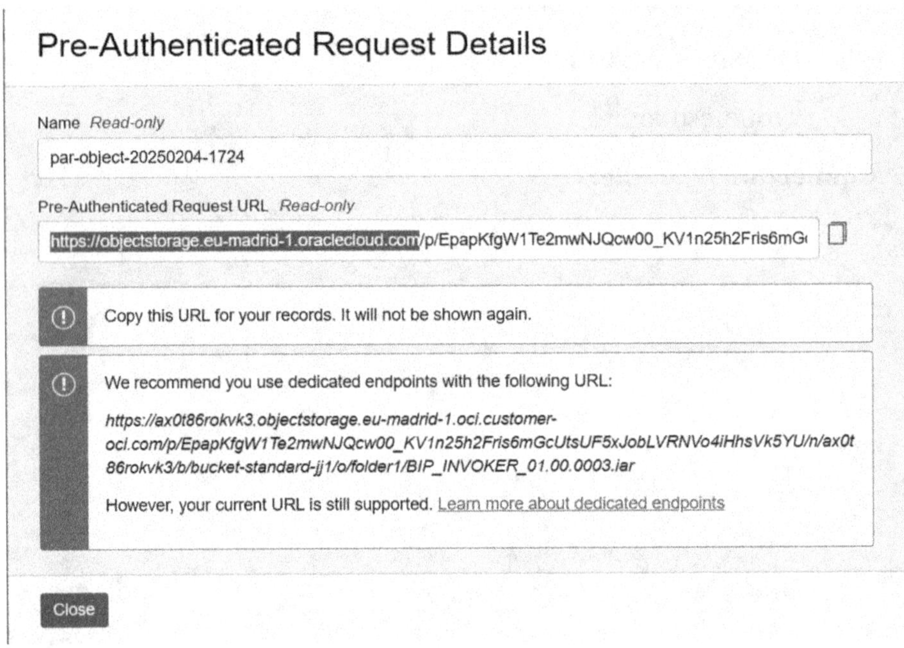

Figure 20-6. *Connection URL Location*

Tenancy OCID

Navigate to Administration ➤ Tenancy Details.

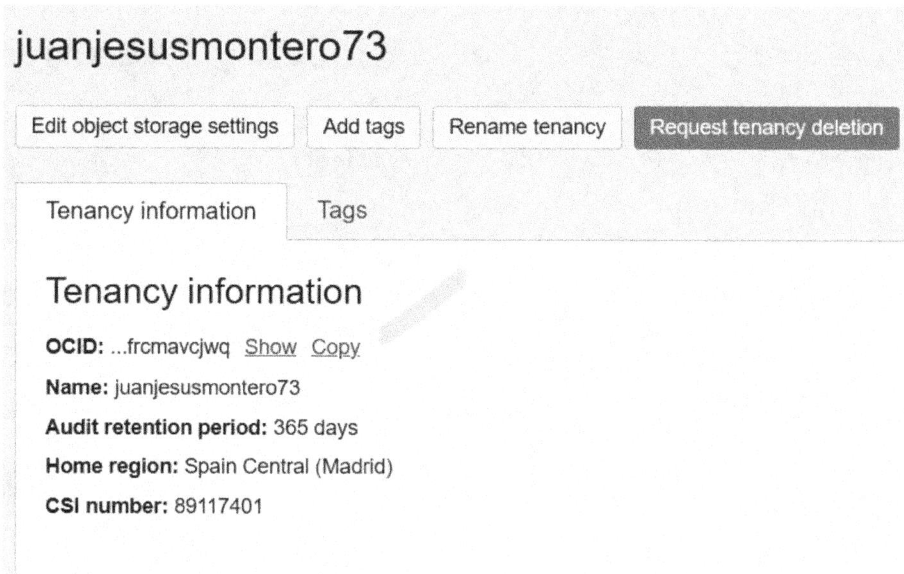

Figure 20-7. *Tenancy OCID Location*

User OCID

Navigate to Identity & Security and then Domains.

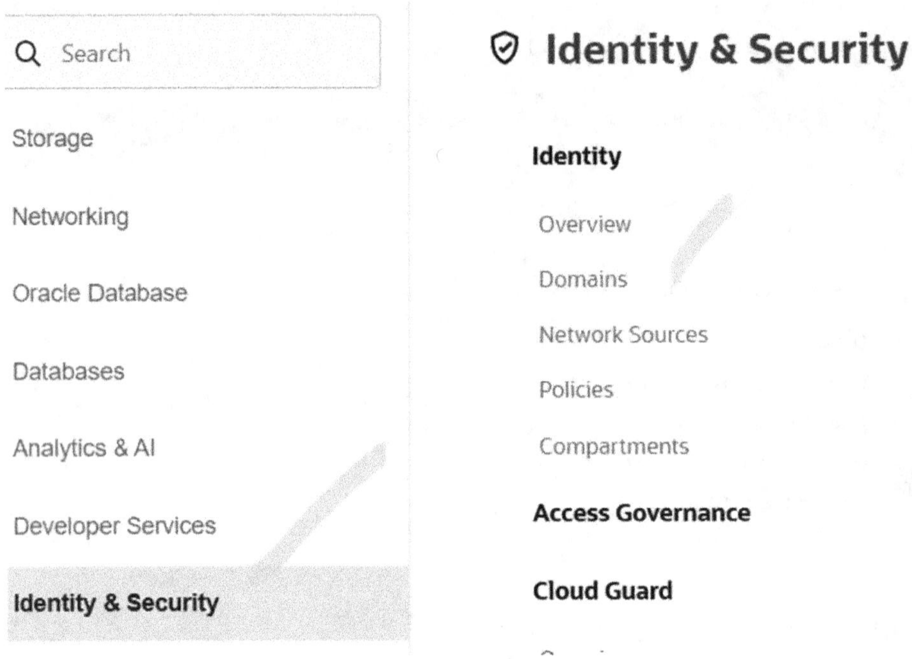

Figure 20-8. *Identity & Security*

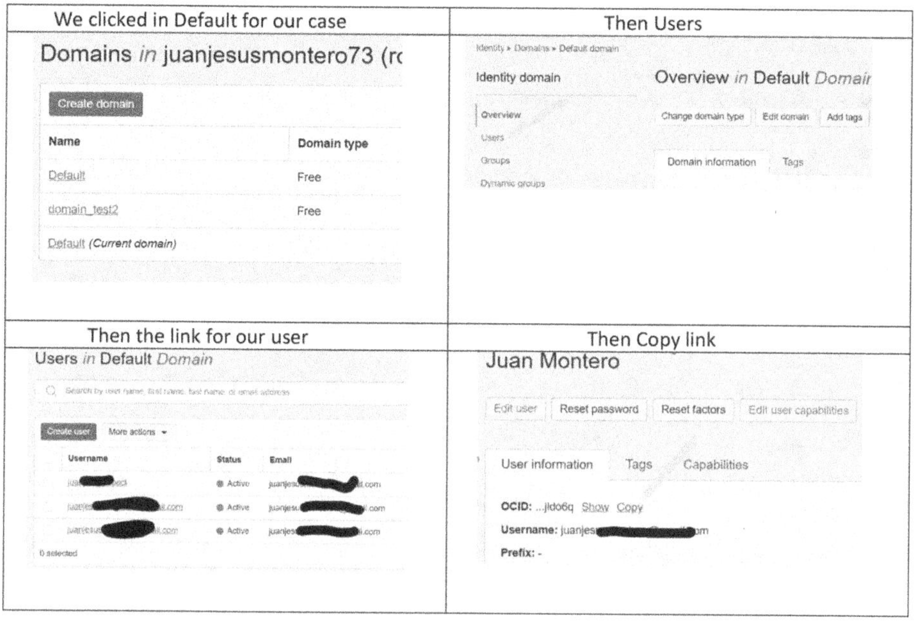

Figure 20-9. *Identity & Security*

API Key and Fingerprint

Navigate to your user profile and select "API Keys".

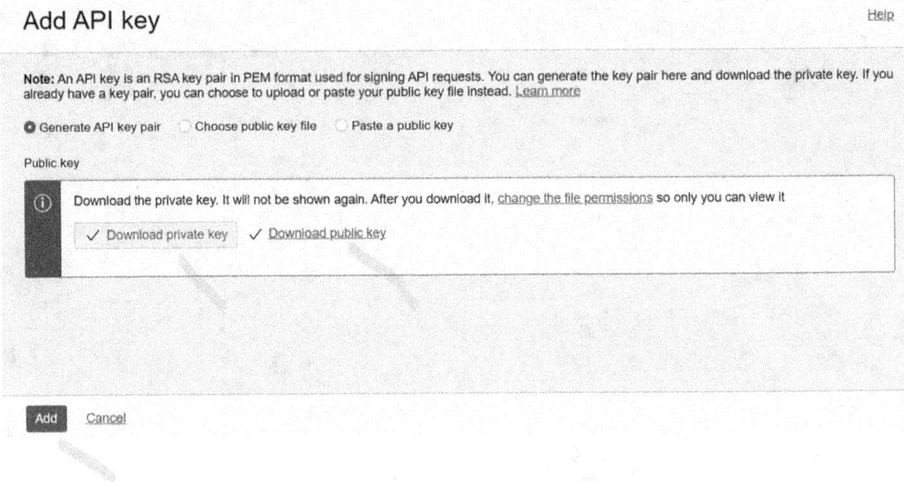

Figure 20-10. *API Keys Section*

You will see the API key configuration screen.

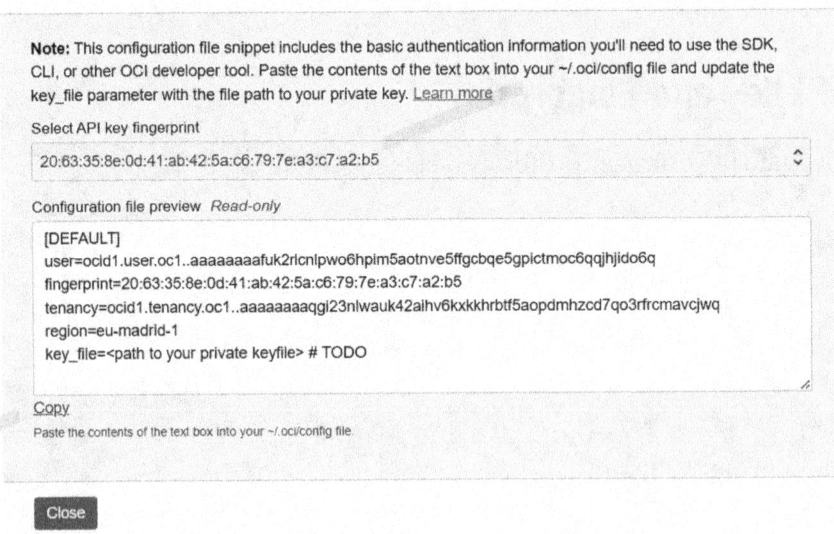

Figure 20-11. *API Key Configuration*

Copy and save the configuration information:

```
[DEFAULT]
user=ocid1.user.oc1..
aaaaaaafuk2rlcnlpwo6hpim5aotnve5ffgcbqe5gpictmoc6qqjhjidddo6q
fingerprint=20:63:35:8e:0d:41:ab:42:5a:c6:79:7e:a3:c7:a2:b5
tenancy=ocid1.tenancy.oc1..
aaaaaaaaqgi23nlwauk42aihv6kddxkkhrbtf5aopdmhzcd7qo3rfrcmavcjwq
region=eu-madrid-1
key_file=<path to your private keyfile>  # TODO
```

Private Key Processing

Download the PEM files and save them securely.

Figure 20-12. *Download PEM Files*

Apply the following OpenSSL command to the private PEM file:

```
openssl rsa -in xxx.xxx@abc.es_2025-02-03T13_33_08.257Z.pem -out
private_zzzz.pem
```

Note Upload the output file (private_zzzz.pem) to your OIC connection.

Integration to Upload a File to Object Storage

Reference Documentation

Rest API for OCI Object Storage

Integration Overview

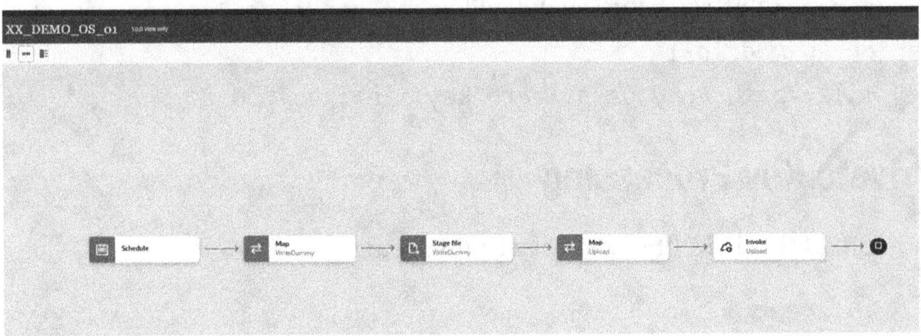

Figure 20-13. *Upload Integration Flow*

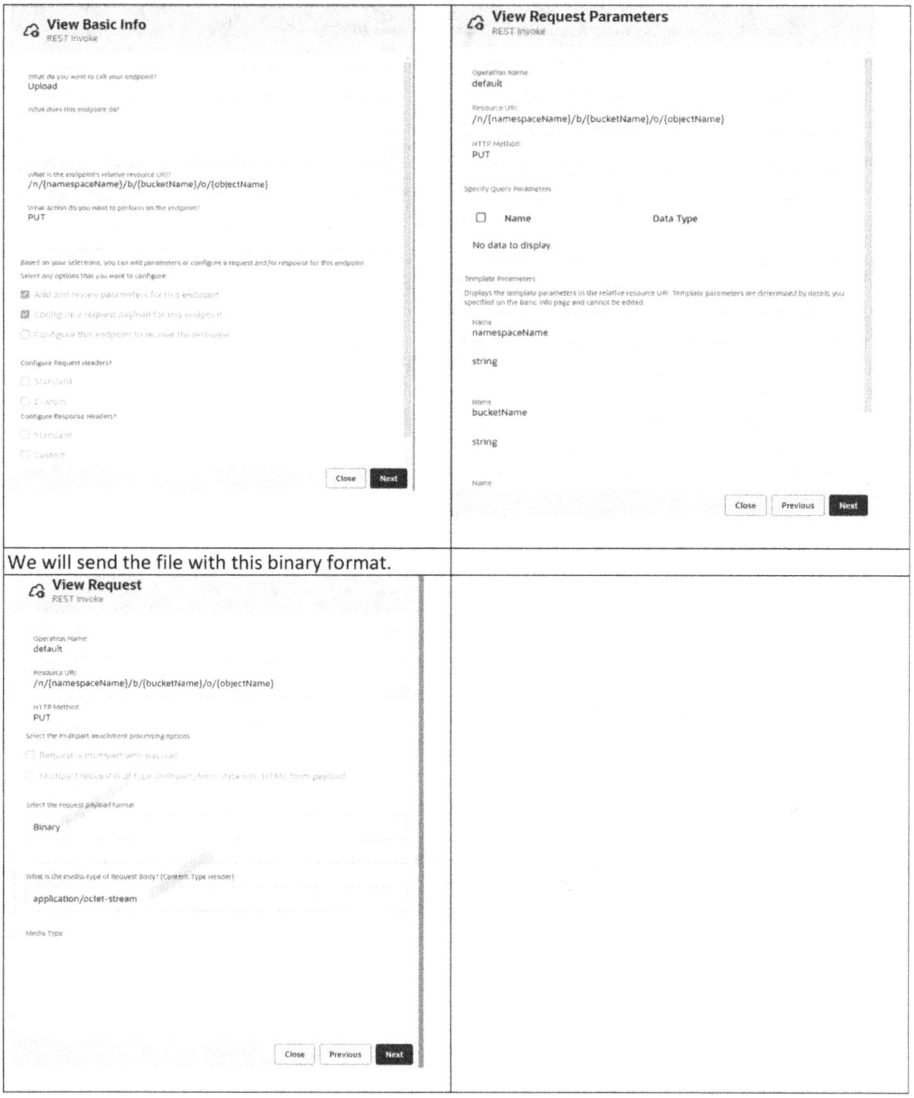

Figure 20-14. *Rest API Configuration*

Mapping Configuration

The mapping should look like this.

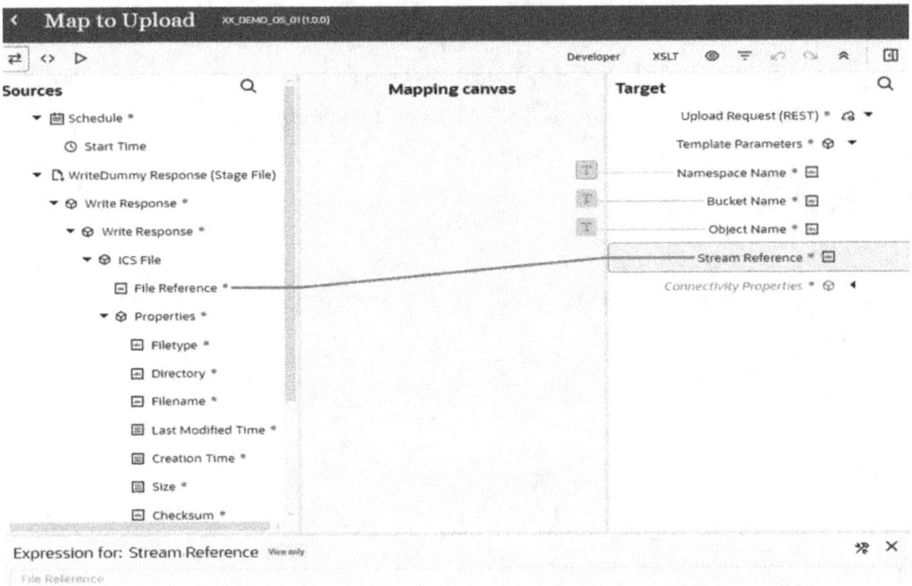

Figure 20-15. *Upload Mapping*

Testing the Integration

Execute a test with the following parameters.

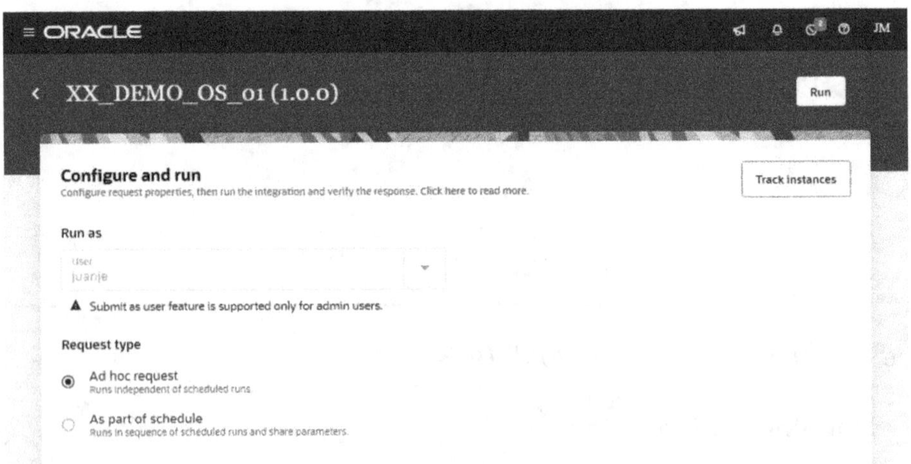

Figure 20-16. *Integration Test Execution*

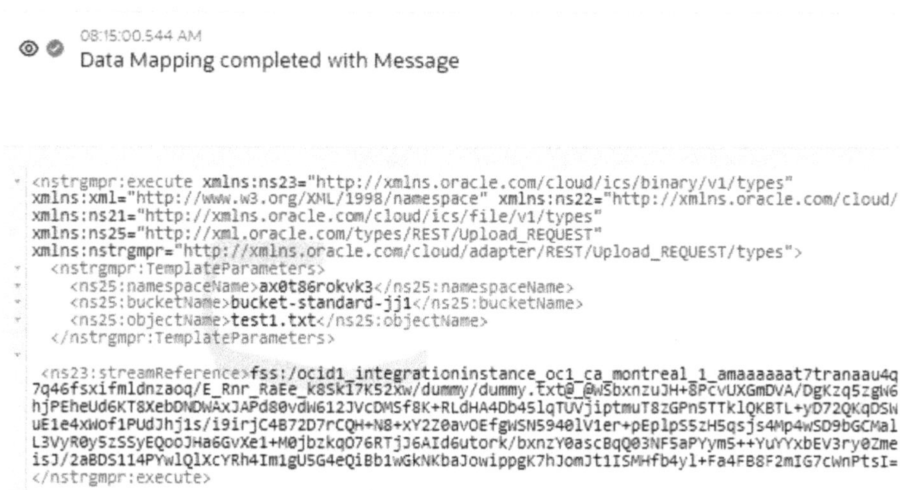


```
<nstrgmpr:execute xmlns:ns23="http://xmlns.oracle.com/cloud/ics/binary/v1/types"
xmlns:xml="http://www.w3.org/XML/1998/namespace" xmlns:ns22="http://xmlns.oracle.com/cloud/
xmlns:ns21="http://xmlns.oracle.com/cloud/ics/file/v1/types"
xmlns:ns25="http://xml.oracle.com/types/REST/Upload_REQUEST"
xmlns:nstrgmpr="http://xmlns.oracle.com/cloud/adapter/REST/Upload_REQUEST/types">
  <nstrgmpr:TemplateParameters>
    <ns25:namespaceName>ax0t86rokvk3</ns25:namespaceName>
    <ns25:bucketName>bucket-standard-jj1</ns25:bucketName>
    <ns25:objectName>test1.txt</ns25:objectName>
  </nstrgmpr:TemplateParameters>

 <ns23:streamReference>fss:/ocid1_integrationinstance_oc1_ca_montreal_1_amaaaaaat7tranaau4q
7q46fsxifmldnzaoq/E_Rnr_RaEe_k8SkI7K52xw/dummy/dummy.txt@_@wSbxnzuJH+8PcvUXGmDVA/DgKzq5zgW6
hjPEheUd6KT8XebDNDWAxJAPd80vdW612JVcDMSf8K+RLdHA4Db45lqTUVjiptmuT8zGPn5TTklQKBTL+yD72QKqDSW
uE1e4xWof1PUdJhj1s/i9irjC4B72D7rCQH+N8+xY2Z0avOEfgWSN5940lV1er+pEplpS5zH5qsjs4Mp4wSD9bGCMal
L3VyR0y5zSSyEQooJHa6GvXe1+M0jbzkqO76RTjJ6AId6utork/bxnzY0ascBqQ03NF5aPYym5++YuYYxbEV3ry0Zme
isJ/2aBDS114PYwlQlXcYRh4Im1gU5G4eQiBb1wGkNKbaJowippgK7hJomJt1ISMHfb4yl+Fa4FB8F2mIG7cWnPtsI=
</nstrgmpr:execute>
```


Figure 20-17. *Test Parameters*

Verification

The uploaded file should appear in the OCI console.

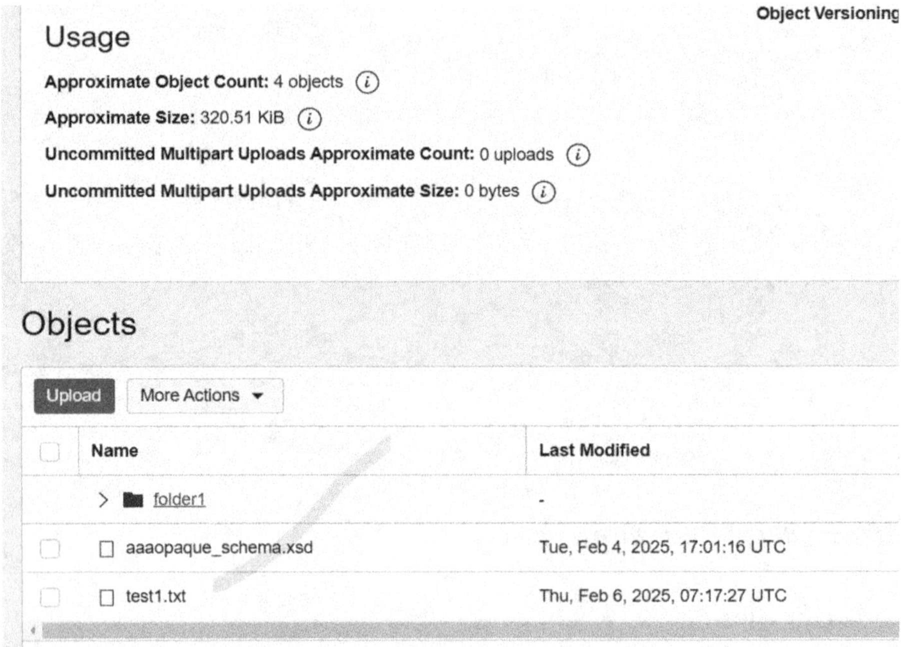

Figure 20-18. *File in the OCI Console*

Technical Reference

Code Example	Comments
XX_OBJECT_STOR_UPLOAD.iar	Integration included in package XX_DEMO_COOKBOOK.par
XX_DEMO_IMP_SUPP_OB_STOR.iar	Integration included in package XX_DEMO_COOKBOOK.par (refer to Chapter 13)
test1.txt	Dummy demo file for testing

CHAPTER 21

Read BI Publisher Reports and Multiple Verbs in REST

Overview

This chapter demonstrates two important OIC features:

1. Reading BI Publisher reports and retrieving data in a manageable format (JSON response)
2. Including multiple REST verbs (operations) in a single REST API call

Reading BI Publisher Reports

Introduction and Goal

Important Consider this demonstration as proof-of-concept for learning purposes.

J. J. Montero Rodríguez and S. Tahseen, *Oracle Integration Cookbook for Oracle ERP Cloud*,
https://doi.org/10.1007/979-8-8688-3020-4_21

This example shows how to

- Run a SaaS/Fusion Applications BI Publisher report with parameters.
- Display the results in a Visual Builder page.

Example Report

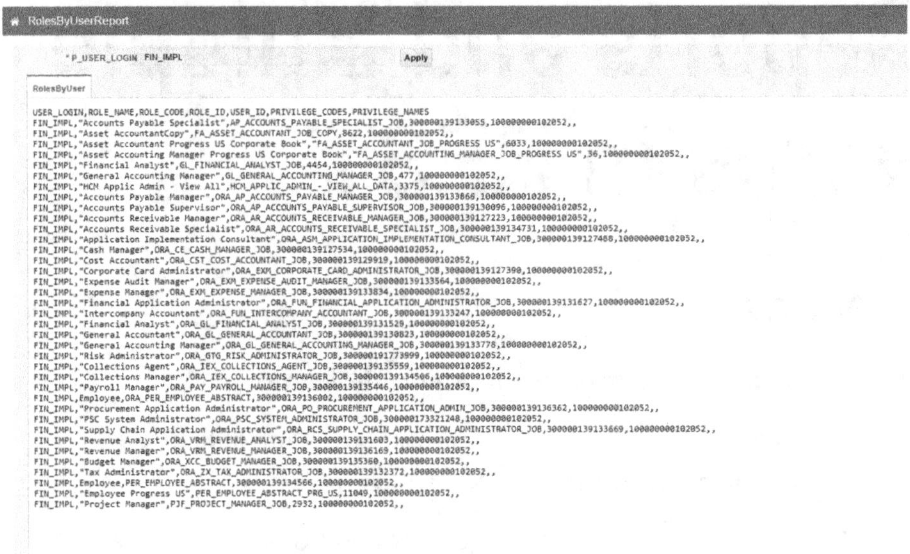

***Figure 21-1.** Sample BI Publisher Report*

The process creates a synchronous flow where

1. Visual Builder calls an OIC integration.
2. OIC retrieves data from the BI report.
3. Results are displayed in Visual Builder.

Figure 21-2. *Visual Builder Display*

Important Considerations

Limitations

- Payload size limits apply to data retrieval.
- Performance is critical—long-running reports or large payloads may cause timeouts.
- This approach works best for small- to medium-sized datasets with quick execution times.

Preparatory Steps

Copy Report Files

Copy the report and data model to this folder: "/Custom/MetricsLic".

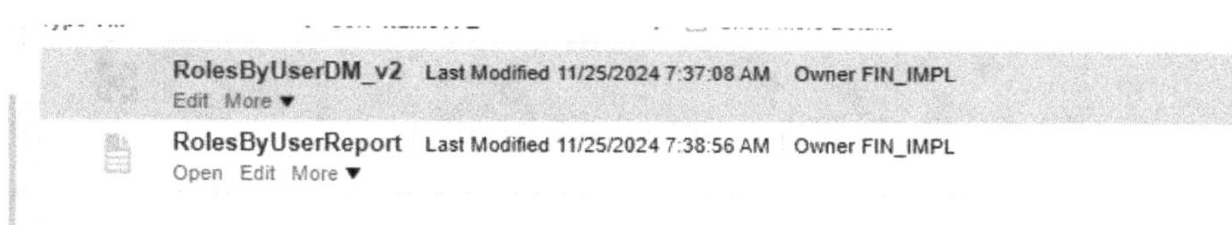

Figure 21-3. *Report Folder Location*

Install OIC Integration

Install the provided OIC integration and configure the connections.

***Figure 21-4.** Required Connections*

REST Connection Configuration

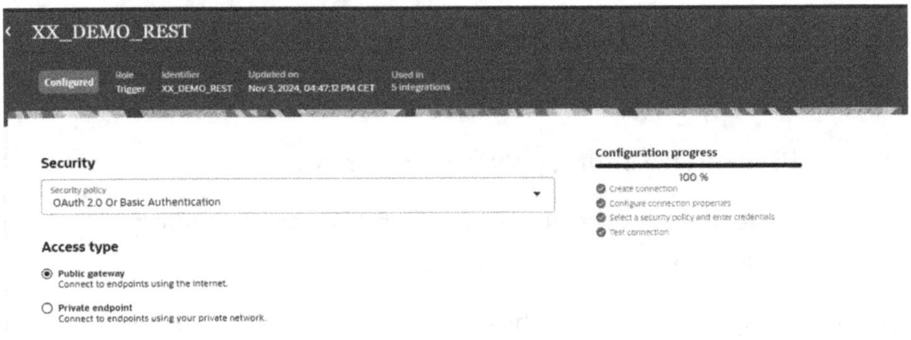

***Figure 21-5.** REST Connection Setup*

SOAP Connection: SOAP ExternalReportWSSService connection (5)

WSDL Endpoint:

`https://fa-xxxx-saasfademo1.ds-fa.oraclepdemos.com/xmlpserver/services/ExternalReportWSSService?WSDL`

Testing the Integration

Select Operation

Choose the "GET_RolesbyUser" operation and provide a test parameter.

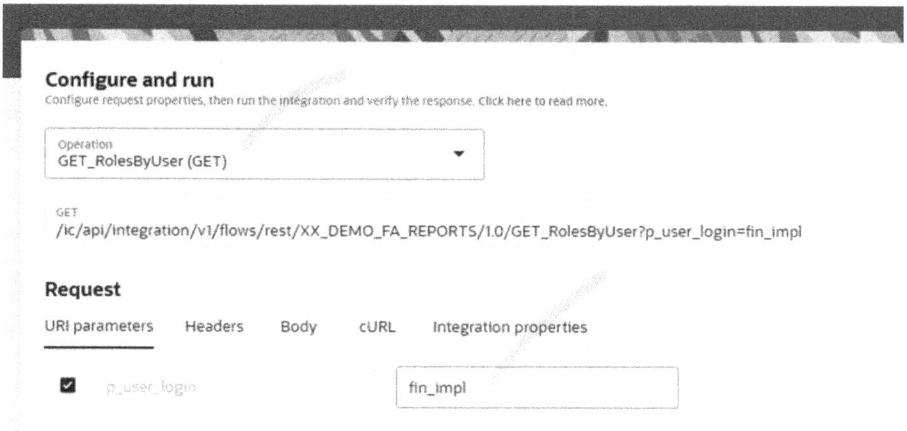

Figure 21-6. Test Operation Selection

Response

The integration returns a JSON response.

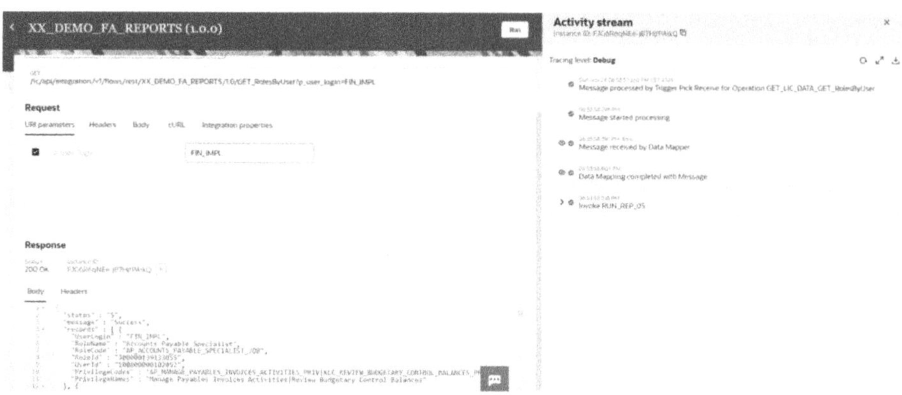

Figure 21-7. JSON Response

REST Endpoint Configuration

The response format is defined in the REST endpoint configuration.

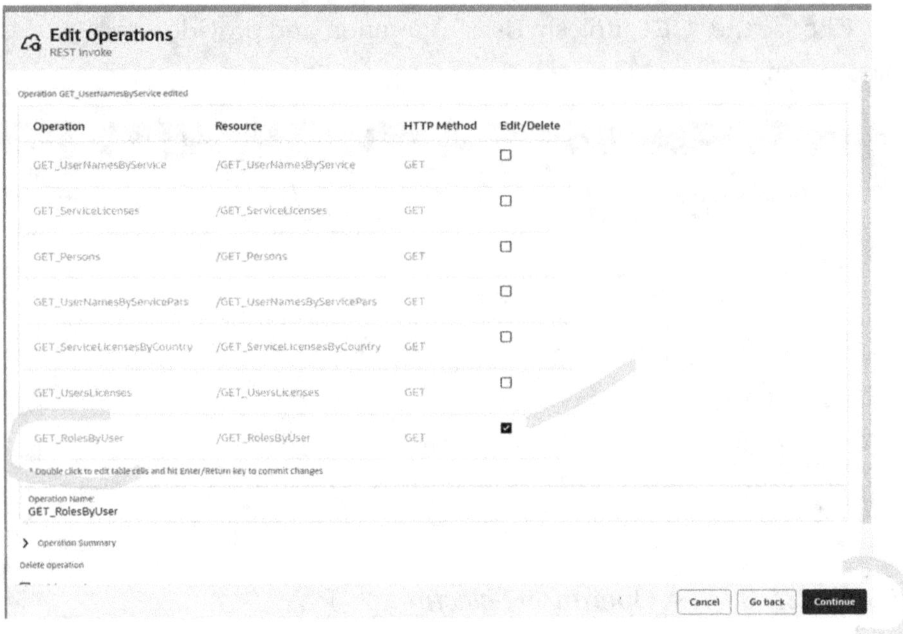

***Figure 21-8.** Response Payload Definition*

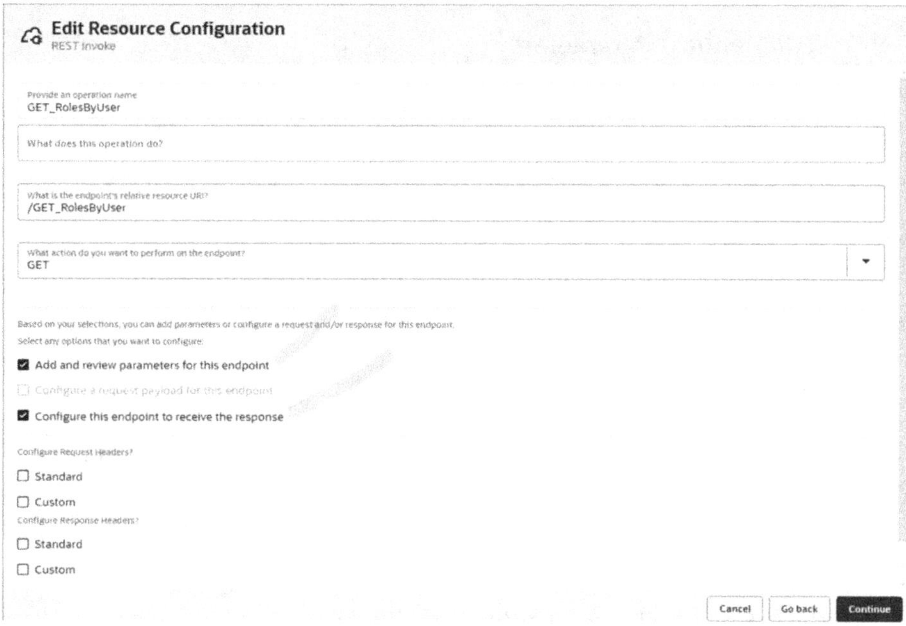

Figure 21-9. *JSON Schema Configuration*

Step 1: Add the Query Parameter

Add the query parameter "p_user_login".

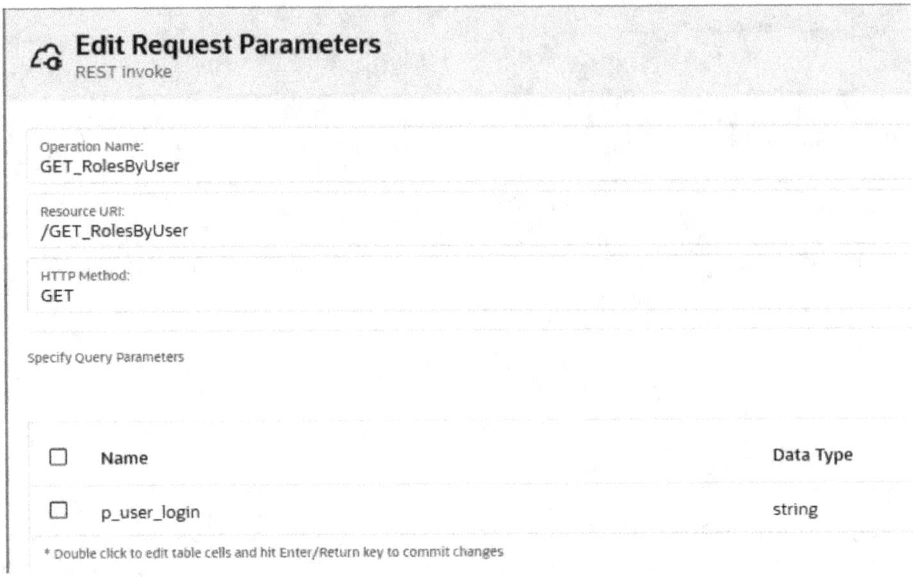

Figure 21-10. *Query Parameter Configuration*

Step 2: Configure Response

Set up the response payload by clicking as shown.

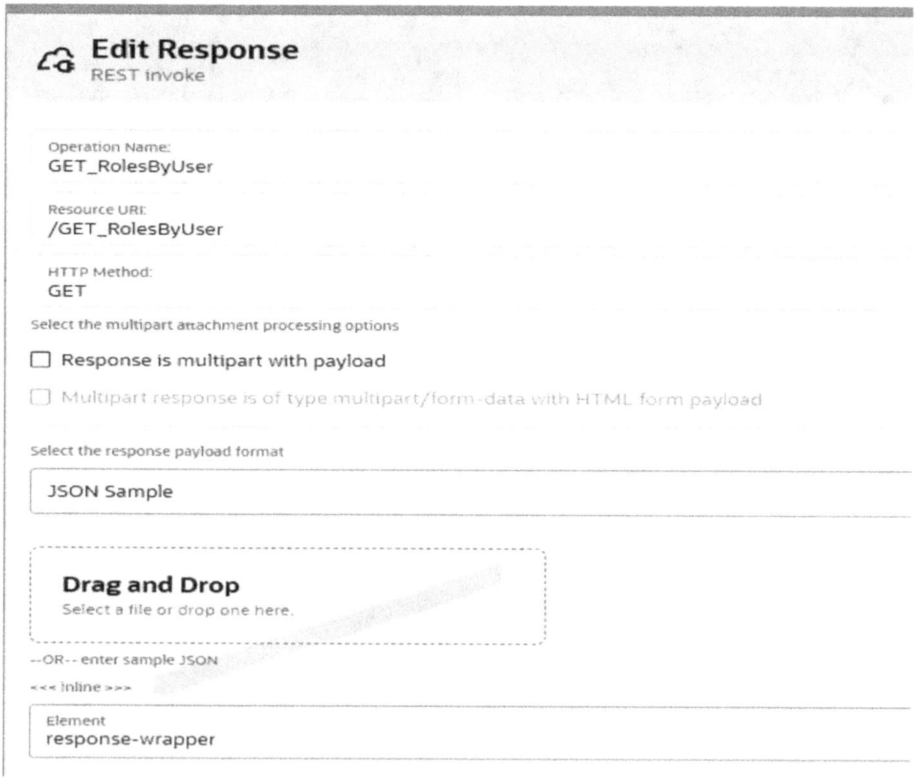

***Figure 21-11.** Response Configuration*

Sample JSON

Available on GitHub as 22_sample.json.

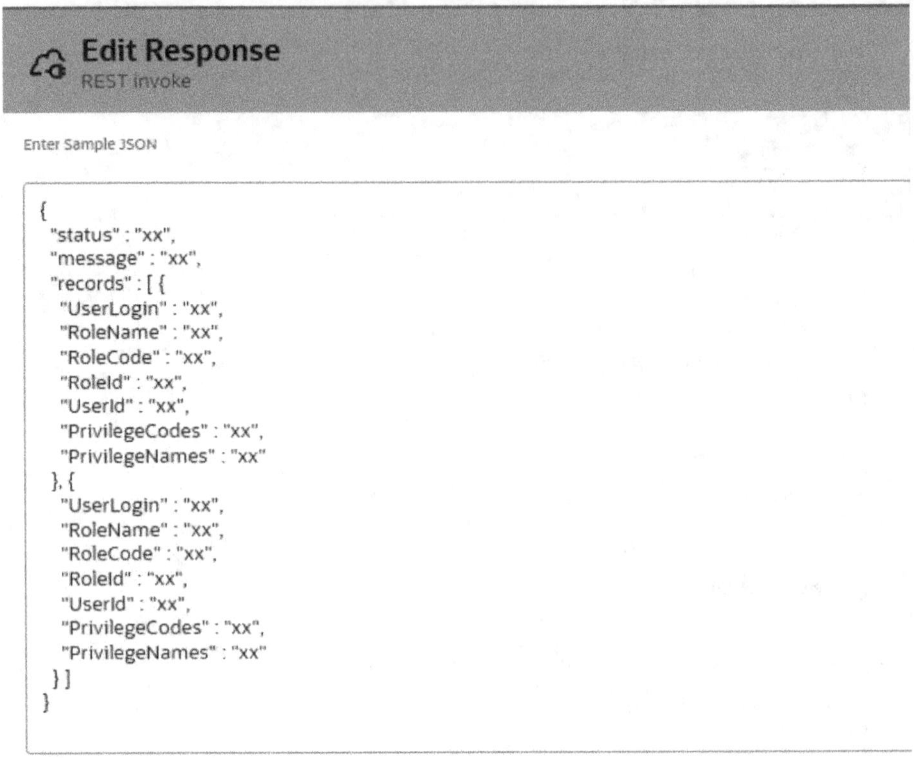

Figure 21-12. *Sample JSON Structure*

Multiple Verbs in REST API

Introduction and Goal

OIC allows up to 11 different verbs (operations) in a single REST API configuration. This feature enables you to create comprehensive APIs that handle multiple operations through one endpoint.

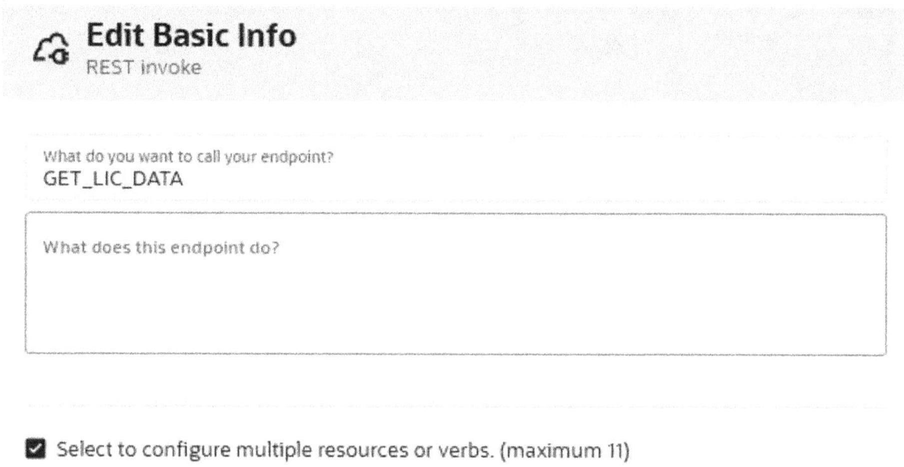

Figure 21-13. *Available REST Verbs*

Configuration

The setup process is straightforward.

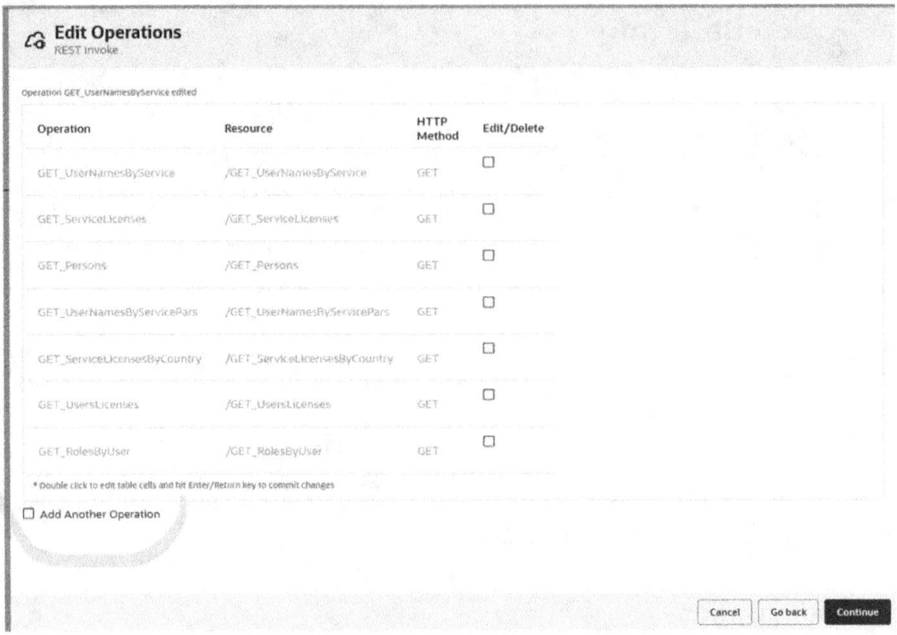

***Figure 21-14.** Multiple Verb Configuration*

Key Points:

- Each verb has its own set of parameters.
- Request payloads can be configured per verb (if applicable).
- Response payloads can be configured per verb (if applicable).

Testing

When testing from OIC, you'll see options for each configured verb.

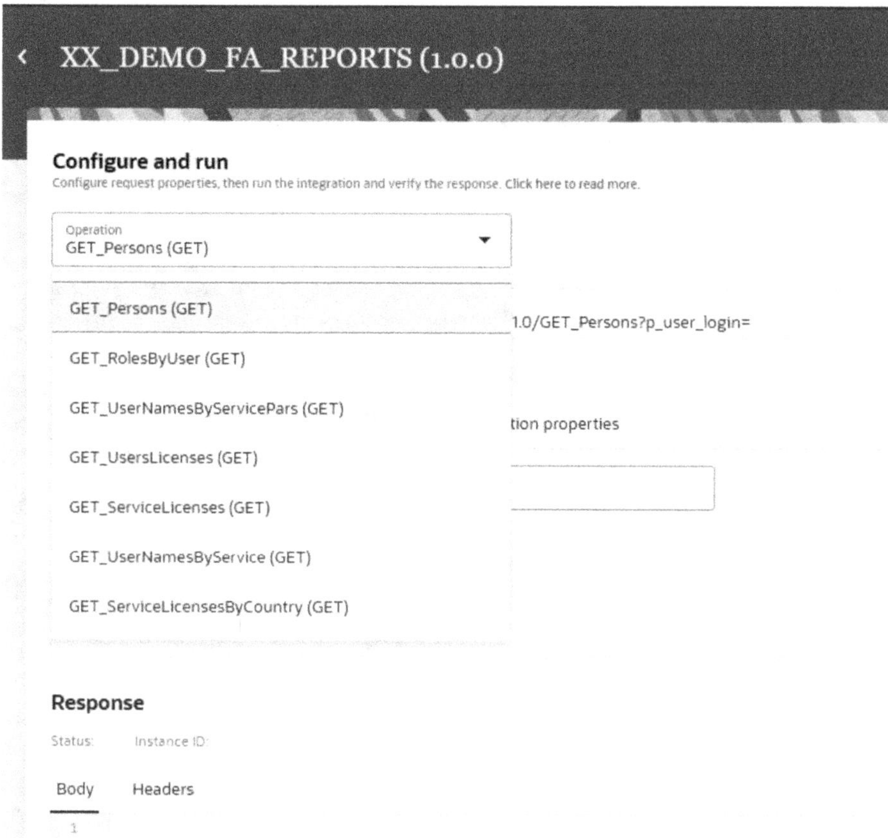

Figure 21-15. Testing Multiple Verbs

Integration Flow

Here's partial overview of the integration (complete code available on GitHub).

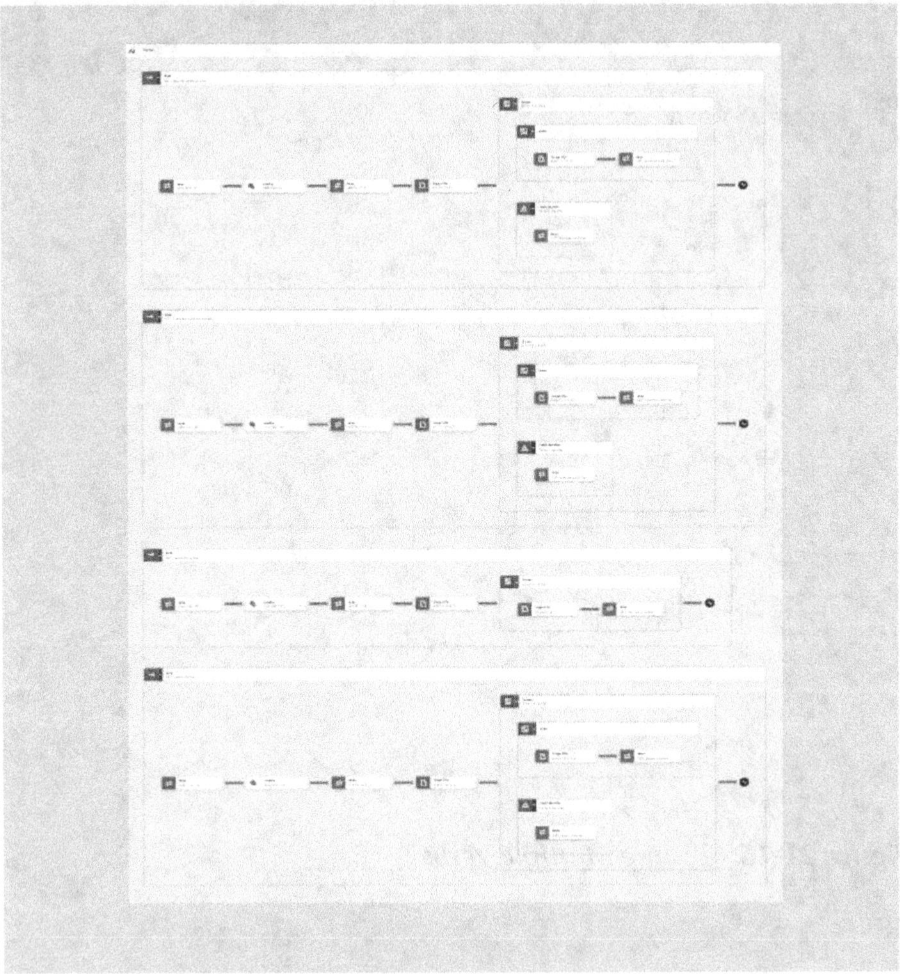

Figure 21-16. *Integration Flow Overview*

Note The sample provided includes one complete branch for learning purposes. Additional branches would follow the same pattern.

Technical Reference

Code Example	Comments
22_RolesByUserDM_v2.xdm.catalog	Data model used in the integration
22_RolesByUserReport.xdo.catalog	Report template
XX_DEMO_FA_REPORTS_01.00.0000.iar	Integration file included in package XX_DEMO_COOKBOOK.par
22_sample.json	Sample JSON response structure

CHAPTER 22

UCM Web Center Download/Upload

Overview

This chapter covers file operations with Oracle Universal Content Management (UCM), which is the content management system used by Oracle ERP Cloud.

Reference Documentation

Download Files from UCM

Download from UCM

Manual Upload for Testing

Step 1: Access File Import/Export

Navigate to the ERP menu.

J. J. Montero Rodríguez and S. Tahseen, *Oracle Integration Cookbook for Oracle ERP Cloud*,
https://doi.org/10.1007/979-8-8688-3020-4_22

Figure 22-1. *ERP Menu Navigation*

Step 2: Select File Import and Export

Choose "File Import and Export" and then select the Upload action.

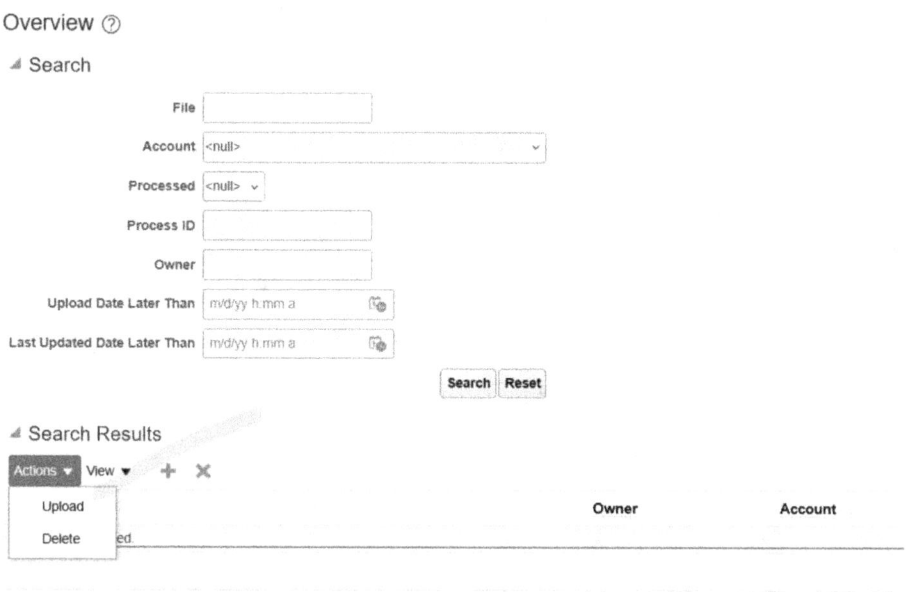

Figure 22-2. *File Import and Export Menu*

Step 3: Upload the File

Select the test file provided in the GitHub repository.

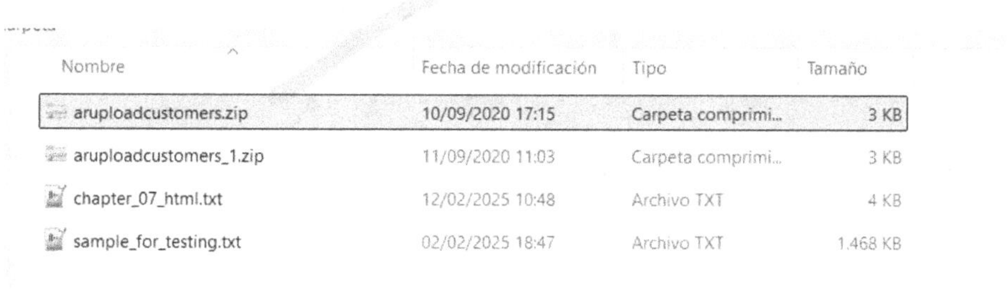

Figure 22-3. *File Selection*

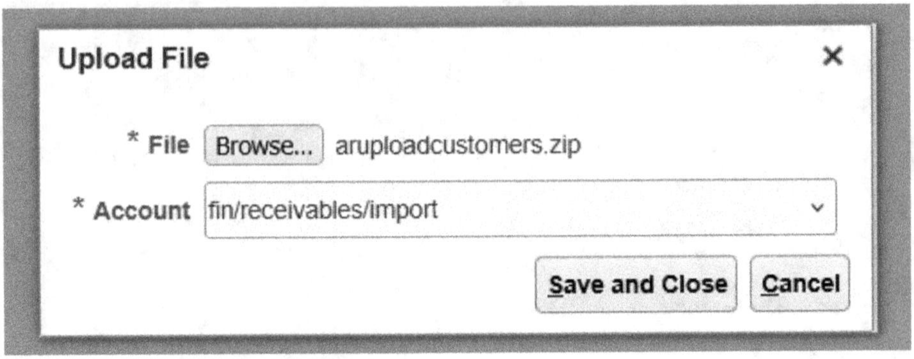

***Figure 22-4.** Upload Confirmation*

Step 4: Verify Upload

The uploaded file should appear in the search results.

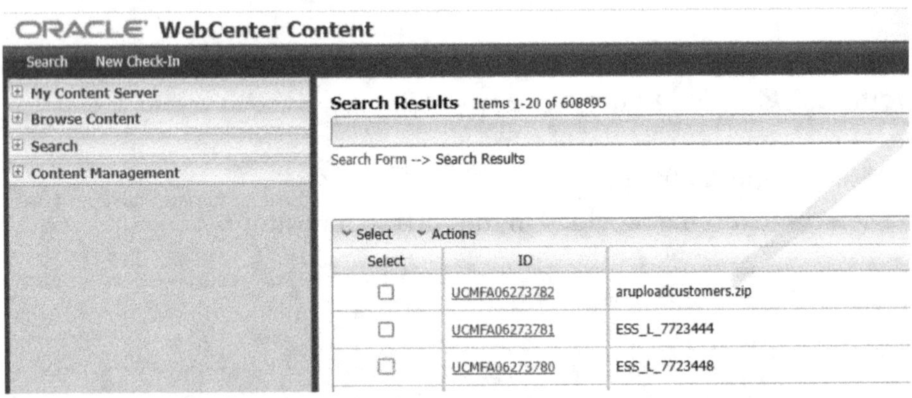

***Figure 22-5.** File Search Results*

UCM Connection Configuration

Connection Details

Connection URL Structure:

- **Prefix:** Your instance POD URL
    - **Example**: `https://fa-petite-saasfademo1.ds-fa.oraclepdemos.com`
- **Suffix:** /idcws/GenericSoapPort?WSDL

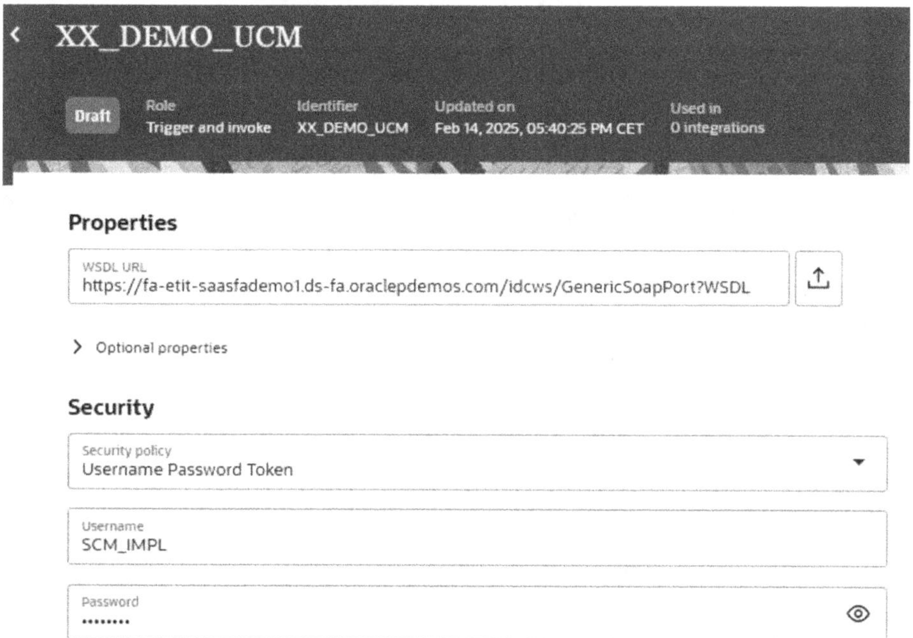

Figure 22-6. *UCM SOAP Connection*

Testing with SoapUI

Create a SOAP project and import the WSDL:

```
https://fa-petit-saasfademo1.ds-fa.oraclepdemos.com/idcws/
GenericSoapPort?WSDL
```

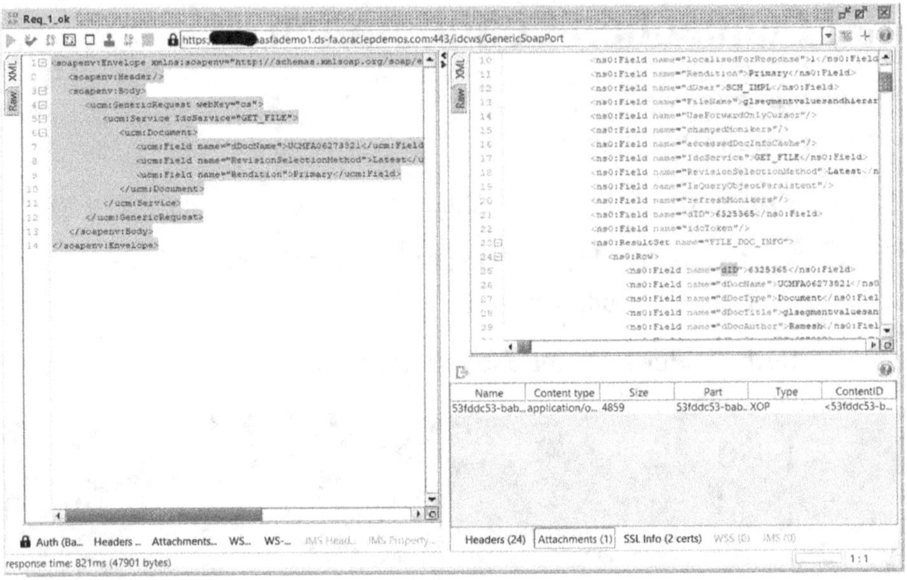

***Figure 22-7.** SoapUI Project Setup*

Sample Request

```
<soapenv:Envelope xmlns:soapenv="http://schemas.xmlsoap.org/
soap/envelope/"
                  xmlns:ucm="http://www.oracle.com/UCM">
  <soapenv:Header/>
  <soapenv:Body>
    <ucm:GenericRequest webKey="cs">
      <ucm:Service IdcService="GET_FILE">
        <ucm:Document>
          <ucm:Field name="dDocName">UCMFA06273821</ucm:Field>
          <ucm:Field name="RevisionSelectionMethod">Latest
          </ucm:Field>
          <ucm:Field name="Rendition">Primary</ucm:Field>
        </ucm:Document>
```

```
      </ucm:Service>
    </ucm:GenericRequest>
  </soapenv:Body>
</soapenv:Envelope>
```

Download Integration Example

Integration Flow

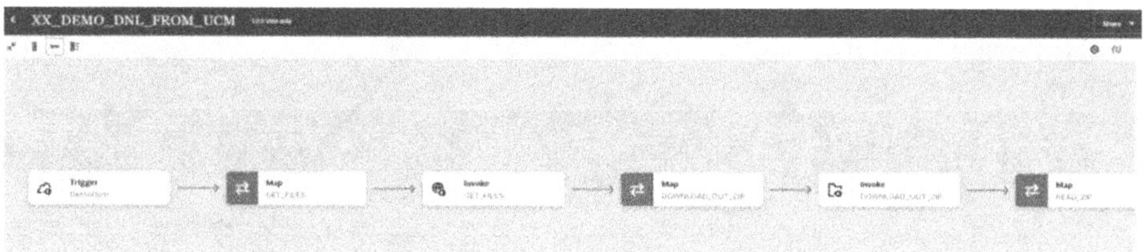

Figure 22-8. *Download Integration Flow*

Steps:

1. Read from UCM using the document name.
2. Download the file.
3. Unzip and copy files to the FTP server.

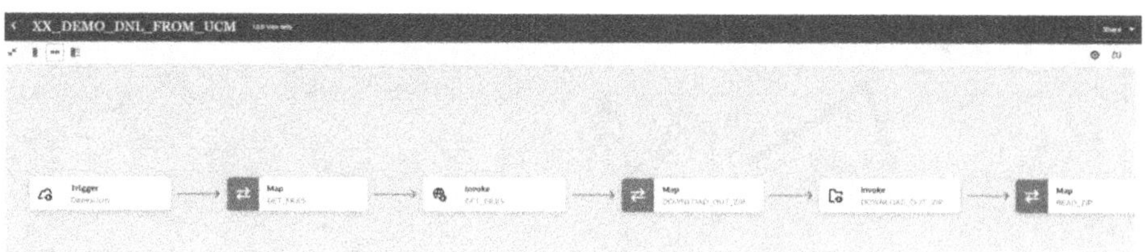

Figure 22-9. *Download Activity*

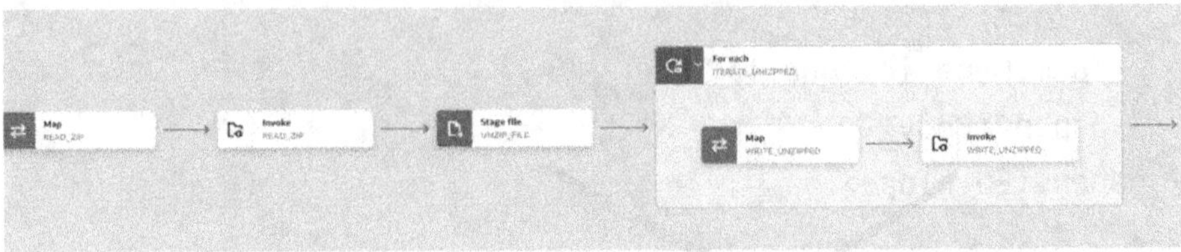

Figure 22-10. *Unzip and Copy to FTP*

Testing

Execute a test run.

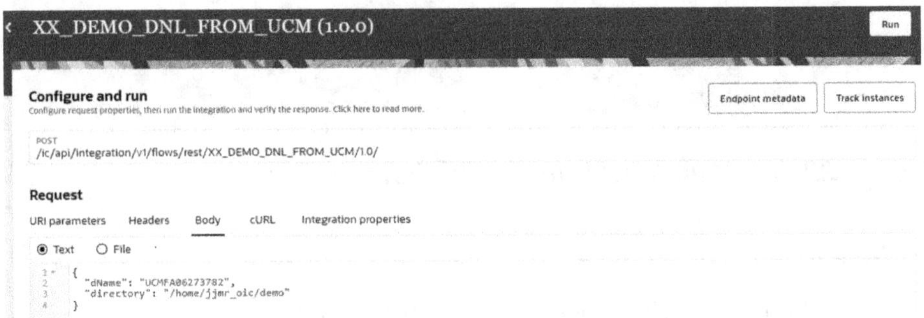

Figure 22-11. *Integration Test Execution*

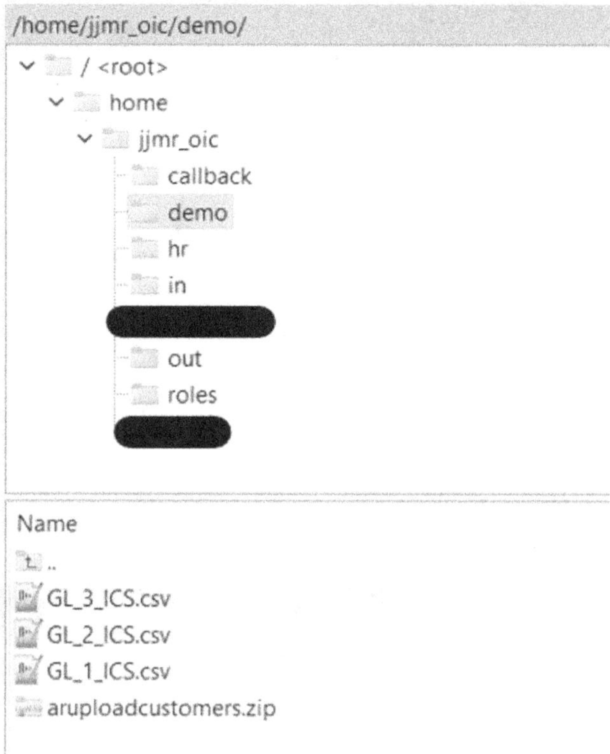

Figure 22-12. *Files on the FTP Server*

Upload to UCM

Integration Overview

For learning purposes, this example creates a file "on the fly" using a Stage activity.

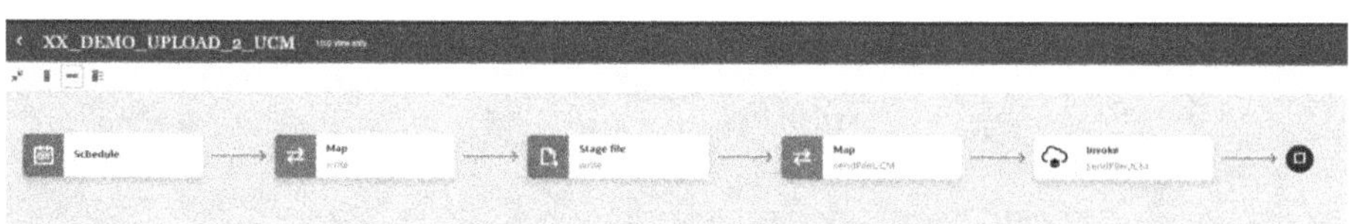

Figure 22-13. *Upload Integration Flow*

Mapping Configuration

The mapping creates file content dynamically.

```
    <xsl:template match="/" xml:id="id_11">
        <nstrgmpr:FileUpload xml:id="id_12">
            <nstrgmpr:docTitle xml:id="id_43">
                <xsl:value-of xml:id="id_44" select="'Demo_cookbook.txt'"/>
            </nstrgmpr:docTitle>
            <nstrgmpr:docType xml:id="id_66">
                <xsl:value-of xml:id="id_67" select="'Document'"/>
            </nstrgmpr:docType>
            <nstrgmpr:docAuthor xml:id="id_64">
                <xsl:value-of xml:id="id_65" select="'FIN_IMPL'"/>
            </nstrgmpr:docAuthor>
            <nstrgmpr:docUser xml:id="id_62">
                <xsl:value-of xml:id="id_63" select="'FIN_IMPL'"/>
            </nstrgmpr:docUser>
            <nstrgmpr:securityGroup xml:id="id_60">
                <xsl:value-of xml:id="id_61" select="'FAFusionImportExport'"/>
            </nstrgmpr:securityGroup>
            <nstrgmpr:docAccount xml:id="id_58">
                <xsl:value-of xml:id="id_59" select="'fin$/generalLedger$/import$'"/>
            </nstrgmpr:docAccount>
            <nstrgmpr:fileReference xml:id="id_41">
                <xsl:value-of xml:id="id_42" select="$write/nsmpr1:WriteResponse/ns27:WriteResponse/file:ICSFile/file:FileReference"/>
            </nstrgmpr:fileReference>
        </nstrgmpr:FileUpload>
    </xsl:template>
</xsl:stylesheet>
```

Figure 22-14. File Content Mapping

Upload Activity

The file is uploaded as a reference.

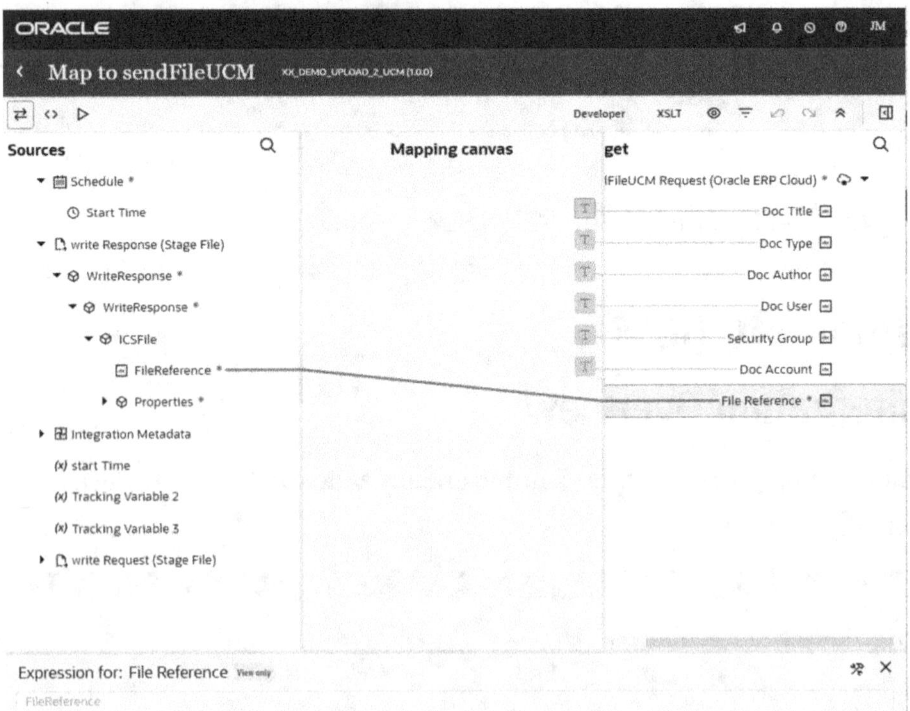

Figure 22-15. Upload Activity Configuration

Testing

Execute the integration test.

Verification in File Import/Export

The uploaded file appears in the tool.

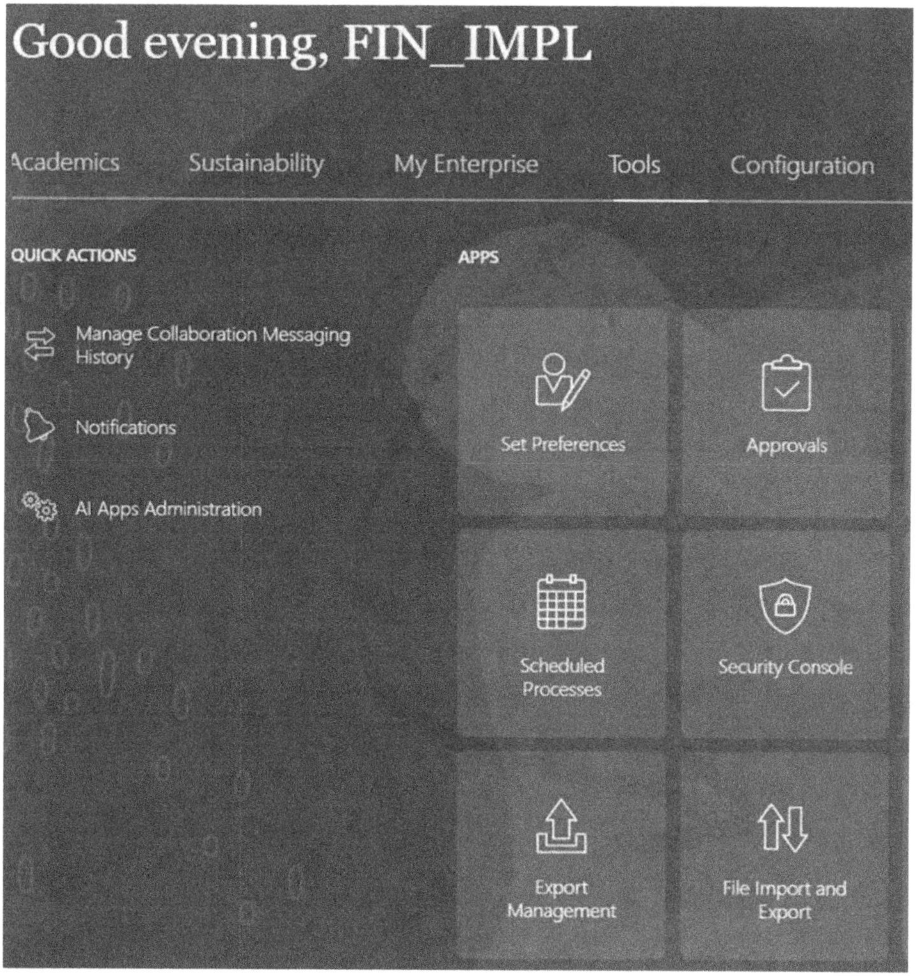

***Figure 22-16.** File in the Import/Export Tool*

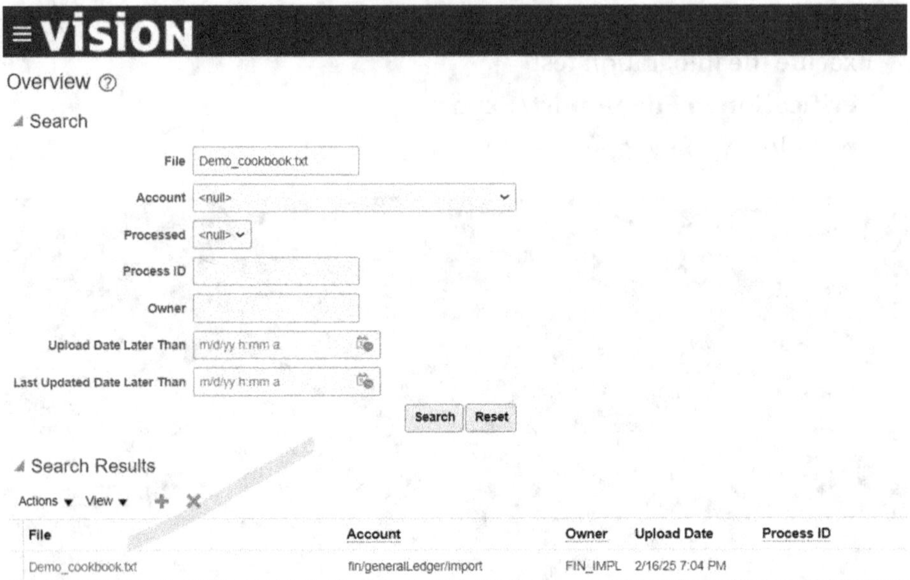

***Figure 22-17.** File Details*

Click the file to download and verify contents.

Verification in the UCM Tool

The file is also visible in the UCM interface.

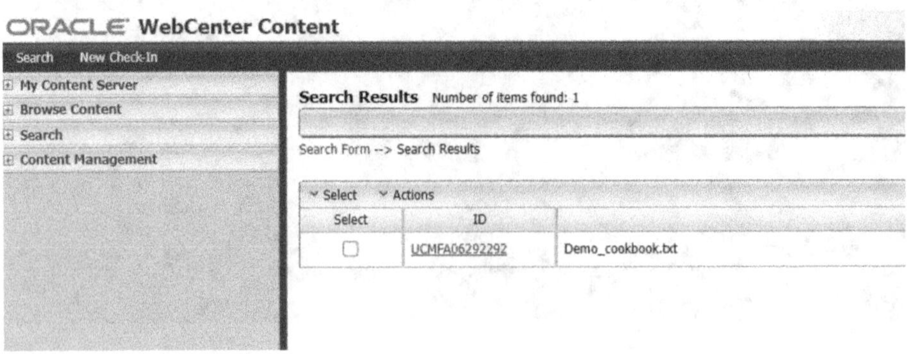

***Figure 22-18.** File in the UCM Tool*

Technical Details

Code Example	Comments
XX_DEMO_DNL_FROM_UCM	Download integration included in package XX_DEMO_COOKBOOK.par
XX_DEMO_UPLOAD_TO_UCM	Upload integration included in package XX_DEMO_COOKBOOK.par

CHAPTER 23

Parallel Activity

Overview

The Parallel activity in Oracle Integration Cloud (OIC) allows you to execute multiple integration flows simultaneously. This chapter demonstrates how to implement parallel processing using both asynchronous and synchronous integrations.

Note Per Oracle Gen3 documentation, a maximum of **ten branches** is supported in a single Parallel action.

Example: Calling Asynchronous Integrations

This example demonstrates the Parallel activity using two previously created integrations. Note that this is a learning exercise, as the two integrations are unrelated in business context.

Integrations Used:

- XX_DEMO_DNL_FROM_UCM
- XX_DEMO_OS_01

Configuration Steps:

1. Adapt the mapping according to your FTP directory and UCM filename requirements.

J. J. Montero Rodríguez and S. Tahseen, *Oracle Integration Cookbook for Oracle ERP Cloud*, https://doi.org/10.1007/979-8-8688-3020-4_23

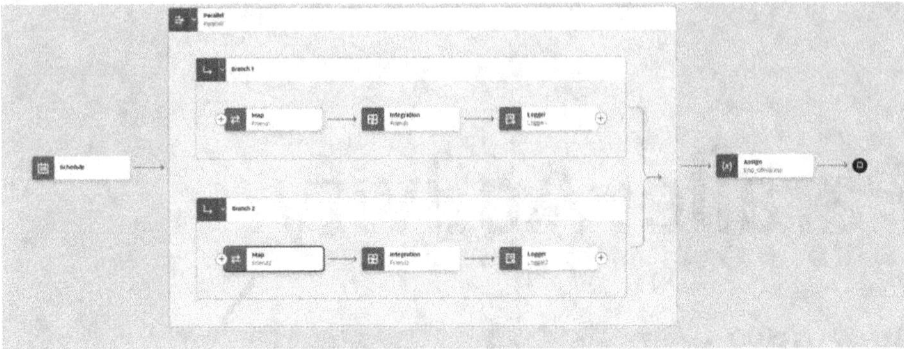

***Figure 23-1.** Parallel Activity Configuration*

2. In the visual representation, both branches display in green, indicating active parallel flows.

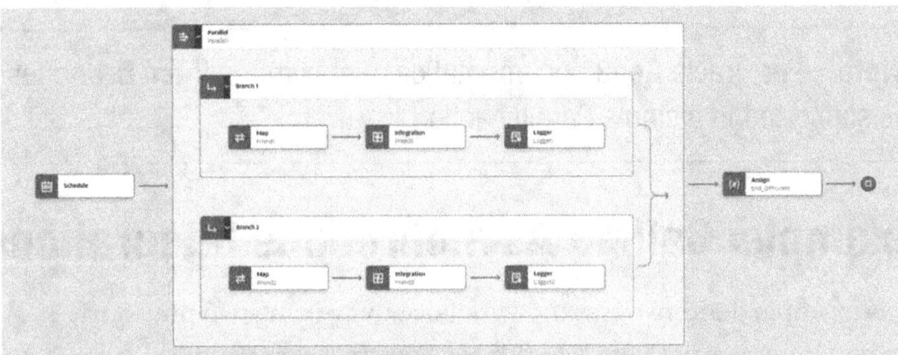

***Figure 23-2.** Parallel Flow Branches*

Important Note About Wait Activity:
Child integrations support the Wait activity.

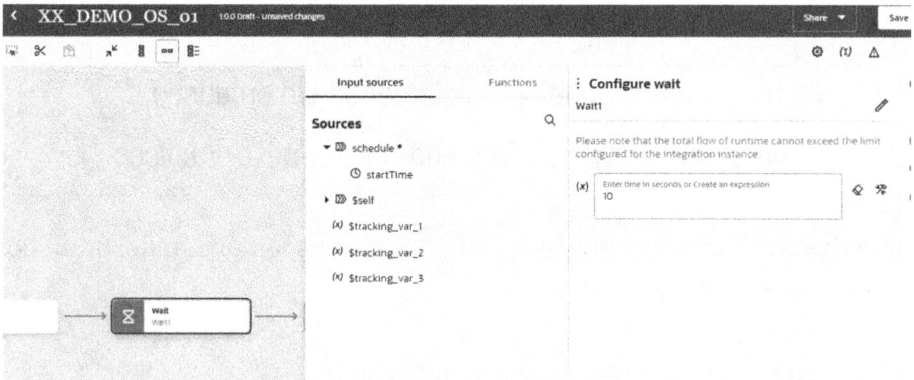

Figure 23-3. *Wait Activity in Child Integration*

However, branch code does not support the Wait activity, as shown in the available actions list.

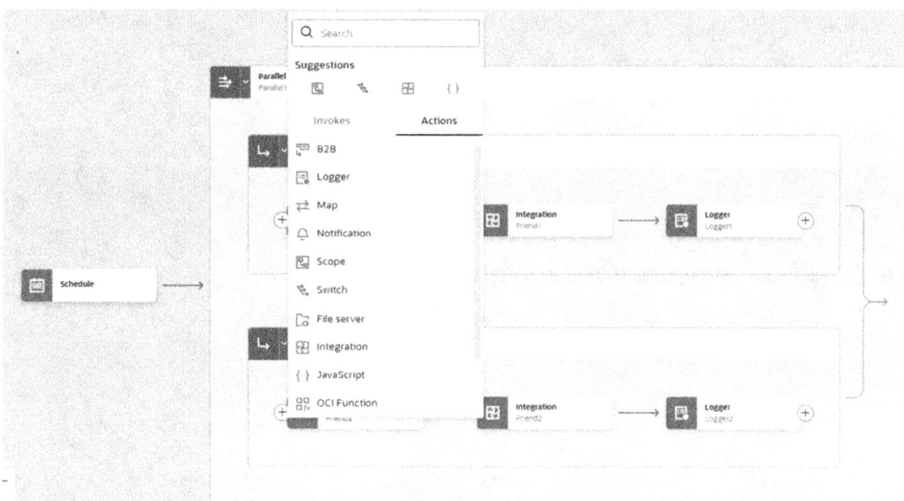

Figure 23-4. *Available Actions in Branch*

Example: Calling Synchronous Integrations

Warning This sample is for learning purposes only. Review the following documentation before implementing in production:

Common-integration-style-pitfalls-and-design-best-practices

Objective: Demonstrate how the integration waits for all parallel branches to complete before proceeding.

Test Setup:

Two dummy integrations have been created:

- **Integration 1**: Contains a one-second Wait activity.
- **Integration 2**: Contains a 20-second Wait activity.

Figure 23-5. Synchronous Integration Setup

General Overview:

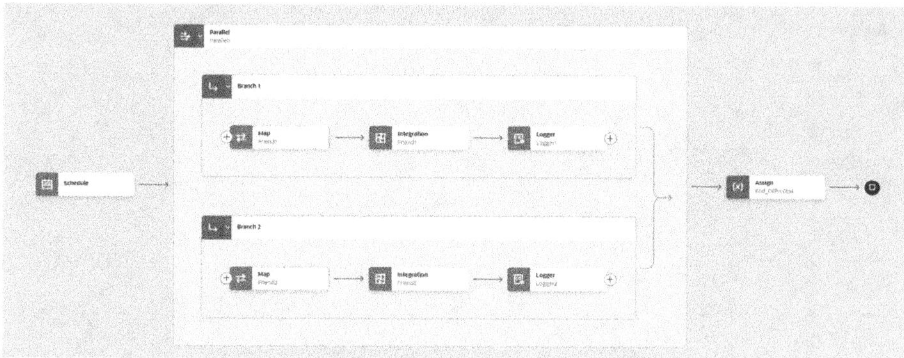

Figure 23-6. *Parallel Synchronous Flow Overview*

Execution Behavior:

When running the parent integration, the child integration that completes first waits for the other to finish before the process continues.

***Figure 23-7.** Execution Wait Behavior*

Technical Reference

Code Example	Comments
XX_DEMO_PARALLEL_SYNC	**Package File**: XX_DEMO_COOKBOOK.par
XX_DEMO_SYNC_1 XX_DEMO_SYNC_2	**Package File**: XX_DEMO_COOKBOOK.par

CHAPTER 24

Data Stitch Activity and Global Variables

Reference Documentation

Oracle Documentation:

Data Stitch Use Cases

Community Resources:

- OIC Basics - Data Stitch
- Append Operation in Data Stitch

Demo Preparation

This demonstration uses the REST API for creating Payables invoices.

Sample Payload: rest_demo_payload_payables_invoice.json (available on GitHub)

J. J. Montero Rodríguez and S. Tahseen, *Oracle Integration Cookbook for Oracle ERP Cloud*,
https://doi.org/10.1007/979-8-8688-3020-4_24

Figure 24-1. *Payables Invoice API Configuration*

API Endpoint:

```
https://xxxx.ds-fa.oraclepdemos.com/fscmRestApi/resources/
11.13.18.05/invoices
```

Sample JSON Payload:

```
{
  "InvoiceNumber": "84300000007",
  "InvoiceCurrency": "EUR",
  "InvoiceAmount": 200,
  "InvoiceDate": "2023-10-01",
  "AccountingDate": "2023-07-01",
  "BusinessUnit": "US1 Business Unit",
  "Supplier": "ABC Consulting",
  "SupplierSite": "ABC US1",
  "InvoiceGroup": "84300000001",
  "Description": "Description XX",
```

```
  "invoiceLines": [
    {
      "LineNumber": 1,
      "LineAmount": 140
    },
    {
      "LineNumber": 2,
      "LineAmount": 60
    }
  ]
}
```

Connection Setup:

Two ERP connections are used to simulate accessing different Oracle ERP instances.

***Figure 24-2.** Dual ERP Connection Configuration*

Global Variables

Standard Assign variables in OIC do not have explicit type enforcement, so numeric operations require explicit type conversion functions like number() or string(). Global variables, by contrast, support explicit type declarations (String, Integer, Boolean, Object, Array, etc.), which is the subject of this chapter.	When we want to work with variables as numbers, we **have to convert using functions** as shown.

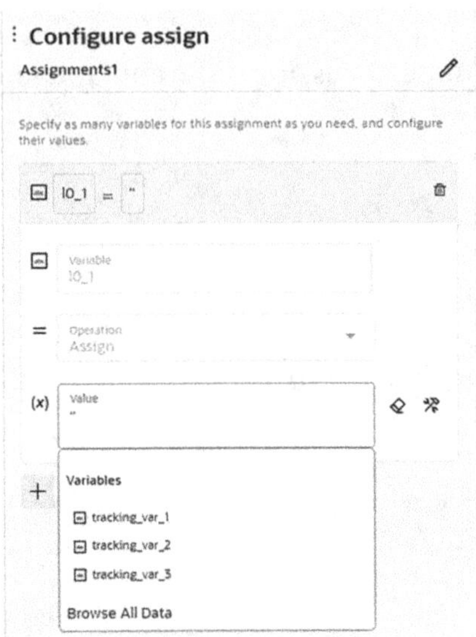

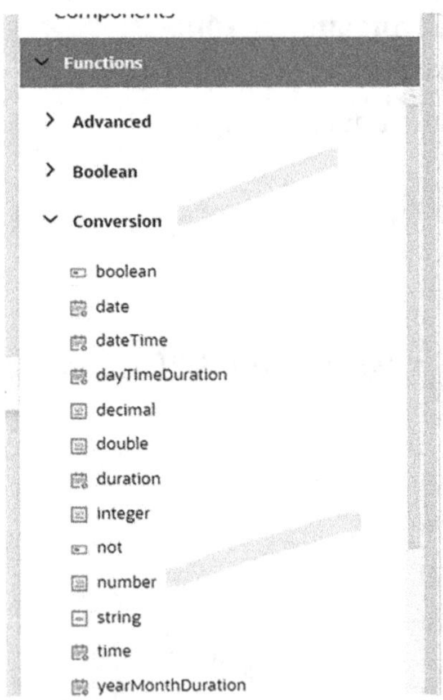

(continued)

For variables requiring complex structures, OIC provides global variables with multiple data types. They are created in the right menu, as shown.

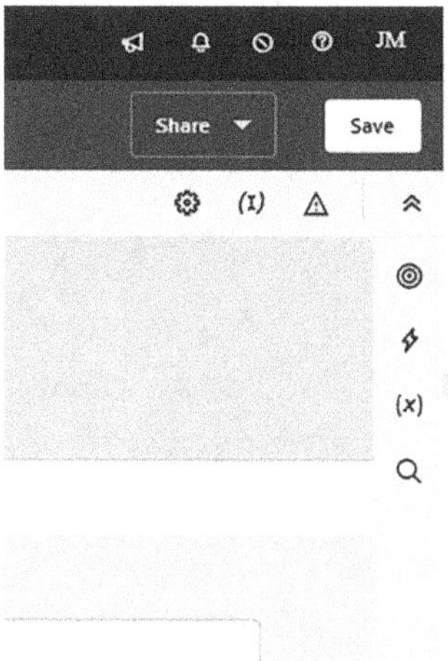

And the available types are the following.

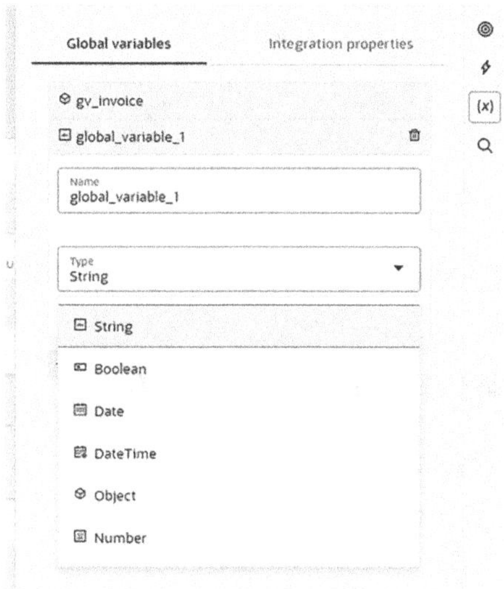

This chapter focuses on **object types** for our examples.

Data Stitch Activity

The Data Stitch activity enables working with complex variable types beyond basic Assign operations.

Business Requirement

Create an invoice using different ERP connections based on payload with some flag in data (currency in this example), with payload modifications based on the selected connection.

Integration Overview:

Figure 24-3. *Data Stitch Integration Overview*

Implementation Steps

Step 1: Receive Payload

Configure REST connection to receive invoice data.

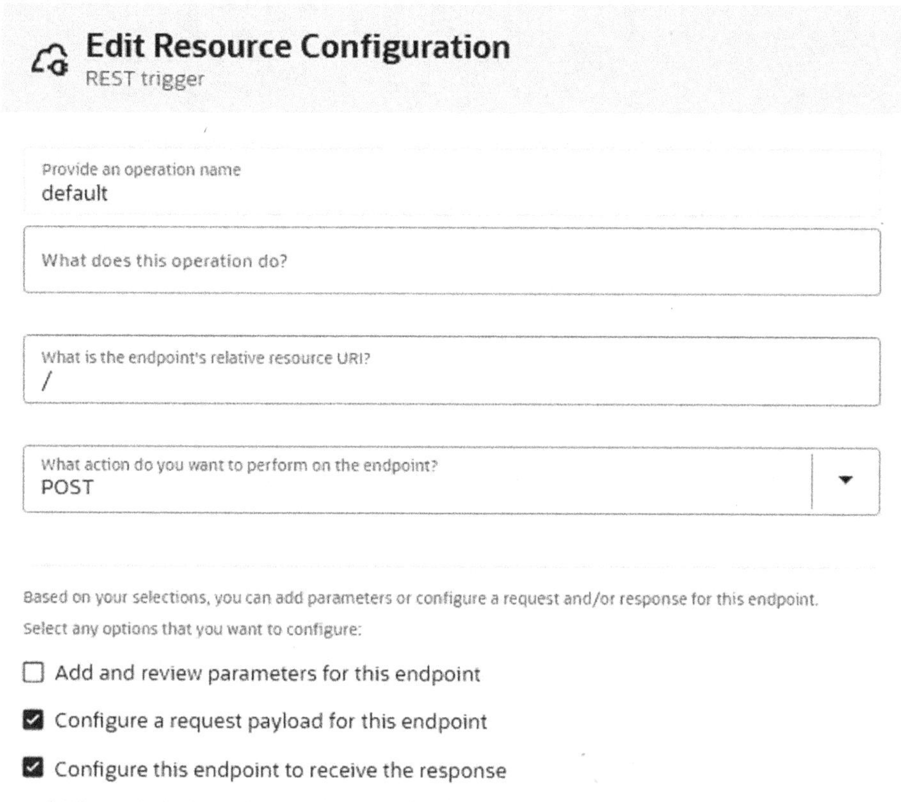

Figure 24-4. *REST Connection Configuration*

Request Payload Structure:

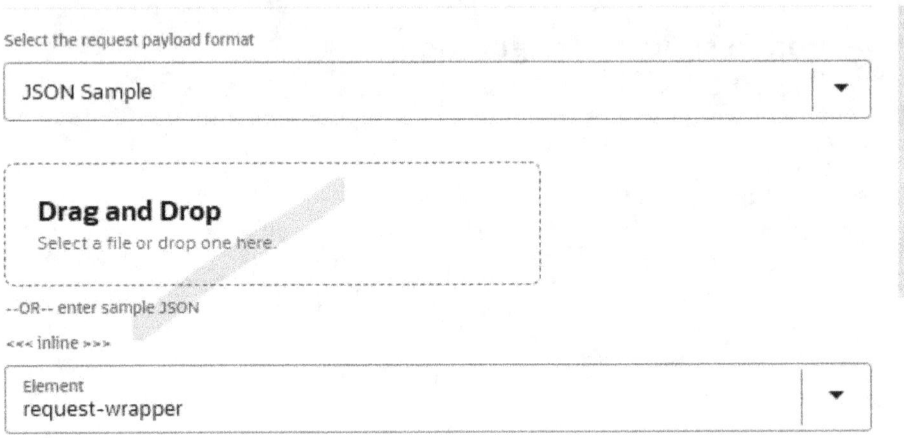

***Figure 24-5.** Request Payload Schema*

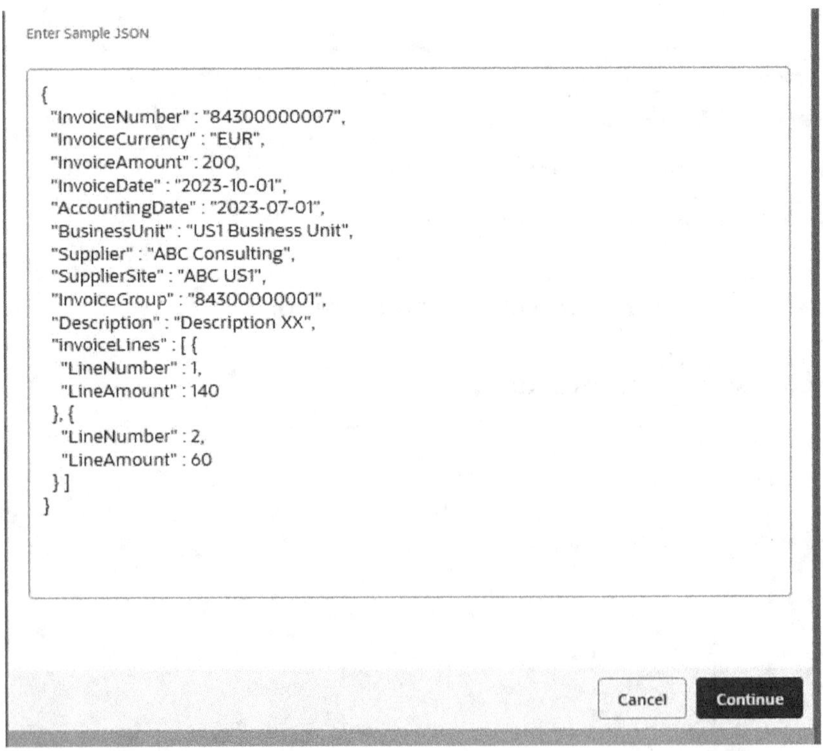

***Figure 24-6.** Request Payload Details*

Response Configuration:

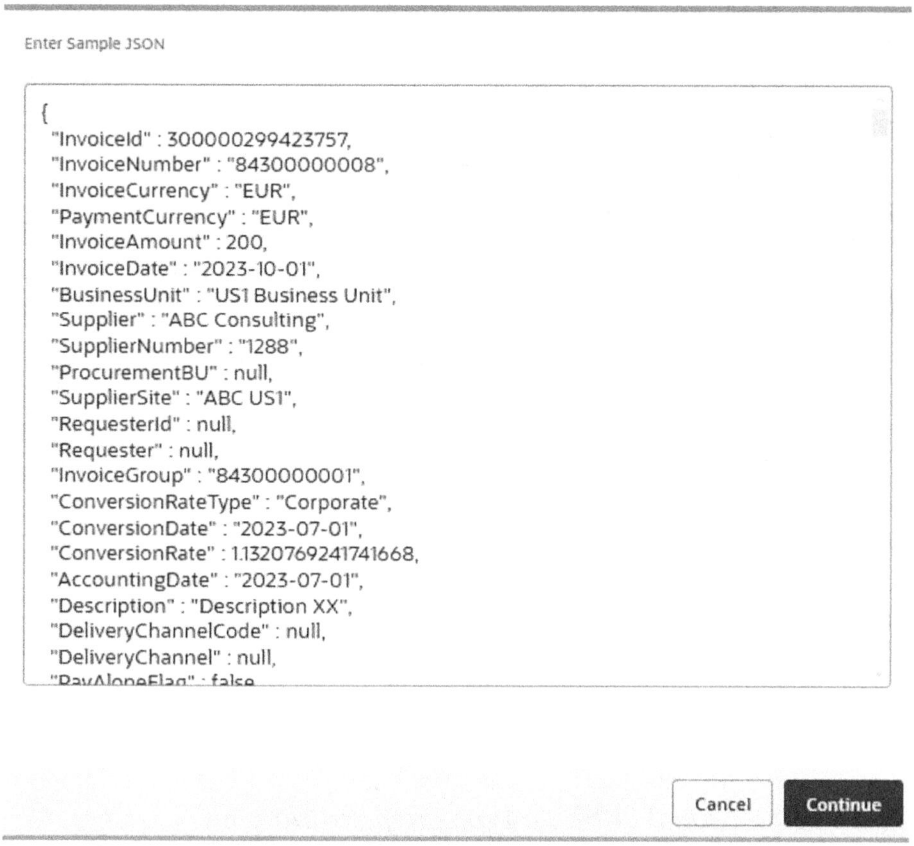

***Figure 24-7.** Response Payload Configuration*

Step 2: Common Mapping

This mapping is positioned before the Invoke c1 (Step 4) to simplify integration maintenance. Benefits include

- Common mapping and making changes using global variables
- Easier maintenance across multiple invokes
- Reduced error potential in complex mappings

Imagine if instead of two invokes we have ten and also if instead of a basic mapping as shown in our example, we have a quite complex mapping with a tree of several nodes and many fields. If we did not play with Stitch and global variables, we would have a lot of work to maintain in case of changes, which is error-prone.

Step 3: Assign to a Global Variable

Create a global variable with c1-invoices type.

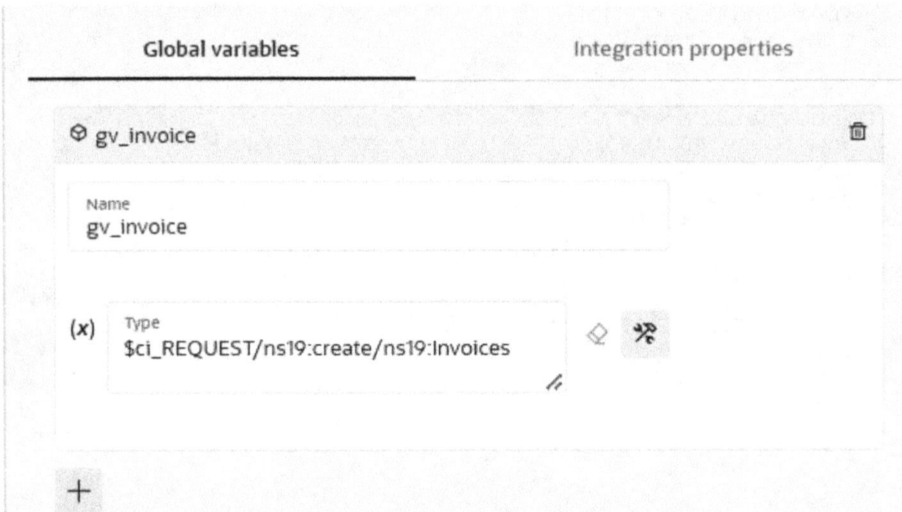

Figure 24-8. *Global Variable Type Configuration*

Assign mapping content to the global variable.

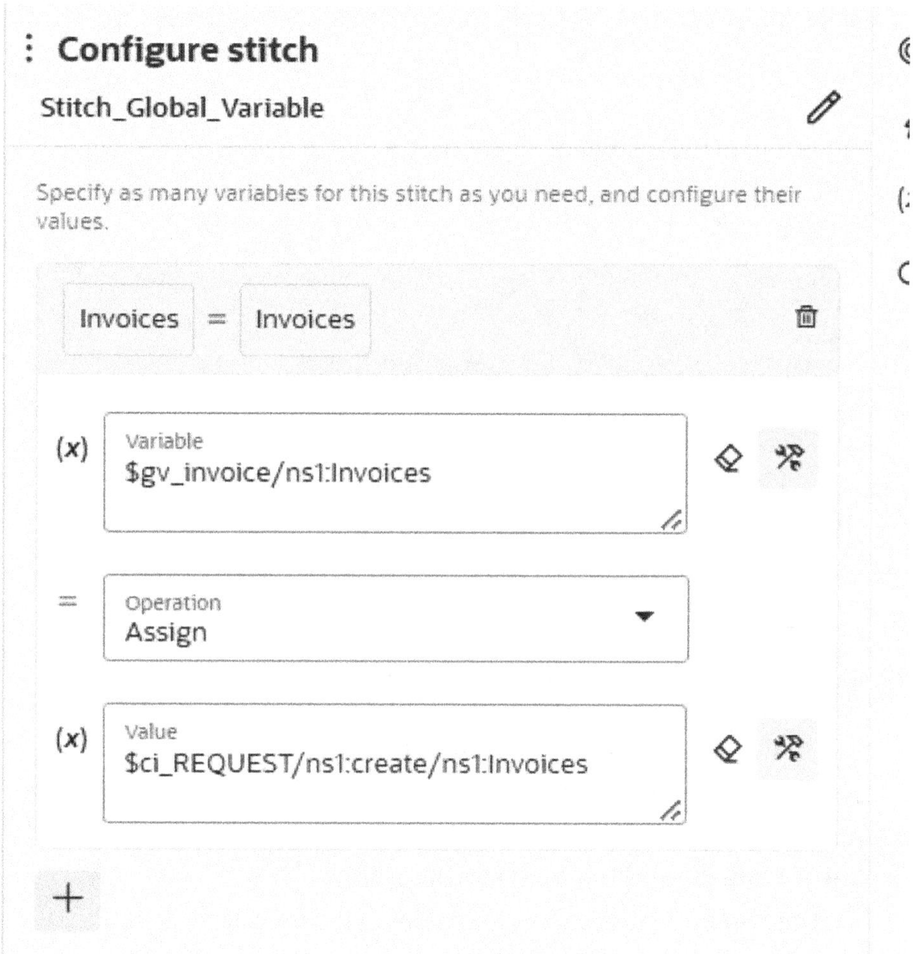

***Figure 24-9.** Global Variable Assignment*

Step 4: Invoke Invoice Creation (Connection 1)

Call invoice creation with default mapping.

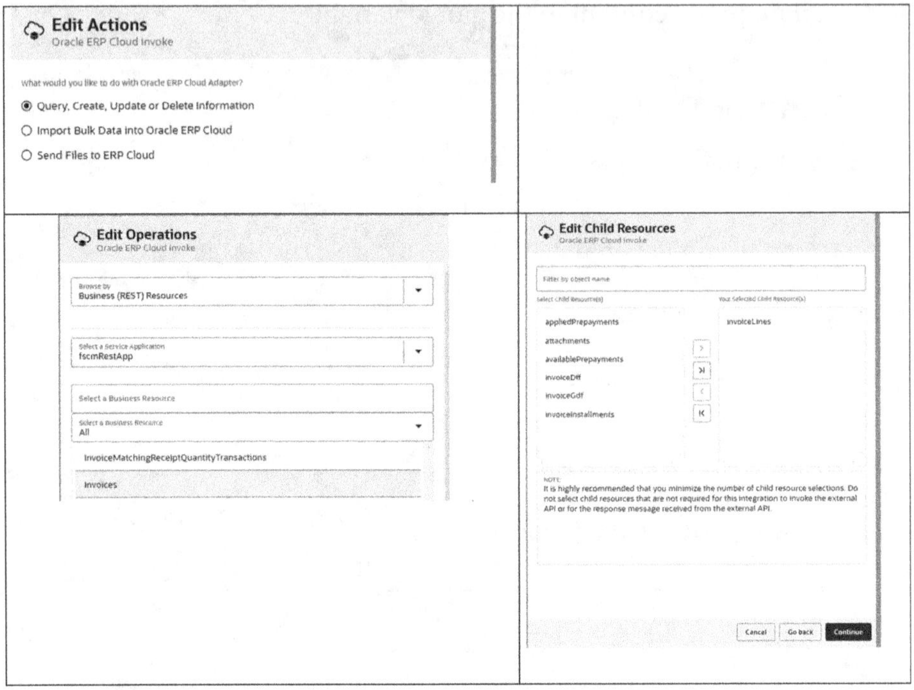

Figure 24-10. *Response Mapping Configuration*

Step 5: Response Mapping (Connection 1)

Create separate response mapping for each connection invoke. This mapping handles the response from Connection 1.

Step 6: Conditional Payload Modification

Use Data Stitch to modify payload when currency is not EUR.

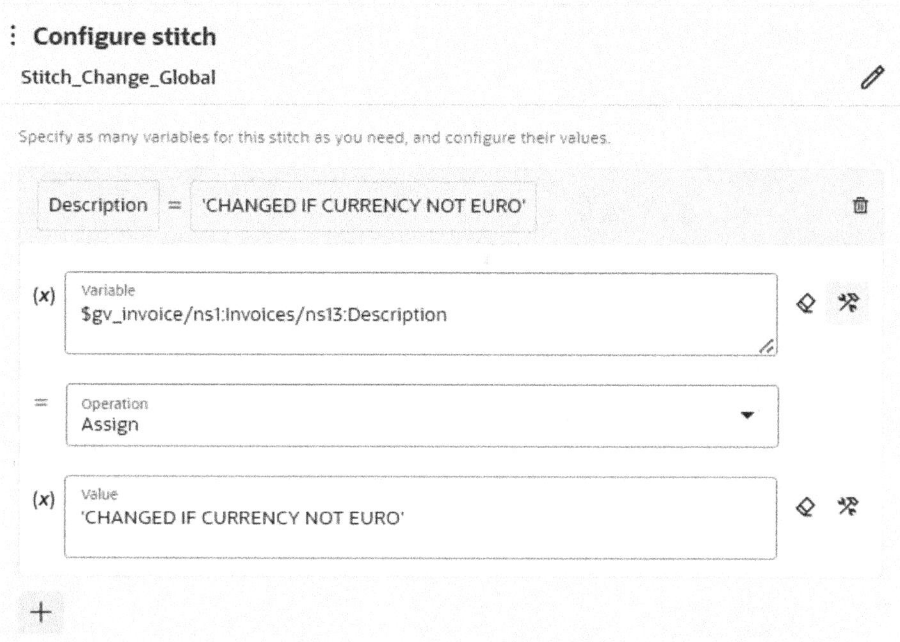

***Figure 24-11.** Data Stitch Conditional Modification*

Modify the global variable based on condition.

Step 7: Assign the Modified Variable

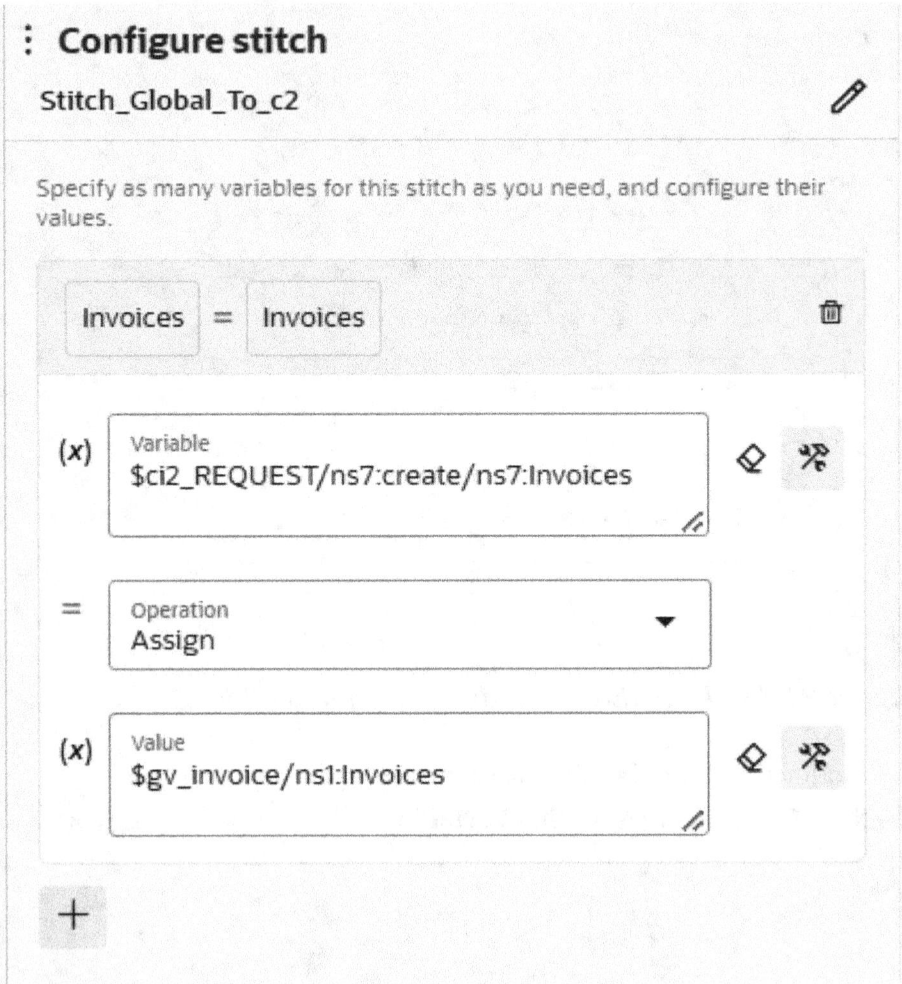

***Figure 24-12.** Assign the Modified Global Variable*

Step 8: Invoke Invoice Creation (Connection 2)
Similar to Step 4, but using the second ERP connection.

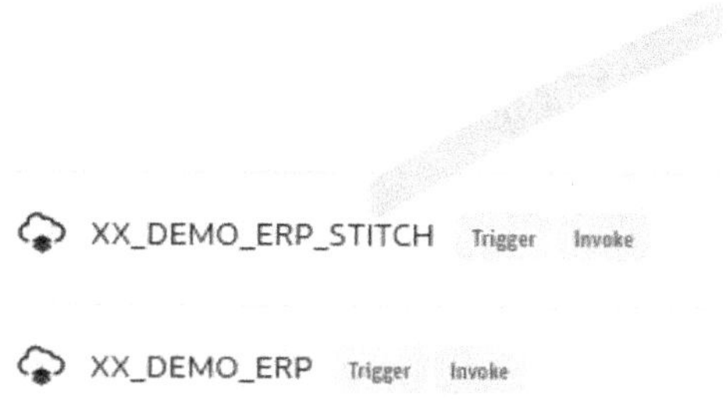

Figure 24-13. *Connection 2 Invoke Configuration*

Step 9: Response Mapping (Connection 2)

Create response mapping for Connection 2 invoke, handling the specific response structure.

Technical Reference

Code Example	Comments
rest_demo_payload_payables_invoice.json	Payload for creating invoices with REST API
XX_DEMO_STITCH_01	**Package File**: XX_DEMO_COOKBOOK.par

CHAPTER 25

REST API Tips

Overview

This chapter provides practical solutions to a common challenge encountered when working with Oracle REST APIs. These tips are based on real implementation experiences and troubleshooting scenarios.

REST Request Headers: Critical Configuration

The Hidden Feature

REST Request Headers are a somewhat hidden but critical feature in OIC REST API calls.

Problem Scenario

When using a standard ERP connection to execute the Validate action for a Payables invoice.

API Documentation:

Oracle Financials 26B—Get Started

J. J. Montero Rodríguez and S. Tahseen, *Oracle Integration Cookbook for Oracle ERP Cloud*,
https://doi.org/10.1007/979-8-8688-3020-4_25

Figure 25-1. *Standard ERP Connection Configuration*

Error Encountered:

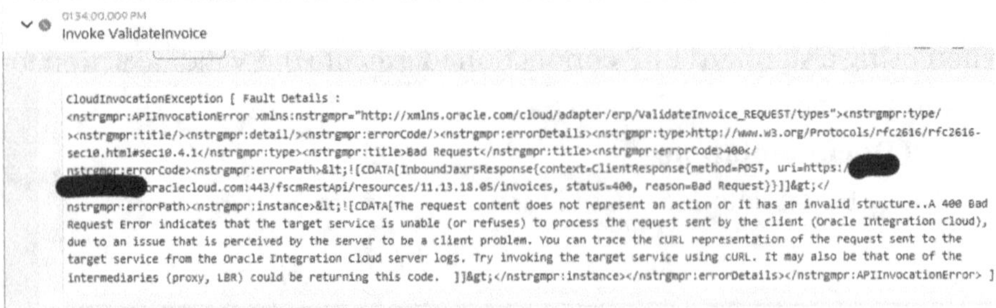

Figure 25-2. *Error Response Without Proper Headers*

Solution Discovery

The REST API documentation reveals a critical requirement.

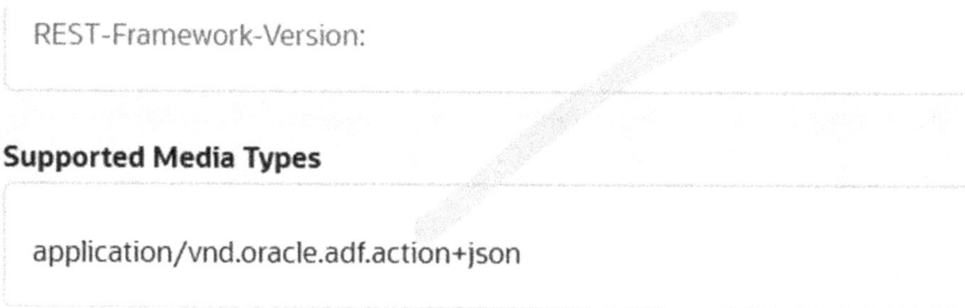

Figure 25-3. *Content-Type Header Requirement in Documentation*

Successful Testing in Postman:

Figure 25-4. *Successful Postman Request Configuration*

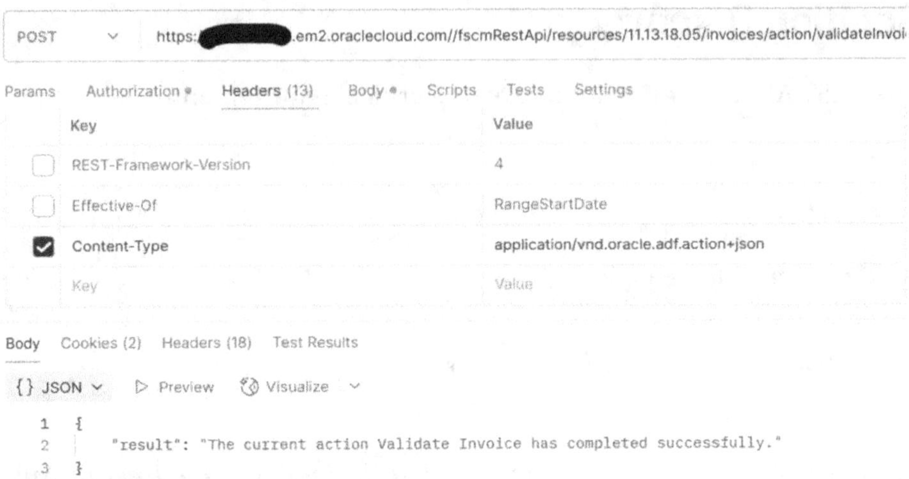

Figure 25-5. *Postman Headers Configuration*

OIC Implementation Fix

Step 1: Change Connection Type

Change from ERP connection type to REST connection type (see Chapter 2 for details).

Note Standard ERP connection type does not provide an option for custom headers.

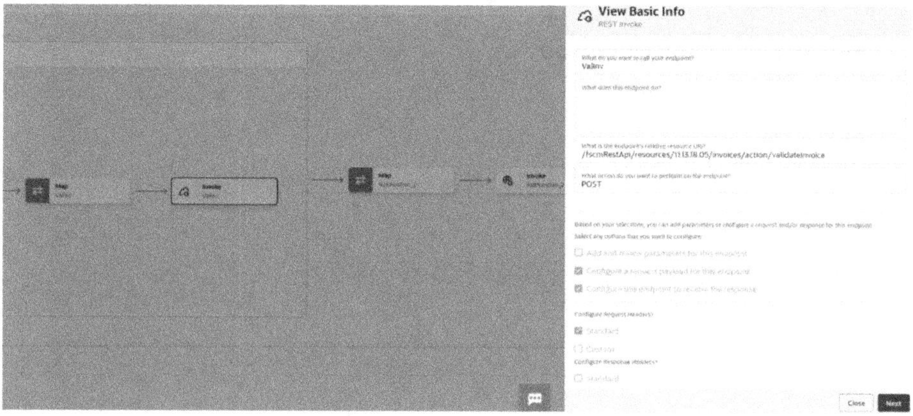

Figure 25-6. *REST Connection Type Configuration*

Sample Request Configuration:

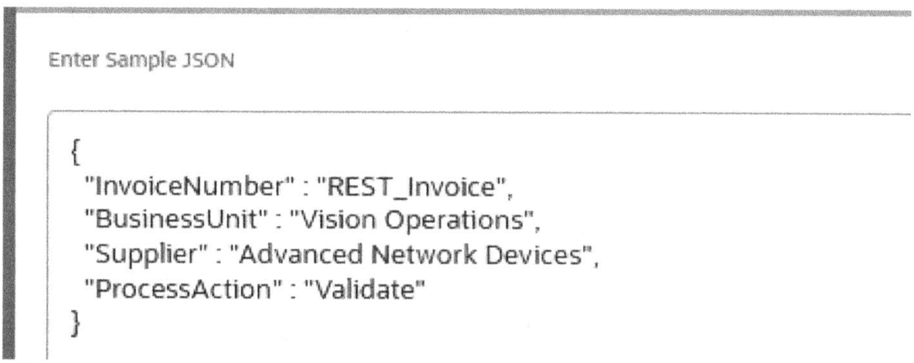

Figure 25-7. *Request Payload Sample*

Step 2: Configure HTTP Header

Open the HTTP Header configuration slot.

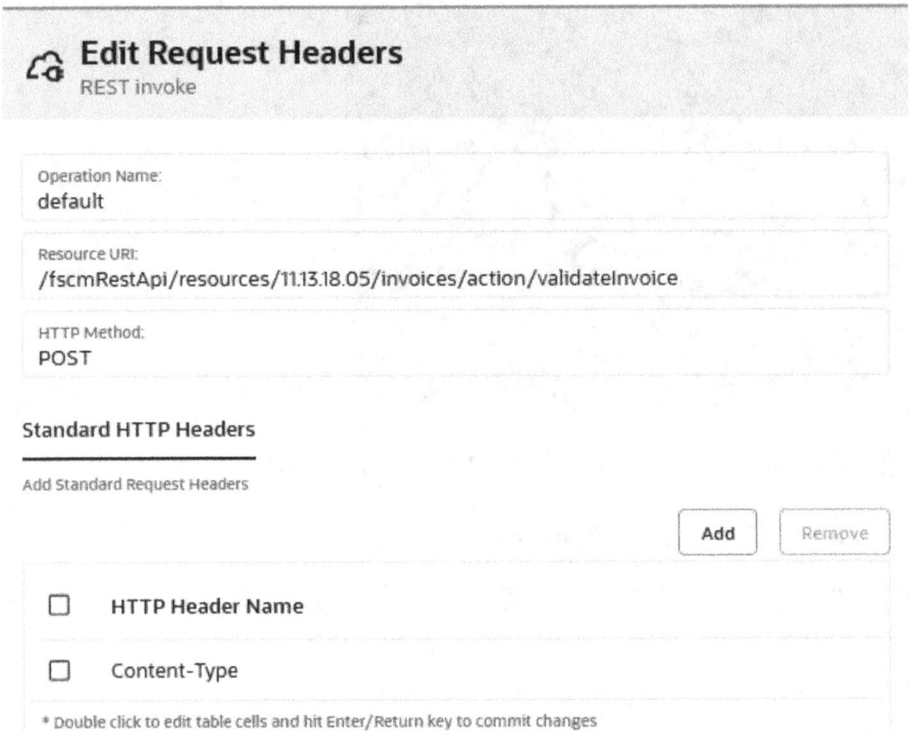

***Figure 25-8.** HTTP Header Configuration Slot*

Response Payload Example:

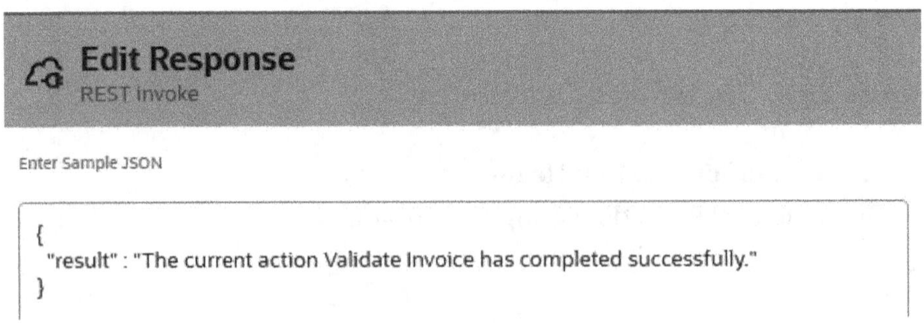

***Figure 25-9.** Response Payload Sample*

Step 3: Map Content-Type Header

Configure the Content-Type header in the mapping.

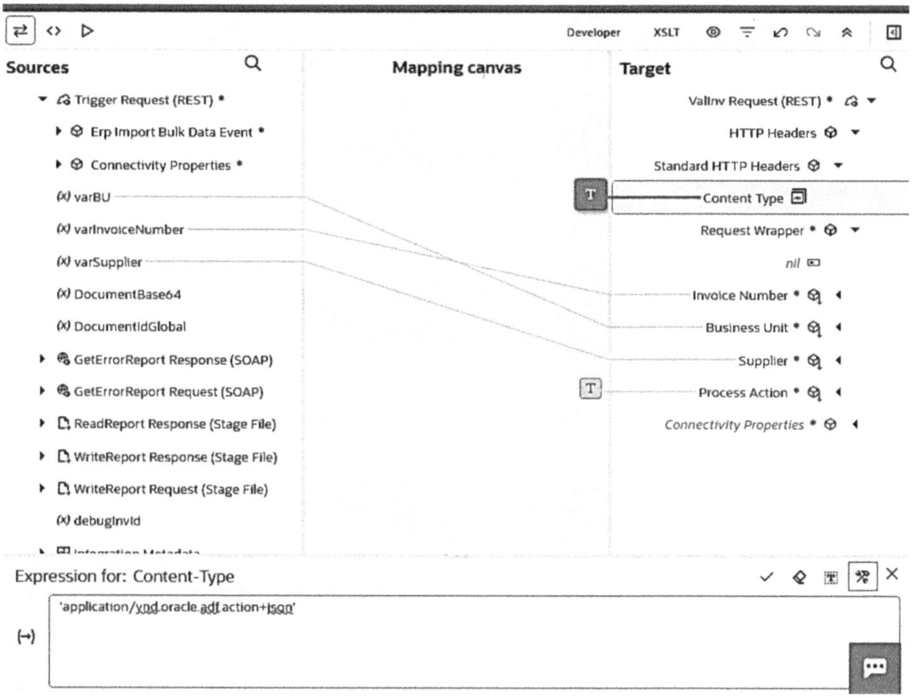

Figure 25-10. *Content-Type Header Mapping*

Expected Request Payload:

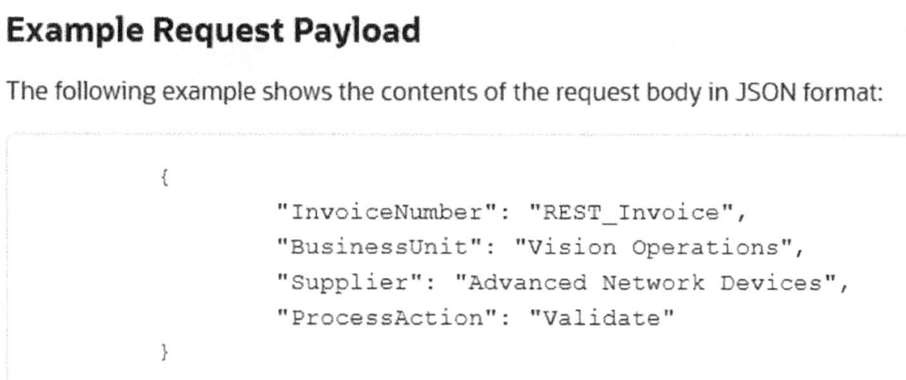

Figure 25-11. *Expected Request Payload Structure*

CHAPTER 26

B2B Basics

Reference Documentation

Oracle Documentation:

- B2B Messages Overview
- B2B Action Schema Reference

Industry Resources:

- B2B Messaging Guide
- B2B Message Best Practices

Introduction

This chapter provides an introductory overview of B2B messaging in Oracle Integration Cloud. Experienced B2B practitioners may skip this section. *(Note: B2B integrations require careful architectural consideration regarding project placement.)*

What Is B2B Integration?

B2B (Business-to-Business) integration focuses on mapping and converting data to standardized formats used for inter-company communication.

J. J. Montero Rodríguez and S. Tahseen, *Oracle Integration Cookbook for Oracle ERP Cloud*, https://doi.org/10.1007/979-8-8688-3020-4_26

Common B2B Scenarios

- **Supplier and Manufacturer:** Exchange of purchase orders, ASNs (Advanced Shipping Notices), and invoices
- **Wholesaler and Retailer:** Product catalogs, orders, and shipping notifications
- **Software Provider and Business Client:** License information, usage data, and billing

Document Types

The B2B landscape includes numerous standardized formats for exchanging:

- Purchase orders
- Sales orders
- Invoices
- Items and product catalogs
- Advanced Shipping Notices (ASNs)
- Price catalogs

OIC B2B Activity

Oracle Integration Cloud simplifies B2B conversions through dedicated B2B activities.

EDI Message Types

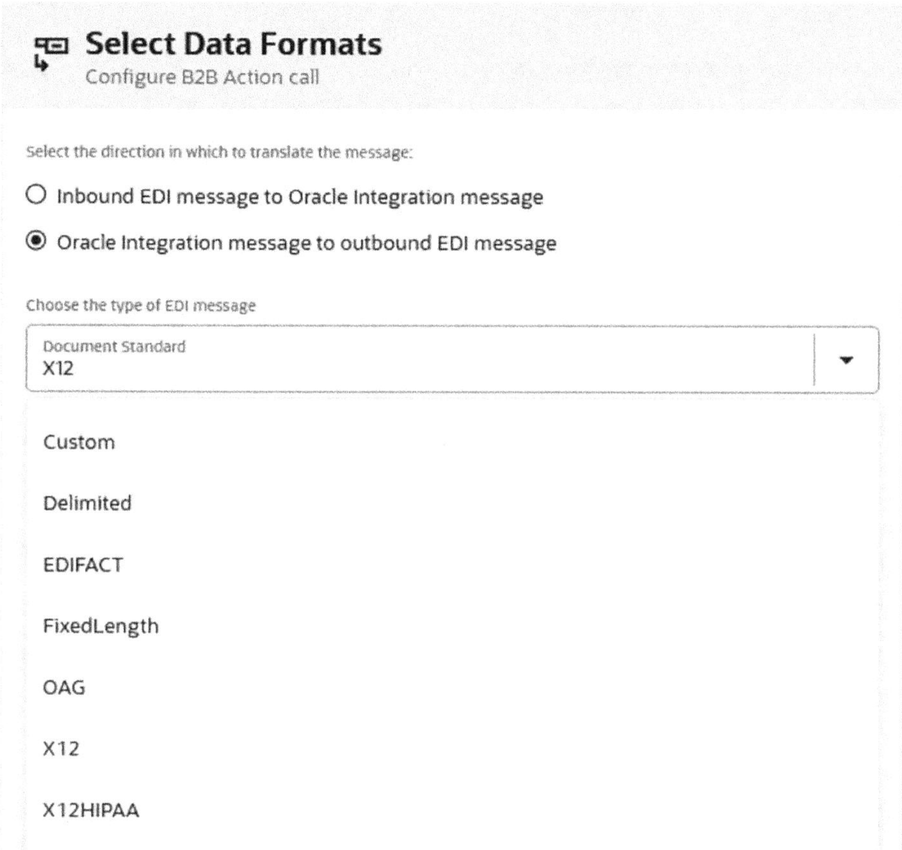

Figure 26-1. EDI Message Type Selection

X12 Document Types

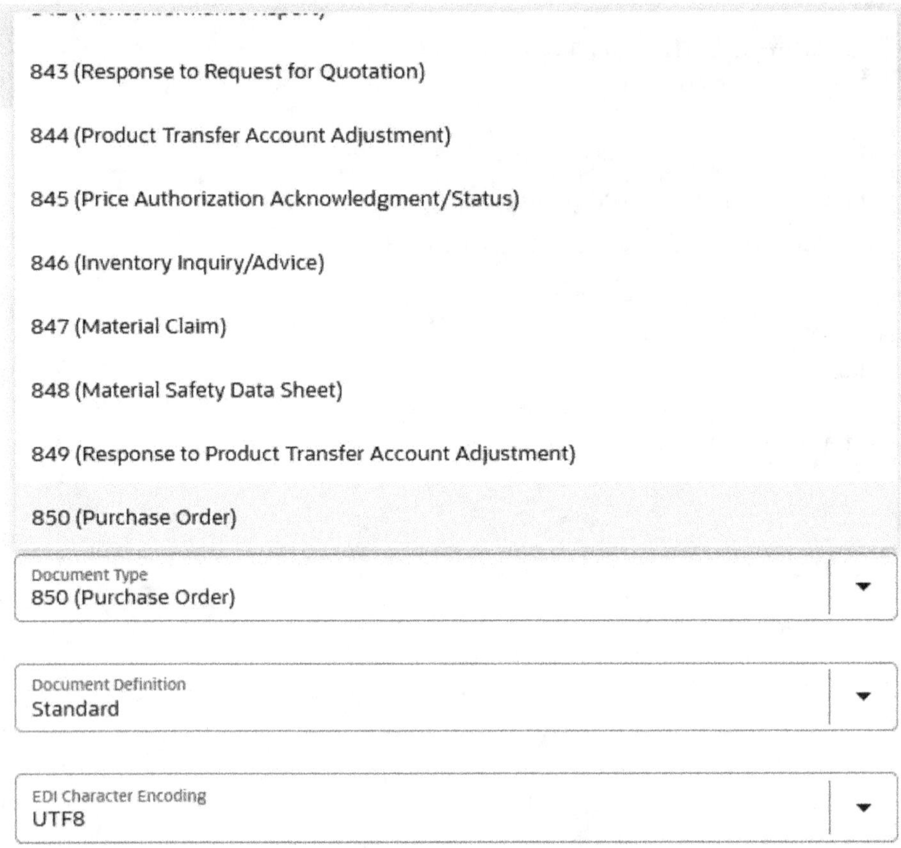

Figure 26-2. *X12 Document Type Selection*

EDIFACT Document Types

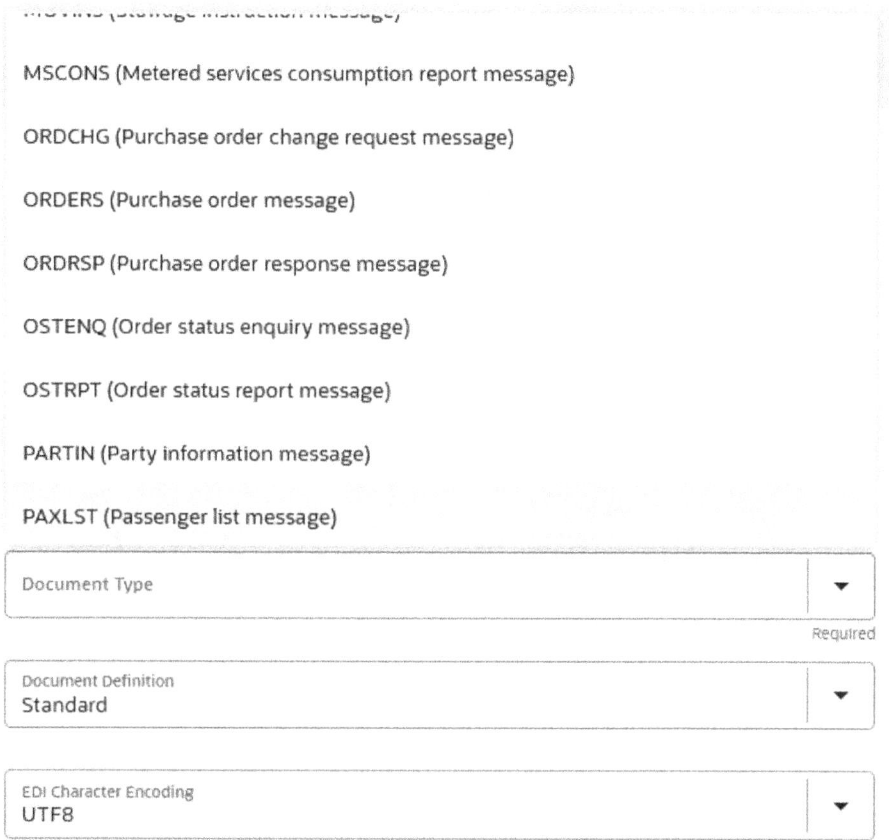

Figure 26-3. *EDIFACT Document Type Selection*

Implementation Steps

Step 1: Prepare Data for Mapping

Figure 26-4. *Data Preparation for B2B Mapping*

Step 2: Add B2B Activity

Insert the B2B activity into your integration flow at the appropriate point.

Step 3: Configure Conversion Details

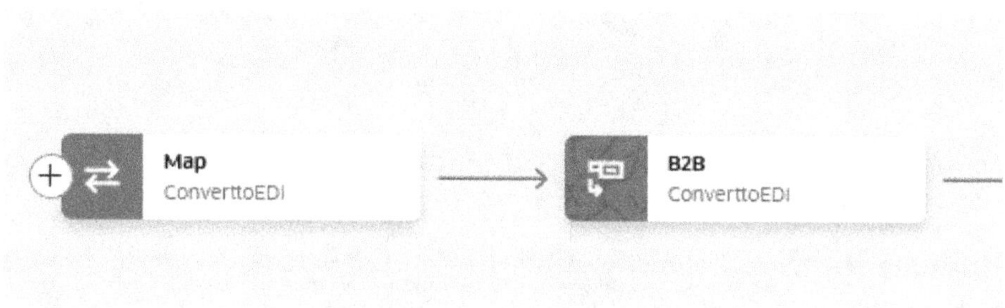

Figure 26-5. *B2B Conversion Configuration*

Pre-built Target Structure:

The B2B activity provides complex pre-built target structures.

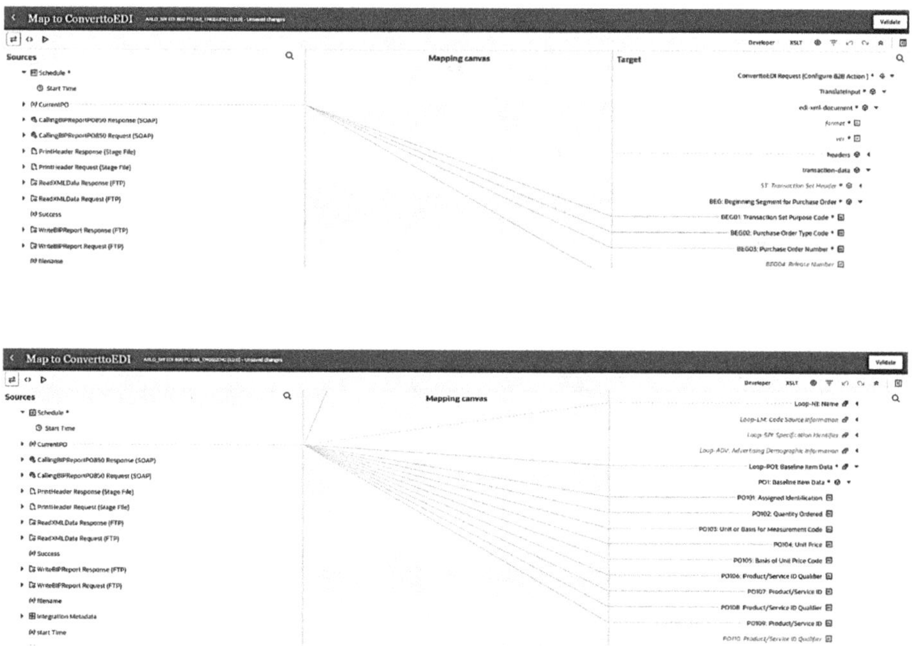

Figure 26-6. *Pre-built Target Structure*

Step 4: Verify Conversion Success

Use response fields to control conversion success and adapt the flow accordingly.

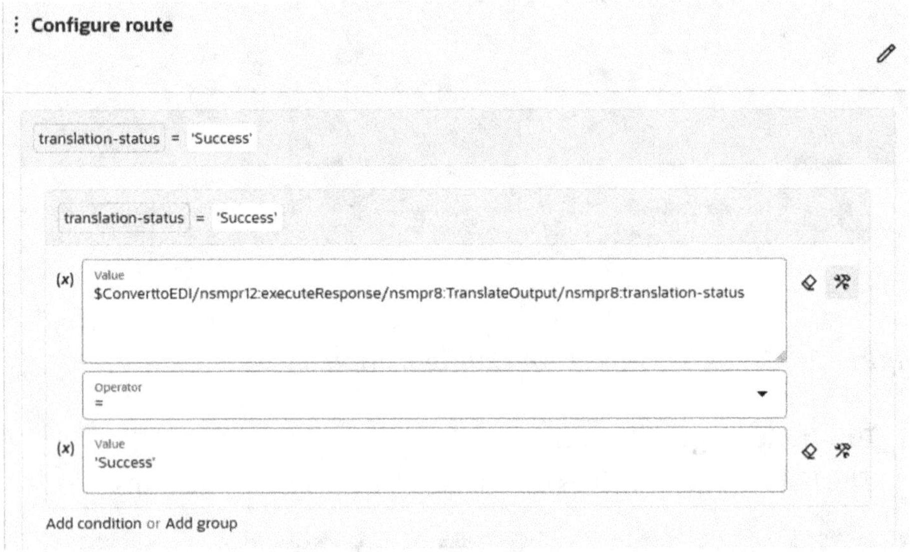

Figure 26-7. *Conversion Status Verification*

Step 5: Handle Success/Error Conditions

Implement appropriate branching logic based on conversion results.

Step 6: Store Output

Common use case is to store the resulting EDI file on an FTP server for partner retrieval.

Note No demo code is provided for this introductory chapter.

CHAPTER 27

Demo Control Dates Between OIC Runs, Using Delta Data Process

Overview

This chapter demonstrates an approach for implementing delta data processing between scheduled OIC runs, particularly useful for scenarios like

- Hourly invoice data synchronization
- Incremental data extraction based on creation dates
- Time-based data filtering

Solution Approach

Rather than building complex custom logic, this solution leverages OIC's built-in scheduling capabilities to manage date ranges automatically.

J. J. Montero Rodríguez and S. Tahseen, *Oracle Integration Cookbook for Oracle ERP Cloud*,
https://doi.org/10.1007/979-8-8688-3020-4_27

General Integration Overview

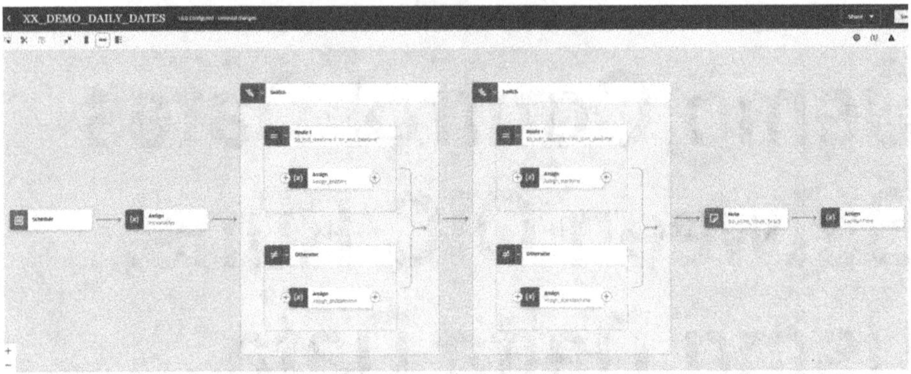

Figure 27-1. *Delta Data Processing Integration Overview*

Integration Tasks:

Your business logic should be implemented in this section.

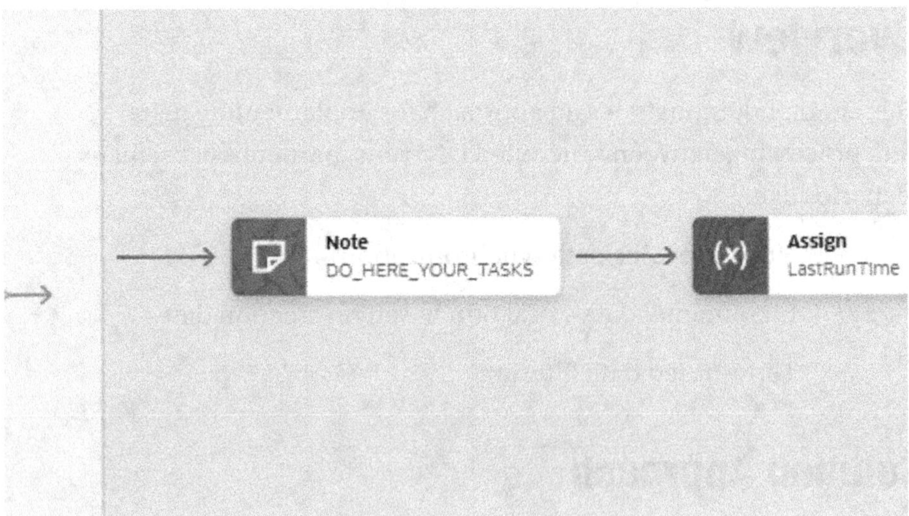

Figure 27-2. *Business Logic Implementation Section*

Key Feature: Schedule Parameters

The integration uses OIC's ability to modify parameters in the scheduled version, enabling automatic date range management.

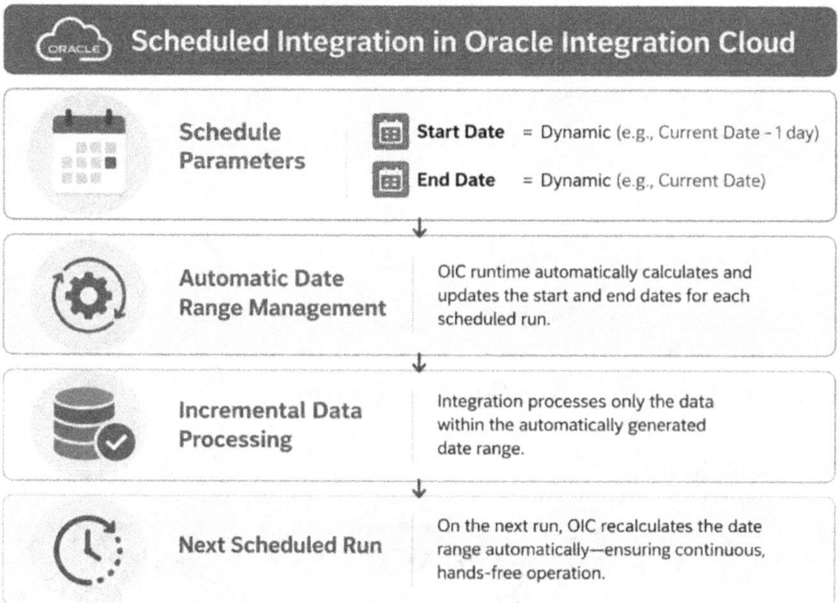

Figure 27-3. *Scheduled Integration in Oracle Integration Cloud*

Testing and Execution

Activation and Scheduling

After activating the integration, schedule it to run at your desired interval (e.g., every ten minutes).

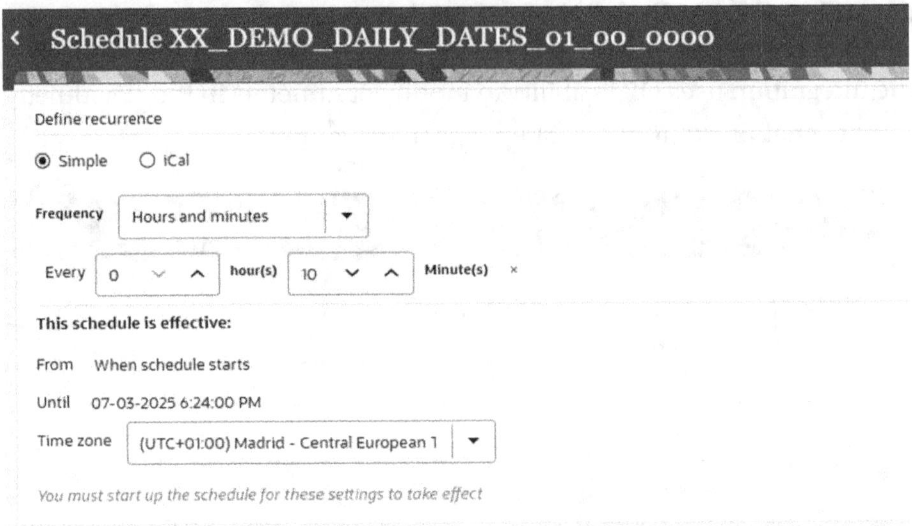

Figure 27-4. *Schedule Execution Configuration*

Start the Schedule:

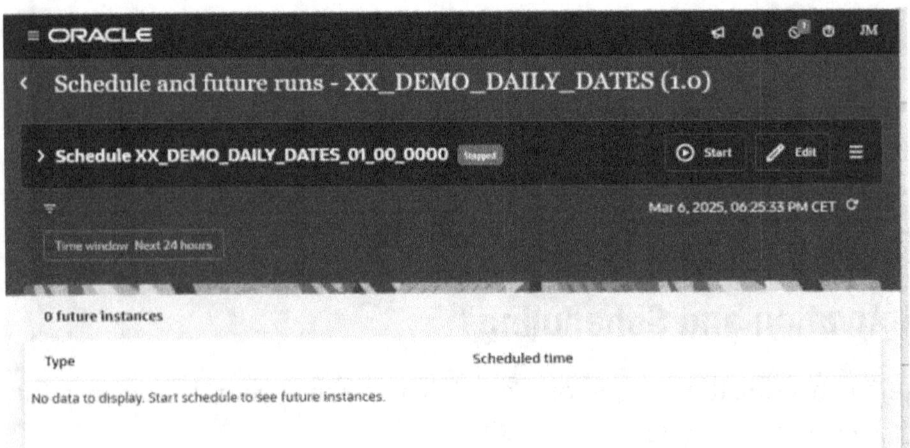

Figure 27-5. *Starting the Schedule*

Default Parameters:

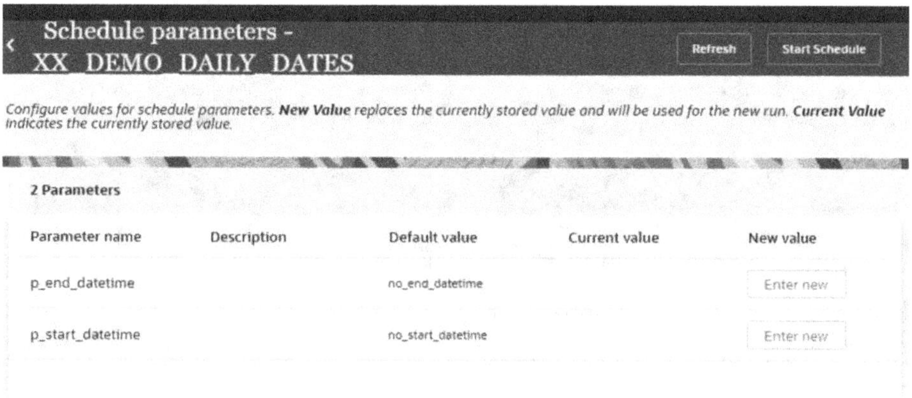

Figure 27-6. *Default Schedule Parameters*

Execution Results

Schedule Runs Overview:

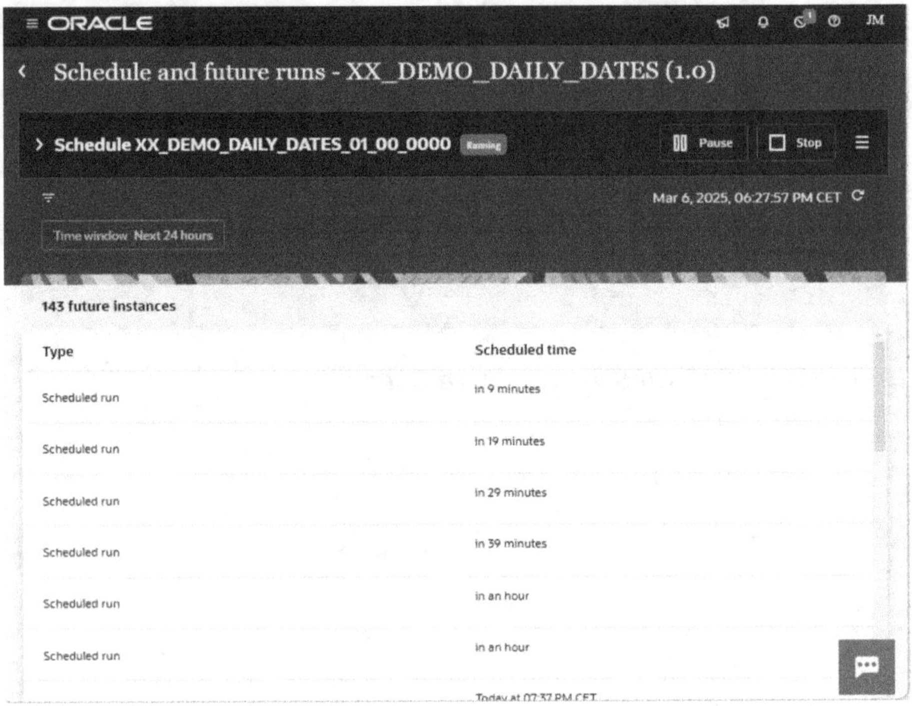

Figure 27-7. *Schedule Runs History*

First Run Results:

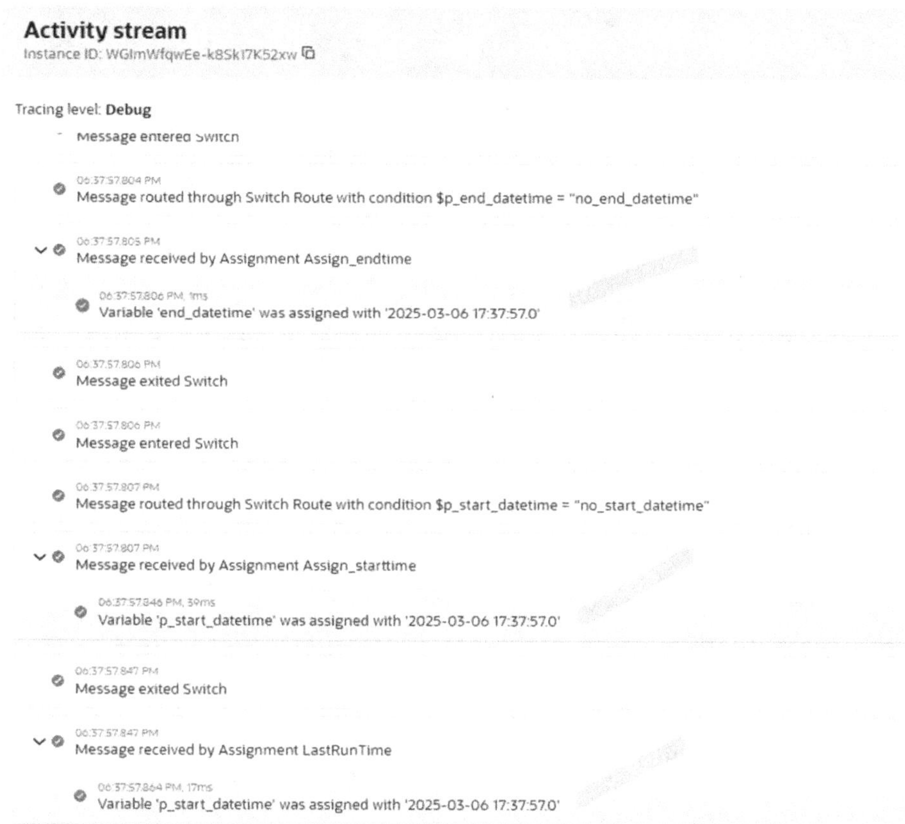

Figure 27-8. *First Run Execution Log*

Second Run Results:

Figure 27-9. *Second Run Execution Log*

Date Range Logic

Key Points:

1. **Start Time (in the Second Run):** Equals the finish time of the previous run

2. **End Time (in the Second Run):** Current date–time when the process executes

3. **Next Start Time:** Set to current end time for subsequent runs

This pattern continues for all subsequent executions, creating automatic delta data windows.

Benefits

The integration automatically manages from-datetime to to-datetime ranges, enabling

- Smart delta data processing
- Automated date range control
- Seamless incremental data extraction
- Reliable data synchronization between systems

Technical Reference

Code Example	Comments
XX_DEMO_DAILY_DATES	**Package File**: XX_DEMO_COOKBOOK_2.par

CHAPTER 28

Oracle ERP Cloud Business Events

Overview

Business events in Oracle ERP Cloud enable real-time integration triggers when Business Object statuses change, such as

- **Payables Invoices**: Created to Validated
- **Receivables Invoices**: Incomplete to Complete
- **Purchase Orders**: Status changes

Reference Documentations:

- ERP Service Catalog Configuration
- Fusion Applications Release 13+
- Enable Payables Invoice Events

Non-Gen3 References:

- Business Events Overview
- Business Events in Saas with OIC
- Business Events in Fusion Saas with OIC with Event Filter Expressions

J. J. Montero Rodríguez and S. Tahseen, *Oracle Integration Cookbook for Oracle ERP Cloud*,
https://doi.org/10.1007/979-8-8688-3020-4_28

Example: Purchase Order Events

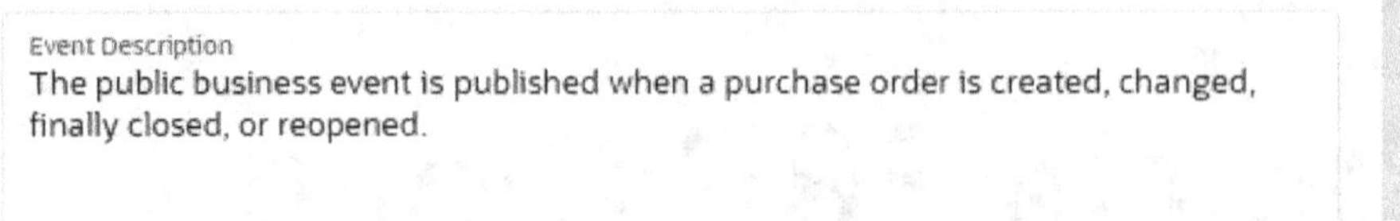

Figure 28-1. *Available Purchase Order Events*

This section demonstrates event-driven integration implementation for purchase orders.

Purchase Order Event Implementation

Setup Configuration

Step 1: Create Event-Driven Integration

Then use the ERP_Cloud_Connection.

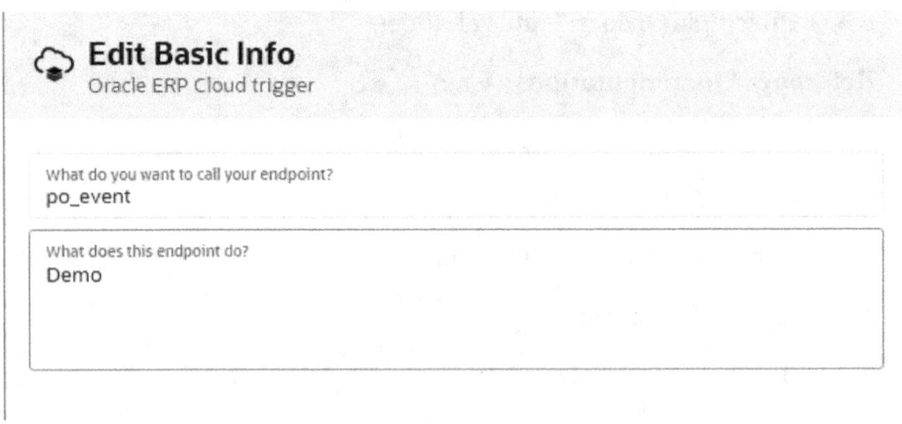

Figure 28-2. *ERP Connection Configuration*

Step 2: Select Event Option

Choose the first option in the wizard.

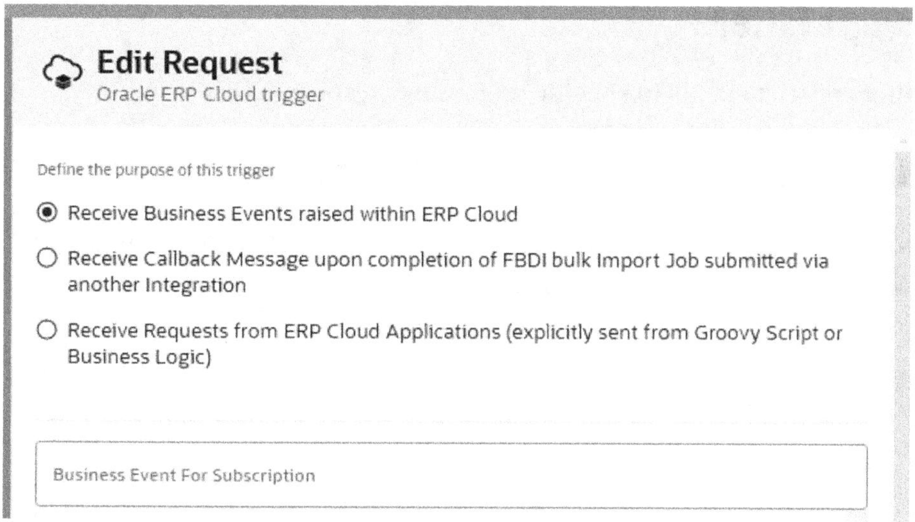

***Figure 28-3.** Event Configuration Wizard—First Option*

Step 3: Select Business Object

Choose the Business Object to monitor.

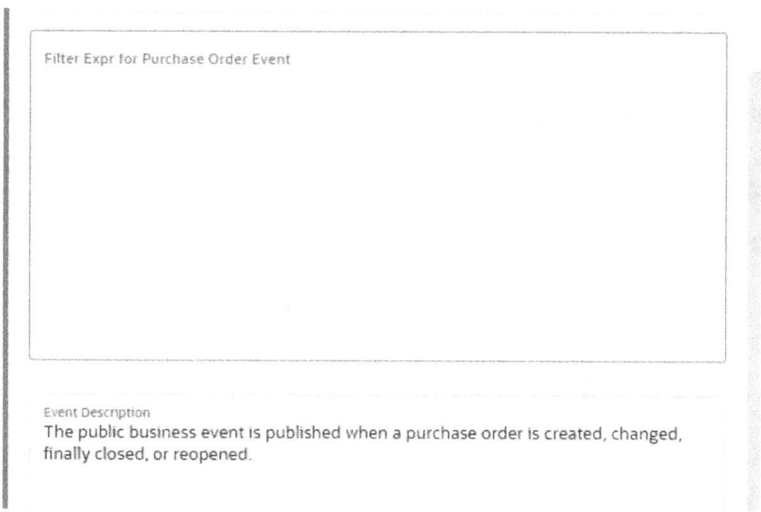

***Figure 28-4.** Business Object Selection*

Event Filters

Filters restrict events to specific criteria using special XPath syntax.

Filter Example 1: Business Unit Filter

```
<xpathExpr xmlns:ns0="http://xmlns.oracle.com/apps/financials/
receivables/shared/model/events">
  $eventPayload/ns0:InvoiceBusinessUnit='BU 1' or
  $eventPayload/ns0:InvoiceBusinessUnit='BU 2'
</xpathExpr>
```

This subscription only triggers when the business unit is 'BU 1' or 'BU 2'.

Filter Example 2: Organization Filter

```
<xpathExpr
  xmlns:ns0="http://xmlns.oracle.com/adf/svc/types/"
  xmlns:ns1="http://xmlns.oracle.com/apps/scm/productModel/
  items/itemServiceV2/"
  xmlns:ns2="http://xmlns.oracle.com/apps/scm/productModel/
  items/itemServiceV2/types/">
  $eventPayload/ns2:result/ns0:Value/ns1:OrganizationId="12345"
</xpathExpr>
```

Filters events for a specific organization ID.

Filter Example 3: Job Name Filter

```
<xpathExpr xmlns:ns0="http://xmlns.oracle.com/apps/financials/
commonModules/shared">
  $inputVariable/ns0:JOBS/ns0:JOBNAME="Load Interface File
  for Import"
</xpathExpr>
```

```
<xpathExpr xmlns:ns0="http://xmlns.oracle.com/apps/financials/
commonModules/shared">
  contains($inputVariable/ns0:JOBS/ns0:DOCUMENTNAME,
  "PROVISION")
</xpathExpr>
```

Filters based on job name and document name containing specific text.

Testing the Integration

Step 1: Activate Integration

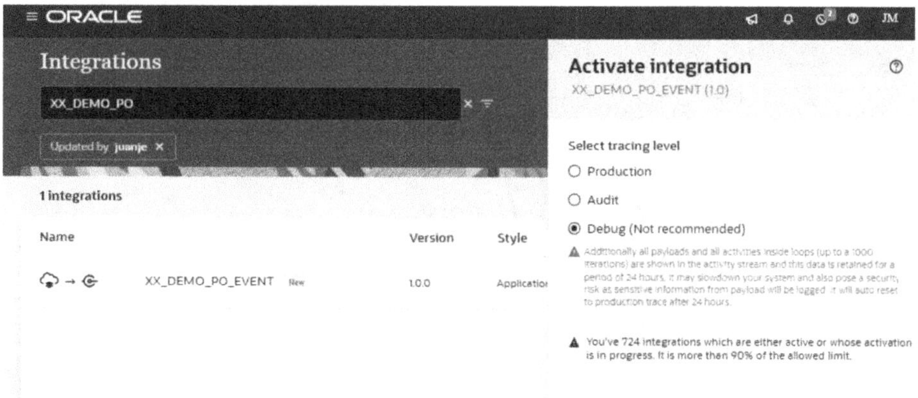

Figure 28-5. *Integration Activation*

Step 2: Trigger Event in ERP

Submit a purchase order in Oracle ERP.

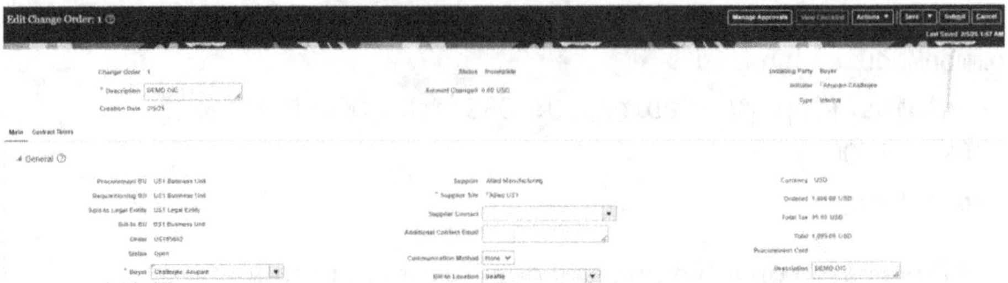

Figure 28-6. *Submit a Purchase Order in ERP*

Step 3: Review OIC Execution

Check integration runs in OIC.

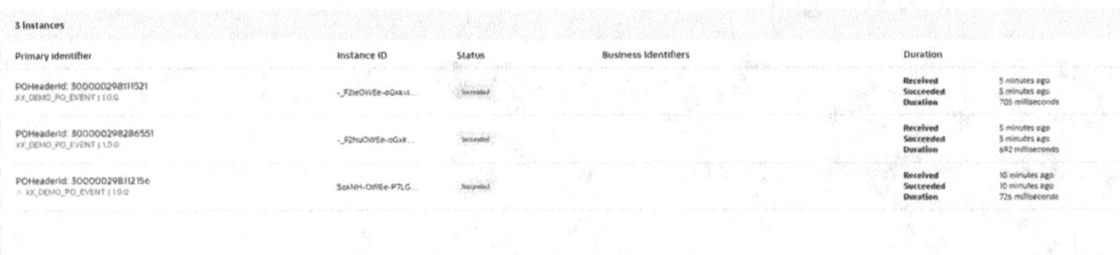

Figure 28-7. *Integration Run History*

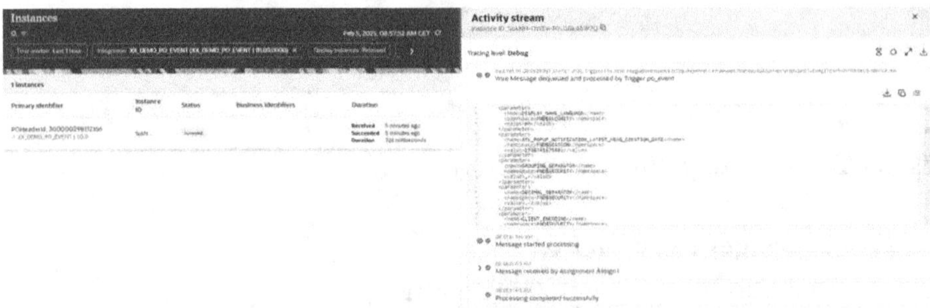

Figure 28-8. *Integration Run Details*

Event Payload Structure

The event payload contains complete purchase order information.

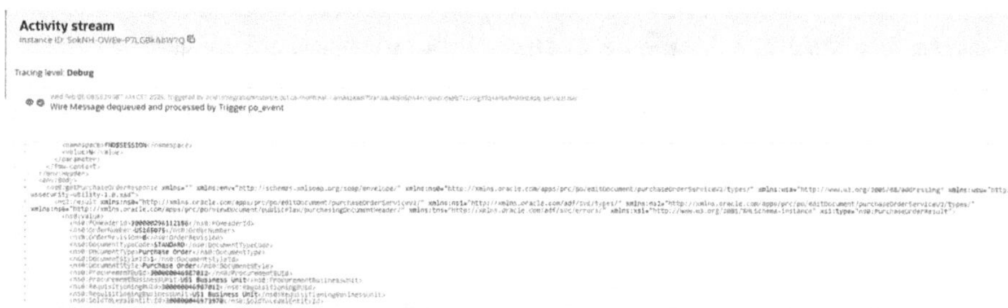

Figure 28-9. *Event Payload Structure*

Integration Actions

With the complete payload, you can implement various actions.

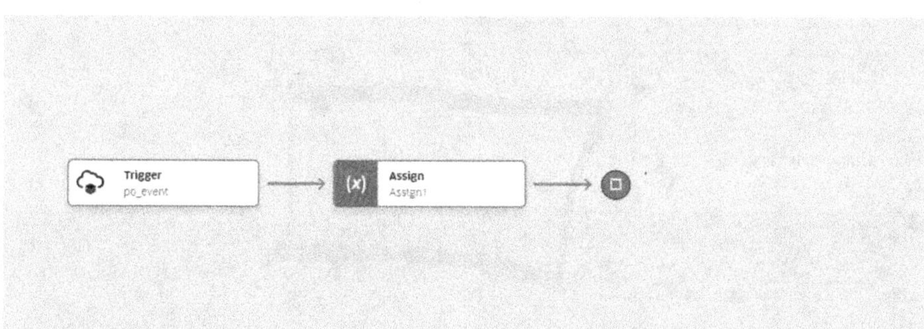

Figure 28-10. *Available Integration Actions*

Common actions include the following:

- Store files in FTP.
- Send notifications.
- Create related documents.
- Update other systems.

Technical Reference

Code Example	Comments
XX_DEMO_PO_EVENT	**Package File**: XX_DEMO_COOKBOOK.par
PO_EVENT_PAYLOAD.xml	Complete event payload sample (available on GitHub)

Payables Invoice Event Implementation

Preparation: Enable Events

Not all Oracle ERP events are active by default. For Payables invoices, enable using this profile option.

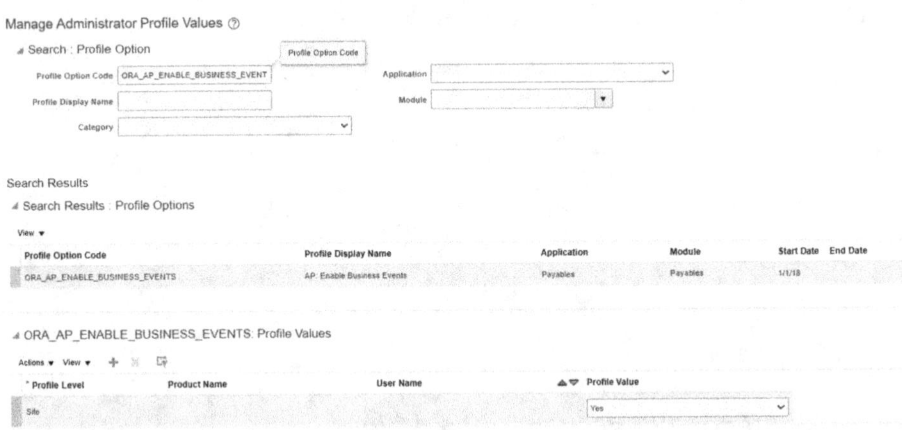

Figure 28-11. *Enable Payables Invoice Events Profile Option*

Integration Setup

Step 1: Create Event-Driven Integration

Then set ERP_Cloud_Connection.

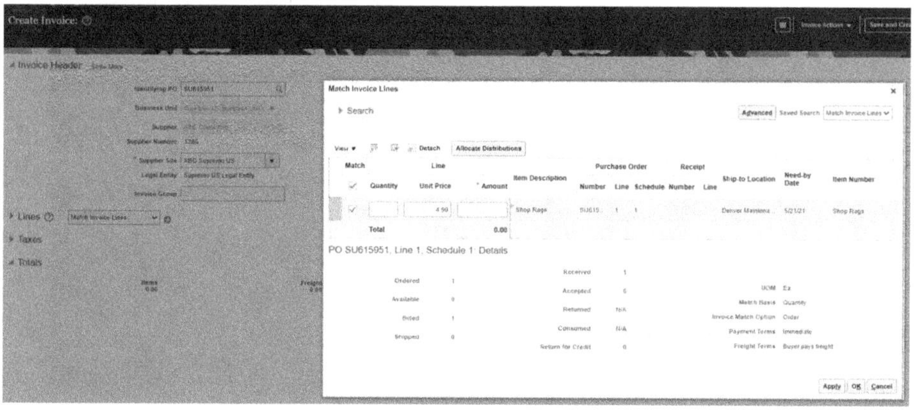

Figure 28-12. *ERP Connection Configuration*

Step 2: Save and Configure

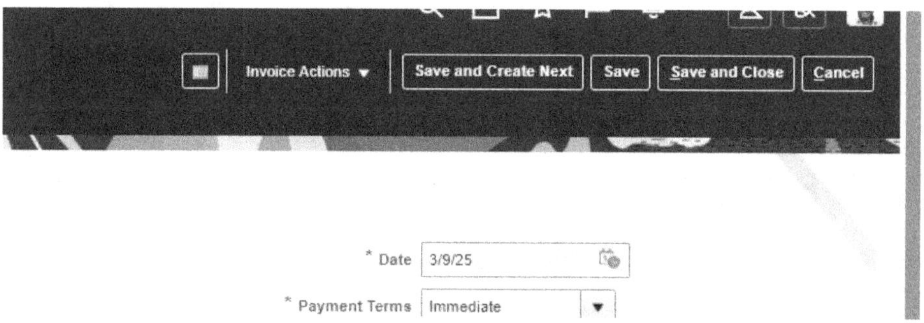

Figure 28-13. *Save Event Configuration*

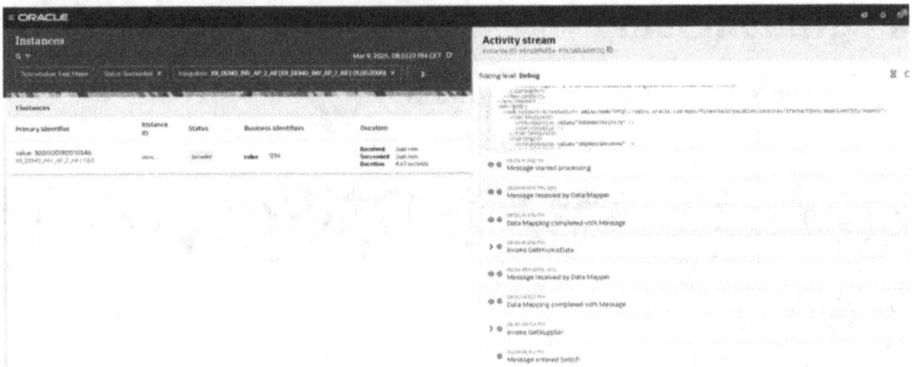

Figure 28-14. *Event Activity Stream*

Integration Overview

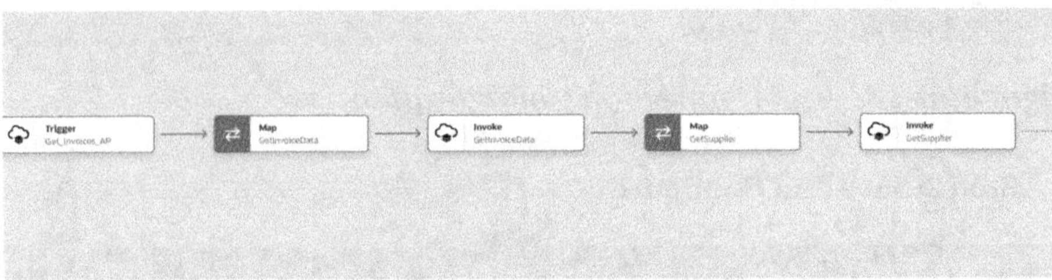

Figure 28-15. *Payables Invoice Event Integration Overview*

Event Payload Information

Step 1: Receive Event Data

Sample Payload Structure:

```
<env:Body>
  <ns0:ApInvoiceCreatedInfo xmlns:ns0="http://xmlns.oracle.com/
  apps/financials/payables/invoices/transactions/model/entity/
  events">
    <ns0:InvoiceId>
      <ns0:newValue value="300000299827479"/>
```

```
  <ns0:oldValue/>
</ns0:InvoiceId>
<ns0:OrgId>
  <ns0:newValue value="300000180010546"/>
  <ns0:oldValue/>
</ns0:OrgId>
<ns0:VendorId>
  <ns0:newValue value="300000075039541"/>
  <ns0:oldValue/>
</ns0:VendorId>
<ns0:VendorSiteId>
  <ns0:newValue value="300000190885035"/>
  <ns0:oldValue/>
</ns0:VendorSiteId>
<ns0:PartyId>
  <ns0:newValue value="300000075039539"/>
  <ns0:oldValue/>
</ns0:PartyId>
<ns0:PartySiteId>
  <ns0:newValue value="300000190884990"/>
  <ns0:oldValue/>
</ns0:PartySiteId>
<ns0:PoHeaderId>
  <ns0:newValue value="300000224842698"/>
  <ns0:oldValue/>
</ns0:PoHeaderId>
<ns0:InvoiceNum>
  <ns0:newValue value="1234"/>
  <ns0:oldValue/>
</ns0:InvoiceNum>
<ns0:InvoiceAmount>
```

```
      <ns0:newValue value="444.00"/>
      <ns0:oldValue/>
    </ns0:InvoiceAmount>
    <ns0:InvoiceCurrencyCode>
      <ns0:newValue value="USD"/>
      <ns0:oldValue/>
    </ns0:InvoiceCurrencyCode>
    <ns0:InvoiceDate>
      <ns0:newValue value="2025-03-09T00:00:00"/>
      <ns0:oldValue/>
    </ns0:InvoiceDate>
    <ns0:InvoiceTypeLookupCode>
      <ns0:newValue value="STANDARD"/>
      <ns0:oldValue/>
    </ns0:InvoiceTypeLookupCode>
  </ns0:ApInvoiceCreatedInfo>
</env:Body>
```

Step 2: Retrieve Invoice Details

Get complete invoice information using the invoice ID.

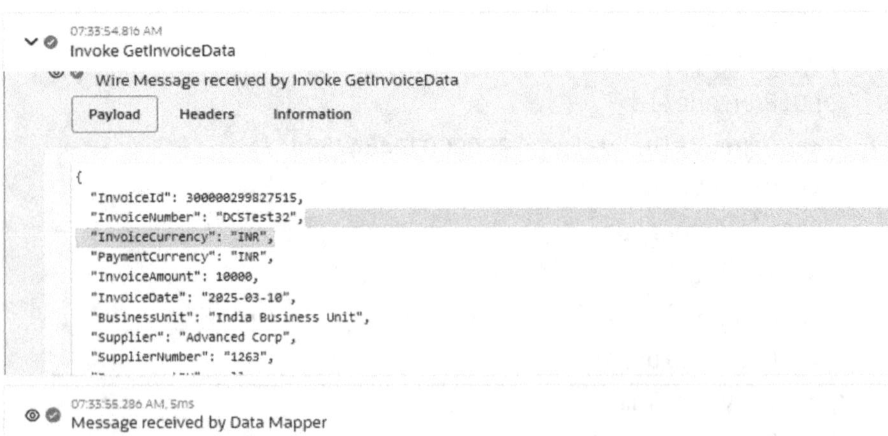

***Figure 28-16.** Retrieve Invoice Details*

Step 3: Retrieve Supplier Details

Get supplier information using the vendor ID.

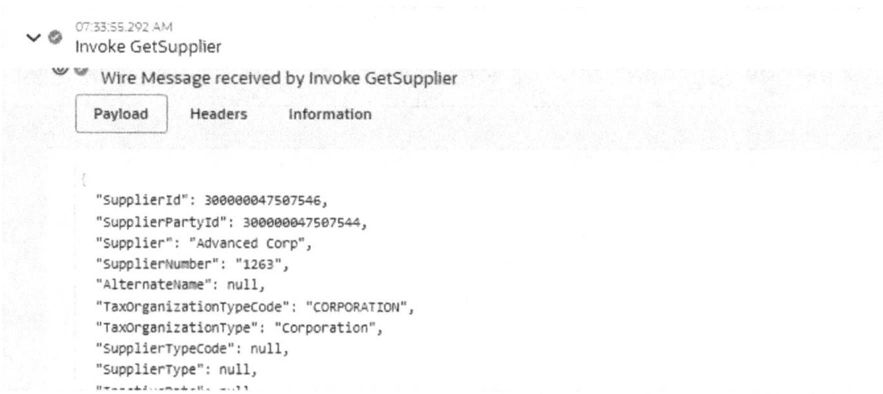

Figure 28-17. *Retrieve Supplier Details*

Step 4: Implement Business Logic

Use the retrieved information for additional actions:

- Create corresponding receivables invoices.
- Send notifications.
- Update external systems.
- Generate reports.

Technical Reference

Code Example	Comments
XX_DEMO_INV_AP_2_AR	**Package File**: XX_DEMO_COOKBOOK_2.par

Receivables Invoice Event Demo

Preparation: Enable Events

Events in Oracle ERP must be enabled for a Payables invoice to use this profile option. **PENDING**

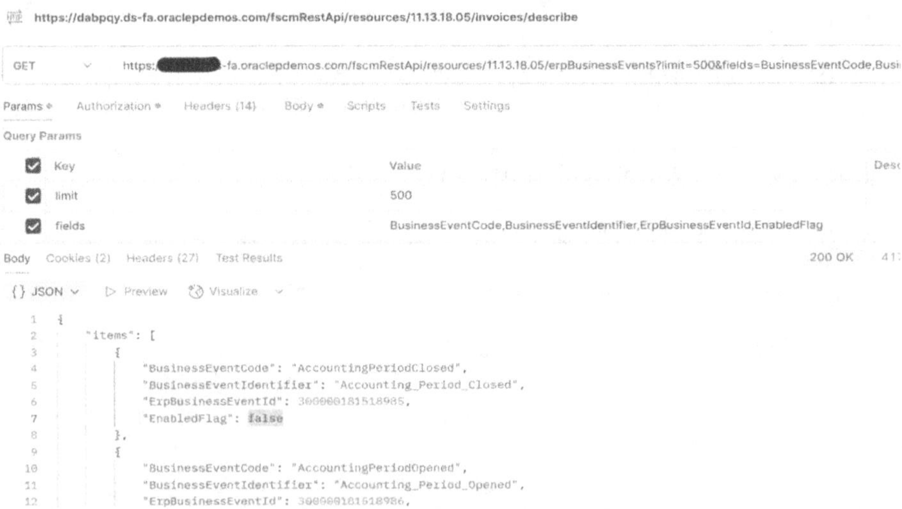

***Figure 28-18.** Configuration for Enabled Flag*

Reference Documentation:

- ERP Business Events API

Available Events:

File: payload_response_events_in_erp.txt


```
{
  "BusinessEventCode": "ReceivablesInvoiceCompleted",
  "BusinessEventIdentifier": "FinArShared_Receivables_Invoice_
  Completed", "ErpBusinessEventId": 100000371405561
},
{
  "BusinessEventCode": "ReceivablesInvoiceIncompleted",
  "BusinessEventIdentifier": "FinArShared_Receivables_Invoice_
  Incompleted", "ErpBusinessEventId": 100000371405562
}
```


Enable Events via PATCH:

Request 1:

```
PATCH
 https://dabpqy.ds-fa.oraclepdemos.com/fscmRestApi/
 resources/11.13.18.05/erpBusinessEvents/100000371405561
{
  "EnabledFlag": true
}
```

Request 2:

```
PATCH
https://dabpqy.ds-fa.oraclepdemos.com/fscmRestApi/
resources/11.13.18.05/erpBusinessEvents/100000371405562

{
  "EnabledFlag": true
}
```

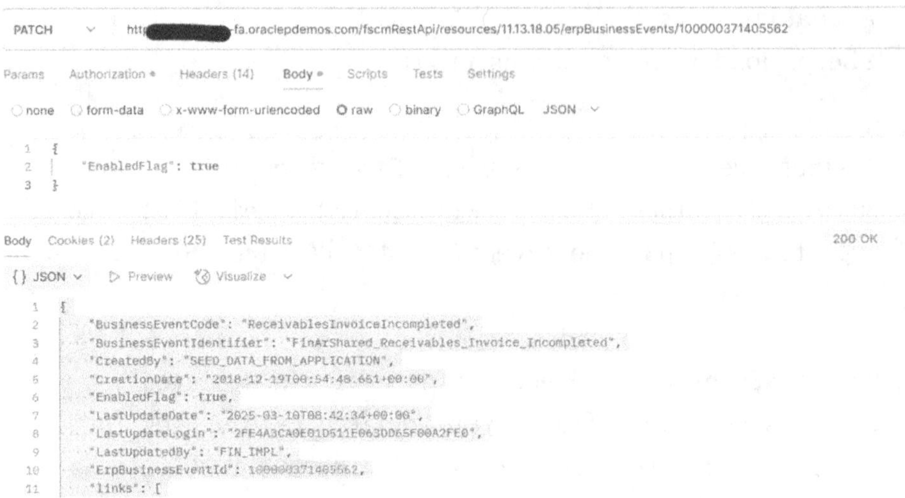

Figure 28-19. Enable Events Using REST API

Integration Configuration

General Overview:

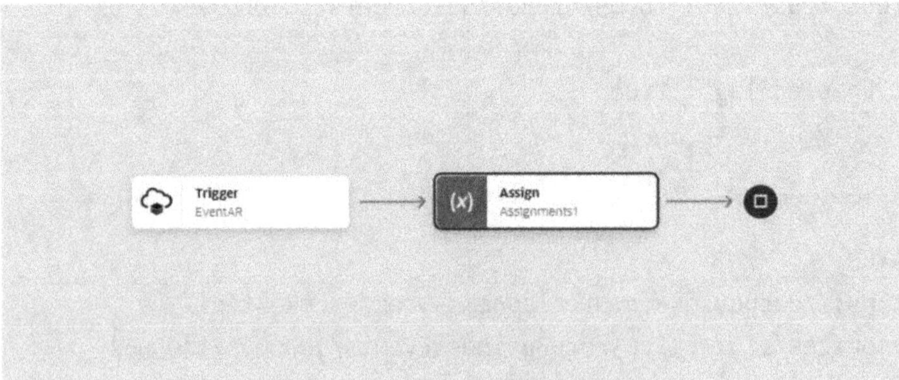

Figure 28-20. Receivables Invoice Event Integration Overview

Connection Setup:

Use “Erp_Cloud_Connection” with the following option.

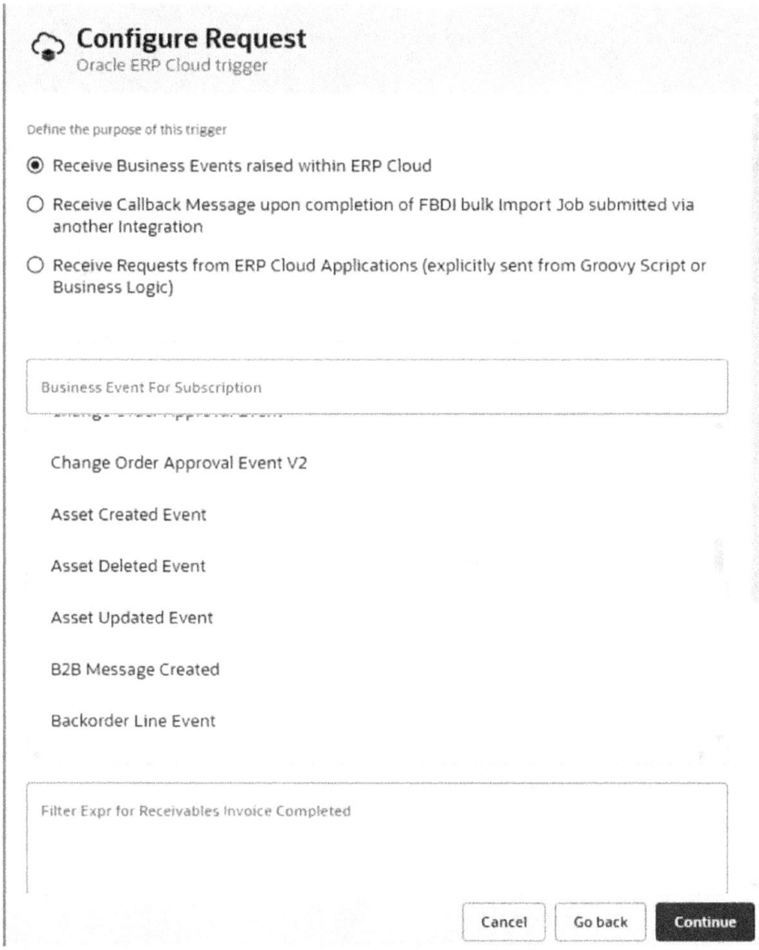

***Figure 28-21.** Event Connection Configuration*

Available Event Data:

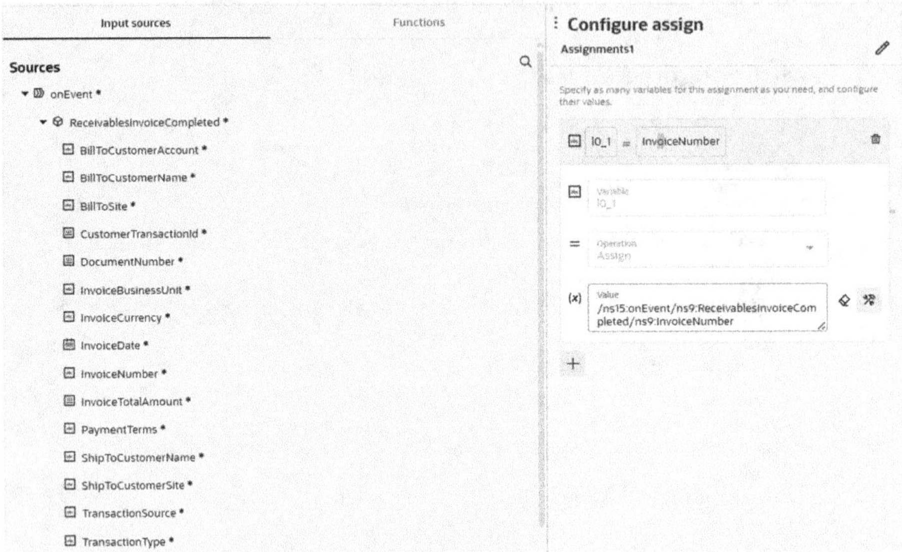

Figure 28-22. Available Event Data Structure

Note Not all transaction information is available directly in the event. Additional REST API calls may be required to retrieve complete details using the provided IDs.

Testing

Complete Invoice in ERP:

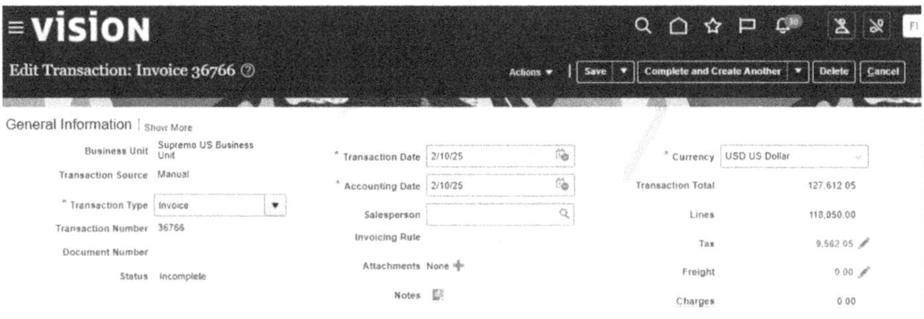

Figure 28-23. *Complete Invoice in Oracle ERP*

After clicking the Complete button, you will receive a confirmation message.

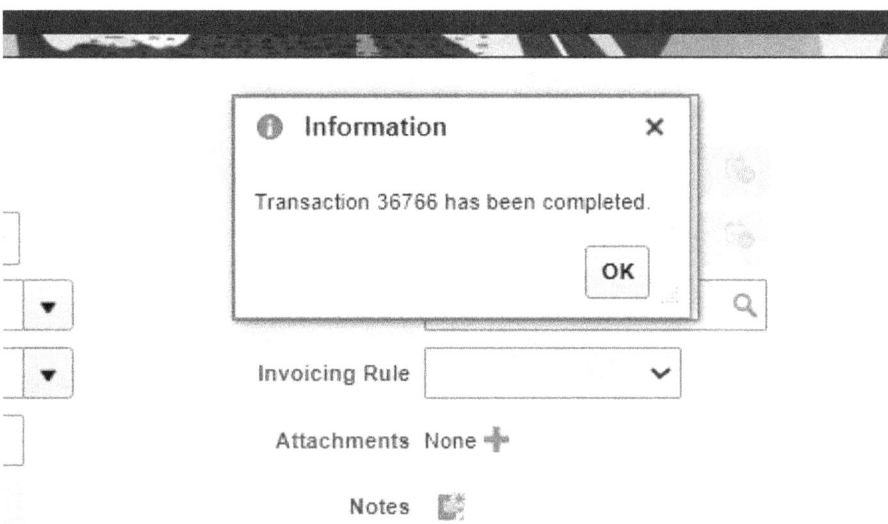

Figure 28-24. *Invoice Completion Confirmation*

Execution Results

After additional testing, check the OIC console for integration runs.

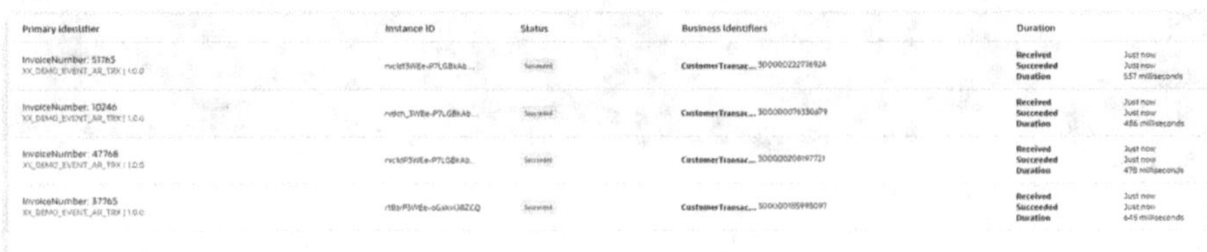

***Figure 28-25.** Integration Execution History in the OIC Console*

Available Event Information

The event provides detailed information for further processing.

```
<env:Body>
  <ns0:ReceivablesInvoiceCompleted xmlns:ns0="http://xmlns.oracle.com/apps/financials/receivables/shared/model/events">
    <ns0:BillToCustomerAccount>60800</ns0:BillToCustomerAccount>
    <ns0:BillToCustomerName>Department of Education</ns0:BillToCustomerName>
    <ns0:BillToSite>Washington</ns0:BillToSite>
    <ns0:CustomerTransactionId>300000222776924</ns0:CustomerTransactionId>
    <ns0:DocumentNumber />
    <ns0:InvoiceBusinessUnit>Progress US Business Unit</ns0:InvoiceBusinessUnit>
    <ns0:InvoiceCurrency>USD</ns0:InvoiceCurrency>
    <ns0:InvoiceDate>2025-02-11</ns0:InvoiceDate>
    <ns0:InvoiceNumber>51765</ns0:InvoiceNumber>
    <ns0:InvoiceTotalAmount>175000</ns0:InvoiceTotalAmount>
    <ns0:PaymentTerms>Net 15</ns0:PaymentTerms>
    <ns0:ShipToCustomerName>Department of Education</ns0:ShipToCustomerName>
    <ns0:ShipToCustomerSite>86896</ns0:ShipToCustomerSite>
    <ns0:TransactionSource>Manual</ns0:TransactionSource>
    <ns0:TransactionType>Invoice</ns0:TransactionType>
  </ns0:ReceivablesInvoiceCompleted>
</env:Body>
</env:Envelope>
```


***Figure 28-26.** Available Event Information for Integration Actions*

This information can be used to implement various business logic:

- Create corresponding documents in other modules.
- Send notifications to stakeholders.
- Update external systems.
- Trigger downstream processes.
- Generate audit trails.

Technical Reference

Code Example	Comments
XX_DEMO_EVENT_AR_TRX	**Package File**: XX_DEMO_COOKBOOK_2.par

CHAPTER 29

Demo with Visual Builder, OIC, FTP, and ATP

Overview

This chapter provides two examples demonstrating how to combine Visual Builder with Oracle Integration Cloud (OIC).

Upload to an FTP Server

Introduction and Goal

This section provides step-by-step instructions to upload files from a Visual Builder page to an FTP server and store them in an ATP database table.

J. J. Montero Rodríguez and S. Tahseen, *Oracle Integration Cookbook for Oracle ERP Cloud*, https://doi.org/10.1007/979-8-8688-3020-4_29

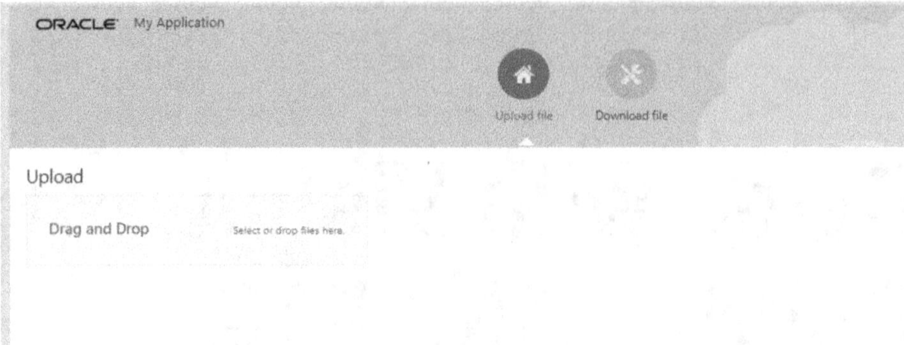

***Figure 29-1.** Visual Builder Upload Interface Showing File Upload Functionality*

Target 1: Send file to FTP server.

***Figure 29-2.** FTP Server Upload Interface*

Target 2: Send file to database as CLOB data type.

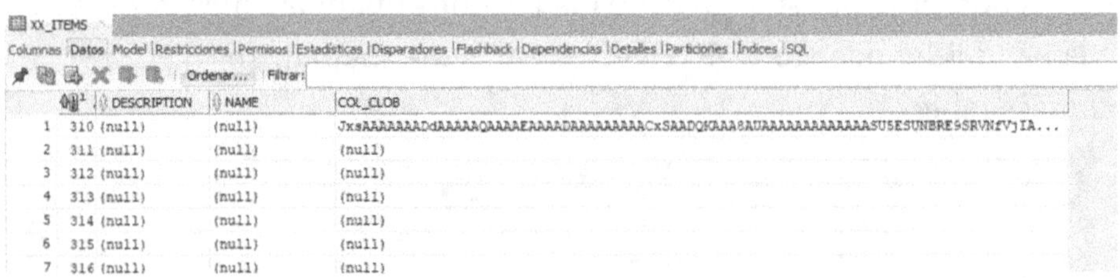

***Figure 29-3.** Database Table Showing CLOB Storage*

Note This is a basic demonstration example for learning purposes. It does not focus on performance optimization or specific production requirements.

Preparatory Steps

You will need the following tools:

- Oracle Integration Cloud (OIC) instance
- FTP server with credentials
- ATP database instance

FTP Server Setup

Ensure you have an FTP server configured with valid credentials.

Figure 29-4. *FTP Server Credentials Configuration*

ATP Database Setup

Configure an ATP database instance. This example uses a personal cloud setup.

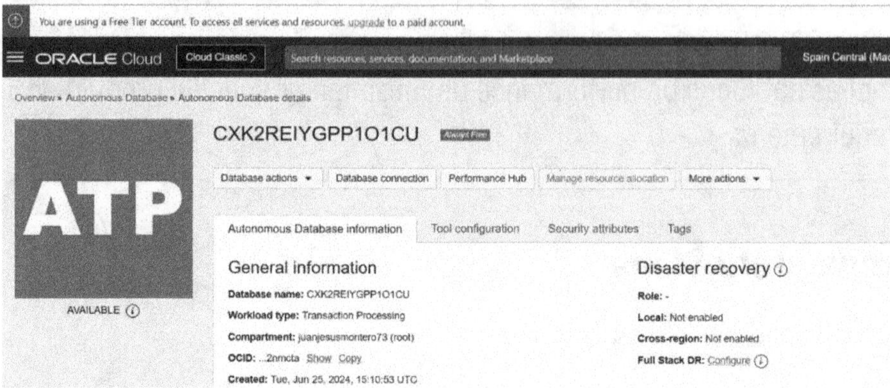

Figure 29-5. *ATP Database Instance Overview*

Database Connection

Create a database connection and table as shown.

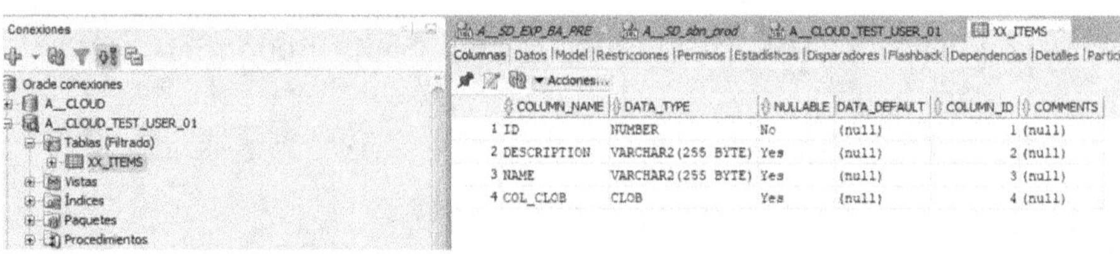

Figure 29-6. *Database Connection Configuration*

Script Reference: 19_sample_0.txt—provided script to create the required table.

Oracle Integration Connections

Configure the following connections in Oracle Integration.

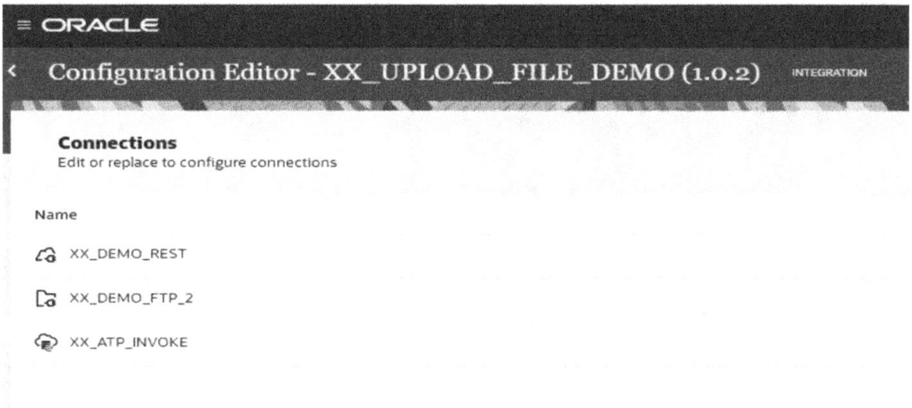

Figure 29-7. Oracle Integration Connections Overview

Refer to Chapter 2 for detailed configuration steps.

Integration Steps

A small integration (code provided) is required to upload files to both the FTP server and database.

High-Level Overview:

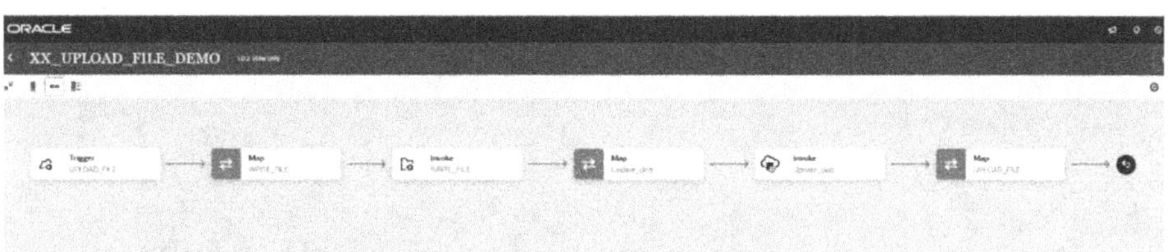

Figure 29-8. Integration Flow Showing the Upload Process

Entry Trigger Configuration:

Configure the entry trigger with Request and Response options activated.

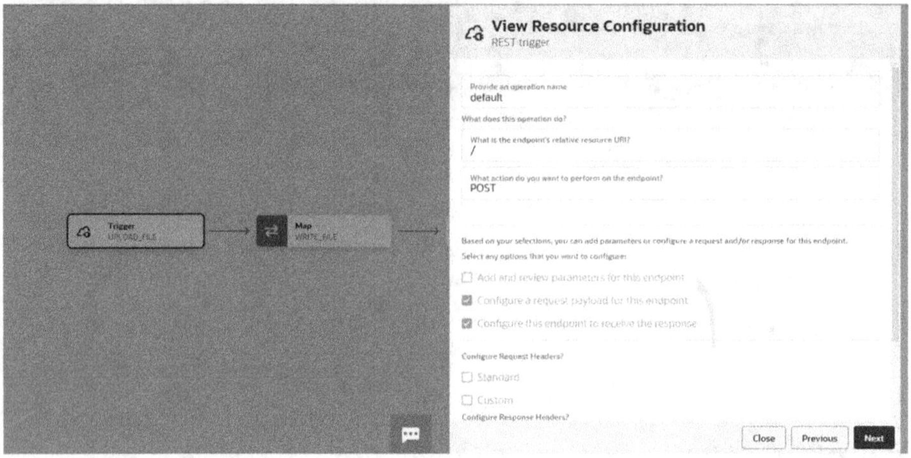

Figure 29-9. Entry Trigger Configuration with Request and Response

Select "multipart/form-data" as shown for request.	These are the parameters for response.
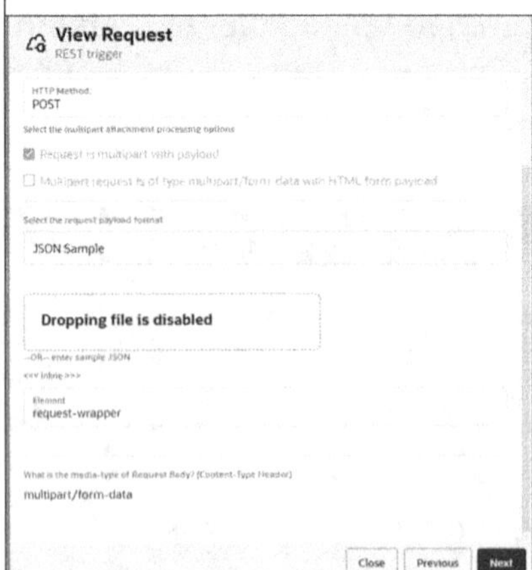	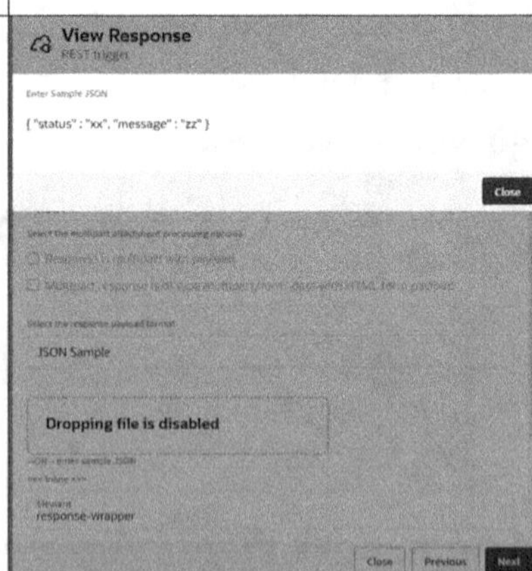

Figure 29-10. REST Trigger multipart/form-data

FTP Server Invoke Activity:

This Invoke activity writes files to the FTP server.

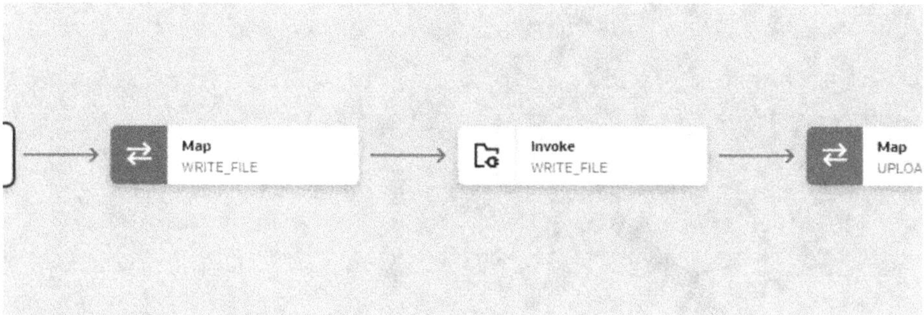

Figure 29-11. *FTP Server Invoke Activity Configuration*

Mapping Configuration:

Configure the mapping as follows.

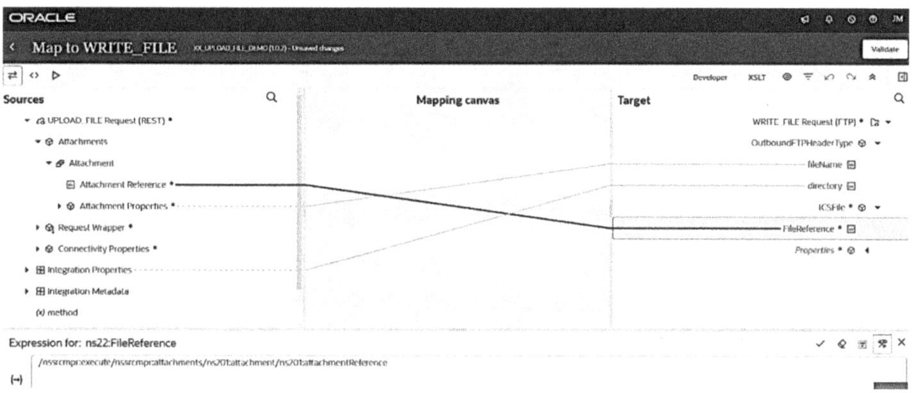

Figure 29-12. *FTP Server Mapping Configuration*

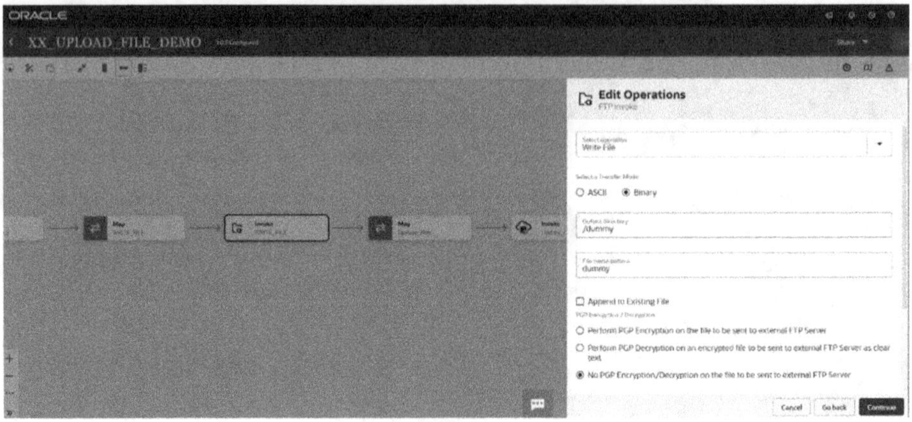

***Figure 29-13.** Detailed View*

Click the **Continue** button to proceed.

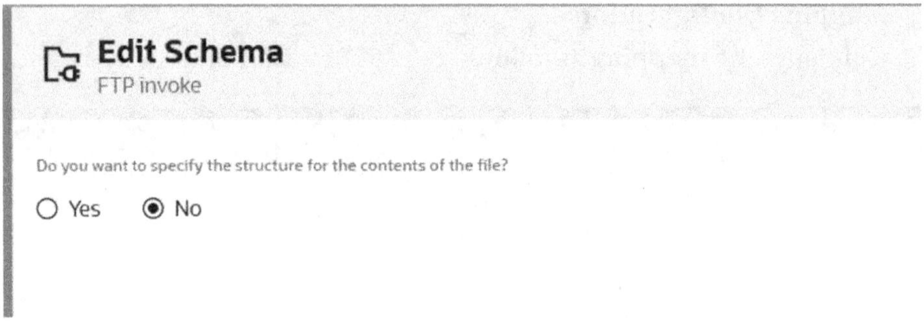

***Figure 29-14.** Continue Button to Proceed with Mapping*

Database Update:

Update a specific row in the table with the Base64 representation of the file. Note: This is a demonstration example only.

Figure 29-15. Database Update Activity

Database Mapping:

Add mapping for the database update. A hardcoded value is used for testing purposes.

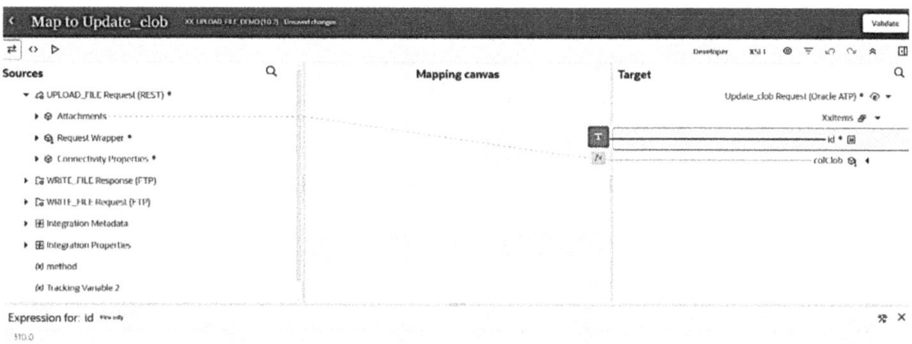

Figure 29-16. Database Mapping Configuration

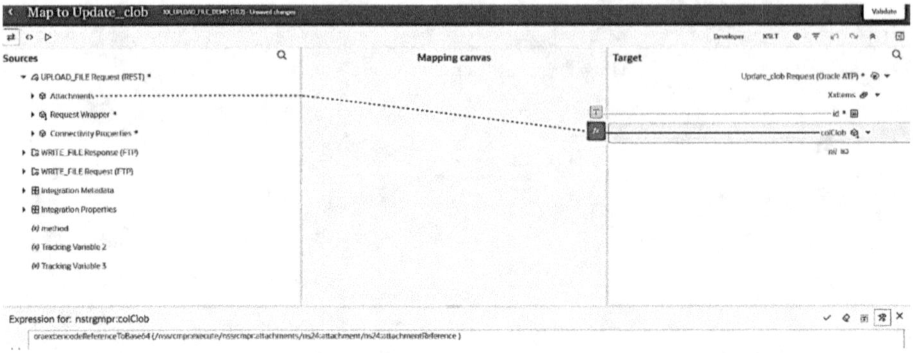

Figure 29-17. *Detailed Database Mapping*

Script Reference: 19_sample_1.txt

```
oraext:encodeReferenceToBase64(/nssrcmpr:execute/
nssrcmpr:attachments/ns24:attachment/ns24:attachmentReference)
```

Select "Update"	Select our table

Figure 29-18. *Update in ATP DB*

Testing from Oracle Integration:

Perform a basic test from the Oracle Integration interface.

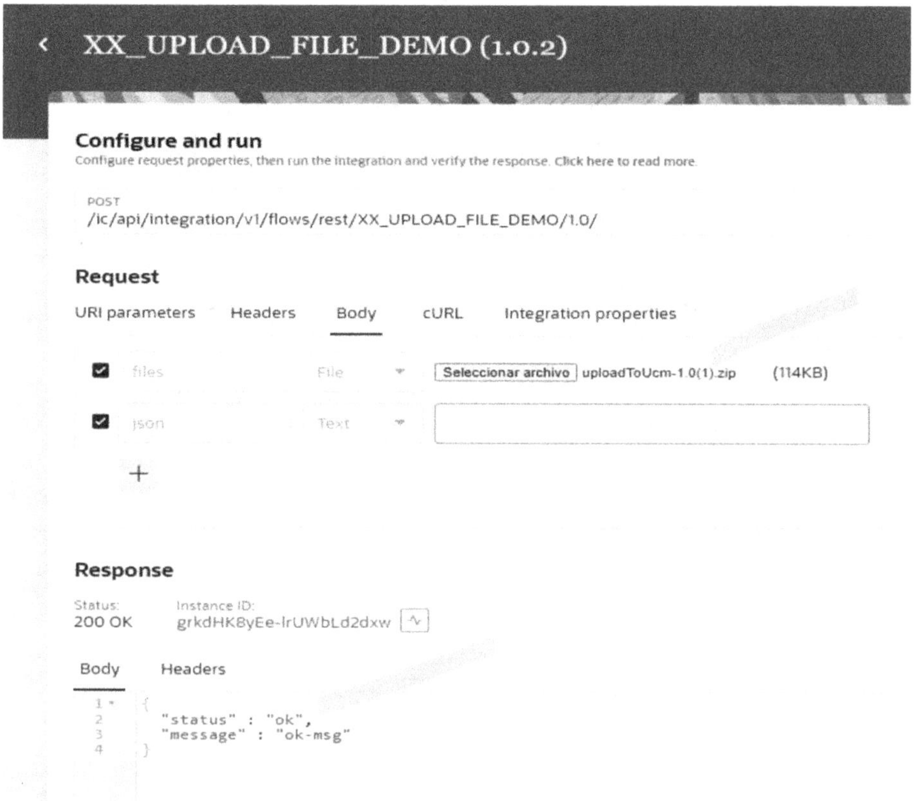

Figure 29-19. Testing Interface in Oracle Integration

FTP Server Result:

Verify the file appears in the FTP server.

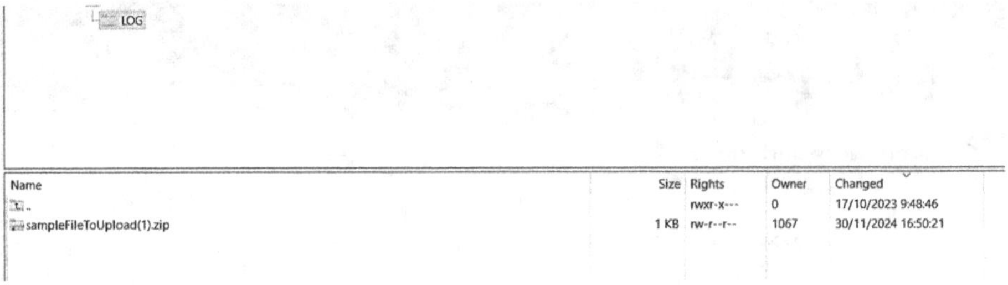

***Figure 29-20.** File Successfully Uploaded to the FTP Server*

Database Result:

Verify the database record with ID=310 has been updated with Base64 data.

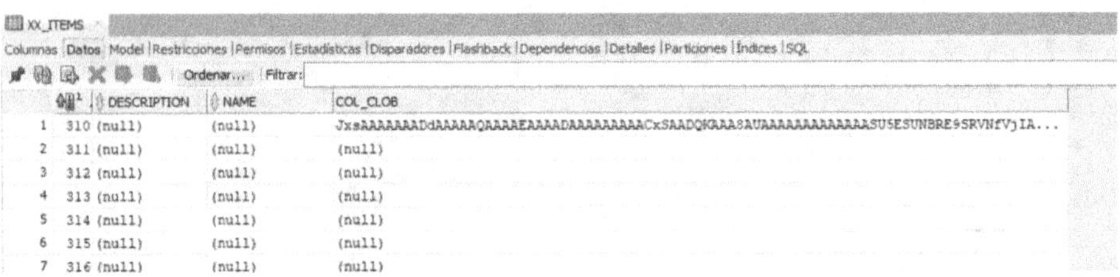

***Figure 29-21.** Database Record Updated with Base64 Data*

Visual Builder Steps

Note Using backends to create connections and access-activated integrations in Oracle Integration is the recommended best practice approach.

At the time of writing, there were intermittent issues in demo instances, requiring connections to be built using "Define by Endpoint".

Warning Use the Define by Endpoint approach for demo purposes only. In production, always use the Backends approach with Delegate Authentication to ensure proper security and credential management.

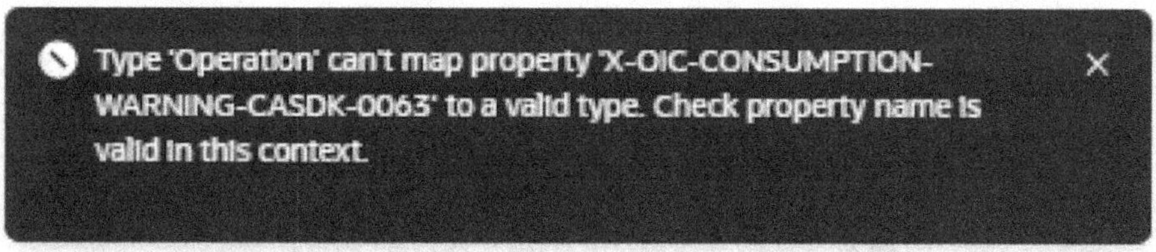

***Figure 29-22.** Define by Endpoint Connection Option*

Connection Configuration:
Build connections using the endpoint approach.

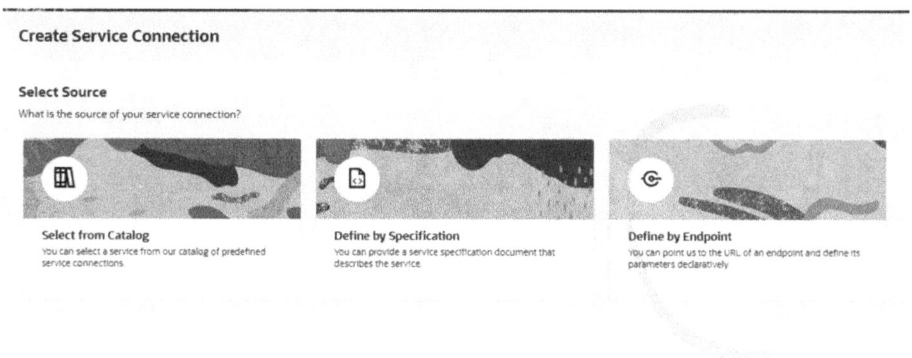

***Figure 29-23.** Connection Configuration Using Define by Endpoint*

OIC URL Configuration:

Retrieve the OIC URL from the integration details.

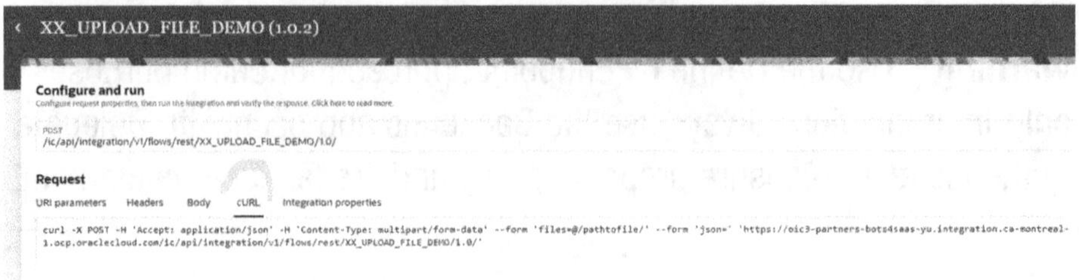

Figure 29-24. Location of OIC URL in Integration Details

URL Format:

`https://oic3-xxxx-redwood_demo-1.ocp.oraclecloud.com/ic/api/integration/v1/flows/rest/XX_UPLOAD_FILE_DEMO/1.0/`

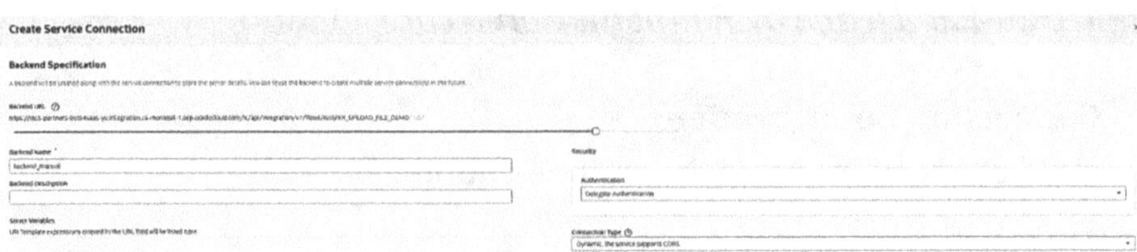

Figure 29-25. Configuring the OIC URL

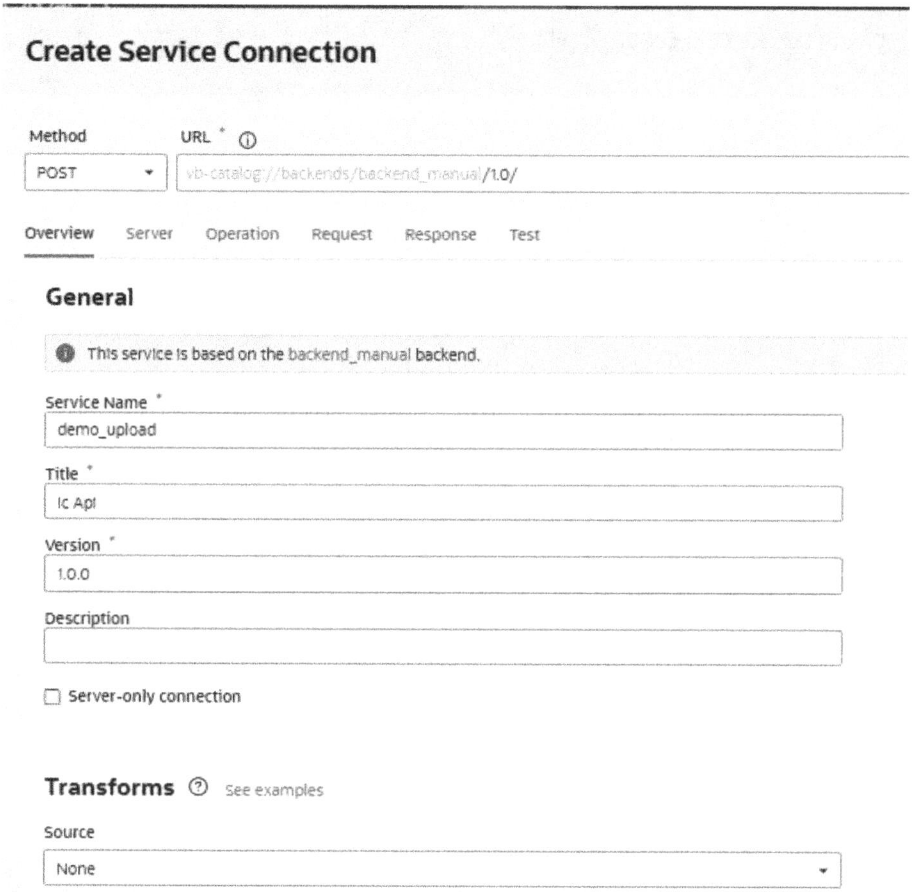

Figure 29-26. *Connection Parameter Configuration*

Important Set **Form-Data** in the request body.

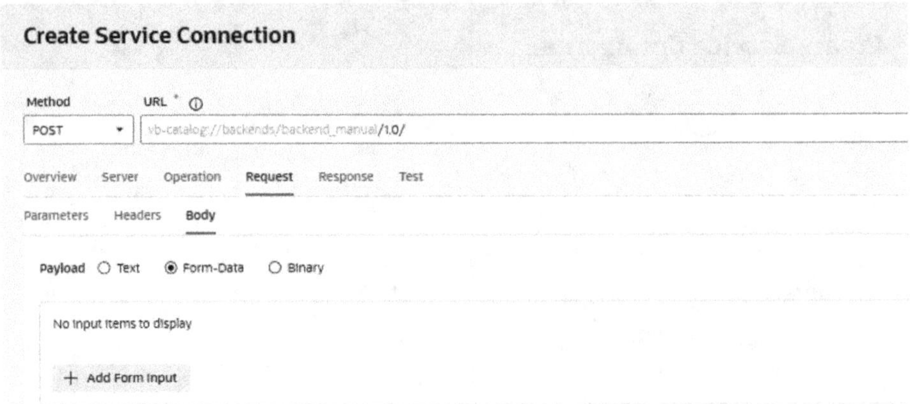

Figure 29-27. *Setting Form-Data in the Request Body*

Response Payload:

Configure the response payload using a JSON sample.

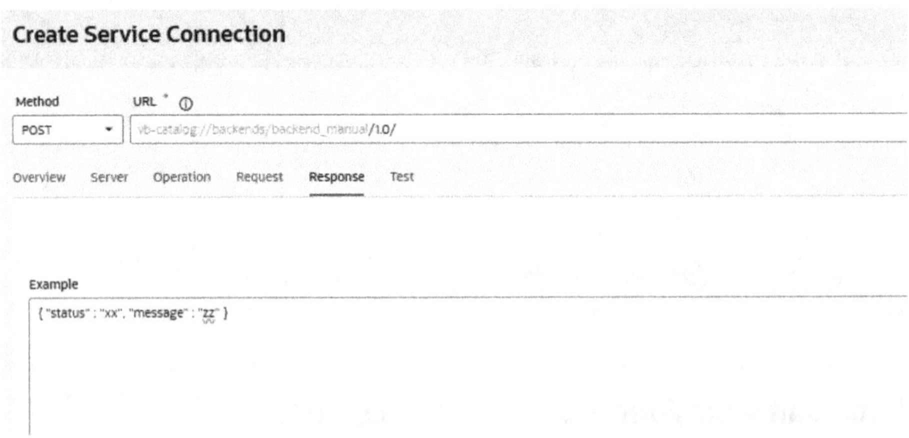

Figure 29-28. *Response Payload Configuration with a JSON Sample*

Page Components:

Drop a File Picker component onto the page.

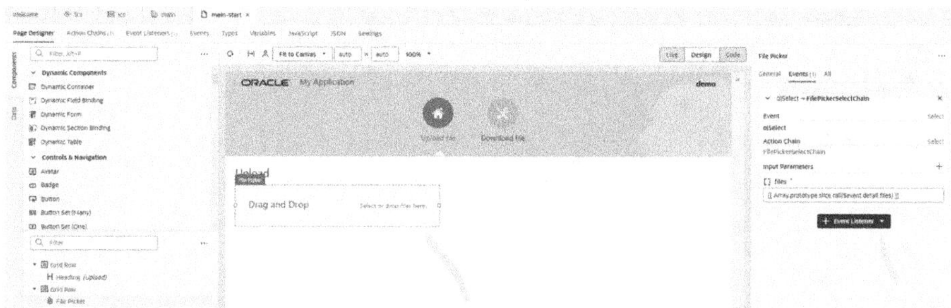

***Figure 29-29.** File Picker Component in Visual Builder*

Action Chain:

Add a linked Action Chain.

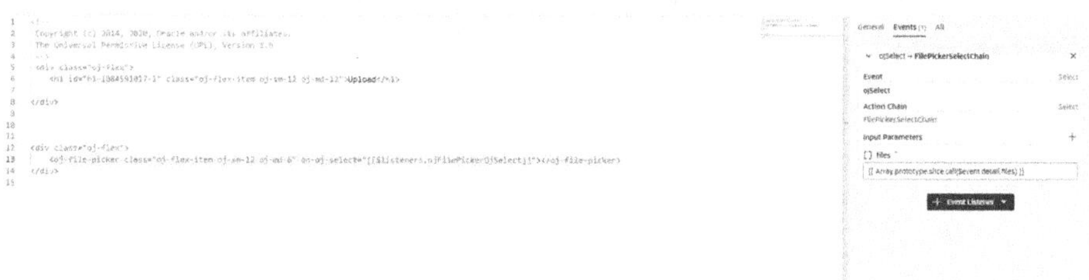

***Figure 29-30.** Action Chain Linked to File Picker*

Parameter Configuration:

Parameter to Send:

[[Array.prototype.slice.call($event.detail.files)]]

Action Chain Code:

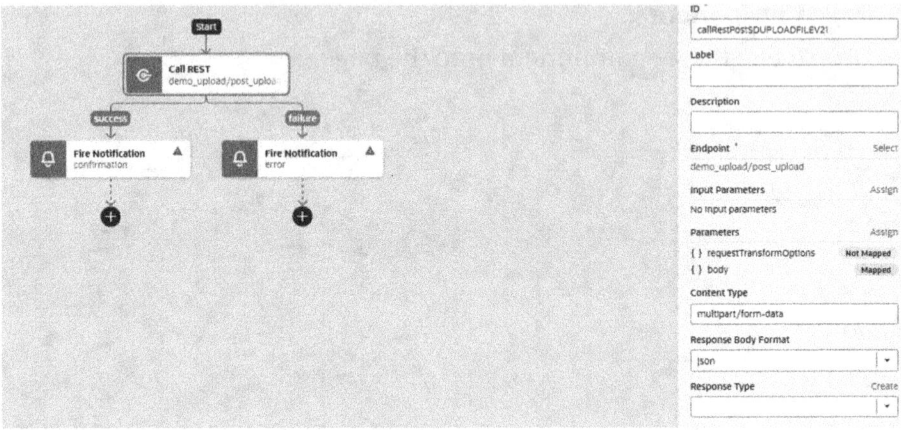

Figure 29-31. *Action Chain Flow Configuration*

Mapping:

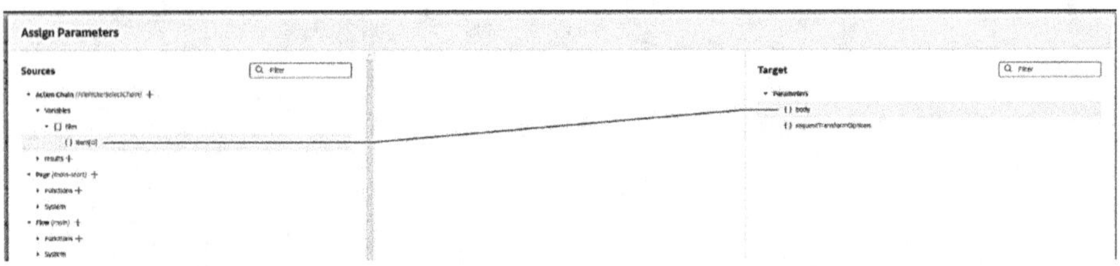

Figure 29-32. *Action Chain Mapping Configuration*

Conclusion

After testing, the file will be successfully uploaded to both the FTP server and the database.

Download from an FTP Server Demo

Introduction and Goal

This section demonstrates how to download files from an FTP server to a client machine using a Visual Builder page.

Figure 29-33. *Visual Builder Download Interface*

When clicking the **Download** button, the file will be downloaded to the local drive.

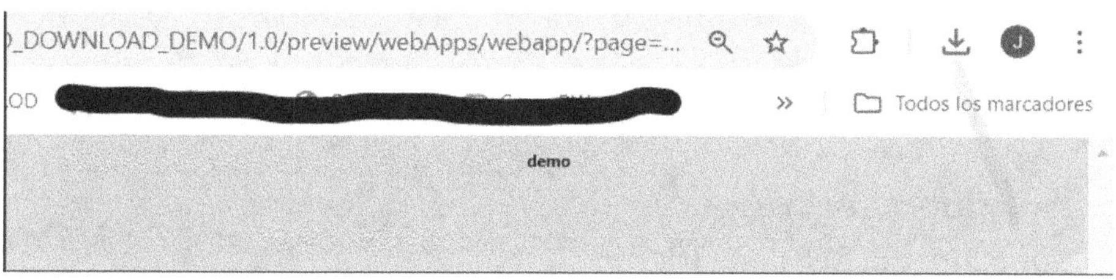

Figure 29-34. *File Download in Progress*

Figure 29-35. *File Successfully Downloaded*

Preparatory Steps

Use the FTP server and Oracle Integration connections from the "Upload to an FTP Server" section.

Oracle Integration Steps

Integration for Download:

Create an integration to download files from the FTP server.

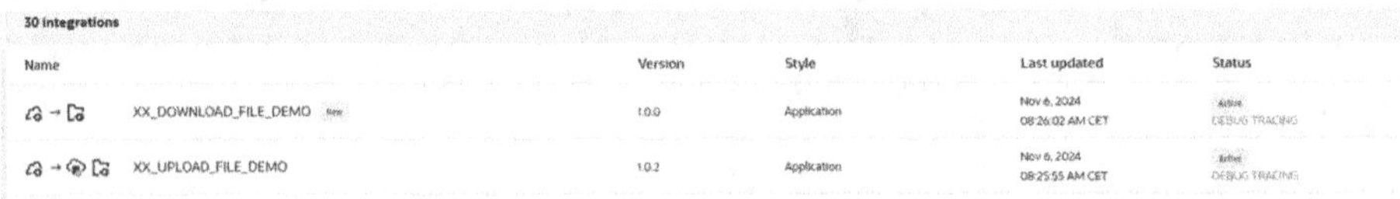

Figure 29-36. *Download Integration Overview*

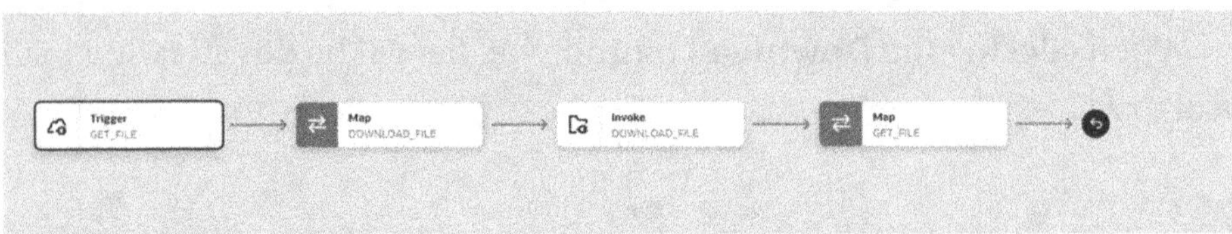

Figure 29-37. *Download Integration Flow*

Entry REST API Trigger:

Configure the REST API trigger.

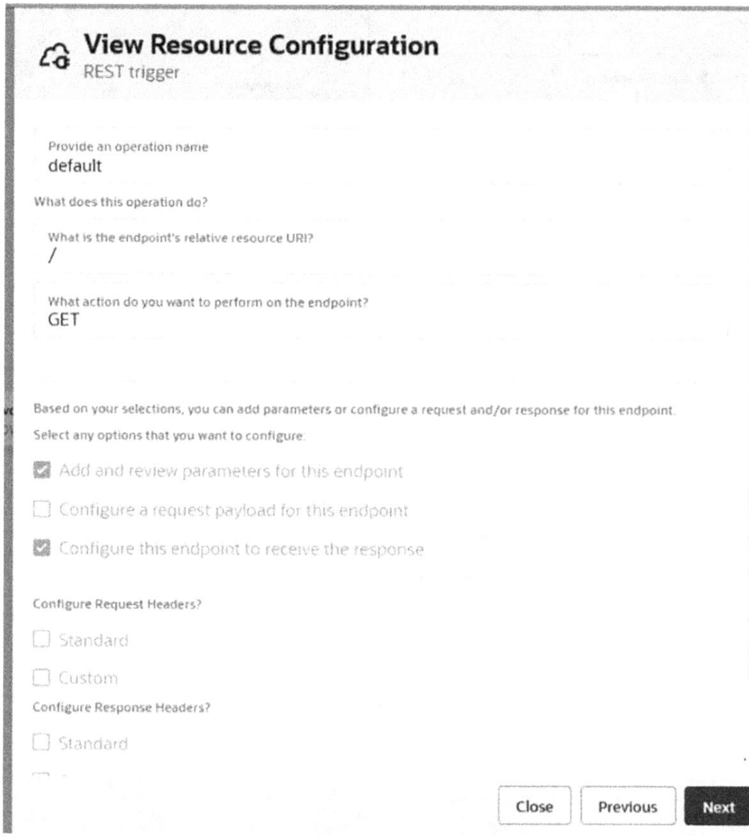

***Figure 29-38.** REST API Trigger Configuration*

Parameters:

Configure parameters as shown.

Parameters.	Click Next.
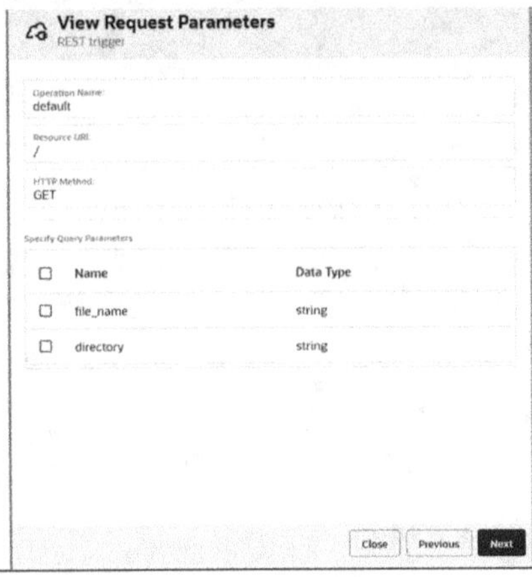	

Figure 29-39. REST Trigger Parameter Configuration

Read-Download File Invoke:

Configure the Invoke activity to read and download the file.

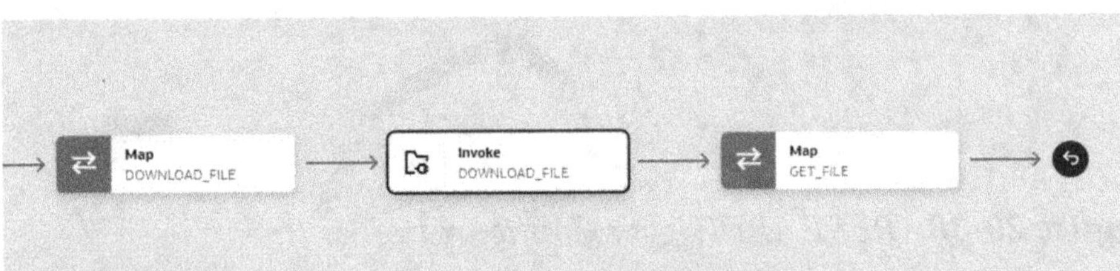

Figure 29-40. Read-Download Invoke Activity

Invoke Definition:

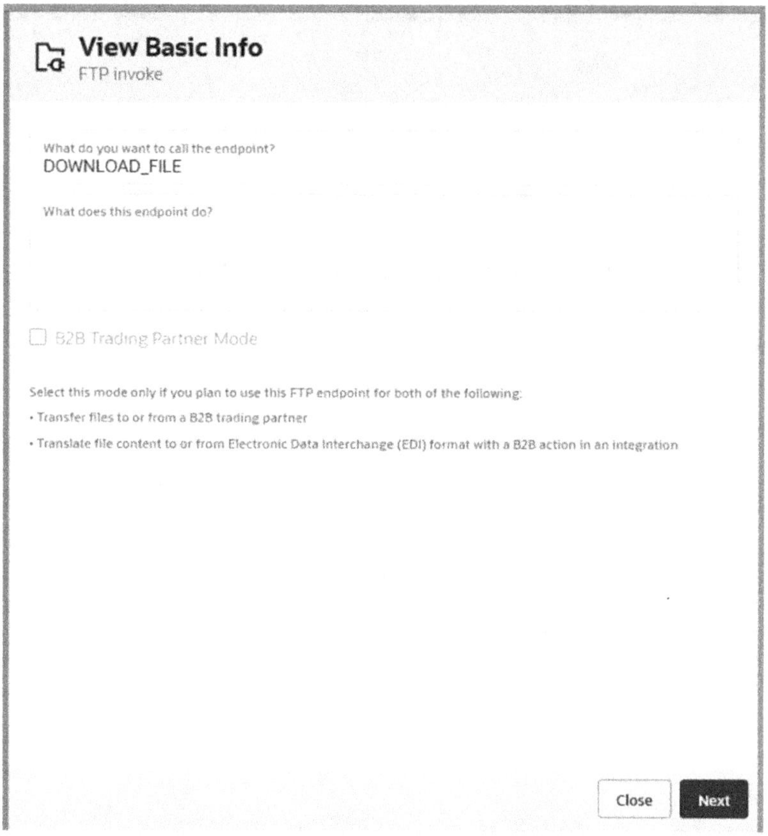

***Figure 29-41.** Invoke Activity Definition*

Click **Next** to continue.

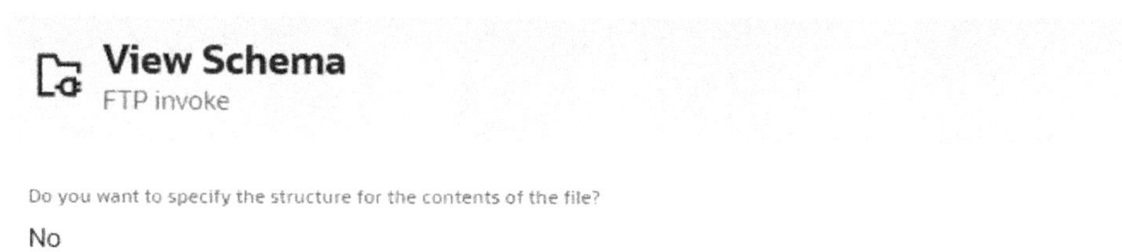

***Figure 29-42.** FTP Invoke Activity*

Read-Download Mapping:

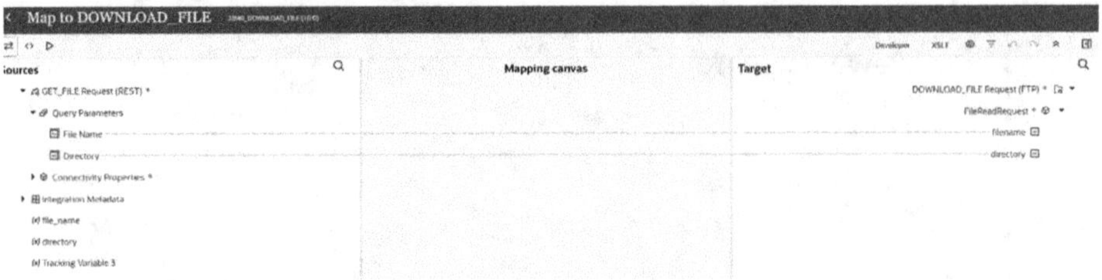

Figure 29-43. Mapping for Read–Download Activity

Final Mapping:

Map the return values.

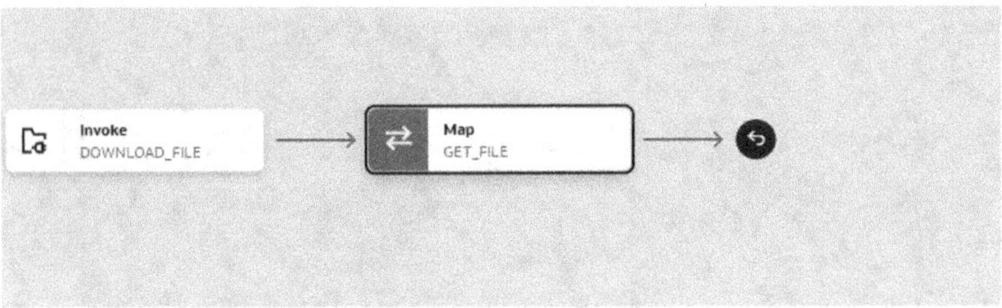

Figure 29-44. Final Mapping to Return Values

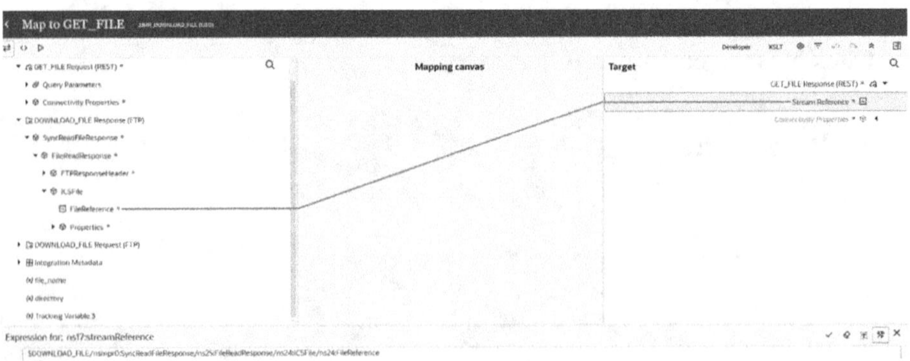

Figure 29-45. Detailed Return Value Mapping

Testing:

Test the integration.

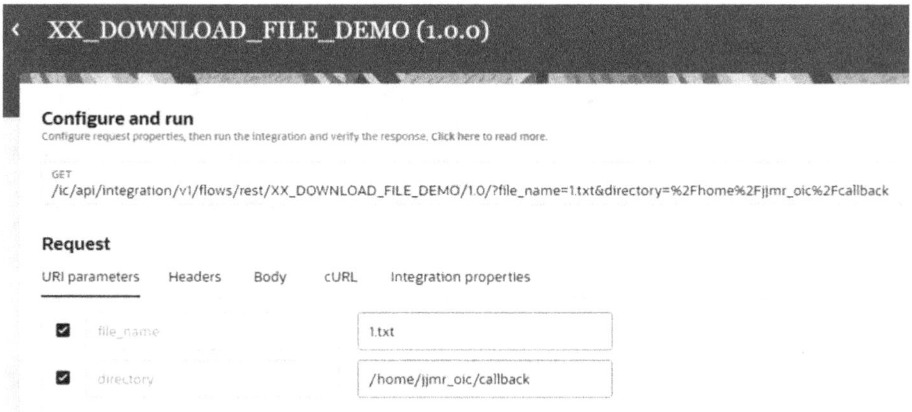

Figure 29-46. *Testing the Download Integration*

Visual Builder Steps

Note Using backends to create connections and access-activated integrations in Oracle Integration is the recommended best practice approach.

At the time of writing, there were intermittent issues in demo instances, requiring manual connection setup.

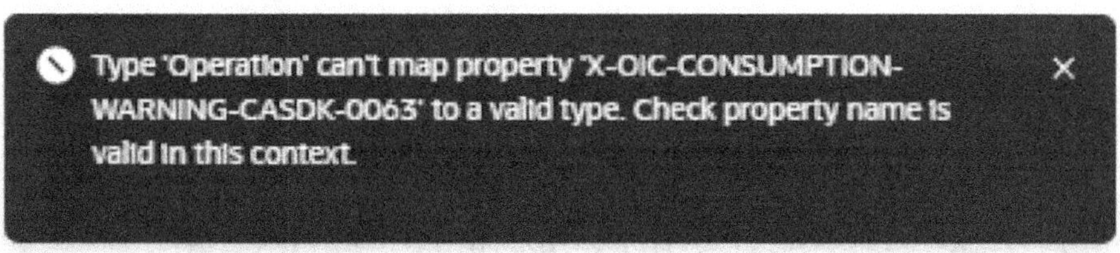

Figure 29-47. *Manual Connection Setup Option*

Build connections using "Define by Endpoint".

Figure 29-48. *Building Connections with Define by Endpoint*

Copy URL from Oracle Integration:

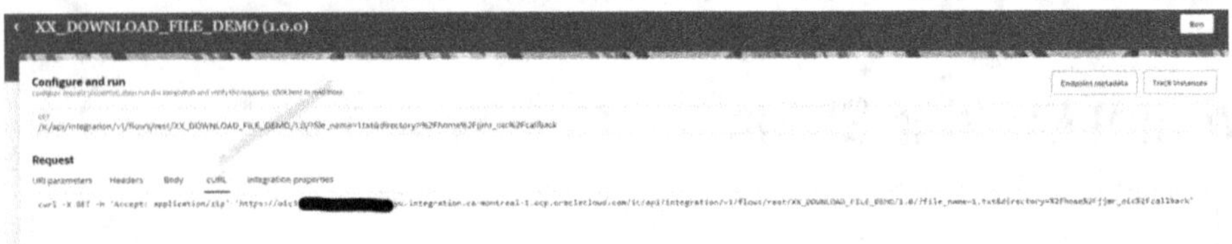

Figure 29-49. *Copying URL from Oracle Integration*

Paste URL:

Paste the URL in the connection configuration.

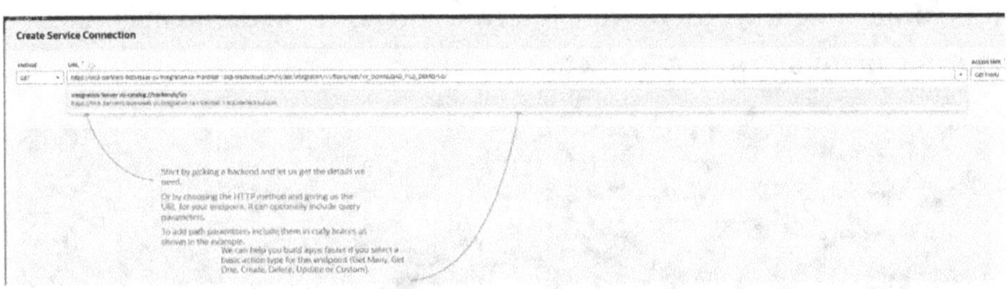

Figure 29-50. *Pasting URL in Connection Configuration*

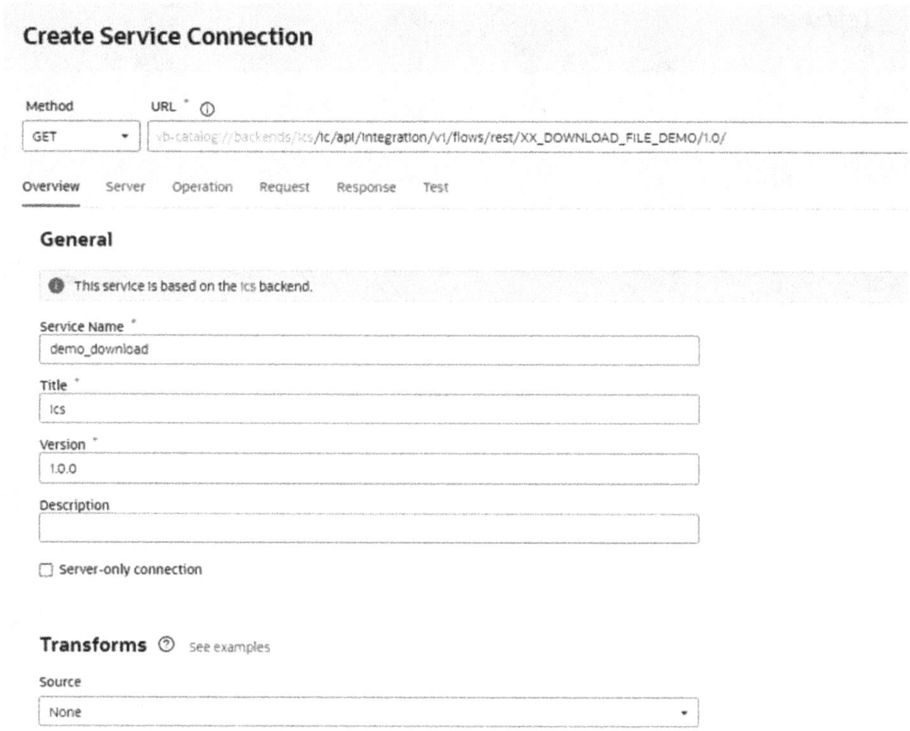

Figure 29-51. *Connection Configuration Details*

Add Parameters:

Add parameters as shown.

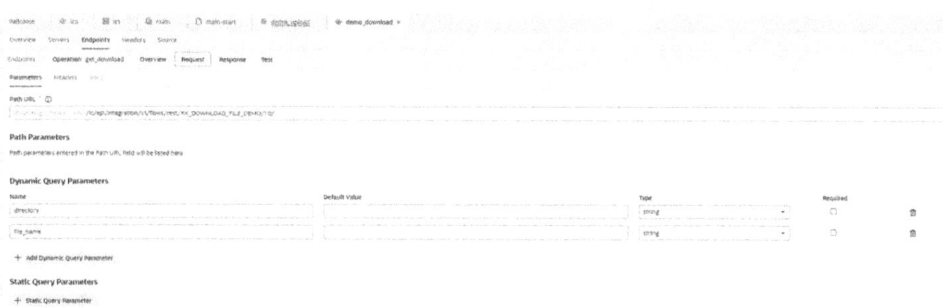

Figure 29-52. *Adding Parameters to the Connection*

Testing:

***Figure 29-53.** Testing the Connection*

JavaScript Code:

Add the following JavaScript code.

Script Reference: 19_sample_2.txt

```
/**
  Copyright (c) 2018, Oracle and/or its affiliates.
  The Universal Permissive License (UPL), Version 1.0
*/

define([], function() {
  'use strict';

  var PageModule = function PageModule() {};
  PageModule.prototype.download = function(fileName,
  specFileContent) {
    // console.log(specFileContent)
    var a = document.createElement("a");
    a.href = specFileContent;
    a.download = fileName;
    a.click(); // Downloaded file
  };
  return PageModule;
});
```

***Figure 29-54.** JavaScript Code in Page Module*

Action Chain Code:

***Figure 29-55.** Action Chain Configuration for Download*

Mapping Configuration:

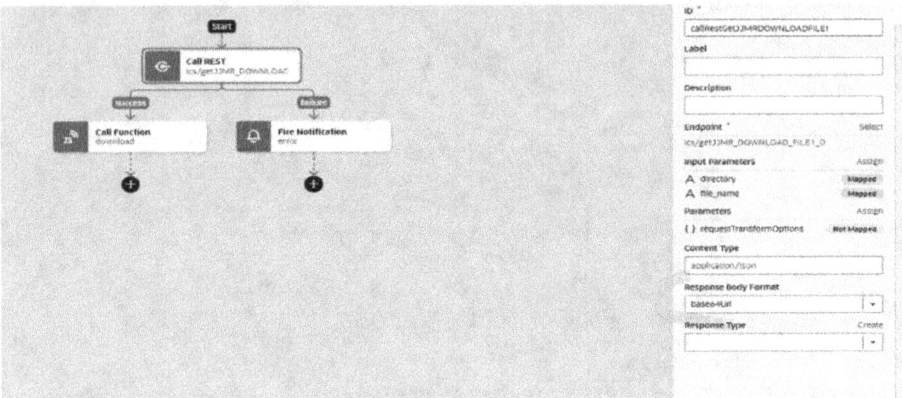

***Figure 29-56.** Mapping Configuration for Download Action*

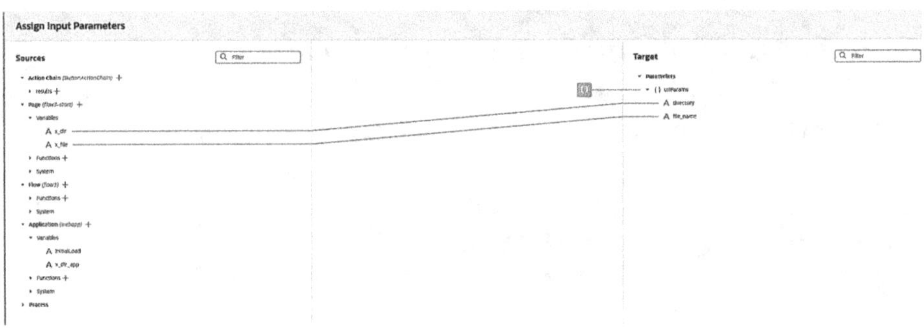

***Figure 29-57.** Detailed Download Mapping*

Conclusion

You can now successfully download files from an FTP server to your local drive using a Visual Builder page.

Technical Reference

Code Example	Comments
XX_UPLOAD_FILE_DEMO_01.iar	Integration for learning purposes to upload files to FTP. **Package File**: XX_DEMO_COOKBOOK.par
XX_DOWNLOAD_FILE_DEMO_01.iar	Integration for learning purposes to download files from FTP. **Package File**: XX_DEMO_COOKBOOK.par
19_UPLOAD_DOWNLOAD_DEMO-1.0.zip	Visual Builder application demo for learning purposes to upload/download files to/from FTP
19_Satish_Kumar_UPLOAD_UCM-1.0.zip	Visual Builder demo for learning purposes to upload files to UCM. Example provided by Satish Kumar
19_sampleFileToUpload.zip	Sample file for testing previous applications

CHAPTER 30

Massive Loads and Deletes in Visual Builder Business Objects: REST API Batch

This chapter explains how to load and delete data from Visual Builder Business Objects using batch operations for improved performance.

Overview

This chapter provides three integrations:

1. Integration to read a file from an FTP server and load into a VB Business Object using a single insert approach

J. J. Montero Rodríguez and S. Tahseen, *Oracle Integration Cookbook for Oracle ERP Cloud*,
https://doi.org/10.1007/979-8-8688-3020-4_30

2. The same process using batch approach for massive loads, utilizing REST API batch functionality

3. Integration to batch-delete from a VB Business Object using REST API batch approach

Not all OIC developers are familiar with **batch** REST calls. This chapter introduces this feature, which provides significantly better performance compared with individual REST calls.

Reference:

- Batch Requests in VBCS
- Perform Batch Actions

Key Implementation Details

One critical requirement for batch operations is using the following HTTP Header:

Content-Type: "application/vnd.oracle.adf.batch+json"

The sample payloads used in batch calls must follow a specific format. See detailed examples below.

Connections

Figure 30-1. *Required Connections for Batch Operations*

Preparation

Import the provided Visual Builder application and refer to Chapter 2 for detailed setup information.

The application is provided as a draft with Business Objects configured.

Note The pages in the provided application are not the primary focus of this exercise. They are work-in-progress and can be customized as needed.

Integration 1: XX_DEMO_FTP_2_DB_VB_SINGLE

General Overview

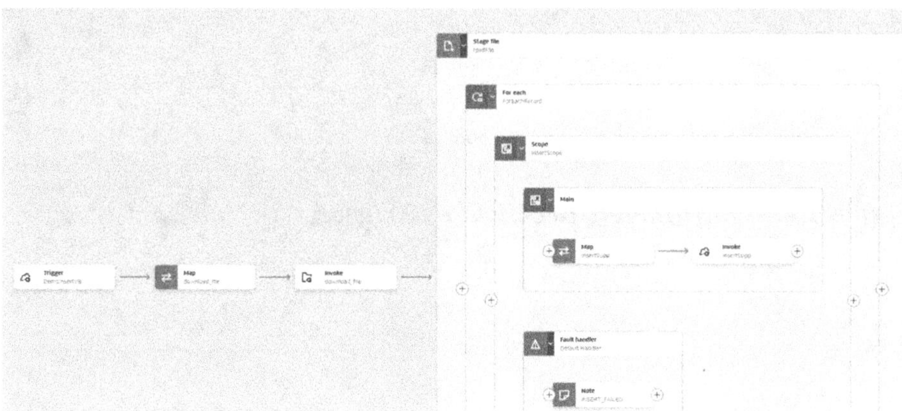

Figure 30-2. Integration Overview for a Single Insert Approach

Setup

Parameters Received by Trigger:

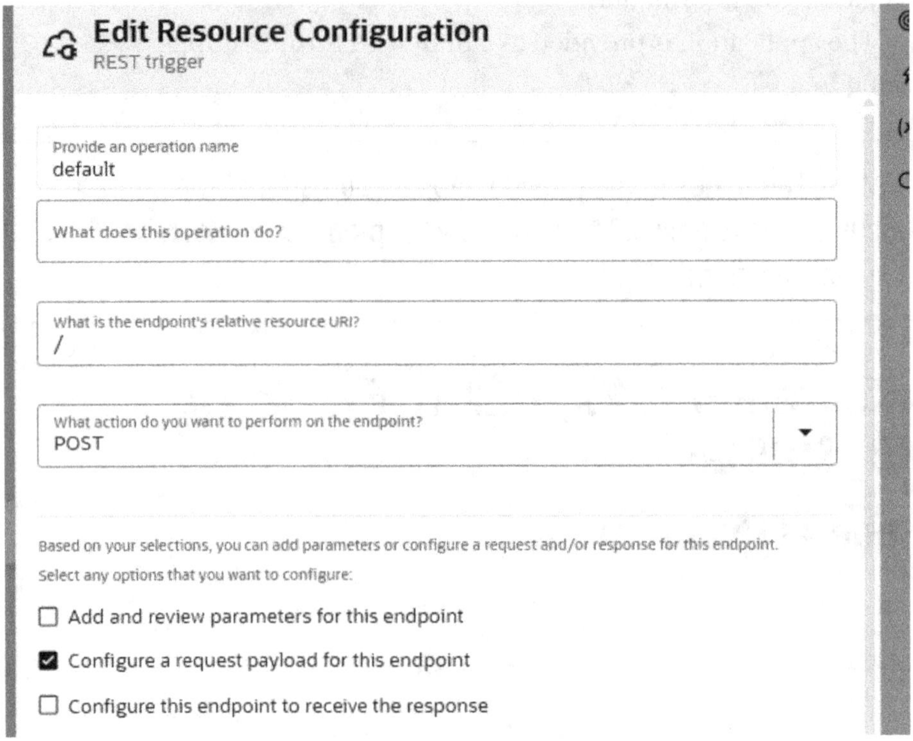

Figure 30-3. *Parameters Received by Trigger*

Request Payload Sample:

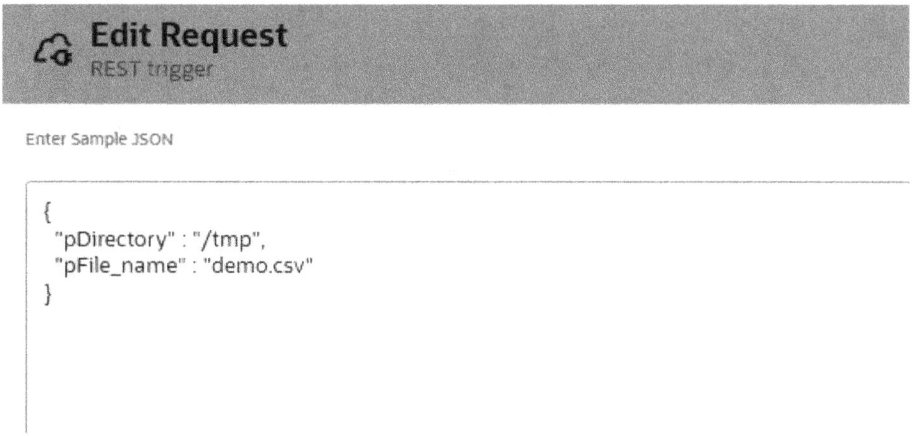

Figure 30-4. *Sample Request Payload*

Download File Activity:

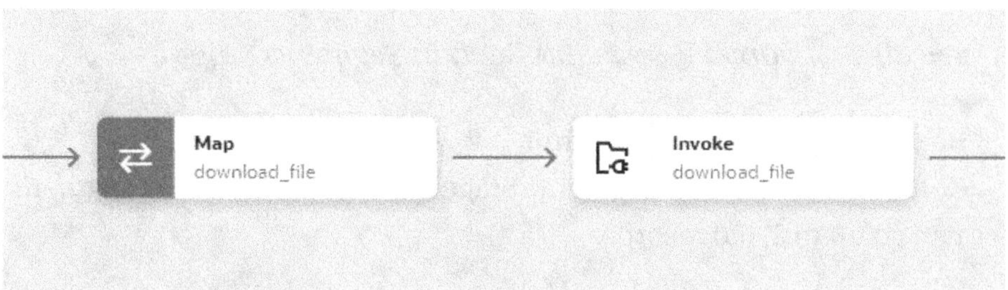

Figure 30-5. *Download File Activity Configuration*

Loop to Insert with Read in Segments:

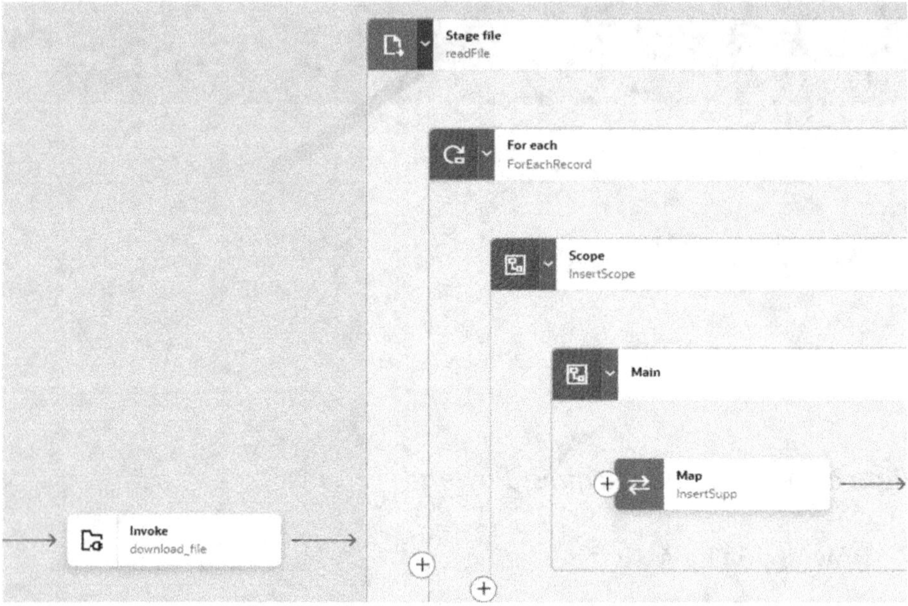

Figure 30-6. *Loop to Insert with Read in Segments Stage*

Read in Segments Stage Setup:

Configure the Read in Segments Stage activity. Note that the segment size can go up to 2,000 records.

Note In Gen2, this was a hardcoded value of 200.

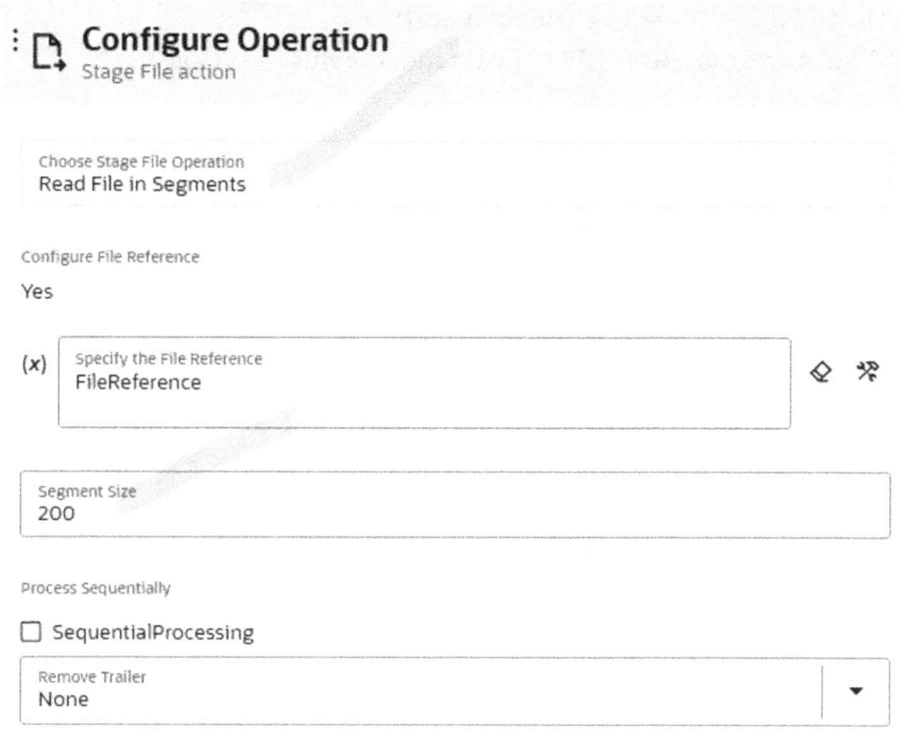

***Figure 30-7.** Read in Segments Stage Configuration*

REST API for Business Object Insert:

Use the regular REST API to insert into the Business Object.

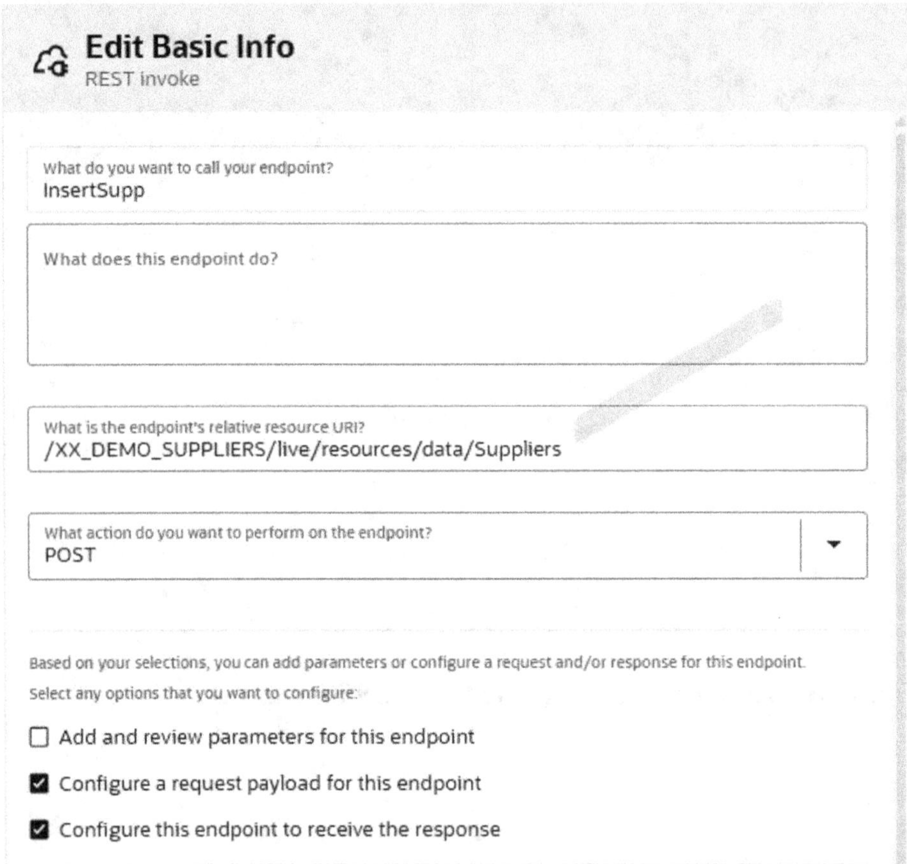

Figure 30-8. *REST API Configuration for Insert*

Sample Request:

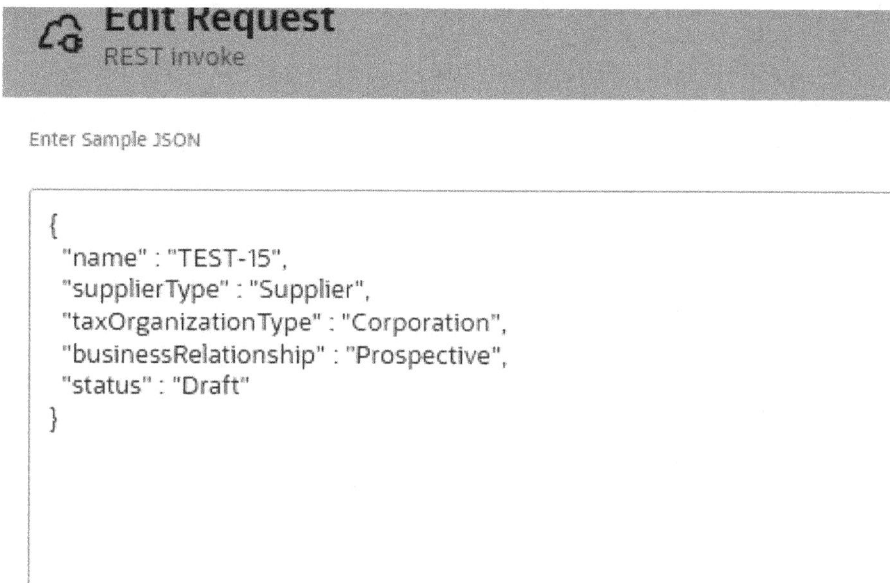

Figure 30-9. *Sample Request for Insert Operation*

Sample Response:

Figure 30-10. Sample Response from Insert Operation

Testing:

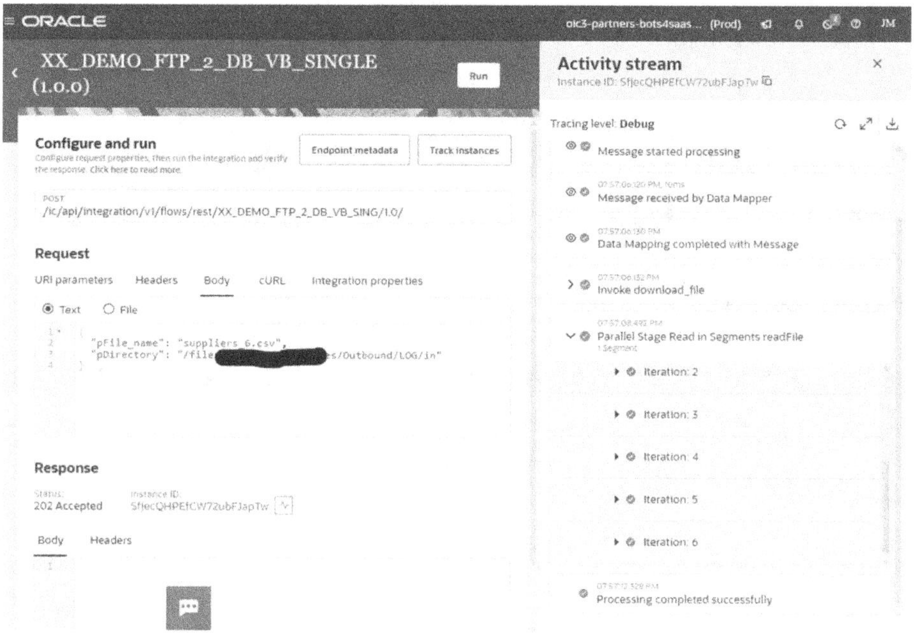

Figure 30-11. *Testing the Integration*

Notice six iterations corresponding to six records in the file.

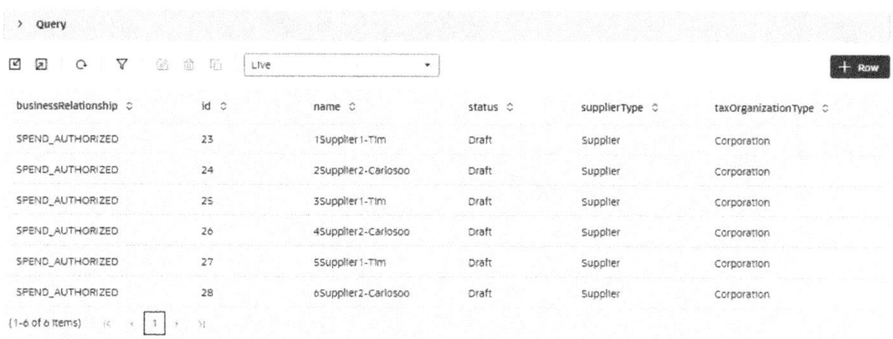

Figure 30-12. *Test Results Showing Iterations*

Question: What can we do if we have to load 1,000,000 records from a file?

Please see Integration 3 in this chapter for the batch approach solution.

Integration 2: XX_DEMO_DB_VB_BATCH_DELETE

General Overview

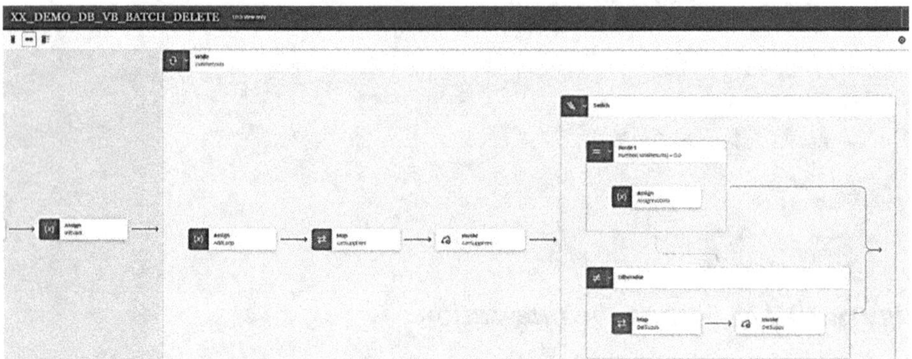

Figure 30-13. *Batch Delete Integration Overview*

Setup of GetSuppliers Activity:

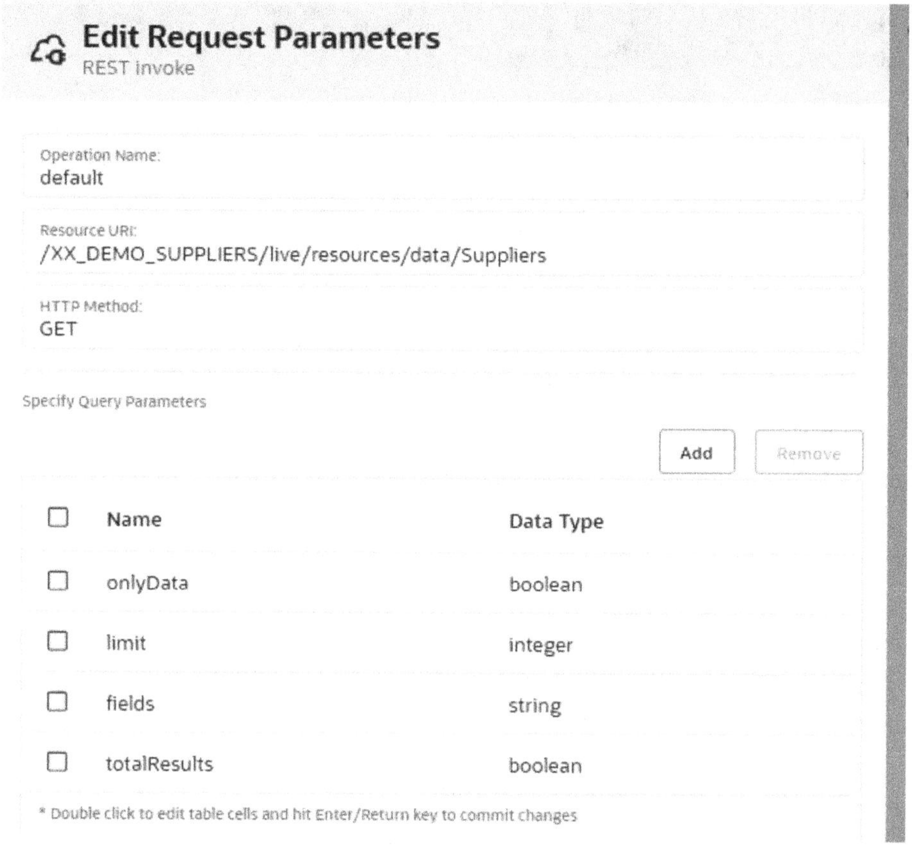

***Figure 30-14.** GetSuppliers Activity Configuration*

Mapping to GetSuppliers:

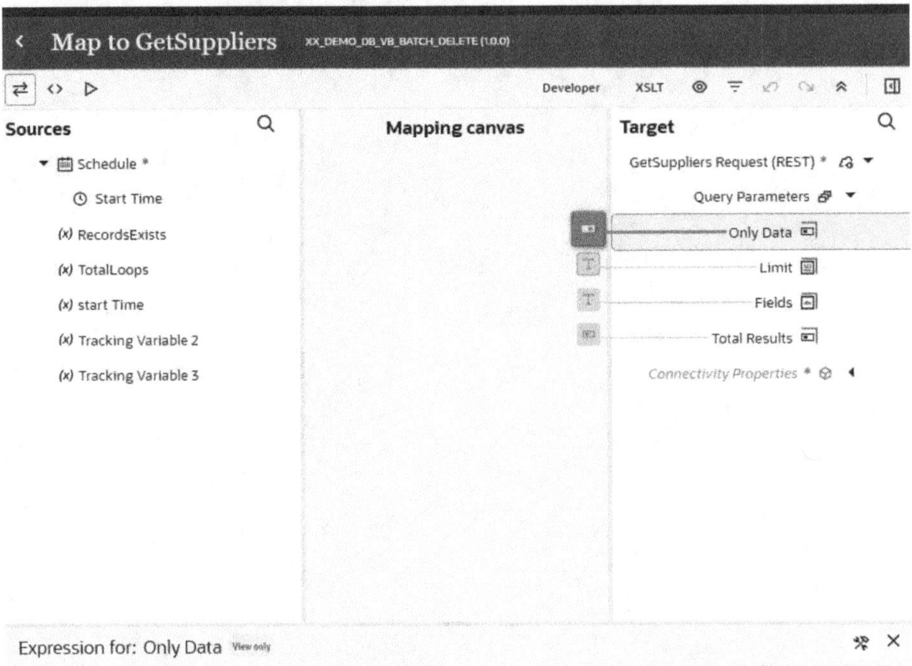

***Figure 30-15.** Mapping Configuration for GetSuppliers*

Detailed Mapping in Code Mode:

```
    <xsl:template match="/" xml:id="id_11">
          <nstrgmpr:execute xml:id="id_12">
                <nstrgmpr:QueryParameters xml:id="id_22">
                      <ns21:onlyData xml:id="id_25">
                            <xsl:value-of xml:id="id_26" select="true ()"/>
                      </ns21:onlyData>
                      <ns21:limit xml:id="id_23">
                            <xsl:value-of xml:id="id_24" select="'500'"/>
                      </ns21:limit>
                      <ns21:fields xml:id="id_27">
                            <xsl:value-of xml:id="id_28" select="'id'"/>
                      </ns21:fields>
                      <ns21:totalResults xml:id="id_29">
                            <xsl:value-of xml:id="id_40" select="true ()"/>
                      </ns21:totalResults>
                </nstrgmpr:QueryParameters>
          </nstrgmpr:execute>
    </xsl:template>
</xsl:stylesheet>
```

***Figure 30-16.** Detailed Mapping in Code Mode*

Delete Action Setup:

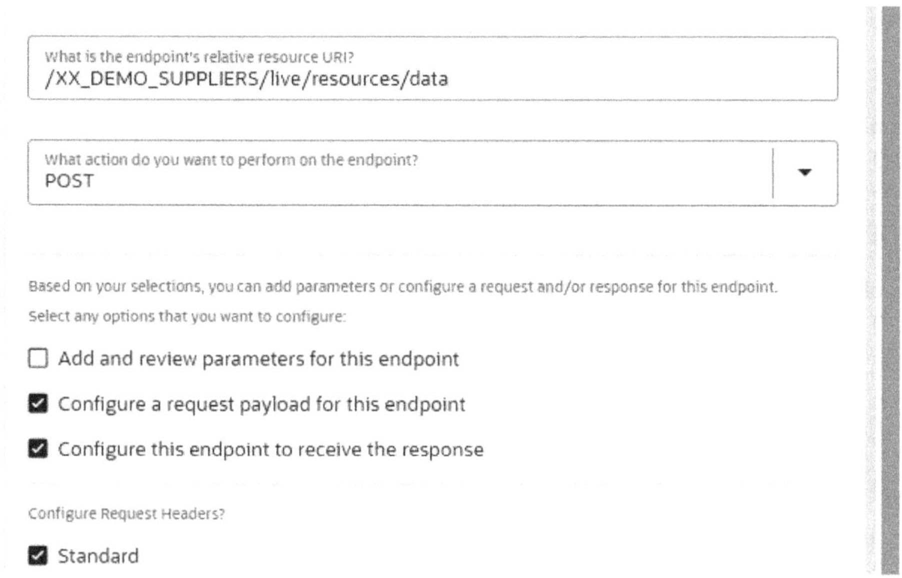

Figure 30-17. *Delete Action Setup*

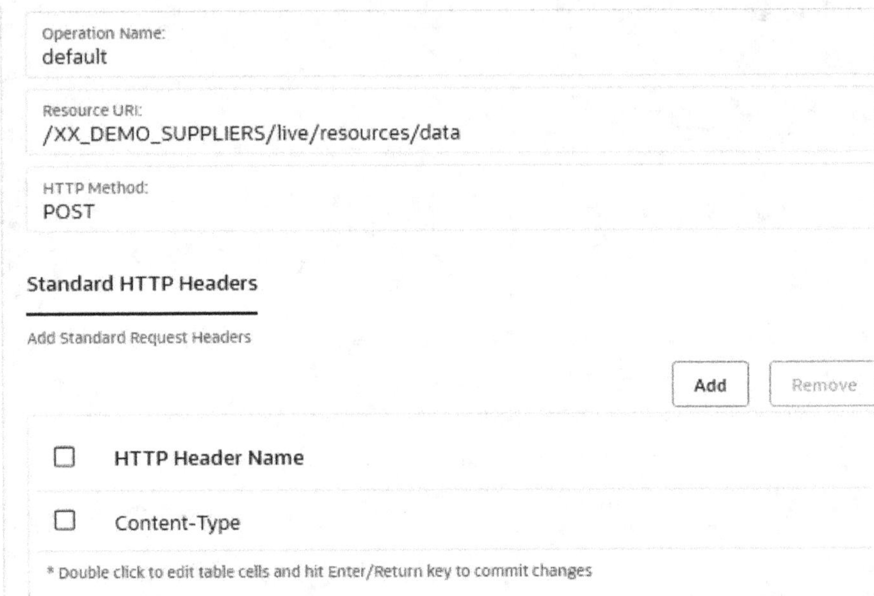

Figure 30-18. *Delete Action Configuration Details*

Mapping to Run Delete Action:

URL Format:

`https://oic-vbcs-xxxx-partners-vb-bots4saas.builder.ca-montreal-1.ocp.oraclecloud.com/ic/builder/rt/XX_DEMO_SUPPLIERS/live/resources/data/Suppliers`

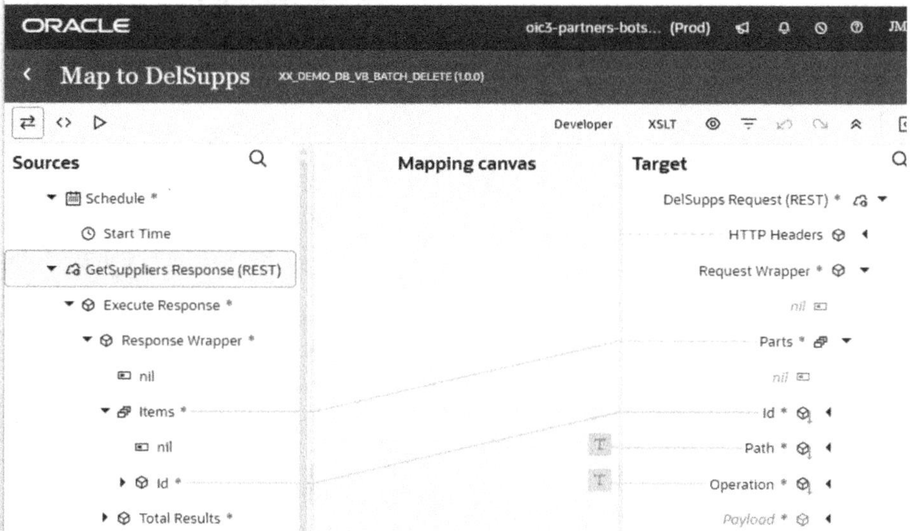

Figure 30-19. Mapping Configuration for Delete Action

Detail Mapping in Code Mode:

```
<xsl:template match="/" xml:id="id_11">
      <nstrgmpr:execute xml:id="id_12">
            <nstrgmpr:HTTPHeaders xml:id="id_39">
                  <ns29:StandardHTTPHeaders xml:id="id_40">
                        <ns29:Content-Type xml:id="id_41">
                              <xsl:value-of xml:id="id_43" select="'application/vnd.oracle.adf.batch+json'"/>
                        </ns29:Content-Type>
                  </ns29:StandardHTTPHeaders>
            </nstrgmpr:HTTPHeaders>
            <ns28:request-wrapper xml:id="id_33">
                  <xsl:for-each xml:id="id_44" select="$GetSuppliers/nsmpr1:executeResponse/ns24:response-wrapper/ns24:items">
                        <ns28:parts xml:id="id_45">
                              <ns28:id xml:id="id_46">
                                    <xsl:value-of xml:id="id_68" select="position ()"/>
                              </ns28:id>
                              <ns28:path xml:id="id_50">
                                    <xsl:value-of xml:id="id_52" select="concat (&quot;/Suppliers/&quot;,ns24:id)"/>
                              </ns28:path>
                              <ns28:operation xml:id="id_48">
                                    <xsl:value-of xml:id="id_49" select="'delete'"/>
                              </ns28:operation>
                        </ns28:parts>
                  </xsl:for-each>
            </ns28:request-wrapper>
      </nstrgmpr:execute>
</xsl:template>
```

Figure 30-20. Detail Mapping in Code Mode

Note the Content-Type value configuration.

Testing the Delete Operation:

When testing, observe the payload sent to the Delete action.

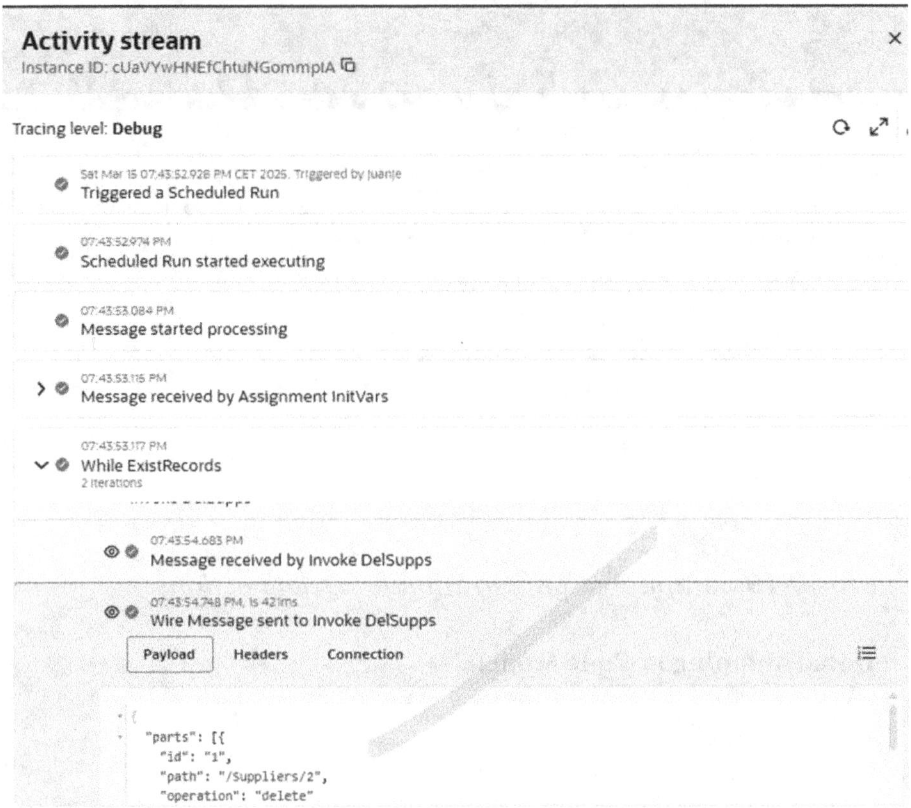

Figure 30-21. Payload Sent During Delete Test

Integration 3: XX_DEMO_FTP_2_DB_VB_BATCH

General Overview

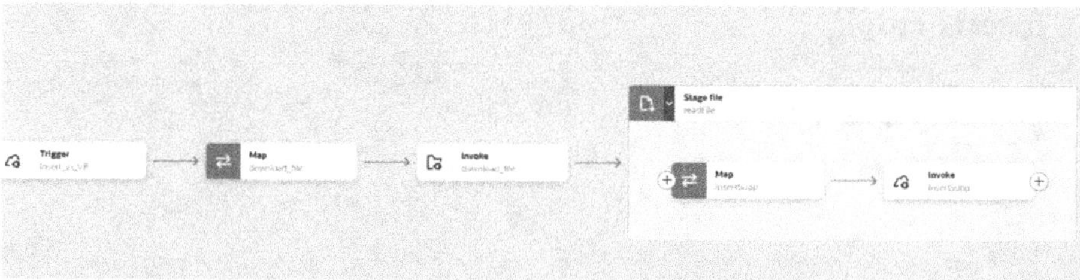

***Figure 30-22.** Batch Load Integration Overview*

For trigger-download configuration, refer to Integration 1 to avoid repetition.

The Key Components

Read in Segments of 2,000 Records:

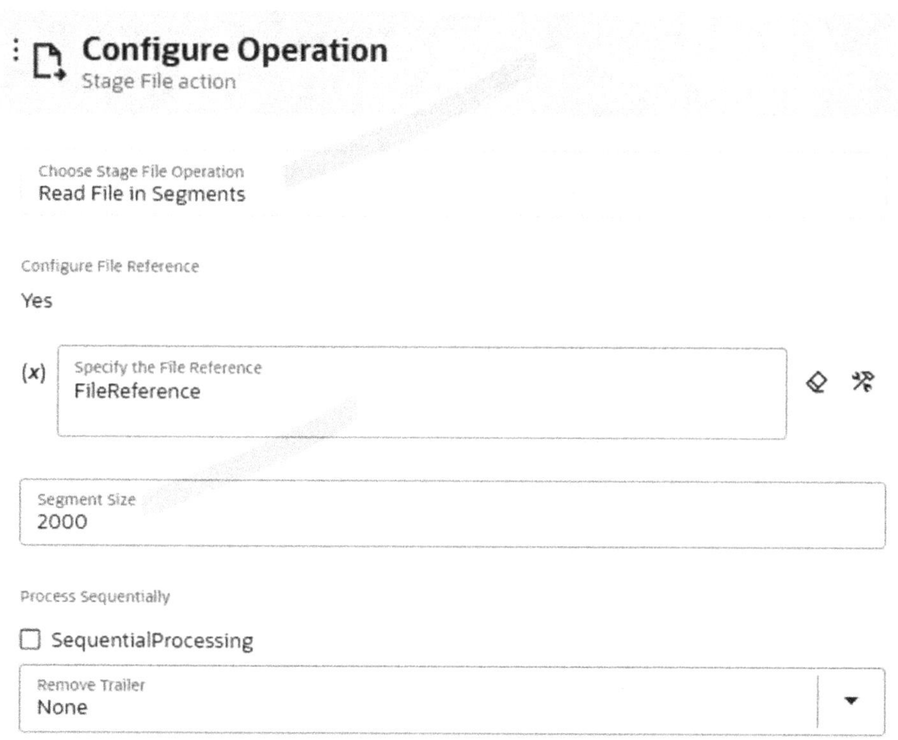

***Figure 30-23.** Read in Segments Configuration for 2,000 Records*

Insert Setup:

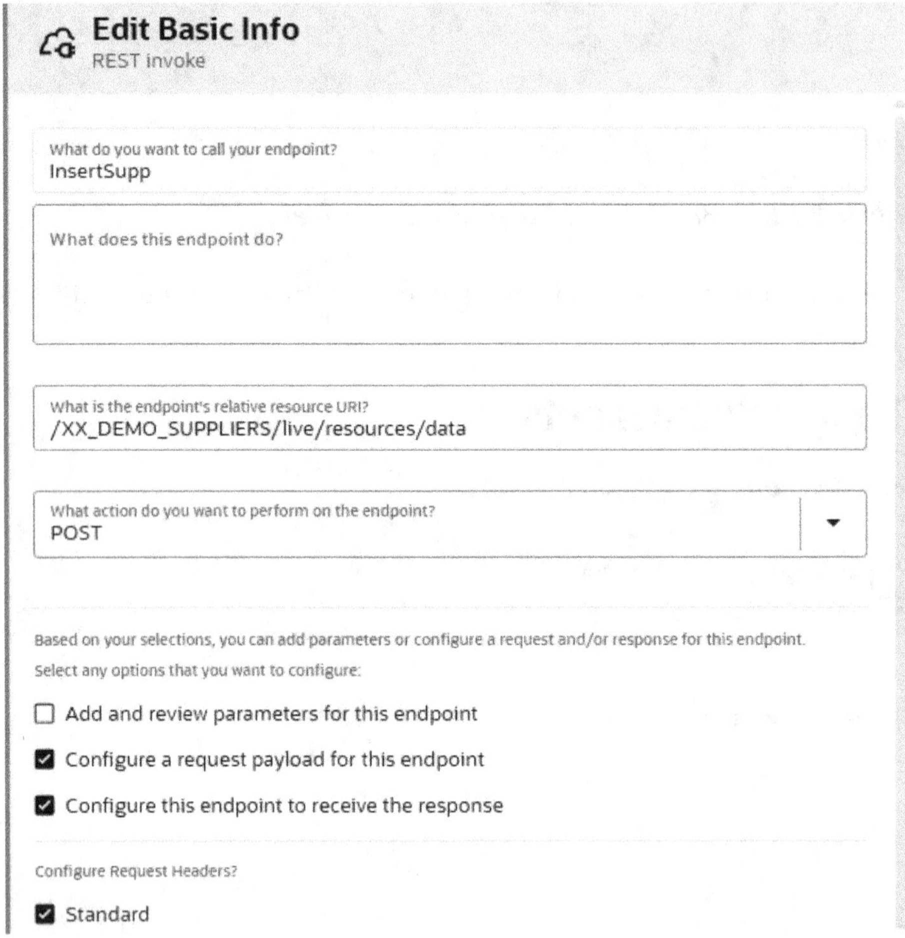

***Figure 30-24.** Batch Insert Configuration*

Payload to Send:

***Figure 30-25.** Payload Configuration for Batch Send*

Important Header Configuration:

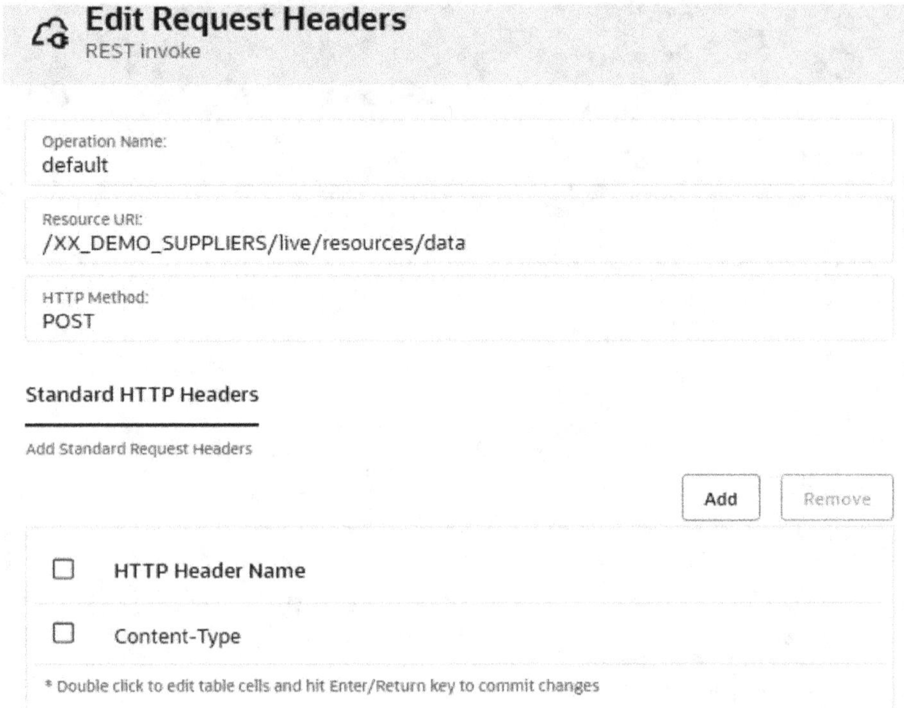

***Figure 30-26.** Critical Header Configuration for Batch Operations*

Payload to Receive:

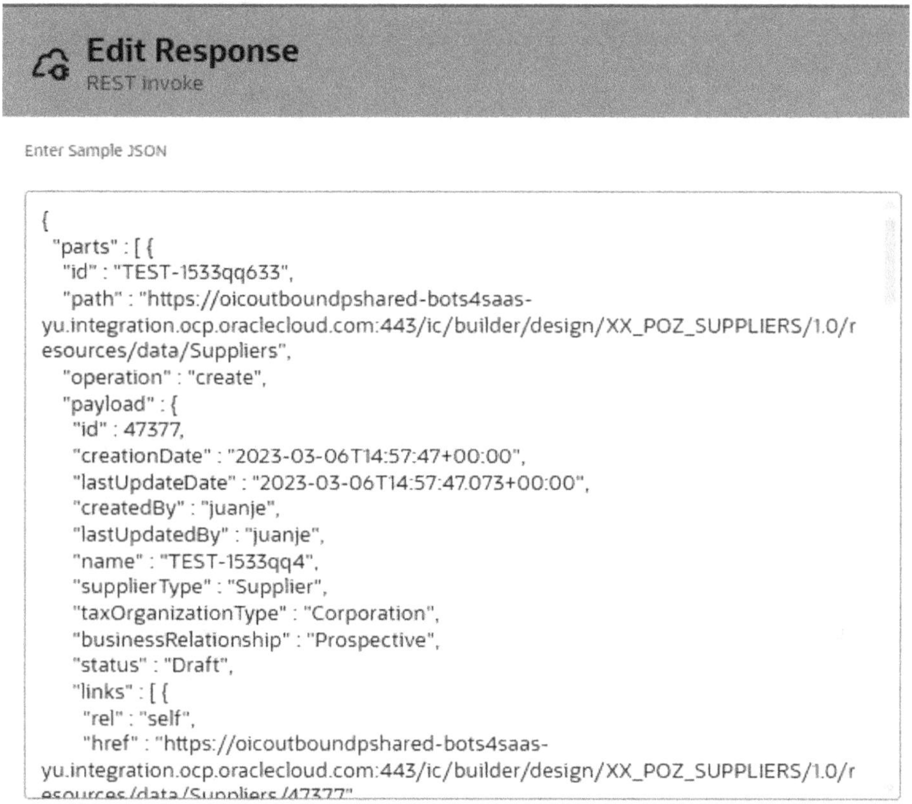

***Figure 30-27.** Payload Configuration for Batch Receive*

Mapping Configuration:

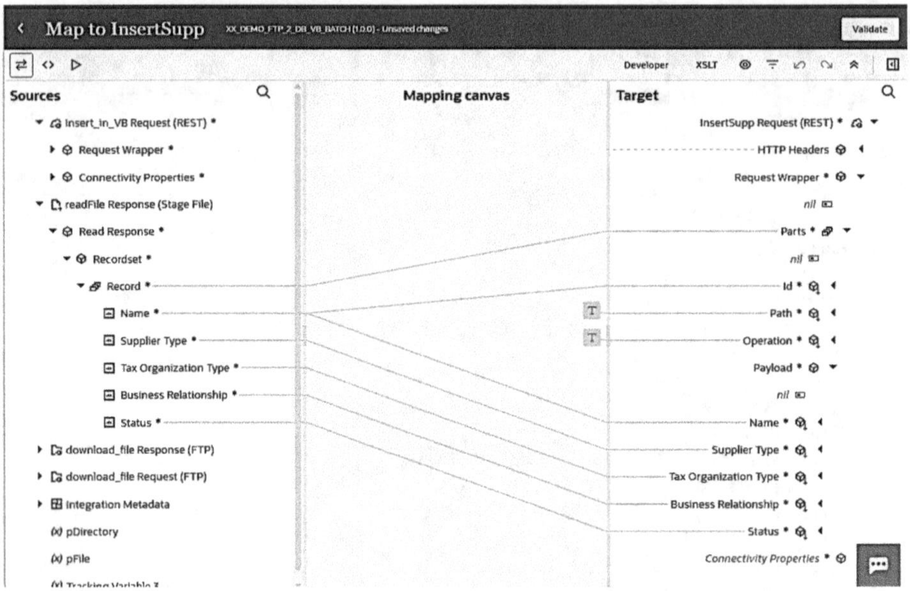

Figure 30-28. Mapping Configuration for Batch Operation

Detailed Batch Mapping in Code Mode:

```
    <xsl:template match="/" xml:id="id_11">
        <nstrgmpr:execute xml:id="id_12">
            <nstrgmpr:HTTPHeaders xml:id="id_75">
                <ns428:StandardHTTPHeaders xml:id="id_76">
                    <ns428:Content-Type xml:id="id_77">
                        <xsl:value-of xml:id="id_79" select="'application/vnd.oracle.adf.batch+json'"/>
                    </ns428:Content-Type>
                </ns428:StandardHTTPHeaders>
            </nstrgmpr:HTTPHeaders>
            <nstrgdfl:request-wrapper xml:id="id_36">
                <xsl:for-each xml:id="id_38" select="$readFile/nsmpr1:ReadResponse/ns25:recordset/ns25:record">
                    <nstrgdfl:parts xml:id="id_39">
                        <nstrgdfl:id xml:id="id_40">
                            <xsl:value-of xml:id="id_41" select="ns25:name"/>
                        </nstrgdfl:id>
                        <nstrgdfl:path xml:id="id_44">
                            <xsl:value-of xml:id="id_45" select="'/Suppliers'"/>
                        </nstrgdfl:path>
                        <nstrgdfl:operation xml:id="id_42">
                            <xsl:value-of xml:id="id_43" select="'create'"/>
                        </nstrgdfl:operation>
                        <nstrgdfl:payload xml:id="id_46">
                            <nstrgdfl:name xml:id="id_47">
                                <xsl:value-of xml:id="id_48" select="ns25:name"/>
                            </nstrgdfl:name>
                            <nstrgdfl:supplierType xml:id="id_49">
                                <xsl:value-of xml:id="id_50" select="ns25:supplierType"/>
                            </nstrgdfl:supplierType>
                            <nstrgdfl:taxOrganizationType xml:id="id_51">
                                <xsl:value-of xml:id="id_52" select="ns25:taxOrganizationType"/>
                            </nstrgdfl:taxOrganizationType>
                            <nstrgdfl:businessRelationship xml:id="id_53">
                                <xsl:value-of xml:id="id_54" select="ns25:businessRelationship"/>
                            </nstrgdfl:businessRelationship>
                            <nstrgdfl:status xml:id="id_55">
                                <xsl:value-of xml:id="id_56" select="ns25:status"/>
                            </nstrgdfl:status>
                        </nstrgdfl:payload>
                    </nstrgdfl:parts>
                </xsl:for-each>
            </nstrgdfl:request-wrapper>
        </nstrgmpr:execute>
    </xsl:template>
</xsl:stylesheet>
```

Figure 30-29. *Detailed Batch Mapping in Code Mode*

Testing with a Large File:

Test using a file with 100,000+ records. A sample file is provided on GitHub for testing.

```
108854-supp,Supplier,Corporation,SPEND_AUTHORIZED,Draft
108855-supp,Supplier,Corporation,SPEND_AUTHORIZED,Draft
108856-supp,Supplier,Corporation,SPEND_AUTHORIZED,Draft
108857-supp,Supplier,Corporation,SPEND_AUTHORIZED,Draft
108858-supp,Supplier,Corporation,SPEND_AUTHORIZED,Draft
108859-supp,Supplier,Corporation,SPEND_AUTHORIZED,Draft
108860-supp,Supplier,Corporation,SPEND_AUTHORIZED,Draft
108861-supp,Supplier,Corporation,SPEND_AUTHORIZED,Draft
108862-supp,Supplier,Corporation,SPEND_AUTHORIZED,Draft
108863-supp,Supplier,Corporation,SPEND_AUTHORIZED,Draft
108864-supp,Supplier,Corporation,SPEND_AUTHORIZED,Draft
```

Figure 30-30. *Test File with 100,000+ Records*

Testing the File:

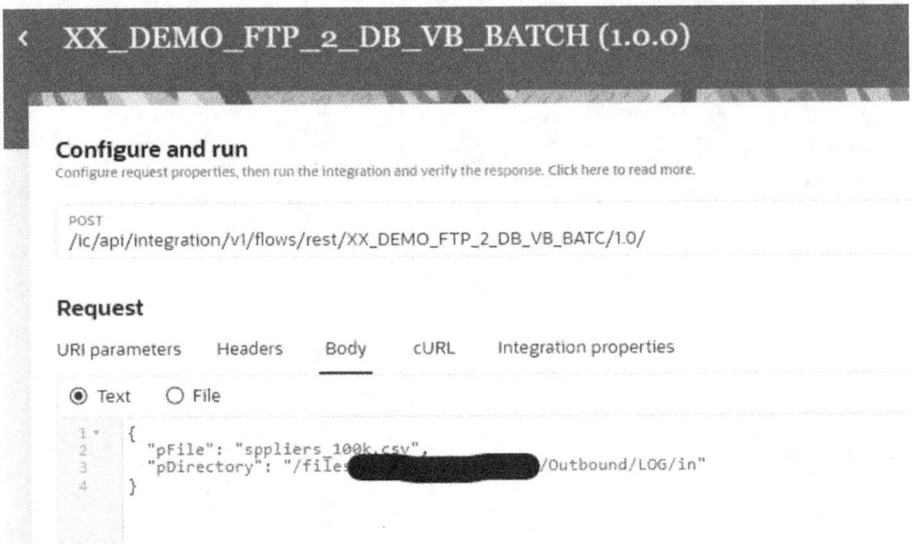

***Figure 30-31.** Testing with a Large File*

OIC Console Results:

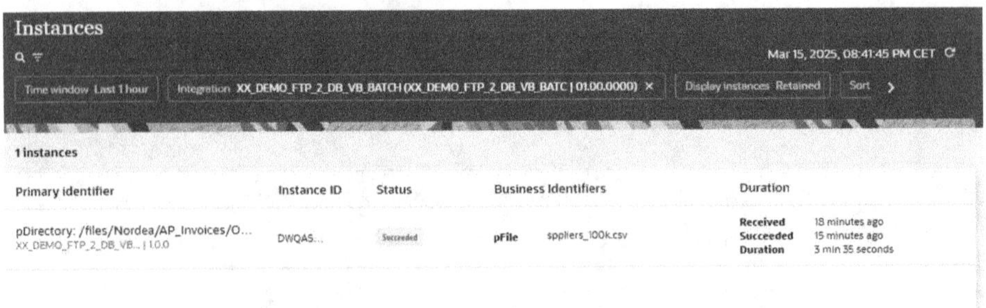

***Figure 30-32.** Results in the OIC Console*

The green indicators show the actual flow followed and the number of iterations.

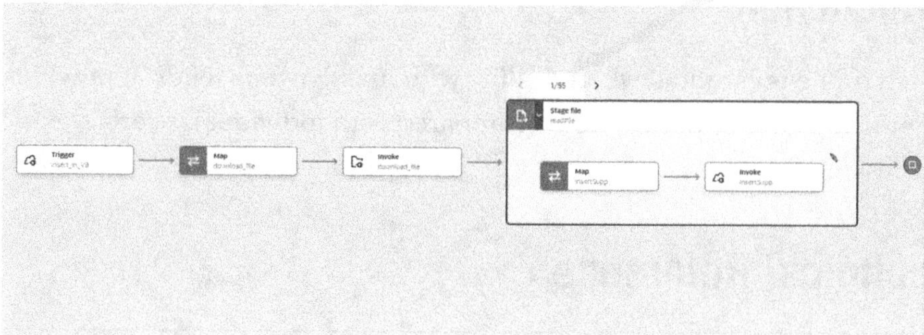

***Figure 30-33.** Details Showing 55 Loops, Each Processing 2,000 Records*

Notice the 55 loops, each processing 2,000 records.

Records Inserted in Visual Builder:

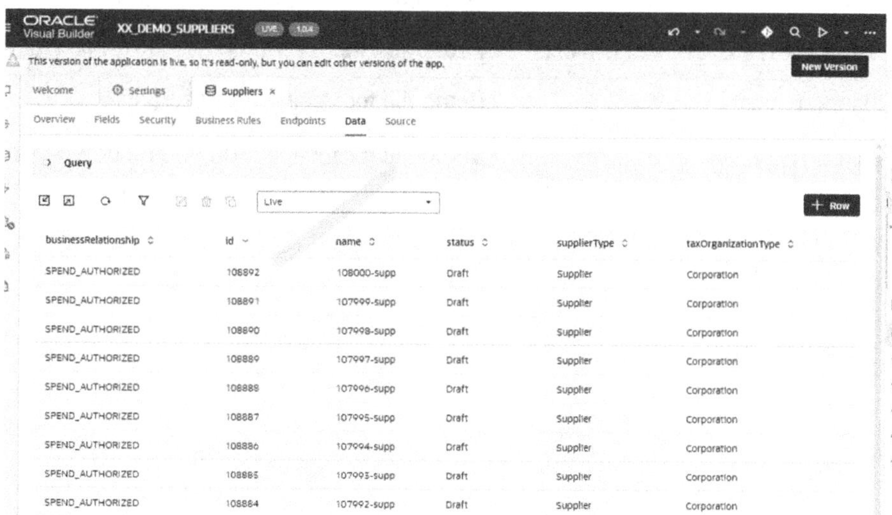

***Figure 30-34.** Records Successfully Inserted in Visual Builder*

Conclusion

Batch mode is essential when dealing with massive data loads. It provides significantly better performance compared with individual record processing.

Technical Reference

Code Example	Comments
XX_DEMO_SUPPLIERS-1.0.4.zip	Visual Builder application with Business Objects
XX_DEMO_FTP_2_DB_VB_SINGLE	**Package File**: XX_DEMO_COOKBOOK_2.par
XX_DEMO_DB_VB_BATCH_DELETE	**Package File**: XX_DEMO_COOKBOOK_2.par
XX_DEMO_FTP_2_DB_VB_BATCH	**Package File**: XX_DEMO_COOKBOOK_2.par
suppliers_6.csv	Demo file for testing (six records)
suppliers_100k.csv	Demo file for testing (100,000 records)

CHAPTER 31

Callback Advanced: Sending FBDI Files + Lookup

Introduction

This chapter builds upon the section "FBDI for Suppliers with Callback (Three Data Sources)" in Chapter 13 as the foundation for this advanced exercise.

Preparation

Refer to Chapter 2 for connection setup details. See the section "REST API for ERP Integrations Connection."

REST API Endpoint:

```
https://xxxx-test.fa.em2.oraclecloud.com/fscmRestApi/
resources/11.13.18.05/erpintegrations
```

This chapter uses the integration from the section "FBDI for Suppliers with Callback (Three Data Sources)" in Chapter 13 to trigger the callback functionality.

J. J. Montero Rodríguez and S. Tahseen, *Oracle Integration Cookbook for Oracle ERP Cloud*,
https://doi.org/10.1007/979-8-8688-3020-4_31

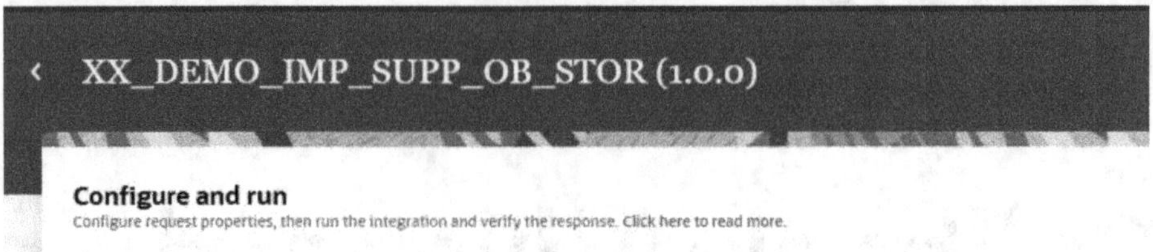

Figure 31-1. Integration to Trigger Callback

Integration 1: XX_DEMO_IMP_SUPP_CB

General Overview

This integration creates a new version of the basic callback integration Refer to Chapter 13, Integration 4, with enhanced features.

Starting Point:

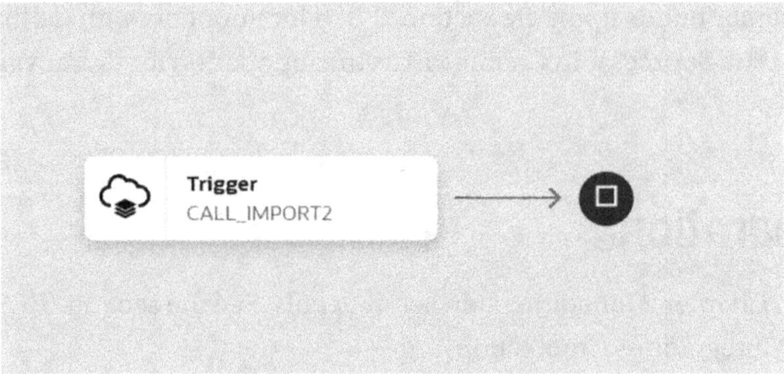

Figure 31-2. Starting Point—Basic Callback Integration

Enhanced Integration:

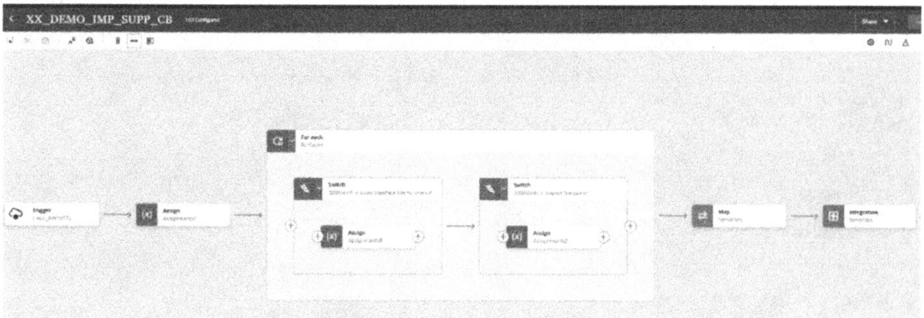

***Figure 31-3.** Goal Integration with Enhanced Features*

The basic integration from Chapter 13 has been improved with additional activities:

1. Capture the result of FBDI jobs, including job ID and result status.
2. Run a secondary integration that sends files related to the FBDI job to the user configured in the lookup.

Payload Received in Callback Integration:

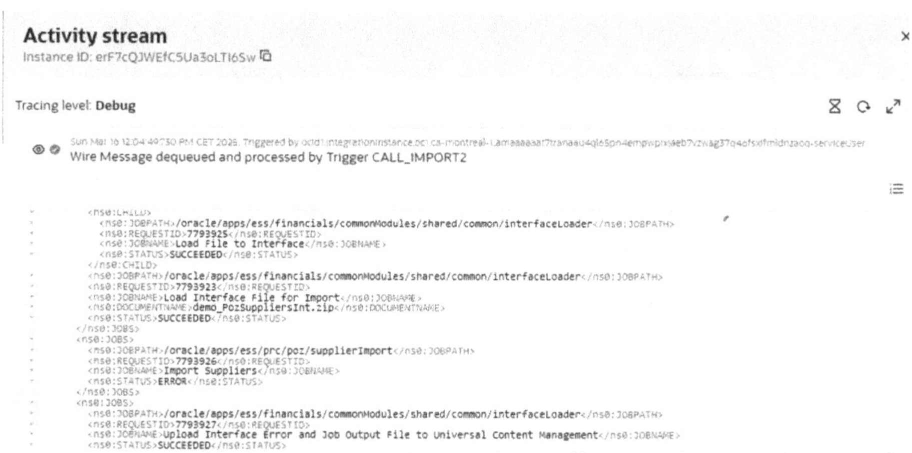

***Figure 31-4.** Payload Received in Callback Integration*

Analyzing Job Data:

The received data can be analyzed to determine job IDs and results.

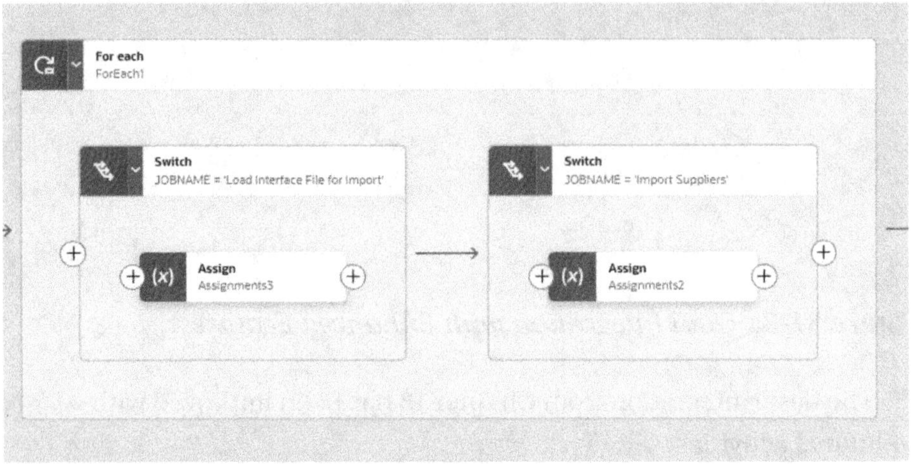

Figure 31-5. *Analyzing Job Data and Results*

Looping Through Jobs:

Loop through jobs and filter for specific jobs of interest.

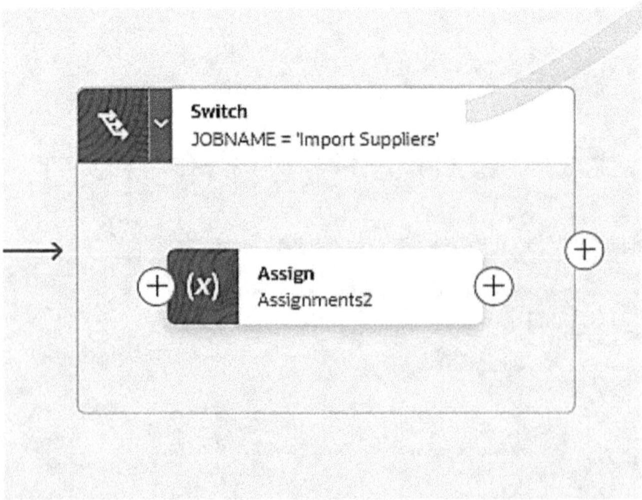

Figure 31-6. *Looping and Filtering Specific Jobs*

Assign Activity:

Store the job ID and status of jobs of interest in the Assign activity.

Running Next Integration:

This activity runs the next integration, sending the required parameters.

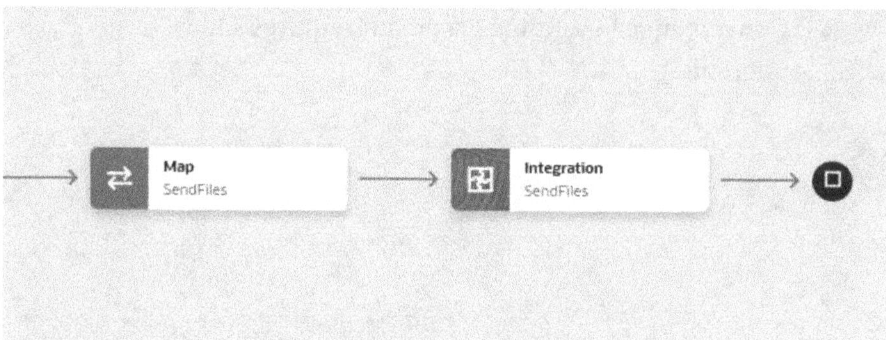

Figure 31-7. *Activity to Run Next Integration with Parameters*

The next integration encapsulates the process of sending FBDI files.

Integration 2: XX_DEMO_SEND_FBDI_FILES

General Overview

Figure 31-8. *Integration Overview for Sending FBDI Files*

Trigger Payload File: rest_payload_XX_DEMO_SEND_FBDI_FILES.json

File Processing

Get File 1:

Retrieve the first file and write to an FTP server for

1. Logging purposes
2. Convenience in sending via email (requires a file reference)

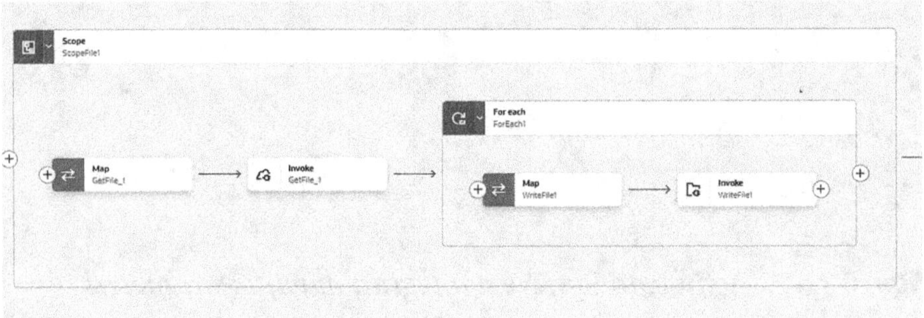

Figure 31-9. Processing the First File

The subprocess for the second file follows a similar pattern.

Read Downloaded Files:

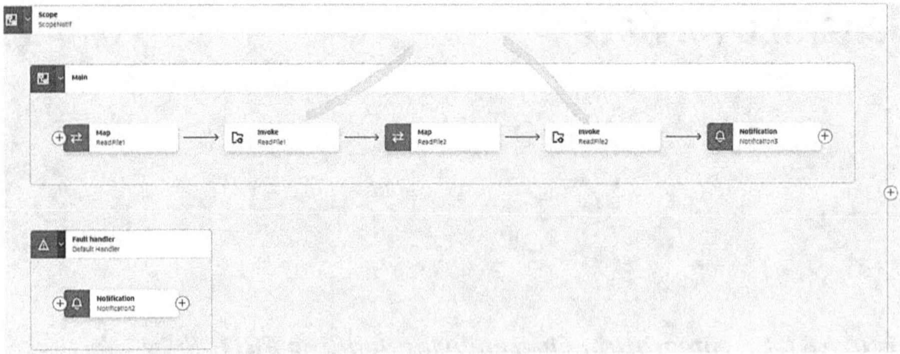

Figure 31-10. Reading Downloaded Files

The goal is to obtain file references for inclusion in the Notification activity.

Notification Activity:

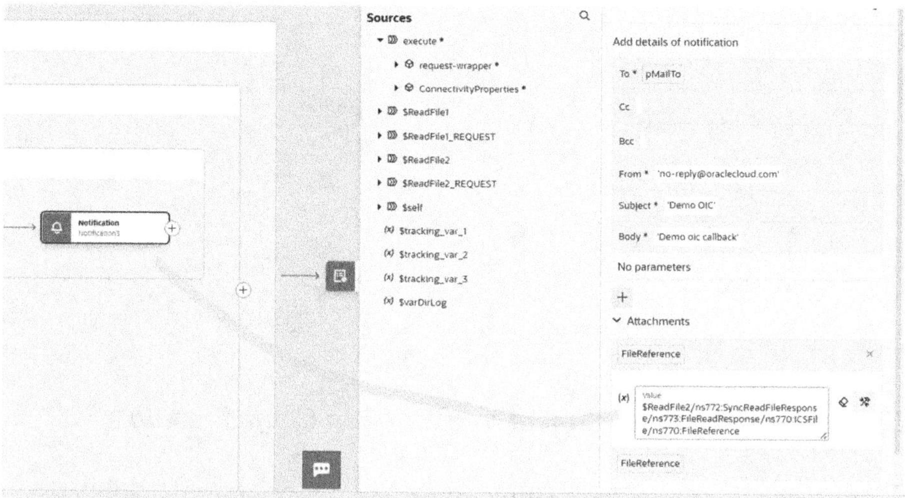

***Figure 31-11.** Notification Activity Configuration*

The email will be sent to the address configured in the lookup, as shown in the callback integration.

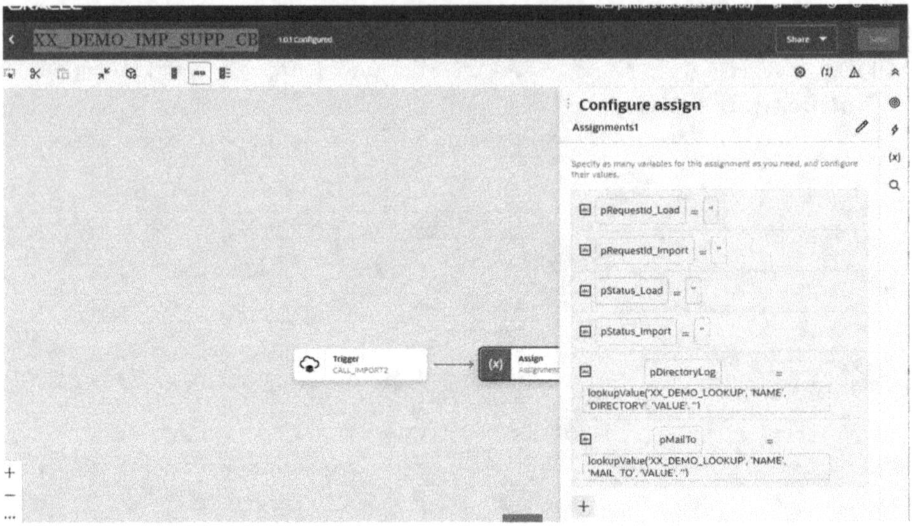

Figure 31-12. *Email Recipient from Lookup Configuration*

This value is passed to the integration as a parameter.

Lookup Setup

Lookup Configuration:

Name	Usage	Domains	mapped	Last updated	Status
XX_DEMO_LOOKUP New	1 integrations	2	2	Mar 16, 2025 11:44:56 AM CET	Configured

Figure 31-13. *Lookup Configuration Overview*

Lookup Values:

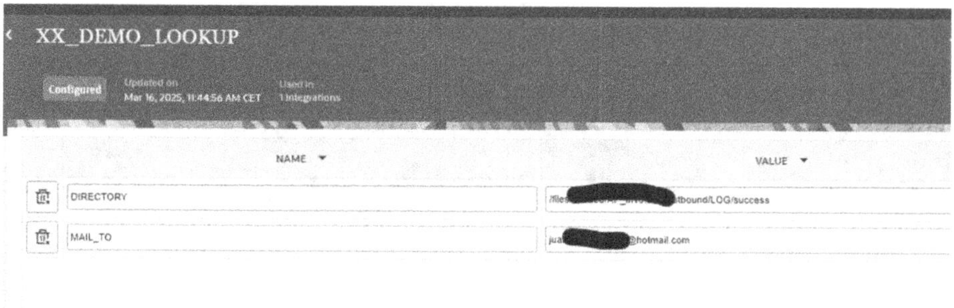

Figure 31-14. *Configured Lookup Values*

Testing

Main Integration Execution

Run the main integration.

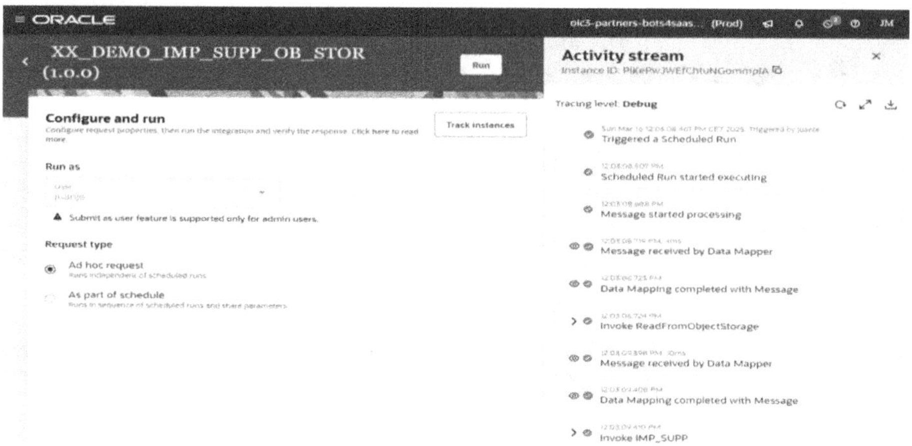

Figure 31-15. *Testing Main Integration*

Callback Integration Execution

The callback integration is automatically triggered.

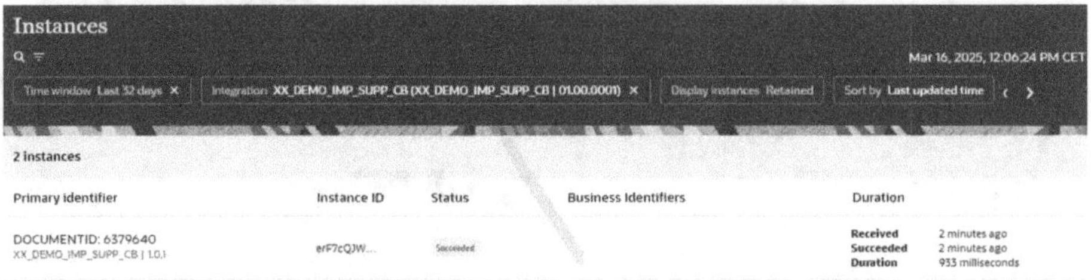

Figure 31-16. Callback Integration Execution

FBDI Files Integration Execution

The FBDI files integration is also executed.

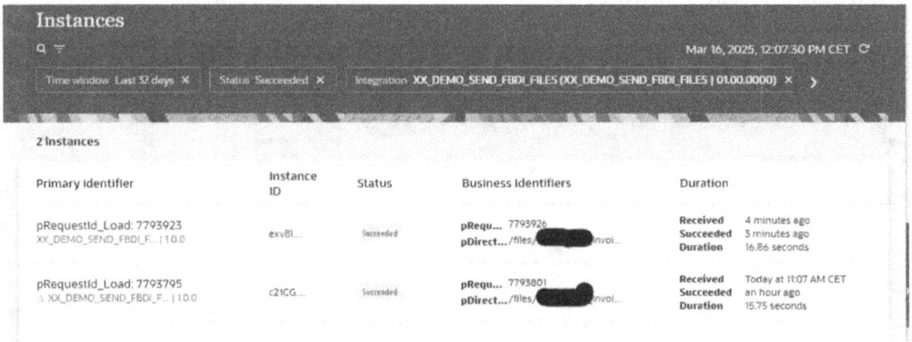

Figure 31-17. FBDI Files Integration Execution

Email Notification

The integration sends an email with attached files.

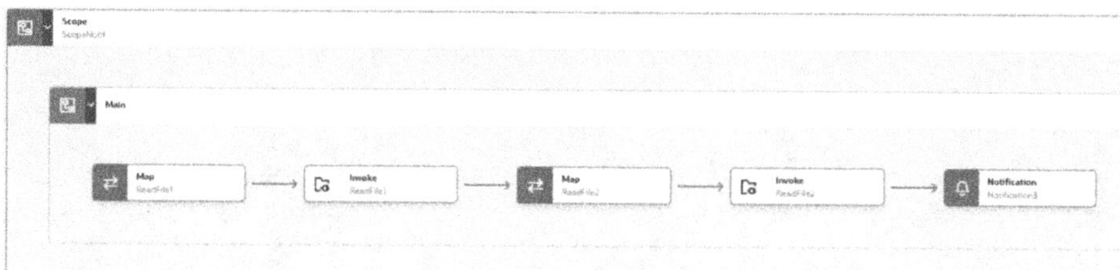

Figure 31-18. *Email Notification Sent Confirmation*

Received Email:

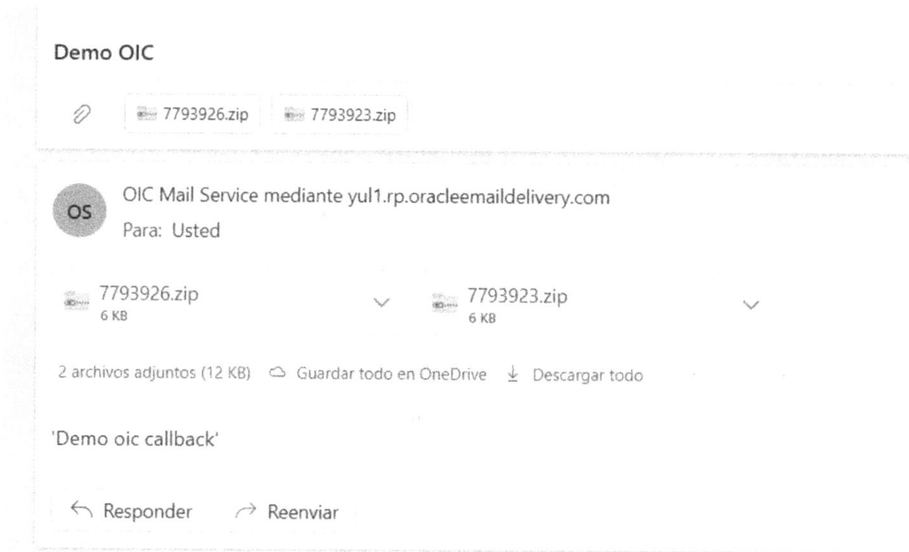

Figure 31-19. *Email Received with FBDI File Attachments*

FTP Server Storage

Files are also stored on the FTP server.

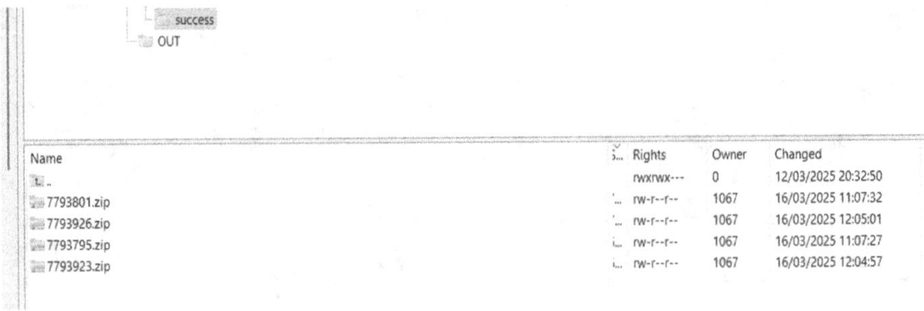

***Figure 31-20.** Files Successfully Stored on the FTP Server*

Technical Reference

Code Example	Comments
XX_DEMO_IMP_SUPP_OB_STOR	**Package File**: XX_DEMO_COOKBOOK_2.par
XX_DEMO_IMP_SUPP_CB Version 1.0.1	**Package File**: XX_DEMO_COOKBOOK_2.par
XX_DEMO_SEND_FBDI_FILES	**Package File**: XX_DEMO_COOKBOOK_2.par
demo_PozSuppliersInt.zip	Demo file for upload
rest_payload_XX_DEMO_SEND_FBDI_FILES.json	Trigger payload file for XX_DEMO_SEND_FBDI_FILES integration

CHAPTER 32

OIC Generation 3 Events

Introduction

The best way to understand how events work in Gen3 is through a practical example that demonstrates the complete publish-subscribe pattern.

Reference Documentation

Publishing and Subscribing to Events (Oracle)

Basic Event Demonstration

Step 1: Create an Event

Navigate to the Events section in the left menu.

J. J. Montero Rodríguez and S. Tahseen, *Oracle Integration Cookbook for Oracle ERP Cloud*,
https://doi.org/10.1007/979-8-8688-3020-4_32

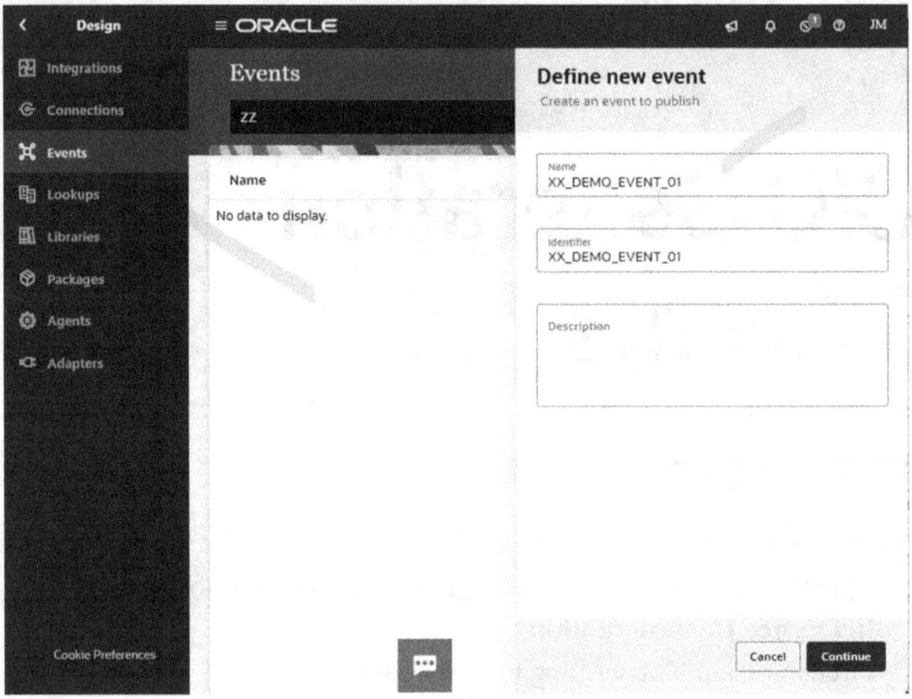

Figure 32-1. *Event Creation Menu*

For learning purposes, we'll use the default payload. Notice it contains different data types.

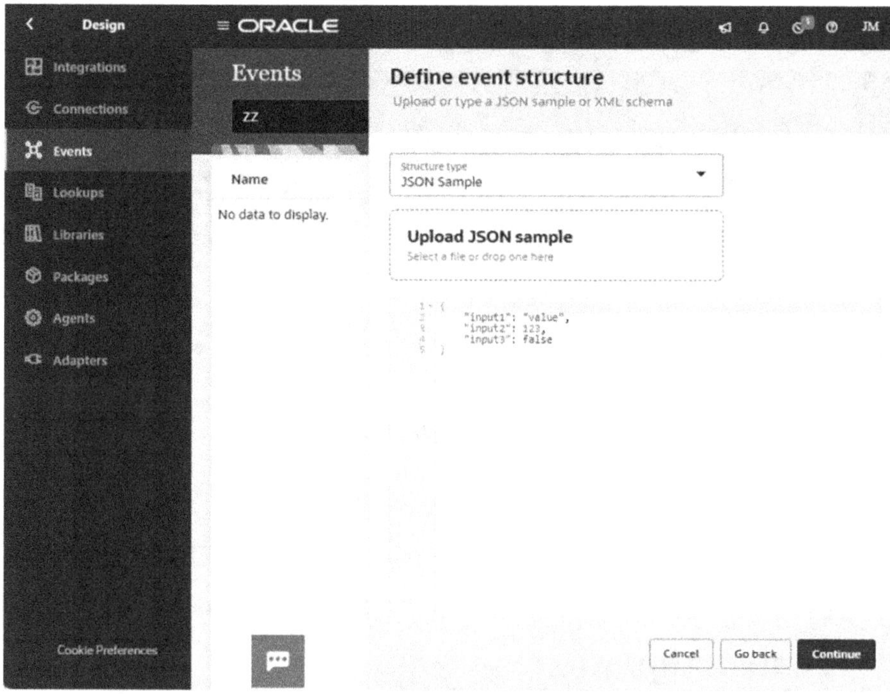

Figure 32-2. *Event Payload Configuration*

Click **Continue.**

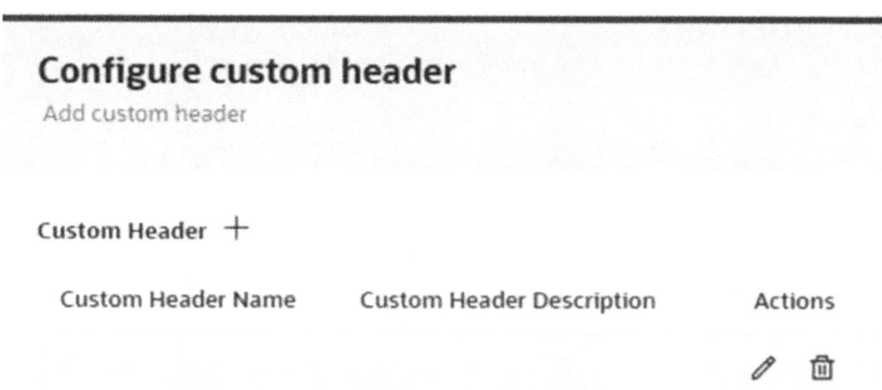

Figure 32-3. *Event Configuration Continued*

Then click **Create**.

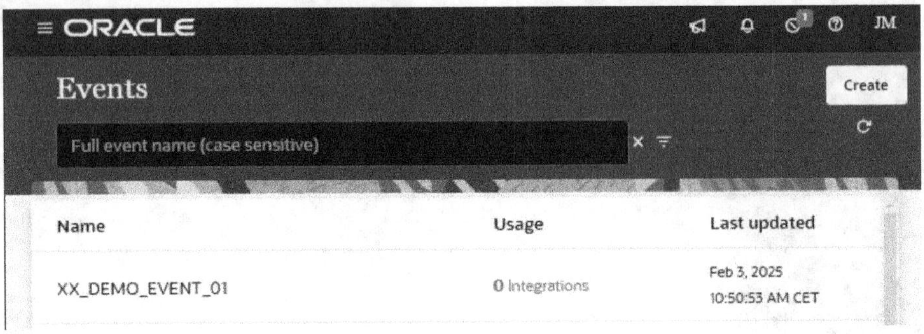

Figure 32-4. *Event Creation Confirmation*

Step 2: Create Publisher Integration

Create a scheduled integration that will publish the event.

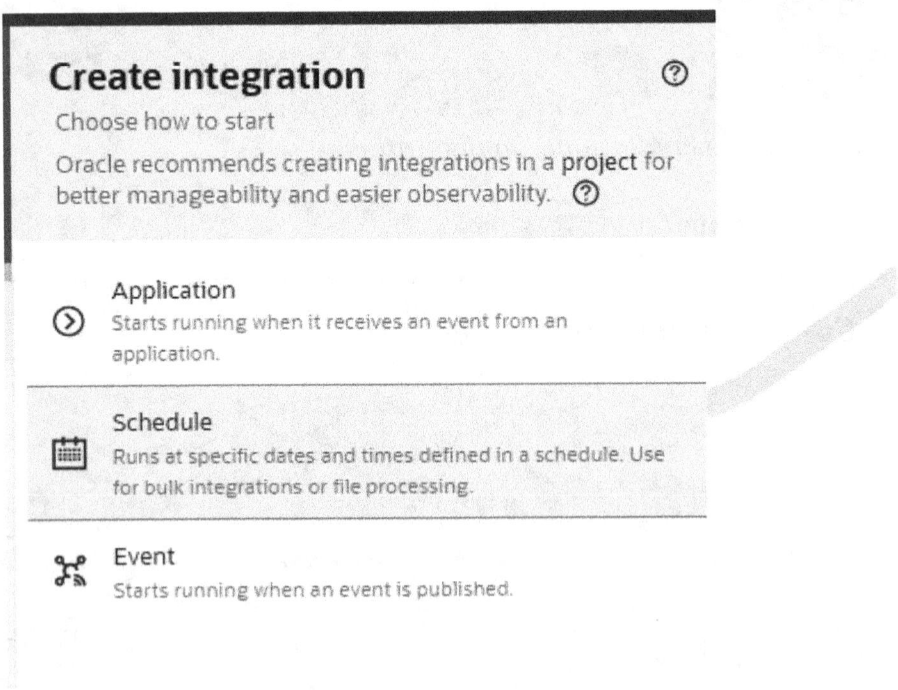

Figure 32-5. *Publisher Integration Creation*

Add a "Call" activity to publish the event.

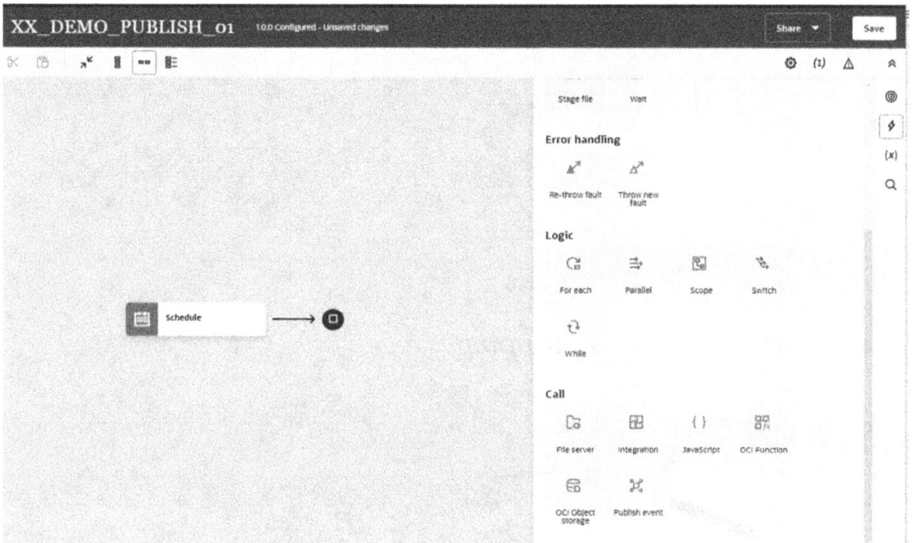

Figure 32-6. *Add Publish Event Activity*

Select the event you created earlier and click **Finish**.

Figure 32-7. *Event Selection*

Map dummy data to the event payload for testing.

```
        <xsl:template match="/" xml:id="id_11">
              <nstrgmpr:execute xml:id="id_12">
                    <ns18:request-wrapper xml:id="id_21">
                          <ns18:input1 xml:id="id_22">
                                <xsl:value-of xml:id="id_23" select="'DEMO PARAMETER 1'"/>
                          </ns18:input1>
                          <ns18:input2 xml:id="id_24">
                                <xsl:value-of xml:id="id_25" select="1000"/>
                          </ns18:input2>
                          <ns18:input3 xml:id="id_26">
                                <xsl:value-of xml:id="id_27" select="true ()"/>
                          </ns18:input3>
                    </ns18:request-wrapper>
              </nstrgmpr:execute>
        </xsl:template>
  </xsl:stylesheet>
```

Figure 32-8. *Event Data Mapping*

Review the complete flow.

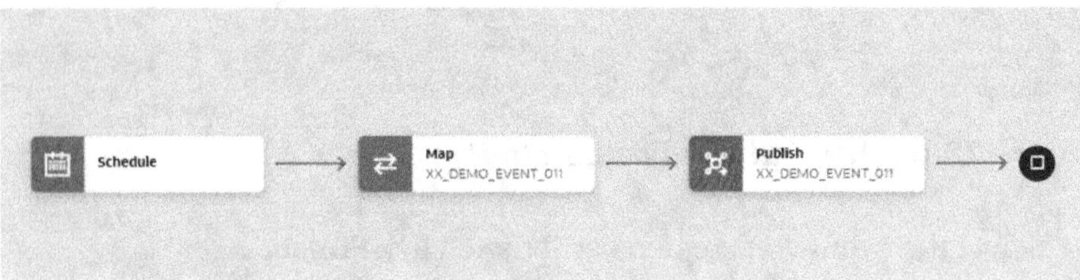

Figure 32-9. *Publisher Integration Overview*

Step 3: Create Subscriber Integration

Create an event-type integration that will subscribe to the event.

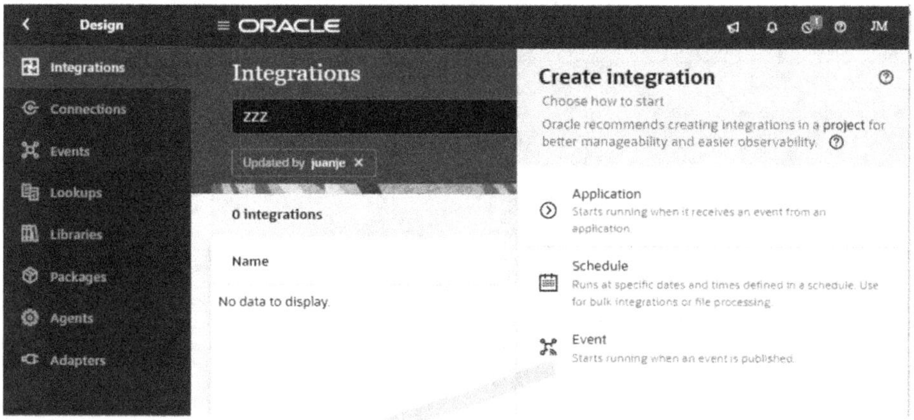

Figure 32-10. *Subscriber Integration Creation*

Assign a name and click **Create**.

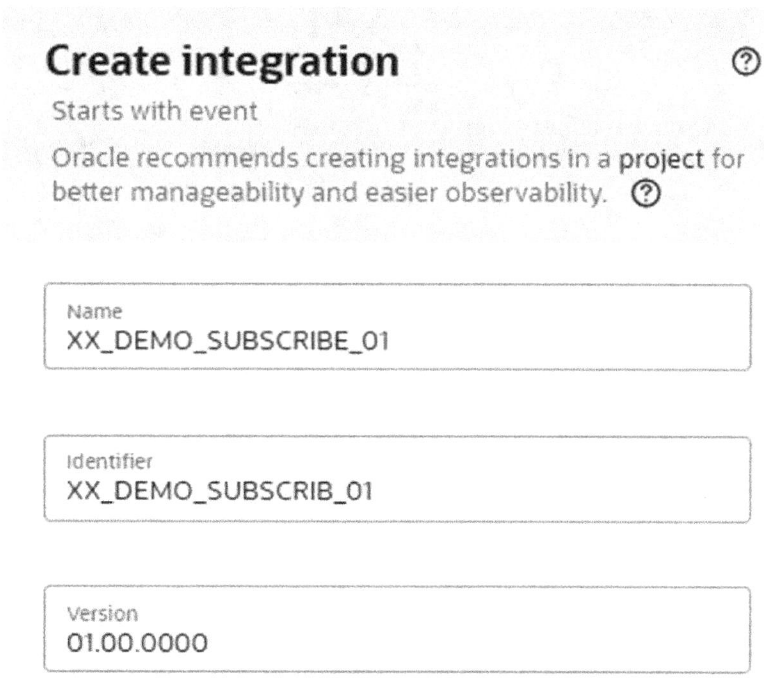

Figure 32-11. *Subscriber Integration Name*

Select the event to subscribe to.

***Figure 32-12.** Subscribe to an Event*

Choose the event and click **Finish**.

Step 4: Configure Business Identifier

You'll encounter an error prompting you to assign a business identifier.

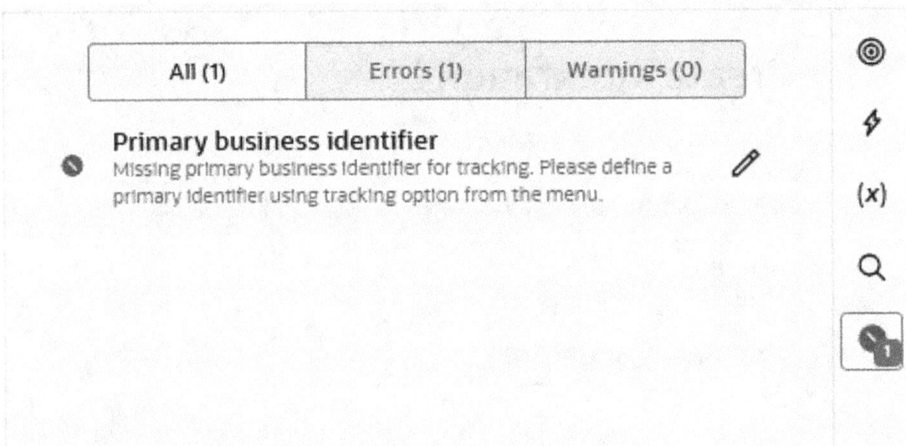

***Figure 32-13.** Business Identifier Error*

Drag and drop a field from the event payload to the Business identifiers section.

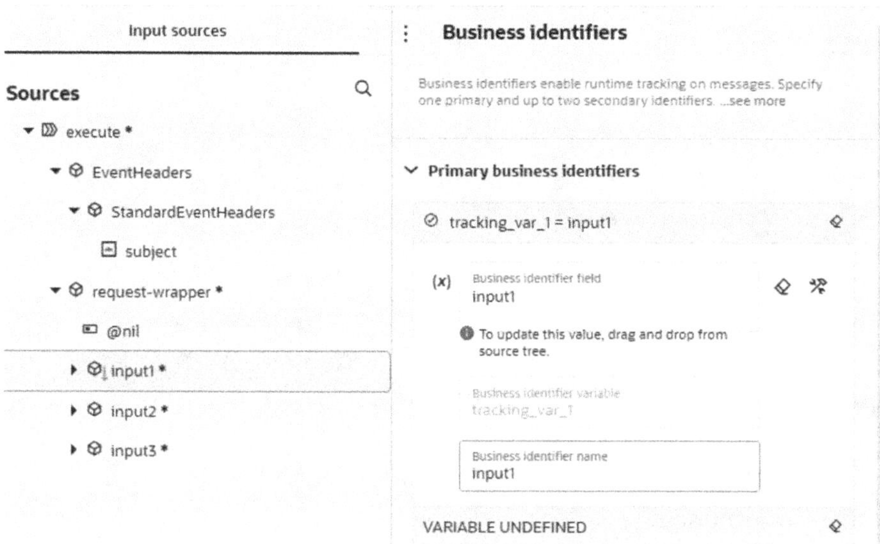

***Figure 32-14.** Assign a Business Identifier*

Testing the Event Flow

After activating both integrations, test by running the publisher integration XX_DEMO_PUBLISH_01.

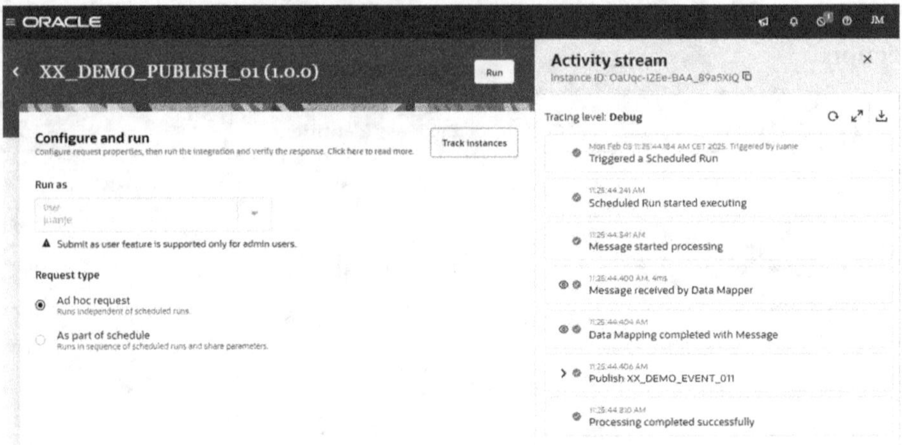

Figure 32-15. *Publisher Execution*

Notice that the subscriber integration XX_DEMO_SUBSCRIBE_01 also executes automatically.

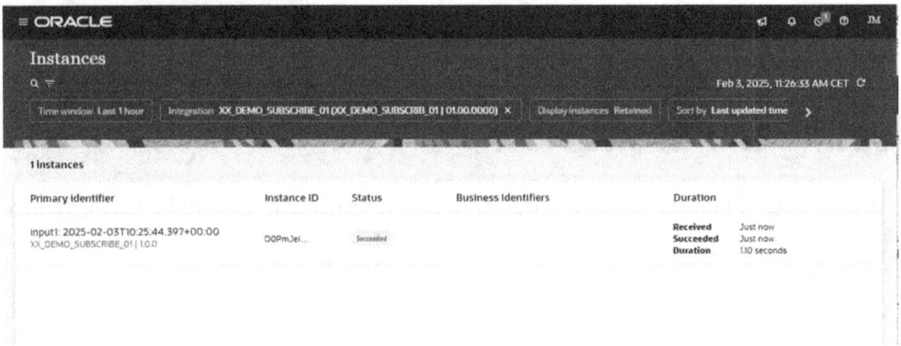

Figure 32-16. *Subscriber Execution*

You can view the event parameters in the activity stream of the subscriber integration.

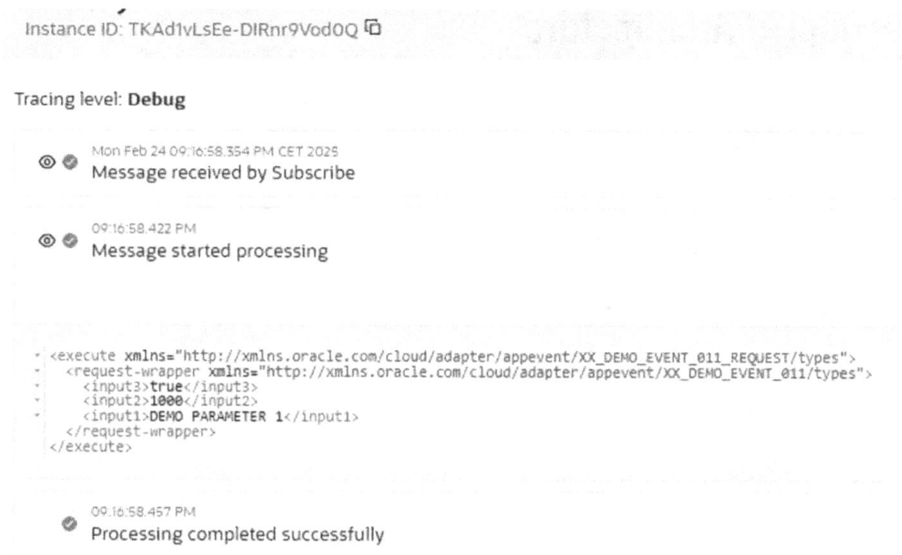

Figure 32-17. *Event Parameters in the Activity Stream*

Understanding Event Use Cases

What Are Events Used For?

Events enable several powerful integration patterns.

One-to-Many Pattern

Link multiple integrations to a single event. When the event is published, all subscribers execute automatically.

Code Reusability

Create a common integration that publishes an event, and then have multiple specialized integrations subscribe to handle different aspects of the business process.

Decoupled Architecture

Publishers and subscribers don't need direct knowledge of each other, improving maintainability and scalability.

Example Scenario

Consider a customer order scenario:

- **Publisher:** Order entry system publishes "Order Created" event.
- **Subscribers:**
    - **Integration 1**: Updates inventory
    - **Integration 2**: Sends confirmation email
    - **Integration 3**: Creates shipping record
    - **Integration 4**: Updates analytics dashboard

Each subscriber can be developed, deployed, and maintained independently.

Events provide a powerful mechanism for building loosely coupled, scalable integration solutions in OIC Gen3.

Important Limitation

A maximum of 50 integrations can subscribe to events per service instance.

Technical Reference

Code Example	Comments
XX_DEMO_EVENT_01	Event definition
XX_DEMO_PUBLISH_01	Publisher integration. **Package File**: XX_DEMO_COOKBOOK.par
XX_DEMO_SUBSCRIBE_01	Subscriber integration. **Package File**: XX_DEMO_COOKBOOK.par

APPENDIX A

REST APIs and Postman

Overview

Postman is a powerful tool for testing and investigating Oracle ERP REST APIs. While it offers numerous features, this guide focuses on the essential functionalities needed for API testing.

Use Case: We use Postman primarily for REST API testing, while SoapUI is reserved for SOAP web services.

Getting Started with Postman

Registration and Setup:

1. Visit `www.postman.com` and register for an account.
2. Create a workspace after account creation.
3. Begin testing your REST APIs.

Reference Documentation:

For detailed information on Oracle REST API documentation, see the following:

Demystifying Oracle REST API Documentation

J. J. Montero Rodríguez and S. Tahseen, *Oracle Integration Cookbook for Oracle ERP Cloud*,
https://doi.org/10.1007/979-8-8688-3020-4

APPENDIX B

SOAP Web Services and SoapUI

Overview

SoapUI is our preferred tool for testing SOAP web services provided by Oracle. While it can also test REST APIs, we use it specifically for SOAP services to maintain consistency in our testing approach.

Getting Started with SoapUI

Download and Installation:

The current version can be downloaded from the official SoapUI website.

J. J. Montero Rodríguez and S. Tahseen, *Oracle Integration Cookbook for Oracle ERP Cloud*, https://doi.org/10.1007/979-8-8688-3020-4

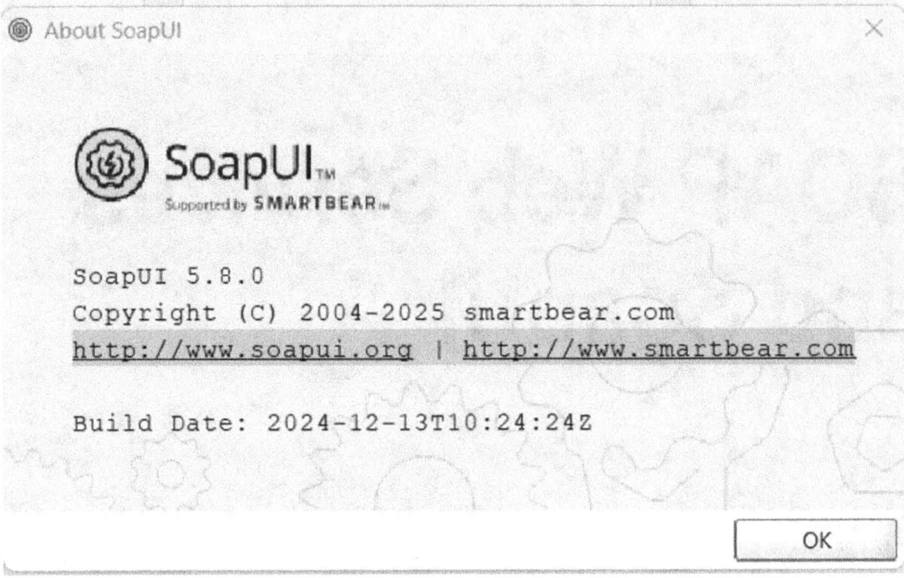

Figure B-1. *SoapUI Download Interface*

Testing SOAP Web Services: Step by Step

Step 1: Locate the WSDL

Example: Supplier SOAP Service (Procurement Module)

1. Navigate to Oracle documentation:
    - **Main Documentation**: Oracle Procurement API 25a
    - **Supplier Service**: Supplier Service Documentation

Figure B-2. *API Documentation Navigation*

2. Find the service WSDL URL in the documentation.

Figure B-3. *WSDL URL in the Documentation*

The WSDL suffix will be

```
https://servername/fscmService/SupplierServiceV2?WSDL
```

Step 2: Compose the Complete WSDL URL

Combine the instance URL (prefix) with the WSDL suffix.

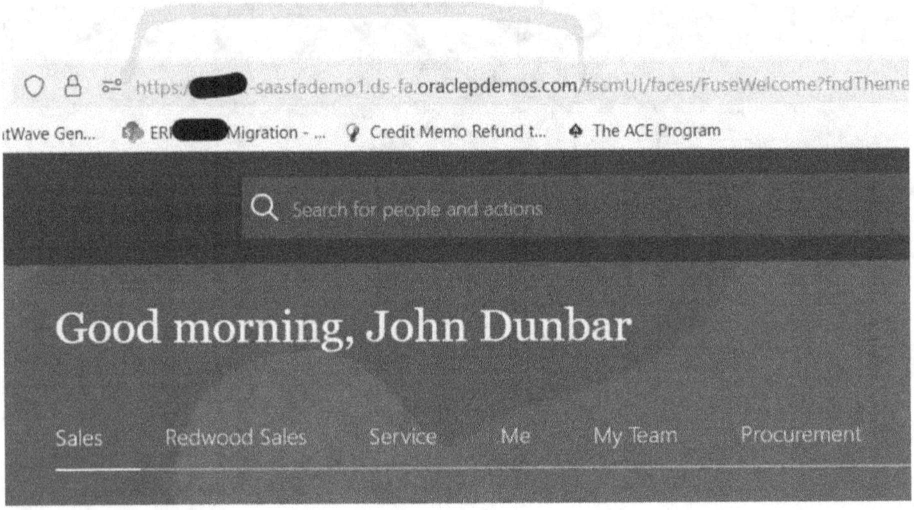

Figure B-4. *Instance URL Configuration*

Complete URL Example:

`https://fa-zzzz-saasfademo1.ds-fa.oraclepdemos.com/fscmService/SupplierServiceV2?WSDL`

Step 3: Create a New SOAP Project

1. In SoapUI, select "New SOAP Project".

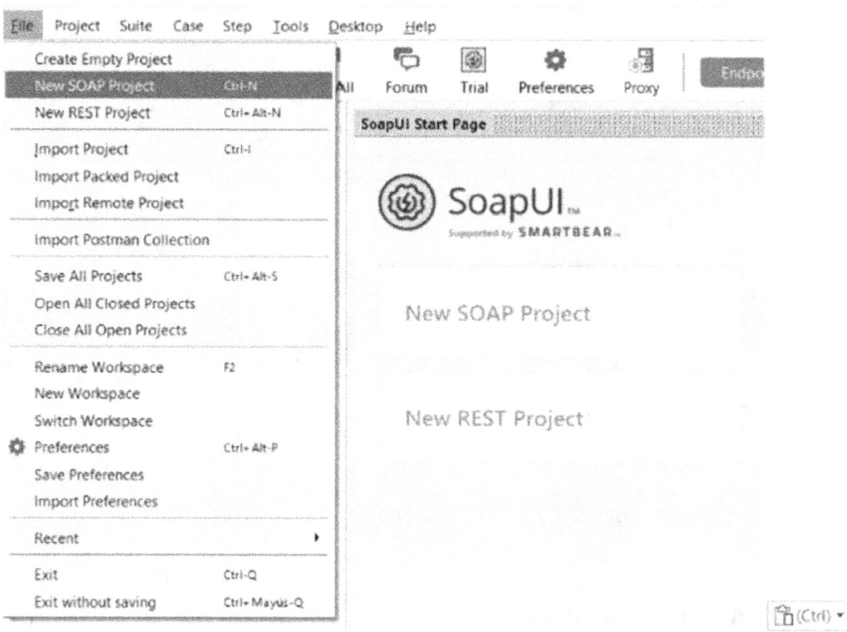

Figure B-5. *Creating a New SOAP Project*

2. Enter the project name and paste the complete WSDL URL.

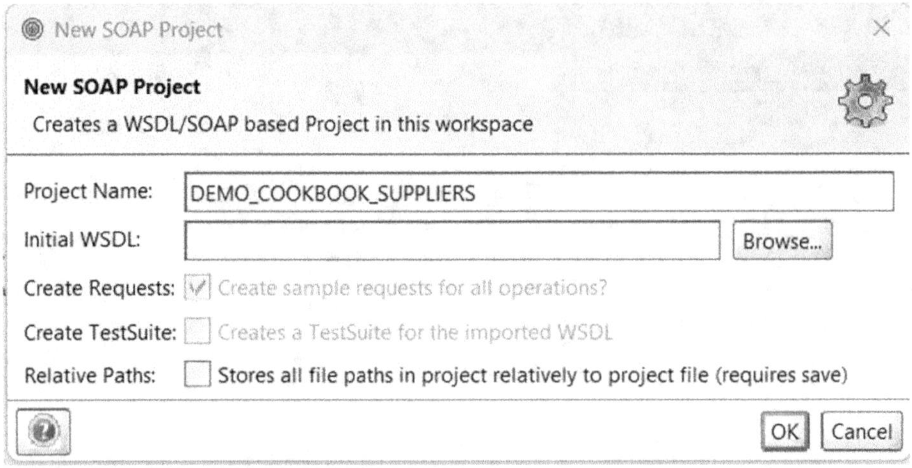

Figure B-6. *Project Configuration Dialog*

Step 4: Configure Authorization

Set up Basic Authorization as shown below. This is the standard method for testing Oracle services.

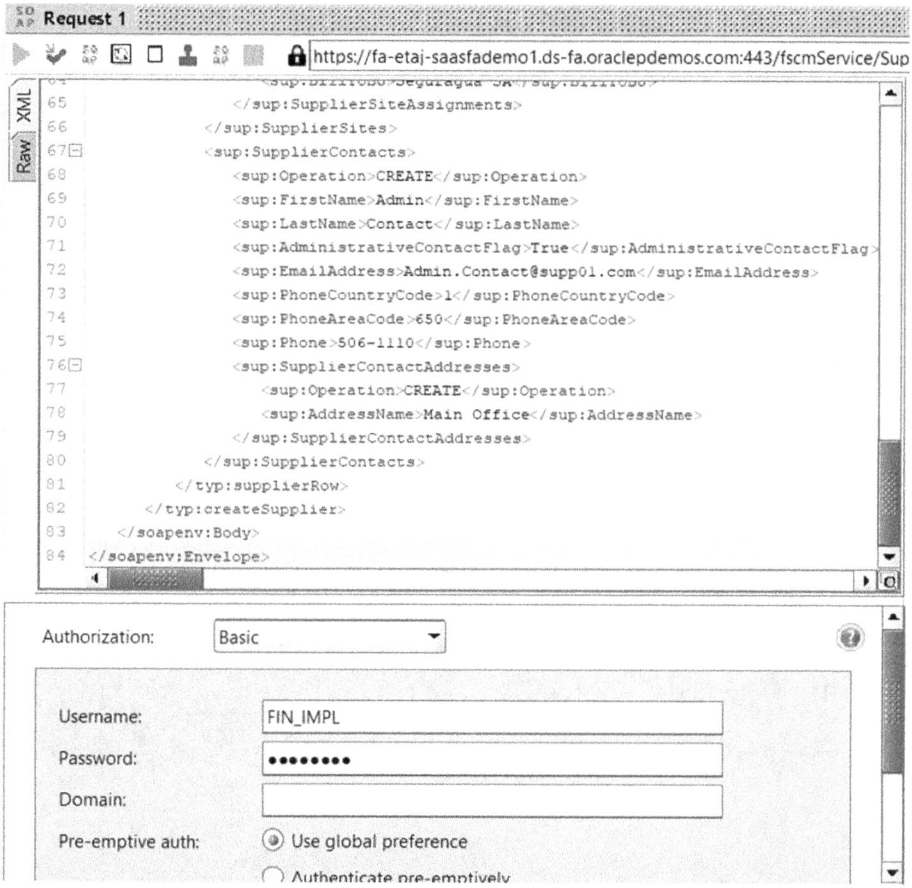

Figure B-7. Basic Authentication Configuration

Step 5: Prepare Your Test Payload

Find a working payload example through

- Internet searches
- Oracle Support documentation
- Appendix C for sample payloads

Note Finding sample payloads can vary in difficulty. Some are readily available, while others require more research.

Step 6: Execute the Test

Use a simplified payload for initial testing.

Figure B-8. *Test Execution Example*

APPENDIX C

SOAP Web Services Samples

Important Disclaimers

⚠ **Deprecation Notice:** Oracle is migrating SOAP web services to REST APIs. Some services listed here may be deprecated by the time you review this document.

⚠ **Version Warning:** Some SOAP services overlap with equivalent REST APIs. For example, SCM Sales Orders SOAP services have been deprecated. Use the REST API version only.

Finding Available SOAP Web Services

Navigation Path:

Main Menu ➤ Tools ➤ Developer Connect

Developer Connect Menu:

J. J. Montero Rodríguez and S. Tahseen, *Oracle Integration Cookbook for Oracle ERP Cloud*, https://doi.org/10.1007/979-8-8688-3020-4

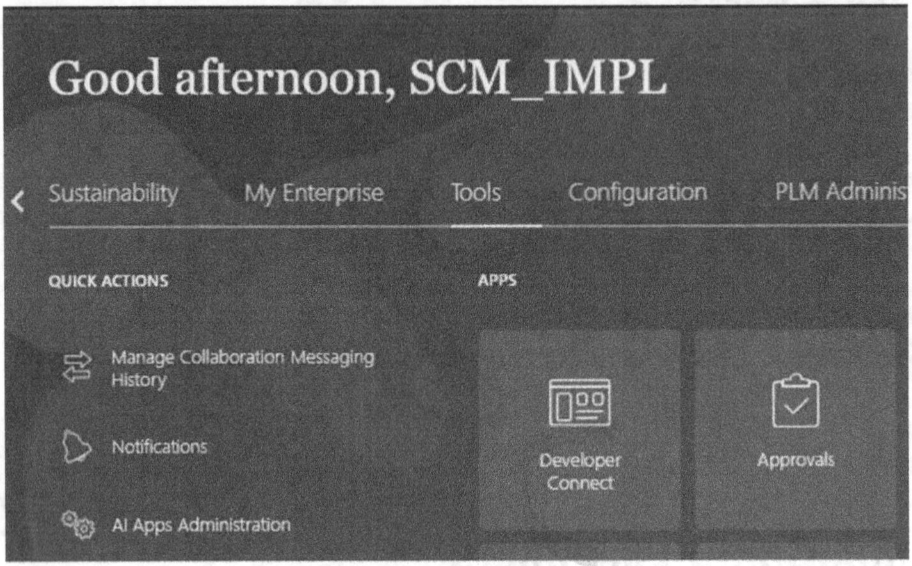

Figure C-1. Developer Connect Navigation

From here you can

1. Download WSDL files for analysis.

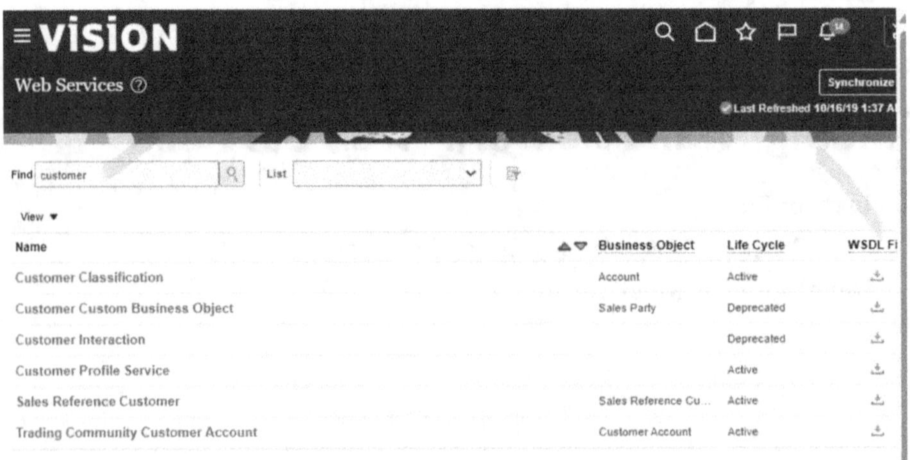

Figure C-2. WSDL Download Interface

2. View detailed service information by clicking the service name.

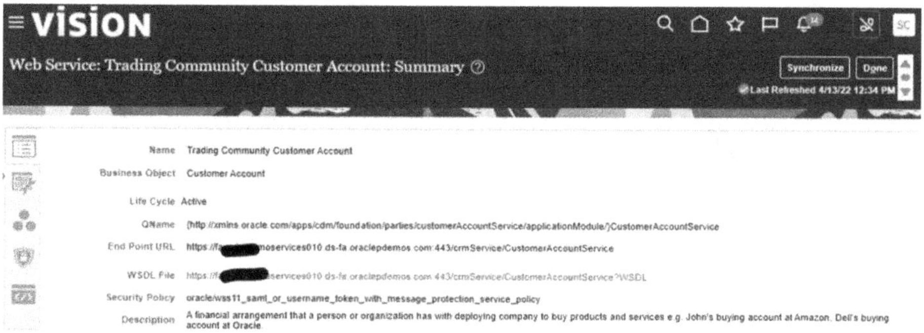

Figure C-3. *Service Details View*

Sample SOAP Payloads

The following samples have been tested and verified. A complete collection of 40+ payloads is available in the GitHub repository.

No.	Sample Payload and WSDL

1	`https://XXXX.ds-fa.oraclepdemos.com/fscmService/ErpObjectDFFUpdateService?WSDL` **ERP Object DFF Update Service**
	`https://xxxx.ds-fa.oraclepdemos.com/fscmService/ErpObjectDFFUpdateService?WSDL`
	`<!--DOCID  METALINK (Doc ID 2546651.1) -->`
	`<!--`
	`https://cloudcustomerconnect.oracle.com/posts/a2489bd8fc`
	`Line Number in User Key A`
	`Invoice Number in User Key B`
	`Business Unit Name in User Key C`
	`Supplier Name in User Key D`

(continued)

No.	Sample Payload and WSDL

```
Supplier Number in User Key E
Supplier Site Name in User Key F
Invoice Identifier in User Key G-VOUCHER NUMBER?
-->
<soap:Body>
<ns1:updateDffEntityDetails xmlns:ns1="http://xmlns.
oracle.com/apps/financials/commonModules/shared/model/
erpIntegrationService/types/">
<ns1:document xmlns:ns2="http://xmlns.oracle.com/apps/
financials/commonModules/shared/model/erpIntegration
Service/">
<ns2:Content>NULL</ns2:Content>
<ns2:FileName>#NULL</ns2:FileName>
<ns2:ContentType>#NULL</ns2:ContentType>
<ns2:DocumentTitle>#NULL</ns2:DocumentTitle>
<ns2:DocumentAuthor>#NULL</ns2:DocumentAuthor>
<ns2:DocumentSecurityGroup>#NULL</ns2:Document
SecurityGroup>
<ns2:DocumentAccount>#NULL </ns2:DocumentAccount>
<ns2:DocumentName/>
<ns2:DocumentId/>
</ns1:document>
<ns1:operationMode>single</ns1:operationMode>
<ns1:object xmlns:ns2="http://xmlns.oracle.com/apps/
financials/commonModules/shared/model/erpIntegration
Service/">
<ns2:EntityName>Payables Invoice Lines</ns2:EntityName>
<ns2:ContextValue>#NULL</ns2:ContextValue>
<ns2:UserKeyA>1</ns2:UserKeyA>
```

(*continued*)

No.	Sample Payload and WSDL

```
<ns2:UserKeyB>TEST00012</ns2:UserKeyB>
<ns2:UserKeyC>ZZZ XXX Spain SAU</ns2:UserKeyC><ns2:UserK
eyD>IBERICA, S.R.L.</ns2:UserKeyD>
<ns2:UserKeyE>11622</ns2:UserKeyE>
<ns2:UserKeyF>ACREEDOR</ns2:UserKeyF>
<ns2:UserKeyG>#NULL</ns2:UserKeyG>
<ns2:UserKeyH>#NULL</ns2:UserKeyH>
<ns2:DFFAttributes>{“ATTRIBUTE4":"123123-1"}
</ns2:DFFAttributes>
</ns1:object>
<ns1:notificationCode>#NULL</ns1:notificationCode>
<ns1:CallbackURL>#NULL</ns1:CallbackURL>
</ns1:updateDffEntityDetails>
</soap:Body>
</soap:Envelope>
```

2 To create records in the Payables invoice interface

https://xxxx.fa.us2.oraclecloud.com:443/fscmService/InvoiceInterfaceService?WSDL

Invoice Interface Service

```
<soapenv:Envelope xmlns:soapenv="http://schemas.xmlsoap
.org/soap/envelope/" xmlns:typ="http://xmlns.oracle.com/
apps/financials/payables/invoices/quickInvoices/
invoiceInterfaceService/types/" xmlns:inv="http://
xmlns.oracle.com/apps/financials/payables/invoices/
quickInvoices/invoiceInterfaceService/">
<soapenv:Header/>
<soapenv:Body>
<typ:createInvoiceInterface>
```

(*continued*)

No.	Sample Payload and WSDL


```
<inv:Source>External</inv:Source>
<inv:OrgId>300000001593038</inv:OrgId><inv:Vendor
Id>300000003756734</inv:VendorId>
<inv:VendorSiteId>300000003756776</inv:VendorSiteId>
<inv:AcctsPayCodeCombinationId>10001</inv:AcctsPay
CodeCombinationId>
<inv:GroupId>999999003</inv:GroupId>
<inv:InvoiceAmount currencyCode="EUR">100</inv:
InvoiceAmount>
<inv:InvoiceCurrencyCode>EUR</inv:InvoiceCurrencyCode>
<inv:InvoiceDate>2024-12-09</inv:InvoiceDate>
<inv:InvoiceNumber>VS_AP_99903</inv:InvoiceNumber>
<inv:InvoiceReceivedDate>2024-12-09</inv:
InvoiceReceivedDate>
<inv:InvoiceTypeLookupCode>STANDARD</inv:InvoiceType
LookupCode>
<inv:LegalEntityId>300000001592008</inv:LegalEntityId>
<inv:PartyId>300000003756732</inv:PartyId>
<inv:PartySiteId>300000003756763</inv:PartySiteId>
<inv:PayGroupLookupCode>Standard</
inv:PayGroupLookupCode>
<inv:PaymentCurrencyCode>EUR</inv:PaymentCurrencyCode>
<inv:PaymentMethodCode>CHECK</inv:PaymentMethodCode>
<inv:PaymentPriority>99</inv:PaymentPriority>
<inv:TermsDate>2024-12-09</inv:TermsDate>
<inv:TermsId>300000001605218</inv:TermsId>
<inv:VendorEmailAddress>test@oracle.com</inv:Vendor
EmailAddress>
```


(*continued*)

No.	Sample Payload and WSDL
	<inv:InvoiceInterfaceLine> <inv:AccountingDate>2024-12-09</inv:AccountingDate> <inv:Amount currencyCode="EUR">100</inv:Amount> <inv:Description>test line by AP Webservice </inv:Description> <inv:DistCodeCombinationId>300000001693009</inv: DistCodeCombinationId> <inv:ItemDescription>TEST ITEM DESCRIPTION JJ991 </inv:ItemDescription> <inv:LineNumber>1</inv:LineNumber> <inv:LineTypeLookupCode>ITEM</inv:LineTypeLookupCode> <inv:OrgId>300000001593038</inv:OrgId> </inv:InvoiceInterfaceLine> </typ:invoiceInterfaceHeader> </typ:createInvoiceInterface> </soapenv:Body> </soapenv:Envelope>

(*continued*)

No.	Sample Payload and WSDL
3	https://abcd-test.fa.em3.oraclecloud.com:443/fscmService/StandardReceiptService https://abcd-test.fa.em3.oraclecloud.com/fscmService/StandardReceiptService?WSDL **Standard Receipt Service** <soapenv:Envelope xmlns:soapenv="http://schemas.xmlsoap.org/soap/envelope/" xmlns:typ="http://xmlns.oracle.com/apps/financials/receivables/receipts/shared/standardReceiptService/commonService/types/ " xmlns:com="http://xmlns.oracle.com/apps/financials/receivables/receipts/shared/standardReceiptService/commonService/" xmlns:act="http://xmlns.oracle.com/apps/flex/financials/receivables/receipts/shared/standardReceiptService/commonService/ActivityApplicationDff/" xmlns:act1="http://xmlns.oracle.com/apps/flex/financials/receivables/receipts/shared/standardReceiptService/commonService/ActivityApplicationGdf/"> <soapenv:Header/> <soapenv:Body> <typ:createActivityApplication> <typ:activityApplication> <com:BusinessUnit>Vision ABC Spain SAU</com:BusinessUnit> <com:ReceiptNumber>REC_JJM_001</com:ReceiptNumber> <com:ReceivableTrxName>Devoluciones a Clientes ZZZ</com:ReceivableTrxName> <com:AmountApplied>20.05</com:AmountApplied> <com:ApplyDate>2021-07-25</com:ApplyDate> <com:ApplyGlDate>2021-07-25</com:ApplyGlDate>

(continued)

No.	Sample Payload and WSDL


```
<com:AppliedPaymentScheduleId>-8</com:AppliedPayment
ScheduleId>
<com:PaymentMethodCode>Transferencia</com:Payment
MethodCode>
</typ:activityApplication>
</typ:createActivityApplication>
</soapenv:Body>
</soapenv:Envelope>
<soapenv:Envelope xmlns:soapenv="http://schemas.xmlsoap.
org/soap/envelope/" xmlns:typ="http://xmlns.oracle.com/
apps/financials/receivables/receipts/shared/standard
ReceiptService/commonService/types/" xmlns:com="
http://xmlns.oracle.com/apps/financials/receivables/
receipts/shared/standardReceiptService/commonService/
" xmlns:act="http://xmlns.oracle.com/apps/flex/
financials/receivables/receipts/shared/standardReceipt
Service/commonService/ActivityApplicationDff/" xmlns:
act1="http://xmlns.oracle.com/apps/flex/financials/
receivables/receipts/shared/standardReceiptService/
commonService/ActivityApplicationGdf/">
<soapenv:Header/>
<soapenv:Body>
<typ:createActivityApplication>
<typ:activityApplication>
<com:BusinessUnit>Vision ABC Spain SAU</com:
BusinessUnit>
```


(*continued*)

No.	Sample Payload and WSDL


```
<com:ReceiptNumber>REC_JJM_0010</com:ReceiptNumber>
<com:ReceivableTrxName>Write-off</com:ReceivableTrxName>
<com:AmountApplied>1</com:AmountApplied>
<com:ApplyDate>2021-08-25</com:ApplyDate>
<com:ApplyGlDate>2021-08-25</com:ApplyGlDate>
<com:AppliedPaymentScheduleId>-3</com:AppliedPayment
ScheduleId>
<!--Optional:
-10 Bills Receivable Fund Recovery
-9 Credit Card Chargeback
-8 Refund
-7 Prepayment
-6 Credit Card Refund
-3 Receipt Write-off-->
</typ:activityApplication>
</typ:createActivityApplication>
</soapenv:Body>
</soapenv:Envelope>
```

APPENDIX D

Technical Tips and Best Practices

Tip 1: Encode/Decode/Base64

Understanding Base64 Encoding

Base64 encoding transforms binary data into printable text, allowing you to transport binary data over protocols that only handle simple text.

Definition: Base64 is used to encode binary data as printable text, enabling transport over protocols that cannot handle binary data formats.

OIC Base64 Functions

Oracle Integration Cloud provides three key functions for Base64 operations.

Base64 Functions:

J. J. Montero Rodríguez and S. Tahseen, *Oracle Integration Cookbook for Oracle ERP Cloud*, https://doi.org/10.1007/979-8-8688-3020-4

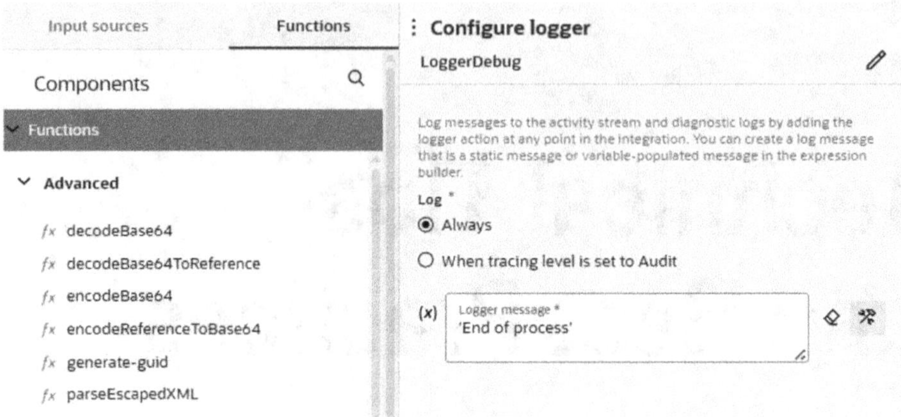

Figure D-1. *OIC Base64 Functions*

Practical Example: XX_FTP_TO_ATP_TO_FTP Integration

This demonstration integration shows how all three Base64 functions work together using an ATP database and an FTP server.

Integration Flow:

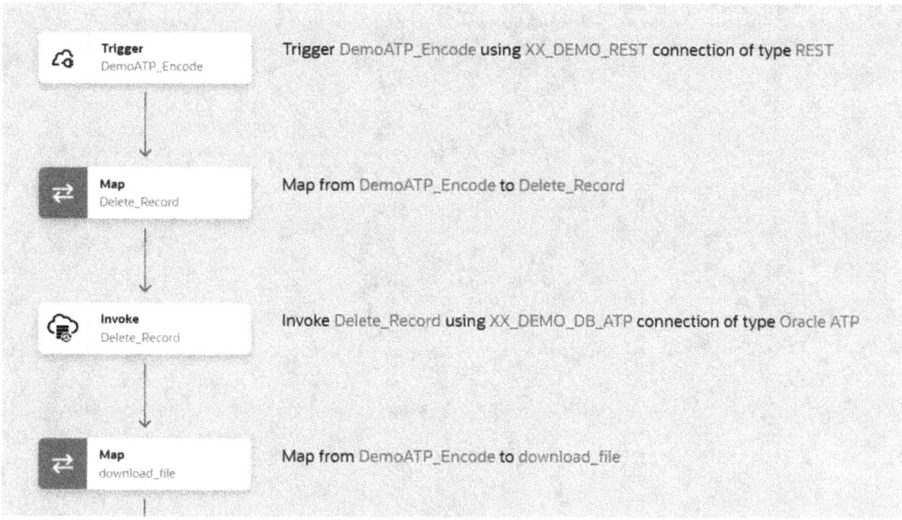

Figure D-2. *Base64 Integration Flow*

Step 1: Download and Encode

Download the file from FTP and insert it into the ATP database as a CLOB.

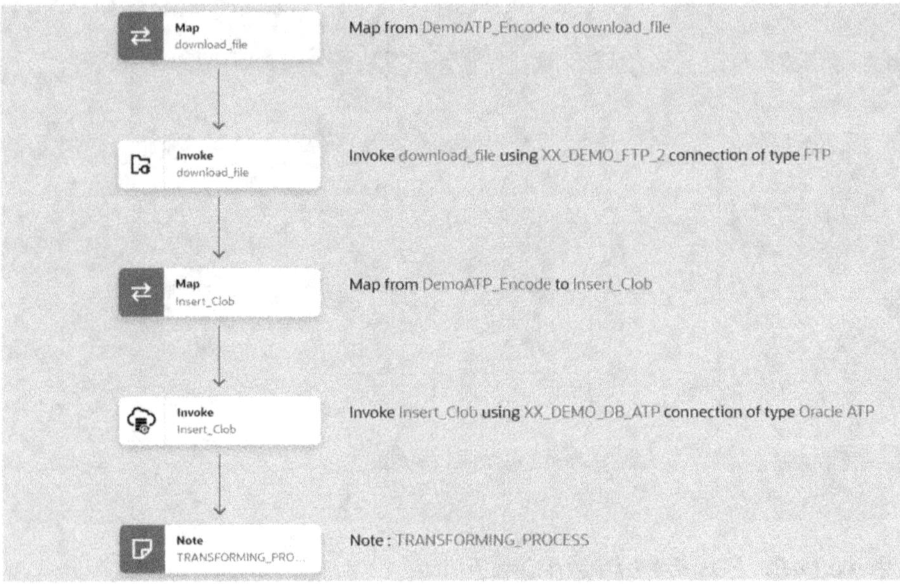

Figure D-3. *File Download and CLOB Insertion*

In the Insert_Clob activity, use encodeReferenceToBase64 to store the file as Base64:

```
oraext:encodeReferenceToBase64(
  $download_file/nsmpr1:DownloadFileToICSResponse/
  ns27:DownloadResponse/ns27:ICSFiles/ns25:ICSFile/
  ns25:FileReference
)
```

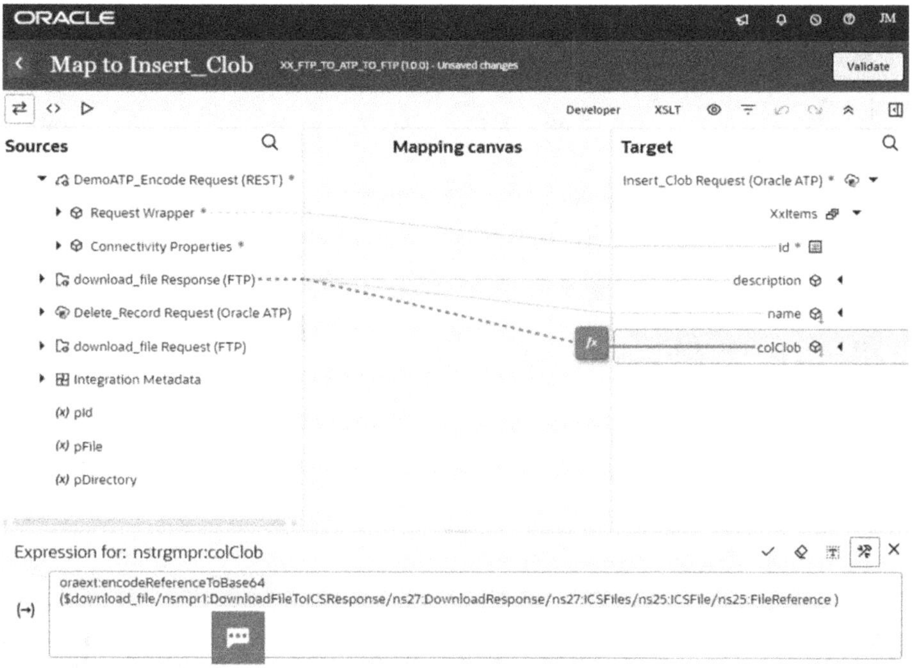

Figure D-4. *encodeReferenceToBase64 Usage*

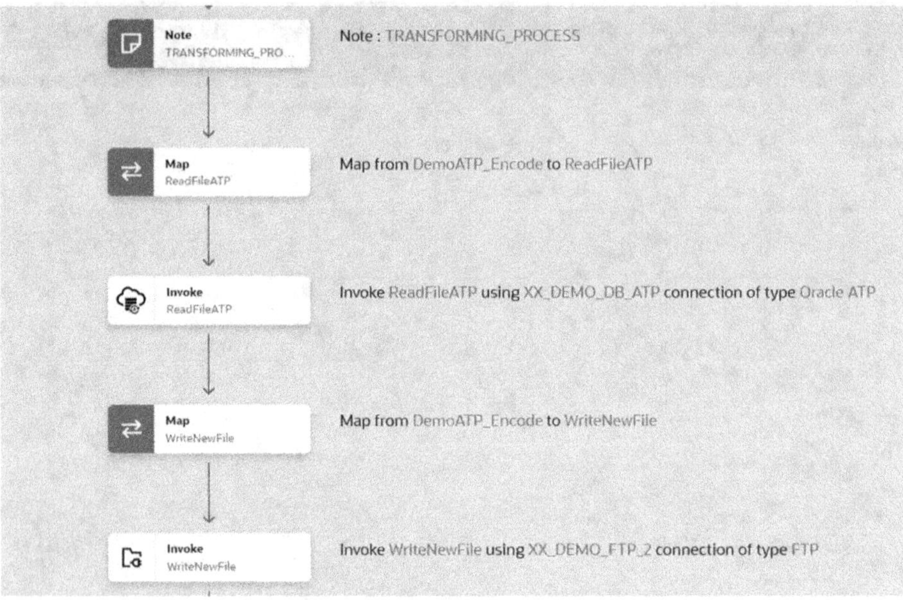

Figure D-5. *Base64 Storage in the Database*

Step 2: Read and Decode

As we have stored the file in the ATP database as Base64 format, we have to decodeBase64ToReference in the WriteNewFile activity; use decodeBase64ToReference because the file operation expects a file reference, not a Base64 string:

```
oraext:decodeBase64ToReference(
  $ReadFileATP/nsmpr7:ReadFileATPOutputCollection/
  nsmpr7:ReadFileATPOutput/nsmpr7:COL_CLOB
)
```

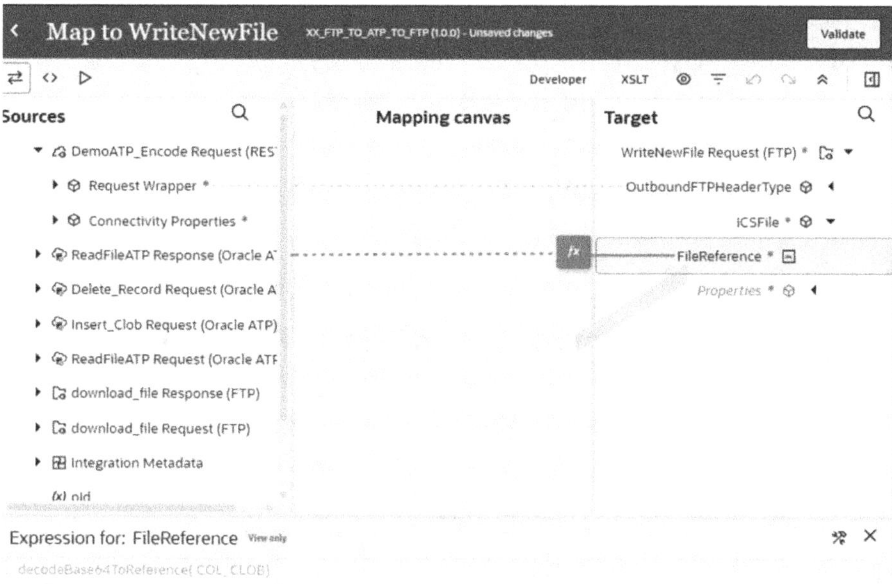

Figure D-6. *File Write Operation Expects File Reference*

Code Reference

Code Example	Comments
XX_FTP_TO_ATP_TO_FTP	Package file XX_DEMO_COOKBOOK.par

Tip 2: Date Formatting

Example 1: Custom Date–Time Format

Create a timestamp in this format: 99YYYYMMDDHHMMSS.

```
fn:concat(
  '99',
  fn:substring(fn:string(fn:current-dateTime()), 1, 4),    /* Year */
```

```
  fn:substring(fn:string(fn:current-dateTime()), 6, 2),    /* Month */
  fn:substring(fn:string(fn:current-dateTime()), 9, 2),    /* Day */
  fn:substring(fn:string(fn:current-dateTime()), 12, 2),   /* Hour */
  fn:substring(fn:string(fn:current-dateTime()), 15, 2),   /* Minute */
  fn:substring(fn:string(fn:current-dateTime()), 18, 2)    /* Second */
)
```

Example 2: Format-DateTime Function

Format a date-time value using XPath 2.0:

```
xp20:format-dateTime(
  /nssrcmpr:schedule/nssrcmpr:startTime,
  "[Y0001]-[M01]-[D01] [H01]:[m01]:[s01]"
)
```

Tip 3: Advanced REST API Techniques

Using Finders

Some REST APIs restrict which fields can be used with the q parameter. Finders define these restrictions.

Example:

```
curl -u "username:password" \
  -H "Content-Type: application/vnd.oracle.adf.
  resourcecollection+json" \
  -X GET \
  https://zzzz-test.fa.em3.oraclecloud.com:443//fscmRestApi/
  resources/11.13.18.05/receivablesInvoices?onlyData=true&
  finder=invoiceSearch;DocumentNumber=aaV18-0030
```

```
&finder=invoiceSearch;DocumentNumber=PTV18-0030
```

Complex Queries with Child Nodes

Filter using child node fields (e.g., SourceOrder):

https://zzzz-dev1.fa.em2.oraclecloud.com:443/fscmRestApi/resources/11.13.18.05/shipments?onlyData=true&q=unpackedShipmentLines.SourceOrder='1241952' and OrganizationCode='IN'

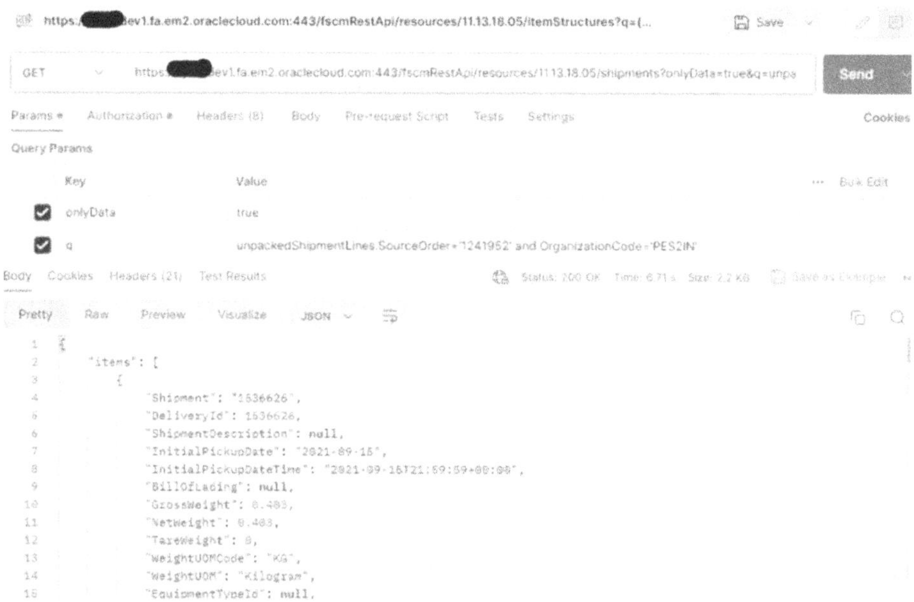

Figure D-7. Filtering with a Child Node

Date Ranges and Child (SourceOrder) Filtering

https://xxxx-dev1.fa.em2.oraclecloud.com:443/fscmRestApi/resources/11.13.18.05/shipments?onlyData=true&q=unpackedShipmentLines.SourceOrder='1241952' and OrganizationCode='aaS2IN' and (ActualShipDateTime BETWEEN '2021-09-14T00:00:00.000%2b00:00' AND '2021-09-16T00:00:00.000%2b00:00')

With Time Component:

```
https://xxxx-dev1.fa.em2.oraclecloud.com:443/fscmRestApi/
resources/11.13.18.05/shipments?q=(ActualShipDateTime BETWEEN
'2023-01-15T00:00:00.000%2b00:00' AND '2023-09-15T00:00:00.000
%2b00:00')&limit=100&onlyData=true
```

Date-Time Filter

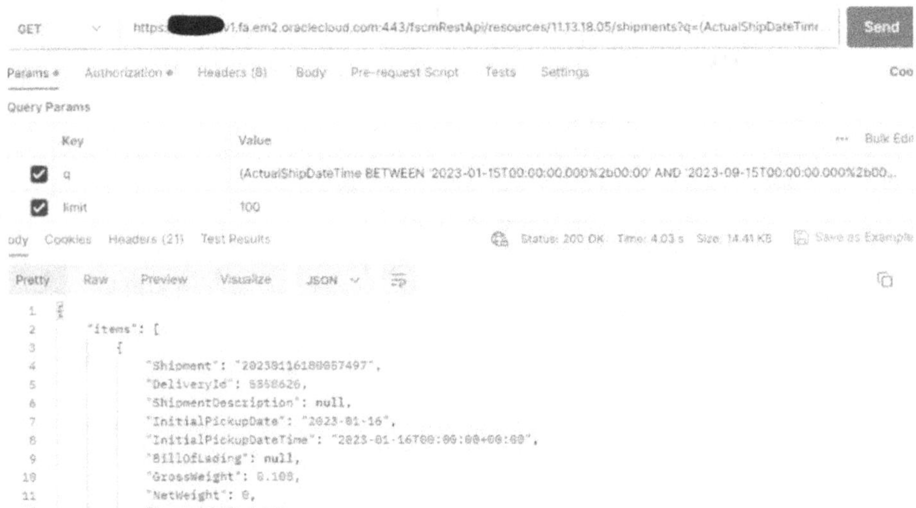

Figure D-8. Date-Time Range Query

Without Time Component:

```
https://xxxx-dev1.fa.em2.oraclecloud.com:443/fscmRestApi/
resources/11.13.18.05/shipments?q=(ActualShipDate BETWEEN
'2023-01-15' AND '2023-09-15')&limit=100&onlyData=true
```

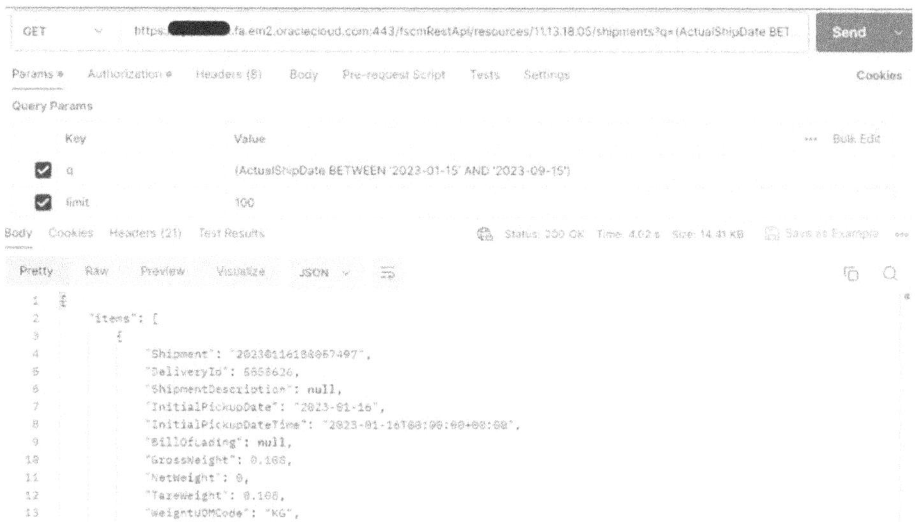

Figure D-9. *Date Range Query*

Expanding Child Collections

Use the expand parameter to include child node data:

```
expand=unpackedShipmentLines&limit=1
```

Or expand all child nodes:

```
expand=all
```

https://abcd-dev1.fa.em2.oraclecloud.com:443/fscmRestApi/resources/11.13.18.05/shipments?onlyData=true&q=unpackedShipmentLines.SourceOrder='1241952' and OrganizationCode='IN' and (ActualShipDateTime BETWEEN '2021-09-14T00:00:00.000%2b00:00' AND '2021-09-16T00:00:00.000%2b00:00')&expand=unpackedShipmentLines&limit=1

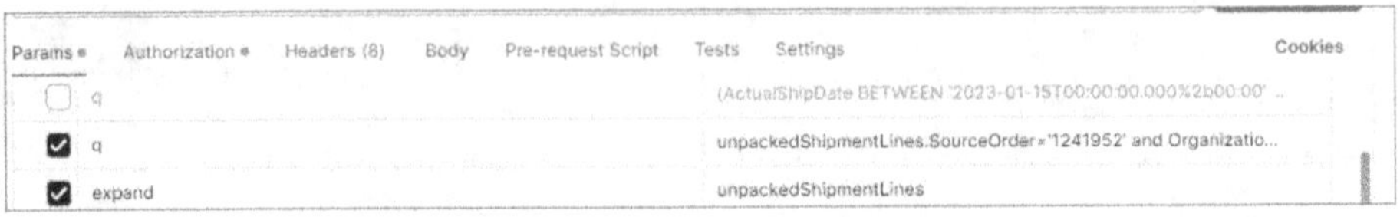

Figure D-10. *Response Showing Expanded Child Nodes*

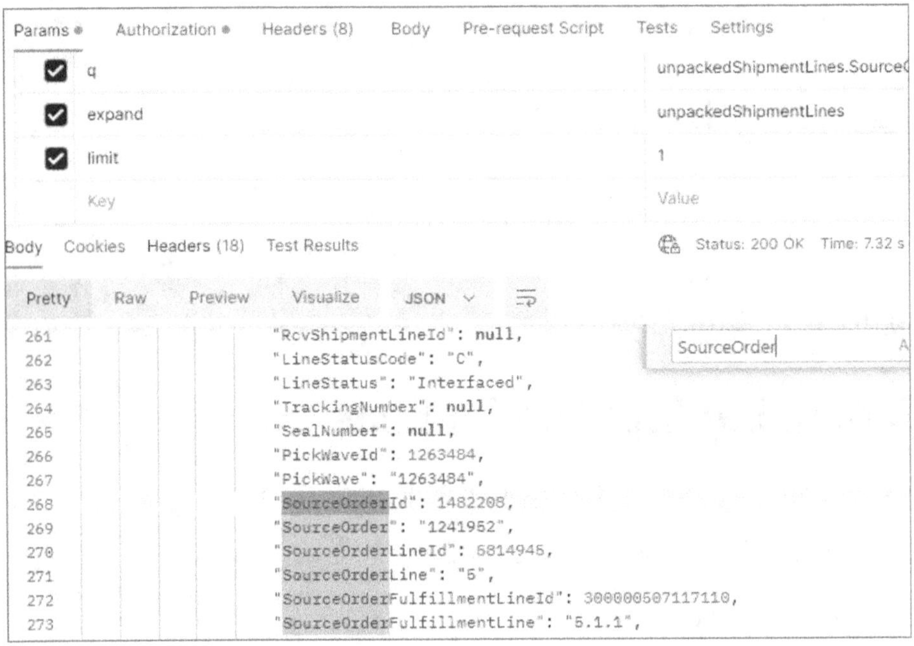

Figure D-11. *Detailed Child Node Data*

REST API Endpoint

This feature will allow as to know what features are available in our REST API.

curl -u "XX:ZZ" -H "Content-Type: application/vnd.oracle.adf.resourcecollection+json" -X GET "`https://abfa.oraclepdemos.com/fscmRestApi/resources/latest/receivablesInvoices/describe`"> a.txt

The response shows for each attribute:

- Can it be updated?
- Is it required?
- Is it queryable?
- Additional metadata

```
{
    "Resources" : {
        "receivablesInvoices" : {
            "discrColumnType" : false,
                "usage" : "BusinessObject",
                    "attributes" : [{
                        "name": "CustomerTransactionId",
                        "type": "integer",
                        "updatable": true,
                        "mandatory": true,
                        "queryable": true,
                        "allowChanges": "inCreate",
                        "precision": 18
```

Figure D-12. *API Describe Response Showing Attribute Properties*

REST API Versions

Issue: Complex queries with AND operators may fail in OIC but work in Postman. Imagine a query like this:

OrderNumber='zzz1000149' AND ProcurementBU='zzzz'

Root Cause: OIC uses a default REST-Framework-Version header value. Queries with AND operators require version 4 or higher.

Solution: Explicitly set the header in OIC.

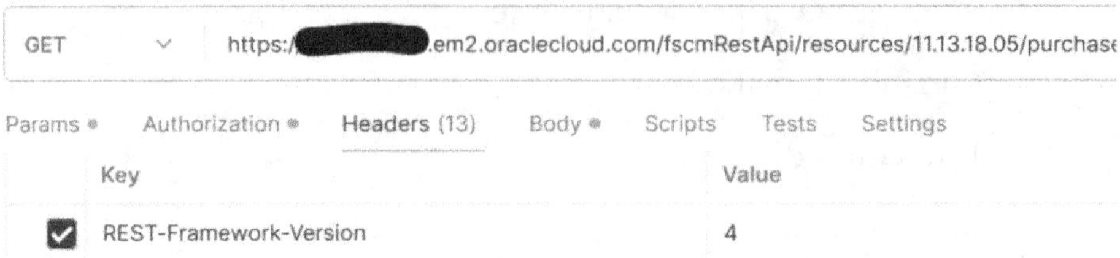

Figure D-13. *REST-Framework-Version in Postman*

OIC Header Configuration

In OIC the default "REST-Framework-Version" is set up by Oracle.

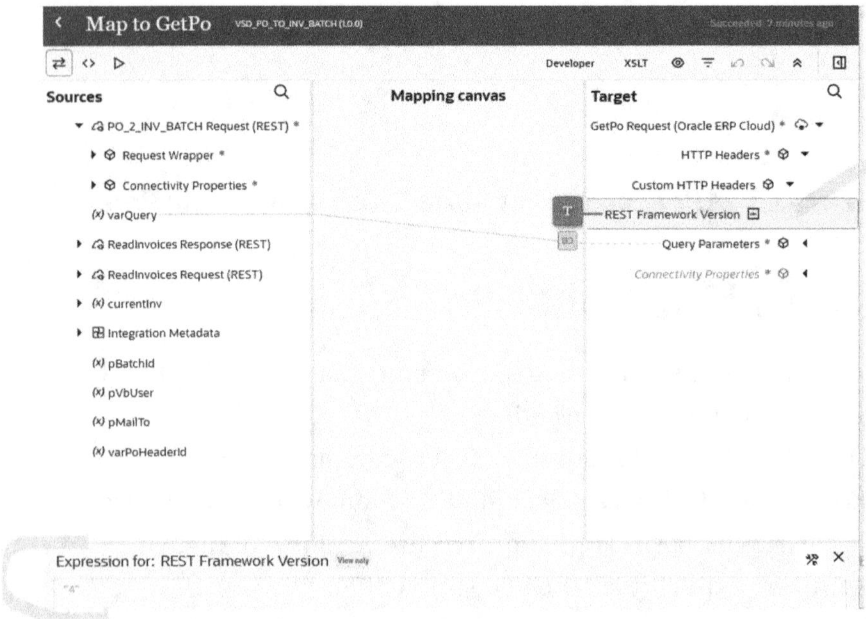

Figure D-14. *Setting REST-Framework-Version in OIC*

Reference Documentation:

Working with REST API Framework Versions

Tip 4: Adding Duration to Dates

Add hours, minutes, or days to date-time values using XSD duration functions.

Example: Add One Hour

```
string(
  fn:current-dateTime() + xsd:dayTimeDuration("PT1H")
)
```

Duration Format:

- PT1H = 1 hour
- PT30M = 30 minutes
- P1D = 1 day
- PT2H30M = 2 hours and 30 minutes

Reference Documentation:

- Date, Time, and Duration Functions
- TechSupper: Date-Time Calculations

Tip 5: Case-Insensitive REST Searches

Perform case-insensitive searches using the UPPER() function with OR logic.

URL Format:

https://abcd.ds-fa.oraclepdemos.com/hcmRestApi/resources/11.13.18.05/publicWorkers?fields=DisplayName,PersonId;assignments:LocationTownOrCity;phones:PhoneNumber&q=((UPPER(DisplayName) LIKE '%cook%') or (DisplayName LIKE '%cook%'))&limit=25&offset=0

Equivalent JSON Query Structure:

```
{
 "op": "$or",
 "criteria": [
  {
   "op": "$co",
   "attribute": "UPPER(DisplayName)",
   "value": "{{ $variables.searchString }}"
  },
  {
   "op": "$co",
   "attribute": "DisplayName",
   "value": "{{ $variables.searchString }}"
  }
 ]
}
```

Important To use OR operators, set REST-Framework-Version to 4 or higher.

Figure D-15. *REST-Framework-Version Header for OR Queries*

Tip 6: OIC Scheduling with iCal

Basic Scheduling

OIC provides a basic scheduling interface for simple scenarios.

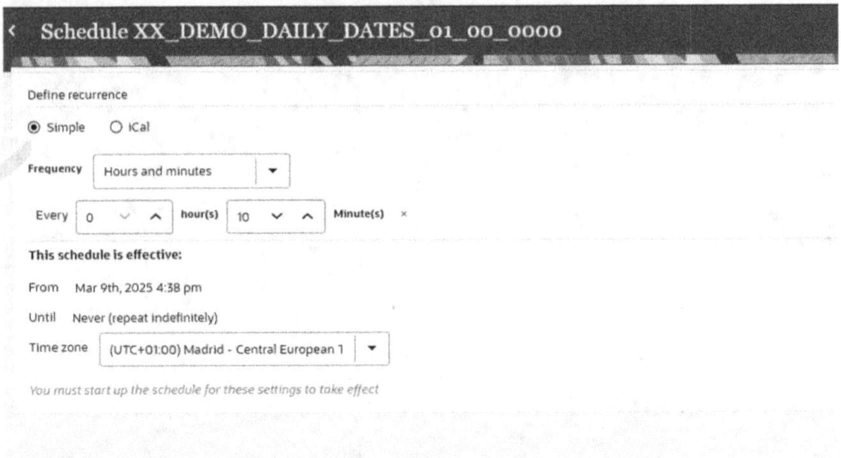

Figure D-16. OIC Basic Scheduling Interface

Advanced Scheduling with iCal

For complex scheduling requirements (e.g., last day of month), use iCal expressions.

Example Goal: Run integration on the last day of every month at 10 AM.

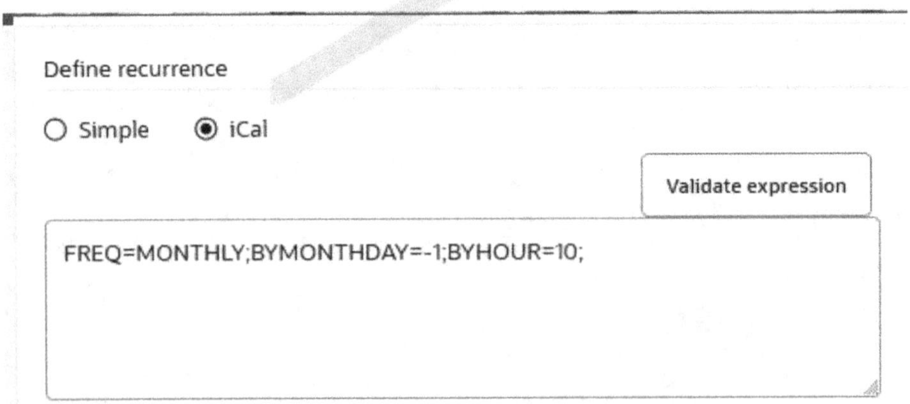

Figure D-17. Last Day of Month Requirement

iCal Expression:

FREQ=MONTHLY;BYMONTHDAY=-1;BYH
OUR=10;

Breakdown:

- FREQ=MONTHLY = Run monthly
- BYMONTHDAY=-1 = The last day of the month (negative values count backward from the end of the month)
- BYHOUR=10 = At 10 AM

Configuration Steps:

1. Select the activated integration in the console.

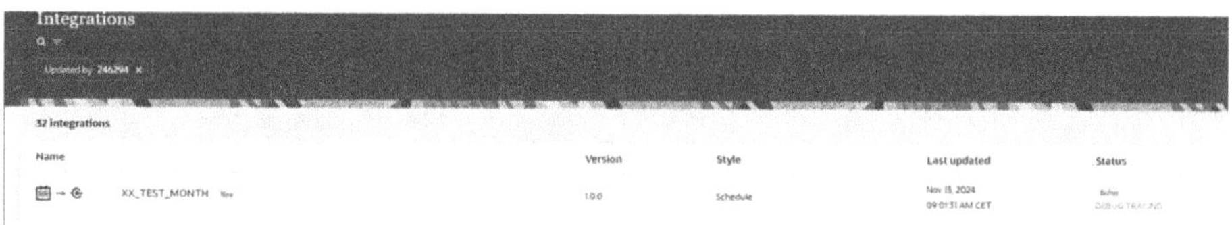

***Figure D-18.** Selecting Integration for Scheduling*

2. Right-click and choose the Schedule option.

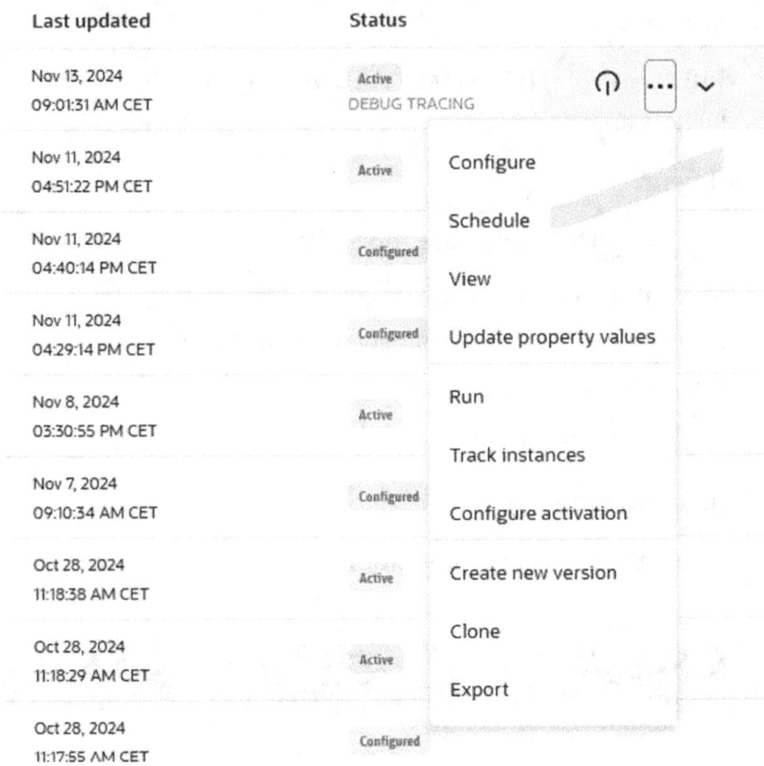

Figure D-19. *Schedule Context Menu*

3. Click "Edit".

Figure D-20. *Edit Button*

4. Enter the iCal expression.

   Use this iCal sentence:

   FREQ=MONTHLY;BYMONTHDAY=-1;BYHOUR=10;

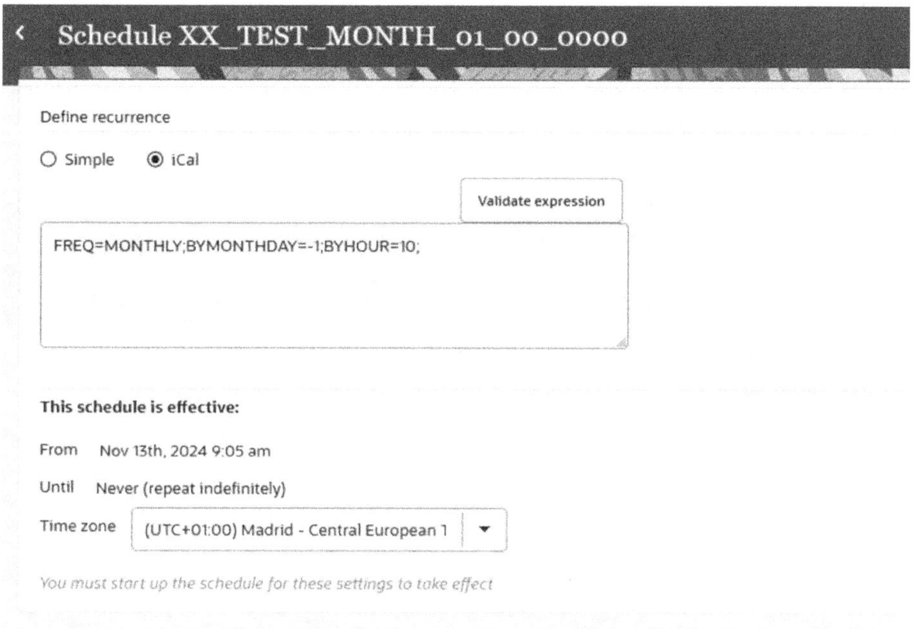

Figure D-21. *Entering iCal Expression*

5. Validate and save, and then click "Start".

***Figure D-22.** Starting the Schedule*

6. View upcoming runs.

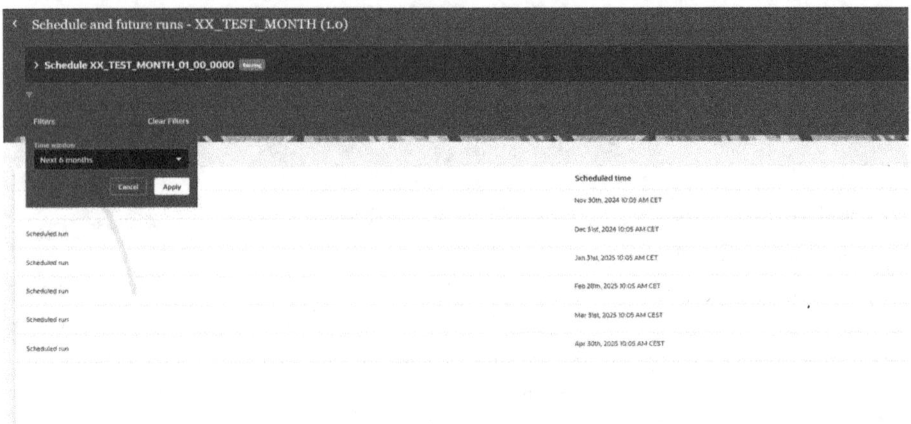

***Figure D-23.** Viewing Scheduled Runs*

Multiple-Day Scheduling

Example 1: First Five Days of the Month

Integration 1:

FREQ=MONTHLY;BYMONTHDAY=1,2,3,4,5,6;BYHO UR=10,11,12,13,14;

Integration 2 (Combine Multiple Schedules with &):

FREQ=MONTHLY;BYMONTHDAY=-1;BYHOUR=10; &FREQ=MONTHLY;BYMONTHDAY=1,2,3,4,5,6;BYHO UR=11,12,13,14,15,16,17,18;

Example 2: Multiple Times Per Day

```
FREQ=DAILY;BYHOUR=17;BYMINUTE=30,40,50;BYSECOND=0;
    &FREQ=DAILY;BYHOUR=18;BYMINUTE=0,10,20,30,40,50;
    BYSECOND=0;
    &FREQ=DAILY;BYHOUR=19;BYMINUTE=0,10,20,30;
    BYSECOND=0;
```

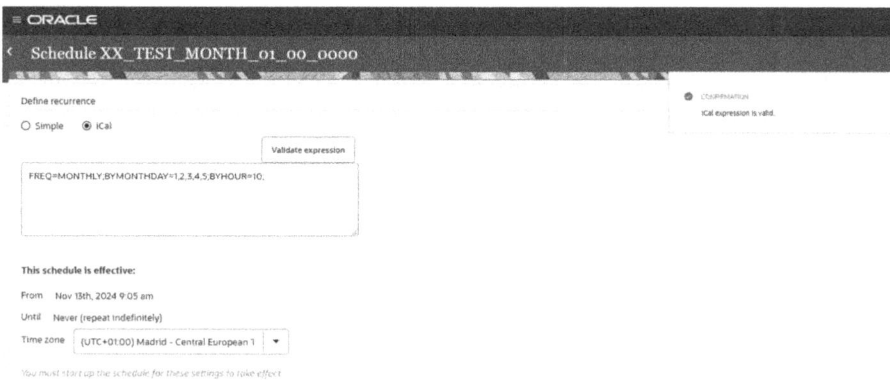

Figure D-24. *Multiple Schedules Configuration*

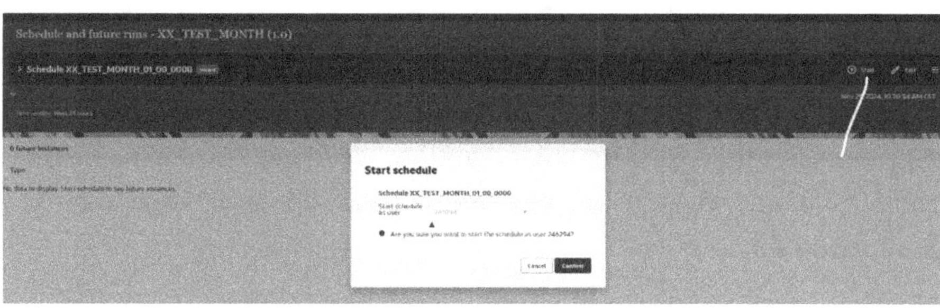

Figure D-25. *Starting Multiple Schedules*

Figure D-26. Viewing Multiple Scheduled Runs

Reference Documentation:

Define Integration Schedule

Tip 7: Get XSD File from Integration to Reuse in Other Integrations

The Problem

Sometimes you need to reuse a format definition from an existing integration, but there's no download option. We always can upload a new format (csv, xml, xsd, etc.), but we cannot download the schema to reuse in other integrations.

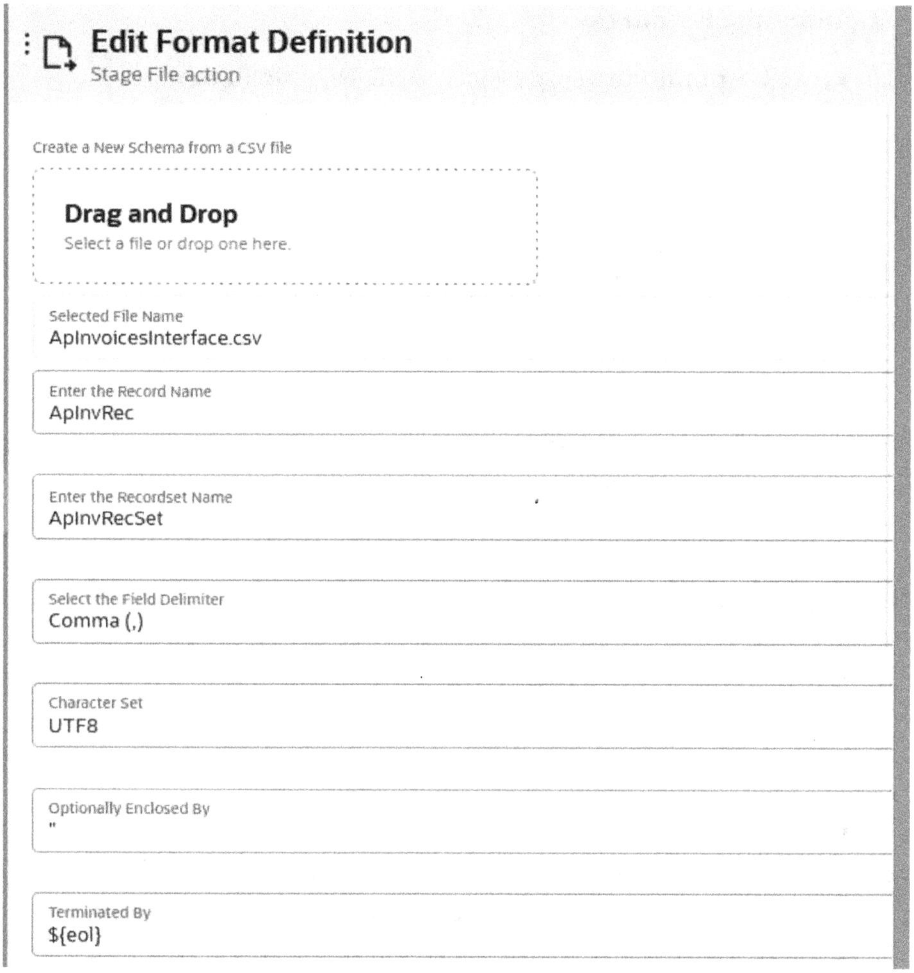

Figure D-27. *Format Definition Without the Download Option*

Manually recreating the XSD can be time-consuming and error-prone.

The Solution

You can extract the XSD from an existing integration and reuse it.

Community Resources:

- OIC Community Discussion – XSD Download Gen3
- OIC Community Discussion – XSD File Download

Tip 8: Cleaning Filenames

The Challenge

Special characters in filenames can cause integration failures. While you should educate users and partners about naming conventions, you may still receive problematic files.

The Solution

Use string manipulation functions to sanitize filenames.

Feel free to adapt to your needs, including to control more characters.

Example:

```
concat (substring (concat (translate (orajs8:replace ($i_
Customer/nsmpr4:Customer/nsmpr4:name, "/", "_" ), " ", "" ),
"_", $date, "_", $i_Customer/nsmpr4:Customer/nsmpr4:invoice,
"_", $self/nsmpr2:metadata/nsmpr2:runtime/nsmpr2:instanceId ),
1, 39 ), ".xml" )
```

This expression

- Replaces forward slashes with underscores
- Removes spaces
- Adds date, invoice number, and instance ID
- Limits the filename to 39 characters
- Adds .xml extension

Tip 9: Handling Quotation Marks in REST Queries

The Problem

When copying query parameters from Postman to OIC, quotation marks can cause syntax errors.

Figure D-28. Query Working in Postman

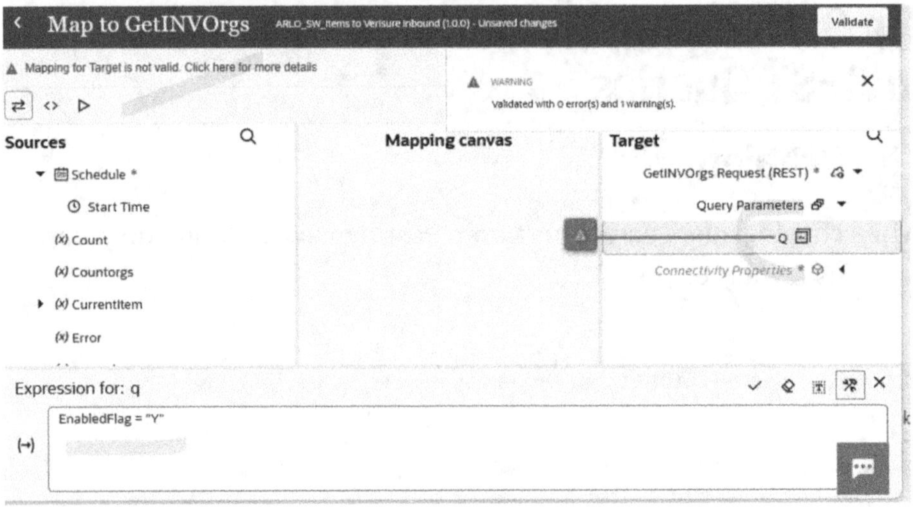

Figure D-29. *Query Error in OIC*

The Solution

Enclose single quotation marks with double quotes using the concat function like below to remove the errors:

```
concat ("EnabledFlag = ", "'", "Y", "'" )
Result: EnabledFlag = 'Y'
```

Glossary

Abbreviation	Definition
API	Application Program Interface
ERP	Enterprise Resource Planning
FA	Fusion Applications (provided as SaaS)
FBDI	File-Based Data Import
OIC	Oracle Integration Cloud
PaaS	Platform as a Service
REST	Representational State Transfer—an architectural API style for developing web services using HTTP
SaaS	Software as a Service (Oracle ERP Cloud)
SOAP	Simple Object Access Protocol
TCM	True Cloud Method—implementation method available from Oracle Cloud Adoption Framework
UCM	Universal Content Management—a document management system based on Oracle WebCenter Content embedded in Oracle Fusion Applications
WS	Web Service
WSDL	Web Services Definition Language

J. J. Montero Rodríguez and S. Tahseen, *Oracle Integration Cookbook for Oracle ERP Cloud*, https://doi.org/10.1007/979-8-8688-3020-4

Glossary

References

Documentation and Resources

1. **OIC Error Messages**
    - Oracle Integration Error Messages PDF
2. **Security Best Practices**
    - OIC Security Overview
    - Enhanced Security in Adapters
    - OIC Security Best Practices
    - OCI Compliance Controls
3. **Rest API Documentation**
    - Demystifying Oracle Rest Api

J. J. Montero Rodríguez and S. Tahseen, *Oracle Integration Cookbook for Oracle ERP Cloud*,
https://doi.org/10.1007/979-8-8688-3020-4

Index

A

Activity stream logs, 98
Adapters
  categories, 6
  definitions, 7
  in Generation 3, 5–6
  Rapid Adapter Builder, 7
  secure connectivity, 7
Advanced flow control
  accumulate the total, 52
  add a For-Each loop action and assign, 49, 50
  add conditional logic with switch, 50, 51
  assignment statement, 53
  assign total to response, 53–55
  conditional logic and loops, 48
  final integration flow, 54
  fn:number() Statement, 52
  For-Each and Switch Configuration, 51
  initialize variables, 49
  number() function, 52
  Switch Variable Initialization, 51
  technical reference, 56
  testing, 54
  Total Calculation Expression, 52
Advanced REST API techniques
  date range query, 521
  date–time range query, 520
  expand child collections, 521–523
  filter, child node fields, 519
  Finders, 518
  OIC header configuration, 524
  REST API versions, 523
  REST-framework-version, Postman, 524
  setting REST-framework-version, OIC, 524
Application integration, 3
  API Endpoint, 35
  connection selection, 38
  create integration dialog, 37
  endpoint configuration, 38
  inside your project, 36
  Postman Test Request, 36
  request and response configuration, 39
  request payload, 39–42
  response data mapping, 42–43
  response payload configuration, 42
  REST API, 35

J. J. Montero Rodríguez and S. Tahseen, *Oracle Integration Cookbook for Oracle ERP Cloud*, https://doi.org/10.1007/979-8-8688-3020-4

Application integration (*cont.*)
the REST Trigger configure, 37
technical reference, 48
testing, 46–48
validate, save, and activate, 44–45
ATP database, 407, 408
ATP query with parameter, 212
ATP invoke, 213
display names, 215
query mapping, 214
query results, 215
run the SQL statement, 213
source data, 216
test execution, 216
connection, 23–27
database script, 205, 206
insert operation, 207
database record, 210
import tables, 207
insert mapping, 208
insert test result, 209
technical reference, 216
update operation, 210
console result, 211
update mapping, 211
updated record, 212
ATP DB, 414
Attachments, Oracle ERP
attachment types, 278
automated attachments, REST APIs, 279
file attachment (*see* File attachment)
manual attachment process, 278, 279
overview, 277
URL attachment (*see* URL attachment)

B

Base64
definition, 511
encoding, 511
Base64 functions
decodeBase64ToReference, 516
encodeReferenceToBase64 Usage, 515
File Download and CLOB Insertion, 514
File Write Operation Expects File Reference, 517
integration flow, 513
storage, database, 516
XX_FTP_TO_ATP_TO_FTP integration, 512, 514
Batch operations, 438
BI report folder structure, 256
Business events, 385
payables invoice event
enable events, 392
integration overview, 394
integration setup, 393, 394
payload information, 394–397
purchase order event, 386
actions, 391

Business Object, 387
ERP_Cloud_Connection, 386
event option selection, 386
filters, 388, 389
integration testing, 389, 390
payload structure, 391
receivables invoice event
enable events, 398–400
integration configuration, 400–402
testing
confirmation message, 403
execution results, 403, 404
information, 404
invoice, 402, 403
Business-to-Business (B2B), 367
activities
EDI message types, 369
EDIFACT document types, 371
X12 document types, 370
document types, 368
implementation
B2B activity, 373
conversion details, 373
conversion status, 374
data preparation, 371, 372
handle success/error conditions, 374
output, 374
target structures, 373
scenarios, 368
trading partner mode, 34

C

callbacks Connection, 16–18
Case-insensitive REST searches, 525
Child node fields, 519
Clean filenames
challenge, 536
solution, 536
CLOB data type, 406
CLOB Storage, 406
Concat function, 538
Connections
ATP database connection, 23–27
callbacks, 16–18
ERP Cloud Connection, 11–16
ERP Cloud events, 16–18
ERP Integrations REST Connection, 31, 32
FTP, 10–11
invoke, 8
object storage connection, 30, 31
OCR Connection, 27, 28
REST, 9
SOAP ErpIntegrationService Connection, 22
SOAP ErpObjectDFFUpdate Service Connection, 21
SOAP ExternalReport WSSService Connection, 19
SOAP ScheduleService Connection, 20

Connections (*cont.*)
trigger, 8
Visual Builder objects
connection, 28–30

D

Database connection, 408
Data Stitch activity, 347
implementation
common mapping, 351
global variable, 352, 353
invoice creation, 353, 354
invoke configuration, 356
modified variable, 355, 356
payload modification, 354, 355
payload structure, 349, 350
response configuration, 351
response mapping, 354, 357
REST connection, 348, 349
integration, 348
Date formatting
custom date-time format, 517
format-datetime function, 518
Date-Time Range Query, 520
Date-time values, 525
decodeBase64ToReference, 516
Delta data process
benefits, 383
data range logic, 382
integration, 376
parameters, 377
results, 380-382
scenarios, 375
solution approach, 375
testing/execution, 377–379
Descriptive flexfields (DFFs), 21
Diagnostic logs, 96
Drag-and-drop mapping, 78

E

Embedded FTP server, 10
End-to-End test
Batch ID, 137, 138
CSV file loading, 137
data editing, 140
data review, 139
ERP cloud, 143
launch application, 136
Load data from file, 138, 139
process execution, 140, 141
results, 142, 143
Enterprise Scheduler Service (ESS), 241
ERP Cloud Connection
Cloud Actions Configuration, 12
configuration, 11
FBDI Import Wizard, 13, 14
import bulk data into Oracle ERP Cloud, 13, 14
operation types, 12
query, create, update, or delete information, 12–13
Send Files to ERP Cloud, 14–16
ERP Cloud events, 16–18

ERP Integrations REST Connection, 31, 32
ErpIntegrationService
  data import/export operations, 242, 243
    importBulkData, 242
    loadAndImportData, 242
    other operations, 243
  document management operations, 242
    uploadFileToUcm, 242
  getESSExecutionDetails operation, 244
  job management operations
    downloadESSJob ExecutionDetails, 242
    getESSExecutionDetails, 242
    getESSJobStatus, 241
    submitESSJobRequest, 241
    submitJobWithOutput, 241
  operations overview, 243
  Oracle ERP Cloud jobs, 241
  Postman, 244
  Postman SOAP Request Configuration, 244
ErpObjectDFFUpdateService
  Oracle ERP cloud setup
    configure DFF context, 266
    deploy Flexfield, 266
    deployment confirmation, 267
    DFF, transaction form, 267
    manage descriptive flexfields, 265
    Postman SOAP Request, 268
    response interpretation, 268
    updated DFF value, 269
  overview, 265
Event-based integrations, 4, 34

F

FBDI, *see* File-Based Data Import (FBDI)
FBDI files + callback
  analyzing job data and results, 468
  integration to trigger callback, 466
  looping and filtering specific jobs, 468
  preparation, 465
  testing
    callback integration, 474
    email notification, 475
    FBDI files integration, 474
    FTP server storage, 476
    main integration, 473
    technical reference, 476
  XX_DEMO_IMP_SUPP_CB
    goal integration with enhanced features, 467
    overview, 466
    payload received, callback integration, 467
    starting point—basic callback integration, 466
  XX_DEMO_SEND_FBDI_FILES

FBDI files + callback (*cont.*)
configured lookup values, 473
email recipient from lookup configuration, 472
file processing, 470
lookup configuration overview, 472
notification activity configuration, 471
overview, 469
reading downloaded files, 470
FBDI file structure
callback, 163
data source approaches, 163
FBDI processing, 163
FBDI ZIP File Contents, 162
properties file contents, 162
required components, 162
FBDI for customers with file management, 178
FBDI for suppliers, callback (three data sources)
FBDI basics, 161
overview, 161
XX_DEMO_AR_IMPORT_CUST
directory file listing, 180
file download/UCM upload, 180
file reference parameter, 181
import process flow, 180
integration overview, 179
mapping configuration, 181
parameter configuration, 179
result handling, 182
sample file, 183
technical reference, 184
test configuration, 183
test results, 184
variable initialization, 179
wait for completion, 182
XX_DEMO_IMP_SUPP_CB
callback event filter, 173
callback integration executions, 174
callback integration flow, 172
callback payload, 175
monitoring integrations, 174
review ERP-SaaS, 177
sample payload structure, 176, 177
succeeded instance details, 175
technical reference, 178
XX_DEMO_IMP_SUPP_FTP
FBDI job submission confirmation, 165
file on FTP server, 164
hardcoded filename configuration, 164
integration flow, 163
test execution, 165
XX_DEMO_IMP_SUPP_NO_FTP
file creation with stage operations, 166

stage-based FBDI
integration flow, 166
test execution, 166
XX_DEMO_IMP_SUPP_OB_
STOR (object storage
approach)
FBDI submit mapping, 170
job, scheduled
processes, 171
object storage configuration,
167, 168
object storage FBDI
integration flow, 167
object storage request
mapping, 169
request ID, activity
stream, 171
FBDI interfaces
AutoInvoice job definition, 190
AutoInvoice parameters,
190, 191
investigation steps, 187, 189, 191
item import job
definition, 191
item import parameters, 192
items import, 191
job definition search, 188
Oracle ERP navigation
steps, 188
overview, 185
parameters, 185
process parameters, 186
setup, 189
scheduled processes
page, 186
payables invoices, 187
receivables invoices, 189
suppliers interface, 186
File attachment
create attachment
activity, 281–283
download file activity, 280, 281
integration flow, 280
mapping configuration
attachment details
mapping, 284
file contents mapping, 285
hardcode the ID value, 285
REST API response, 287
transaction ID mapping,
283, 284
transaction ID using
REST API, 286
transaction with
attachment, 288
File-Based Data Import (FBDI),
2, 161
Filter, 519
Finders, 518
FTP Connection, 10–11
FTP server
credentials configuration, 407
download
client machine, 423
in progress, 423
successfully, 423

FTP server (*cont.*)
 Visual Builder Download Interface, 423
 file successfully uploaded, 416
 invoke activity, 411
 invoke activity configuration, 411
 mapping configuration, 411
 preparatory steps, 407
 send file, 406
 upload files, 405–407
 upload interface, 406
FTP server and Stage activity
 basic file download integration, 195
 return mapping, 197
 trigger parameters, 195, 196
 date calculation/date function, 201
 date comparison, 202
 definition, 193
 file filtering mapping, 201
 FTP server connection, 198
 FTP server *vs.* Stage operations, 194
 FTP to database integration, 197, 198
 integration overview, 199
 key differences, 194
 log results, 202
 parameter configuration, 199
 request sample, 200
 sample request access, 200
 technical reference, 203
 test directory, 203
 test results, 203

G, H

Gen3, 100
Global variables, 346, 347

I

Integration configuration
 file contents, 252
 FTP server contents, 251
 integration design
 job details, Oracle ERP cloud, 247
 job execution details, 247
 integration flow overview, 248
 integration test results, 250, 251
 required integration connections, 246
 technical reference, 252
 write activity mapping, 250
 write activity properties, 249
Integration flow design
 inbound parameters, 119
 integration activities
 error handling, 123, 124
 invoice creation, 120
 mapping, 123
 ProcessData, 120
 response design, 125

test execution, 126, 127
testing, 125
UpdateInvData, 121, 122
overview, 119
Integration setup
getAllJobInstanceIDs
Operation, 260
getAllScheduledReportHistory
Operation, 261
getDocumentData
Operation, 262
Get Job Instance Step, 262
Get Report ID Step, 263
getScheduledJobInfo
Operation, 259
getScheduledReportOutputInfo
Operation, 261
getScheduledReportStatus
Operation, 260
getXMLData Operation, 260
Get XML Data Step, 262
integration output
variables, 264
integration test execution, 259
schedule integration type, 258
technical reference, 264–265
Integration Style Selection
Screen, 3
Integration types
application, 3
event-based, 4
schedule, 4
Invoke connection, 8

J, K

JavaScript libraries
confirmation, 74
example, 71
file selection, 72
import/manual upload, 71, 72
JavaScript functions,
integrations
assign activity, 75
function selection, 75
test execution results, 76
HTML configuration, 134
JSON configuration, 133
library configuration, 73
menu location, 70
technical reference, 76

L

Lookups, 147
API response format, 153
implementation steps
column values, 159
CSV file, 157–159
file reference, 155–157
read data, 154, 155
testing, 159, 160
integration design, 154
table-based access, use
cases, 160
tables
challenge, 150

Lookups (*cont.*)
solution
implementation, 151–153
use case, 151
use cases
complex mapping, 149, 150
hardcoded values, 148, 149
value mapping, 147, 148

M

Monitoring/troubleshooting, OIC Gen3
Gen3, 100
OIC Gen2 monitoring interface, 99
Monitor/troubleshoot, OIC Gen3
activity stream (instance tracking), 95, 96
alerts, 96, 98, 99
automation, 98, 99
diagnostic logs, 96
Gen2 *vs.* Gen3 monitoring comparison, 99
notifications, 96
Observability Dashboard, 94
Observe subtab, 94, 95
OCI Cloud console, 98
OCI logging analytics, 98
OIC service metrics, 98
replay and testing capabilities, 97
Multiple verbs, REST API
available REST verbs, 317
goal, 316
integration flow overview, 320
multiple verb configuration, 318
technical reference, 321
testing, 319

N

Notification
activity configuration, 62
attachments, 67, 68
configuration fields, 62
details, 64
email body options, 63
execution flow, 67
FlowId location, 66
HTML body configuration, 66
HTML body with parameters, 63
integration flow setup, 64
overview, 61
parameter mapping, 65
sample email output, 67
technical reference, 68

O

Object Storage
connection, 30, 31
REST API-based storage service, 291
upload integration flow, 302
Object Storage structure
Bucket Contents, 293
connection parameters

API Keys, 299, 300
connection URL, 296
Identity & Security, 298, 299
private key processing, 301
Tenancy OCID, 297
Namespace Location, OCI Console, 294
Object Storage Buckets, 293
Object Storage hierarchy, 293, 294
OCI console access, 292
REST Connection, 295
OCR, *see* Optical Character Recognition (OCR)
OCI Console Navigation, 25
OCI logging analytics, 98
OCR Connection, 27, 28
OIC Base64 Functions, 511, 512
OIC Gen3, 93
integration patterns, 34–35
projects, 33–34
OIC Generation 3 events
add publish event activity, 481
assign business identifier, 485
business identifier error, 484
create an event, 477
event creation confirmation, 480
event creation menu, 478
event data mapping, 482
event payload configuration, 479
event selection, 481
publisher integration creation, 480
publisher integration overview, 482
subscriber integration creation, 483
subscriber integration name, 483
subscribe to an event, 484
OIC implementation fix
connection type, 362, 363
Content-Type header, 364, 365
HTTP Header configuration, 363, 364
OIC Integration setup
configuration, 273
integration flow overview, 270
integration test results, 272
mapping configuration, 271
mapping, code mode, 271
oracle support notes, 275
payables DFF payload details, 274
payables invoice DFF update, 273
payables invoice lines example, 273
select an update operation, 270
technical reference, 275
verified update, ERP Cloud, 272
OIC scheduling with iCal
advanced scheduling, 528, 529, 531

OIC scheduling with iCal (*cont.*)
basic scheduling, 527, 528
multiple-day scheduling, 532–534
OIC URL Configuration, 418
Optical Character Recognition (OCR)
integration test, 109
OCR API response, 104
OIC integration components, 105, 106, 108
Postman, 102
body configuration, 103
headers configuration, 103
to OIC, 105
sample PDF demonstration, 104
service registration, 102
technical reference, 110
tools, 101
Oracle, 71, 86, 501
Oracle Cloud Infrastructure (OCI) Object Storage, 291
Oracle ERP Cloud, 1
Oracle Integration, 2, 69, 114
code provided, 409
database mapping, 413–414
database record updated with Base64 data, 416
database update activity, 412, 413
detailed return value mapping, 428
download integration, 424
entry trigger configuration, 410
final mapping, 428
FTP invoke activity, 427
FTP server, 416
FTP server and database, 409
FTP server invoke activity, 411
high-level overview, 409
invoke activity definition, 427
mapping configuration, 411, 412
mapping for read-download activity, 428
read-download invoke activity, 426
read-download mapping, 428
REST API, 135, 136
REST API trigger configuration, 424, 425
REST Trigger multipart/form-data, 410
REST trigger parameter configuration, 425, 426
testing, 415, 429
upload process, 409
Oracle Integration Cloud (OIC), 1–3, 511
Oracle Integration configuration
connections, 409
OIC, 115
REST, 118
SaaS/Fusion applications, 118
VB business object connection, 115–117
Oracle integration limits
design strategies, 90

no one-size-fits-all solution, 90
OIC limits, 89
requirements, 89, 90
service limits, 89
synchronous *vs.* asynchronous integrations, 91
Oracle SOA Suite, 1
Oracle SOA tools, 1
Oracle's reference documentation, 3
OR operators, 526

P

Packages (Pre-Gen3), 84
context menu, 86
project creation, 86, 87
Page-Level JavaScript Code, 134
Parallel activity, 337
asynchronous integration
configuration, 337, 338
integrations, 337
Wait activity, 339
synchronous integration
execution, 341, 342
objective, 340
overview, 341
test setup, 340
Payables invoices
API configuration, 344
API endpoint, 344
connection setup, 345
JSON, 344, 345
payload, 343
Postman, 102, 244, 491, 537
report execution, Oracle ERP Cloud, 258
schedule report payload, 257
schedule report request, 257
Projects
access control, 84
deployment, 85
Gen3 evolution, 84
limitations, 85
migration challenges, 85
monitor, 85
OIC Gen3, 83
recommendation, 86
versions, 85
Proof-of-concept (POC), 111, 145

Q

Query error, OIC, 538

R

Read BI Publisher reports
copy report files, 309
goal, 308
install OIC integration, 310
JSON response, 311
JSON schema configuration, 313
limitations, 309
Query parameter configuration, 314
report folder location, 309
response configuration, 315

Read BI Publisher reports (*cont.*)
response payload
definition, 312
REST connection setup, 310
sample, 308
sample JSON structure, 316
test operation selection, 311
visual builder display, 309
Receivables transaction
auxiliary integration
connection, 225
flexfield data, 223
mapping, 225
overview, 224
parameters, 224
purpose, 224
SOAP invoke, 225
main integration
attachments, 236
create invoice, 227, 231, 232
flexfield updation,
233, 235–236
original transaction, 233–235
overview, 226
read transaction, 227,
229, 230
receive parameters, 227, 228
return response, 237
preparation
add attachment, 219
ATTRIBUTE1, 223
Deploy Flexfield, 223
descriptive flexfield, 220–222
editing, 222
sample transaction, 219
transaction ID, 220
requirements, 217, 218
testing, 237–239
Redwood Guided Process
error handling, 144, 145
file selection, 112
launch page, 112
process review, 143, 144
REST API–based file
attachments, 279
REST API batch, 438
REST APIs, 2
REST Connection, 9
REST-framework-version header,
OR queries, 527
REST Request Headers
feature, 359
problem, 359, 360
solution, 361, 362
Retry mechanism
complete integration, 57
"controlled" action, 58
execution results after three
retries, 59
FTP server, 57
graphical view of retry
attempts, 60
technical reference, 60
test execution, 59
testing, 58–60
while loop configuration, 58
Role-based access
control (RBAC), 84

S

Scheduled integration, 4
ScheduleService
  delivery service, 255, 256
  document and data operations, 255
  job history management, 254
  overview, 252
  report information retrieval, 254, 255
  schedule management, 253, 254
SCM Sales Orders SOAP services, 501
Scope component, definition, 56–57
Service-Oriented Architecture (SOA), 1
SOAP ErpIntegrationService Connection, 22
SOAP ErpObjectDFFUpdateService Connection, 21
SOAP ExternalReportWSSService Connection, 19
SOAP ScheduleService Connection, 20
SOAP web services, 2
  API documentation navigation, 495
  compose the complete WSDL URL, 495
  configure authorization, 498, 499
  create new SOAP Project, 496, 497
  Developer Connect Navigation, 502
  instance URL configuration, 496
  locate the WSDL, 494
  project configuration dialog, 498
  samples, 501–503
  sample SOAP payloads, 503
  Service Details View, 503
  test execution example, 500
  test payload, 499
  WSDL Download Interface, 502
  WSDL URL, documentation, 495
SoapUI, 493
SoapUI download interface, 494
Stage activity, 193
Standard functions vs. custom JavaScript, 70
Suppliers interface, 186
Synchronous integrations, 90
Synchronous *vs.* asynchronous integrations, 91

T

Test event flow
  event parameters, activity stream, 486, 487
  event use cases
    code reusability, 487
    decoupled architecture, 488
    one-to-many pattern, 487
  example scenario, 488

Test event flow (*cont.*)
  limitation, 488
  publisher execution, 486
  subscriber execution, 486
  technical reference, 489
Trigger, 8

U

UCM, *see* Universal Content Management (UCM)
UCM connection configuration
  connection URL structure, 327
  download integration flow, 329
    download activity, 329
    integration test execution, 330
    unzip and copy to FTP, 330
  files, FTP server, 331
  SoapUI project setup, 328
  UCM SOAP connection, 327
Universal Content Management (UCM), 323
  download
    ERP menu navigation, 324
    file import and export menu, 325
    file search results, 326
    file selection, 325
    upload confirmation, 326
  upload
    activity configuration, 332
    file content mapping, 332
    file details, 334
    file, Import/Export Tool, 333
    file, UCM Tool, 334
    integration flow, 331
    technical details, 335
UPPER() function, 525
URL attachment
  attachment type, 288, 289
  integration flow, 288
  mapping configuration, 288
  technical reference, 290
  transaction, 290
  URL mapping, 289

V

VB Business Object
  applications, 439
  batch operations, 438
  XX_DEMO_DB_VB_BATCH_DELETE, 448–454
  XX_DEMO_FTP_2_DB_VB_BATCH, 454–463
  XX_DEMO_FTP_2_DB_VB_SINGLE, 439–448
Virtual File System (VFS), 155
Visual Builder
  action chain, 421, 422
  action chain configuration, 433
  add parameters, 431
  business objects, 437
  connection configuration, 417, 431
  connection parameter configuration, 419

copying URL from Oracle integration, 430
"Define by Endpoint", 417, 430
detailed download mapping, 434
File Picker Component, 421
JavaScript Code in Page Module, 432, 433
manual connection setup, 429
mapping configuration, 434
OIC URL Configuration, 418
page components, 421
pasting URL in connection configuration, 430
response payload configuration with a JSON, 420
setting form-data in the request body, 420
testing, 432
upload to an FTP server, 405–407
URL format, 418
Visual Builder (VB) configuration, 113
Business Object, 132
connections
backend, 128, 129
OIC service, 129, 130
testing, 130, 131
Visual Builder objects connection, 28–30

W

While loop, 57–58

X, Y, Z

XSD duration functions, 525
XSD file, 534, 535
XSLT (Extensible Stylesheet Language Transformations)
best practices, 82
code editing, 81
Code Editor, 82
code mode, 82
constructs, 80
construct selection, 81
constructs menu, 80
definition, 77
example complex mapping requirements, 79–80
manual XSLT transformation example, 79
mapping editor interface, 78
simple *vs.* complex mappings, 78
switch to code view, 81
XX_DEMO_DB_VB_BATCH_DELETE
batch delete integration, 448
delete action configuration, 452
delete action setup, 451
delete mapping in code mode, 453
detailed mapping in code mode, 450
GetSuppliers activity configuration, 449
mapping configuration for delete action, 452, 453

XX_DEMO_DB_VB_BATCH_DELETE (*cont.*)
- mapping configuration for getsuppliers, 450
- payload sent during delete test, 453, 454
- URL Format, 452

XX_DEMO_FTP_2_DB_VB_BATCH
- batch load integration, 455
- detailed batch mapping in code mode, 461
- header configuration for batch operations, 458
- insert configuration, 456
- mapping configuration for batch operation, 460
- OIC console results, 462
- payload configuration for batch receive, 459
- payload configuration for batch send, 457
- read in segments of 2,000 records, 455
- records inserted in VB, 463
- test file with 100,000+ records, 461, 462
- trigger-download configuration, 455

XX_DEMO_FTP_2_DB_VB_SINGLE
- download file activity configuration, 441
- loop to insert with read in segments stage, 442
- parameters received by trigger, 440
- read in segments stage configuration, 442, 443
- REST API configuration for insert, 444
- sample request for insert operation, 445
- sample request payload, 441
- sample response from insert operation, 446
- single insert approach, 439
- testing, 447

GPSR Compliance
The European Union's (EU) General Product Safety Regulation (GPSR) is a set of rules that requires consumer products to be safe and our obligations to ensure this.

If you have any concerns about our products, you can contact us on

ProductSafety@springernature.com

In case Publisher is established outside the EU, the EU authorized representative is:

Springer Nature Customer Service Center GmbH
Europaplatz 3
69115 Heidelberg, Germany

www.ingramcontent.com/pod-product-compliance
Lightning Source LLC
LaVergne TN
LVHW052209200926
848481LV00001B/65
* 9 7 9 8 8 6 8 8 3 0 1 9 8 *